The NGRC Greyhound Racing Yearbook 1995

**Edited by
Paul Fry**

Published by Ringpress Books Limited

PO Box 8, Lydney, Gloucs. GL15 6YD

First published 1995

© Ringpress Books 1995

ISBN 186054 010 4

Printed and bound in Great Britain by
BPC Hazell Books Ltd
A member of
The British Printing Company Ltd

ACKNOWLEDGEMENTS

A NUMBER of people have been key to the production of this book and I would like to take this opportunity to thank them. First and foremost the expertise, experience and knowledge of **Paul Millward** and **Mike Palmer**, of the Racing Post.

Peter Meldrum toiled long and hard over a hot computer to produce the many facts and figures included.

I would also like to thank the many track officials for their assistance with the Directory section, the core component of the book, with its extensive track facts and race records section.

Steve Nash, the sport's premier photographer, has once again generously given us the run of his extensive picture library.

The NGRC have been instrumental contributors and I thank **Geoffrey Thomas** and **Archie Newhouse** for their assistance and patience.

Thanks to all of our other contributors, and to **John**, **Julia**, **Nick** and **Julie** at Ringpress for their unflagging support.

And, last but by no means least, to **Dawn**, **Zoe** and **Stefanie**.

PAUL FRY
February 1995

PUBLISHER'S NOTE

WELCOME to the *NGRC Greyhound Racing Yearbook*, a worthy successor to the *Greyhound Factfile*, whose three editions were publishing landmarks in the history of the sport.

The *Factfile* flourished, first with the help of the *Daily Mirror* and latterly Ladbrokes, but lack of sponsorship meant that it has not appeared since 1992.

Its resurrection as *The Yearbook* is due to the foresight and generosity of our new sponsor, The British Greyhound Racing Fund. If you are one of those who ask "what does the Fund do for me?" one answer is right in front of you. Without the BGRF backing, this book would have cost you at least half as much again.

The *NGRC Greyhound Racing Yearbook* contains many new features as well as a wealth of information updated from the last *Factfile*. The new publication also has a new editor in Paul Fry, who earned his spurs on *The Sporting Life*, and a new design which will make it much easier to use than its predecessor. One or two old friends have gone, notably the Independent track directory, the inclusion of which would have been inappropriate under our new banner.

Most importantly, we have an assured future for a book which is indispensable to greyhound racing people – so much so that the first thing most people do with their copy is to write their name on it!.

At least if your book vanishes under the attentions of a "borrower", you won't have to wait so long for a replacement. Now we can say with confidence: "See you next year".

Xspell's 'xtraordinary year!

1993 – B.W.R.A. STRAIGHT CHAMPIONSHIPS	– SUPREME DOG
1993 – N.W.R.F. STRAIGHT CHAMPIONSHIPS	– SUPREME DOG
1993 – B.W.R.A. BEND CHAMPIONSHIPS	– SUPREME DOG
1993 – WHIPPET NEWS TOP TEN	– WINNER
1993 – N.W.R.F. TOP FIVE	– WINNER
1993 – HIGHLAND DERBY 2nd. OVERALL	– TOP DOG
1993 – N.W.R.F. DEVON OPEN 2nd. OVERALL	– TOP DOG
1993 – N.W.R.F. BEND DERBY	– FINALIST
1993 – B.W.R.A. JACK CADMAN FINALIST	– ONLY DOG IN FINAL

Mark Pettitt says "Gill & I set **'Ross'** some tough targets in 1993 but he never once let us down. We believe in attention to detail both in his training and in his feeding so regular use of **SA-37** with extra vitamin E is an integral part of his programme."

sa-37e
for champions

Pack sizes:
100 g and 2 kg available from your usual supplier of Animal Health Products

(Intervet)

For further information:
INTERVET U.K. LIMITED
Science Park, Milton Road,
Cambridge CB4 4FP
Tel: 0223 420221
Fax: 0223 420751

INTERVET (IRELAND) LTD.
Ballyboggan Industrial Estate
Ballyboggan Road,
Finglas, Dublin 11
Tel: 01-309446/309012

THE GREYHOUND AND WHIPPET SHOP

For all racing requirements

WORLDWIDE WINNERS

288 Chingford Road,
London E17, England

Tel: 0181 527 7278
Fax: 0181 527 3425

HOME OF THE BEST PRICES AROUND ON ALL THE BIG NAME PRODUCTS IN GREYHOUND RACING, INCLUDING . . .

THE MASTER SERIES

THE DRAGMASTER: Ideally suited for pups as its upright design allows for maximum overview. Geared for easy acceleration (it will do 200 yards in 10 seconds) as well as having a free-wheeling brake control, this manually operated unit is proving time and again that it cannot be beaten as a schooling aid or indeed as a major player at any lure coursing event.

THE TRAPMASTER: Once again ideally suited for schooling young dogs through that most stressful period of their novice careers. Now you control their rate of progress. Familiarity breeds confidence. Ensure all your dogs stay trap sharp throughout their racing lives with this sturdy, built-to-last unit. Available as both a single or double set.

FOR MORE INFORMATION ON THESE FINE PRODUCTS AS WELL AS A PRICE LIST OF THE COMPLETE RANGE OF GOODS AVAILABLE, CALL OR VISIT . . .

THE GREYHOUND AND WHIPPET SHOP

STILL THE ONLY ONE THAT'S GOT IT ALL!

Shop hours: 10am to 5pm Early closing Thurs: 3pm Sat: 4pm

Contents

Preface

9 **INTRODUCTION** By Lord Kimball

Features

12 **THAT WAS THE YEAR THAT WAS.** A look back at all the big races of 1994

39 **THE CLASS OF '95.** Seven to follow. Jonathan Kay

43 **A YEAR IN POLITICS:** Greyhound racing's image on the line. Mike Palmer

46 **TRAINER PROFILE:** Secrets of Nick Savva's success. Mike Palmer

56 **BYRNES' UNIT:** Spotlight on an Irish greyhound racing dynasty. John Martin. Plus Irish Derby report.

60 **WILD ABOUT HARRY:** Outspoken, a real livewire — Harry Findlay's coming to a screen near you. Jonathan Hobbs

64 **CONFESSIONS OF A GIANT-KILLER:** Meet ebullient Jock McNaughton, of Henlow. Mike Palmer

72 **SALUTE TO ALAN FEARN:** Senior Steward's reflections on a lifetime in greyhound racing.

Contents

75 FOUR WEDDINGS AND A RACECARD: A look at what's cooking in the nation's track restaurants. Paul Fry

97 A DAY IN THE LIFE OF SIS: The inside story. Errol Blythe

99 MORAL VICTORY: Derby report and results Jonathan Hobbs

68 UNHAPPY RETURNS: Analysis of 1994's Tote and attendance returns.

334 BREEDING: Litter numbers trend under the spotlight. P R Saward

Statistics

109 OPEN RACE STATISTICS Peter Meldrum

132 A-Z OF OPEN RACE WINNERS 1994

178 COMPARATIVE TIMES AT OPEN TRACKS

Listings

162 COMPLETE FIXTURES, 1995

181 NGRC TRACK DIRECTORY

281 TRAINERS AND OWNER TRAINERS

369 IRISH TRACK DIRECTORY

TALKING GREYHOUNDS

A veterinary advice video with
Dr JOHN KOHNKE BVSc RDA
Dr REG HOSKINS BVSc MASVSc
A video that no greyhound man should be without. It shows the correct way to feed a greyhound and shows injury examination and clinical examples of injuries. The accompanying 116 page book expands in detail the full content of the video. This is a really essential reference guide for everyone who wishes to get the best from their greyhounds.

TRAINER'S TIP

Reduce walking to half or three-quarters of a mile daily once a greyhound is fit. (Walk to stretch the limbs and empty the bowels). Fitness is maintained more easily by regular short hand gallops of 150 to 200 yards two or three times a week or by racing once per week.

This outstanding package is not to be missed and costs only

£22.95 including p & p

Please send cheque/postal orders to:
Romar Video
Torne Gatehouse, Epworth,
Doncaster DN9 1LE

Preface

By LORD KIMBALL

The British Greyhound Racing Fund is approaching its second birthday. Contributions from the off-course bookmakers are edging ahead. There is still a distorted understanding of the word 'voluntary'. This does not apply to the sum to be collected: it has already been given back to the bookmakers.

The Fund's task over the period covered by this useful publication is to add a further £1m. to its annual total: that is the target before the next publication of the NGRC Greyhound Racing Yearbook.

KIMBALL

Introduction

The British Greyhound Racing Fund

The British Greyhound Racing Fund began its work at the beginning of 1993. Since that time it has collected nearly £4 million as a result of the decision to reduce betting levy by a quarter percent and successfully distributed this money to the advancement of and for the benefit of greyhound racing in this country.

The Fund has concentrated its spending on three areas: integrity services, adding value to the sport and prize money.

Integrity Services

The integrity of greyhound racing is not only crucial to the success of the Sport but represents the only area, after betting duty, in which the Government have a continuing role. The Home Secretary has an ultimate responsibility for the integrity of the public's bet.

For these reasons the Fund:

- refunds the NGRC's forensic testing programme at Newmarket.

- pays for the NGRC flying squad.

- contributes towards the costs of the pre-race chromatography.

- assists with track veterinary and licensed paddock security costs.

Value Added

National promotion of greyhound racing is reliant on the sport being able to meet the ever-increasing demands for better leisure facilities from racecourses. It is the stated aim of the Fund to seek to extend its powers in the future to include the ability to make loans to tracks in order to provide better facilities for the public.

At present, the Fund is seeking to secure the infrastructure of the sport and at the same time to assist in all aspects pertaining to the welfare of the racing greyhound.

Grants towards new kennel blocks, better drainage, track surfaces, new traps and enhanced lighting have been given.

Introduction

Moreover, the Fund has increased threefold its support for the Retired Greyhound Trust, making it possible for the RGT to find homes for a record number of ex-racers in 1994.

Prize Money

With the prospect of Sunday racing in 1995 and the ever-spiralling demand for more races, greyhound racing needs to attract owners into the Sport. To this end, the Fund has looked to provide substantial help in increasing graded prize money.

The sight of BGRF kennel sweepstakes across NGRC race cards is now common and there is little doubt that the Funds contribution to prize money including the National Intertrack competition is vital to the future prospect of greyhound racing.

The Future

The Sporting Life runs a feature called *Personality Profile* which asks 'What Would You do If You Were Lord Kimball?'. Ask Lord Kimball himself and the answer would be clear. Given the full support of his Board and within the legislative restraints hanging over the sport his aim is to:

- obtain a full return of the duty given back to bookmakers by the Chancellor.

- maximise the Fund's revenue by establishing a loan fund within the Fund in a form agreed and advised by the Revenue.

- increase the public awareness of greyhound racing by encouraging more personalities, owners and greyhounds.

- assist in the removal of any further restraints which stop greyhound racing achieving its full potential.

Review of 1994

Goodbye to all that!

Paul Millward and Mike Palmer reflect on a memorable 12 months of triumph and tragedy on the track.

1993 was an exceptional year for Hall Green trainer Tony Meek, the highlight of which was the superb Derby victory by the trailblazing Ringa Hustle. It would have been a brave man, therefore, who would have predicted even greater success for him in 1994.

But greater it was, thanks mostly to Moral Standards, who gave Meek his second successive Derby win.

JANUARY

The year was just days old when Meek signalled his intent, steering Tammys Delight to victory in the **Embassy Marathon Gold Cup** over 825 metres at Hackney, the first Category One event ever held at the track under the Fleetfoot Racing banner.

A gamble, on and off-course, saw Theo Mentzis' Lisnakill Move backed from 20-1 down to 6-1, but this was not be her night and she eventually came home third behind Tammys Delight, who won by more than two lengths from Kilpipe Bibi in 54.44sec., 10 spots inside the track record set earlier in the competition by the previous season's Cesarewitch winner, Killenagh Dream.

Indeed, it was he who disputed much of the early running with Tammys Delight, but Charlie Lister's dog was struck into at the fifth bend and that virtually put paid to his chances. The incident enabled Tammys Delight to go clear and she was never threatened thereafter. Tony Meek was on his way again . . .

WIMBLEDON Sporting Life Juvenile Championship

AYR FLYER came to London with a big reputation but those who

Review of 1994

AYR FLYER: Came with big reputation and justified it brilliantly.

had taken odds of 7-2 on Dawn Wheatley's dog landing the spoils had a few anxious moments in the Juvenile, over 460 metres.

This Wimbledon annual has produced some superb encounters down the years but 1994 threatened to produce one of the biggest shocks in the history of the competition when Ayr Flyer was knocked sideways at first bend by reserve runner Dashboard Flight.

A lesser hound would have swallowed it there and then but Ayr Flyer rode the bump well and charged down the back straight as if nothing had happened. Showing superb middle pace, he was soon clear of Dashboard Flight and Chakalak Zeus and, by the time he hit the last bend, it was all academic.

Ayr Flyer had put an incredible five lengths between himself and Dashboard Flyer and his time of 27.63sec. on a track estimated to be running .30sec. fast would have been a good deal quicker but for that early setback. Dawn Wheatley confirmed after the race that the dog's major objective for the year would be the Derby and how well this outstanding greyhound performed in reaching the final.

After the Derby he went to Dundalk and was a highly-impressive winner of the International.

WIMBLEDON John Smith's Gold Cup

HOVE'S Island Doe was an unlucky greyhound, injuries throughout his career unquestionably denying him the many victories he so richly deserved. But there was one race he won which will live long in the memory of all those who saw it, the 660 metres John Smith's

Review of 1994

Gold Cup. Starting 6-4 favourite, Derek Knight's dog had an epic battle with local runner Bularine Slippy, so much so that after the race Knight chirped 'it was a shame there had to be a loser'.

But while Bularine Slippy ended up as bridesmaid, his connections prided themselves in the knowledge that their dog had played a major role in one of the best races seen at Plough Lane for years.

Bularine Slippy got away to a flying start and streaked clear going to the first turn. Island Doe, meanwhile, broke moderately in comparison but he displayed a tremendous turn of early foot to claw back the local runner at the winning line on the first circuit.

From there it was nail-biting stuff with Bularine Slippy refusing to give best and he ranged up alongside Island Doe at the fifth. He chose to challenge on the inside at this point but the leader slammed the door in his face, forcing Philip Rees' runner to check.

But still he refused to quit and forced his way through on the inside at the final turn. Momentarily he snatched back the lead but Island Doe, who lost ground by drifting wide at the last bend, dug deep into his reserves and got back up on the line to win by a short-head in 40.59sec. (.15sec. fast).

It was wonderful and, with a huge sigh of relief as the result was announced, Knight said: 'What a race!' He can say that again.

WALTHAMSTOW Pepsi Cola Marathon

WALTHAMSTOW in January was a happy hunting ground for that outstanding trainer, Charlie Lister. Less than three weeks after steering Monard Wish to victory there in the Bookmakers Invitation 640, he struck gold again with Sunhill Misty in the 820m Marathon. The race looked a match—or at least that's how the bookmakers saw it—between her and Weave Macgregor, the Irish-owned bitch who was cheered on in vain by her connections who made the mad dash from Naas races to Walthamstow early on Saturday evening.

Michael Fortune, the Racing Post's Irish correspondent, came over with his wife, Rita, Weave Macgregor's former trainer, Brian Cross, and Paddy and Anne Meehan, the other part owners.

Meanwhile, Sunhill Misty's owners, Robert Wallis and Sandy McKenzie had travelled down from Scotland to cheer on their runner and the journey was not a wasted one.

Star Girl took them along early but she could never shake off My Texette and at the fifth bend there was little to choose between the pair with Sunhill Misty now looming up ominously in third. Weave Macgregor, as usual, was in rear but

CHARLIE LISTER: Struck gold again.

Review of 1994

looked dangerous when changing up a gear in the back stretch on the final circuit.

Rounding the last two bends, they all began to bunch but Weave Macgregor ran into the back of Roan Sean and was clobbered again as they swung for home. It was not to be her night and the Irish drowned their sorrows.

Up front My Texette tried valiantly to keep Sunhill Misty at bay but the line came just a little too late and Lister's bitch got up to score by half a length in 52.80sec.

If it was going to be a good year for Tony Meek, then it was also the start of a splendid 12 months for Lister.

FEBRUARY

IMPERIAL TOBBACO are greyhound racing's biggest sponsors, backing competitions throughout the country and, for the first time at the new track in Northern Ireland, Ballyskeagh.

They also came up with a new competition at **Sunderland,** the 450m **Regal £10,000**, and it was a race which at long last gave Carrigeen Blaze his first major success. Runner-up in the Irish Derby and third in the Eclipse at Nottingham in 1993, Ron Hough's dog seemed fated not to win a big one but it all came right on that cold night in the North-East.

Overcoming a track to which he was not particularly suited and a niggling wrist injury, Carrigeen Blaze then recovered from a poor start, displaying tremendous early speed which carried him into a first-bend lead.

Less than fluent on the corners, he looked to be in trouble when the powerful local runner, Killila Place, ranged up on his inside along the back straight and there was precious little between the two from there on. But when they straightened up for home, the Sheffield dog held Killila Place to the line, winning by a head in 27.72sec.

After the race Hough showered Carrigeen Blaze with praise. 'He's the best middle-distance dog I've ever had and he deserved to win this after Shelbourne and Nottingham.'

The morning after the race, Carrigeen Blaze was sore again in the wrist and precious little more would be seen of him.

WIMBLEDON   John Henwood Springbok Trophy

THE disappointment of losing his training position at Oxford some months earlier was a distant memory for trainer Bernie Doyle at Wimbledon in February where

BERNIE DOYLE: Rush job at Plough Lane.

Review of 1994

the chirpy Glaswegian enjoyed one of his best career wins in the Springbok Trophy over 460m.

As usual in this major annual for novice hurdlers—entries must be maidens over the sticks up until the start of the year—there were shocks galore throughout but, come final night Doyle's Avoid The Rush was the star of the meeting. Nearer last than first in the early stages as the 2-1 favourite and local runner Steady Major bowled along in front, Avoid The Rush came late on the scene to snatch victory, and how deserved it was.

Doyle had been schooling the dog over hurdles for fully three months, in fact since back in the previous September at Oxford, where immediately he took an instant liking to the jumping game. The dog recorded a staggering 28.30sec. in his first-ever trial at the Cowley track, a run which prompted Doyle to say: 'I knew he was something special right away.'

Famous last words indeed.

HACKNEY A R Dennis Middle Park Puppy Cup

IT WAS an eventful year for trainer John McGee, the champion handler sitting it out on the sidelines after the High Court upheld a seven-month ban imposed by the NGRC after a prohibited substance was found in his Peterborough Derby finalist, Rabatino.

That he retained his title as champion speaks volumes for his natural talent with greyhounds and he kicked off 1994 in the manner now familiar, lifting an early-season big race, the Middle Park. McGee's representative was Druids Elprado, who was out to reverse semi-final form with Dave Conway's Anhid Blaze, who beat him by a comfortable distance in that penultimate round.

But it was a different ball game when it mattered most and Druids Elprado, after tracking Super Bridge, forged ahead on the run-in as the pacemaker's stride began to shorten. McGee's runner put just over a length between himself and the runner-up, clocking what was really a moderate 29.60sec., but the victory signalled what was to come for Druids Elprado.

The punters at Hackney mostly got it wrong for they allowed the winner to drift out to 2-1 (from 6-4) as they plunged on Anhid Blaze from 7-4 to 11-10. But the favourite backers soon knew their fate as Anhid Blaze missed his break.

After the race, McGee beamed: 'I think this is the best start to a year I've ever had.' Few would argue with that but if it was his best start it was certainly his worst finish, that High Court ruling putting McGee out of action from late December until June 30 this year.

CRAYFORD Ladbroke Golden Jacket

COULD the 1993 Greyhound of the Year, Heavenly Lady, crown a magnificent career by landing the Ladbroke Golden Jacket final for

Review of 1994

a second time? This was the question they were all asking at Crayford.

Magnificent when taking this 714 metres event 12 months earlier, it was asking an awful lot for her to give a repeat performance, despite the fact that she held the track record and was unbeaten in the preliminaries.

There were, however, several others in there with major claims, including Derek Knight's classy runner, Wexford Minx, and The Great Gonzo. Nevertheless, there was considerable ante-post support for Linda Mullins' bitch in the week leading up to the final with Ladbrokes' liability alone in excess of £40,000.

Yet she was still among the unfancied runners in the market but what a brave effort she produced, going to the front at the first bend to the roars of her many supporters. The noise level was maintained until it was clear approaching the seventh bend that the distress signals were going out.

JOHN McGEE: Best start.

Wexford Minx, who was soon tucked in behind Heavenly Lady in what eventually turned out to be a match between the pair, took command down the back stretch second time round and went away for what proved to be a comfortable success.

Heavenly Lady held off Jubilee Rebecca for second and was darling of the crowd but Crayford racegoers had seen an outstanding performance by Wexford Minx, who landed a first Golden Jacket for Hove trainer Derek Knight and owners Eamon and Carol Furlong, great supporters of the sport in this country.

MARCH

HEAVENLY LADY had failed to defend her Ladbroke Golden Jacket crown at Crayford but made no mistake just a couple of weeks later in the 660m **W J & J E Cearns Memorial** final at Wimbledon.

So impressive when taking the title 12 months earlier at Plough Lane, she faced a tough rival this time in the shape of Mary Harding's local runner, First Defence, who shared 11-8 favouritism with Heavenly Lady. If the bookmakers thought it was close between the pair, the race was run in totally different contrast, with Heavenly Lady going clear while First Defence completely missed

Review of 1994

her break and trailed the field going Into the first bend. Badly crowded at that initial turn, First Defence's task looked impossible. However, she weaved her way through the field and while there was no catching Heavenly Lady, It speaks volumes for her reserves of stamina that she eventually ran second, albeit four and a half lengths behind the 40.46sec. (+20sec.) winner.

After the race there was considerable debate between Lady's trainer, Linda Mullins, and owner Tony Head, over the bitch's future. She was getting no younger and while there was talk of the Trainers' championship at home track Walthamstow, where she was never at her best , and the Regency at Hove.

The end of a great career was only weeks away.

OXFORD Arthur Prince Pall Mall

LASSA JAVA, *below,* was one of the fastest greyhounds of recent years and also one of the most unlucky. Laurence Blunt's dog suffered more than his share of injuries during his career but Tony Meek waved the magic wand once more when he ran the dog in the 450m Pall Mall.

With the £5,000 Embassy Gold Cup trophy already on the trainer's mantelpiece thanks to Tammys Delight, here was another £5,000 competition heading the way of Meek and his highly-talented team of runners.

None too well away, Lassa Java showed good early pace but it was the ill-fated Salcombe, with the advantage of the rails, who led the pack around the first bend. Java was in touch as they entered the back straight and, with Ashford Boy also improving, it was virtually three abreast going into the third turn. Then Salcombe and Ashford Boy came together, spoiling each other's chances.

Lassa Java side-stepped the pair on the outside and took a decisive lead. Keeping on well, he crossed the line with just under two lengths to spare over the rallying Ashford Boy in 27.17sec.

With yet another title under his belt, Meek was now turning his attention towards the Derby and was particularly sweet about the chances of one particular greyhound in his kennels. The name? Moral Standards.

WALTHAMSTOW Racing Post Arc

A STAR of immense proportions was born in the final of the Arc at Walthamstow in March when Westmead Chick landed the first of four titles in 1994 and, in the process genuinely established herself as one of the greatest bitches of all time. Immense in stature and

Review of 1994

ability, Westmead Chick, another outstanding product of the Dunstable kennels of Nick and Natalie Savva, was always going to win the Arc, despite a super-game effort by Arthur Boyce's Catford runner, Paradise Slippy.

He went clear at the first bend and was still in the van as they turned for home but Westmead Chick, *right*, who flew down the back straight and swept past Ardilaun Bridge, had the Catford runner clearly in her sights as they turned for home and, in a driving finish got up to pip Paradise Slippy by a neck in a flying 28.73sec.

Nick Savva made the bold statement that Westmead Chick could prove to be 'as good as her mother'. When you consider that was the magnificent Westmead Move, you will see how much Nick thought of Chick at this early stage.

The only regret on a memorable Arc night was that the winner's owner, Bob Morton, cut short his holiday to attend the final, only to be taken ill during the evening and miss the big occasion.

HALL GREEN Daily Mirror/Sporting Life Grand National

LINDA MULLINS likes a hurdler or two and was doubly represented in the National over Hall Green's 474 metres. The Walthamstow handler sent out Heavenly Dream and Super Spy but neither had an answer to Randy Savage, the Kevin O'Connor Canterbury dog who, despite starting at long odds, turned the race into a procession.

His cause was greatly assisted by trouble at the first flight which virtually put paid to the chances of four of the runners, including the favourite, Gis A Smile, who rallied to take third behind Randy Savage and Heavenly Dream. But Jaimsie Cotter, Super Spy and Hi Brazil Sam never recovered from the incident and came home fourth, fifth and sixth behind the 29.50sec. winner.

A fast start by Randy Savage carried him clear of trouble and he was never headed in beating Heavenly Dream, the only other runner to gain a clear run, by two lengths.

APRIL

BANNER-WAVING half-wits as the BBC's Desmond Lynam described them, delayed the start of the **BBC Television Trophy** final at Sunderland but they did not spoil the night and fans throughout the country were treated to a vintage performance by Jubilee Rebecca. Animal rights protesters, acting in the wake of

Review of 1994

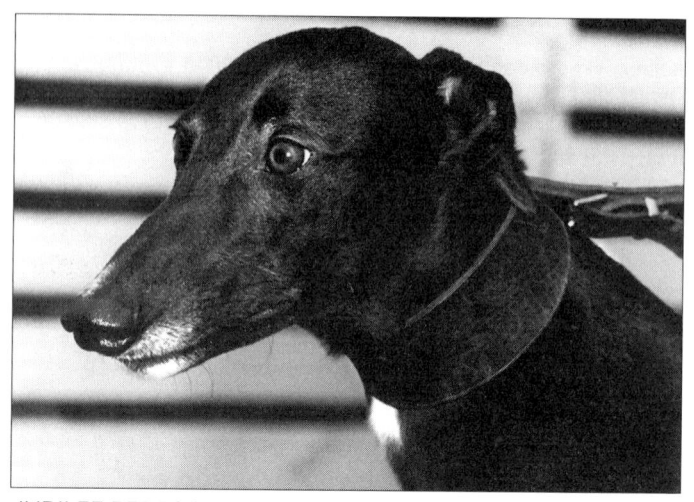

JUBILEE REBECCA: Found top gear to land the TV Trophy

the *On The Line* documentary, jumped onto the track as the signal was given to start the hare for the final.

The goons were quickly bundled out of the track and, having been checked again by the vet, the runners were returned to traps eight minutes behind schedule. Charlie Lister's Killenagh Dream, who had finished lame in the Ladbroke Golden Jacket final, was first to show in the 827m showpiece and looked set fair following trouble behind.

However, Jubilee Rebecca, trained at nearby Brough Park by Gordon Rooks, found top gear on the second circuit and, sweeping past Killenagh Dream at the seventh bend, drew right away to win by almost eight lengths in 53.13sec. Favourite Newry Town, who had looked a cinch for the competition in the weeks leading up to the big race, ran disappointingly. He was balked at the first bend and was rather one-paced, finishing a well-beaten fourth.

WEMBLEY Wendy Fair Blue Riband

OWNER Peter Dellow was beginning to think he would never win a big-race final until, that is, Ardilaun Bridge went to Wembley for the £7,500 Blue Riband decider over 490 metres.

When Ardilaun Bridge ran third in the *Racing Post* Arc at Walthamstow the previous month, it was Dellow's 13th consecutive final defeat but the big black dog stopped the rot in no uncertain style on a bitterly cold night at Wembley.

After some inspired performances in the qualifying rounds and a perfect trap one draw for this bang railer, Ardilaun Bridge settled the issue in a matter of strides, bolting from the traps and racing clear to the first bend. He was not going to be caught after such a flying start and the Chris Duggan-trained runner ran home almost

Review of 1994

four lengths clear of Drovers Road in 29.08sec. 'The pressure of having the favourite was pretty noticeable,' recalled Dellow. 'I handled it in the days leading up to the final but in the last five minutes before the race my stomach turned over a thousand times.'

The Blue Riband is normally a valuable guide to the Derby but none of the finalists covered himself in glory three months later at Wimbledon. Druids Elprado, who would go further than all of them at Wimbledon and started second favourite in the Riband, was knocked over at the first bend and took a horrible tumble.

READING The Masters

DRUIDS ELPRADO became only the third greyhound to better the 28.00sec. barrier at Reading when winning the £20,000 Bookmakers Masters final on the last Saturday In April.

The 465m competition drew a high-class entry and there were some outstanding performances, although controversy surrounded the semi-finals when the track heavily favoured wide runners. Consequently five seeded runners made their way through to the decider and the odd man out was Druids Elprado who, on going with no hint of bias, held a big advantage as the only railer.

And the John McGee-trained dog made not a single mistake, despite breaking only fifth. But, running the first bend superbly and aided by the fact that Micks Rover in two moved off and collided with Salthill Champ, Druids Elprado set off in pursuit of early leader Farmer Patrick and, showing superb middle pace, challenged the leader at the third bend, from which point it was as good as over.

Druids drew clear and won by almost three lengths from Longvalley Manor in 27.99sec.

HOVE Courage Olympic

WESTMEAD CHICK did not set the world on fire in the preliminary rounds of the Olympic over Hove's 515 metres but like so many Nick and Natalie Savva runners, she got it right when it mattered.

Local hope Roving Bunnie made a brave effort to make all the running but the writing was on the wall for John Rouse's bitch when Chick turned second and, displaying that tenacious middle-distance pace, swept past the Bunnie at the third bend. The Arc winner drew away off the last corner and beat Roving Bunnie by almost two lengths in 30.55sec. and thus landed the second of her four famous wins of 1994. Headleys Bridge ran on to take third while there was no luck for Pepsi Joe who, although beaten at the time, lost more ground when carried wide on the run-in and finished fifth.

MAY

HE lined up with the two fastest qualifying times to his credit, was the sole wide seed with an automatic trap six draw. No wonder that

Review of 1994

Ireland's Droopys Sandy was considered the proverbial good thing for the £20,000 **Regal Scottish Derby** over Shawfield's galloping 500 metres.

But not even the biggest optimist in the business could have predicted a performance such as the one Francie Murray's hound produced—and against a field which included the subsequent English Derby winner, Moral Standards.

It took little time for Droopys Sandy to sew things up, breaking quickly along with Sure Fantasy. The latter is no slouch but the Irish dog showed the better early pace, dived inside at the first bend and turned it into a procession. At the line Droopys Sandy had nine lengths to spare over the outsider, So I Heard.

A deafening silence descended as the vociferous Glaswegian crowd awaited the winning time. Had he broken the clock was the big question and the answer was an emphatic yes. In fact, Droopys Sandy smashed the record set four years ealier by Westmead Harry by an incredible 23 spots, recording 29.39 sec.

As for Moral Standards, he was in all kinds of trouble early and finished fifth, but the 'judges' at Shawfield that night were confident he would have finished higher but for those early setbacks. Afterwards, a leading odds-compiler said that Droopys Sandy would have been an automatic favourite for the English Derby but Wimbledon did not feature in Murray's plans.

Shawfield have announced that in 1995 the Scottish Derby trip will be over the shorter journey of 480 metres, 'to encourage a better class of entry,' said a track spokesman. Recent winners include Westmead Harry, Phantom Flash, New Level and, of course, Droopys Sandy. They don't come any classier than that, do they?

WALTHAMSTOW Mistley Trojan Puppy Stakes

THIS always attracts a quality field of youngsters. Locally-trained In The Zim was sent off a warm favourite for the final after completing his sixth consecutive victory in the penultimate round.

However, a mistimed start by Chris Duggan's dog meant he was always fighting a losing battle as Lacken Prince and Gamblers Sport made the best of their smart breaks. In The Zim showed tremendous early pace and attempted to force his way past the early leaders at the corner but there was nowhere to go and he was forced to check and lost ground again. Entering the back straight, Lacken Prince raced into a lead of some two lengths but back again came In The Zim and at the third it looked like he would pull his way to the front. But once again the door was slammed in his face and he had no alternative but to check again. Lacken Prince needed no second chance and he raced away to win by just under two lengths in a calculated 29.11sec. for the 475 metres.

Frank Wright trained the winner but a few days after the race the dog was purchased by Danny Dhamnia and went on to chase home Westmead Chick in the Midland Flat final at Hall Green.

Review of 1994

HOVE Regency

WITH two prestigious 'away' victories to her credit in the Ladbroke Golden Jacket final and the E Coomes Greenwich Cup, Hove fans were hoping Wexford Minx would produce more of the same in the £5,000 Regency decider at her home track in May.

Very much the darling of the Hove supporters, it looked as if their prayers had been answered when Wexford Minx, showing tremendous acceleration, raced clear of the pack on the dash to the first. But another buzz went up from stands as the heavily-backed favourite, Decoy Cougar, slipped into second just out of the first bend—and she was going ominously well.

There was crowding at the first bend which effectively handed the race on a plate to the front two but a local win looked a strong possibility when, at the fourth bend, Derek Knight's bitch shut out Decoy Cougar as she was about to challenge. But British-bred Decoy Cougar recovered well from the setback and stormed past Wexford Minx at the fifth bend and pulled away to win comfortably. Decoy Lynx, who made good progress after a rough early passage, almost made it a 1-2 for the late Trevor Cobbold.

JUNE

WOLF MAN landed the first of the season's championships for home-breds when running away with the **48th Two-Year-Old Produce Stakes** final over 460 metres at Bristol.

WEXFORD MINX: Hove upset.

Mica Pugh's Hall Green runner, the strongest finisher in the field, was expected to have to work hard from behind to win but he defied all when flying from the traps. It was a procession from there on with Wolf Man pulling clear with every stride to win by more than seven lengths from Super Dominee in 27.82sec, two spots inside Hencliffe Ben's track record.

The main rival to the winner, on paper at least, was See Jays Tiger, but he lost his chance when moving wide and into trouble on the run to the first bend. Indeed, apart from the first two home, there were excuses for them all for being beaten after Wolf Man's uncharacteristic fast start.

HOVE National Hurdles

LONG-STANDING Hove owner Jimmy Jupp could not hide his delight when Master Westlands landed the 515m National Hurdles.

Review of 1994

SMART victory: Ernie Gaskin Snr with Smart Decision, winner of Hall Green's Invitation Marathon.

Trained by Bill Masters, Master Westlands flew from the traps and, within a matter of strides, settled the issue. With trouble behind, he powered away to win by just over five lengths in 30.83sec. (.40sec. fast).

The victory emulated that of his sire, Lord Westlands, in the competition six years earlier and Jupp said: 'I was jumping up and down with excitement right through the race. I'm so proud of him.'

HALL GREEN Bookmakers Invitation Marathon

WHILE all the middle-distance stars in June were busy battling for Derby honours at Wimbledon, long-distance runners took centre stage over Hall Green's 815m.

Three of the protagonists had met in the same heat three days earlier and the wonderful consistency of greyhound racing was demonstrated once again when Ernie Gaskin's Smart Decision again came from behind Newry Town to land the spoils.

Candid Black made the early running, five lengths clear of Newry Town with Smart Decision in mid-division on the first circuit. Along the back straight for the final time, Newry Town and Smart Decision moved up strongly and the beaten TV Trophy favourite briefly hit the front at the seventh bend, just as he had in their mid-week encounter. But once again he had no answer to Smart Decislon's awesome strength and Gaskin's bitch ran right away for a six-lengths plus victory in 52.17sec.

WALTHAMSTOW Carling Black Label Test

REDWOOD GIRL, the Grand Prix winner over course and distance the previous October but who suffered a nasty leg injury early in

Review of 1994

1994, bounced back to her best at her home track. One of the three runners from Ernie Gaskin's yard, she recovered from a slow start to take up the running at the second bend and was never seriously challenged. Favourite Ballygown Lilly was first to show but the eventual winner's litter sister, Redwood Pippin, showed sizzling early pace and barged her way past Ballygown Lilly at the first bend, a move which gave Redwood Girl a glorious run through.

The family now looked to have it to themselves and by halfway it was the Grand Prix heroine who had bolted clear. As the race began to unfold, Danny Talbot's Ballygown Lilly gradually got back into the act and at one stage looked a threat to the leader.

Approaching the fifth bend she was very much in contention but was forced to check at the final turn, which gave Redwood Girl the opportunity she needed and, while Ballygown Lilly rallied going for home, Gaskin's runner held her by just under a length in 39.60sec.

HOVE   Brighton Belle

ANOTHER greyhound to emulate one of her parents by winning a Hove competition last year was the magnificent Westmead Chick who, after landing the Arc in March and the Olympic at Hove the following month, returned to the Sussex track for the £1,000 Brighton Belle in June.

Starting 7-4 ON for the final, Nick and Natalie Savva's outstanding bitch turned the race into a procession, going clear at the first turn and romping home three lengths ahead of Silver Low in 29.86sec., just 13 spots outside the 515 m track record held by the 1988 Derby winner, Hit The Lid.

Wexford Minx, beaten in the Regency final, was on the receiving end again, breaking slow and eventually finishing fourth.

Westmead Chick followed In the footsteps of her mother, Westmead Move, who won the Belle seven years earlier. Already the new Savva sensation had won three titles, but there was still more to come in 1994

JULY

THE owner/trainer team of Danny Dhamnia and John McGee were on the winner's rostrum again when Rabatino ran away with the Courage-sponsored **Scurry Gold Cup** over 385 metres. But as the lids went up, a convincing victory for Rabatino looked anything but likely as Ar Dream bolted out and was a length clear in a matter of strides.

However, such was the earlier speed Rabatino had showed, McGee's dog overhauled the Reading runner by the first turn and after that it was a procession.

Clear down the far side as the remainder bunched round the first two turns, Rabatino got home by a rapidly-diminishing length and three-quarter from Highway Leader, who at one stage was six lengths adrift of the winner after tangling with Rickys Mate at the

Review of 1994

first bend. Mike Bacon's runner, as game as ever, rallied magnificently but he had lost too much ground to get that close to the 23.57sec. winner after so much trouble speaks volumes for his ability.

ROMFORD Champion Stakes

THE early lead changed hands several times but there was never a serious doubt about the outcome, with Pat Ryan's Perry Barr raider, Heres Seanie, eventually obliging quite comfortably. Simply Free, the Select Stakes winner at Wembley the previous year, went on at the first bend but Mountain Wish took it up at the second.

That effort did not last long either for Heres Seanie, who gave his fans a fright with a very slow start, roared after them and took command at the third. He increased his lead, eventually winning by nearly five lengths from Simply Free in 35.22sec.

Silver Glow, who was badly crowded at the first bend, stuck to his guns and ran third while Wexford Minx, as she did in the Brighton Belle final behind Westmead Chick, placed fourth.

Wimbledon Wey Plastics Tony Stanton Memorial

TONY MEEK must have been wondering whether Greenane Squire would ever win a big race. The dog reached the Derby final in 1993 and the semi-final stage 12 months later yet still a major prize eluded him.

Run over the Derby trip of 480 metres and held four Saturdays after the Classic final, the memorial saw Greenane Squire a firm favourite to lose his maiden tag, despite the presence of Pearls Girl, Moaning Lad and Stylefield Law.

And this was to be his big night. Pearls Girl played a part in opening up the race for John Jefford and Jim Wenman's dog. The local broke fractionally in front but seemed to lose her footing and simultaneously impeded Moaning Lad as she stumbled. The incident enabled Greenane Squire to seize the initiative but he was quickly joined on the run to the bend by Philip Rees' local runner, Doreens Hope.

But taking a rails slot, Greenane Squire eased Doreens Hope aside at the bend and opened up a clear advantage turning into the back straight. Lengths clear, perhaps as many as four, Meek's runner looked home and hosed but favourite supporters had reckoned without the power finish of Stylefield Law, who closed ominously approaching the third bend.

Turning for home it looked like Greenane Squire would again. be denied a major victory but he got home by a neck in 28.62sec. With £6,000 in the kitty, the next target was the Dundalk International. That he never got there is now history, the dog dying shortly after arriving in Ireland. It was thought heat stress set off that tragic chain of events.

Review of 1994

JUST CHAMPION: Heres Seanie, a clear winner at Romford.

WALTHAMSTOW Tetley Yorkshire Bitter Circuit

THE withdrawal, lame, of Snow Flash took a bit of shine off the race but it nevertheless turned out to be a memorable decider with Connells Cross breaking the 475m track record on the Stow's new all-sand surface.

Back for another bite at a Walthamstow cherry was Paradise Slippy, the Arc runner-up here in March and later beaten in a £1,500 competition at the track, while Moynevilla Echo and Ticos Lodge completed the four-runner line-up.

As usual when there are depleted fields, the race went without incident, much to the surprise of favourite backers, who lumped on Moynevilla Echo. But he had no answer to the all-round speed of Connells Cross.

BELLE VUE Northern Flat

SUNDERLAND racegoers have few greater favourites than Gold Doon, Eddie Palmer's dog whose wins at the north-east circuit have been plentiful over the past two years. He seldom travelled away for the major competitions but Palmer's decision to enter him for the Northern Flat at Belle Vue paid off handsomely.

Pond Hamlet, his Sunderland trackmate, went off second favourite behind Drovers Road but both encountered crowding at the first bend while Gold Doon had flown the nest. Soon going clear and capitalising on that early congestion, Gold Doon comfortably held Pond Hamlet while Drovers Road stayed on for third.

Gold Doon clocked 28.02sec., a splendid effort from a grey-

Review of 1994

hound who was just three months short of his fourth birthday when landing this, the biggest success of a magnificent career.

AUGUST

HIGHWAY LEADER showed just how unlucky he had been in Catford's Scurry Gold Cup with a superb run through the **Q8 Peterborough Derby**. A fast-finishing second to Rabatino at Catford, Mike Bacon's dog was out to avenge that defeat and did so in no uncertain fashion.

Breaking the track record twice in the preliminaries, it was clear that Highway Leader was now at his peak and, in front of a packed Fengate stadium crowd, he once again demonstrated that, at his best, he rates among the top performers in the land.

Drawn none too well, in five for the £10,000 showdown, he looked to be in trouble when breaking only moderately behind Chadwell Charmer, who pinged the lids, Nice Melody and Witches Dean. But Nice Melody did Highway a big favour heading across to the rails and that gave Bacon's dog room to operate. Nipping clear of Nice Melody, he took control on the inside and a comfortable victory looked in prospect.

But you can never write off Witches Dean, who went in pursuit with the rest tailed off thanks to Nice Melody's dive to the inside. Down the back stretch he and Highway Leader raced nip and for one second it looked like Peter Rich's dog might just pinch it. But Highway Leader held Witches Dean to the line, winning by nearly two lengths in 25.47sec.

Bacon's dog had taken his revenge over Rabatino, who had no chance after that first-bend trouble, and was now setting his sights on the Edinburgh Cup at Powderhall.

GREAT, HARRY: Frank Bruno joins the party after Highway Leader's brilliant win.

Review of 1994

SHEFFIELD William Stones Silver Collar

TOUCH AGAIN, born and bred in Ireland but raced solely in England, proved a highly-popular local winner of the William Stones Silver Collar over 500 metres at Sheffield in August.

Trained by Harry Crapper, the son of Ravage Again appeared to have one main rival in the form of Alans Wonder but as that one struggled in mid-division, the local star ran home in splendid isolation in 29.83sec. Touch Again's performances at Sheffield are in total contrast to his 'away efforts' and Crapper explained: 'While Sheffield is a super track with long straights and easy bends, it's one of the worst to school a puppy on.

'It's too easy to run so when you take a dog away and run him elsewhere, more often than not he gets completely lost. Touch Again has never won a puppy open away from Sheffield but now he's in an all-aged final here and I reckon he's got a chance second to none.'

Prophetic words indeed.

WALTHAMSTOW A R Dennis Silver Collar

SILBURY CLOUD had the Walthamstow bookmakers rubbing their hands in glee after landing a shock 20-1 victory.

Soundly beaten in the two qualifying rounds, punters gave her little chance but she saved a very special effort for the big night and, 20-1 or not, the result was never in serious doubt.

Market fancies Simply Free and Gallys Lady lost their chance when failing to get away to their usual smart breaks. Not so Silvery Cloud. Ann Finch's runner got a flyer. Lyons Double came out of the pack at the third bend and looked dangerous and almost reached the leader by the fifth bend. But just as in the preliminaries, he could not find any extra going home, failing by just over a length behind the 39.80sec. winner.

HACKNEY Embassy Imperial Cup

ANN HAYWARD said she was in 'hysterics' after her Pretty Lively had floored the odds on Coolmona Road.

'We came here just for the giggle,' she beamed. 'We hoped he wouldn't be last but anything else was a bonus—how could we have possibly hoped to beat Coolmona Road?'

But beat him she did, the 12-1 shot pinging the lids and carrying himself clear of a first-bend melee which involved the 5-2 ON Coolmona Road. Although Pretty Lively tired on the run-in, she held on by over a length from Gallys Lady in 40.73sec. with Coolmona Road, who was later to be withdrawn off-colour from the St Leger, out of contention.

It was one of those nights for favourite backers and the final

Review of 1994

straw came when the 10-1 ON Smart Decision was well beaten in the 825 metres supporting marathon by Sunhill MIsty.

Oxford   Oxfordshire Gold Trophy

JUST for once Tony Meek drew a blank in a big-race final when Glenholm Tiger ran into all kinds of trouble.

Owned by Eddie Shotton, whose Mailcom company last year withdrew its sponsorship of the Northern Puppy Derby at Sunderland, the Tiger was in trouble on the run-up, again at the first bend and was in the wars at the third turn, eventually finishing fifth. But it did not detract from the smart victory by Freds Flyer, whose signalled the start of a splendid run on the open scene for Hove's Bill Masters.

Freds Flyer was also in trouble on the first corner but he rode it well, to beat Decoy Gold in a smart 27.29sec.

SEPTEMBER

CATFORD'S **John Humphreys Gold Collar** has produced some memorable finals down the years and the 1994 running was no exception, eventually going to the Oaks and Wey Plastics champion of 1993, Sam Sykes' magnificent bitch, Pearls Girl.

Brilliantly-fast starting was a feature of her performances in the earlier rounds and it was the same again in 555 metres final, worth, thanks to sponsor John Humphreys, £7,500 to the winner. Horribly drawn, or seemingly so in trap six, Pearls Girl got away to a flyer as the rest of the pack either bumped or crowded at the first corner.

The pile-up enabled Pearls Girl to build an unassailable lead and, to the roars of her army of supporters, she came home in fashion, although Decoy Cheetah had reduced the gap to an ever-diminishing neck at the line. But her time of 34.82sec. made the other returns on the night look pedestrian.

Champion Stakes wInner Heres Seanie ran third, Decoy Holly was fourth while Westmead Mystic ran fifth. And yet again there was no big-race luck for Paradise Slippy, Arthur Boyce's dog who ran second In the Arc in March and was now out to land a major victory on home soil.

Paradise Slippy had the best of the draw in trap one but suffered more than most at the first bend and was never at the races.

WEMBLEY   Foster's Select Stakes

MOANING LAD will long be remembered as one of the unluckiest greyhounds of 1994. Immensely talented, he often found himself in the wrong place at the wrong time.

Trainer Theo Mentzis was hopeful he would eventually break the ice in the Select Stakes over Wembley's 490m—but once again he was to be thwarted. This time it was Snow Flash who spoilt the

Review of 1994

UNLUCKY AGAIN: Moaning Lad had to give best to Snow Flash in the Fosters Select Stakes at Wembley.

party. Colin Dolby's dog, who won the Derby consolation race at Wimbledon in June, bolted from the traps and, on a rain-soaked track, was always a step ahead of the field.

Moaning Lad's ground-eating stride saw him move up ominously at the last bend but he could never quite get to Snow Flash, who beat him a length in 29.71sec., indicative of the poor underfoot conditions. The Blue Riband winner here in April, Ardilaun Brldge, was bumped at the first bend and finished fourth while Pearls Girl, who just two nights earlier won the Gold Collar at Catford was also bumped at the initial turn and finished fifth.

WIMBLEDON **Puppy Derby**

LOCAL trainer Terry Dartnall produced an amazing feat by sending out not only the wlnner, Bonmahon Darkie, but also the second and third, Droopys Joe and Deenside Dean.

At the break, it was Dartnall's thlrd string, Droopys Joe, who was first to show with Bonmahon Darkie boring across to the middle of the track from trap five into the back straight, Bonmahon Darkie closed ominously on his kennel mate and ranged up at halfway. Droopys Joe tried valiantly to keep him at bay but Darkie forced his way to the front at the third bend and came home just under two lengths to the good in 27.70sec.

POWDERHALL **Regal Edinburgh Cup**

A MODERATE break followed by crowding out of the traps would have been enough to dampen the enthusiasm of most greyhounds but not so Highway Leader. Mike Bacon's dog who, despite starting favourite, looked to have it all to do in the 465 Regal Edinburgh

Review of 1994

Cup final. But the game Highway Leader, brushing aside those early setbacks, threw himself into the lead at the first bend to end any thoughts of a shock result.

Seeing out the trip well, the Peterborough Derby winner scored by four lengths from Faultless Buddy in a smart 28.08sec. to put himself well in the running for the Greyhound of the Year Oscar.

After the race, Bacon revealed that Highway Leader had been treated for a shoulder injury. 'I think he did it when he cannoned into the hare trolley in the first round,' he said. 'But he's a very brave dog and I knew he'd come out of the first bend in front when he was with them going into it!'

ROMFORD   Essex Vase

LISA MY GIRL justified solid ante-post support when running away the £5,000 Essex Vase over Romford's 575m course, John Coleman's Walthamstow bitch beating Solva Flame by almost four lengths in 35.69sec.

Two outstanding wins in the first and second rounds followed by a missed break and defeat in the semi-finals but she made no such mistake when the money was down.

JOHN COLEMAN

Showing good early speed, she was impeded at the first bend as first Solva Flame and then Harrys Lion shared the donkey work up front.

Lisa My Girl avoided further trouble and came to take it up from Harrys Lion at the last bend. She won going away.

Solva Flame held on to second spot with Gortmore Express making good late progress into third. Pepsi Pete, from the John McGee/Danny Dhamnia partnership, came home last but there was some consolation when that fine bitch, Urgent Meeting, took a 400m supporting open in a speedy 24.12sec.

YARMOUTH   East Anglian Derby

FRANKS DOLL gave trainer Justin Scott an unforgettable thrill when winning the £10,000 East Anglian Derby final at a damp and

Review of 1994

miserable Yarmouth. Callahow Daly started a shade odds-on for them 462 metres showdown but he finished last of the five and was later reported 'very lame in the shoulder' by trainer Charlle Lister.

At the business end, Franks Doll had flown the boxes, outpaced Psycho City on the dash to the bend and was a good five lengths up on the chasing pack down the far side. Tornaroy Copper, who was forced to check at the first bend, came with a big finish but he was never going to catch Franks Doll, who ran the race of his life.

BELLE VUE   Fosters Cesarewitch

SANDOLLAR LOUIE, originally sent to trainer Kevin Connor to be schooled over hurdles, produced one of the big race shocks of the year when landing the Cesarewitch.

Going off a 10-1 chance, he showed ahead at the traps but Double Polano's superior early pace took him to the front at the second bend. He maintained the lead until moving off at the fifth where First Defence nipped through on the rails with what seemed a potentially race-winning challenge.

Sandollar Louie was always in close contention and loomed up rounding the couple of turns, his head in front again off the last. However, it is a long run-in at Belle Vue and with Decoy Lynx, in trouble early, finally extricating herself from the pack, she was eating up ground. But Sandollar Louie prevailed by a neck with First Defence thlrd to the 55.20sec. winner.

It was turnlng out to be quite a year for Connor, who in Aprll won the Grand Natlonal with Randy Savage. Perhaps that's why Rebecca Bowden, the owner of Sandollar Louie, sent him to Connor for hurdles schooling!

OCTOBER

HAVING fielded first, second and third in the Puppy Derby on his home patch, Terry Dartnall now switched his attentions to the **Ike Morris Laurels.** And while the incredible success of his runners in the youngsters showpiece would have been nigh impossible to repeat, Terry was more than happy to field just the winner, Deenside Dean.

Dartnall popularly has a low opinion of the Press and, while his attitude has perhaps made that feeling mutual, his record on the track speaks for itself. Most, however, felt that the Laurels was destined to be Moaning Lad's. Unlucky in the Derby final draw, and in the Stanton Memorial final draw, he had now been luckless with the draw in the Laurels final. But he had the pace if just, just for once, the gaps appeared.

Unfortunately for Theo Mentzis they did not. Deenside Dean, so pacey into the bend was soon in command and landed the event from Dancing Lance by four and a half lengths. It meant more Plough Lane success for Dartnall and had those at the track hoping

Review of 1994

JOHN MCGEE with his formidable 1994 line-up

that in his delight owner Roger Waters, formerly of Pink Floyd, would stage an impromptu comeback!

Testimony to Justright Melody's ability and reputation was that while though still a raw puppy, he started odds-on favourite to land Nottingham's Coldseal Classic final in August. His opposition had included Callahow Daly and Simply Free, a formidable duo. Still the bookies kept faith in youth, favouring Tom Robinson's runner. Callahow Daly triumphed, but among his own age group in the Richard McGuire Puppy Championship at Powderhall he was always likely to take the world of beating. And he did, winning from Cheeky Hero in the final to lift the £2,500 prize and justify substantial ante-post interest in the process.

HALL GREEN British Breeders' Forum Produce Stks

WESTMEAD MERLIN and Westmead Chick headed Nick and Natalie Savva's powerful assault and, while early betting favoured Chick, it was Merlin who landed the £10,000 prize.

The event, switched from Wembley following Madonna's untimely visit to the stadium, has now settled in Birmingham. Come final night the Savvas, too, were smiling, Westmead Merlin (28.33sec.) only four spots off what was then the 474m record when outgunning Sandford Star by five and a quarter lengths.

NOTTINGHAM Peter Derrick Eclipse

LIKE the Produce Stakes, the Eclipse has had a nomadic existence,

Review of 1994

BALLARUE MINX: Class all the way in the St Leger final.

originally contested at Coventry before switching to Nottingham in 1987. Then last year Westmead Merlin, fresh from Hall Green attempted an audacious and quick-fire double in the 500 metres four-bender. He was joined in the preliminaries by Chick. But it was the appearance of Moral Standards that brought most to Colwick Park for the first round.

The English Derby winner looked less than 100 per cent when taken across the water for the Irish version. And it showed. But a flying near track-record trial before the Eclipse proved he was back,

Or was he? Moral Standards made the semi-finals but was a shadow of his Wimbledon self and, following diagnosis of a stress fracture, was finished for the year. While that was disappointing, the Eclipse final went some way to compensate. Credit, once more, goes to sponsor Peter Derrick.

Jimmy Gibson's Coalbrook Star (Charlesworth Stayers Stakes), Tony Meek's On The Bounce (Keith Tomlin Puppy Cup) and Linda Jones' Fernhill Tiger (Bill Bright Sprint) were the supporting stars on a night of four major finals. And the fourth? Well the Westmeads had it sewn up, did they not? The betting certainly favoured them.

In the ring, it was 5-4 Westmead Chick, 5-2 Westmead Merlin, 4-1 Sure Fantasy, and the rest nowhere. But from the lids it was Spit It Out who broke clear andwas still clear by five as the remainder crowded. Joy for Mick Bacon and joy for his owner, the enthusiastic Stuart Southgate.

'In Ireland, he was a world beater,' Southgate said. 'But he had problem after problem whe: first over here, and he rally just took

Review of 1994

time to settle.' But Spit It Out scored from Westmeads Chick and Merlin, in 29.80sec.

SUNDERLAND Dransfield Northern Puppy Derby

A FEW HUNDRED miles north of Nottingham, TV's newest double act, Harry Findlay and Barry Silkman were proving that greyhound racing still has television appeal, producing as good a job off the track for Sky TV as Justright Melody did on the track to win the Dransfield Northern Puppy Derby.

WEMBLEY   Wendy Fair St Leger

THE LEGER was packing them in, with ante-post favourite Coolmona Road taking time to come to the boil. Beaten in the first two rounds as Redwood Girl, Browside Pat, Flashing Support and Liberal Idea took the early plaudits, Derek Knight's runner produced the goods in the semis.

So too, though, did Clongeel Fern. It is not often Catford fields a Classic finalist but in the Ray Peacock-trained runner— a fastest-of-the-event 39.58sec. semi-final winner—south London had an opportunity to redress the balance. Clongeel Fern's chance was enhanced when Coolmona Road failed to make the final. Knight reported that he was struggling with a bug at his kennels. A number were already showing symptoms but he crossed his fingers that Coolmona Road missed it. He did not. On the morning of the race the son of Ardfert Sean was struck down and pulled out.

Clongeel Fern started 2-1 favourite, while Twin Rainbow, sister of Moral Standards, was out to strike where her brother, seemingly a Leger natural until his injury, was unable to. Ballarue Minx was left to fly the Hove flag in the absence of Coolmona Road.

In the end, it was the last-gasp effort of Bill Masters' bitch, backed down to 7-2, that landed the £10,000 spoils. Here was no flash-in-the-pan St Leger winner — Ballarue Minx was from the top drawer. However, subsequent events were to cloud the remainder of the year for John McGee and his leading owner Danny Dhamnia but, free to run Lemon Rob in the Guineas final at Hackney after a successful (albeit temporary) high court injunction against his NGRC ban, consolation awaited as the 6-1 chance ran away with the Hackney competition.

On to Wimbledon and an event rejuvenated following the arrival of a new sponsor, commission agents Larrys Racing Services of Couldon. Their backing of the Puppy Oaks, with a new format and increased prizemoney, attracted a high class field of puppy bitches, including the much-touted Irish entry Droopys Fergie. And Sean Dunphy's bitch looked to have the race at her mercy after waltzing through the event, her best time of 27.52sec. in the semis by far the quickest. She started 1-5. But it's a funny old game . . . up popped Charlie Savoury's Stay Going (33-1) to steal the limelight.

Review of 1994

CHICK FANS: Westmead Chick with owner Bob Morton's sons (from left) Edward, Andrew, Robert and Charlie, with kennelhand Bob Hannan after the Oaks win at Wimbledon.

NOVEMBER / DECEMBER

WHILE Witton Star (Harry Holmes Memorial— Sheffield) and Sodas Slippy (Manchester Puppy Cup— Belle Vue) were grabbing the headlines in the north, Nottingham-based John Wileman headed south, to Catford, with a bitch who was to make her British debut in the **William Hill First For Services Stayers Stakes**.

Last Action was her name and those who backed her at 10-1 ante-post were laughing all the way to the bank as the bitch, who was to top her class by the end of the year, justified favouritism in the final. Even now, her heat win from way of the pace— and after trouble— has to be seen to be believed.

HALL GREEN Foster Midland Flat

TWO DAYS later, the culmination of some fine action at Hall Green saw the Westmeads bid to plunder more glory at the Birmingham. But this time it was Westmead Chick who outgunned Westmead Merlin and company to strike it lucky in the Midland Flat final. The

Review of 1994

race had seen the track record, held by Faultless Mouse fall by the wayside as Westmead Chick produced one the great runs of the year, a flying 28.20sec in the semis. It would take something special to halt the Savva bitch, although Lacken Prince ran with credit in the final to finish seond

BROUGH PARK
All-England Cup

1994, the Derby-winning antics of Moral Standards aside, belonged largely to the Westmeads and greyhound racing's answer to Billy The Kid and Pat Garrett were ready to shoot their rivals down once more, Westmead Merlin looking to plunder the All England Cup at Brough Park and Westmead Chick the Oaks at Wimbledon.

LACKEN PRINCE: second

The All England Cup final was a cracker. Westmead Merlin started 4-6 favourite but with crack youngster Justright Melody, Derby finalist Callahow Daly and the Jim Morris-Jim Gibson-backed Moral Director in the field, it would take some winning and Moral Director led the way home to thwart the favourite.

WIMBLEDON   St Mary's Hospital Oaks

CONSOLATION for the Savvas was to come at Wimbledon where Chick headed the bookmakers' lists from the off.

And while that is not to detract from a field which included the likes of Droopys Fergie, Twin Rainbow and Coomlogane Euro, her runaway win in the Oaks final was awesome.

Ostensibly, the year concluded with the ever-popular Boxing Day Marathon at Catford. They hung for the rafters at the south London track and the traditional yuletide showpiece. And with Wexford Minx edging out Ballarue Minx and Senlac Rose, the first salvos for the coming year— destined to be a vintage one for the stayers— had been fired.

● *Open Race winners and 1994 statistics, page 109.*

SEVEN To Follow

Can you spot a potential winner in the crowd? **JONATHAN KAY** is our man with the binoculars and the crystal ball as he forecasts the track's likely Stars of '95.

My Magnificent Seven

This forecasting game is never easy. And everyone has his own opinion. But there are clues to be spotted in the quest to get ahead of the game. And, after careful consideration and whittling down of an initial list of candidates, here are my seven hopefuls for 1995.

ARDCOLLUM FLASH *(bk d Phantom Flash-Seventh Dynamic Oct92)*

THIS dog has the potential to dominate the sprinting scene this year. Trained by Patsy Byrne, he first came to prominence at Nottingham in December with an eye-catching run behind Longvalley Manor. His next run was disappointing but he showed

SEVEN To Follow

that form to be all wrong with an impressive win at Hove's first Sunday meeting in January when slamming a useful field which included the classy Fast Copper.

Another win at Hove, plus one at Wimbledon followed and there seems no reason why he should not continue to pick up similar races with monotonous regularity.

He will probably be kept to sprinting for the time being but, come the warmer weather in summer, he should find a sharp four bends such as Catford or Romford well within his compass.

AUTUMN TIGER (be bd d Coalbrook Tiger-Queenies Fire May93)

RARELY has such a young dog left the impression that this fellow did when winning at Sheffield in December. Sue Cliff's dog was out with the washing early on but produced a storming finish to get up close home over four bends and he was a mile clear at the drop.

Stepped up to six bends next time at Monmore, he scrambled home by a short-head but was more impressive subsequently back at Sheffield when beating a field that included Aglish Blaze and TV Trophy heroine Jubilee Rebecca.

He has a handy combination of early pace and stamina and, with a litter sister already having won over eight bends, it is not beyond the realms of possibility that he will stay futher himself in time.

DECOY COUGAR (bk b Slaneyside Hare-Easy Bimbo Jly92)

WINNER of last year's Regency at Hove, Pam Cobbold's bitch could prove to be a major force in eight-bend races this time around.

Seasonal rest ruled her out of the big events in summer and autumn last year but she really found her feet round Christmas time, winning a Romford competition and then posting a flying calculated time for 820m at Walthamstow.

The more she races over marathon trips, the stronger she will get and, unlike many around on the eight-bend scene at the moment, she has decent early pace and can dominate from the front.

That can be a potent weapon as the slower starters tend to find all the trouble going and, nature permitting, Decoy Cougar should be a major player in the TV Trophy and Cesarewitch.

MISSION TRIO (w f d April Trio-Powerhouse Jewel Jly93)

DAVID PRUHS has had some good dogs through his hands over the years so when he says this one could be better than any of them, you should really sit up and take notice. His early form does

SEVEN To Follow

CHARLIE LISTER: Recently took charge of Suncrest Sail, who looks one to watch in six-benders this year.

not amount to an awful lot but it was the manner of a debut Nottingham win that had the purists purring as he left any amount on the track but still came through to take the spoils.

He followed up in style on a slow track at Reading, not leading until the final bend but pulling six lengths clear of a field that included useful juvenile On The Bounce.

The one nagging doubt about the dog with regards to Classic

SEVEN To Follow

pretentions is a possible failing in the early pace department but there is no doubting his overall ability.

SEANS DEPOSIT *(w bk d Murlens Hawk-Night Angel Jne93)*

EVERY list of greyhounds to follow should have an unknown quantity and this is it. At the time of writing, Ernie Gaskin's dog has had just three graded runs at Walthamstow and has won the lot, progressing to a smart 28.97sec. (calc) in the last of them.

His best line of form in Ireland was a half length second behind a 29.38sec. Cork winner and he has continued to go the right way over here.

He has fair early pace, certainly enough to keep him out of trouble, but it is along the back straight that he really opens up. Walthamstow is as good a grade as you will find anywhere in the country and this dog really could be anything.

STAPLERS JO *(w bk d Dempsey Duke-Perfect Rhythm Jne93)*

NICK SAVVA'S dog needs to learn to trap. If he does, he could go to the very, very top. His pace once his feet hit the ground has to be seen to be believed.

But it is one thing giving fellow pups a couple of lengths start from the boxes and still beating them to the bend. It will be altogether harder against the top all-aged company.

That said, trapping is an art than can be learnt and this is a dog that will not be led to the bend if coming away level. He is that fast.

It is true that he was coming back to his field over 500m at Nottingham, and again when winning over 475m at Walthamstow. But I'd rather have a dog out in front and there to be shot at than one who needs luck to pick his way through the field.

SUNCREST SAIL *(be bd d Low Sail-Sarahs Surprise Aug92)*

LOOKED set for the top last year only for lameness to force him out of the Grand Prix semi-finals at Walthamstow when one of the leading fancies Has recently joined Charlie Lister and is likely to be placed to win plenty of six-bend opens.

Has good early pace for a stayer, as shown by a number of flying trials over 474m at Hall Green where he has clocked times faster than many opens over the trip are won in.

But he stays well too and it is not inconceivable that he might actually get a marathon trip if connections fancy trying it.

In the meantime, he is definitely one to keep on the right side when running in six-bend company where his pace should see him able to dominate from the outset.

The Year in POLITICS

Year the sport's image was on the line

Mike Palmer sees hope amid the accusations that tarnished greyhound racing's reputation.

THERE were some magnificent performances on the track in 1994 but it will go down as a year when greyhound racing was, on more than one occasion, dragged through the mill. There was plenty of controversy too, not least the ban imposed by the NGRC which saw the sport's champion trainer sidelined for seven months at the end of last year.

John McGee was stood down after a prohibited substance was discovered in his Peterborough Derby finalist, Rabatino, last August. McGee took it to the High Court and the stewards were relieved to find their actions were upheld.

Drugs were very much at the centre of three media features covering, as ever, the so-called seedy side of greyhound racing. The most damaging was BBC2's *On The Line* in January.

Film of live kills, dilapidated conditions in Spanish kennels and an interview with a former NGRC trainer who claimed he could come by any drug imaginable simply by picking up the telephone, were the main themes.

That *On The Line* did untold damage to greyhound racing is undeniable, that the sport spent the rest of the year trying to recover from that is equally undeniable.

A scathing attack on the sport in a Sunday tabloid, though it bordered on the world of fantasy, nevertheless did nothing for our image and neither did the *London Programme*, where allegations of doping and race-fixing at Hackney were also made.

Those allegations centred around John McGee and his leading

REDMAN MEDICAL

Sales, rentals & repairs
for injury problems
with your dog

**ULTRASOUND, MAGNETIC FIELD THERAPY,
INJURY POINT
LOCATOR, GEL, MUSCLE TONER,
MAGNETO BLANKET, LASER,
INTERFERENTIAL**

**SECOND HAND EQUIPMENT BOUGHT
AND SOLD**

**YOU'VE TRIED THE REST
NOW TRY THE BEST!**

High quality, unbelievable
prices, all goods with
warranty

WE TAKE ACCESS AND ADVICE IS FREE

**FOR MORE
INFORMATION
PLEASE PHONE
01527 878536**

The Year in POLITICS

owner, Danny Dhamnia. All have been denied but to this day McGee believes the programme helped to influence the stewards and their action over the Rabatino affair. Regrettably the media, television especially, has a fetish about greyhound racing. it more often than not sensationalises what it feels are the shady areas of the sport, and appears to derive immense satisfaction in doing so.

One day there will be a programme showing the world what it is really like, a business for some, a hobby for others but, at the end of the day, an industry bursting to the seams with enthusiastic owners and dedicated kennel staff.

They do not do it for the money, there is very little of it in greyhound racing in this country, but because of their sheer love of the sport and the greyhound breed.

It is this kind of message that Geoffrey Thomas , the new man in charge of the British Greyhound Racing Board, will be seeking to get across to the public. Greyhound racing is fun, exciting and a darn sight more respectable than dozens of other sports I could name.

While there is a new chief at the BGRB, there is also a new senior steward at the NGRC, Bill Cook. An owner, once a home-finder, he has seen most sides of the sport and took with him to Camden Town a refreshing new approach .

If he lives up to early form he will prove a worthy successor to Alan Fearn, who retired at the end of the year (see page 300).

He might make one of his priorities solid guidelines on the drugs and food chain issue. In June, trainers' association chairman, Paddy Milligan made a breakthrough when the NGRC stated, in so many words, that trainers whose greyhounds were found to contain traces of residue drugs through the food chain would be treated more sympathetically.

> *One day a programme will show what the sport is really like — a business bursting with enthusiastic owners and dedicated kennel staff*

There was an outcry in November when the NGRC fined trainer Mal Thomas £500 for withdrawing two runners from a Reading meeting in August. In his opinion, the going was unsatisfactory and, acting in the interests of their welfare decided his dogs would not run.

There was an enormous amount of public sympathy for Thomas and the issue raised once again the subject of track surfaces and their safety or otherwise. We will doubtless be hearing a lot more about this in 1995.

After a failed attempt to form an advisory committee, a second attempt promises to deliver. The seven-man committee represents all sides of greyhound life, from promoters to owners, a trainer, a

The Year in POLITICS

vet, an NGRC steward and a chief racing manager.

This working party will strive to come up with a blueprint for safer surfaces but, at the end of the day, the answer to the problem is proper maintenance. It is pointless if the committee make ' recommendations that are soon forgotten.

Greyhound racing is coming under closer inspection from animal welfare groups. and it is of paramount importance that we get our act together— and keep it together!

'We should make no mistake,' says Geoffrey Thomas. 'Any sport or any commercial activity involving animals will 'increasingly come under the welfare microscope. The attitude to animals in our society is changing and greyhound racing must be prepared to change with it.'

Thomas, in his new role as British Greyhound Racing Board executive director, will have plenty to keep him occupied this year as the BGRB takes on the responsibility, among other things, of industry commercial matters.

It covers a large area, from promoting greyhound racing, to playing its part in securing a levy from off-course bookmakers— which Thomas confidently expects will happen—and to successfully launch the exciting new prospect of track-to-track betting.

A track-to-track 'committee' has been formed which will accustom people to the principal and technology of this new phenomenon, which next year could see the first £1 million jackpot.

'Yes, our aim is a £1m. jackpot but I don't think it will happen this year,' says Thomas. 'But this part of the deregulation package I believe will fundamentally change the face of an evening's greyhound racing. It will give the sport two major advantages. Firstly it will add to the product for soon people will not just go to a track and watch 12 races. Instead, they will have the opportunity of seeing, hearing and betting on races beamed from other tracks.

'Just imagine, if 30 tracks race on a Saturday night and punters at those tracks can invest in one big jackpot pool, the sky's the limit. The returns could, and probably will, be astronomical.

'If you have a sizeable bet at present on the tote you are, in effect, buying your own money. But all this will change with track-to-track betting, pools will be so strong.

'But we must be very careful not to make our jackpot pool like the National Lottery. To be guaranteed of winning that, you need to buy 14 million tickets. This will not be the case in greyhound racing, our jackpots will be far less difficult to scoop.'

There could be more than 30 tracks racing on Saturday nights In future for with new venues opening at Harlow and Sittingbourne — better late than never Sittingbourne — there will be more and more opportunities for everyone, owners, trainers and, last but by no means least, the people who keep this great sport of ours going, the racegoers.

Hopefully by the time you read this, the track at Sittingbourne will be up and running, and what a track it looks. A superb gallop

The Year in POLITICS

with first-class facilities, once the financial side has been sorted that is, Sittingbourne could prove to be one of greyhound racing's success stories.

And so too could Harlow, a smaller circuit but one which former trainer Toni Nicholls has designed and has designed and built virtually with his own hands. Toni spent seven years looking for a site to fulfil his lifetime ambition, a track of his own.

The man's enthusiasm is amazing and with this kind of dedication at the top, Harlow can only go one way. Quite what kind of affect it will have on nearby Rye House remains to be seen but I never did hear yet of competition doing any harm.

And what of the much talked about new track at Basildon? If It gets off the ground, and I've been given no reason to believe it will do otherwise, then it too could be a super stadium. The plans are impressive to say the least but it is some way behind Sittingbourne and Harlow in terms of reality.

There has been considerable talk of a regular television spot for greyhound racing, with Sky the probable favourites to secure contract to broadcast live some of our major meetings.

The stumbling block appears to be finance, Sky has been reported to want £10,000 for every broadcast to cover production costs. It is an awful lot of money but must be weighed against the virtues of national exposure on a weekly basis.

I am not so sure the industry can afford, indeed should afford £500,000 a year to cover televislon costs. If the exposure generates advertising and sponsorship, then a few promoters might disagree with me but, while I'm a firm believer in the old adage that you must speculate to accumulate, I am not convinced that speculation would be superseded by accumulation. But that is one for Geoffrey Thomas and his colleagues to think about.

A lot of thought has gone into the first exciting breakthrough in greyhound racing this year, the introduction of Sunday racing. Several tracks began earlier than expected on January 8, including Hove, where the initial Sabbath card was an unqualified success.

Peterborough did well, too, while cheeky Mildenhall stole some of the media glamour with the first-ever Sunday greyhound race with betting — at one minute past midnight on Sunday morning!

My view is that Sunday racing is here to stay but promoters do not need me to tell them that they must continue to work hard at it. Keeping the customer satisfied is the hardest part of greyhound racing but early signs indicate they are extremely satisfied.

Mention of Hove earlier reminds me that it lost its most famous son in 1994, the magnificent Ballyregan Bob. The old dog laid down and died at the age of ten and with him died a legend.

Forget television coverage, or any other kind of media exposure, what Ballyregan Bob did for greyhound racIng in the 1980s is unlikely to be equalled, let alone surpassed. He was a magnificent hound. He left us with many magnificent memories.

Trainer PROFILE

The Nick Savva Story

By Mike Palmer of the Racing Post

HARD though it is to imagine, when Nick Savva packed his bags and left his beloved Cyprus for Britain more than 40 years ago, he didn't know one end of a greyhound from the other. Now however, thanks to the total dedication of his wife Natalie, who actually holds the training licence, the name of Savva is synonymous with all that is good in greyhound racing in this country.

As breeders of greyhounds with the Westmead prefix, they have established themselves as one of the most successful breeding and training partnerships the sport has ever known and the success shows no sign of decline.

The Irish say they breed the best and fastest greyhounds in the world but there are many who would challenge that claim for the Savvas seem to have a never-ending production line of home-bred champions.

But it all looked so different back in 1951 when Nick, then a young man, set off in search of fame and fortune in London. Labouring in an engineering factory for £2.50 a week was the starting point.

Simply the best: from hired hand to master of an empire of greyhound racing champions

"To say I did the donkey work there is an understatement," recalls Nick in that charming Anglo-Cypriot tongue of his. He didn't stay there too long and soon after doubled his wage when working in a kitchen for a fiver a week.

"Then I got a job as a waiter in a restaurant and that was when the money started to come in, at least a lot more compared with what I was earning before," he says. "Working in the restaurant

GLITTERING PRIZES: It has been that sort of year for Nick Savva.

allowed me to have a drink and a smoke and also have a bit of money for a bet on the dogs."

And that's where the Savva success story was born for, in 1952, he took an interest in greyhounds which was to lead him to the pinnacle of the greyhound training profession and also recognition as the country's most knowledgeable spokesman on track surfaces.

"Yes, I followed the dogs from then on and spent most of my time at Harringay, which still has to rate as one of my favourite tracks. Shame isn't it, they always seem to close down the best

NGRC Greyhound Racing Yearbook 1995

Trainer PROFILE

DARLING OF THEM ALL: The brilliant Westmead Chick

tracks," he lamented. "As purely a racing fan, I saw some great dogs in the Fifties, like Pigalle Wonder, Clonalvy Pride and Galtree Cleo. I'm lucky to say that I've seen the best ever since then and still love my racing today as much as I did all those years ago.

But Young Savva the punter wanted more out of greyhound life, though any attempt, as he puts it, "to get closer to the dogs" was a virtual impossibility.

"I wanted to get a job as a kennel hand but it was a closed shop in those days, while trying to get a position in the GRA's training establishment at Northaw was more difficult than getting into Fort Knox!"

With the experience of that disappointment, Nick made a vow to himself. He became involved in the dressmaking industry, determined to make enough money "to get out of London one day" and start his own kennels. "I started as a presser in a dressmaking firm

Trainer PROFILE

ARC LEADING LIGHTS: Savva and winner Westmead Chick

and then took a chance and started my own workshop. Before I started the workshop, I was earning decent money but never really had any in my pocket, so that gave me an extra incentive to be my own boss and make good."

He made good too in 1957 when he met Natalie in London and they were married five years later. Meanwhile, the workshop was flourishing and, when Savva was satisfied he could sell the business for enough money to keep him comfortably for the rest of his life, he bought the kennels.

"Ever since the day I went into greyhound racing, I have continued to plough money back into the kennels and it has paid off. I have what I consider perfect rearing and training facilities here at Dunstable. But don't run away with the idea that running a greyhound kennel is a doddle.

"It's far from it" he continued. "Natalie and I work 12 hours a

Trainer PROFILE

day and longer when we're out racing. Sure, we're devoted to greyhounds and have enjoyed a lot of success, but an awful lot of it depends on luck, and we've had plenty of that too. Mind you, in this game you're entitled to a little bit of good fortune from time to time, it makes up for some of the heartaches it brings."

One of those heartaches was the broken hock suffered by Westmead County when he had the 1972 St Leger final at his mercy. He hobbled home on three legs as Ramdeen Stuart came through to snatch a rather fortunate victory.

But, six years later, in the same race at Wembley, it was a different story entirely, when Westmead Power, an odds-on chance, came storming through to land the prize, sponsored in those days by Ladbrokes.

In 1986, the magnificent Westmead Move—as effective these days as a brood bitch—followed her Catford Gold Collar success with victory in the Grand Prix at Walthamstow while Westmead Power, the year before he won the Leger, also took the Catford Classic.

Westmead Harry and Special Account won Scottish Derbys for the Savvas, Balligari, the Laurels, and scores of other outstanding home-bred champions won a multitude of other events, far too many to mention here.

> *I now have the perfect set-up. But don't get the idea that training is a doddle—far from it!*

Last year though, we saw probably the best greyhound ever to come out of the Savva camp, the remarkable Westmead Chick. Wins in the Racing Post Arc at Walthamstow, the Olympic at Hove and the Midland Flat at Hall Green stamped her as one of the greatest bitches of all time, probably the best since the halcyon days of Dolores Rocket.

Indeed, her brilliant victory in the Oaks as Wimbledon makes her comparable with the best there has ever been. Not only is she an incredible racetrack performer, her potential in the breeding paddocks is beyond belief. The bloodlines are quite simply the best and each generation seems to improve.

So, is Westmead Chick the best the Savvas have ever had? "I don't really know, there have been so many good ones it's difficult to make comparisons," says Nick. "Mind you, I think she is very, very good."

The Savvas favourite tracks are pretty easy to predict if, that is, you follow the fortunes of the husband and wife team. "I like big, galloping tracks, the type where a greyhound has every chance to run to his best form, tracks like Hove, Shawfield, Nottingham and Swindon.

"Wembley would also be one of my favourites but for the fact

Trainer PROFILE

MAGIC MOMENT: Westmead Merlin with Savva and proud owners Ian and Glenda Broom

that the straights there are narrow these days and the bends unbanked. Nevertheless, it's not a bad circuit by any manner of means."

Considering the success the Savvas have achieved, you could be forgiven for thinking they would encourage newcomers to the sport into the world of training greyhounds, but not Nick.

"If they just wanted to keep a couple of greyhounds for fun then fine, I'd wish them all the best. But to set up commercial kennels in this country these days would be a nightmare; it would cost a fortune. money you'd have little chance of recovering," he said.

"Training greyhounds as a profession is a very hard way to make a living, in fact some trainers have found it impossible to make it pay. I was very lucky when I sold my dressmaking company, I had a cushion; something to rely upon come a rainy day."

"The system in this country is all wrong and things are very difficult to change here. Owners and trainers in England are expected

NGRC Greyhound Racing Yearbook 1995

Trainer PROFILE

to provide greyhounds to tracks for the love of it, I ask you, how can this be right? In truth, training greyhounds here should be a hobby."

As for the NGRC rules, Nick, like many others in the business, is sometimes confused. "There's been so much said about the rules that they don't make sense any more. And I find it particularly unsatisfactory that a trainer is ultimately responsible for the care of every greyhound in his kennel at all times.

"It's okay for me and Natalie, we have a comparatively small kennel and if one of our dogs was ever interfered with, then I would only have myself to blame. I would have employed the culprit and therefore I would be considered a bad judge.

"But you have to sympathise with those trainers with a large kennel, where turnover of staff is frequent. It is impossible for them to keep check on everything 24 hours a day, and the rule should be looked at by the NGRC."

Savva, along with the rest of us, is well aware that greyhound racing in Britain could be in a far healthier state.

The salvation of the sport is in the hands of a tote monopoly, with tracks ploughing profits into prize money

"A lot could be done to improve the situation, like a levy from off-course bookmakers. That, after all, seems only fair. But the salvation of the sport as we know it would be a tote monopoly.

"Let's do away with the bookmakers and have tote betting only, just as they do in America and Australia.

"Comparatively speaking, greyhound racing is thriving in those countries and the reason is that tracks plough back into prize money the profits from the tote."

"It generates first class prize money, better facilities, both for the greyhounds and the customers and consequently it is a far superior product."

Nick and Natalie have two daughters, Lisa and Nicola. "They showed an interest in the dogs when they were children but as they grew up gradually lost interest.

"Now it's down to my staff and especially Natalie, without whose tremendous support, well, you wouldn't have heard of me.

"I shall keep going in greyhound racing for as long as I can and, do you know, I enjoy winning a low grade race just as much as I do a major competition. I just love the game."

The Savva story will be the envy of any aspiring young owner or trainer. As for me—I'm about to enrol at dressmaking college! ●

K9 PRODUCTS

STRIDE
The nutrient for finishing power

Proven to allow greyhounds maintain maximum speeds for extended distances

BOOST
The second wind for greyhounds

High quality Vitamin B tonic also containing Lysine to allow more oxygen to get to active muscles

RESTORE
The solution to dehydration

Multi electrolyte and vitamin supplement to prevent dehydration

KLEAR
The power to heal

Sulphur rich solution which acts rapidly on cuts and quicks

JOINT LUBE
The natural lubricant for joints

Helps to prevent toe injuries. Lubricates sore joints, especially for arthritic dogs or those with bad wrists or toes.

THE BEST VALUE IN QUALITY SUPPLEMENTS

For information contact:
(0582) 457742, (081) 527 7278, (0429) 221809
(0698) 359241 or K Flex Ltd, 17 Balally Park, Dundrum, Dublin 16. Tel (101 353-1) 295 4630

BE FIRST PAST THE POST...

with these great Greyhound Racing book and video offers...

Books

Veterinary Advice for Greyhound Owners
£14.99 (plus £2.50 post and packing)
Practical, easy-to-follow advice from **JOHN KOHNKE**, the vet who is Greyhound racing's leading columnist dealing with greyhound ailments. Covers everything from the treatment and prevention of injuries to vital information on nutrition.

1994 Greyhound Stud Book
£20 (plus £2.50 post and packing)
The breeder's bible

George Curtis: Training Greyhounds
£17.50 (plus £2.50 post and packing)
Secrets of the maestro. The essential, classic guide for all those with an interest in Greyhounds. It chronicles the training methods of the great George Curtis, who came from the slums of pre-war Portsmouth to become Britain's leading trainer.

The Complete Book of Greyhounds
£17.50 (plus £2.50 post and packing)
Edited by **Julia Barnes** and written by the world's TOP experts on every facet of the breed.
JOHN KOHNKE on **PHYSIOLOGY, FEEDING** and **NUTRITION; NICK SAVVA** on **BREEDING** and **REARING; MALCOLM WILLIS** on **GENETICS; PATRICK SAWARD** on **BLOODLINES; GEOFF DE MULDER, LINDA MULLINS** and **MICHAEL O'SULLIVAN** compare **TRAINING** methods with leading American and Australian handlers

Videos

GREAT RACES OF 1994 (£19.99)
The video of the year – a must
1994 GREYHOUND DERBY (£19.99)
Every race from the premier classic
Training Greyhounds with George Curtis (£19.99)
Unique insights into his methods

Order the Curtis book and video together for £27.49 – SAVE £10!

To order, send a cheque or money order to:
Ringpress Books, PO Box 8, Lydney, Glos., GL15 6YD
Access/Visa orders phone **0594 563800**. Prices are UK only. Eire add £2 per item.

Irish PROFILE

Byrne's unit is working overtime

They live in Stepaside. But they don't do that too often. **JOHN MARTIN**, of the Irish Independent, reports on a prolific greyhound racing dynasty.

SHELBOURNE Park. Traps open. An orange blur. Trap five leads the pack into the first bend and stretches away off the second turn. The bare form figures of the Glasskenny runner had made very little appeal. Yet, Dermot Byrne had said not to leave her out.

These days, in Dublin, you leave a runner with the Glasskenny prefix out at your peril. There are not many or them. The family kennel never houses more than six inmates. Often, on the breading side, they do not jump off the programme at you and demand support. Yet, they win. Time and again. The strike-rate is phenomenal. You have to ask why.

The late Harry Allen was the doyen of local greyhound correspondents. Just like his son Michael does today, Harry filed the Dublin returns to the Irish newspapers. He know his stuff, did Harry. As owner, trainer, punter; Harry knew the game inside out. And Harry once said that there was no point in bringing a dog to Dublin, or anywhere else for that matter, if it was not fed properly.

Perhaps that's the reason! The actual licence holder in the Byrne family from Stepaside, a village at the foot of the mountains outside Dublin, is largely irrelevant. Father Mick, sons Dermot and Tony—they have all held it at some time or other. It just so happens that Tony is taking the plaudits at the moment.

Only Ken (26), a budding musician, of Mick's four sons does not have an active interest in the longtails. And Ken, too, is alone in not being accomplished— indeed qualified— in the culinary arts. Dermot (40), Colin (37) and Tony (35) are all chefs by trade.

In this respect, Tony is the most high profile in that he dons his white hat in the canteen of RTE, the national television network. While Tony feeds the TV stars by day, father Mick, a sprightly 70

NGRC Greyhound Racing Yearbook 1995   57

Irish PROFILE

years old, oversees the round-the-clock diet of the canine stars. Retired after 46 years as a laboratory technician in the Veterinary College, Mick has a crucial role in all of this.

The Byrnes have Harry Allen's basics right. The dogs are fed well. None are fed better. When it comes to sporting animals, it is not always easy to say why one person has an edge over another. Short Interviews ram 29.40 for Cork's 525 yards at 14 months and was one of the first winners of the Sporting Life Juvenile Championship for Tommy Johnstone at Wembley.

It was Mick Byrne who diagnosed Short Interview as a 'chronic creeper' and had the know-all and the cure to keep him going, He had that great indefinable—the knack.

> 'When Tony said we should buy a £70 dog for £180, I thought he was gone off his head'

Mick Byrne also built his reputation on spotting relatively inexpensive greyhounds and turning over an instant profit. In 1981, Thanks Kev was purchased for £1,400 and immediately beat the much-vaunted Millbowe Sam to win the £5,000 Bookmakers Stake, recording 29.24sec. for the 525 yards at Shelbourne Park.

It is only in more recent years that the Byrne family have concentrated on training, rather than merely being middlemen in the business of shrewd purchasing and profitable selling .They are not afraid to questions one another's judgment. Who's Lots was bought at public auction for £70 and was running accordingly.

'When Tony said we should buy a £70 dog for £180, I thought he was gone off his head,' recalls Mick. 'I could not see what he saw in him.' Who's Lots was to win 10 races and the Irish Grand National, beating Kildare Slippy which had recorded a phenomenal 29.10sec. for 525 yards over the sticks. The 1992 Shelbourne Park decider saw Who's Lots turn around a seven-length semi-final deficit.

It was Dad who turned the tables in 1994. 'Colin reckoned that Glasskenny Echo was the ugliest-looking dog he had ever seen,' reports Mick who, however, beheld something else when he gave £350 for him at four months of age.

On a famous Friday in October, Glasskenny Echo turned £350 into a £7,000 profit with victory in the Red Mills Racer Irish Puppy Derby at Harolds Cross. The times for the 525 yards of 28.80 just failed by .02 of a sacond to better the track record held jointly by Where's Carmel and Pulse Tube since 1985.

When Glasskenny Echo goes to Wimbledon for the English Derby, backers will ignore him at their peril—and a little £550 dog called Lego Man, too.

The Byrnes' recipe for success says that there is no truth in the adage about there being 'too many cooks'

Irish DERBY REPORT

Meanwhile, in the Emerald Isle's big race of the year...

Joyful Tidings and Kerry gold!

JOYFUL TIDINGS was an accommodating winner of the 1994 Respond Irish Derby over 550 yards (503m) at Dublin's Shelbourne Park in September. The victory of the 5-2 second favourite facilitated many of the punters present but was also favourable to the Kerry Group, sponsors of the £50,000 premier Irish classic, *John Martin writes*.

Having backed the event for three years, the dairying giant and producers of Respond greyhound feed, have been operating on a year-to-year basis. What better to put them into a positive frame of mind for 1995 than a triumph for a dog from their own heartland.

Joyful Tidings is owned by Michael Carmody, a publican from Tarbert and was trained by Donal O'Regan, of Ardfert. The only non-County Kerry connection was the breeder, Tipperaryman Donal O'Connor. A cruelly ironic fact was that Joyful Tidings is a son of Whisper Wishes, who died during the course of the Derby, weeks before his September 92 son (ex-Newmans Mall) was to cement his reputation.

The death of Whisper Wishes was to continue a tragic trend in Irish breeding and the connections of Joyful Tidings were ideally placed to fill the void. The notion of immediately retiring a champion is one which does not well with the racegoers but, in the case of the Derby winner, it was perfectly understandable. He had only turned two but few felt that he could fail in the breeding paddocks. The owner was not averse to selling the dog but since there had been a number of big-money transfers—including Helen Roche's purchase of English Derby winner Moral Standards—most of the major players had spent their dough.

There was little doubt that Joyful Tidings would be patronised in Co. Kerry and Ireland as a whole. The Derby story of the winner of the £5,000 Lee Strand 550 at Tralee started with a preliminary round defeat. However, Joyful Tidings was only coming back from toe trouble. Subsequent to that defeat he never looked back.

The unbeaten Reggie Roberts-owned Old Maid went off favourite but missed her break. It was left to Michael's Machine, owned by English-based Jimmy O'Connor, to make a race of it to the first bend. Joyful Tidings went to his outside off the first two turns, took up the running and it as all over. Old Maid ran on in fourth place to pick up a £10,000 breeding bonus for trainer-breeder Roberts who had entered her for the classic as a whelp.

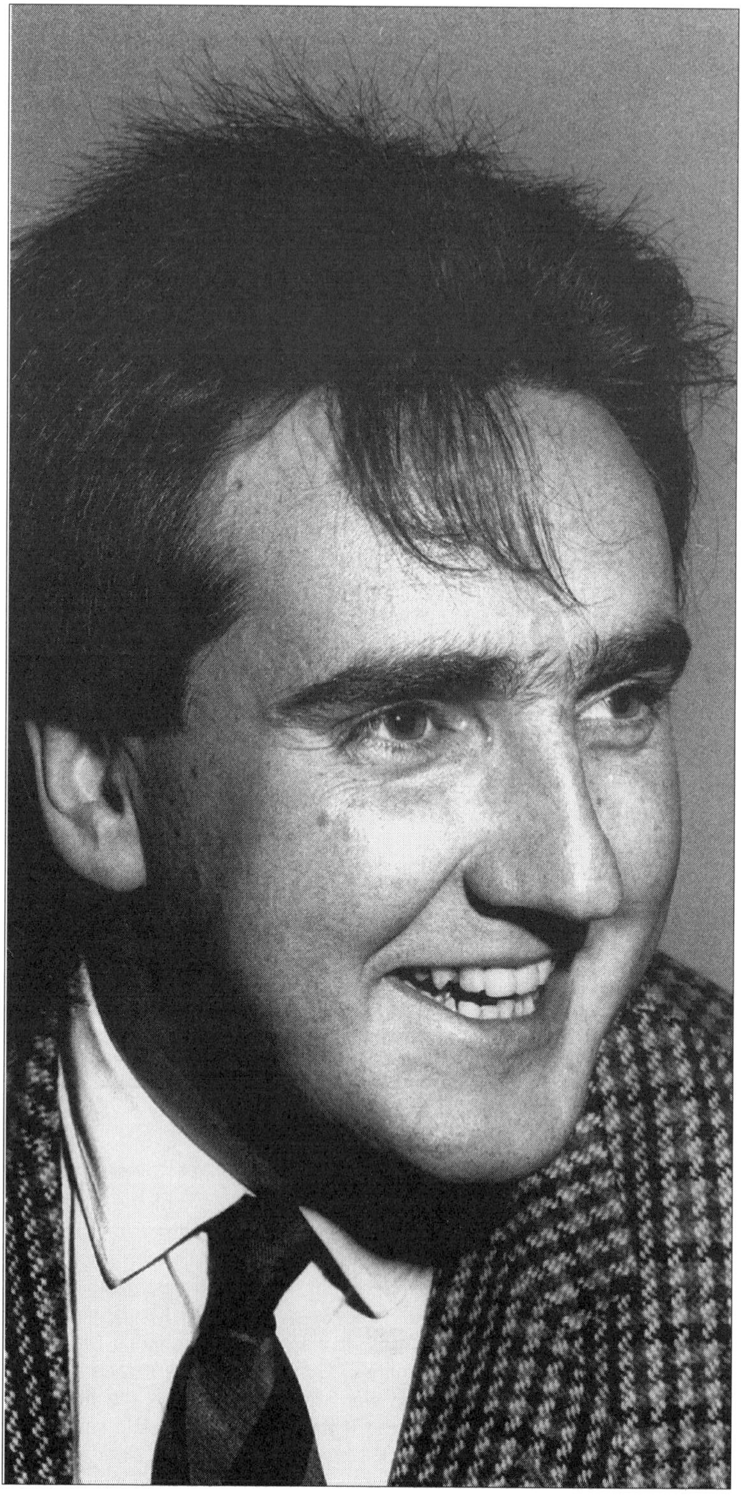

Owner PROFILE

Sky's the limit in '95 for 'Cheeky' chappie!

Larger than life, that's Harry Findlay. Owning Chicita Banana, among others, raised his profile. Now, as **JONATHAN HOBBS** reports, he's coming to a screen near you. Watch out . . .

There is no question that 1995 promises to be Harry Findlay's year in greyhound racing. This larger-than life character is set to strike back on two fronts, as a Sky TV presenter for the satellite station's new greyhound programme—and as a successful owner, once more.

Findlay, whose brilliant staying bitch Chicita Banana first catapulted him into the limelight in the heady days of the late 80's when six-bend performers such as 'Cheeky', Waltham Abbey and Sail On Valerie thrilled racegoers, feels now might be the right time to 'return' to ownership.

Not that he has ever really been away.

A regular visitor to tracks the length and breadth of the country, he has an interest in litters of pups produced by Chicita Banana. But it is a while since he entered the market for a prized possession, although after the success he enjoyed with Cheeky perhaps that is hardly surprising.

'It was a glorious time for six-bend dogs then,' he said. 'We had had Ballyregan Bob and Scurlogue Champ and just when you thought it couldn't get better, up popped Cheeky, Sail On Valerie, Waltham Abbey. They were all top class, brilliant dogs and I was part of it.

'They were great days. Myself and John (McGee) had some

Owner PROFILE

wonderful trips. We went everywhere. But the truth is that those three stayers, Cheeky included, were head and shoulders above anything that has appeared since and I'm including Bobs Regan here.'

Findlay feels that only now has the calibre of staying races—his favourite—reached the heights of Chicita Banana's era. 'Last Action, Ballarue Minx, Wexford Minx, Flashing Support, Suncrest Sail, Jubilee Rebecca, First Defence, Senlau Rose. They're all brilliant. And I could go on'

He would dearly love to be part of it again but if a deal cannot be struck, he at least has the consolation of fronting a programme the sport's equivalent of Sky's *Winning Post*, starting on May 26, during which it is hoped to feature the likes of the aforementioned high-class staying clique.

> 'The new McCririck? As a punter I can boast a far better record!'

The programme kicks off with Daily Mirror/Sporting Life Derby from Wimbledon, clearly high-quality fare. 'But we must make sure it continues,' says Harry.

'The press, promoters and Sky have to ensure the programmes feature really top-class racing. That's what we all want. That's what it needs to be success.'

Findlay is sure, certain even, that greyhound racing on Sky will be a success. To use its own slogan, there's No Turning Back. And he is fully aware how important TV is to greyhound racing.

'We have to show people what they're missing. Greyhound racing is the best thing in the world. It's exciting and can make for brilliant TV—if it's done right.'

The BBC's erstwhile interest in the Greyhound Derby and its continued patronage of the TV Trophy have been celluloid high points for the sport. But those aside, there have been few occasions to cheer and a majority of the time TV coverage of the sport has been used as a vehicle to snipe.

Findlay and the Sky crew have so far been mainly confined to fishing, snooker and darts. Greyhound racing is his first love and the sport is lucky to have someone who will lobby hard for a pastime he adores.

And it is not just talk. He really does intend to spread the word. During the World Darts Championship featured on Sky earlier this year, Findlay managed to persuade the crew to film an interview with one of the players at John McGee's schooling track.

'His name was Dennis Smith, and his father in law is Peter Swadden, the Bristol trainer,' Findlay explained.

'Obviously, like me, he is mad keen on the dogs and I thought

Owner PROFILE

BALLARUE MINX: Raising profile of the stayers, says Findlay.

we'd go down to John's for the morning. The weather was bloody awful but the interview worked and we featured some of Cheeky's pups schooling.'

And, of course, his performance in front of the cameras for Sky at the final of the Northern Puppy Derby at Sunderland was brilliant. His 'double act' with Barry Silkman was a joy to behold and resulted in rave reviews for what was the 'Harry and Barry' show!

A self-confessed sport and sports' betting-addict, Findlay originally made his name as a professional punter and can recount numerous stories involving bet—large bets—he has had with the bookmakers, some successful, some not so.

'I always get the feeling people think I'm a millionaire, but half the time I'm skint!' he laughs.

He is renowned for playing the heavy odds-on bets and fondly recalls his first visit to the National Coursing Festival in Clonmel as an 18-year-old.

'They bet on head-to-heads there: 1-10 chances, and all that. Clonmel runs in February but after what I drew, I thought it was Christmas all over again!' he bellows.

He recalls a bet he had on Stephen Hendry in snooker's World Championship. The odds? 1-25! 'But the guy he was playing was a 10,000-1 chance in my book. It just had to be taken. Of course, from time to time the odds-on chances get beaten. But that's life!' he reasons.

A likeable character and the most sociable of men you would care to meet, he is made for TV. Comparisons with the equally 'loud' John McCririck regularly do the rounds but, according to Findlay, they are futile.

'He's a racing man, I'm a dog man. And as a punter I can boast a far better record!'

Track Boss PROFILE

Confessions of a giant-killer

Mike Palmer meets Jock McNaughton, owner of Henlow, the surprise 1994 Inter-Track champions

HENLOW boss Jock McNaughton is one of the newest promoters in the business. Yet already he believes he has enjoyed his finest hour. That was the memorable night at Wembley last November, when the Berdfordshire track won the National Intertrack Championship against Stainforth.

It was like a fairy tale for McNaughton, who had been in the Henlow hotseat less than a year when his minnows, after disposing of Romford, Walthamstow, Wembley and then Portsmouth, completed what was surely the greatest giant-killing act greyhound racing has known.

'I don't know what it meant to anyone else but it gave me one helluva buzz,' he enthused. 'Throughout the competition I couldn't think of anything else. I even used to dream about it — that's how involved I was.

'And I swear that in the two weeks leading up to the final I didn't sleep a wink. It was marvellous. Just marvellous. My owners and trainers got a real thrill too, and also a nice few quid out of it!'

But McNaughton, a 51-year-old native of Burnpark in Strathclyde, believes the title will not be going back to Henlow, the small permit track four miles from Hitchin.

'Not in my lifetime, anyhow,' he added. 'I believe the rules will change a bit this year and imagine the big tracks will think seriously about insisting their trainers make available for the competition their open race runners. But it was great while it lasted— a moment that everyone involved in the event will cherish for as long as they live.'

One or two will also recall their hangovers— around 200 Henlow supporters returned from Wembley to their track to celebrate. McNaughton's wife had prepared a massive buffet and while

WEMBLEY GLORY NIGHT: McNaughton's proud moment as he shows off the Intertrack Trophy after a memorable triumph.

the first batch of supporters started to drift away at 4.30 on Saturday morning many were still going strong as dawn broke two hours later!

McNaughton has been through the card, as it were, in greyhound racing. He has been an owner, trainer and now a promoter, taking over the helm at Henlow in January 1994 from the Smith family.

'I once trained under permit at Rye House and then trained at Henlow before I took the place over,' he recalls. His first involvement in the sport was as a young lad, when he paraded runners for a friend.

> **The Wembley win gave me a helluva buzz. I even used to dream about it, that's how involved I was**

'He raced at Blantyre in Hamilton. I suppose you could say it was there that I first got the taste for the sport,' he said. 'We had lots of fun but I later decided to go in search of fame and fortune in Canada.' That was in 1964 when, aged just 21, he went to Toronto. 'By this time I had worked at various jobs in Scotland, but found nothing suitable,' McNaughton recalls.

However, Canada did not suit him and he was back in Scotland in less than

Track Boss PROFILE

There's too much racing. I find after seven or eight races the punters get bored and start to drift away

a year, and journeyed south a few months later. I just couldn't get on with Canada, although I owe a great debt to a friend I met over there, an American footballer who was a giant of a man— at least six feet six and close on 23 stones. But he was very good to me.

'I was a bit of a tearaway in those days but he took me to one side, had a word in my ear and told me a few things I shall never forget.'

Three years after McNaughton upped roots again and moved to England he became involved with greyhounds again, this time having a few graders with Josh Hedley at Hackney. From there he took out his own permit licence and, after a spell at Rye House, moved to Henlow to begin his love affair with the Bedfordshire track.

The Intertrack success apart, it has not all been sweetness and light as a promoter. 'I'd love to improve the facilities here in a big way but the track is not getting the support it once did,' says McNaughton.

'It's difficult, therefore, to make a long-term commitment. I don't know why it should be but it seems the smaller tracks suffer more when times are hard. Hopefully things will pick up soon and I can start thinking about brightening the place up.'

He believes greyhound racing is running the risk of overkill and that there are too many tracks putting on too many races. 'Of course they race too much,' he says. 'If they're on a three meetings a week schedule then they should only be staging eight races. I find that after seven or eight races punters begin to drift away. They get bored after a couple of hours or so.

'Having said that, I still believe the sport can only go one way— and that's forward. You only have to go to Walthamstow and see

RECIPE FOR SUCCESS; Jock's wife gives him a cake for his 50th birthday

66 NGRC Greyhound Racing Yearbook 1995

Track Boss PROFILE

CHAMPION LINE-UP: The winning Henlow team enjoy their moment of Inter-Track glory at Wembley Stadium.

all the young children there. These are the people who will be greyhound racing in the next century. For my part at Henlow, I'm working on ways to attract youngsters in. I'm going round all the clubs giving away passes.

'If you attract ten people to the track and say two or three come back for more then it has been a successful manoeuvre.'

McNaughton thinks Sunday racing is the way forward. But he is less convinced that early January was the correct time to introduce racing on the Sabbath.

'Indeed it was the wrong time of year to start but, in time, I think Sunday racing will prove very worthwhile.'

Of the NGRC, he says they are a necessary body but feels they can be too strict on minor breaches of the rules. 'Some of the rules need to be re-written, there's no question about it,' he claims.

One pet hate he has is the 'unnecessary cost' to trainers for kennel inspection by NGRC stipendary stewards. 'You could have the best, cleanest kennels in the world but still they insist on twice-yearly inspections and the trainer has to pay both times.'

John McNaughton pulls no punches and I wouldn't mind betting that one day he will pull Henlow into shape and make it one of the leading lights on the permit scene.

If dedication and a love of greyhound racing are necessary requirements to achieve this, he can't fail.

Tote STATISTICS 1994

Greyhound racing has never been promoted or marketed better, whihc makes the NGRC's 1994 returns the more difficult to swallow . . .

Renewed call for levy as tote and crowd figures dive

The NGRC repeated its call for a statutory levy from off-course bookmakers after making public its survey of tote and attendance records early in the New Year. The survey showed that attendances dipped on average by 3.3 per cent and tote turnover dived by 4.9 per cent at NGRC tracks in 1994.

The only good news was that prize money was up almost 20 per cent thanks to the near £2m a year 'donations' by the betting shop fraternity gathered by the British Greyhound Racing Fund.

For Geoffrey Thomas, executive director of the BGRF, the figures made largely depressing reading. He told Bob Betts, of *The Sporting Life*: 'A year which started off so hopefully ended with disappointing tote and attendance figures.

'Reflecting the competitiveness of the leisure industry and the ever-increasing competition for the gambling pie, the 1994 figures demonstrate how difficult it is to get people to come greyhound racing and to encourage them to bet when they are there.

'Several tracks have posted useful figures and appear to be bucking the trend.'

He cited solid performances from Hall Green, Catford, Crayford, Hull, Belle Vue, Mildenhall, Oxford, Peterborough, Portsmouth, Ramsgate and Yarmouth and said they could face 1995 with some optimism.

'However, although it is possible to balance the 1994 statistics by recognising the positive and adding a number of factors to explain the wider picture, there is no escaping the stark realisation that we are struggling to stand still.

'This is despite the fact that the sport is now better promoted and mar-

Tote STATISTICS 1994

TOTE TURNOVER PER MEETING

94	93	Track	1989	1990	1991	1992	1993	1994	%+/-
1	1	Walthamstow	108,000	103,600	88,100	84,700	75,700	72,800	-3.8
2	2	Wimbledon	85,000	80,100	68,000	60,000	55,300	50,900	-7.9
3	3	Hall Green	31,000	33,500	33,200	32,200	32,400	32,700	+0.9
4	4	Catford	43,100	36,600	35,300	32,000	31,400	32,500	+2.9
5	5	Romford	43,400	44,700	35,700	33,000	31,000	27,500	-11.3
6	6	Belle Vue	27,400	28,700	29,100	29,500	28,800	30,900	+7.3
7	8	Hove	36,100	34,300	28,300	22,900	24,000	23,300	-3.0
8	7	Wembley	43,700	36,200	29,500	26,800	24,400	22,200	-9.0
9	9	Crayford	16,600	18,100	16,700	15,700	13,500	13,400	-0.7
10	10	Sheffield	12,600	10,800	11,800	12,700	12,400	12,800	+3.2
11	13	Sunderland	—	13,300	11,100	10,300	10,300	10,100	-1.9
12	15	Portsmouth	10,500	10,700	9,600	8,300	9,300	10,000	+7.5
13	=17	Peterboro	4,500	5,200	5,300	6,800	8,500	9,400	+10.6
14	14	Yarmouth	11,300	11,900	11,300	10,100	9,400	9,100	-3.2
=15	11	Perry Barr	-	10,800	11,100	12,300	12,300	8,700	-29.3
=15	12	Shawfield	14,200	11,900	12,000	11,400	10,500	8,700	-17.1
17	=17	Monmore	10,300	9,600	8,500	8,200	8,500	8,300	-2.3
18	16	Reading	9,500	9,600	9,500	9,400	8,700	7,800	-10.3
=19	19	Brough Park	9,100	7,600	8,000	8,400	8,300	7,700	-7.2
=19	23	M Keynes	11,200	10,500	8,300	7,200	7,200	7,700	+7.0
21	21	Oxford	12,200	11,300	9,700	8,500	7,600	7,600	—
22	20	Powderhall	14,700	12,000	9,100	7,400	8,100	7,200	-11.1
23	22	Ramsgate	11,400	11,000	9,900	8,200	7,400	7,000	-5.4
24	27	Hackney	4,900	5,100	4,600	3,700	4,700	6,200	+32.0
=25	24	Bristol	4,900	5,100	4,600	5,200	5,900	5,300	-10.1
=25	25	Stainforth	—	—	—	—	5,400	5,300	-1.9
27	26	Nottingham	4,100	4,800	5,100	5,300	5,200	4,900	-5.8
28	28	Swindon	6,300	5,700	4,900	5,200	4,500	4,400	-2.2
29	33	Hull	5,300	3,900	5,100	3,600	3,400	3,900	+14.8
30	=29	Canterbury	6,800	8,200	6,800	5,000	4,300	3,800	-11.7
31	=29	Rye House	6,700	6,200	5,300	4,400	4,300	3,300	-23.2
32	31	Cradley Hth	3,990	4,300	4,000	3,900	3,600	3,100	-13.9
33	32	Henlow	5,200	5,300	4,400	3,400	3,500	2,900	-17.1
34	34	Midd'boro	2,900	2,800	3,300	3,400	3,100	2,800	-9.7
35	35	Swaffham	3,900	3,700	3,200	3,200	2,900	2,500	-13.9
36	37	Mildenhall	—	—	2,900	2,500	1,100	1,900	+72.7
37	--	Dundee	—	—	—	—	-	0,510	—

'The 1994 figures demonstrate how difficult it is to get people to come greyhound racing and to encourage them to bet when they are there.'
— Geoffrey Thomas, BGRF

Tote STATISTICS 1994

CLIVE FELTHAM

keted than at any time in the past. That the national position is not more bleak is due to the efforts of people like Peter Shotton, Gordon Bissett, Clive Feltham, Kevin Wilde, Rex Perkins, Kevan Hedderly and Jon Carter who remain at the cutting edge.'

Thomas was upbeat about the hike in prize money, however. 'It was most encouraging. Full credit must go to the BGRF, whose substantial contribution to prize money should not go unrecognised.

'We also hope that the money raised by tracks (for charities) will top £1m in 1995. Last year we were just £4,000 adrift.'

Geoffrey Thomas pointed to the changes which will allow inter-track totalisator betting to come to reality in 1995. 'This should make for a very different and very exciting on-course betting market,' he said.

The type of help the Horserace Levy Board is able to give its sport was singled out by Thomas as 'the biggest single factor in explaining the decline in greyhound attendances'.

'The steady increase in off-course betting turnover on greyhound racing has been at the expense of dog racing betting on-course.

'Horseracing got its levy in 1961. Greyhound racing is looking for 1995 as the year it gets its own levy,' he said.

Catering facilities were now at the leading edge for many tracks in their attempts to woo back fans and attract new customers.

Sunday racing and the continual development at established tracks and the building of new ones served to dispel some of the blackest clouds.

Mildenhall (see table, below) led the way in the tote turnover stakes, and is a sign that better days are ahead.

Promoter Richard Borthwick said: 'I've been especially encouraged by Sunday racing.'

ATTENDANCE AND TURNOVER FIGURES

	Attendances	Tote turnover	Meetings	Races
1993 (37 tracks)	3,859,498	88,170,111	6,054	70,493
1994 (37 tracks)	3,911,447	87,885,471	6,393	73,138
+/- on 1993	-3.3%	4.9%	4.8%	+3.8%

Tote STATISTICS 1994

TOTE TURNOVER COMPARISONS

Track	1994 £	£1993 £	Mtgs 1994	1993
Hall Green	5,362,104	5,253,442	164	162
Perry Barr	2,285,133	1,902,770	251	155
Brighton	5,022,073	5,119,748	215	214
Bristol	***1,091,199	1,216,128	205	206
Canterbury	(est) 778,088	882,275	204	205
Cradley Heath	320,482	366,518	104	102
Crayford	2,784,522	2,775,235	208	205
Dundee	*11,200	0	*22	0
Powderhall	1,117,783	1,303,237	155	161
Shawfield	2,228,312	2,665,568	255	254
Henlow	572,445	444,600	200	126
Hull	421,915	353,507	109	104
Belle Vue	4,788,192	4,579,486	155	159
Middlesbrough	450,499	94,475	159	158
Mildenhall	198,371	97,927	105	88
Milton Keynes	844,294	709,117	110	99
Brough Park	1,791,153	1,867,195	231	226
Nottingham	757,706	810,403	155	155
Oxford	1,549,700	1,545,335	205	204
Peterborough	1,953,811	1,754,275	208	206
Portsmouth	1,586,672	1,459,270	158	157
Ramsgate	1,196,763	1,293,515	171	174
Reading	1,235,903	1,373,859	158	157
Romford	6,444,861	7,218,562	234	232
Rye House	**89,271	55,154	**27	128
Sheffield	2,119,876	1,935,404	165	156
Stainforth	873,516	632,472	154	117
Sunderland	1,897,544	1,934,577	188	188
Swaffham	381,854	36 427	151	157
Swindon	678,515	684,719	155	151
Yarmouth	1,387,021-	1,472,310	153	156
London tracks				
Catford	5,073,607	4,875,779	156	155
Hackney	2,165,153	542,700	348	114
Walthamstow	12,814,342	- 12,792,314	176	169
Wembley	3,282,911	3,291,898	148	125
Wimbledon	10,647,193	11,454,253	209	207

* Opened October 1994
** Closed, January-October 1994
*** Capacity and turnover reduced by fire damage

NGRC Spotlight

Evergreen Fearn signs off

Senior Steward **Alan Fearn** reflects on his long and distinctive career at the NGRC

ALAN FEARN can take a more detached view of greyhound racing this year after his recent retirement as Senior Steward of the NGRC. He held the post for six and a half years prior to being succeeded by Bill Cooke. Naturally he has seen many changes during his stewardship. The sport has grown far more than he could have imagined when he first became a steward in 1972.

'No-one could have thought then that the tracks would be racing four or even five times a week with programmes of 12 or 14 races,' Alan told Alan Lennox of *The Sporting Life*. 'For over 60 years greyhound racing had been shackled by restrictive legislation to virtually two meetings a week. Thank goodness the NGRC was able to persuade the Government to deregulate the number of racedays in 1985.

'I understand the feelings of some people when they say that there is too much racing, but I think it will find its own level eventually.' Even in retirement at home in Rochdale, Alan Fearn remains a staunch ally of his former employers, saying that those who criticise the NGRC should remember that the body exists for the good of the sport. It should be judged on its achievements, he says.

He could never be accused of not knowing what he was saying. The 70-year-old Fearn has owned around 100 greyhounds in his long association with the sport, and trained 25 when he held an owner-trainer licence between 1968 and 1972.

One of those was the renowned stayer Booked Six., voted Dog of the Year in 1969, when he finished runner-up in the St Leger. Alan's heavy business commitments at the time, as a dentist in Hyde, Cheshire, meant that he couldn't enjoy the experience fully. Indeed, his wife Barbara often had to take the runners racing because he was so busy. Eventually this pressure led to Alan

ALAN FEARN, in one of his more favourite roles— a presentation to Bernard Shannon in recognition of his wife Ann's work with retired greyhounds

putting Booked Six into pro hands, with Billy France at Belle Vue and later Jimmy Jowett at Clapton.

Alan's political inclinations—five times he stood unsuccessfully for the Conservatives in the North West—saw him gravitate towards the sports governing bodies. In 1972, while on a working party, he was instrumental in changing the ruling on greyhounds' birthdays. Working with the Retired Greyhound Trust in the North West, he noticed that with all dogs having an official birthday on January 1, those born towards the end of the year were denied a puppy season.

He is especially pleased to see Bolton in the NGRC fold. He first experienced the sport there and at other independents in the Fifties. 'I'd like to see more smaller tracks finding their way into the NGRC,' he says.

He ends his official ties with greyhound racing at an exciting, promising time, though he is experienced enough to counsel caution: 'Promoters and the authorities must be careful not to over-egg the pudding.' For now, though, he can spend more time with the family—two daughters and four grandchildren.

CORAL ROMFORD STADIUM

GREYHOUND RACING

Mondays, Wednesdays, Fridays at 7.30 p.m.
& Saturdays at 7.15 p.m.
Also some Tuesday & Thursday afternoons

With daily specials, a la carte menu & extensive wine list

TOTE MESSENGER SERVICE

FAST FOOD OUTLETS

RACE SPONSORSHIP

A NIGHT YOU'LL REMEMBER!

CHILDRENS PLAYGROUND

CHARITY EVENINGS

CELEBRATION PACKAGES

BARS

Mondays & Wednesdays
MOST DRAUGHT PINTS
99p

GLASS OF HOUSE WINE
99p

..... *plus excellent greyhound racing*

CORAL ROMFORD STADIUM
London Road, Romford, Essex, RM7 9DU
For further details Tel: (01708) 762345
Restaurant reservations Tel: (01708) 725213

CORAL BRIGHTON & HOVE STADIUM

GREYHOUND RACING

Tuesdays & Thursdays at 7.30 p.m.
Saturdays at 7.15 p.m.
& Sunday afternoons
Also Wednesday afternoons

Tuesdays & Thursdays
CARLING BLACK LABEL &
WORTHINGTON BEST BITTER
99p

..... *plus excellent greyhound racing*

CORAL BRIGHTON & HOVE STADIUM
Nevill Road, Hove, East Sussex, BN3 7BZ
For further details Tel: (01273) 204601

Track FOOD GUIDE

Four Weddings and a Racecard

From Sunday roasts to corporate fun nights and wedding breakfasts. **PAUL FRY** discovers how the greyhound tracks of the Nineties are catering for a new public as well as the diehard punters.

Track FOOD GUIDE

GREYHOUND RACING means business. Big business. And the fast-changing public perception of the sport is beginning to whet the appetites of track bosses. A big slice of a typical track's business today is served up by the catering operation.

Indeed, many marketing managers will admit that without the significant revenue from their restaurants and bars, some tracks not survive at all.

The public's largely outdated, down-market, cliched image of the sport is becoming increasingly dispelled thanks to innovative managements who are coming to terms with the growing demands on their businesses and with the new markets and challenges that lay ahead.

Top of the menu for managements to salivate over last autumn was Sunday racing. A month after its introduction they are still picking over the bones and digesting the commercial implications of the revolution it promises.

All tracks have a unique local appeal and as such have different targets and priorities. Some, like Birmingham's Perry Barr, have such a busy race schedule that they are not contemplating Sundays for the moment. Instead they are busy wooing big corporate customers.

Others, such as Peterborough and Hove couldn't wait to join in the bonanza and have seen an immediate effect on business, with new customers filling their tables—customers who might otherwise be taking Sunday lunch in a local pub.

And there are other tracks who are watching events with keen interest. Perhaps, like Romford, they are committed to BAGS on Mondays until the contract is up this summer, but essentially itching to take advantage of an exciting new business opportunity.

Whatever their stance, there is little doubt that managements are having to try harder. Open a restaurant of any quality—and there is no shortage of that at tracks all over the country—and you find yourself in a whole new market.

'We're up against not just sports venues, but everything from bingo to bowling and fancy French restaurants to Pizza Hut'

As Robina Gibbs, marketing manager at Romford says: 'We see ourselves as a leisure facility, and we're up against not just sports venues, but everything from bingo to bowling, and fancy French restaurants to Pizza Hut.'

Romford can cater for 240 people at a sitting in the Chase Restaurant. It is very popular. And, with an outstanding set menu on Mondays and Wednesdays for only £9.99, including track admission, you can see why. Robina says: 'At most restaurants set

Track FOOD GUIDE

MODERN OUTLOOK: Walthamstow's Ascot Suite corporate box.

menus come with a very limited choice, but we offer 10 starters as well as around 11 main courses and eight desserts.

'On Fridays and Saturdays, for £12.99, there are three filling courses and you can go a la carte for a small supplementary charge. Good value for money is an important factor—especially if you want repeat business.' The stadium's competition is ever-changing. 'And it will change again if we race on Sundays. At the moment we are contracted to put on BAGS races every Monday. But clearly we are looking at Sunday as a business option. It's got huge potential.'

The Chase features a different theme night each month, most recently an Italian menu — and you could say Romford are pasta masters at this sort of thing. The restaurant was specially decked out in green and red, while it was all stars and stripes for the popular American night, the previous month, when burgers and wings were washed down in great quantities by an assortment of lite beers. 'These theme nights are very important to us. They bring in a different sort of customer, someone who wants good food, but as part of an overall package of entertainment. People have so much choice now, and we have to compete very hard.'

Wembley is widely recognised as providing some of the best food at any of the nation's tracks. Perhaps not suprisingly as the caterers, National Leisure Catering, are performing at the country's premier sports venue. The Food of Legends?...

Catering manager Joan Spearing says the diversity of sports functions and the quite different crowds that each attracts, each with its different demand, provides the job's biggest challenge.

Keeping track, as it were, is the key. Mrs Spearing explains:

Track FOOD GUIDE

AIRY SPLENDOUR: Dining at Sheffield's Owlerton Stadium and, inset, an executive suite at Stainforth.

'We have a very detailed analysis of the catering at each event we host. We look at what sells and why, taking into account every factor we can think of, from the time and date to the weather and so on. The analysis helps us undoubtedly to both run the business better and to provide a better service for our customers.' Quality is very much the watchword.

The restaurant's crowds on Mondays, Wednesdays and Fridays (only briefly on Sundays) vary little. And the £14.99 Chef's Special, offering a choice of three starters, main courses and desserts, has long proved a popular selection.

At Hove they can seat up to 470 in the main restaurant, there are two fast-food bars and a 200-seat cocktail lounge that is often booked by corporate clients. It is clearly a massive operation and requires 160 full- and part-time staff. Staff training and maintaining quality are manager Teresa Lyne's biggest worries.

A £9.99 midweek menu that includes coffee is pulling them in. Trade is buoyant and the Sunday lunches are being consumed in huge quantities. 'We were mobbed on the first Sunday,' said Teresa. 'And the bookings are coming in fast. It's great to see so many new faces here. You still get the diehards with their grandchildren, but we are getting a lot of families.'

Richard Perkins, a director at Peterborough, says the track—like most—would struggle financially without the catering operation. 'Our restaurant turned over something like £200,000 last year,

Track FOOD GUIDE

so you can see it is a very serious consideration for us. 'But we are increasingly optimistic, especially with the advent of Sunday meetings. We started as soon as we could and have found we are getting a different crowd on Sundays. It's great to see so many families. They come in for the roasts, and they're finding that we also offer a good racecard. There's not a great deal on offer for families on Sundays in our area—except for the neighbouring 14-screen cinema—and we're delighted with the response so far.

'The competition has changed, which is an important factor. We're now up against the pubs, with their popular lunch trade. We have to compete on quality and price—but the racing then becomes an edge in itself.

'We're getting customers new and old. I met one chap the other night who had not been racing for 24 years. He was very pleasantly surprised how things had changed. There is no doubt that the sport has had an image problem, but Sunday racing could well prove our best ally yet.

> *'I met one punter who had not been here for 24 years. He couldn't believe how much things had changed for the better'*

'We offer a choice of roast dishes each Sunday, plus a vegetarian dish. I have eaten here—so it can't be too bad!

'I had a very good salmon and broccoli mornay the other evening and it was a credit to the staff.'

Service at Peterborough is very good, and the management works hard at cutting down waste. With cash flow likely to receive a boost from Sunday racing, the track may soon be able to consider developing corporate facilities, something on which the Perkins family owners are particularly keen.

At Perry Barr, where there are no immediate plans to race on Sundays the corporate market has been an important element for just over a year and the response very satisfying, says Marketing Manager Jane Madden.

'It's all new business for us and the spin-off has been a fair number of repeat customers. Once people come they like what they see and say they'll look forward to coming again. The big problem is getting them here in the first place.

'People have a certain picture in their minds of what to expect, but they find a much more up-market reality. We have to market ourselves quite aggressively, with brochures and advertising.'

The Birmingham track offers conference and private function room facilities. They have even had afternoon wedding parties in function suites. Once the breakfast and those nerve-wracking speeches are out of the way, the party stay on to relax and watch the racing.

Track FOOD GUIDE

Then there are conferences. There might not be all the 21st century conference technology available, but companies can bring along their own overhead projectors and other kit.

'Some companies have their conferences at nearby hotels, then come racing as part of an organised evening coach outing,' Jane says. 'We offer a full a la carte service if people want it, and at a fair, competive price. Business has been very good and we are hopeful of further growth.'

Stainforth is one of the few tracks so far not to be overwhelmed with the effect of Sunday racing. Initial response was very good, comfortably filling their 160-seater restaurant, but they fear the novelty may wear off a little and are monitoring demand.

But what about the food? A whistle-stop tour to sample the nation's trackside fayre reveals it's far from being quick-fire pie and mash, and chips with everything.

Teresa Lyne is not alone among catering bosses in striving to kill off that myth. 'I came to Hove Stadium from a hotel background. I was worried that I would not be able to produce the sort of quality food you can in a hotel catering for, say, 50.

'But we have a wonderfully talented and dedicated team here, and I think we produce food of a consistently high standard — and certainly the punters seem to agree.'

Hove is a favourite haunt of holiday punters, but people come from miles to sample the speciality of the house, the Dover Sole. In fact the fish offerings are as good as you would expect at a coastal venue. 'The great thing about my job is that, although we're owned by Bass, who have a number of restaurant outlets and tend to do things the same wherever you go, I get a lot of leeway with the way I do things. For example, we do trout, but in an Italian marinade.'

Some tracks are branching out into theme venues. Walthamstow, for example, offers a new American-style Classic Diner for those looking for something different to the food on offer in its main restaurant. The progressive management have also added the wonderfully modern-looking Ascot Suite corporate box. It all serves to widen the stadium's appeal.

And, with the increasing distractions of life today, broadening the customer base remains a growing objective—one which, on current evidence, is being tackled head-on at NGRC tracks.

A year to savour for Savva!

Nick Savva in typical 1994 pose — with an armful of prizes.

Moral victory

DERBY DELIGHT for Tony Meek (inset, bottom right with jubilant connections) as Moral Standards gets up late to beat Ayr Flyer (6) and Moaning Lad (5)

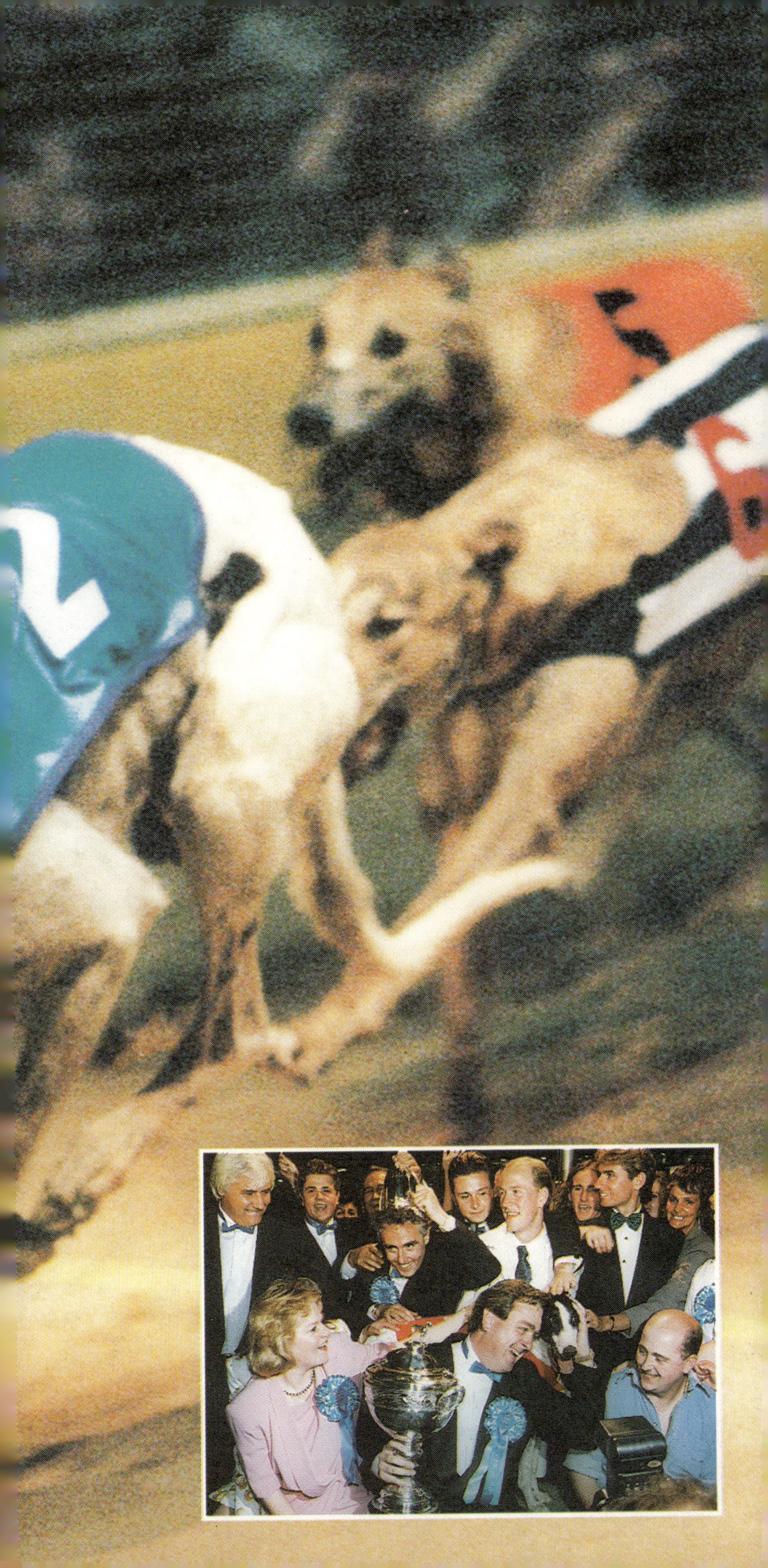

Reasons to be cheerful
(Part One)

**Now here's a man to enliven any presentation ceremony! John McCririck hands Nick Savva the trophy after Westmead Chick's Racing Post Arc triumph.
Meanwhile, another big star of 1994, Wexford Minx, shows off the Ladbroke Golden Jacket for Derek Knight.**

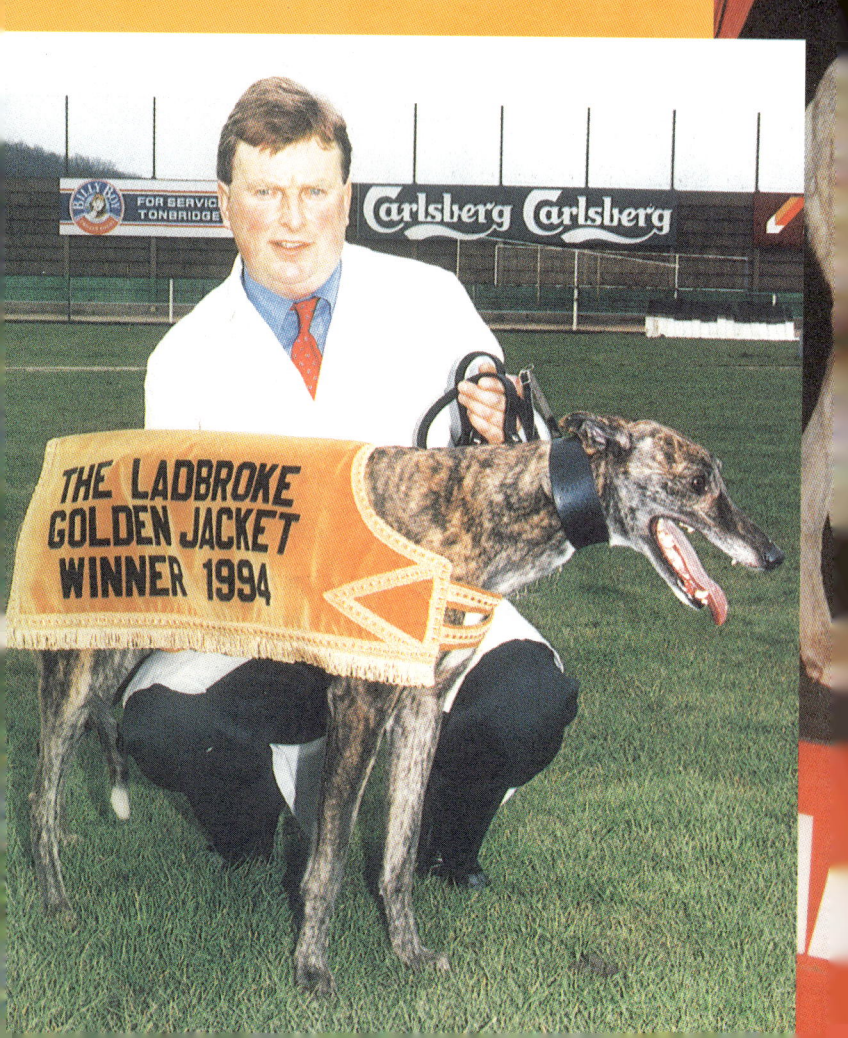

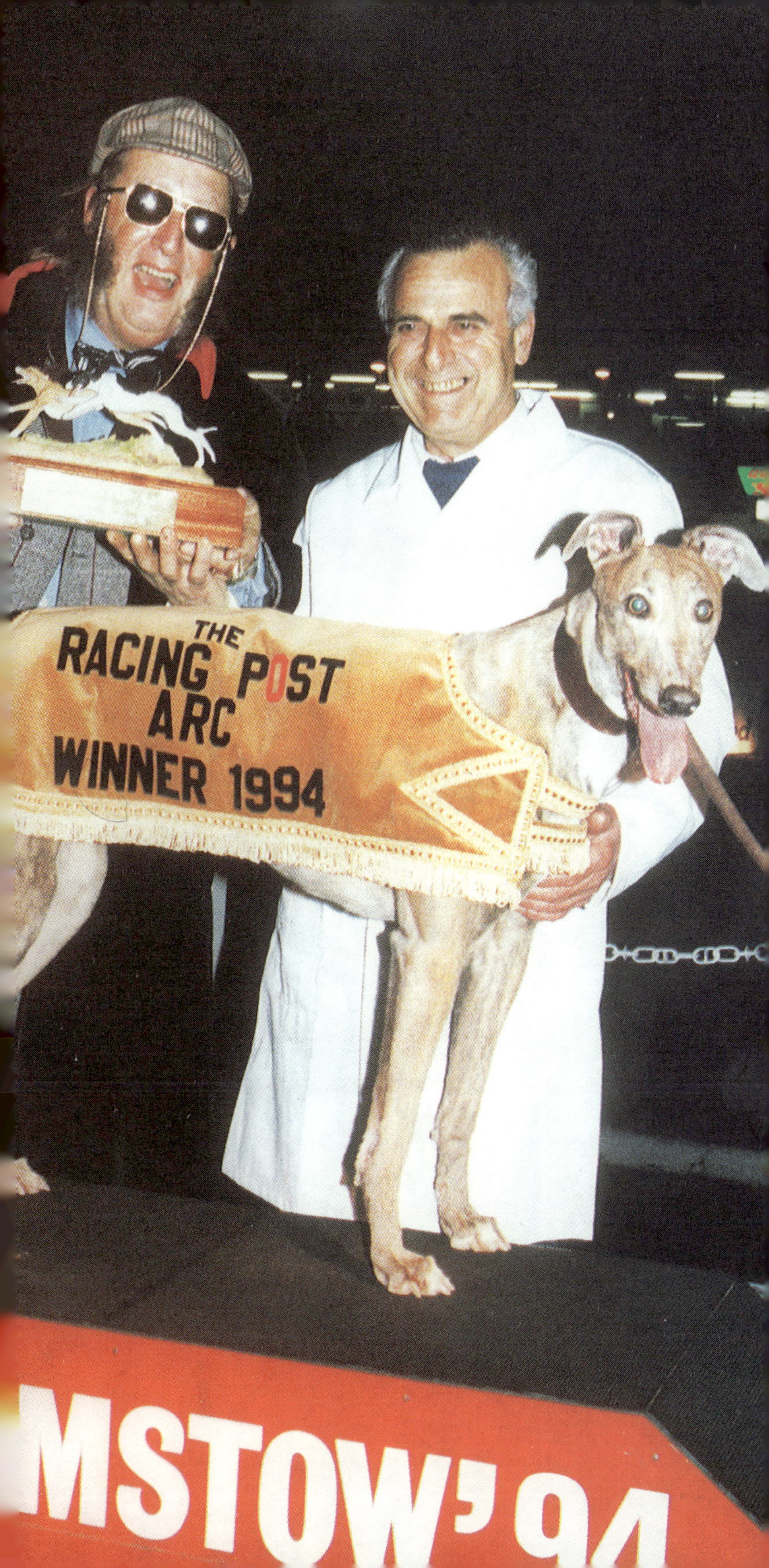
THE
RACING POST
ARC
WINNER 1994
MSTOW'94

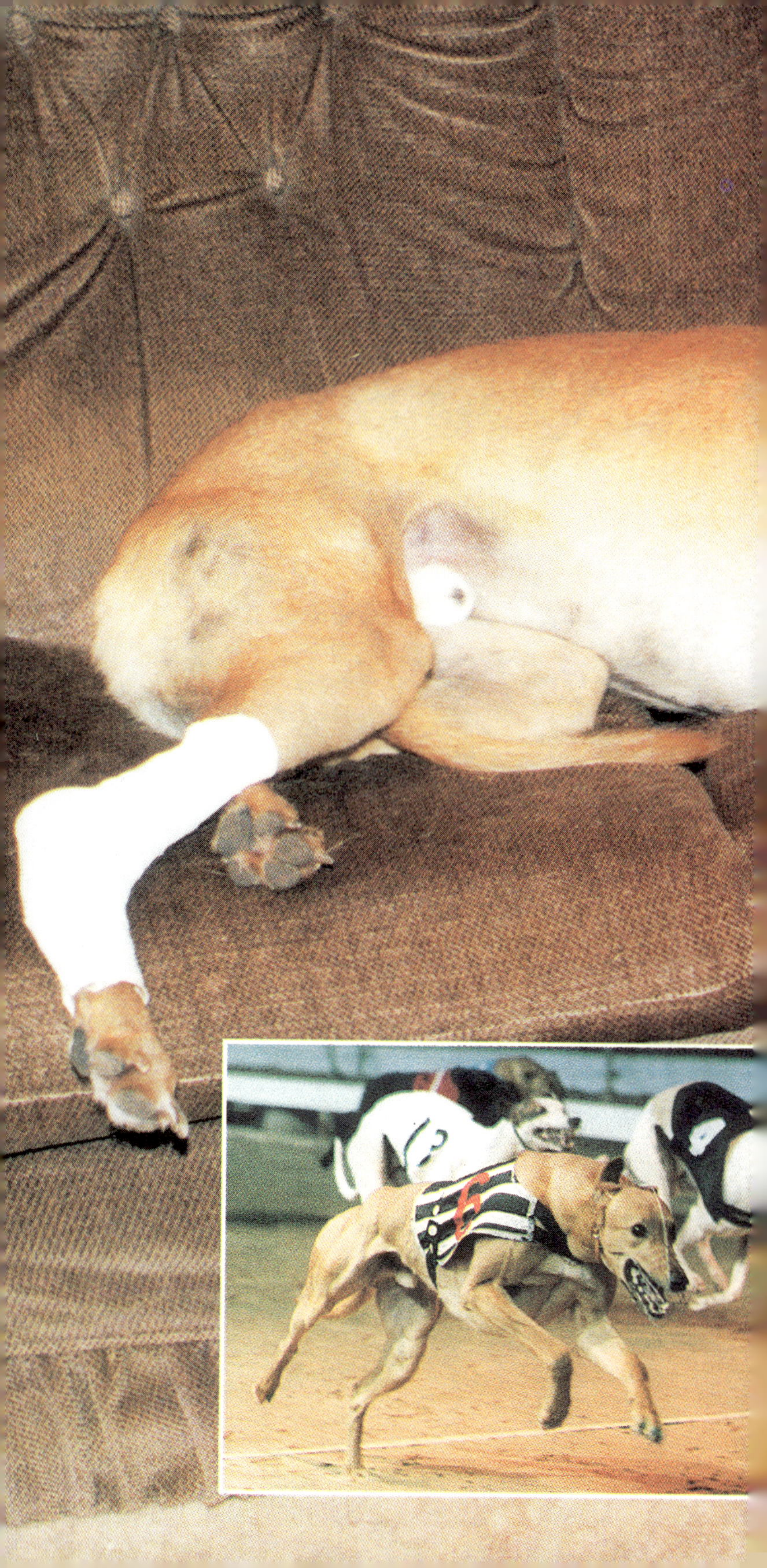

It's a dog's life on the easy list!

LASSA JAVA, thrilling winner of the Pall Mall, left, makes himself at home on Tony Meek's sofa as he recovers from a broken hock. Naturally, we all wish him a speedy recovery.

All dressed up...
and ready to go

It has long been a venue for quality greyhound racing, but the Venue of Legends has never looked better in its new all-seater guise. As well as regular meetings, last season Wembley hosted the Inter-track final, won famously by little Henlow, a memorable night for all concerned.

Reasons to be cheerful (Part Two)

In the pink . . . that's former Pink Floyd guitarist Roger Waters, co-owner with wife Priscilla of Ike Morris Laurels winner Deenside Dean, right. Above, it's party time for connections of Pearls Girl, winner of the John Humphreys Gold Collar.

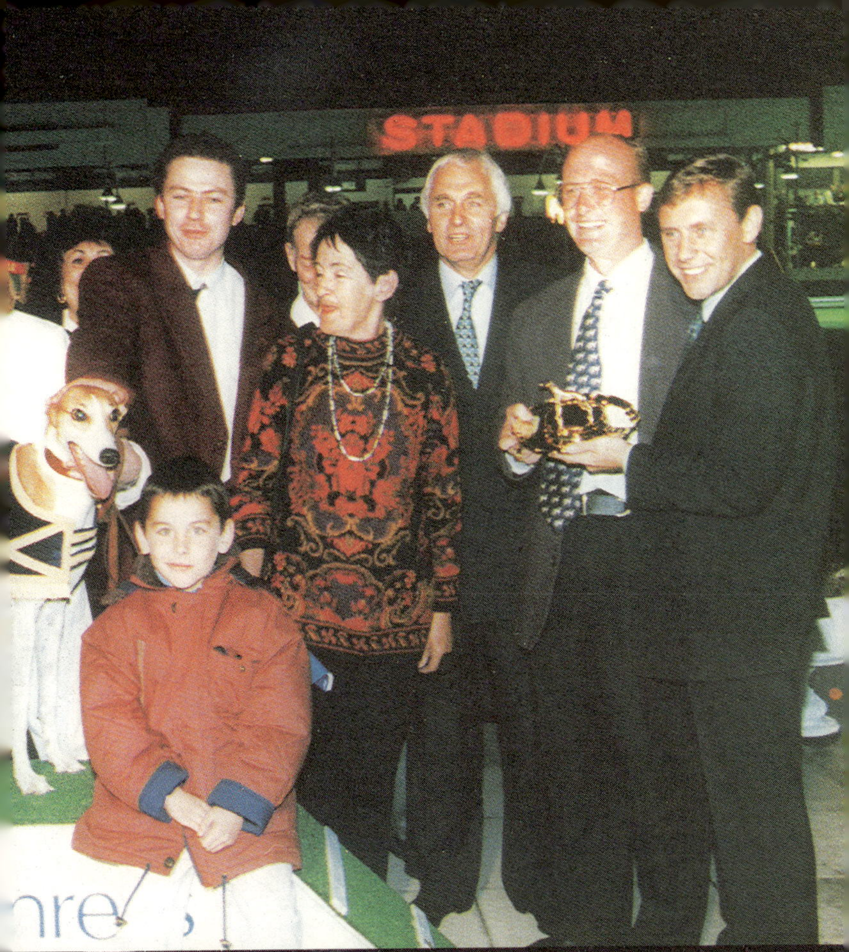
STADIUM

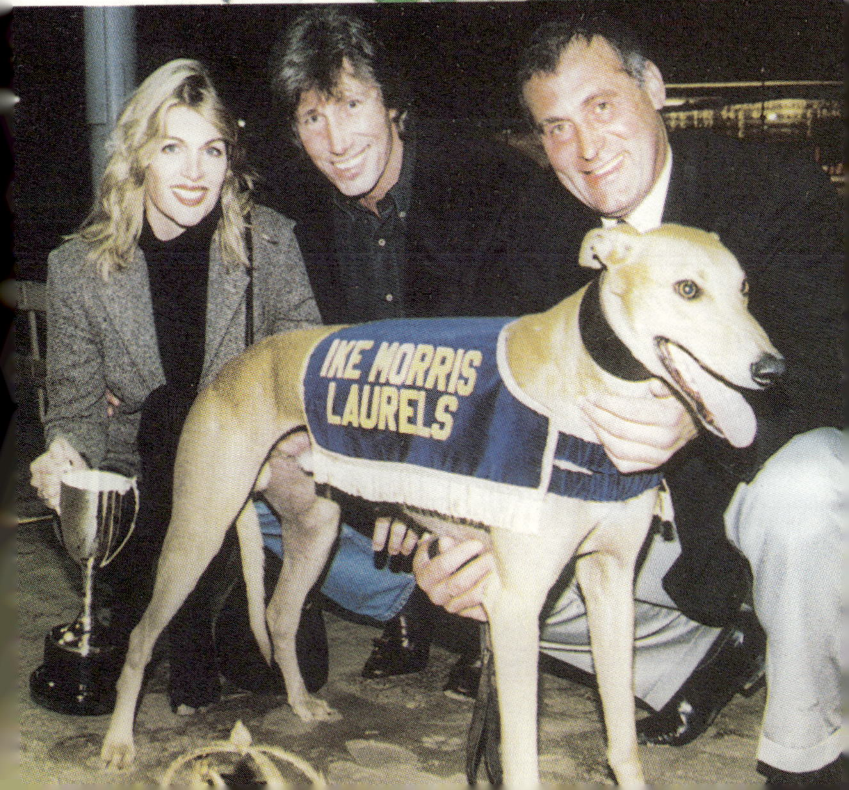
IKE MORRIS
LAURELS

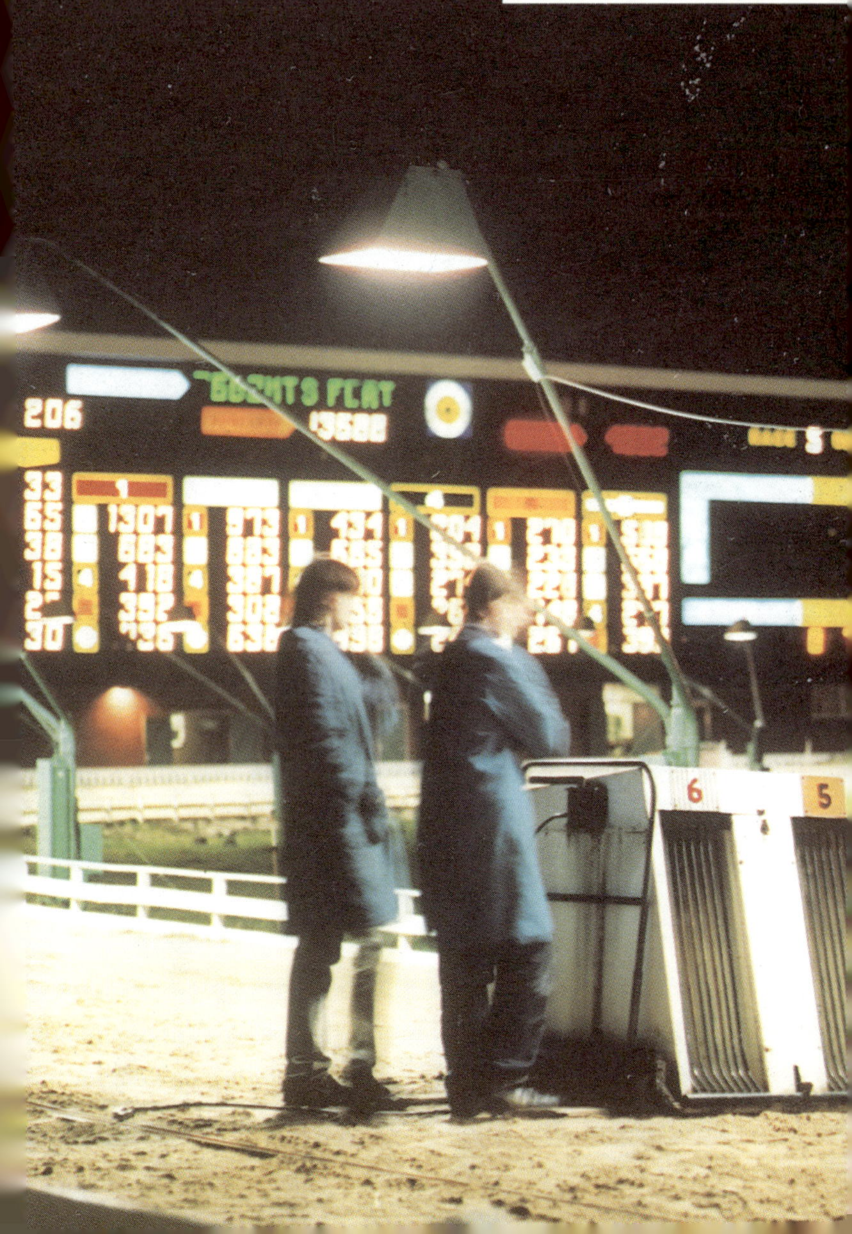
206
6
5

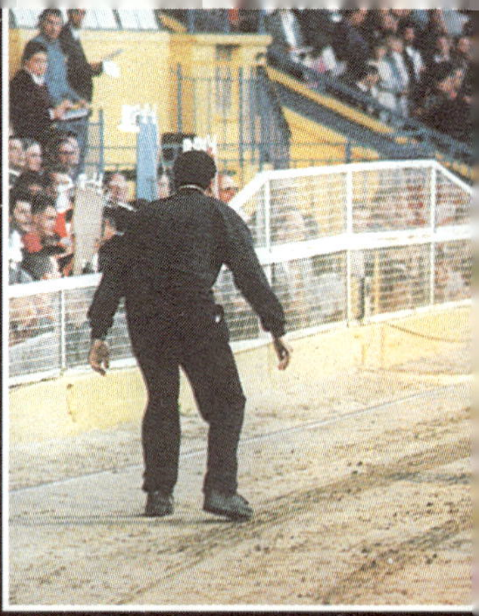

Back-stage stalwarts

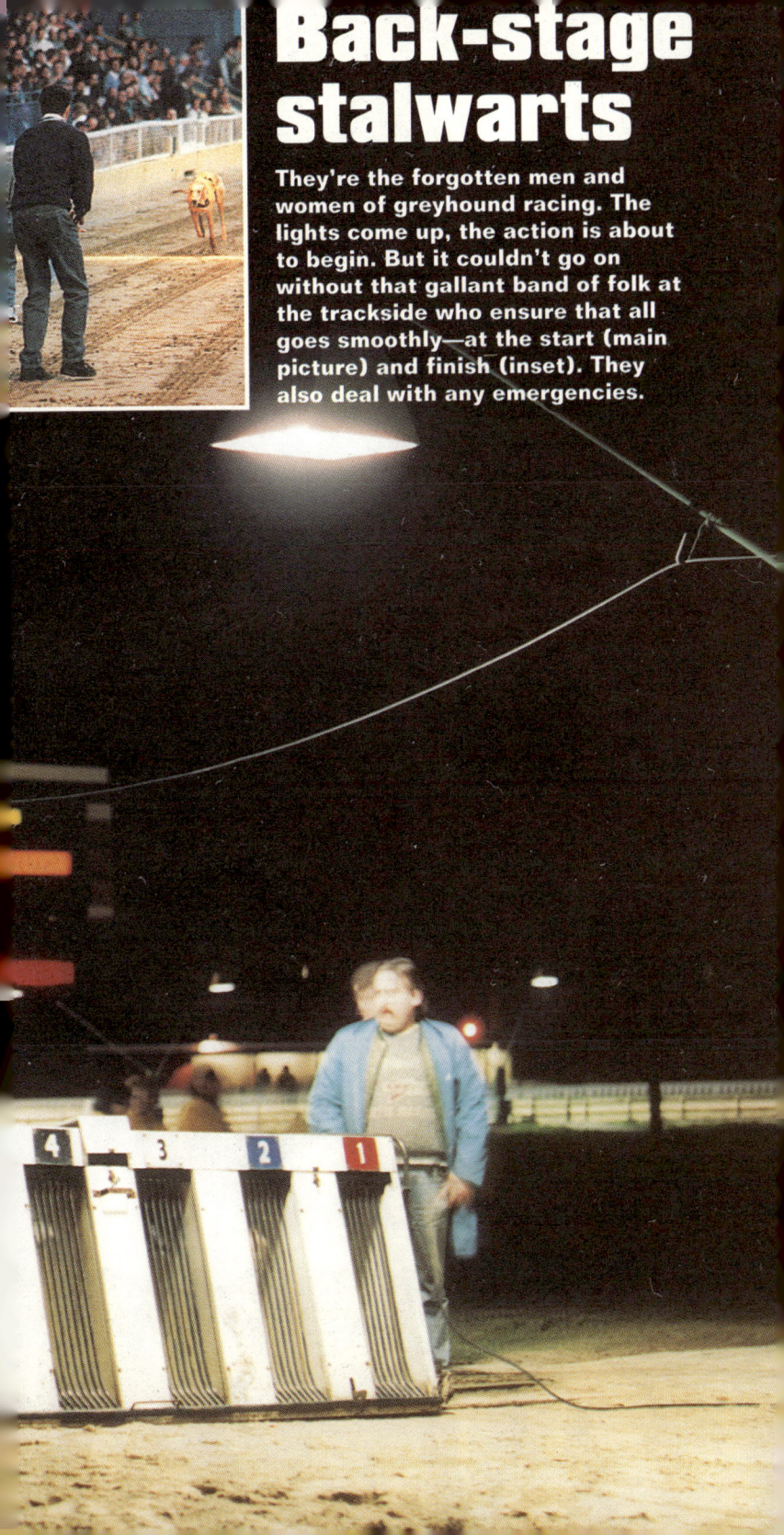

They're the forgotten men and women of greyhound racing. The lights come up, the action is about to begin. But it couldn't go on without that gallant band of folk at the trackside who ensure that all goes smoothly—at the start (main picture) and finish (inset). They also deal with any emergencies.

THE
LAURENT PE
CHAMPAG
GRAND P
WINNER

WENDY FAIR
BLUE
RIBAND

Reasons to be cheerful (Part Three)

Champagne time for Redwood Girl's connections after the Laurent-Perrier Champagne Grand Prix at Walthamstow. The bubbly was doubtless flowing, too, for the owners of Ardilaun Bridge, winner of the Blue Riband.

Reasons to be cheerful (eight of them)

Spot the champion of the future... Well, if they take after dad, they've got a chance. Dad's name? Derrycool Fire.

IN CONTROL: SIS technicians keeping punters in the picture

Feeding time

The growing role of SIS. By Errol Blyth

AS revolutions go, it all started fairly modestly. The date: May 6, 1987 — a Tuesday. That was when Satellite Information Services beamed the first live pictures of racing at Chester and greyhound racing action from Hackney to around a hundred betting offices in Bristol and Colchester.

More impressive was that it took SIS just eight months to complete its roll-out plan to over 10,000 outlets in the UK and Ireland, switching them on to live pictures of the day's racing and up-to-the-minute betting information.

There is no doubting the impact of the revolution, which has done much to influence people's lifestyles and betting habits.

For greyhound racing, the changes in the afternoon service transmitted by SIS and supplied by BAGS has been profound. When SIS began live coverage, only seven tracks were on the service. In 1995, 14 tracks will be supplying the action.

A record 14 tracks will be part of SIS's expanded live service for punters in 1995

It's a far cry from 1987, when BAGS was the subject of much hostility. This year Walthamstow and Wimbledon, unlikely support-

A Day in the Life of SIS

ers in years gone by, will be part of the BAGS action. The promoters and bookmakers have become harmonious with the advent of the British Greyhound Racing Fund (BGRF). And, to illustrate further how the cold war has thawed between certain camps, 1995 will see the first Greyhound Derby to go out live to the nation's betting shops.

So why, eight years down the track, do we need more television coverage for the betting shops? There are several factors, notably the extension of betting shop opening hours to include evenings and now, for the first time, Sundays. In 1987-88, seven tracks staged 542 BAGS meetings and 5,180 races. In 1994-95, 14 tracks will stage 889 meetings and 9,650 races.

With the advent of SIS, it quickly became apparent that, to keep the casual punter interested in greyhound racing, more variety was needed, rather than the formula of 10 races over 460m. The result: eight-dog races, handicap racing, hurdles and six-bend contests spiced up the regular diet of one-lap events.

Racecards have lengthened. Meetings are staged at lunchtimes on Fridays and during big festival weeks such as Cheltenham and Ascot. Saturday morning cards from Hackney and Crayford have expanded from eight-race programmes to 10-race cards, and the exposure given to the BAGS events by SIS can only serve to encourage more people to experience greyhound racing first-hand.

It certainly converted me. When I joined SIS in December 1986 I knew precious little about the sport. But, after a fact-finding mission at Hackney later that month I soon became hooked.

These days, after I have commentated on 24 greyhound races during the afternoon at the SIS offices in London, people find it a little odd that I go on to enjoy a night of greyhound racing at Wembley or some other track.

But it is a great way to relax and unwind, and there is nothing more exciting than being able to cheer on a winner after a busy day spent giving a balanced viewpoint on the day's racing for SIS.

So what of the future? With the advent of track-to-track tote betting on the horizon and therefore big jackpot pools, SIS must be in a position to be able to provide pictures from the meetings at the centre of the action that night.

As a foretaste to that, SIS transmitted the 1993 Greyhound Derby to 36 NGRC tracks to test the cost-effectiveness of the scheme. Thus, the futures of both SIS and greyhound racing are very much inter-twined.

Greyhound DERBY REVIEW

Victory for the People's Champion

1994 Derby Review. By Jonathan Hobbs

TO BE at Wimbledon on Saturday June 25, 1994, was to rejoice in what our sport, so often berated by the ignorant, is all about. The atmosphere; the excitement; the sheer elation of victory. It warmed the hearts of the converted and educated the uninitiated. It was more 'feelgood' than Forrest Gump.

The reason? Simply, Moral Standards.

Christened the People's Champion by the sporting press, no other greyhound since the halcyon days of Ballyregan Bob and Scurlogue Champ captured the imagination quite like Moral Standards. Why? Because he was the greyhound who confounded us all. He was not suited to Wimbledon. He started too slowly to be considered a serious Derby contender. And even if he were to reach the final, history told us the winner would lead from trap to line, not win from far off the pace. Of course, we were wrong. But did we care?

The road to Wimbledon for Moral Standards had seen him triumph at Hackney in the Gimcrack and reach the final of the Scottish Derby at Shawfield. On galloping tracks such as these, it was expected his best would be on show. But Wimbledon? Even his trainer, Tony Meek, had reservations.

He knew more than most what was required at Plough Lane, having guided Ringa Hustle to glory 12 months earlier. Ringa Hustle was early-paced, a front runner who ultimately proved too tough for his rivals to dislodge once in front.

The background to the 1994 *Daily Mirror/Sporting Life* Derby, though, was shrouded by events which followed the BBC's *On The Line* expose. Its repercussions were felt by most, notably Ger McKenna. Animal cruelty allegations levelled at McKenna and his son Owen resulted in the pair being banned from the Derby. And with compatriot Matt O'Donnell similarly banned, Wimbledon was without two famous faces. Both had tasted English Derby glory,

Greyhound DERBY REVIEW

REVELLING IN SUCCESS: For the second year running Tony Meek celebrates a Derby win, this time with Moral Standards

McKenna with Parkdown Jet (1981) and Lartigue Note (1989), and O'Donnell with Farloe Melody (1992). Always a force, the Irish this year had to look to the likes of Up The Junction, trained by the unassuming Pat Norris. The dog arrived with a tall reputation and was the Emerald Isle's principal hope. He started well, winning his first round by almost seven lengths in 28.90 sec. But it was Moral Standards (28.52) and Westmead Chick (28.57) who led the way.

The second round, with eight heats apiece, left racegoers with a feeling of *deja vu*, as Lassa Java, the 1993 finalist and Pall Mall hero, raced to a fastest of the session 28.72sec. Kennelmate Moral Standards left it late in his heat but a storming run up the home straight moved him over two lengths clear of Egmont Joan in 28.80. Roving Bunnie and Druids Omega were among the casualties here, while on the Saturday the likes of Simply Free, Jurassic Park, Highway Leader, Witches Dean and Glenholm Tiger succumbed. But not Moaning Lad, who drew clear from the first bend to win by nine lengths in 28.99sec (-35), emerging as star material.

Ayr Flyer was faultless, three spots quicker as he led home Flag The Fawn and Ardcollum Hilda . On rain-softened going, Greenane Squire also emerged as a leading contender. He posted 29.22 (-35) to pay testimony to the Moaning Lad's effort.

The third round produced several memorable ties: Moaning Lad versus Ardcollum Hilda; Greenane Squire versus Callahow Daly; Moral Standards versus Pearl's Girl. Who can forget Ayr Flyer and Snow Flash racing neck-and-neck from the second bend, with Druids Elprado in pursuit in the same heat. Knocked out of contention at the first bend, a ten-lengths deficit at the second became less than a length at the line. Up The Junction's success brought a huge response from his large army of south-London based followers. He was now the Derby favourite. But Moaning Lad was still the fastest, outgunning Gold Collar champion Ardcollum Hilda. The

Greyhound DERBY REVIEW

third round showed the down side of the game when Tony Meek, buoyed by the performances of Moral Standards and Greenane Squire, was left nursing Lassa Java, whose broken hock ended a champion career. At least he was saved. Salcombe was not so fortunate. Images of Jack Wilson's black injured in front of the stands in his quarter-final overshadowed the round.

But another marvellous performance from Moaning Lad thrilled the Wimbledon faithful. His demolition of Ayr Flyer was awesome. He clocked 28.41, just seven spots off Lodge Prince's long-held record, the fastest of the event. And with the likes of Ayr Flyer, Druids Elprado and Westmead Chick (eliminated) behind him. 'He's still very green, too,' said his trainer.

Greenane Squire (28.61) edged out Callahow Daly in the quarter-final, with Up The Junction the evens favourite in third. Longvalley Manor continued his steady progress while Moral Standards looked an unlikely qualifier at half-way in the final tie of

Greyhound DERBY REVIEW

the round. Checking at the first bend, he was left contesting last place down the far side but his now-familiar turn of speed brought him into contention with 20 metres to travel. He swept past Doreens Hope and Flag The Fawn for the spoils.

To the semi-finals, and another headline-grabbing performance from the greyhound who was clearly intent on rewriting the record books. Moral Standards' success over Up The Junction and Flag The Fawn in his customary last-gasp style inspired the most apt analogies in the Racing Post.

'Such an audacious tackle from behind would have probably earned Moral Standards a red card in the World Cup.' wrote Jeff Piper. The Irish hope, perhaps inspired by Ray Houghton's goal against Italy in New York moments earlier, led at the first bend. But once more moral Standards devoured the ground to win by half a length in 28.58sec.

Flag The Fawn secured his Derby final place in third, denying Magnetic Dancer, Fermaine Monarch and Doreens Hope. Hindsight shows the 5-1 offered about Ayr Flyer in the second semi-final was a steal. But his comprehensive defeat by Moaning Lad in the last round and the appearance of Greenane Squire in the line-up meant that pair dominated the market. But it was all Ayr Flyer from the traps, blasting clear from six and making all in 28.70sec.

Callahow Daly chased him home while Moaning Lad prevailed in his back-straight duel with Greenane Squire to make the final. Longvalley Manor and Druids Elprado also bowed out, the last exceeding himself on a track to which he is unsuited.

Martin Pipe, the champion National Hunt trainer was now charged with sealing the finalists' fate in the draw at the Derby lunch at Wimbledon. Live into the betting shops via SIS, Pipe said his father, a bookie, used to combine the White City Derby with the Irish Derby and the Pitmen's Derby in a special treble.

'It's always been a special weekend for me,' said Pipe. But what about the runners? Dawn Wheatley already knew her fate. Ayr Flyer as the sole wide seed would occupy six. As a youngster, Flyer had won the Manchester Cup and the Sporting Life Juvenile. He ended the season as winter favourite for the Derby and was an impressive greyhound — such that Nottingham promoter Terry Corden, on behalf of his friend Helen Roche, purchased a half-share in the February 1992 whelp. Helen owned the 1991 winner Ballinderry Ash. Absent for the final then and having to resort to commentary via mobile phone while on a pilgrimage to Lourdes, Helen now shared ownership with Helen and John Halbert.

Neil Morrice, the Racing Post's Lambourn man, had 'won' Flag The Fawn in an auction and was clearly enjoying every minute. None of this could be imagined when the greyhound badly injured a hock in the Reading Masters. Patsy Byrne feared he had run his last race. 'I had Pa doing the novenas!' he quipped. The prayers of head man Pa Fitzgerald were answered as Flag The Fawn lined up

Greyhound DERBY REVIEW

in the shadow of his sire, Druids Johno, the 1990 Derby runner-up. Asked by Blyth where he'd like to see his dog drawn, Fitzgerald smiled: 'Four lengths in front!'

Owners Jimmy Elias, Kevin Baily and George Cowle had, in Moaning Lad, what many believed the fastest of the finalists The only one who could beat Moral Standards in a straight two-dog race over 480 metres. He had been bought by Theo Mentzis from Ireland at the backend of the previous year. Notified of a potential champion, Mentzis arranged for three of his owners to meet. The trio knew each other but were not friends as such. But they took Mentzis at his word and pooled resources. The April fawn arrived and was now just over 28sec away from a £50,000 windfall.

Irish trained but English owned, Up The Junction was intent on landing a popular success. Grant Firminger, his ebullient owner, promised a coachload of support and this £550 purchase as a puppy from John Davis, of Farlow Melody fame, had support to rival that of Moral Standards. He had winning form at Waterford, Harolds Cross and Kilkenny, the last a brilliant 29.08sec for the Red Mills Cup. Trainer Pat Norris had been camped with Geoff de Mulder for the duration and was hoping some of the Meriden handler's Derby experience would rub off. Moral Standards now faced the acid test. Five straight wins in the event meant an unprecedented Wimbledon Derby-winning sequence was in prospect. Owned by Jim Wenman and John Jefford, or more precisely their wives Suzy and Rita, Moral Standards was purchased on the recommendation of Clonmel racing manager Gus Ryan.

He chalked up four wins from four in Ireland, and Ryan, having also 'spotted' Greenane Squire for the same partnership, a Derby final night double courtesy of the Squire in the Consolation final would have been a dream for the Romford-based businessmen.

For Callahow Daly, it was just another race. With 72 races under his belt and at three years five months the oldest finalist, supporters were hoping his experience would reap dividends. But for Charlie Lister and owner Martin Rogers, this was all new.

The draw was:
T1 Up The Junction T2 Moral Standards T3 Flag The Fawn
T4 Callahow Daly T5 Moaning Lad T6 Ayr Flyer.

Jimmy Wenman ordered 100 blue rosettes for supporters of Moral Standards but it looked as though he'd seriously under-ordered. In the ring, bookmakers were swamped with money for the People's Champion. He opened 7-2 but closed 9-4 favourite.

Lister had some pre-race excitement. He was told by police that he didn't have the right passes and would not be allowed in. He protested, saying he had a Derby finalist in the back of the van. The policeman did not believe him until Callahow Daly barked!

Enjoyable performances from Decoy Lynx in the eight-bender, Gis A Smile in the hurdle, Galleydown Boy in the six-bender and Greenane Squire in the Consolation Derby set the scene for a

Greyhound DERBY REVIEW

memorable night. The Derby roar was deafening. Up The Junction and Ayr Flyer bolted from the traps. So, too, did Moral Standards. He had got away better than at any time in the Derby and turned third. Already they were celebrating.

With Moaning Lad missing the start and Flag The Fawn and Callahow Daly bumping out of the traps it was Ayr Flyer and Up The Junction racing toe-to-toe down the far side. Moral Standards wound up for his move into the third and the stadium erupted.

But then, as Up The Junction found Ayr Flyer too tough and the latter went on, Moral Standards was stopped in his tracks as he converged on the pair. His stride shortened and hearts missed a beat or more. But he steadied and then pounced.

Carving his way between Ayr Flyer and Up The Junction, he struck the front in sight of the winning line. Wimbledon was delirious. Hordes invaded the track, wanting to be part of one of the greatest Derby finals and be close to one of its greatest winners.

And we were.

Results in Full

Daily Mirror/Sporting Life Greyhound Derby **1st Round** May 25

Heat 1
1 TULLIG PHANTOM 5-1 (3)
2 Super Bridge   7-4jf (4)
3 Moral Director 3-1 (2)
4 Stylefield Law 7-4jf (1)
5 Rio Remember   12-1 (5)
6 My Little King 25-1 (6)
29.21 (N) 1, hd, $1^{3}/_{4}$, $2^{1}/_{4}$, hd
Hitch (Wimbledon)

Heat 2
1 TOMS CABIN KING 7-4 (2)
2 Salcombe   4-5F (4)
3 Pollysbrae Boy 10-1 (5)
4 Tain Billy   33-1 (1)
5 Laganore Spark 8-1 (6)
6 Creation   14-1 (3)
28.97 (N) $2^{1}/_{4}$, $1^{3}/_{4}$, $3^{3}/_{4}$, sht-hd, $3^{3}/_{4}$
Knibb (Milton Keynes)

Heat 3
1 COLORADO FLAME 7-1 (4)
2 Gamblers Sport 9-4F (6)
3 Arrancourt Gem 5-2 (2)
4 Rio Gold   3-1 (5)
5 Mount Trader   16-1 (1)
6 Chakalak Zeus   7-2 (3)
29.36 (N) $1^{3}/_{4}$, 3, $1^{3}/_{4}$, hd, nk
Silkman (Canterbury)

Heat 4
1 GAFFERS DASHER Ev   (2)
2 Glenholm Tiger 4-5F (6)
3 Little Hammer   25-1 (4)
4 Rocket Symphony 50-1 (3)
5 Movealong Mascot 50-1 (1)
6 Cosmic Man   50-1 (5)
28.74 (N) 5, $3^{1}/_{4}$, 4, $2^{1}/_{2}$, $4^{1}/_{2}$, $1^{1}/_{4}$
Rees (Wimbledon)

Heat 5
1 PARQUET PADDY   8-11F (3)
2 Bayside   2-1 (4)
3 Farewell Slippy 8-1 (2)
4 Forest Rocket   20-1 (6)
5 Mollys Maid   33-1 (5)
6 Armiger   10-1 (1)
28.89 (N) nk, $1^{1}/_{4}$, $2^{1}/_{4}$, 3, $^{1}/_{2}$
Hitch (Wimbledon)

Heat 6
1 ARDILAUN BRIDGE 3-1 (5)
2 Mucky Budd   EvF (1)
3 Our Timmy   4-1 (2)
4 Able Ramon   10-1 (4)
5 Milltown Talent 12-1 (6)
6 Autumn Barry   10-1 (3)
29.01 (N) $4^{3}/_{4}$, $3^{1}/_{2}$, $^{3}/_{4}$, hd, dis.
Duggan (Walthamstow)

Heat 7
1 MAGNETIC OCEAN 1-3F (6)
2 Sure Fantasy   11-4 (3)
3 Connells Cross 12-1 (1)
4 Im Home Maid   33-1 (5)
5 Magical Chief   33-1 (4)
6 Spiral Web   50-1 (2)
28.81 (N) $1^{1}/_{2}$, $^{1}/_{2}$, $1^{1}/_{2}$, 3, $3^{3}/_{4}$
Byrne (Hackney)

Heat 8
1 LASSA JAVA   1-2F (4)
2 Be My Pal   3-1 (5)
3 Fangio Dragon   50-1 (3)
4 Westlake Wonder 8-1 (6)
5 Gorse Green   66-1 (2)
6 Spring Welcome 14-1 (1)
28.93 (N) $1^{3}/_{4}$, $^{3}/_{4}$, $1^{1}/_{2}$, nk, $5^{1}/_{4}$
Meek (Hall Green)

Greyhound DERBY RESULTS in full

Heat 9
1 LONGVALLY MANOR 4-5F (5)
2 Green Bell 5-1 (3)
3 Spiral Zee Zee 7-4 (2)
4 Ballinderry Chet 16-1 (1)
5 Loaded Weapon 20-1 (4)
Trap Vacant (6)
28.94 (N) $1^{3}/_{4}$, $^{3}/_{4}$, $1^{3}/_{4}$, $7^{3}/_{4}$
Coleman (Walthamstow)

Heat 10
1 WESTMEAD CHICK 4-6F (2)
2 Ballywalter Sir 7-1 (6)
3 Pams Silver 7-1 (4)
4 Coast Is Clear 8-1 (5)
5 Moynevilla Echo 5-1 (3)
6 Rugby Wishes 6-1 (1)
28.57 (N) $6^{1}/_{4}$, $1^{3}/_{4}$, hd, $^{3}/_{4}$, $2^{3}/_{4}$
Savva (Walthamstow)

Heat 11
1 BEAU TOIT 3-1 (1)
2 Druids Elprado 4-9F (3)
3 Tullig Mouse 8-1 (4)
4 Barny Rubble 33-1 (2)
5 Westmead Mack 50-1 (6)
6 Jackies Phantom 8-1 (5)
28.84 (N) $1^{1}/_{4}$, $3^{1}/_{4}$, 1, 4, $2^{1}/_{2}$
Towner (Canterbury)

(May 27) Heat 12

1 RINGSIDE RETURN 8-11F (2)
2 Pepsi Pete 10-1 (1)
3 So I Heard 10-1 (4)
4 Roslo Speedy 8-1 (6)
5 Franks Doll 9-4 (3)
6 Friars Hero 20-1 (5)
28.83 (N) $1^{1}/_{4}$, $2^{3}/_{4}$, $2^{1}/_{4}$, $2^{1}/_{2}$, nk
Osborne (Bristol)

Heat 13
1 ROVING BUNNIE 5-4F (1)
2 Ticos Lodge 8-1 (6)
3 Lester 25-1 (4)
4 Trade Union 6-4 (5)
5 Kyle Judge 20-1 (3)
6 Westmead Hazzard 5-1 (2)
28.81 (+10) 9, $2^{3}/_{4}$, 1, nk, $^{3}/_{4}$
Rouse (Hove)

Heat 14
1 NOIR BANJO 2-1 (1)
2 Fermaine Monarch 4-1 (4)
3 Ballygown Hero 20-1 (3)
4 The Other Style 20-1 (5)
5 Bond End Damsel 7-4F (6)
6 Ardnacrohy Blue 7-2 (2)
28.79 (+10) $5^{1}/_{4}$, $1^{3}/_{4}$, $3^{1}/_{4}$, 1, $2^{1}/_{2}$
Wileman (Monmore)

Heat 15
1 MORAL STANDARDS 11-10 (2)
2 Simply Free EvF (5)
3 Duffys Legend 12-1 (1)
4 Van Die Queen 7-1 (4)
5 Craker Clipper 50-1 (6)
NR Billys Idea (Trap 3 Vacant)
28.52 (+10) $5^{3}/_{4}$, $1^{1}/_{2}$, $3^{1}/_{2}$, $1^{3}/_{4}$
Meek (Hall Green)

Heat 16
1 MOANING LAD 2-1F (2)
2 Always Good 7-1 (5)
3 Winsor Dan 5-2 (6)
4 Salthill Champ 7-2 (4)
5 Tyrian Blue 8-1 (3)
6 Alans Wonder 7-1 (1)
29.08 (+10) 1, sht-hd, hd, 1, $^{3}/_{4}$
Mentzis (Milton Keynes)

Heat 17
1 CAREYS FAULT 7-2 (3)
2 Muls Cheerful 20-1 (5)
3 Darragh Fox 50-1 (4)
4 Mr Tan 4-1 (1)
5 Michaels Machine 4-5F (2)
6 Jamie Jim 8-1 (6)
28.84 (+10) $2^{3}/_{4}$, 2, sht-hd, 1, $^{3}/_{4}$
Sykes (Wimbledon)

Heat 18
1 AYR FLYER 4-7F (4)
2 Dennys Bar 5-2 (6)
3 Battstreet Benny 20-1 (3)
4 Off Our Minds 25-1 (5)
5 Rosstemple Pride 14-1 (2)
6 Colorado Green 7-1 (1)
28.76 (+10) $1^{1}/_{4}$, $4^{3}/_{4}$, $1^{3}/_{4}$, $1^{1}/_{4}$, $1^{1}/_{4}$
Wheatley (Nottingham)

Heat 19
1 GREENANE SQUIRE 11-8F (3)
2 Westmead Merlin 7-4 (2)
3 Witches Dean 4-1 (5)
4 Killila Place 20-1 (4)
5 Droopys Craig 5-1 (1)
6 Westmead Blue 50-1 (6)
28.71 (+10) $^{3}/_{4}$, 1, $1^{1}/_{2}$, hd, dis.
Meek (Hall Green)

Heat 20
1 SONIC BLUE 7-2 (2)
2 Perrys Charmer 4-6F (1)
3 Woodview Brandy 9-2 (3)
4 Welsh Wizard 14-1 (4)
5 Droopys Ayrton 10-1 (5)
6 Fairmile Fox 50-1 (6)
28.94 (+10) $3^{1}/_{4}$, $3^{3}/_{4}$, $^{3}/_{4}$, $2^{3}/_{4}$, $1^{1}/_{2}$
Hitch (Wimbledon)

Heat 21
1 RINGSIDE CYCLONE 5-1 (5)
2 Copelands Cut 7-1 (6)
3 Star Of Tyrone 11-10F (3)
4 Spiral Dancer 7-2 (1)
5 November Jet 16-1 (2)
6 You Lead 7-2 (4)
28.88 (+10) 8, $1^{3}/_{4}$, $^{3}/_{4}$, hd, $2^{3}/_{4}$
Osborne (Bristol)

Heat 22
1 FLAG THE FAWN 3-1 (3)
2 Ceader Mountain 4-9F (5)
3 Highway Leader 8-1 (4)
4 Glengar Fred 33-1 (6)
5 Fifis Monkey 50-1 (2)
NR Geinis Champion (Trap 1 Vacant)
28.87 (+10) $2^{1}/_{4}$, $1^{1}/_{4}$, $2^{3}/_{4}$, $1^{1}/_{4}$
Byrne (Hackney)

Greyhound DERBY RESULTS in full

(May 28) Heat 23
1 MURLENS SON 10-1 (6)
2 Lughill Slippy 12-1 (3)
3 Pearls Girl 1-1F (5)
4 Sandanita 7-4 (2)
5 Droopys Curtis 7-1 (4)
6 Droopys Doyle 10-1 (1)
29.09 (+10) ½, sht-hd, 1¾, 2¾, 2½
Hitch (Wimbledon)

Heat 24
1 CARRAIG PAWS 4-7F (1)
2 Battstreet Ivy 7-1 (2)
3 Rockglen Dasher 12-1 (5)
4 Fred The Needle 20-1 (3)
5 Ballinora Lucky 2-1 (4)
6 Hard Nut 100-1 (6)
29.03 (+10) sht-hd, 3, 2¼, 3¼, dis.
Black (Reading)

Heat 25
1 CRAFTY FONTANA 11-8 (1)
2 Picture Gold 6-1 (6)
3 Rathcannon Lodge 10-11F (2)
4 Prove The Point 20-1 (3)
5 Esha Ness 7-4F (5)
Trap 4 Vacant
28.85 (+10) 2½, 2, 1½, 3½
Mullins (Walthamstow)

Heat 26
1 BALLINDERRY SUE 2-1JF (3)
2 Patriot Sail 5-2 (1)
3 Listen To Dan 12-1 (5)
4 Knockrour Bruno 8-1 (2)
5 Fearless Cougar 2-1JF (6)
6 Jaffa Line 50-1 (4)
28.66 (+10) 5¼, 1½, 3, sht-hd, 2¼
Tasker (Unattached)

Heat 27
1 CANT BE SERIOUS 3-1 (3)
2 Havoc House EvF (4)
3 Faultless April 5-1 (6)
4 Spiral Grand 6-1 (2)
5 Bowmans Arrow 6-1 (1)
6 Arrogant Prince 20-1 (5)
29.03 (+10) 2, 4¼, hd, 2½, sht-hd
Byrne (Hackney)

Heat 28
1 ARDCOLLUM HILDA 9-4 (2)
2 Callahow Daly 4-7F (1)
3 Kane 20-1 (3)
4 Johnos Magic 10-1 (6)
5 Astis Account 10-1 (4)
6 Ginger Brian 25-1 (5)
28.88 (+10) 2¾, 6, nk, ¾, 1½
Byrne (Hackney)

Heat 29
1 JURASSIC PARK 7-2 (1)
2 Druids Tycoon 4-1 (4)
3 Powys Gold 3-1 (5)
4 Fast Off 2-1F (3)
5 Blissful Style 6-1 (6)
6 Bills Prince 20-1 (2)
29.19 (+10) nk, sht-hd, sht-hd, 1¼, 5¾
Byrne (Hackney)

Heat 30
1 UP THE JUNCTION 4-6F (2)
2 Timeless Pragada 50-1 (1)
3 Druids Omega 4-1 (5)
4 Spit It Out 25-1 (4)
5 Kenaloe 50-1 (3)
6 Greenane Slippy 9-4 (6)
28.90 (+10) 6¾, 1¼, hd, 2¼, 5¼
Norris (Ireland)

Heat 31
1 EGMONT JOAN 5-2 (2)
2 New York Express 14-1 (5)
3 Urgent Meeting 2-1 (4)
4 Want To Be 20-1 (3)
5 Redwood Walk 50-1 (6)
6 Ballyard Rush 6-4F (1)
28.90 (+10) 4¾, 1, 2¼, 4¼, d.n.f
Lister (Peterborough)

Heat 32
1 PARTNERS IN HOPE 9-2 (6)
2 Orizontals Best 3-1 (1)
3 Rabatino 4-1 (2)
4 Affadown Tony 20-1 (5)
5 Home From Home 6-4F (4)
6 Pirates Gold 12-1 (3)
29.00 (+10) 1¼, 1¼, ½, 2¾, ½
Lawlor (Oxford)

Heat 33
1 SNOW FLASH EvF (2)
2 Doreens Hope 12-1 (3)
3 Witches Billy 5-1 (6)
4 New Inn Ranger 8-1 (1)
5 Pepsi Joe 2-1 (4)
6 Kings Seskin 14-1 (5)
28.65 (+10) 3¼, 4, 1¾, ½, 3¼
Dolby (Hackney)

2nd Round (June 3) Heat 1
1 DOREENS HOPE 10-1 (2)
2 Beau Toit 6-4 (1)
3 Witches Billy 20-1 (5)
4 Gaffers Dasher EvF (4)
5 Lughill Slippy 6-1 (3)
6 Pams Silver 10-1 (6)
29.04 (N) 1½, 2¾, 2¾, nk, 4¼
Rees (Wimbledon)

Heat 2
1 WESTMEAD MERLIN 4-7F (2)
2 Green Bell 4-1 (1)
3 Fermaine Monarch 5-1 (5)
4 New York Express 16-1 (6)
5 Our Timmy 10-1 (3)
6 Tullig Mouse 20-1 (4)
29.06 (N) ½, 1, 2, 1½, hd
Savva (Unattached)

Heat 3
1 DRUIDS ELPRADO 6-4 (1)
2. Parquet Paddy EvF (2)
3 Carraig Paws 4-1 (4)
4 Lester 50-1 (3)
5 Listen To Dan 10-1 (5)
Trap 6 vacant
28.98 (N) ¾, 1, 1, 4¼
McGee (Unattached)

NGRC Greyhound Racing Yearbook 1995

Greyhound DERBY RESULTS in full

Heat 4
1 UP THE JUNCTION 4-6F (1)
2 Sure Fantasy 5-2 (3)
3 Super Bridge 10-1 (2)
4 Ticos Lodge 25-1 (5)
5 Roving Bunnie 4-1 (4)
6 Faultless April 66-1 (6)
28.81 (N) 2, 6, nk, 1/4, 3/4
Norris (Ireland)

Heat 5
1 LASSA JAVA 6-4 (6)
2 Magnetic Ocean 4-6F (4)
3 Colorado Flame 40-1 (2)
4 Sonic Blue 12-1 (1)
5 Pollysbrae Boy 50-1 (5)
6 Farewell Slippy 12-1 (3)
28.72 (N) 3 1/2, 61/4, sht-hd, 11/2, 1
Meek (Hall Green)

Heat 6
1 CALLAHOW DALY 7-4 (3)
2 Pearls Girl 4-5F (1)
3 Perrys Charmer 14-1 (2)
4 Partners In Hope 14-1 (6)
5 Winsor Dan 50-1 (4)
6 Muls Cheerful 12-1 (5)
29.18 (N) hd, sht-hd, 21/4, 1/2, 33/4
Lister (Peterborough)

Heat 7
1 TOMS CABIN KING 10-1 (1)
2 Ringside Return 9-4 (2)
3 Moral Director 14-1 (3)
4 Bayside 9-4 (6)
5 Cant Be Serious 12-1 (4)
6 Druids Omega 2-1F (5)
28.98 (N) 1, 2, 1 1/2, sht-hd, 3/4
Knibb (Milton Keynes)

Heat 8
1 MORAL STANDARDS 4-7F (1)
2 Egmont Joan 3-1 (2)
3 Longvalley Manor 5-1 (6)
4 So I Heard 20-1 (3)
5 Mucky Budd 14-1 (4)
6 Rabatino 33-1 (5)
28.80 (N) 21/4, 3/4, nk, sht-hd, 3/4
Meek (Hall Green)

(June 4) Heat 9
1 HAVOC HOUSE 9-2 (3)
2 Urgent Meeting 10-3 (5)
3 Battstreet Ivy 9-2 (2)
4 Jurrasic Park 9-2 (1)
5 Be My Pal 6-4F (6)
6 Little Hammer 33-1 (4)
29.34 (-30) 23/4, sht-hd, 11/2, nk, 11/2
Sykes (Wimbledon)

Heat 10
1 AYR FLYER 4-7F (5)
2 Flag The Fawn 9-2 (1)
3 Ardcollum Hilda 5-2 (2)
4 Highway Leader 14-1 (3)
5 Duffys Legend 33-1 (4)
6 Battstreet Benny 66-1 (6)
28.96 (-30) 23/4, 63/4, 11/2, 43/4, d.n.f.
Wheatley (Nottingham)

Heat 11
1 POWYS GOLD 3-1 (5)
2 Salcombe 7-4 (1)
3 Darragh Fox 50-1 (6)
4 Ringside Cyclone 11-10F (2)
5 Kane 20-1 (3)
6 Arrancourt Gem 14-1 (4)
29.44 (-30) 3/4, 2, 31/2, 1, 11/2
Meek (Hall Green)

Heat 12
1 WESTMEAD CHICK 1-2F (3)
2 Always Good 7-1 (6)
3 Picture Gold 8-1 (5)
4 Patriot Sail 10-1 (2)
5 Orizontals Best 25-1 (4)
6 Pepsi Pete 7-1 (1)
29.04 (-30) 41/4, 3/4, 13/4, nk, 2 1/2
Savva (Hackney)

Heat 13
1 ARDILAUN BRIDGE 2-1 (1)
2 Ballinderry Sue 4-6F (6)
3 Copelands Cut 40-1 (2)
4 Tullig Phantom 7-1 (5)
5 Murlens Son 20-1 (4)
6 Connells Cross 14-1 (3)
29.30 (-35) 2, 5 1/2, 11/4, nk, 1
Duggan (Walthamstow)

Heat 14
1 MOANING LAD 7-2 (2)
2 Timeless Pragada 50-1 (3)
3 Gamblers Sport 14-1 (4)
4 Simply Free 4-5F (1)
5 Glenholm Tiger 7-4 (5)
6 Ballygown Hero 33-1 (6)
28.99 (-35) 9, 1 1/2, 1/2, 1 3/4, d.n.f.
Mentzis (Milton Keynes)

Heat 15
1 GREENANE SQUIRE EvF (3)
2 Snow Flash 5-2 (2)
3 Dennys Bar 4-1 (5)
4 Druids Tycoon 16-1 (6)
5 Star Of Tyrone 12-1 (1)
6 Crafty Fontana 12-1 (4)
29.22 (-35) 21/4, 13/4, nk, 3/4, 1 1/2
Meek (Hall Green)

Heat 16
1 NOIR BANJO 5-2 (2)
2 Careys Fault 7-4F (1)
3 Woodview Brandy 50-1 (3)
4 Witches Dean 9-4 (4)
5 Rockglen Dasher 20-1 (6)
6 Ballywalter Sir 5-1 (5)
29.43 (-35) 1/2, 11/2, hd, 3/4, 3/4
Wileman (Monmore)

3rd Round (June 11) Heat 1
1 ALWAYS GOOD 5-1 (6)
2 Havoc House 6-4 (1)
3 Woodview Brandy 25-1 (4)
4 Noir Banjo 5-4F (3)
5 Toms Cabin King 7-2 (5)
Trap 2 Vacant
28.92 (+10) 21/4, 33/4, 3/4, sht-hd
Hodson (Hove)

NGRC Greyhound Racing Yearbook 1995

Greyhound DERBY RESULTS in full

Heat 2
1 MOANING LAD   5-4JF   (5)
2 Ardcollum Hilda   5-4JF   (2)
3 Battstreet Ivy   7-1   (1)
4 Copelands Cut   66-1   (3)
5 Super Bridge   8-1   (6)
6 Careys Fault   12-1   (4)
28.52 (+10) 4³/₄, 5, 2³/₄, sht-hd, ³/₄
Mentzis (Milton Keynes)

Heat 3
1 GREENANE SQUIRE   8-11F   (4)
2 Ballinderry Sue   7-4   (6)
3 Doreens Hope   16-1   (1)
4 Gamblers Sport   66-1   (5)
5 Green Bell   10-1   (2)
6 Egmont Joan   7-1   (3)
28.78 (+10) 1, 4, ³/₄, 2, 1
Meek (Hall Green)

Heat 4
1 UP THE JUNCTION   11-10F (3)
2 Westmead Chick   9-4   (4)
3 Fermaine Monarch   33-1   (6)
4 Ringside Return   8-1   (5)
5 Ardilaun Bridge   5-2   (1)
6 Timeless Pragada   100-1   (2)
28.75 (+10) 4¹/₄, 1¹/₄, 1, nk, 4
Norris (Ireland)

Heat 5
1 CALLAHOW DALY   3-1   (1)
2 Dennys Bar   10-1   (4)
3 Salcombe   10-1   (3)
4 Witches Billy   66-1   (6)
5 Urgent Meeting   5-1   (2)
6 Lassa Java   4-6F   (5)
28.79 (+10) 4¹/₂, 1¹/₂, hd, 2, dis.
Lister (Peterborough)

Heat 6
1 AYR FLYER   4-7F   (5)
2 Snow Flash   5-2   (1)
3 Druids Elprado   5-1   (2)
4 Picture Gold   33-1   (6)
5 Colorado Flame   100-1   (3)
6 Beau Toit 20-1   (4)
28.89 (+10) ¹/₂, nk, 2³/₄, 2¹/₂, 2³/₄
Wheatley (Nottingham)

Heat 7
1 MORAL STANDARDS   10-1   (3)
2 Flag The Fawn   9-4   (1)
3 Moral Director   14-1   (4)
4 Pearls Girl   9-4   (2)
5 Carraig Paws   12-1   (5)
6 Darragh Fox   2-1F   (6)
28.78 (+10) 3¹/₂, sht-hd, ³/₄, ³/₄, 1
Meek (Hall Green)

Heat 8
1 LONGVALLEY MANOR   10-1   (3)
2 Westmead Merlin   4-1   (6)
3 Magnetic Ocean   6-4   (4)
4 Parquet Paddy   5-4F   (1)
5 Perrys Charmer   25-1   (2)
6 Powys Gold   20-1   (5)
28.79 (+10) 2, ³/₄, ¹/₂,³/₄, 2³/₄
Coleman (Walthamstow)

Quarter Finals June 14
1 LONGVALLEY MANOR   11-4   (2)
2 Magnetic Ocean   6-4F   (4)
3 Fermaine Monarch   16-1   (6)
4 Moral Director   5-1   (1)
5 Westmead Merlin   7-2   (5)
6 Salcombe   8-1   (3)
28.70 (+20) 2³/₄, 1¹/₄, hd, 1³/₄, d.n.f.
Coleman (Walthamstow)

1 MOANING LAD   6-4   (2)
2 Ayr Flyer   11-10F (6)
3 Druids Elprado   7-1   (4)
4 Westmead Chick   9-2   (5)
5 Woodview Brandy   50-1   (1)
6 Havoc House   20-1   (3)
28.41 (+20) 5¹/₂, 1, nk, 2¹/₂, sht-hd
Mentzis (Milton Keynes)

1 GREENANE SQUIRE   5-2   (2)
2 Callahow Daly   14-1   (3)
3 Up The Junction   EvF   (1)
4 Dennys Bar   33-1   (5)
5 Ballinderry Sue   4-1   (6)
6 Snow Flash   10-1   (4)
28.61 (+20) ³/₄, 4¹/₂, 1, 5¹/₄, 1³/₄
Meek (Hall Green)

1 MORAL STANDARDS   4-5F   (1)
2 Doreens Hope   20-1   (4)
3 Flag The Fawn   3-1   (2)
4 Ardcollum Hilda   3-1   (5)
5 Always Good   12-1   (6)
6 Battstreet Ivy   33-1   (3)
28.85 (+20) ³/₄, ³/₄,³/₄, hd, ³/₄
Meek (Hall Green)

Semi Finals June 18
1 MORAL STANDARDS   2-1   (4)
2 Up The Junction   8-11F   (3)
3 Flag The Fawn   8-1   (1)
4 Magnetic Ocean   7-1   (6)
5 Fermaine Monarch   66-1   (5)
6 Doreens Hope   33-1   (2)
28.58 (+20) ¹/₂, nk, 2³/₄, ³/₄, 4¹/₂
Meek (Hall Green)

1 AYR FLYER   5-1   (6)
2 Calahow Daly   20-1   (5)
3 Moaning Lad   6-4   (3)
4 Druids Elprado   12-1   (4)
5 Greenane Squire   5-4   (1)
6 Longvalley Manor   14-1   (2)
28.70 (+20) ³/₄, 2, 5, 1, 2¹/₂
Wheatley (Nottingham)

Final June 25
1 **MORAL STANDARDS** 9-4F   (2)
  wbk d Flag Star-No Way Jose May 92
2 Ayr Flyer   3-1   (6)
  bd d Ardfert Sean-Slaneyside Glory Apr 92
3 Moaning Lad   7-2   (5)
  f d Kyle Jack-Lady Bellamy Apr 92
4 Up The Junction   3-1   (1)
  bd d Slippys Quest-Elf Arrow Feb 92
5 Flag The Fawn   16-1   (3)
  f d Druids Johno-Almond Blossom Jul 91
6 Calahow Daly   12-1   (4)
  f d Daleys Gold-Ahaveen Fever Jan 91
28.59 (+20) 1¹/₄, ¹/₂, sht-hd, 1¹/₂, 1¹/₂
Meek (Hall Green)

NGRC Statistics

Open Races 1994

Reproduced by kind permission of the *Racing Post*. Compiled by *Peter Meldrum*

Open Race winners: Category 1

DATE	RACE	PURSE	WINNER
15-Jan	Embassy Marathon, Hackney	£5,000	Tammys Delight
22-Jan	Fosters Gold Cup, Wimbledon	£5,000	Island Doe
4-Feb	Embassy Permit Derby, Hackney	£5,000	Annamore Kyle
16-Feb	A R Dennis Middle Park Puppy Cup Final, Hackney	£5,000	Druids Elprado
19-Feb	Regal 10,000, Sunderland	£10,000	Carrigeen Blaze
26-Feb	Ladbroke Golden Jacket, Crayford	£6,000	Wexford Minx
5-Mar	Racing Post Arc, Walthamstow	£5,000	Westmead Chick
19-Mar	Pall Mall, Oxford	£5,000	Lassa Java
30-Mar	Daily Mirror\Sporting Life Grand National, Hall Green	£5,000	Randy Savage
04-Apr	Wendy Fair Blue Riband, Wembley	£7,500	Ardilaun Bridge
06-Apr	BBC Television Trophy, Sunderland	£6,000	Jubilee Rebecca
14-Apr	Courage Greyhound Olympic, Hove	£3,000	Westmead Chick
30-Apr	Reading Masters, Reading	£20,000	Druids Elprado
21-May	Regal Scottish Greyhound Derby, Shawfield	£20,000	Droopys Sandy
21-May	The Regency Final, Hove	£5,000	Decoy Cougar
11-Jun	48th Courage 2-Y-0 Produce Stakes, Bristol	£5,000	Wolf Man
25-Jun	Daily Mirror\Sporting Life Greyhound Derby, Wimbledon	£50,000	Moral Standards
9-Jul	Tetley Yorkshire Bitter Circuit Walthamstow	£2,500	Connells Cross
22-Jul	Coral Romford Champion Stakes, Romford	£10,000	Here's Seanie
23-Jul	Wey Plastics, Wimbledon	£6,000	Greenane Squire
4-Aug	Sussex Cup Final, Hove	£3,000	Unique Bay
6-Aug	Peterborough Derby	£10,000	Highway Leader
13-Aug	A R Dennis Silver Collar, Walthamstow	£3,000	Silbury Cloud
15-Aug	Carlsberg Vase, Crayford	£3,000	Ashfield Arrow
2-Sep	Stadium Bookmakers Essex Vase, Romford	£5,000	Lisa My Girl
3-Sep	Edinburgh Cup, Powderhall	£7,500	Highway Leader
15-Sep	East Anglian Derby, Yarmouth	£10,000	Franks Doll

NGRC Statistics

Category 1 (cont)

DATE	RACE	PURSE	WINNER
17-Sep	John Humphreys Gold Collar, Catford	£7,500	Pearls Girl
24-Sep	Fosters Cesarewitch, Belle Vue	£10,000	Sandollar Louie
24-Sep	Surrey Racing Puppy Derby Wimbledon	£3,500	Bonmahon Darkie
29-Sep	Ansells Birmingham Cup, Perry Barr	£6,000	Here's Seanie
8-Oct	Laurent Perrier Champagne Grand Prix, Walthamstow	£7,500	Redwood Girl
15-Oct	Breeders Forum Produce Stakes, Hall Green	£10,000	Westmead Merlin
15-Oct	Ike Morris Laurels, Wimbledon	£7,500	Deenside Dean
28-Oct	Bailey Racing Golden Sprint, Romford	£3,000	Witches Dean
29-Oct	Peter Derrick Eclipse, Nottingham	£10,000	Spit It Out
29-Oct	Dranesfield Northern Puppy Cup, Sunderland	£5,000	Justright Melody
11-Nov	Wendy Fair Greyhound St Leger, Wembley	£12,000	Ballarue Minx
26-Nov	Foster Midland Flat Championship, Hall Green	£5,000	Westmead Chick
10-Dec	All England Cup, Brough Park	£5,000	Moral Director
17-Dec	St Mary's Hospital Oaks Final, Wimbledon	£6,000	Westmead Chick

DEAN OF WIMBLEDON!: Ike Morris Laurels winner Deenside Dean after his victory at Plough Lane.

SPEEDFORM 1995

A COMPREHENSIVE GUIDE TO GREYHOUND RACING AT NGRC TRACKS

Compiled by
PETER MELDRUM

QUOTES FROM SPORTING PRESS

Racing Post – **"Speedform 1995 is heartily recommended to anyone with more than a token interest in Greyhound Racing"**

Odds on Magazine, Jonathan Hobbs – **"Crammed full of facts and figures – A real Bookie Basher"**

£7.99 (plus £1 postage & package)

Please send me .... copies of **SPEEDFORM 1995**

Name

Address

Post Code .... Telephone

I enclose cheque/money order for £ .... made payable to:

PETER MELDRUM, 11 KINGSMOOR CLOSE, NOTTINGHAM NG5 9RE
Telephone 0602-763875

NGRC Statistics

Open Race winners: Category 2

DATE	RACE	PURSE	WINNER
14-Jan	Tony Williams Coronation Cup, Romford	£1,000	Smile Rose
27-Jan	Northumberland Gold Cup, Brough Park	£2,000	Droopys Slave
29-Jan	Pepsi Cola Marathon, Walthamstow	£2,000	Sunhill Misty
4-Feb	William Hill Cup, Catford	£1,000	Blackstairs Boy
5-Feb	Jim Davis Stakes, Walthamstow	£1,000	Loch Bo Anchor
0-Feb	A R Dennis Triumph Hurdle, Hackney	£1,500	Gis A Smile
19-Feb	John Henwood Springbok Trophy, Wimbledon	£2,300	Avoid The Rush
12-Mar	J & J E Cearns Memorial Trophy, Wimbledon	£2,000	Heavenly Lady
12-Mar	Carlsberg Midland Puppy Derby, Monmore	£1,750	Mr Tan
26-Mar	Scottish St Leger, Powderhall	£1,000	Droopys Evelyn
8-Apr	William Hill Steel City Cup Final, Sheffield	£2,000	Anhid Blaze
9-Apr	Peterborough Puppy Derby, Peterborough	£1,000	Pams Silver
14-Apr	Embassy London Grand National, Hackney	£2,500	Heavenly Dream
16-Apr	NGRC Strewards Cup, Walthamstow	£2,000	Ballygown Lilly
20-Apr	Whitbred Flying Childers, Hackney	£2,500	Fast Copper
30-Apr	Coomes Greenwich Cup Final, Catford	£3,000	Wexford Minx
7-May	Scottish Grand National, Powderhall	£1,000	Heavenly Dream
12-May	Master Brewer Trophy Final, Ramsgate	£1,000	Patriot Sail
13-May	Quicksilver Stakes Final, Romford	£1,250	Decoy Gold
14-May	Mistley Trojan Puppy Stakes, Walthamstow	£1,500	Lacken Prince
21-May	Fosters Midland Oaks, Hall Green	£1,000	Active Summer
26-May	Catford Bookmakers National, Catford	£1,500	Bayview Blaze
28-May	Peterborough Cesarewitch, Peterborough	£1,000	Gortmore Express
7-Jun	Carling Black Label Test, Walthamstow	£2,000	Redwood Girl
24-Jun	Swaffham Derby, Swaffham	£2,000	Drovers Road
25-Jun	William Hill Champion Hurdle, Wimbledon	£2,000	Gis A Smile

NGRC Statistics

Category 2 (cont)

DATE	RACE	PURSE	WINNER
5-Jun	Con John Trophy, Bristol	£1,000	Scintillas Pansy
2-Jul	Regal Mild Final, Stainforth	£1,500	Super Bridge
2-Jul	Regal Filter Final, Stainforth	£1,500	Toybox Schooner
2-Jul	Regal King Size Sprint Final Stainforth	£1,500	Tawny Flash
6-Jul	William Hill Trophy Final, Hall Green	£1,000	Billys Idea
7-Jul	Ladbroke Midland Gold Cup Monmore	£3,000	Droopys Craig
9-Jul	Fosters Scurry Gold Cup, Catford	£2,500	Rabatino
9-Jul	July Cup, Crayford	£2,000	Wexford Minx
9-Jul	Midland St Leger, Monmore	£1,500	Kerogue Ivy
16-Jul	Demmy Racing Northern Flat Belle Vue	£2,000	Gold Doon
23-Jul	Guys & Dolls, Crayford	£3,000	Gun Fighter
23-Jul	Ron Bazell Puppy Stakes Walthamstow	£1,500	Barny Rubble
06-Aug	Golden Crest, Bristol	£1,500	Decoy Gold
12-Aug	William Stones, Sheffield	£2,000	Touch Again
18-Aug	Summer Cup, Milton Keynes	£2,000	Toms Cabin King
20-Aug	Oxfordshire Gold Cup, Oxford	£2,500	Freds Flyer
20-Aug	Ernest Thornton Smith Trophy, Bristol	£1,600	Decoy Lynx
20-Aug	Ladbroke 1,000 Guineas, Perry Barr	£1,050	Telford Boy
27-Aug	Embassy Imperial Cup, Hackney	£3,000	Pretty Lively
29-Aug	Coldseal Classic Final, Nottingham	£3,000	Callahow Daly
24-Sep	John Bull Thanet Gold Cup, Ramsgate	£2,000	Bunmahon Lad
15-Oct	Richard Mcguire Scottish Puppy Championship, Powderhall	£2,500	Justright Melody
15-Oct	Regal Stayers Trophy, Sunderland	£2,000	Aglish Blaze
28-Oct	John Power Anniversary Cup Final,m Hackney	£2,000	Trade Exchange
12-Nov	Hackney Guineas Final, Hackney	£2,500	Lemon Rob
19-Nov	Larrys Puppy Oaks, Wimbledon	£2,000	Stay Going
23-Nov	John Power Puppy Nursery Hackney	£2,000	Kilmacsimon Wave
25-Nov	Triumph Hurdle, Romford	£1,300	Mr Ossy
26-Nov	Wm Hill First For Services Stayers' Final, Catford	£1,500	Last Action
26-Nov	Countrywide Steels Goodwood Cup, Walthamstow	£1,000	Countrywide Fox
08-Dec	Puppy Cup Final, Romford	£2,000	Welfare Panther
15-Dec	Holts Marathon, Walthamstow	£1,000	Senlac Rose

NGRC Statistics

Category 2 (cont)

DATE	RACE	PURSE	WINNER
16-Dec	Dransfield Novelty Christmas Cup Final, Sheffield	£2,000	Corries Tim
20-Dec	Schweppes Christmas Vase Hurdle Final, Wimbledon	£1,000	Westlake Wonder
24-Dec	Peter Derrick Christmas Cracker, Nottingham	£2,500	Fast Copper
26-Dec	Ray Dean Boxing Day Marathon Catford	£1,250	Wexford Minx

Leading Open Race winners

Key to table: Figs in columns on second line indicate Win distances: S: Shortest; L: Longest; A: Average; W: No. of wins; R: No. of runs.

	Greyhound	Trainer	Track	Breeding				
1	SMART DECISION	Gaskin	Walthamstow	wbd b	Carters Lad-Knockshe Dream			
				Whelped	S	L	A	W	R
				May-91	790	925	843	23	34
2	CARRAIG PAWS	Black	Reading	bd d	Castlelyons Gem-Push Open			
				Jul-91	380	480	450	20	33
3	GIS A SMILE	Rees	Wimbledon	wf d	Flashy Sir-Desert Pearl			
				Apr-91	385	484	462	19	30
4	PARADISE SLIPPY	Boyce	Catford	bk d	Will Dannagher-Paradise Whisper			
				Jul-91	465	555	485	19	44
5	DECOY LYNX	Cobbold P	Unattached	bk b	Slaneyside Hare-Easy Bimbo			
				Jul-92	640	880	812	18	27
6	WESTMEAD CHICK	Savva	Walthamstow	bd b	I'm Slippy-Westmead Move			
				Jan-92	474	515	486	17	33
7	WEXFORD MINX	Knight	Hove	bd b	Manorville Major-Ballarue Suzy			
				Aug-91	480	740	603	17	33
8	FREEWHEEL KYLO	McGee Jr	Rye House	bd d	Kyle Jack-Shanavulin Girl			
				Oct-90	460	675	601	17	33
9	GLIDEAWAY FOX	Compton	Unattached	f d	Greenpark Fox-Cute Betty			
				Dec-91	255	420	293	16	26
10	WITCHES DEAN	Rich	Romford	bk d	Lyons Dean-Witches Betty			
				Feb-92	275	475	401	16	35
11	DECOY LION	Cobbold P	Unattached	bk d	Slaneyside Hare-Easy Bimbo			
				Jul-92	480	665	611	16	45
12	JUSTRIGHT MELODY	Robinson	Unattached	f d	Farloe Melody-Farloe Mineola			
				Dec-92	450	500	468	15	28
13	BUNMAHON LAD	Rich	Romford	bk d	Druids Johno-Bunmahon Ese			
				Apr-92	260	450	376	15	28
14	MICKS ROVER	Pruhs	Peterborough	bk d	Greenpark Fox-Lowfield Wishes			
				Aug-91	400	500	427	15	29
15	ACE CHOICE	Knight	Hove	wbd d	Fearless Ace-Worthy Choice			
				Aug-91	400	575	522	15	33
16	REDWOOD GIRL	Gaskin	Walthamstow	bd b	Ardfert Sean-Redwood Sue			
				Mar-91	640	655	643	14	27

NGRC Statistics

Leading Open Race winners

	Greyhound	Trainer	Track	Breeding				
17	SUPER BRIDGE	Conway	Stainforth	bd d	Adraville Bridge-Anhid Cross			
				Whelped	S	L	A	W	R
				Mar-92	420	484	460	14	31
18	GALLYS LADY	Gaskin	Walthamstow	wbk b	Kilcannon Hero-Babs Pet			
				Aug-91	490	685	634	14	34
19	UNIQUE BAY	Mullins	Walthamstow	wf d	Castlelyons Gem-Kenmare Bay			
				Apr-91	450	590	498	14	35
20	ARDILAUN BRIDGE	Sams	Crayford	bk d	Adraville Bridge-Cecelia One			
				Nov-91	462	655	497	14	36
21	COOLMONA ROAD	Knight	Hove	bd d	Ardfert Sean-Westpark Tee			
				May-92	640	695	664	13	20
22	BLACKSTAIRS BOY	Clemenson	Hove	bk d	Midnight Hustle-Lighthouse Lou			
				Aug-90	460	555	504	13	21
23	NEWRY TOWN	Mullins	Walthamstow	bk d	Flag Star-Lady Tico			
				Feb-90	660	827	788	13	22
24	ALANS ACE	Foster	Wimbledon	f d	Alans Champion-Parsons Echo			
				Nov-91	385	515	460	13	24
25	HIGHWAY LEADER	Bacon	Perry Barr	bk d	Leaders Best-Highway Mystery			
				Nov-91	290	465	427	13	25
26	BALLARUE MINX	Masters	Hove	wbd b	Greenpark Fox-Ballarue Suzy			
				May-92	640	792	713	13	27
27	WESTMEAD MERLIN	Savva	Walthamstow	bd d	Murlens Slippy-Westmead Hannah			
				Sep-92	474	515	483	13	27
28	FAST COPPER	Burrows	Reading	bk d	Ballyard Hoffman-Parkswood Magpie			
				May-91	260	438	313	13	27
29	LACKEN PRINCE	McGee Jr	Rye House	be d	Live Contender -Afternoon Blue			
				Sep-92	475	575	532	13	30
30	HEAVENLY DREAM	Mullins	Walthamstow	f d	Whisper Wishes-Sail On Jenny			
				Jul-90	420	515	479	13	36
31	DECOY GOLD	Cobbold P	Unattached	bd d	Daleys Gold Slaneyside Holly			
				Dec-91	400	484	438	13	38
32	GREAT HOUSE	Conway	Stainforth	f d	Dukes Lodge-Shirleys Opinion			
				May-92	458	500	489	13	39
33	HEAVENLY SPIRIT	Mullins	Walthamstow	bk b	Daleys Gold Black Sancisco			
				Oct-91	475	660	607	13	51
34	MORAL STANDARDS	Meek	Hall Green	wbk d	Flag Star-No Way Jose			
				May-92	480	500	485	12	18
35	CALLAHOW DALY	Lister	Peterborough	f d	Daleys Gold-Ahaveen Fever			
				Jan-91	450	500	480	12	27
36	SIMPLY FREE	Shearman	Unattached	bk b	Daleys Gold-Rooskey Critic			
				Apr-91	500	640	575	12	29
37	DRUIDS OMEGA	McGee Jr	Rye House	wbd d	I'm Slippy-Druids Dalroy			
				Mar-92	480	500	492	12	32
38	APRIL SUPER	McGee Jr	Rye House	bd d	Ardfert Sean-Fairy Wings			
				Apr-89	385	465	420	11	21
39	STAR OF TYRONE	Smith B	Hall Green	dkbd d	Leaders Best-Aldens Support			
				Aug-91	462	575	482	11	22
40	SHROPSHIRE NICK	Silkman	Unattached	f d	Slippy Blue-Chocolate Satin			
				Oct-90	509	675	639	11	24
41	ANHID BLAZE	Conway	Stainforth	bk d	Adraville Bridge-Anhid Cross			
				Mar-92	480	666	508	11	26

NGRC Greyhound Racing Yearbook 1995

NGRC Statistics

Leading Open Race winners (cont)

	Greyhound	Trainer	Track	Breeding				
42	DROVERS ROAD	Wheatley	Nottingham	bd d	I'm Slippy-Slaneyside Glory			
				Whelped	*S*	*L*	*A*	*W*	*R*
				Mar-91 460	500	491	11	29
43	RINGSIDE RETURN	Osborne	Bristol	wbkd	Daleys Gold-No Way Jose			
				Aug-91 250	480	340	11	29
44	TERRYDRUM BLUE	Riches	Hackney	f d	Glenpark Dancer- Farloe Mineola			
				Apr-91 450	515	475	11	29
45	DROOPYS CRAIG	Tasker	Perry Barr	bkw d	Moral Support-Droopys Aliysa			
				May-92 484	509	493	11	30
46	KEELEYS BANANA	McGee Jr	Rye House	bd d	Flashy Sir-Chicita Banana			
				Oct-91 640	660	645	11	32
47	LOTS OF JOLLY	Baker	Yarmouth	bd d	Whisper Wishes-Fair Hill Rose			
				Oct-91 220	450	354	11	32
48	MILES DEMPSEY	McGee Jr	Rye House	f d	Dempseys Whisper-Coppertone			
				Feb-92 590	718	674	11	33
49	WESTMEAD PADDY	Wileman	Monmore	bk d	Airmount Grand-Westmead Move			
				Sep-90 480	685	619	11	33
50	FERNDALE LODGE	Conway	Stainforth	bd d	Druids Lodge-Ferndale Mo			
				Sep-91 480	500	494	11	39
51	MISS PIGGY	Compton	Unattached	bd b	Deenside Spark-Miss Irene			
				May-92 700	868	799	10	18
52	JUBILEE REBECCA	Rooks	Brough Park	bkw b	Pond Mirage-Lively Bide			
				Mar-91 580	827	716	10	19
53	HEAVENLY COMET	Haynes	Wembley	bk b	Daleys Gold- Black Sancuco			
				Oct-91 400	484	474	10	20
54	SURE FANTASY	Lister	Peterborough	bk d	Phantom Flash- Lively Spark			
				Sep-90 474	500	494	10	22
55	FLY WISH	Barlow	Hall Green	bk b	Whisper Wishes-Slippy Toots			
				Apr-92 259	484	322	10	22
56	PEARLS GIRL	Sykes	Wimbledon	fw b	Flashy Sir-Desert Pearl			
				Apr-91 385	555	497	10	23
57	TROMORA MAYOR	Steels	Swaffham	bebd d	Manorville Major-Born To Race			
				Feb-91 440	605	540	10	23
58	SUNHILL MISTY	Lister	Peterborough	bd b	Kyle Jack- Game Misty			
				Oct-91 820	932	840	10	24
59	MOANING LAD	Mentzis	Rye House	f d	Kyle Jack- Lady Bellamy			
				Apr-92 460	555	485	10	24
60	PARQUET PADDY	Hitch	Wimbledon	wbd d	I'm Slippy-Bangor Style			
				Aug-91 460	515	477	10	24
61	GLENHOLM TIGER	Meek	Hall Green	bd d	Manorville Majo-Quare Gold			
				Dec-91 450	484	470	10	25
62	DECOY CHEETAH	Cobbold P	Unattached	bk b	Slaneyside Hare- Easy Bimbo			
				Jul-92 380	686	539	10	26
63	SQUIRE DELTA	Andrews	Belle Vue	bd d	Easy And Slow-Squire Jenny			
				Apr-90 555	650	615	10	26
64	AGLISH BLAZE	Tidswell	Stainforth	wbd d	I'm Slippy-Crossfield Spec			
				Mar-92 631	747	660	10	27
65	SILVERHILL SUE	Pickett	Hackney	bd b	Hyper-Silverhill Lass			
				Mar-92 484	655	556	10	28
66	TINAS DEPOSIT	Wileman	Monmore	bd b	Kildare Ash-Cheerful Deposit			
				Jun-91 655	815	715	10	30

NGRC Statistics

Leading Open Race winners (cont)

	Greyhound	Trainer	Track	Breeding				
67	**SPENWOOD MAGIC**	Hough	Sheffield	bk b	Westmead Claim-Loopy Lill			
				Whelped	S	L	A	W R
				Jun-91	631	710	670	10 30
68	**TOYBOX SCHOONER**	Williams	Sunderland	bd d	Odell Schooner-Pond Jemina			
				Oct-91	480	500	490	10 31
69	**CORA HILL**	Vine	Canterbury	wbe d	Glenpark Dancer-Quare Mint			
				Sep-91	260	400	311	10 31
70	**PATRIOT SAIL**	Cantrell	Reading	bd d	Manorville Major-Touch The Sail			
				Jul-91	465	645	588	10 32
71	**LONGVALLEY MANOR**	Coleman	Walthamstow	wbk d	I'm Slippy-Longvalley Lady			
				Jul-91	310	484	460	10 32
72	**BLACKCHURCH ALF**	Pugh	Hall Green	bk d	Slaneyside Hare-Congeel Liz			
				Jul-92	400	575	474	10 32
73	**DECOY JAGUAR**	Cobbold P	Unattached	bk d	Slaneyside Hare-Easy Bimbo			
				Jul-92	440	515	485	10 39
74	**GREENANE SQUIRE**	Meek	Hall Green	bd d	Manorville Major-Endless Game			
				Jun-91	480	480	480	9 13
75	**NIGHT OF THE FOX**	Pett	Canterbury	bd d	Greenpark Fox-Easy Journey			
				Nov-91	480	480	480	9 14
76	**STOUKE TANIA**	Dartnall	Wimbledon	wbk b	Darragh Commet-Stouke Pet			
				Apr-91	465	650	588	9 15
77	**FEARLESS LINX**	De Mulder	Hall Green	bd b	Fearless Mustang-Daniels Dolly			
				Aug-92	474	665	630	9 17
78	**BYE BYE GARRY**	Sykes	Wimbledon	bk d	Druids Johno-Up The Ladder			
				Jul-91	385	460	428	9 20
79	**BAYVIEW BLAZE**	McEllistrim	Wimbledon	wbk d	Dutch Delight-Ask Helen			
				Jun-91	385	475	448	9 21
80	**KILLENAGH DREAM**	Lister	Peterborough	wbd d	Dads Bank-Killeenagh Lady			
				Mar-90	686	827	762	9 21
81	**DECOY COUGAR**	Cobbold P	Unattached	bk d	Slaneyside Hare-Easy Bimbo			
				Jul-92	640	750	713	9 23
82	**IZA POSER**	Luckhurst	Crayford	wbk d	Ransom Crackers-Thats A Lady			
				Mar-92	480	540	502	9 23
83	**REDWOOD PIPPIN**	Gaskin	Walthamstow	bd b	Ardfert Sean-Redwood Sue			
				Mar-91	640	825	688	9 25
84	**SALTHILL CHAMP**	Peckover	Unattached	wbd d	Druids Lodge-Park Na Veena			
				Jul-91	465	515	485	9 26
85	**URGENT MEETING**	McGee Jr	Rye House	wbe b	Daleys Gold-Coragh Lady			
				Jan-92	278	480	414	9 27
86	**DUTCH FLYER**	Holland	Swaffham	bk d	Dutch Prince-Catch Ruby			
				Nov-91	480	659	595	9 27
87	**SONIC BLUE**	Hitch	Wimbledon	bebd d	Daleys Gold-Drom Echo			
				May-91	480	660	608	9 29
88	**PEPSI PETE**	McGee Jr	Rye House	bd d	I'm Slippy-Pepsi Princess			
				Jan-92	484	575	529	9 29
89	**BACK BEFORE DAWN**	Fletcher	Canterbury	bkw b	Moneypoint Coal-Fashion Fever			
				Sep-91	675	880	820	9 32
90	**TELL THE YARN**	Mullins	Walthamstow	fbd d	I'm Slippy-Duchess Of Erin			
				Aug-91	640	710	687	9 33
91	**SATIN FLASH**	McGee Jr	Rye House	bk b	Phantom Flash-Chocolate Satin			
				Sep-91	620	714	666	9 34

NGRC Statistics

Leading Open Race winners (cont)

	Greyhound	Trainer	Track		Breeding				
92	**CRAFTY FONTANA**	Counsell	Unattached	bk d	Druids Lodge-Crafty Winter				
				Whelped	*S*	*L*	*A*	*W*	*R*
				Aug-91	465	490	478	9	39
93	**GORTMORE EXPRESS**	Linzell	Romford	bk d	Nightpark Lad-Eugenes Girl				
				Jan-90	575	640	596	9	39
94	**CREAMERY BRIDGE**	Linzell	Romford	wbd d	I'm Slippy-Creamery Wish				
				Jan-92	484	640	555	9	40
95	**I'M JOE**	Linzell	Romford	bk d	I'm Slippy-Minnies Siren				
				Oct-92	400	484	432	8	14
96	**BALLYGOWN LILLY**	Talbot	Unattached	wbk b	Track Man-Bar Doll				
				Aug-91	640	663	648	8	15
97	**WITTON STAR**	Rowell	Brough Park	bd d	Macs Lock-Pond Juliet				
				Apr-92	460	640	500	8	19
98	**NOT MY LINE**	Walden	Reading	bd b	Adraville Bridge-Odd The Line				
				Sep-92	440	490	471	8	19
99	**CITY CLASS**	Milligan	Sunderland	wf d	Arrow House-Alexa				
				Feb-92	255	310	284	8	20
100	**POWYS GOLD**	Meek	Hall Green	f d	Daleys Gold-Diamias Damsel				
				May-91	450	490	478	8	21

TOP MEN: (from left) Tony Meek Ernie Gaskin and Geoff de Mulder

Leading Trainers

Pos.	Trainer	Track	wins	points
1	**McGEE**	Unattached	197	634
2	**LISTER**	Peterborough	149	502
3	**MULLINS**	Walthamstow	167	481
4	**MEEK**	Hall Green	83	479
5	**SAVVA**	Walthamstow	63	417
6	**KNIGHT**	Hove	86	340
7	**GASKIN**	Walthamstow	112	325
8	**MASTERS**	Hove	36	261
9	**COLEMAN**	Walthamstow	67	223
10	**BACON**	Perry Barr	31	222
11	**RICH**	Romford	71	212
12	**CONWAY**	Stainforth	66	193
13	**GIBSON**	BelleVue	33	176
14	**COBBOLD P**	Unattached	62	173
15	**COBBOLD T**	Unattached	54	171
16	**DARTNALL**	Wimbledon	26	165
17	**WILLIAMS H**	Sunderland	57	165
18	**BYRNE**	Hackney	62	160
19	**PRUHS**	Peterborough	69	147
20	**LINZELL**	Romford	68	144
21	**REES**	Wimbledon	41	142
22	**CONNOR**	Canterbury	15	139

NGRC Statistics

Pos.	Trainer	Track	wins	points
23	DUGGAN	Walthamstow	42	136
24	SYKES	Wimbledon	39	133
25	RYAN	Perry Barr	9	132
26	WILEMAN	Monmore	50	121
27	ROBINSON	Unattached	21	118
28	MULLINS D	Catford	40	113
29	WHEATLEY	Nottingham	21	111
30	FOSTER	Wimbledon	50	107
31	DE MULDER	Hall Green	44	105
32	FINCH	Swindon	25	92
33	CLEMENSON	Hove	39	90
34	PARKER	Stainforth	23	89
35	HOUGH	Sheffield	14	87
36	FAINT	Rye House	40	83
37	COMPTON	Unattached	40	82
38	ROOKS	Brough Park	15	82
39	RICHES	Hackney	33	81
40	HODSON	Hove	44	79
41	PALMER	Sunderland	22	77
42	DOLBY	Wembley	27	72
43	TASKER	Perry Barr	21	72
44	PUGH	Hall Green	26	71
45	PICKETT	Hackney	23	71
46	COPPLESTONE	Reading	28	71
47	HAYNES	Wembley	27	68
48	SAMS	Crayford	29	65
49	JONES L	Unattached	38	64
50	WALSH J	Unattached	8	64
51	SCOTT	Canterbury	4	64
52	MENTZIS	Rye House	21	62
53	MURRAY	Ireland	3	62
54	McELLISTRIM	Wimbledon	27	62
55	HITCH	Wimbledon	29	58
56	SILKMAN	Canterbury	31	57
57	McGEE Jnr	Rye House	19	54
58	REYNOLDS	Crayford	19	54
59	BLACK	Reading	21	52
60	CRAPPER	Sheffield	17	51
61	CANTRELL	Reading	15	51
62	BURROWS	Reading	12	50
63	TOWNER	Canterbury	28	49
64	BOYCE	Catford	21	49
65	TIDSWELL	Stainforth	10	47
66	AMYES	Unattached	19	47
67	STEELS	Peterborough	27	46
68	CALVERT	Brough Park	25	46
69	PEACOCK	Catford	20	45
70	DARNELL	Swaffham	16	44
71	LITTLE	Sunderland	20	43
72	ROUSE	Hove	19	42
73	SHEARMAN	Unattached	11	41
74	BURRIDGE	Portsmouth	18	40
75	MILLIGAN P	Catford	18	40
76	CATCHPOLE	Unattached	9	38
77	SAUNDERS	Belle Vue	14	38
78	TAYLOR	Swaffham	8	37
79	BEAUMONT	Sheffield	7	37
80	TALBOT	Unattached	9	36
81	DOYLE	Reading	10	36
82	STRINGER	Monmore	14	35
83	HANCOX	Hall Green	19	34
84	BUCKLAND	Monmore	16	34
85	WHEELER	Unattached	7	34

NGRC Greyhound Racing Yearbook 1995

LEADING TRAINERS

NGRC Statistics

Pos.	Trainer	Track	wins	points
86	**DICKSON**	Wembley	17	33
87	**THWAITES**	Ramsgate	5	33
88	**PETT**	Canterbury	14	32
89	**WALDEN**	Reading	13	32
90	**ROWELL**	Brough Park	8	32
91	**WRIGHT**	Cradley Heath	8	32
92	**ANDREWS**	Belle Vue	16	31
93	**PECKOVER**	Unattached	11	31
94	**KNIBB**	Milton Keynes	8	31
95	**BARLOW**	Hall Green	16	30
96	**MILLEN**	Sittingborne	14	30
97	**DAVIS**	Oxford	8	30
98	**DENNIS**	Romford	13	29
99	**DOUGLASS**	Hackney	14	28
100	**OSBORNE**	Bristol	13	28

Leading Prize Winning Dogs

	Greyhound	Trainer	Track	Breeding			
1	**MORAL STANDARDS**	Meek	Hall Green	wbk d	Flag Star-No Way Jose		
			Whelped	Ave win	W/R		Total
			May-92	£3,129	12	18	£56,325
2	**DRUIDS ELPRADO**	McGee Jr	Rye House	bdw d	I'm Slippy-Druids Dalroy		
			Mar-92	£1,170	8	22	£25,750
3	**DROOPYS SANDY**	Murray	Ireland	bk d	Ardfert Sean-Droopys First		
			May-92	£5,000	3	4	£20,000
4	**HIGHWAY LEADER**	Bacon	Perry Barr	bk d	Leaders Best-Highway Mystery		
			Nov-91	£769	13	25	£19,225
5	**HERES SEANIE**	Ryan	Perry Barr	f d	Ardfert Sean-Mindys Miracle		
			Jul-92	£1,066	7	16	£17,050
6	**WESTMEAD MERLIN**	Savva	Walthamstow	bd	d Murlens Slippy-Westmead Hannah		
			Sep-92	£410	13	27	£11,060
7	**SANDOLLAR LOUIE**	Connor	Canterbury	bk d	Manorville Magic-I'm A Survivor		
			Dec-91	£371	6	28	£10,395
8	**SPIT IT OUT**	Bacon	Perry Barr	bk d	Phantom Flash-Ivalog		
			May-92	£517	5	20	£10,345
9	**CARRIGEEN BLAZE**	Hough	Sheffield	bk d	Adraville Bridge-Carrig Lucky		
			May-91	£1,144	3	9	£10,300
10	**FRANKS DOLL**	Scott	Canterbury	bd d	Kilbarry Slippy-Come On Mandy		
			Dec-91	£536	4	19	£10,190
11	**JUSTRIGHT MELODY**	Robinson	Unattached	f d	Farloe Melody-Farloe Mineola		
			Dec-92	£312	15	28	£8,730
12	**ARDILAUN BRIDGE**	Sams	Crayford	bk d	Adraville Bridge-Cecelia One		
			Nov-91	£239	14	36	£8,615
13	**GREENANE SQUIRE**	Meek	Hall Green	bd d	Manorville Major-Endless Game		
			Jun-91	£650	9	13	£8,450
14	**DEENSIDE DEAN**	Dartnall	Wimbledon	f d	Willie Joe-Deenside Sunset		
			Oct-92	£788	4	10	£7,875
15	**RANDY SAVAGE**	Conner	Canterbury	bk d	Randy-Sooty Foot		
			May-91	£355	6	18	£6,395
16	**GIS A SMILE**	Rees	Wimbledon	wf d	Flashy Sir-Desert Pearl		
			Apr-91	£210	19	30	£6,310
17	**HEAVENLY DREAM**	Mullins	Walthamstow	f d	Whisper Wishes-Sail On Jenny		
			Jul-90	£173	13	36	£6,245

NGRC Statistics

Leading Prize Winning Dogs (cont)

	Greyhound	Trainer	Track	Breeding			
18	FAST COPPER	Burrows	Reading	bk d	Ballyard Hoffman-Parkswood Magpie		
				Whelped	Ave win	W/R	Total
				May-91	£230	13 27	£6,220
19	MORAL DIRECTOR	Gibson	Belle Vue	wbd d	Double Bid-Moral Shadow		
				May-92	£226	6 27	£6,115
20	LASSA JAVA	Meek	Hall Green	f d	Lassana Champ-Fawn Java		
				Jun-91	£413	7 14	£5,775
21	ANNAMORE KYLE	Glaister	Portsmouth	bk d	Kyle Jack-Velvet Doll		
				Nov-90	£232	7 24	£5,575
22	WOLF MAN	Pugh	Hall Green	bk d	Slaneyside Hare-Clongeel Liz		
				Jul-92	£316	3 16	£5,050
23	FREEWHEEL KYLO	McGee Jr	Rye House	bd d	Kyle Jack-Shanavulin Girl		
				Oct-90	£145	17 33	£4,800
24	DROVERS ROAD	Wheatley	Nottingham	bd d	I'm Slippy-Slaneyside Glory		
				Mar-91	£156	11 29	£4,525
25	BUNMAHON LAD	Rich	Romford	bk d	Druids Johno-Bunmahon Ese		
				Apr-92	£161	15 28	£4,495
26	UNIQUE BAY	Mullins	Walthamstow	wf d	Castlelyons Gem-Kenmare Bay		
				Apr-91	£128	14 35	£4,470
27	BONMAHON DARKIE	Dartnall	Wimbledon	bdw d	Carmels Prince-Debs Tick		
				Oct-92	£405	6 11	£4,450
28	WITCHES DEAN	Rich	Romford	bk d	Lyons Dean-Witches Betty		
				Feb-92	£125	16 35	£4,370
29	DROOPYS CRAIG	Tasker	Perry Barr	bkw d	Moral Support-Droopys Aliysa		
				May-92	£144	11 30	£4,315
30	CALLAHOW DALY	Lister	Peterborough	f d	Daleys Gold-Ahaveen Fever		
				Jan-91	£157	12 27	£4,250
31	LACKEN PRINCE	McGee Jr	Rye House	be d	Live Contender-Afternoon Blue		
				Sep-92	£140	13 30	£4,205
32	ISLAND DOE	Knight	Hove	f d	John Doe-City Border		
				Mar-91	£418	6 10	£4,175
33	SNOW FLASH	Dolby	Wembley	wbk d	Phantom Flash-Airport Lady		
				Sep-91	£447	5 9	£4,025
34	AGLISH BLAZE	Tidswell	Stainforth	wbd d	I'm Slippy-Crossfield Spec		
				Mar-92	£149	10 27	£4,010
35	POND HAMLET	Williams	Sunderland	bd d	Tapwatcher-Pond Mosquito		
				Apr-92	£172	8 23	£3,950
36	DECOY GOLD	Cobbold P	Unattached	bd d	Daleys Gold-Slaneyside Holly		
				Dec-91	£98	13 38	£3,725
37	ACE CHOICE	Knight	Hove	wbd d	Fearless Ace-Worthy Choice		
				Aug-91	£103	15 33	£3,410
38	PRETTY LIVELY	Thwaites	Hackney	bk d	Live Contender-Solas An Maiden		
				Jul-92	£300	4 11	£3,295
39	PATRIOT SAIL	Cantrell	Reading	bd d	Manorville Major-Touch The Sail		
				Jul-91	£103	10 32	£3,280
40	CARRAIG PAWS	Black	Reading	bd d	Castlelyons Gem-Push Open		
				Jul-91	£99	20 33	£3,265
41	GUN FIGHTER	Masters	Hove	bd d	I'm Slippy Strange Manner		
				Jul-92	£271	3 12	£3,250
42	RABATINO	McGee Jr	Rye House	f d	Poor James-Hymenstown Rose		
				Jan-92	£109	6 29	£3,175

NGRC Greyhound Racing Yearbook 1995

NGRC Statistics

Leading Prize Winning Dogs (cont)

	Greyhound	Trainer	Track	Breeding			
43	TRADE EXCHANGE	Taylor	Swaffham	bd d	Greenpark Fox-Trade Gold		
				Whelped	Ave win	W/R	Total
				Nov-92	£194 7	16	£3,110
44	ANHID BLAZE	Conway	Stainforth	bk d	Adraville Bridge-Anhid Cross		
				Mar-92	£114 11	26	£2,975
45	FERNDALE LODGE	Conway	Stainforth	bd d	Druids Lodge-Ferndale Mo		
				Sep-91	£76 11	39	£2,975
46	CONNELLS CROSS	Gaskin	Walthamstow	bk d	Adraville Bridge-Ballydrisheen		
				Sep-91	£117 6	25	£2,925
47	FREDS FLYER	Masters	Hove	wbk d	Whisper Wishes-Roving Linda		
				Jul-92	£188 5	15	£2,825
48	LEMON ROB	McGee Jr	Rye House	wbk d	Daleys Gold-Lemon Miss		
				Nov-92	£350 4	8	£2,800
49	WELFARE PANTHER	Wheeler	Unattached	bk d	Balalika-Sappys Susie		
				Jan-93	£187 4	15	£2,800
50	CRAFTY FONTANA	Counsell	Unattached	bk d	Druids Lodge-Crafty Winter		
				Aug-91	£72 9	39	£2,800
51	SUPER BRIDGE	Conway	Stainforth	bd d	Adraville Bridge-Anhid Cross		
				Mar-92	£88 14	31	£2,725
52	GOLD DOON	Milligan	Sunderland	f d	Top Flash-Doon Duchess		
				Oct-90	£113 8	24	£2,700
53	MR TAN	Catchpole	Unattached	bdw d	Murlens Slippy-Without Equal		
				Jun-92	£84 6	31	£2,600
54	AVOID THE RUSH	Newman	Hackney	bd d	Manorville Star-Smokey Snowdrop		
				Jul-90	£118 5	22	£2,585
55	DROOPYS SLAVE	Louth	Swaffham	bd d	Manorville Major-Twilight Slave		
				Feb-91	£115 7	22	£2,525
56	CHADWELL CHARMER	Kearney	Unattached	bk d	Fly Cruiser-Slippery Moth		
				Jul-92	£146 7	17	£2,475
57	TOYBOX SCHOONER	Williams	Sunderland	bd d	Odell Schooner-Pond Jemina		
				Oct-91	£80 10	31	£2,475
58	WITTON STAR	Rowell	Brough Park	bd d	Macs Lock-Pond Juliet		
				Apr-92	£129 8	19	£2,455
59	BLACKSTAIRS BOY	Clemenson	Hove	bk d	Midnight Hustle-Lighthouse Lou		
				Aug-90	£117 13	21	£2,450
60	BAYVIEW BLAZE	McEllistrim	Wimbledon	wbk d	Dutch Delight-Ask Helen		
				Jun-91	£114 9	21	£2,390
61	TOMS CABIN KING	Knibb	Mil Keynes	f d	Surge Home-Timmies One		
				Apr-91	£103 6	23	£2,375
62	COOLMONA ROAD	Knight	Hove	bd d	Ardfert Sean-Westpark Tee		
				May-92	£118 13	20	£2,365
63	DECOY LION	Cobbold P	Unattached	bk d	Slaneyside Hare-Easy Bimbo		
				Jul-92	£52 16	45	£2,360
64	TELL THE YARN	Mullins	Walthamstow	fbd d	I'm Slippy-Duchess Of Erin		
				Aug-91	£70 9	33	£2,320
65	PARADISE SLIPPY	Boyce	Catford	bk d	Will Dannagher-Paradise Whisper		
				Jul-91	£51 19	44	£2,265
66	KILMACSIMON WAVE	Wearing	Hackney	bk d	Ninth Wave-Honky Tonk Lady		
				Jan-93	£271 3	8	£2,165
67	GLENHOLM TIGER	Meek	Hall Green	bd d	Manorville Major-Quare Gold		
				Dec-91	£86 10	25	£2,150

NGRC Statistics

Leading Prize Winning Dogs (cont)

	Greyhound	Trainer	Track	Breeding			
68	CORRIES TIM	Beaumont	Sheffield	bebd d	Aghadown Timmy-Hard To Start		
				Whelped	Ave win	W/R	Total
				Sep-92	£304	3 7	£2,125
69	TAWNY FLASH	Parker	Stainforth	bk d	Lartigue Note-Flashy Fiona		
				Mar-92	£121	7 17	£2,050
70	WELSH WIZARD	Riches	Hackney	f d	Westmead Havoc-Fortune Princess		
				Mar-92	£56	7 36	£2,025
71	TOUCH AGAIN	Crapper	Sheffield	f d	Ravage Again-Westmead Kara		
				Jun-92	£105	4 19	£2,000
72	NEWRY TOWN	Mullins	Walthamstow	bk d	Flag Star-Lady Tico		
				Feb-90	£89	13 22	£1,960
73	SURE FANTASY	Lister	Peterborough	bk d	Phantom Flash-Lively Spark		
				Sep-90	£88	10 22	£1,925
74	KILLENAGH DREAM	Lister	Peterborough	wbd d	Dads Bank-Killenagh Lady		
				Mar-90	£91	9 21	£1,905
75	DROOPYS ALFIE	Gibson	Belle Vue	bkw d	'Im Slippy-Droopys Aliysa		
				Aug-91	£70	4 27	£1,900
76	GORTMORE EXPRESS	Linzell	Romford	bk d	Nightpark Lad-Eugenes Girl		
				Jan-90	£48	9 39	£1,880
77	ASTIS ACCOUNT	Lister	Peterborough	f d	Ard Knock-Paceys Gold		
				Sep-91	£75	6 24	£1,805
78	AYR FLYER	Wheatley	Nottingham	bd d	Ardfert Sean-Slaneyside Glory		
				Feb-92	£192	6 9	£1,725
79	TELFORD BOY	Wilkinson	Perry Barr	f d	Penny Less-Fawn Music		
				Jan-91	£88	7 19	£1,665
80	BARNY RUBBLE	Amyes	Unattached	bd d	Glenpark Dancer-Bay Road Jill		
				Aug-92	£79	3 21	£1,665
81	DELMONTE LANE	Milligan	Sunderland	bd d	Nine Thirty-Gods Lane		
				May-92	£66	6 25	£1,650
82	DANS BANANA	McGee Jr	Rye House	bk d	Flashy Sir-Chicita Banana		
				Oct-91	£150	4 11	£1,645
83	MILES DEMPSEY	McGee Jr	Rye House	f d	Dempseys Whisper-Coppertone		
				Feb-92	£50	1 33	£1,640
84	FEARLESS COUGAR	De Mulder	Hall Green	bdw d	Slaneyside Hare-Daniels Dolly		
				Nov-91	£58	8 28	£1,625
85	LOCH BO ANCHOR	McGee Jr	Rye House	wbd d	Murlens Slippy-Loch Bo Cheeky		
				Mar-90	£229	3 7	£1,600
86	MR OSSY	Puzey	Walthamstow	bd d	Curryhills Gara-Alley Lady		
				Jun-91	£50	3 32	£1,600
87	FEARLESS ATLAS	Lucas	Hove	bk d	Randy-Dresden Lady		
				Jul-91	£88	7 8	£1,585
88	STAR OF TYRONE	Smith B	Hall Green	dkbd d	Leaders Best-Aldens Support		
				Aug-91	£72	11 22	£1,580
89	GLIDEAWAY FOX	Compton	Unattached	f d	Greenpark Fox-Cute Betty		
				Dec-91	£61	16 26	£1,580
90	APRIL SUPER	McGee Jr	Rye House	bd d	Ardfert Sean-Fairy Wings		
				Apr-89	£75	11 21	£1,565
91	MICKS ROVER	Pruhs	Peterborough	bk d	Greenpark Fox-Lowfield Wishes		
				Aug-91	£54	15 29	£1,560
92	POWYS GOLD	Meek	Hall Green	f d	Daleys Gold-Diamias Damsel		
				May-91	£74	8 21	£1,550

NGRC Statistics

Leading Prize Winning Dogs (cont)

	Greyhound	Trainer	Track	Breeding			
93	**KEELEYS BANANA**	McGee Jr	Rye House	bd d	Flashy Sir-Chicita Banana		
				Whelped	*Ave win*	*W/R*	*Total*
				Oct-91	£48	11 32	£1,550
94	**HARRYS LION**	McGee Jr	Rye House	f d	Skelligs Tiger-Maggies Wishes		
				Nov-91	£48	8 32	£1,535
95	**SONIC BLUE**	Hitch	Wimbledon	bebd d	Daleys Gold-Drom Echo		
				May-91	£52	9 29	£1,515
96	**COALBROOK STAR**	Gibson	Belle Vue	bk d	Coalbrook Tiger-Floridian Magic		
				Apr-92	£94	2 16	£1,500
97	**BENS COURT**	Mullins D	Catford	wbk d	Flashy Sir-Rose Boquet		
				Mar-91	£45	6 3	£1,475
98	**RINGSIDE RETURN**	Osborne	Bristol	wbk d	Daleys Gold-No Way Jose		
				Aug-91	£50	11 29	£1,450
99	**DRUIDS OMEGA**	McGee Jr	Rye House	wbd d	I'm Slippy-Druids Dalroy		
				Mar-92	£45	12 32	£1,450
100	**BYE BYE GARRY**	Sykes	Wimbledon	bk d	Druids Johno-Up The Ladder		
				Jul-91	£72	9 20	£1,440

WEXFORD MINX leads home Heavenly Lady in the Golden Jacket Final. She won over £11,000 in 1994.

Leading Prize Winning Bitches

	Greyhound	Trainer	Track	Breeding			
1	**WESTMEAD CHICK**	Savva	Walthamstow	bd b	I'm Slippy-Westmead Move		
				Whelped	*Ave win*	*W/R*	*Total*
				Jan-92	£637	17 33	£21,010
2	**BALLARUE MINX**	Masters	Hove	wbd b	Greenpark Fox-Ballarue Suzy		
				May-92	£615	13 27	£16,600
3	**WEXFORD MINX**	Knight	Hove	bd b	Manorville Major-Ballarue Suzy		
				Aug-91	£347	17 33	£11,450
4	**REDWOOD GIRL**	Gaskin	Walthamstow	bd b	Ardfert Sean-Redwood Sue		
				Mar-91	£410	14 27	£11,075
5	**PEARLS GIRL**	Sykes	Wimbledon	fw b	Flashy Sir-Desert Pearl		
				Apr-91	£396	10 23	£9,100

NGRC Statistics

Leading Prize Winning Bitches

	Greyhound	Trainer	Track	Breeding			
6	**JUBILEE REBECCA**	Rooks	Brough Park	bkw b	Pond Mirage-Lively Bid		
				Whelped	Ave win	W/R	Total
				Mar-91	£384 10	19	£7,300
7	**TAMMYS DELIGHT**	Lister	Peterborough	wbk b	Waltham Abbey-Lulus Moth		
				May-91	£401 5	16	£6,420
8	**SMART DECISION**	Gaskin	Walthamstow	wbd b	Carters Lad-Knockshe Dream		
				May-91	£186 23	34	£6,310
9	**DECOY COUGAR**	Cobbold P	Unattached	bk b	Slaneyside Hare-Easy Bimbo		
				Jul-92	£253 9	23	£5,815
10	**LISA MY GIRL**	Coleman	Walthamstow	wbd b	Murlens Slippy-Longvalley Lady		
				Mar-92	£444 5	12	£5,325
11	**DECOY LYNX**	Cobbold P	Unattached	bk b	Slaneyside Hare-Easy Bimbo		
				Jul-92	£191 18	27	£5,160
12	**SUNHILL MISTY**	Lister	Peterborough	bd b	Kyle Jack-Game Misty		
				Oct-91	£167 10	24	£4,000
13	**ASHFIELD ARROW**	Masters	Hove	f b	Slippys Quest-Elf Arrow		
				Feb-92	£232 4	16	£3,710
14	**SILBURY CLOUD**	Finch	Swindon	f b	Whisper Wishes-Ferndale Class		
				May-92	£161 6	22	£3,550
15	**MOS IMP**	Parker	Stainforth	bk b	Whisper Wishes-Celt Country		
				Jun-91	£96 8	34	£3,275
16	**BALLYGOWN LILLY**	Talbot	Unattached	wbk b	Track Man-Bar Doll		
				Aug-91	£203 8	15	£3,040
17	**HEAVENLY COMET**	Haynes	Wembley	bk b	Daleys Gold-Black Sancuco		
				Oct-91	£138 10	20	£2,750
18	**HEAVENLY LADY**	Mullins	Walthamstow	bk b	Manorville Sand-Black Sancisco		
				Jun-90	£354 5	7	£2,475
19	**CUB HUNTER**	Rees	Wimbledon	f b	Moneypoint Coal-Slaneyside Ivy		
				Jan-92	£127 5	18	£2,285
20	**MONARD WISH**	Lister	Peterborough	bd b	Whisper Wishes-Solas An Maiden		
				Aug-91	£76 7	27	£2,060
21	**STAY GOING**	Savory	Sheffield	bk b	Murlens Hawk-Neat Dish		
				Dec-92	£146 2	14	£2,050
22	**LAST ACTION**	Wileman	Monmore	bd b	Chet-Sunshine Penny		
				Oct-92	£340 4	6	£2,040
23	**FEARLESS LINX**	De Mulder	Hall Green	bd b	Fearless Mustang-Daniels Dolly		
				Aug-92	£117 9	17	£1,985
24	**KEROGUE IVY**	Russell	Powderhall	bk b	Lartigue Note-Kerogue Wish		
				Apr-92	£139 5	14	£1,940
25	**SODAS SLIPPY**	Barrett	Cradley Heath	bkw b	Aulton Slippy-Springfield Soda		
				Dec-92	£133 6	14	£1,855
26	**GALLYS LADY**	Gaskin	Walthamstow	wbk b	Kilcannon Hero-Babs Pet		
				Aug-91	£54 14	34	£1,825
27	**DROOPYS EVELYN**	Williams	Sunderland	wbkb	Game Ball-Immoral Support		
				Jul-90	£83 7	20	£1,650
28	**CANALSIDE ANNE**	Ridley	Perry Barr	be b	Glencorby Celt-Wolseleys Yarn		
				Mar-91	£60 7	27	£1,625
29	**SILVERHILL SUE**	Pickett	Hackney	bd b	Hyper-Silverhill Lass		
				Mar-92	£57 10	28	£1,590
30	**KILDAGON KITTY**	Reynolds	Crayford	bk b	Waltham Abbey-Poor Kitty		
				Feb-92	£116 6	13	£1,510

NGRC Statistics

Leading Prize Winning Bitches

	Greyhound	Trainer	Track	Breeding			
31	SCINTILLAS PANSY	Stringer	Monmore	bd b	Murlens Slippy-Scintillas Queen		
				Whelped	Ave win	W/R	Total
				Apr-91	£68	6	22 £1,495
32	NOT MY LINE	Walden	Reading	bd b	Adraville Bridge-Odd The Line		
				Sep-92	£75	8	19 £1,425
33	HEAVENLY SPIRIT	Mullins	Walthamstow	bk b	Daleys Gold-Black Sancisco		
				Oct-91	£28	13	51 £1,415
34	DELTA DUCHESS	Clemenson	Hove	bd b	Zanzibar-Bangor Style		
				May-92	£61	8	23 £1,410
35	EGMONT JOAN	Lister	Peterborough	f b	Daleys Gold-Egmont Biddy		
				May-92	£60	6	23 £1,375
36	FIRST DEFENCE	Harding	Wimbledon	bk b	Easy And Slow-Fast Pace		
				Feb-92	£58	8	23 £1,345
37	TINAS DEPOSIT	Wileman	Monmore	bd b	Kildare Ash Cheerful Deposit		
				Jun-91	£45	10	30 £1,335
38	REDWOOD PIPPIN	Gaskin	Walthamstow	bd b	Ardfert Sean-Redwood Sue		
				Mar-91	£51	9	25 £1,270
39	WEAVE MCGREGOR	Byrne	Hackney	bk b	Manorville Magic-Cute Pigeon		
				Jul-91	£63	6	20 £1,250
40	KISH GALE	Clarke	Nottingham	bk b	Randy-Kishquirk Linda		
				Apr-92	£66	3	18 £1,195
41	MISS PIGGY	Compton	Unattached	bd b	Deenside Spark-Miss Irene		
				May-92	£66	10	18 £1,185
42	ACTIVE SUMMER	Saunders	Belle Vue	f b	Greenpark Fox-Active Touch		
				Apr-91	£107	3	11 £1,175
43	SATIN FLASH	McGee Jr	Rye House	bk b	Phantom Flash-Chocolate Satin		
				Sep-91	£35	9	34 £1,175
44	DECOY CHEETAH	Cobbold	Unattached	bk b	Slaneyside Hare-Easy Bimbo		
				Jul-92	£43	10	26 £1,120
45	SPENWOOD MAGIC	Hough	Sheffield	bk b	Westmead Claim-Loopy Lill		
				Jun-91	£37	10	30 £1,100
46	SENLAC ROSE	Knight	Hove	wf b	Satharn Beo-Liberal Girl		
				Sep-92	£273	2	4 £1,090
47	ARDCOLLUM HILDA	Byrne	Hackney	f b	Druids Johno-Seventh Dynamic		
				May-91	£63	4	17 £1,075
48	SIMPLY FREE	Shearman	Unattached	bk b	Daleys Gold-Rooskey Critic		
				Apr-91	£37	12	29 £1,065
49	PENNYS DIANA	Robinson	Ireland	bk b	Adraville Bridge-Colorado Holly		
				Jul-91	£1,000	1	1 £1,000
50	SMILE ROSE	Coleman	Walthamstow	bk b	Kyle Jack-Feedwell Rose		
				Apr-91	£333	1	3 £1,000
51	RAMBLING HEATHER	Dolby	Wembley	be b	Airmount Grand-Rambling Delight		
				Jul-91	£44	5	22 £975
52	URGENT MEETING	McGee Jnr	Rye House	wbe b	Daleys Gold Coragh Lady		
				Jan-92	£35	9	27 £940
53	PAT YOUR BACK	Wiley	Romford	wbk b	Flag Star-Take The Wean		
				Aug-91	£52	7	18 £930
54	BACK BEFORE DAWN	Fletcher	Canterbury	bkw b	Moneypoint Coal-Fashion Fever		
				Sep-91	£29	9	32 £930
55	MISS SANDRA	Jones L	Unattached	bk b	Ballyard Hoffman-Every Second		
				Sep-91	£66	3	14 £925

NGRC Statistics

Leading Prize Winning Bitches

	Greyhound	Trainer	Track	Breeding			
56	STOUKE TANIA	Dartnall	Wimbledon	wbk b	Darragh Commet-Stouke Pet		
				Whelped	Ave win	W/R	Total
				Apr-91	£59	9 15	£890
57	DARRAGH BEAU	Marlow	Romford	bkw b	Balalika-Quarry Heather		
				Sep-91	£11	4 27	£800
58	CLOVERHILL DREAM	Sams	Crayford	bd b	Moneypoint Coal-Cloverhill Daisy		
				Jan-92	£67	5 12	£800
59	KILLILA PLACE	Miller	Unattached	f b	Ardfert Sean-Adams For Peace		
				May-91	£30	8 27	£800
60	CLONGEEL FERN	Peacock	Catford	bk b	Whisper Wishes-Ferndale Class		
				May-92	£31	8 24	£755
61	KILLOURAGH LUCY	Milligan	Catford	bd b	Murlens Slippy-Singside Lady		
				Aug-92	£10	6 37	£740
62	SILVER GLOW	Knight	Hove	bdw b	I'm Slippy-Frisly White		
				Feb-92	£37	6 20	£735
63	LEADERS SMILER	Adams	Henlow	bd b	Leaders Best-Ballyboggan Lady		
				Jul-91	£35	7 20	£700
64	STAR GIRL	Gaskin	Walthamstow	bd b	Ballyard Hoffman-Star Approach		
				Oct-91	£27	7 26	£700
65	DEMESNE DAISY	Young	Hove	f b	Tipi Tip-Demesne Joy		
				Jun-92	£58	4 12	£690
66	WHISPERING ROSE	Hancox	Hall Green	wbd b	Murlens Slippy-Elegant Dream		
				May-92	£36	6 19	£680
67	MINOR CRYSTAL	Massey	Oxford	bk b	Bold Rabbit-Newmans Mall		
				Oct-90	£84	6 8	£675
68	BENRO BILLIE	Douglass	Hackney	bd b	Greenpark Fox-Minstrel Lady		
				Feb-93	£10	8 46	£650
69	CLONBRIN BLACK	McGee Jr	Rye House	bk b	Moral Support-Shining Bright		
				Nov-90	£28	5 23	£645
70	DANCERS JOY	Mann	Swindon	bd b	Celtic Dancer-Black Spray		
				Jul-92	£46	7 14	£640
71	BOND END DAMSEL	Meek	Hall Green	bk b	Daleys Gold-Damiens Damsel		
				May-91	£46	6 14	£640
72	DRUIDS ELLYMAY	McGee Jr	Rye House	wbd b	I'm Slippy-Druids Dalroy		
				Mar-92	£40	5 16	£635
73	PEMBURY GIFT	White H	Hackney	bdw b	Farncombe Black-Proud To Run		
				Oct-91	£31	6 20	£625
74	GOOD LUCK CHARM	Walsh D	Hove	bd b	House Hunter-California Belle		
				Aug-90	£30	2 21	£620
75	MOLLIES DREAM	Savigar	Perry Barr	bd b	Carters Lad-Knocksme Dream		
				May-91	£21	5 29	£620
76	LEMON NELL	Green	Nottingham	bk b	Greenpark Fox-Lemon Chill		
				May-92	£31	5 20	£610
77	SUNGLEN DOLLAR	Pruhs	Peterborough	bd b	Satharn Beo-Ardrine Fluff		
				Jun-92	£50	5 2	£605
78	ASHGROVE MAID	Andrews	Mildenhall	bd b	Daleys Gold-Orchard Fairy		
				Jul-90	£50	6 12	£600
79	WATH BLUBELL	Little	Sunderland	bew b	Ballygalda Glory-Wath Duchess		
				Oct-92	£50	5 12	£600
80	PHANTOM ROSIE	Rees	Wimbledon	bk b	Phantom Flash-Tullig Rosie		
				Apr-92	£38	3 16	£600

NGRC Greyhound Racing Yearbook 1995

NGRC Statistics

Leading Prize Winning Bitches

	Greyhound	Trainer	Track	Breeding			
81	**WINETAVERN CELT**	Hodson	Hove	bk b	Ardfert Sean-Pamar Celt		
				Whelped	Ave win	W/R	Total
				Jul-92	£39	5 15	£590
82	**BAYSIDE**	Coleman	Walthamstow	bk b	Daleys Gold-Foretop		
				May-92	£24	5 25	£590
83	**DONGADONG**	Duggan	Walthamstow	bd b	Deenside Spark-Celtic Cracker		
				Apr-92	£45	5 13	£585
84	**JOESITA**	Bergin	Hackney	wf b	Bankers Benefit-Margarets Joy		
				Nov-91	£34	5 17	£585
85	**EARLY ROSE**	Simmons	Unattached	f b	I'm Slippy-Winsor Aird		
				Aug-92	£72	4 8	£575
86	**COME ON HONEY**	Rich	Romford	bd b	Lartigue Note-Queen Of Country		
				Feb-92	£26	6 22	£575
87	**TOMBRICK LIKA**	Duggan	Walthamstow	bkw b	Rockmount Toff-Lika Rip		
				May-91	£26	5 22	£575
88	**AMERICAN HOT**	Byrne	Hackney	bd b	Tain Solas-Kelsos Slinkey		
				May-92	£25	4 23	£575
89	**SANDOLLAR SOPHIE**	Hubble	Unattached	wbd b	Manorville Magic-I'm A Survivor		
				Dec-91	£30	4 19	£570
90	**MEENG FLYER**	Tompsett	Crayford	bk b	Whisper Wishes-Fortune Citizen		
				Mar-91	£29	4 20	£570
91	**WHOS MINNIE**	Sams	Crayford	bd b	Tipi Tip-Greenfield Madam		
				Aug-92	£47	4 12	£560
92	**AR DREAM**	Yeates	Reading	wbd b	Satharn Beo-Wendys Dream		
				Nov-91	£34	7 16	£550
93	**MIDWAY BEO VIEW**	Douglas	Hackney	bd b	Satharn Beo-Review		
				Jul-92	£53	4 10	£525
94	**DUSTY IMAGE**	Finch	Mildenhall	bk b	Big City-Dryland Dusty		
				Jun-92	£48	5 11	£525
95	**KILCOMMON PET**	Crapper	Sheffield	bd b	Lavally Oak-Alfos Pal		
				Jun-91	£48	3 11	£525
96	**KILPIPE BIBI**	Mullins	Walthamstow	wbd b	Manorville SandAnother Cheer		
				Sep-90	£28	4 19	£525
97	**MOSSFIELD SCOTTY**	Kinsey	Perry Barr	wf b	Catunda Flame-Mossfield Terror		
				Oct-90	£52	3 10	£525
98	**NANNY STAGE**	Dennis	Romford	be b	Ballygrowman Jim-Blue Stage		
				May-91	£8	1 6	£500
99	**ANNES SWAN**	Douglass	Hackney	wbk b	Greenpark Fox-Exclusive Lady		
				Jun-92	£33	4 15	£500
100	**SPINNING SUN**	Gaskin	Walthamstow	bd b	Whisper Wishes-KS Expressions		
				May-92	£25	3 20	£500

Leading Sires

Sire	wnrs	R/W	Prize Money
I'M SLIPPY	126	369	£97,500
GREENPARK FOX	65	201	£42,415
DALEYS GOLD	63	234	£36,490
MURLENS SLIPPY	57	149	£34,585
WHISPER WISHES	55	179	£34,975
SKELLIGS TIGER	45	87	£12,070

NGRC Statistics

Leading Sires (cont)

Sire	wnrs	R/W	Prize Money
MANORVILLE MAJOR	39	139	£37,790
SATHARN BEO	36	85	£9,865
ADRAVILLE BRIDGE	35	114	£36,590
FLASHY SIR	34	110	£27,095
ARDFERT SEAN	32	133	£62,575
TAPWATCHER	26	68	£10,030
KYLE JACK	24	89	£21,765
DOUBLE BID	23	50	£10,605
PHANTOM FLASH	21	67	£21,870
CARTERS LAD	21	63	£10,935
ARROW HOUSE	21	38	£4,155
SLANEYSIDE HARE	20	110	£26,420
DRUIDS JOHNO	20	68	£11,095
AIRMOUNT GRAND	20	61	£6,690
RANDY	19	49	£12,955

HIT THE LID (front): modest success, with five winners last year.

DRUIDS LODGE	18	60	£9,900
LIVE CONTENDER	18	48	£11,750
CURRYHILLS GARA	18	31	£4,925
WESTMEAD HAVOC	17	40	£5,930
WALTHAM ABBEY	17	39	£10,790
GLENPARK DANCER	16	48	£6,045
MANORVILLE SAND	16	39	£6,475
MANORVILLE MAGIC	16	33	£13,930
FLY CRUISER	15	40	£5,920
KILDARE ASH	15	34	£3,695
BALALIKA	15	30	£5,825
DEENSIDE SPARK	14	45	£4,685
MURLENS HAWK	14	33	£5,830
LEADERS BEST	12	47	£24,685
SLIPPY BLUE	12	36	£3,855
LARTIGUE NOTE	11	37	£7,080
CARMELS PRINCE	11	29	£6,710
MACS LOCK	11	29	£4,545

NGRC Statistics

Leading Sires (cont)

Sire	wnrs	R/W	Prize Money
AULTON SLIPPY	11	28	£5,160
MONEYPOINT COAL	10	29	£4,865
GLENCORBRY CELT	10	22	£3,105
CASTLYONS GEM	9	55	£10,025
EARLY VOCATION	9	12	£1,455
BALLYARD HOFFMAN	8	35	£9,775
EASY AND SLOW	8	35	£3,860
MORAL SUPPORT	8	30	£6,370
BANKERS BENEFIT	8	23	£2,155
LODGE PRINCE	8	22	£2,520
WILLIE JOE	8	19	£9,495
AGHADOWN TIMMY	8	15	£3,575
RAVAGE AGAIN	8	14	£3,090
FLAG STAR	7	43	£60,425
BOLD RABBIT	7	25	£2,555
COALBROOK TIGER	7	21	£4,050
SLIPPYS QUEST	7	16	£5,335
TICO	7	11	£1,365
ALPINE MINISTER	7	11	£1,085
GALTYMORE LAD	7	11	£905
LYONS DEAN	6	24	£5,170
WESTMEAD CLAIM	6	24	£2,365
PENNY LESS	6	22	£4,220
FEARLESS ACE	6	22	£4,050
DUTCH DELIGHT	6	20	£3,755
NIGHTPARK LAD	6	20	£3,015
DARRAGH COMMET	6	20	£2,745
KYLEHILL CHEETA	6	18	£1,845
CATUNDA FLAME	6	13	£1,705
BALLYMADOE BEN	6	11	£1,045
POND MIRAGE	5	19	£8,210
HYGARD	5	17	£1,665
ZANZIBAR	5	16	£2,250
HELLO BLACKIE	5	13	£1,600
BALLYREGAN BOB	5	12	£1,515
AMENHOTEP	5	11	£1,390
THE OTHER RISK	5	10	£920
HIT THE LID	5	7	£705
ODELL KING	5	7	£680
MANX TREASURE	5	7	£610
GREEN GORSE	5	6	£520
FEARLESS CHAMP	5	5	£670
CURRYHILLS SPECL	5	5	£475
MANX MARAJAX	4	18	£2,075
ALANS CHAMPION	4	17	£1,815
BROWNIES OUTLOOK	4	16	£1,900
TRACK MAN	4	15	£4,415
DEMPSEYS WHISPER	4	15	£2,165
RANSOM CRACKERS	4	14	£1,415
BIG CITY	4	13	£1,315
BALLYGALDA GLORY	4	12	£1,650

Leading Dams

Dam	wnrs	R/W	Prize Money
SPECIAL GAMBLE	7	11	£1,050
EASY BIMBO	6	68	£15,275
WESTMEAD MOVE	6	38	£23,415
DRUIDS DALROY	6	36	£28,900
CHICITA BANANA	6	26	£4,355
YELLOW RIBAND	6	17	£1,580

NGRC Statistics

LEADING DAMS

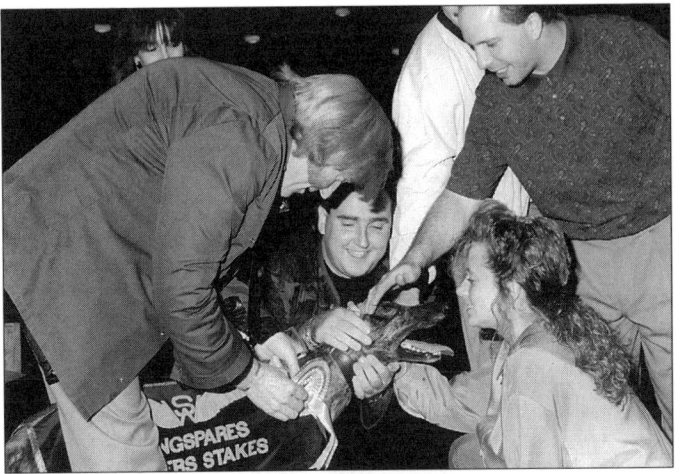

CHICITA BANANA . . .huge success on the track and now six winners to her name as a dam in 1994.

TOBYS DELIGHT	6	12	£1,475
LANRIGG LASSIE	6	12	£1,275
FARLOE MINEOLA	5	37	£10,590
BLACK SANCISCO	5	30	£6,840
SLANEYSIDE HOLLY	5	30	£5,525
DANIELS DOLLY	5	28	£5,355
FERNDALE CLASS	5	25	£5,300
BANGOR STYLE	5	23	£2,655
POND MOSQUITO	5	21	£5,400
ALWAYS GRUMBLING	5	14	£1,470
KILLEENAGH LADY	5	13	£2,400
HOME ALONE	5	11	£1,325
GREEN GODDESS	5	11	£1,215
LULUS MOTH	5	10	£7,145
SPRING SEASON	5	7	£1,775
SYNONE CREST	5	5	£1,550
COOLELAN GRAND	5	5	£425
BALLARUE SUZY	4	36	£28,690
CHOCOLATE SATIN	4	23	£2,515
GAME MISTY	4	19	£4,855
MISS IRENE	4	19	£1,990
LEMON MISS	4	18	£4,990
FAIR HILL ROSE	4	17	£1,450
CORAGH LADY	4	16	£1,740
POND JEMIMA	4	15	£3,025
ROVING LINDA	4	12	£3,380
WATH DUCHESS	4	12	£1,650
LEMON CHILL	4	12	£1,365
DENVER MINNIE	4	11	£1,130
ZEE ZEE	4	10	£1,280
WESTMEAD CHLOE	4	10	£1,050
TRACY BUDD	4	10	£990
MARGARETS JOY	4	9	£930
I'M UGLY	4	8	£1,705
TINY CATCHER	4	6	£1,210
COLORADO HOLLY	4	5	£1,360

NGRC Greyhound Racing Yearbook 1995

A-Z STATISTICS

How They Ran

KEY: Table of Open Race winners in 1994, showing the greyhound's breeding, date whelped, number of wins, and runs in the year, total prize money won (£), average winning distance and the date of its last win.

Greyhound	W	R	£	Ave D	Last Win
ABBEYFEALE HOPE bd b Slaneyside Hare-Pineapple Manor Apr-92	1	6	150	475	7-Jun
ABLE RAMON wf d Kildare Ash-Hillville Blonde Aug-91	2	17	225	485	13-May
ACADEMIC f d lm Slippy -Satharn Lady Feb-93	5	9	360	423	5-Dec
ACE CHOICE wbd d Fearless Ace-Worthy Choice Aug-91	15	33	3,410	523	21-Nov
ACTIVE PRINCE f d lm Slippy -Active Touch Jul-92	7	16	620	477	9-Nov
ACTIVE SUMMER f b Greenpark Fox-Active Touch Apr-91	3	11	1,175	474	21-May
ADAMSTOWN KING bd d Manorville Major-Sam Snipe Jun-92	2	13	350	530	27-May
ADVANCE PARTY bk d lm Slippy-Siahg Aug-91	2	8	325	372	29-Mar
AFFADOWN ROSIE bd b Aghadown Timmy-High Corner Nov-91	2	17	200	260	23-Sep
AGHADOWN FIONA bk b Ballyard Hoffman-Aghadown Heather Nov-90	1	5	75	375	18-Nov
AGLISH BLAZE wbd d lm Slippy-Crossfield Spec Mar-92	10	27	4,010	660	15-Dec
AGLISH MAXI bd b Yes Speedy-Ballybrack Charm Oct-91	3	12	415	461	8-Mar
AGLISH RAMBLER wbk d Whisper Wishes-Crossfield Spec Jun-91	2	7	230	647	15-Jun
AIR MAX bd d Double Bid-Cheerful Heart Jan-92	3	17	250	498	1-Dec
AISLING WHISPER bk dBalalika-Ees Whisper Aug-91	2	16	195	505	1-Sep
ALANS ACE f d Alans Champion -Parsons Echo Nov-91	13	24	1,390	460	27-Jun
ALANS WISH bk d Blue Baron-Fairy Lawn Sep-89	1	10	200	640	24-Mar
ALANS WONDER bk d Satharn Beo-Lady Lawn Apr-91	3	19	100	488	27-Aug
ALBERTO BLUE be d Penny Less-Silver Dipsi Nov-92	1	4	50	375	10-Oct
ALEXS BERTIE bk d Adraville Bridge-Summer Express Jun-92	1	9	120	420	16-Nov
ALFA POSTED be b Glengar Ranger-On Deposit Feb-92	5	17	465	545	17-Dec
ALLGLAZE WIZARD bk d Ballyregan Bob-Allglaze Grace Dec-91	2	19	215	686	15-Oct
ALLY DASH bk d Right Move-Westmead Chloe Aug-92	2	5	275	565	5-Dec
ALMOST NEW bk b Satharn Beo-Gortbofinna Lady Feb-90	2	8	615	484	31-Mar
ALPHAS MIRAGE bk d Pond Mirage-Ariadne Jun-91	2	11	210	465	20-Jun
ALWAYS GOOD bk d Skelligs Tiger-Always Grumbling Apr-92	7	26	695	556	11-Oct
ALWAYS GRAND bk b Skelligs Tiger-Roving Linda Nov-90	1	9	100	480	31-Jan
ALWAYS SKINT bd d Skelligs Tiger-She Sings Jan-93	1	3	100	480	9-Dec
AMBER CHAD f d Bold Rabbit-Lost Energy Jun-91	3	21	250	651	10-Nov
AMBLESIDE BOY wbk d Nightpark Lad-Run For Pleasure Jul-91	6	17	450	408	14-Dec
AMBLESIDE GOLD wbk d Nightpark Lad -Run For Pleasure Jul-91	1	2	75	480	22-Jul
AMERICAN HOT bd b Tain Solas-Kelsos Slinkey May-92	4	23	575	719	2-Sep
AMIGO RUNNER f d Fly Cruiser-Stainsby Girl Sep-91	1	4	50	663	26-Aug
AMY LADY bk g Powerstown Polo-Lady Amy Oct-91	1	7	175	663	18-Apr
ANGELS WHITE wf d Aulton Slippy-Madam Rosa Feb-91	2	10	250	650	15-Feb
ANHID BLAZE bk d Adraville Bridge-Anhid Cross Mar-92	11	26	2,975	508	1-Dec
ANNALEE MILLER wbk d Satharn Beo-Proud Adventure Nov-91	1	3	0	500	6-Aug
ANNAMORE KYLE bk d Kyle Jack-Velvet Doll Nov-90	7	24	5,575	552	24-Nov
ANNES SWAN wbk b Greenpark Fox-Exclusive Lady Jun-92	4	15	500	663	16-Jun
ANNS ABBEY bd b Waltham Abbey-Dellatoe Wonder Mar-92	3	11	275	677	4-May
ANNSBORO MAJOR dkbd d Manorville Major-Endless Game Jun-91	1	3	100	290	21-May
ANOTHER BOGEY f d Glenpark Dancer-Hazel Kitty Jun-91	1	10	100	400	28-Oct
ANOTHER FOREST f d Manorville Sand-Green Goddess Oct-92	4	13	355	475	9-Dec
ANOTHER GLOSS wbd b Fearless Ace-Carmencita Oct-91	2	11	240	880	22-Apr
ANOTHER MOMENT bd d Coalbrook Tiger-Firm Mist Aug-92	5	15	350	476	19-Nov
ANOTHER REJECT bd d Concentration-Storms Vixen Aug-92	2	7	130	420	28-Mar
ANOTHER SKYLARK wbd d Double Bid-Cathys Air Oct-92	2	14	170	645	25-Nov
APPLEBY GEM f d Tapwatcher-Appleby Blue Sep-92	2	14	210	457	13-Aug

A-Z STATISTICS

Greyhound	W	R	£	Ave D	Last
APRIL SUPER bd d Ardfert Sean-Fairy Wings Apr-89	11	21	1,565	420	28-Nov
AQUADUCT FOXY f b Greenpark Fox-Aquaduct Gypsy Mar-92	2	8	210	548	26-Apr
AQUAVITA fw b Daleys Gold-Foretop May-92	1	6	75	440	6-May
AR DREAM wbd b Satharn Beo-Wendys Dream Nov-91	7	16	550	422	6-Dec
ARAZIE bk d Skelligs Tiger-Woodford Magic Oct-91	2	10	235	468	17-Nov
ARDAN PRINCESS fw b lm Slippy -Gabriel Lucy Apr-90	1	4	110	380	11-Jun
ARDCOLLUM HILDA f b Druids Johno-Seventh Dynamic May-91	4	17	1,075	458	28-May
ARDCOLLUM MICK bk d Druids Johno-Seventh Dynamic May-91	2	6	200	275	10-Jun
ARDERA SUPPORT wbd d Moral Support-Bar Snowie Jun-92	3	6	285	560	17-Nov
ARDFERT WILLY f d Ardfert Sean-Slippy Hart Oct-91	1	7	0	500	31-Mar
ARDILAUN BRIDGE bk d Adraville Bridge-Cecelia One Nov-91	14	36	8,615	499	9-Dec
ARDMORE MAC wbk d Lartigue Note-Dainty Susan Jun-91	1	9	100	480	4-Oct
ARDNACROHY BLUE be d Balalika-Ferbane Skippy Sep-91	1	12	75	484	4-May
ARMIGER wf d Daleys Gold-What If Mar-92	3	20	220	507	5-Sep
ARNIES HOPE bebd d Alans Champion-Kilpatrick Wren Jun-92	1	2	150	458	1-Dec
ARRANCOURT GEM f d The Other Barrie-Lacca Ita May-91	4	20	430	515	26-Apr
ARRANCOURT LORD bkw d Ardfert Sean-Kilmorna Pearl Jun-91	2	10	250	714	19-Feb
ARRIGLE LIGHT bk d Glenpark Dancer-Lanigans Light Nov-92	1	2	75	480	30-Sep
ARROGANT PRINCE f d Ballinderry Ash-Proverbia Aug-92	1	4	500	460	25-Jun
ARTHURS ACE dkbd d Chnoc An Ein-Shuttle Smash Nov-91	1	11	120	484	16-Sep
ASHFIELD ARROW f b Slippys Quest-Elf Arrow Feb-92	4	16	3,710	544	26-Dec
ASHFORD BOY fw d Murlens Hawk-Supreme Peg Jun-91	7	13	950	433	22-Apr
ASHGROVE COMMET wbk d Darragh Commet-Lovely Sand Sep-91	1	7	40	555	28-Mar
ASHGROVE MAID bd b Daleys Gold-Orchard Fairy Jul-90	6	12	600	362	16-Nov
ASHTOWN HERO bd d Macs Lock-Hi Brazil Gypsy Apr-92	3	26	300	450	16-May
ASTIS ACCOUNT f d Ard Knock-Paceys Gold Sep-91	6	24	1,805	473	28-Oct
ASTROSYN CARESS f b Ravage Again-Astrosyn Kate Jun-92	2	16	240	515	29-Apr
ASTROSYN DRIVE bdw d Fryers Well-Astrosyn Trace Aug-91	1	4	175	655	28-Apr
ASTROSYN RAVAGE bk d Ravage Again-Astrosyn Kate Jun-92	1	15	140	555	24-Nov
ASTROSYN STEPPER bdw d Fryers Well-Astrosyn Trace Aug-91	1	14	120	695	4-Jan
ATE THE MEAT f d Ben G Cruiser-Kizzys Baby Jan-91	2	24	200	815	1-Nov
ATTITUDE PROBLEM wf d Satharn Beo-Much Adored Jul-91	2	10	0	500	14-May
AUREOLE TIGER wbd d Skelligs Tiger-Lady Serina Oct-90	1	4	200	278	28-Jan
AUSTERLITZ bd d Deenside Spark-Typical Torment Jul-93	1	2	100	450	30-Nov
AUTUMN AMBER bd d Deenside Spark-Miss Irene May-92	5	18	420	481	1-Jun
AUTUMN BARRY bew d Fly Cruiser-Paper Slippy Aug-91	5	26	820	490	3-Nov
AUTUMN TIGER bebd d Coalbrook Tiger-Queenies Fire May-93	2	4	265	574	16-Dec
AUTUMN TURBO bd d Moral Support-Miss Do Jun-90	1	7	100	450	12-Apr
AVOID THE RUSH bd d Manorville Star-Smokey Snowdrop Jul-90	5	22	2,585	464	19-Mar
AWBEG CAPTAIN bd d Captain Villa -Fast Girl Jan-92	1	5	150	278	8-Sep
AYR FLYER bd d Ardfert Sean-Slaneyside Glory Feb-92	6	9	1,725	477	18-Jun
AYRTON bk d Daleys Gold-Lightly Row Jun-92	2	6	185	420	2-Jun
BABY BIANCA bk b Murlens Slippy -Cassiebiancababy Dec-92	1	6	75	460	12-Nov
BABY DAN bew d Ballygalda Glory-Wath Duchess Oct-92	5	17	450	459	8-Oct
BACARDI QUEEN wf b Hit The Lid-Off To Lloyd Jul-91	1	8	75	220	17-Dec
BACK BEFORE DAWN bkw b Moneypoint Coal-Fashion Fever Sep-91	9	32	930	820	16-Nov
BACK FROM RIO wbd b lm Slippy-Life Policy Apr-91	1	10	120	285	9-Aug
BAGGYWRINKLE bk d Lyons Dean-Belindas Way Oct-91	1	5	100	640	22-Feb
BALAS BANKER bk b Balalika-Lauragh Pride Apr-91	1	6	120	605	21-Nov
BALLARUE HOVE bd d Curryhills Fox-Ballarue Suzy Jan-90	5	10	540	550	28-Mar
BALLARUE MINX wbd b Greenpark Fox -Ballarue Suzy May-92	13	27	16,600	713	19-Dec
BALLINDERRY SUE wbd b lm Slippy-Ballinderry Sand Jan-92	1	9	100	480	28-May
BALLINORA BEN bd d Satharn Beo-Yellow Riband Sep-92	3	12	270	473	12-Dec
BALLINORA LUCKY bd d Daleys Gold-Yellow Riband Nov-91	4	17	300	280	30-Jun
BALLYBRACK GROVE f d Arrow House-Ballybrack Dream Apr-92	1	4	100	260	2-Nov
BALLYCASTLE ECHO wbd d Murlens Slippy-Ballycastle Lady Jan-93	1	5	85	440	24-Nov

A-Z STATISTICS

Greyhound	W	R	£	Ave D	Last Win
BALLYCASTLE HUT f d Daleys Gold-Ballycastle Gold Nov-89	1	10	150	235	6-Aug
BALLYGOWN BARBIE bew b Track Man-Barbary Doll Aug-91	3	16	340	751	20-Jun
BALLYGOWN HERO bd d Willie Joe-Lissaniskea Gold Feb-91	1	4	100	465	7-Apr
BALLYGOWN LILLY wbk b Track Man-Bar Doll Aug-91	8	15	3,040	648	2-Jul
BALLYGOWN MUSIC wbd d Murlens Slippy-Beel Des Champ Feb-93	1	8	40	400	30-Nov
BALLYGUIRY CHAMP bd d Waltham Abbey-Ballyhane Lodge Jun-92	1	6	75	545	10-Jan
BALLYHACK PRINCE bd d Manorville Sand-Eyrehill Queen Jun-90	3	16	390	502	23-Apr
BALLYHANE ABBEY wbk d Waltham Abbey-Ballyhane Lodge Jun-92	1	3	100	647	9-Aug
BALLYHEA DREAMER f d Curryhills Ron-Anna Maria Mar-92	2	10	75	480	17-Jun
BALLYMACODA LINE bd d Manorville Major-Future Wishes Nov-90	1	5	75	440	25-Jan
BALLYMAH HOPE f b Tapwatcher-Ballymah Fawn Aug-90	1	4	50	260	31-Mar
BALLYREGAN WALLY bk d Murlens Hawk-Ballyregan Eve Aug-91	5	22	450	464	12-Sep
BALLYSHANE WIND wf d Slippy Blue-Ballyshane Belle Jun-91	1	9	200	484	7-Apr
BALLYWALTER SIR bk d Glenpark Dancer-Idle Chat Mar-92	5	23	575	482	17-Dec
BANGOR JENNY w b Zanzibar-Tims Lady Linda Aug-90	1	7	100	700	28-Mar
BANGOR LOU wbd b Zanzibar-Bangor Style May-92	3	15	340	637	14-Nov
BANGOR VALE f b Zanzibar-Bangor Drew Mar-92	3	9	300	660	24-Dec
BANJO BOY f d Kildare Ash-Dirty Nelly Oct-91	1	6	120	484	19-May
BANKERS CREDIT bw b Bankers Benefit-Margarets Joy Nov-91	2	13	150	634	30-Mar
BANKERS DIVIDEND bd d Bankers Benefit-Margarets Joy Nov-91	1	7	120	666	28-Feb
BANTES BLUE be d Alpine Minister-Corelish Susan Sep-92	1	10	100	500	10-Oct
BAREFOOT EXPRESS bk d Tico-Beclare Maid May-90	1	8	200	484	14-Mar
BAREFOOT RULER wbk d Polnoon Chief-Cheeky Carmaur Jan-93	1	2	40	400	30-Nov
BAREFOOT STAG f d Polnoon Chief-Cheeky Carmaur Jan-93	1	5	40	400	30-Jan
BARKED MY GIRL b b Carters Lad-Maggies Friend Sep-92	1	2	100	620	26-Dec
BARN LANE b d Odell Supreme-Daybreaks Wish Jul-90	3	9	300	529	31-Mar
BARNY RUBBLE bd d Glenpark Dancer-Bay Road Jill Aug-92	3	21	1,665	512	10-Dec
BARRELS CROSS dkbd d Manorville Major-Borne Misty Nov-92	2	5	175	375	24-Oct
BASHFUL CHIPS bd d Bold Rabbit-Bashful Tanya Oct-91	4	19	470	459	19-Sep
BASSIANO bef d Daleys Gold-Paint And Powder Oct-91	5	39	465	538	14-Oct
BATSFORD BOY bd d Hit The Lid -Midnight Cassim Oct-89	1	2	75	509	3-Aug
BATTERSEA BANDIT wbd d Druids Lodge-Park Na Veena Jul-91	1	5	75	490	25-Mar
BATTSTREET BENNY bd d Double Bid-Moral Shadow May-92	1	8	100	400	22-Apr
BATTSTREET IVY f b Oran Blonde-Movealong Mabel Jun-91	2	17	200	575	24-Jun
BAWNOGUE BLUEY bebd d Im Slippy-Penny Mead Jan-92	3	16	300	255	7-Sep
BAY ROAD GLEN bd d Glenpark Dancer-Bay Road Jill Aug-92	2	11	185	530	1-Dec
BAY ROAD GOLD f d Daleys Gold-Audrey Rose May-91	1	3	50	474	12-Nov
BAYSIDE bk b Daleys Gold -Foretop May-92	5	25	590	501	11-Jul
BAYVIEW ABBEY bk d Waltham Abbey-Longcross Lucy Aug-90	2	5	220	853	10-Feb
BAYVIEW BLAZE wbk d Dutch Delight-Ask Helen Jun-91	9	21	2,390	448	16-Dec
BE MY PAL bk d Parquet Pal-Cavecourt Bet Mar-92	3	19	550	397	25-Aug
BEAMING LUCKY f d Slippy Blue-Mummies Glory Sep-91	1	8	80	318	20-May
BEAU LUCKY bd b Fly Cruiser-Slippery Maid Apr-92	1	14	100	275	11-Nov
BEAU TOIT bkw d Fly Cruiser-Slippery Maid Apr-92	2	30	200	480	13-Sep
BEAVERWIND WOOD f d Galtymore Lad-Im Cruising Jan-93	1	6	100	480	10-Dec
BECK ROW PRINCE bd d Tapwatcher-Coolelan Grand Mar-93	1	4	75	375	28-Sep
BECKYS QUEST bd b Slippys Quest-Old Court Aug-92	1	13	150	655	19-Sep
BEECHROW FOX bkw d Merlins Wonder-Mullawn Darling Feb-92	1	4	75	545	7-Feb
BELINDAS ECHO bd d Echo Spark-Belindas Beauty May-91	1	6	100	450	28-Feb
BELINDAS TRAVLES bk d Echo Spark-Belindas Beauty May-91	1	8	100	275	28-Feb
BELLVIEW DUKE bd d Mr John Dee-Cold Climate Aug-91	4	9	490	636	12-Mar
BENRO BILLIE bd b Greenpark Fox-Minstrel Lady Feb-93	4	6	650	684	26-Dec
BENS COURT wbk d Flashy Sir -Rose Boquet Mar-91	6	33	1,475	370	29-Apr
BETTYS WISH f b Beautiful Rory-Hot Betty Mar-93	3	4	245	447	22-Dec
BEYOND CALL f d Druids Johno-Yorkville Beauty Sep-91	6	17	600	260	2-Sep
BIFOCAL CHAMP wbd d Im Slippy-Frisky White Feb-92	6	20	550	454	28-Jul

A-Z STATISTICS

Greyhound	W	R	£	Ave D	Last
BIG CYRIL wbd d lm Slippy-Bangor Style Aug-91	1	3	100	465	27-Aug
BILLYS IDEA f d Ballyard Hoffman-Pride Of Barna Oct-91	5	13	1,330	487	25-Jul
BIMBOS SPARKY bd d Tico-Keltic Bimbo Oct-91	2	12	200	440	17-Jun
BIT OF GAME bk d Druids Johno-Ormond Blossom Jul-91	2	14	240	484	24-Oct
BLACK ALL OVER bk d Whisper Wishes-Oaklawn Lass Aug-89	3	18	700	481	7-Oct
BLACK DUSK bk b Glencorbry Celt-Tiny Catcher Jun-92	1	4	75	480	6-Oct
BLACK EMO bk d Airmount Grand-Kilemy Cindy May-92	1	4	100	450	5-Sep
BLACK MIRAGE bk d Manorville Major-August Morning Sep-90	2	17	140	480	2-May
BLACK TOGA bk d Guiding Hope-Saratoga Miss Sep-91	1	1	75	375	19-Oct
BLACKCHURCH ALF bk d Slaneyside Hare -Congeel Liz Jul-92	10	32	795	474	5-Dec
BLACKPARK JAMES bk d Fionntra Highway-Lady Viking Aug-92	1	2	100	450	21-Jun
BLACKSTAIRS BOY d Midnight Hustle-Lighthouse Lou Aug-90	13	21	2,450	506	16-Nov
BLACKSTAIRS LENA f b Alans Champion-Blackstairs Lady Mar-92	1	5	125	640	5-Mar
BLACKWATER STILE wbk d Glenpark Dancer-Idle Chat Mar-92	1	17	50	515	26-Jul
BLAKES WISDOM fw d Adraville Bridge -Mailroad Star Sep-91	1	5	200	484	24-Feb
BLISSFUL STYLE wbd d Zanzibar-Bangor Style May-92	1	8	100	450	7-Jun
BLUE PETER be d Tico-Burgess Fonda Jan-90	1	1	100	275	28-Feb
BLUE SERGE be d Tapwatcher-Ambridge Lady Mar-92	4	21	375	418	16-Sep
BLUEGRASS GIN bd d Tipi Tip-Bluegrass Belle Jul-92	2	3	200	450	26-Jul
BLUEGRASS SEAN f d Hello Blackie-Lovely Wish Jan-92	3	5	450	298	8-Apr
BOBS DUKE bd b Skelligs Tiger-Junior Miss Jan-91	1	9	70	645	19-Apr
BOCONNELL EVE bk b lm Slippy-Dolls Baby Feb-92	1	6	100	660	3-Mar
BODYSHOP JOY bd b Fly Cruiser-Doonbeg Fugitive Aug-91	1	7	125	640	17-Jun
BOGGRA CHAMP bkw d Curryhills Ron-Kilowen Magpie Jan-92	2	4	150	680	13-Dec
BOHER WILLIE f d Willie Joe -Bomber Hall May-91	1	23	150	640	17-Feb
BOND END DAMSEL bk b Daleys Gold-Damiens Damsel May-91	6	14	640	449	18-May
BONMAHON DARKIE bdw d Carmels Prince-Debs Tick Oct-92	6	11	4,450	460	15-Oct
BONUS MARKS f d Ben G Cruiser-Another Whisper Feb-91	1	8	75	659	22-Aug
BOOS UP f d Boo Favourite-Slippy Canogue Sep-90	2	11	300	388	21-Sep
BOOZED LIGHTNING bk d Balalika-Rising Sun Oct-92	1	3	50	500	9-Dec
BORCULO bd b Curryhills Gara-Try Pry Girl Oct-90	1	11	100	660	7-Jun
BORDER LAD bd d Ravage Again New Kid Jan-93	1	2	125	480	3-Nov
BORDER PRINCE bebd d Carmels Prince-Lake Princess Sep-92	1	9	115	484	29-Oct
BORIS f d Adraville Bridge Wispa Oct-92	2	5	150	480	10-Dec
BORIS CHEETA dkbd d Kylehill Cheeta-Borris Little May-92	1	3	100	575	30-Sep
BORRIS HEATHER be b Kylehill Cheeta-Borris Little May-92	2	10	170	557	14-May
BOSHEEN MIST bk b Early Vocation-Saratoga Miss Nov-92	1	3	75	545	28-Sep
BOSSY BOOTS BOY bd d Hyper-Silverhill Lass Mar-92	1	4	125	640	26-Dec
BOURBON JACK bk d Princes Pal-Ritya May-91	3	7	250	453	2-Aug
BOVEY TRACEY bd b Waltham Abbey-Burmese Princess Sep-90	1	9	150	827	12-Mar
BOW WOW BENNY f d Lartigue Note-Riglis Rosa Aug-91	3	24	530	441	14-Apr
BOWER SWINGER bk d Adraville Bridge-Bower Bee Aug-91	1	8	100	465	10-Mar
BOWMANS ARROW wf d Arrow House-Greenfield Lass Mar-92	1	4	125	490	5-May
BOY LAD wf d lm Slippy -Maggies Friend Oct-91	4	14	425	396	24-May
BRACKEN HEATH bd b Tapwatcher-Game Sabre Jun-92	2	3	185	530	29-Dec
BRANDY SODA wbd d Double Bid-Catsrock Bubble May-92	4	15	370	445	10-May
BRANTHILL BLUE be d Green Gorse-Curraduff Bambi Jul-90	2	5	245	474	30-Mar
BREAGAGH MANOR bk d Curryhills Gara-Springwell Julia Aug-91	2	13	250	470	24-Mar
BREDAS SPARK bebd d Deenside Spark-Bredas Opinion Aug-92	1	5	100	275	23-Sep
BRENASH PRINCESS f b Slippys Quest-Yale Princess May-92	1	7	75	265	30-Nov
BRENNIES MAGIC wbd d Satharn Beo-Tullykeel Susie Dec-92	1	3	50	490	7-Nov
BRIDGE OFFICER bk d Adraville Bridge-Miss Jessica Sep-92	1	2	500	460	9-Dec
BRIDIES SECRET f b Whisper Wishes -Kalamity Kelly Nov-90	1	3	100	610	25-Mar
BROADOAK DENZL bk d Westmead Havoc-Wally May Aug-91	4	14	515	400	26-Aug
BROCKAGH FANTASY bd b Curryhills Gara-Coolagh Fantasy Oct-91	1	1	100	270	6-Aug
BROKEN HORSESHOE bk d Greenpark Fox-Lakeview Wispa Oct-92	1	4	75	630	17-Dec

A-Z STATISTICS

Greyhound	W	R	£	Ave D	Last Win
BROOM DANCER bk b Druids Johno-Willowbrook Peg Nov-92	1	2	100	310	12-Dec
BROTHERS PET bd d Manorville Major-Anything Fresh Nov-90	1	7	45	476	9-Feb
BROWSIDE JULIE bk b Burntoak Champ-Another Viking May-92	1	2	40	474	14-May
BROWSIDE PAT wbd b Im Slippy-Druids Dalroy Mar-92	6	18	470	635	21-Nov
BRUCES BANANA bd b Flashy Sir-Chicita Banana Oct-91	1	6	100	660	1-Dec
BRUNSWICK BANKER bd d Bankers Benefit-M Joy Jan-93	2	3	200	480	19-Dec
BULARINE SLIPPY wbk d Im Slippy-Belclare Maid Jul-91	2	14	290	660	5-Apr
BUNAGLANNA bk d Waltham Abbey-Suir Sharon Oct-92	1	7	75	545	29-Aug
BUNMAHON LAD bk d Druids Johno-Bunmahon Ese Apr-92	15	28	4,495	370	5-Dec
BURCOTT BOSH bk d Carters Lad -Aulton Blacky Sep-92	2	5	200	565	24-Nov
BURCOTT SPIRIT bk d Carters Champ-Aulton Blacky Sep-92	1	14	100	620	29-Aug
BURNPARK ALFED bd d Kildare Ash-Burnpark Lisa Sep-92	1	3	100	465	15-Dec
BURNPARK BEANO bd d Kildare Ash-Burnpark Lisa Sep-92	1	5	100	465	17-Nov
BURNPARK RASCAL bd d Green Gorse-Burnpark Lisa May-91	1	2	50	484	10-Feb
BURNTOAK PATCH wbk d Arrow House-Annjo Sep-90	1	2	150	460	16-Nov
BURWOOD ROSE f b Ardfert Sean -Lady Viking Mar-91	1	3	110	645	26-Jul
BUSHVILLE DUKE f d Daleys Gold-Black Sancisco Oct-91	1	3	100	250	14-Jun
BUTTERBRIDGE AMY bd b Waltham Abbey -Ballycarney Ann Apr-92	3	10	245	611	18-Jul
BYE BYE GARRY bk d Druids Johno-Up The Ladder Jul-91	9	20	1,440	428	13-Dec
CACTUS TAMMY wbd b Carters Lad-Silver Mac Sep-92	1	5	110	645	29-Nov
CAHARA CRAZE bk b Randy-Colla Craze May-89	1	2	100	675	2-Dec
CALIFORNIA DOT bd b Alpine Minister-California Blue Jul-92	1	9	100	480	28-Feb
CALLAHOW DALY f d Daleys Gold-Ahaveen Fever Jan-91	12	27	4,250	480	17-Oct
CAMBERWEL PRINCE wf d Daleys Gold -Centrefold Jul-91	2	12	275	377	3-Mar
CANADA CALL bd b Manorville Major-Slippy Helen Nov-91	1	22	50	640	27-Sep
CANALSIDE ANNE be b Glencorbry Celt-Wolseleys Yarn Mar-91	7	27	1,625	630	2-Jul
CANDID BLACK bk b Fly Cruiser -Queenies Fire Apr-92	4	15	480	716	23-Jun
CANDLE FLASH bk d Floating Champ-Orient Queen Mar-92	3	14	270	440	11-Nov
CANNY CHOICE w bk d Murlens Slippy-Knockelly Dawn Feb-93	1	11	100	450	22-Oct
CANNY DEAL bd d Ardfert Sean-Coolclar Mover May-92	1	4	75	480	26-Apr
CANOVA w bd d Randy-Trap To Line Oct-91	2	14	150	659	3-Oct
CANT BE SERIOUS wbk d Druids Lodge-Cant Clean Ash Oct-91	1	5	100	480	28-May
CANT KNOCK ASH wbd d Druids Lodge-Cant Clean Ash Oct-91	4	7	415	278	3-Dec
CAPENOR BOOGIE bd b Druids Lodge-Grannys Black Apr-91	1	5	100	450	12-Mar
CAPOLLA TOM bdw d Murlens Slippy-Off The Line Sep-91	6	18	790	629	11-Jul
CAPOOLA MAC bk d Easy And Slow-Mabeline Jun-91	1	11	75	480	10-Jun
CAPTAIN BAGGI bk d Captain Villa-Nancy Myles May-90	1	5	150	290	27-May
CARALEE BLUE be d Daleys Gold-Coragh Lady Jan-92	1	7	200	400	21-Apr
CARANNAHS SAND wbd b Greenpark Fox-Ballarue Suzy May-92	1	3	100	660	15-Dec
CAREYS FAULT bd b Greenpark Fox-Tracy Budd Mar-92	1	12	100	480	27-May
CARITA f b Fearless Ace-Murlens Tansy May-91	1	2	100	660	27-Jan
CARKER CLIPPER bd d Hondo Audacious-Fawn Whisper Sep-90	1	15	100	465	26-Jul
CARLOWAY DANCER bkw d Greenpark Fox-Prize Dancer Aug-91	3	8	350	487	15-Nov
CARRADUFF DUKE bd d Slippy Blue-Curraduff Pearl Mar-92	1	2	100	270	25-Jun
CARRAIG PAWS bd d Castlelyons Gem-Push Open Jul-91	20	33	3,265	446	16-Jul
CARRICK KING wbk d Daleys Gold-Shang Apr-91	2	6	150	375	24-Jan
CARRIGEEN BLAZE bk d Adraville Bridge-Carrigeen Lucky May-91	3	9	10,300	450	19-Feb
CARRIGEEN ROMEO f d Adraville Bridge-Carrigeen Lucky May-91	1	11	200	278	25-Mar
CARRIGEEN STAG f d Adraville Bridge-Carrigeen Lucky May-91	2	18	200	310	30-May
CARRIGEEN TOWER f d Ballinderry Ash-Carrigeen Lucky Mar-92	1	12	100	450	12-Oct
CARROW CONTENDER bk d Live Contender-Clonea Style Jun-92	1	5	60	450	15-Sep
CARROW STAR bkw d Live Contender-Clonea Style Jun-92	3	19	380	473	3-Dec
CARTOON CHAMP bk d Liosgarbh Miller-Dancers Record Jun-92	1	1	50	420	28-Mar
CASTLE CALL bdw d Manorville Sand-Angel Passing Feb-91	1	6	200	825	24-Feb
CASTLE LEWIS bd d Murlens Slippy-Yellow Carmaur Dec-90	3	6	310	573	8-Aug
CASTLELYONS ICE wbd d Castlelyons Gem-Alans Rosey Feb-93	3	8	200	413	30-Dec

A-Z STATISTICS

Greyhound	W	R	£	Ave D	Last
CATCH ME NOW bd d Deenside Spark-Tiny Catcher Feb-93	1	2	100	490	16-Sep
CEADER MOUNTAIN f d Greenpark Fox-Kevalling Kwik Jul-91	5	20	535	496	10-May
CEILI HOUSE wf Quare Rocket -Sugar Pill Oct-91	1	5	40	460	15-Mar
CENTURY ANGEL bd b Fly Cruiser-Century Sunset Apr-92	1	5	115	484	19-Feb
CERTAIN BLACK bk d Adraville Bridge-Moral Certainty Apr-92	2	10	240	484	2-Dec
CHADWELL CHARMER bk d Fly Cruiser-Slippery Moth Jul-92	7	17	2,475	456	12-Oct
CHAIRMAN MATT bd d Whisper Wishes-Wendys Dream Jul-90	3	12	330	314	26-Nov
CHAKALAK ZEUS bd d lm Slippy-Mountleader Emer Mar-92	3	20	225	407	25-Jul
CHAMPS GOLD bk b Childrens Champ-Barraduff Gold May-91	1	5	100	420	17-Jan
CHANCE AGAIN bd d Kylehill Cheetam-Golden Mar-92	7	34	680	459	9-Dec
CHARNES CHAMP bkw d Flashy Sir-Macs Jeanie Feb-91	1	6	125	640	14-Jun
CHASING MAD bk b Lyons Dean-Boveens Rose Apr-92	1	15	10	0	660 15-Sep
CHEEKY HERO wbe d Fionntra Highway-Classy Chic Mar-93	4	9	1,150	471	22-Nov
CHEEKY MOVE bk d Right Move-Cheeky Sparrow Feb-93	1	2	100	620	19-Dec
CHILHAM LASS bd b Carters Lad-Chilham Jet Jun-91	2	13	200	480	6-Sep
CHILTERN MICK bk d Flashy Sir-Chiltern Sarah May-91	2	5	170	440	24-Feb
CHLOES WHISPER f d Never Issued-Im Not Sarah Nov-92	3	13	290	447	29-Sep
CHOICE WHISPER bd b Whisper Wishes-Bold Hope Jun-92	1	5	100	400	13-May
CHURCH LANE wbd b Skelligs Tiger-Always Grumbling Apr-92	3	17	325	653	2-Dec
CILL DUBH LAD bd d Live Contender-Cill Dubh Villa Apr-92	1	4	100	590	31-Oct
CILL DUBH LIVE be bd d Live Contender-Cill Dubh Villa Apr-92	1	17	125	640	19-May
CITIZEN WONDER bk d Arrow House-Kiskeam Slippy Jul-90	1	6	200	256	9-Sep
CITY CLASS wf d Arrow House-Alexa Feb-92	8	20	650	284	19-Dec
CLANWILLIAM LASS bd b Ballygarvan Jet-Luminous Seven Mar-92	1	12	100	640	31-Oct
CLAPAWAY KEVIN fw d Balalika-Roses Wise Jul-91	1	5	40	545	28-Nov
CLAREMOUNT PARK bk d Glenpark Dancer-Wish Miss Sep-90	1	3	75	245	2-May
CLASHROE FRANCO bdw d Ardfert Sean-Dark Alley Aug-92	3	11	400	607	12-Nov
CLEAR PORT bd d Druids Lodge-Dancing Way Nov-90	1	10	200	484	24-Feb
CLEVER ANKWIK bk b Whisper Wishes-Quick Respond Mar-92	2	6	200	465	8-Feb
CLIFF HOUSE bebd b Mr John Dee-Own Return Aug-91	1	4	200	710	7-Mar
CLOHEENA STAR fw d Catunda Flame -Movealong Mabel Apr-90	1	12	75	685	16-Mar
CLONBRIN BLACK bk b Moral Support-Shining Bright Nov-90	5	23	645	755	6-Jun
CLONBRIN MOON bk d Soda Fountain-Shibumi Sep-91	2	9	150	545	24-Jan
CLONGEEL FERN bk b Whisper Wishes-Ferndale Class May-92	8	24	755	680	7-Nov
CLONKEEN DUCHESS bd b Kylehill Cheeta-Clonkeen Sandy Mar-92	2	9	150	545	28-Mar
CLONLUSK DEGREE bk b Alpine Minister-Clonlusk Chic Feb-92	1	4	120	385	23-Jun
CLONPRIEST JET bd d Manorville Major-French Belle Apr-91	1	3	120	515	22-Jan
CLOONTY BOY f d Master Hardy-Clountie User Mar-92	2	13	320	555	28-Nov
CLOTH CAP wbd d lm Slippy-Gulleen Dasher Sep-91	2	7	150	280	27-May
CLOVER TOM f d Manorville Magic-Lights Are Sep-91	3	12	375	640	18-Nov
CLOVERHILL DREAM bd b Moneypoint Coal-Cloverhill Daisy Jan-92	5	12	800	664	4-May
CLOVERS REWARD wf d Daleys Gold-Small Goods Mar-92	1	6	100	480	13-May
CLOYNE CLIPPER bd b lm Slippy-Siagh Aug-91	1	7	200	610	9-Sep
CO PILOT wbk d Catunda Flame-Relekas Beau Dec-91	3	7	485	647	15-Apr
COAL BREAKER bk b Moneypoint Coal-Roman Princess Aug-91	2	6	160	355	10-Feb
COALBROOK STAR bk d Coalbrook Tiger-Floridian Magic Apr-92	2	16	1,500	700	29-Oct
COAST IS CLEAR f d Glenpark Dancer-Quiet Welcome May-91	3	16	425	490	21-Mar
COLORADA QUEEN wbd b Roseville Jackie-Amazon Queen Jun-90	2	4	175	751	8-Nov
COLORADO FLAME bk d Airmount Grand-Denver Minnie Jul-91	5	20	550	489	8-Sep
COLORADO LAURA wf b Airmount Grand-Denver Minnie Jul-91	1	14	75	509	23-Mar
COLORADO ROSE bd b Carters Lad-Round Tower Rita Feb-89	1	4	100	450	12-Apr
COLOUR STORM f d lm Slippy-Fryers Storm Jul-91	1	3	125	260	10-Feb
COLUMBUS CHAMP bd d reenpark Fox-Merry Moments Jan-93	1	7	100	465	17-Dec
COLWELL PREDATOR bd d Westmead Havoc-Latchstring Jan-92	5	18	520	596	13-Dec
COMAVILLE STAR wbd d Satharn Beo-Mystique Model Sep-91	2	11	280	850	11-Jun
COME ON GERJOE wf d Galtymore Lad-Come On Princess Jun-91	1	4	100	260	16-Jun

A-Z STATISTICS

Greyhound	W	R	£	Ave D	Last Win
COME ON HONEY bd b Lartigue Note-Queen Of Country Feb-92	6	22	575	576	4-Nov
COME ON JAMIE wf d Galtymore Lad -Come On Princess Jun-91	1	5	125	400	24-Mar
COME ON REBEL bk d Odell Supreme-Silver Linda Aug-90	2	8	150	270	6-May
COME WHAT MAY wbd d Carmels Prince-Toora Sprite Jun-92	3	14	300	450	7-Nov
COMING HOME wbd d Flashy Sir-Daisys Queen Sep-91	2	13	200	450	3-Oct
COMMONS EAST f d Arrow House-Round Tower Rita Apr-92	2	3	200	250	15-Nov
CONNELLS CROSS bk d Adraville Bridge-Ballydrisheen Sep-91	6	25	2,925	514	18-Aug
CONSULTATION bk d Balalika-Ballyhaden Queen May-91	2	12	175	488	17-Feb
COOL JIM bd d Tapwatcher-Coolelan Grand Mar-93	1	3	75	220	28-Sep
COOL TESS be bd b Tapwatcher-Coolelan Grand May-92	1	8	100	700	10-Oct
COOLMONA ROAD bd d Ardfert Sean-Westpark Tee May-92	13	20	2,365	664	30-Dec
COOLROE JOAN wbd b Double Bid-Daily Express Oct-91	2	12	210	633	25-Oct
COOLROE SOCKS f b Alans Champion-Blazing City Jan-92	2	6	150	528	30-Dec
COOM CRUISER wbk d Arrow House-Coom Cross Aug-92	1	8	100	490	7-Oct
COOMLOGANE EURO bd b Arrow House-Lanrigg Lassie Mar-92	5	14	410	474	13-Dec
COOMLOGANE QUEEN bd b Arrow House-Lanrigg Lassie Nov-92	1	7	100	545	5-Oct
COPPER STEP f d Aghadown Timmy-Lilliput Lil Jun-91	2	16	275	268	27-Jul
CORA HILL wbe d Glenpark Dancer-Quare Mint Sep-91	10	31	975	311	4-Nov
CORBAL SKITT wbk d Satharn Beo-Ashcarne Magic Apr-92	1	3	100	450	12-Jan
CORKWOOD BLADE f d Ballymadoe Ben-Distant Form Aug-92	1	12	125	420	4-Jul
CORKWOOD CRYSTAL f b Ballymadoe Ben-Distant Form Aug-92	1	6	125	400	27-Jan
CORKWOOD FORM f b Ballymadoe Ben-Distant Form Aug-92	1	10	125	400	3-Mar
CORKWOOD GOLD f d Ballymadoe Ben -Celtic Swallow Jan-92	5	14	445	531	2-Dec
CORKWOOD MISTRAL bd b Ballymadoe Ben-Celtic Swallow Jan-92	1	3	75	465	1-Jan
CORNER FLIGHT bd d Manorville Sand-Another Cheer Sep-90	1	4	100	680	9-Apr
CORNER MAGIC bebd d Im Slippy -Nikita Feb-91	1	2	175	820	16-Apr
CORNER TIP wf b Thorny Tip-Stakehill Fox Aug-92	1	8	110	540	11-Jul
CORRIES TIM be bd d Aghadown Timmy-Hard To Start Sep-92	3	7	2,125	500	16-Dec
COSMIC MAN wbd d Ardfert Sean-Savin Rose Feb-92	3	24	285	447	29-Aug
COSMOJO bd d Carmels Prince-Most Jo Oct-92	1	7	100	460	16-Sep
COTTON SOCKS bk b Inchy Sand -Salthill Daisy Jun-91	1	1	250	666	28-Jan
COUNTRYWIDE FOX bk d Greenpark Fox -Quare Wish Feb-92	6	15	1,400	450	26-Nov
COUNTRYWIDE GIRL bk b Carters Lad -Fair Damsel Aug-91	2	13	200	575	27-May
COUNTRYWIDE MAN wf d Skelligs Tiger-Bold Belle Apr-92	1	3	150	475	8-Nov
COURTLOUGH DELL wbd d Murlens Slippy-Glenclare Oct-91	2	16	300	483	5-Mar
COURTMAN MANDY bdw b Skelligs Tiger-Slippys Jenny Apr-91	1	3	150	484	10-Feb
COVERT CYCLONE f b Slippy Blue-Covert Streak Sep-92	1	12	200	484	5-May
COWBOY JOE f d Willie Joe-Sneaky Snake Jul-89	3	26	320	778	26-Dec
CRAFTY ABILITY wbk b Curryhills Gara-Plough Support Sep-91	4	9	460	491	12-Aug
CRAFTY FONTANA bk d Druids Lodge-Crafty Winter Aug-91	9	39	2,800	478	14-Sep
CRAGAKNOCK JACK bk d Kyle Jack-Sandy Fan Jan-90	1	3	200	484	24-Mar
CREAMERY BRIDGE wbd d Im Slippy -Creamery Wish Jan-92	9	40	1,195	555	9-Dec
CREE CROSS wbk d Airmount Grand-Purple Boots Feb-91	3	9	300	490	7-Nov
CRICKETS CORNER f d Kyle Jack -Castle Bess Apr-91	2	7	200	283	24-Jan
CROPPY HEATHER bb b Tapwatcher-Drive On Lucky Apr-93	1	5	150	385	24-Nov
CROPPY LANCER bd d Tapwatcher-Cranley Primrose Aug-91	6	18	775	265	23-Aug
CRORY MAJOR bd d Manorville Major-Crory Flavor Sep-89	2	12	200	260	11-Apr
CRUISERS ODELL bd d Odell Schooner-Skip It Fluff Apr-91	2	9	200	250	25-Jan
CUB HUNTER f b Moneypoint Coal-Slaneyside Ivy Jan-92	5	18	2,285	499	22-Oct
CUCKOO SKY bk d Poor James -Twist Sand Jul-91	1	4	120	680	6-Apr
CURRYHILLS CATCH bdw d Macs Lock-Westpark Algeria Jun-92	2	11	175	269	15-Oct
CURRYHILLS FANCY bd d Deenside Spark-Westpark Schull Aug-92	3	10	250	463	17-Dec
CURRYHILLS LOCK bd b Macs Lock-Westpark Algeria Jun-92	1	7	50	420	28-Mar
CURRYHILLS LOVE be b Meeniyan Prince-Curryhills Brave Jun-92	1	4	200	640	21-Apr
CURRYHILLS QUEEN bd b Manorville Sand-West Jet Off Aug-91	1	6	50	484	22-Mar
CURRYHILLS YAQUT wbd d Im Slippy-Westpark Algeria Oct-91	6	14	500	263	10-Dec

A-Z STATISTICS

Greyhound	W	R	£	Ave D	Last
CURRYHILLS ZINK f d Manorville Sand-Jetoff Aug-91	5	31	555	635	1-Nov
CUSACK BUSH bd d Deenside Spark-Cusack Light Sep-91	1	2	50	460	6-Dec
CUSHIE MISCHIEF bk b Cushie Supreme-Rathdaniel Black Dec-91	1	2	80	620	17-May
CUSHIE TIM wf d lm Slippy -Cushie Wini Nov-91	2	14	225	326	4-Nov
DADDY ROCHE bd d Early Vocation-Saratoga Miss Nov-92	1	4	100	460	16-Sep
DADS OPINION bd d Express Opinion-Just A Fact May-90	1	5	150	750	11-Feb
DALEYS DENIS wbd d Daleys Gold-Lisnakill Flyer Oct-90	2	3	610	484	29-Apr
DAMIENS SPEED wbk d Double Bid -Festival Wonder Jul-92	2	9	175	450	27-Sep
DANCE RIKIE f d Manorville Magic-Tracy Charm Feb-92	1	5	80	660	29-Mar
DANCERS JOY bd b Celtic Dancer-Black Spray Jul-92	7	14	640	691	10-Nov
DANCING LANCE bk d Adraville Bridge -Westpark Coppeen Jul-92	3	18	300	468	24-Sep
DANESFORT PAL f b Manorville Magic-Tracton Pal Aug-91	2	12	240	714	15-Jan
DANESFORT SLIPPY f d Slippy Blue-Noras Gold Jul-92	5	14	500	408	21-Oct
DANGEROUS TIMES bd d Odell Schooner-Pond Spitfire Jun-92	7	25	750	431	28-Jun
DANS BANANA bk d Flashy Sir-Chicita Banana Oct-91	4	11	1,645	488	9-Dec
DARKLAWN CORBY bk d Glencorby-Celtdarklawn Mist May-90	1	6	100	450	20-Sep
DAROMA DAME wf b Daleys Gold Small Goods Mar-92	1	5	100	480	14-Mar
DARRAGH BEAU bkw b Balalika-Quarry Heather Sep-91	2	7	800	750	28-Dec
DAVCLIFF MASTER wbd d New Level-Starlight Airway Mar-93	4	10	300	485	10-Dec
DEANPARK CAPTAIN bk d Airmount Grand-Hong Kong Girl Oct-91	5	24	500	255	1-Oct
DECOY APACHE wf d Daleys Gold-Slaneyside Holly Dec-91	6	26	375	393	4-Nov
DECOY BONNIE wbd b Catsrock Dan-Decoy Princess Feb-92	4	20	400	813	19-Aug
DECOY CHEETAH bk b Slaneyside Hare-Easy Bimbo Jul-92	10	26	1,120	539	22-Nov
DECOY COMMANCHE bd d Daleys Gold-Slaneyside Holly Dec-91	4	14	650	471	12-Apr
DECOY COUGAR bk b Slaneyside Hare-Easy Bimbo Jul-92	9	23	5,815	713	28-Dec
DECOY EAGLE f d Satharn Beo-Decoy Regan Lass May-92	3	16	355	808	7-Oct
DECOY GOLD bd d Daleys Gold-Slaneyside Holly Dec-91	13	38	3,725	437	27-Sep
DECOY HOLLY bd d Daleys Gold-Slaneyside Holly Dec-91	3	20	350	523	21-Nov
DECOY JAGUAR bk d Slaneyside Hare-Easy Bimbo Jul-92	10	39	445	485	6-Dec
DECOY LION bk d Slaneyside Hare-Easy Bimbo Jul-92	16	45	2,360	602	24-Nov
DECOY LYNX bk b Slaneyside Hare-Easy Bimbo Jul-92	18	27	5,160	799	22-Oct
DECOY OSPREY f d Satharn Beo-Decoy Regan Lass May-92	1	9	115	484	26-Feb
DECOY PANTHER wbk d Slaneyside Hare-Easy Bimbo Jul-92	5	18	375	566	23-Dec
DECOY SIOUX wbk b Daleys Gold-Slaneyside Holly Dec-91	4	16	425	404	18-Nov
DEENSIDE DEAN f d Willie Joe-Deenside Sunset Oct-92	4	10	7,875	460	15-Oct
DEENSIDE FIRE f d Placid Son-Deenside Echo Feb-91	1	12	120	900	14-Jun
DEENSIDE JOE f d Willie Joe-Deenside Sunset Oct-92	3	10	300	512	22-Dec
DELMONTE LANE bd d Nine Thirty -Gods Lane May-92	6	25	1,650	355	30-Aug
DELMONTE STREET wbd d Dereen Star-Nells Mink May-92	5	23	300	406	29-Nov
DELTA DUCHESS bd b Zanzibar-Bangor Style May-92	8	23	1,410	570	23-Sep
DEMESNE DAISY f b Tipi Tip-Demesne Joy Jun-92	4	12	690	796	23-Dec
DEMOLITION DOG bd d Manorville Major Quiet Welcome Oct-92	3	13	250	467	1-Dec
DEN MARK DITTO bd d Tapwatcher-Hide High Mar-92	2	7	200	355	2-Aug
DENNY STREET f d Westmead Wish-O'Hickey Silver Apr-90	1	1	150	655	31-Jan
DENNYS BAR dkbd d Slippys Quest-Old Court Daid Aug-92	5	10	800	498	2-Jul
DENNYS MELODY bd b Ardfert Sean-Dennys Favourite Apr-92	2	8	175	617	26-Sep
DENNYS SLIPPY bew d lm Slippy-Dennys Daisy Feb-91	1	8	125	480	21-Feb
DERBY GRAND bk d Airmount Grand-Flames Of Joy Feb-92	1	3	120	440	4-Nov
DERRYLOUGH GOLD bk d Adraville Bridge-Ballycastle Gold Feb-91	1	6	100	310	3-Jan
DIAMOND CARA bk d Glencorby Celt-Local Madam Mar-91	2	16	160	463	24-Mar
DIAMOND DOUBLE bd d Manorville Sand-Sheer Velvet May-92	1	8	100	640	1-Aug
DIAMOND SAPPHIRE wbd b Murlens Slippy-Louise Champion Sep-91	5	37	500	480	8-Nov
DILLYS SON f d Strange Dilly -Roslea Hero Jun-92	7	13	625	267	16-Sep
DINAN PRINCE bk d Murlens Post -Lisbealad Spark Apr-93	1	5	100	400	21-Nov
DINGLE BAY f d Dingle Greatest-Pulsars Girl Oct-91	1	11	120	484	23-Sep
DIRECT FORTUNE bk d Bardev Magic-Mandys Charm Sep-91	1	2	100	480	14-Jun

A-Z STATISTICS

Greyhound	W	R	£	Ave D	Last Win
DISRAELI fw d Flashy Sir-Hogans Kizzy Jan-92	1	12	0	460	2-Jun
DONGADONG bd b Deenside Spark-Celtic Cracker Apr-92	5	13	585	392	17-Sep
DOON SAND bdw d Moral Support-Sand Deposit Nov-91	1	10	100	580	23-Jan
DOREENS HOPE wbd b lm Slippy-Gold Goblet Sep-92	2	13	225	480	16-Jul
DOUBLE DANCE bd d Double Bid-Hazelwood Shadow Nov-91	1	18	75	277	3-Aug
DOUBLE DOSE bk d Double Bid-Zee Zee Oct-91	3	14	300	501	18-Apr
DOUBLE POLANO bk d Double Bid-Polano Jul-92	2	15	230	835	26-Nov
DRAGON PRINCE wbk d Whisper Wishes-Supreme Miss Apr-93	2	2	235	470	29-Dec
DREAM LOVER f b Flashy Sir-Hogans Kizzy Jan-92	1	11	100	640	12-May
DREGHORN SHELL wf d Druids Lodge-Churchtown Star Oct-91	1	17	120	695	18-Jun
DROOPYS ALFIE bkw d lm Slippy-Droopys Aliysa Aug-91	4	27	1,900	496	30-Jul
DROOPYS AYRTON bd b Curryhills Gara-Bunnys Star Apr-92	4	15	375	482	30-Dec
DROOPYS CRAIG bkw d Moral Support-Droopys Aliysa May-92	11	30	4,315	493	17-Oct
DROOPYS CURTIS bk d Ardfert Sean-Droopys First May-92	1	12	100	484	20-Apr
DROOPYS DOYLE fw d lm Slippy -Ballyard Monroe Feb-92	5	21	380	550	17-Nov
DROOPYS EVELYN wbk b Game Ball-Immoral Support Jul-90	7	20	1,650	587	3-May
DROOPYS FERGIE bk b Manx Treasure-Star Approach Feb-93	3	7	235	467	10-Dec
DROOPYS FLASH bk d Phantom Flash-Droopys Stranger Jan-92	2	3	500	484	17-Feb
DROOPYS JOANNE f b Coalbrook Tiger-Astral Breeze Oct-92	3	8	310	614	25-Nov
DROOPYS LANNY bkw d Ardfert Sean-Droopys First May-92	6	19	745	456	21-Nov
DROOPYS LARRY wbk d lm Slippy-Ballyard Monroe Feb-92	4	11	350	625	13-Aug
DROOPYS SANDY bk d Ardfert Sean-Droopys First May-92	3	4	20,000	500	21-May
DROOPYS SLAVE bd d Manorville Majo-Twilight Slave Feb-91	7	22	2,525	494	24-May
DROOPYS STAN be d Live Contender -Afternoon Blue Aug-92	2	6	185	430	8-Aug
DROVERS ROAD bd d lm Slippy -Slaneyside Glory Mar-91	11	29	4,525	491	24-Dec
DRU AGAIN bebd d Slippy Blue-Druids Dalroy Sep-90	2	4	270	515	14-Apr
DRUIDS ELLYMAY wbk b lm Slippy-Druids Dalroy Mar-92	5	16	635	472	10-Dec
DRUIDS ELPRADO bdw d lm Slippy-Druids Dalroy Mar-92	8	22	25,750	468	3-Jun
DRUIDS OMEGA wbd d lm Slippy-Druids Dalroy Mar-92	12	32	1,450	492	22-Nov
DRUIDS TYCOON wbd d lm Slippy-Druids Darley Mar-92	3	11	325	370	21-Jun
DRUMCOO MOTH bd b Lodge Prince-Olympic Moth May-92	4	21	385	448	25-Aug
DRUMSNA bk d Manorville Major -Slieve Sand Jul-91	5	24	375	519	21-Oct
DRUMSNA BEAUTY bd b Carters Lad -Tinrah Slippy Oct-91	1	1	100	675	13-May
DRUMSNA SLIPPY bd b Carters Lad -Tinrah Slippy Oct-91	1	13	150	400	3-Feb
DUE TO TRAVEL bebd d Skelligs Tiger -Ginger String Jan-93	1	7	50	440	14-Nov
DUFFYS LEGEND bk d Balalika-Ma Hand Jan-92	3	14	320	452	23-Jul
DUNFIELD DANNY bkw d Whisper Wishes-Ferndale Class May-92	2	8	200	660	18-Oct
DUNMAIN DUKE wbe d Daleys Gold-No Sale Jan-92	1	9	100	465	27-Aug
DUNMURRY LAKE bd d Live Contender-Dunmurry Rose May-92	2	115	484	24-Nov	
DUNROAMIN PRIDE bd b Fly Cruiser-Dower Celt Aug-91	1	5	0	462	13-Jun
DUSKY SOUND bew d Concentration -High St Special Sep-92	1	11	100	465	1-Dec
DUSTY BLUEBELL be b Big City-Dryland Dusty Jun-92	3	7	300	730	19-Oct
DUSTY IMAGE bk bBig City-Dryland Dusty Jun-92	5	11	525	841	8-Dec
DUSTY LONER bk d Big City-Dryland Dusty Jun-92	1	1	75	843	13-Dec
DUSTY ROVER wbk d Big City-Dryland Dusty Jun-92	4	12	415	641	6-Oct
DUTCH BOOSTER bk d Dutch Prince -Zogarnici Oct-90	3	12	230	440	3-Nov
DUTCH FLYER bk d Dutch Prince-Catch Ruby Nov-91	9	27	650	595	29-Dec
EAGLE CREEK bd b Amenhotep-Tobys Delight Aug-92	1	3	175	820	29-Oct
EAGLE RACING bd d Balalika-South Salonica Sep-92	2	9	175	398	23-Nov
EARLY ROSE f b lm Slippy-Winsor Aird Aug-92	4	8	575	468	12-May
EASY BLACK bk d Easy And Slow-Sailing Island Apr-91	3	9	320	580	20-Sep
EASY LODGE wbd d Druids Lodge-Ant Ese Sep-91	7	31	520	563	29-Sep
EBONY CHIEFTAIN bk d Chief Canary-Jerpoint Eva May-92	1	3	250	484	14-Apr
EDDIES VENTURE wbd b lm Slippy-Seldom Mary Oct-92	1	3	115	440	16-Dec
EDWORTH CHAMP wbd b Seafield Quest-Down Your Way Apr-92	1	7	150	1102	22-Jul
EGMONT DESSIE f d Satharn Beo-Egmont Betty Jul-92	3	17	275	392	31-Oct

A-Z STATISTICS

Greyhound	W	R	£	Ave D	Last
EGMONT JOAN f b Daleys Gold-Egmont Biddy May-92	6	23	1,375	450	8-Aug
EGMONT POPEYE bd d Curryhills Lemon -Egmont Biddy Jan-91	2	11	75	480	17-Jun
EGMONT SCOBY bkw d Satharn Beo-Egmont Betty Jul-92	5	14	475	472	21-Sep
EGMONT ZAG bk d Whisper Wishes-Courtenay Gold May-91	2	18	150	275	27-Apr
ELAINAS SLIPPY wf d lm Slippy-Whip Express Sep-91	1	7	125	640	4-Feb
ELEGANT BRANDY bd d Murlens Slippy-Elegant Dream May-92	5	17	620	483	15-Dec
ELEGANT SWALLOW bd b Murlens Slippy-Elegant Dream May-92	3	9	300	580	25-Apr
ELLA DEE bk b Fly Cruiser-Bettys Lark Feb-92	1	4	100	647	26-Jul
ELUSIVE MAIDEN bk b Whisper Wishes-Newhill Abbey Apr-92	1	2	85	440	10-Nov
ESHA NESS bk d Phantom Flash-Matrons Sue Apr-92	2	14	200	480	1-Jul
ESSENTIAL NEEDS wbd d Carters Lad-Classiebawn Sand May-91	1	2	100	620	13-Jan
ETTRICK BETSY bd b Catunda Flame-Jubilee Rosy Nov-91	1	3	100	580	10-Aug
EUROPEAN MANAGER wbd d lm Slippy-Leeview Jill Dec-90	1	3	100	278	17-Feb
EUROPEAN PRINCE wbk d lm Slippy-Princess Alanna Nov-90	2	16	75	460	10-Jun
EVANGALISTA bd b Curryhills Gara-Girls Band Oct-91	1	5	80	620	6-Aug
EXIT SPRING bebd d Chief Ironside-Spring Exit Aug-91	1	11	200	278	25-Mar
FAIR PENNY bd d Penny Less-Fawn Music Jan-91	1	13	750	575	25-Mar
FAIRY BELLE bd b Grey Wolf-My Alanna Nov-90	1	13	125	640	3-Jun
FAIRY WATCHER bd b Tapwatcher-Westmead Fairy Sep-92	3	18	285	553	23-Dec
FANCY MAJOR bk d Airmount Grand-Denver Minnie Jul-91	4	18	405	475	13-Dec
FAREWELL SLIPPY be d lm Slippy-Moneypoint Wit Dec-91	2	13	225	560	7-Jul
FARLOE BENEFIT bd d Bankers Benefit-Farloe Mineola Oct-91	5	16	465	504	21-Sep
FARLOE BOLD bk d The Other Risk-Mineola Tina Sep-91	5	23	500	254	18-Oct
FARLOE DUCHESS bd b lm Slippy-Westmead Sarra Jan-93	3	7	275	553	25-Nov
FARLOE RISK bkw d The Other Risk-Mineola Tina Sep-91	1	14	0	277	24-Nov
FARLOE SESSION f d Fearless Ace-Mineola Kylie Jul-92	1	4	0	462	13-Jun
FARLOE WHISPERS bk d Whisper Wishes-Im A Duchess Sep-88	1	1	100	420	21-Mar
FARMER PATRICK f d Murlens Hawk-Hawkfield Music Oct-91	3	15	250	407	5-Jul
FARRIERS CHOICE fw d Ballyard Hoffman-Pride Of Barna Oct-91	1	9	50	545	17-Oct
FASHION SETTER wbd d Greenpark Fox-Rikie Apr-92	1	9	250	484	17-Mar
FAST AND FOXY bd d Greenpark Fox-Coragh Lady Nov-92	3	13	300	372	17-Aug
FAST COPPER bk d Ballyard Hoffman-Parkswood Magpie May-91	13	27	6,220	313	24-Dec
FAST FITZ PETE bkw d Lartigue Note-Kerogue Wish Apr-92	4	17	550	603	21-Nov
FAST OFF bd b Murlens Hawk-Hawkfield Music Oct-91	3	12	400	488	15-Oct
FAST VOCATION bk d Early Vocation-Lakeshore Rose May-93	1	2	100	400	21-Nov
FAULTLESS BUDDY bd d Murlens Slippy-Tracy Budd Oct-90	2	20	100	475	6-Aug
FAULTLESS JOE bd d Greenpark Fox-Tracy Budd Mar-92	1	3	100	252	24-Aug
FAUX PAR bk d Randy-Trans Linda Aug-91	2	10	200	563	8-Sep
FAWN FORTUNE f d April Trio-Velvet Girl Nov-92	1	3	100	278	11-Aug
FEAR FAIRE bd d Kyle Jack-Game Misty Oct-91	1	8	100	465	22-Feb
FEARLESS ATLAS bk d Randy -Dresden Lady Jul-91	7	18	1,585	595	27-Jul
FEARLESS COUGAR bdw d Slaneyside Hare-Daniels Dolly Nov-91	8	28	1,625	384	26-Dec
FEARLESS LEADER f d Fearless Mustang-Daniels Dolly Aug-92	6	16	625	476	12-Oct
FEARLESS LINX bd b Fearless Mustang-Daniels Dolly Aug-92	9	17	1,985	636	21-Dec
FELTHAM DONALD wbk d Summerhill Super-Westmead Dominee Jun-92	5	14	585	601	25-Oct
FERBANE REYNARD be d Balalika-Ferbane Skippy Sep-91	6	26	550	500	18-Aug
FERMAINE MONARCH f d Flashy Sir-Westmead Hustler Jul-91	5	21	600	450	27-Apr
FERNDALE ARROW f d Arrow House-Drominagh Sally Nov-91	1	4	120	490	3-Feb
FERNDALE LODGE bd d Druids Lodge-Ferndale Mo Sep-91	11	39	2,975	494	11-Jul
FERNHILL TIGER bd d Coalbrook Tiger-Bright Future Apr-92	7	15	1,425	276	9-Nov
FIERY FRANCES wbk b Whisper Wishes-Silver Shoes May-90	1	3	100	465	15-Sep
FIFTHOFNOVEMBER f d Skelligs Tiger-Maggies Wishes Nov-91	1	9	300	484	3-Mar
FINAL EDITION bk b Druids Johno-Flying Carmel Jul-91	1	5	100	460	7-Feb
FINBARRS BREE bk d Whisper Wishes-Slippy Linda May-92	3	16	650	595	19-Nov
FINE MIST bk b Portrun Flier-Blackmans Wish Apr-92	1	7	100	545	14-Oct
FIRERAY STAR bd d Slaneyside Hare-Westmead Sarra Apr-92	3	19	300	352	2-Nov

NGRC Greyhound Racing Yearbook 1995

A-Z STATISTICS

Greyhound		W	R	£	Ave D	Last Win
FIRM JOLLY bd d Double Bid-Limekiln Pet Jul-89		2	5	300	460	25-Nov
FIRST DEFENCE bk b Easy And Slow-Fast Pace Feb-92		8	23	1,345	708	17-Dec
FIRST EMPEROR f d Yellow Emperor-Balmy Blond Jun-90		1	13	40	385	12-Sep
FIRST NAME BART f d Westmead Wish-Saga Miss Jan-90		2	15	215	634	2-Jul
FLAG STYLE bk d Flag Star-Fast Blast Aug-92		1	5	100	660	2-Aug
FLAG THE FAWN f d Druids Johno-Almond Blossom Jul-91		4	19	445	485	2-Dec
FLASHING SUPPORT bd b Low Sail-Sahara Surprise Sep-92		6	17	455	614	4-Nov
FLASHING SWORD wbd d Fearless Champ-Quainton Sabre Oct-88		1	1	300	484	17-Mar
FLESK BRIGG f d Oughter Brigg -Annamore Velvet Mar-92		2	17	260	590	10-Mar
FLY COMIC fw d Galtymore Lad-Come On Whisper Mar-92		2	9	175	450	11-Oct
FLY DOUR LEO f d Adraville Bridge-Coolnasmear Lady Mar-91		2	13	50	492	22-Feb
FLY PRIDE wbk d Curryhills Fox-Lauragh Pride Apr-90		1	22	0	484	5-Apr
FLY WISH bk d Whisper Wishes -Slippy Toots Apr-92		10	22	930	322	21-Oct
FLYING BIRD bd b Echo Spark-Silrin Sue May-91		3	8	435	657	26-May
FLYING EIGHT f d Glencorbry Dawn-Hurry On Misty Feb-92		3	8	325	695	17-Dec
FLYING FANTASY bkw d Whisper Wishes-Rapid Lady Nov-90		1	15	125	260	4-Mar
FLYING SEAL bkw d Whisper Wishes-Yellow Suzy Oct-91		5	27	550	296	17-Oct
FOREIGN CANARY bd d Manorville Major-Champagne Lady Mar-91		2	4	825	575	11-Feb
FOREST JADE f d Manorville Sand-Green Goddess Oct-92		2	2	195	483	14-Dec
FOREST KING bk d Skelligs Tiger-Green Goddess Nov-91		1	6	300	484	14-Apr
FOREST PRINCESS bk b Skelligs Tiger-Green Goddess Nov-91		1	9	50	655	31-Oct
FOREST ROCKET be d Skelligs Tiger -Green Goddess Nov-91		3	12	315	504	25-Nov
FOREVER MANX b d Manx Marajax -Genevey Slippy Jul-92		6	16	480	650	17-Dec
FORTUNES GIRL bd b Whisper Wishes-Roving Linda Jul-92		2	7	150	495	8-Aug
FOTA FLASH f b Flashy Sir -Annies Last Aug-91		1	7	100	610	25-Mar
FOUR YEARS ON wbk d Another Flag-Greenview Mary Jan-93		1	3	75	480	23-Sep
FOXCOVER GEM f b Airmount Grand-Burnpark May May-93		1	5	85	440	26-Dec
FOXCOVER GIRL bd b Money Matters-Rocksan Sep-91		1	3	100	660	27-Jan
FOXDALE SWIFT bd d Lisamote Dawn-Modern Fiction Jul-92		1	7	100	580	7-Sep
FRANKS DOLL bd d Kilbarry Slippy -Come On Mandy Dec-91		4	19	10,190	457	30-Dec
FREDS FLYER wbk d Whisper Wishes-Roving Linda Jul-92		5	15	2,825	457	5-Oct
FREE KICK wbd b Greenpark Fox-Lyns Fli Jan-92		1	4	100	450	9-Mar
FREE TIME wbd d Skelligs Tiger-Primrose Moon Aug-92		1	4	50	515	28-Jun
FREEWAY STATE wf d Dads Bank-Brazen Bibi Aug-91		1	3	115	484	16-Apr
FREEWHEEL KYLO bd d Kyle Jack -Shanavulin Girl Oct-90		17	33	4,800	603	19-Nov
FREIGHDUFF MAC wbk d Adraville Bridge-Kilbarry Lady Jun-91		3	9	480	407	17-Mar
FRISBY FAITHFUL bk d Flashy Sir-Frisby Fortina Jun-92		1	12	50	474	29-Jun
FRISBY FLY bkw d Im Slippy-Fly Smasher Jun-92		3	12	320	441	24-May
FROM THE QUARRY bdw d Kildare Ash-Ever Loving Doll Aug-92		2	4	75	274	24-Nov
FUN OF CORK bk d Handsome Dan-How Sad Jan-92		4	16	415	375	17-Dec
FUNNY ENOUGH bd d Odell Yankee-Ready Rubbed Jul-92		2	7	100	500	13-Aug
GAFFERS DASHER bd d Ardfert Sean-Glynn Gold Sep-91		2	4	200	480	25-May
GALLEYDOWN BOY f d Flashy Sir-Annies Last Aug-91		4	13	820	593	25-Jun
GALLYS LADY wbk b Kilcannon Hero-Babs Pet Aug-91		14	34	1,825	633	19-Nov
GALTEE ORIGIN bd d Kildare Ash -Mogelly Dawn Jan-93		1	9	100	465	11-Aug
GALTYMORE DAWN wf b Lodge Prince-Borris Chat Jul-90		1	4	100	660	6-Jan
GALTYMORE MIST f d Moneypoint Coal-Borris Chat May-92		1	21	100	714	4-Jul
GAMBLERS LOU wbd d Castlelyons Gem-Gamblers Gold Jun-92		1	5	100	610	9-Sep
GAMBLERS SPORT wbk d Castlelyons Gem-Gamblers Gold Jun-92		7	27	930	509	29-Oct
GAME CASCADE bd b Kyle Jack-Game Misty Oct-91		3	11	300	643	10-Dec
GAME EASY f d Willie Joe-Game Flo Jul-92		1	2	100	255	29-Oct
GARRETS AISLING bk d Randy-Shanavulin Rose Aug-91		1	11	100	590	27-Jan
GARRYGLASS SUSIE f b Trip To Arran-Garryglass Rose Aug-91		1	9	150	460	4-Feb
GEINIS CHAMPION wbd d Druids Lodge-Geinis Pride Oct-92		2	21	205	470	30-Jul
GEM PRINCESS bd b Greenpark Fox-Rosewood Lass Dec-91		1	6	75	509	26-Jan
GENEROUS JET bd d Castlelyons Gem-Mogelly Dawn Mar-92		3	11	330	426	8-Dec

A-Z STATISTICS

Greyhound	W	R	£	Ave D	Last
GENEROUS LION wbd d Greenpark Fox -Urban Princess Apr-92	1	9	75	484	5-Mar
GENOTIN LAURA bk b lm Slippy -Solas An Maiden Jul-91	4	15	480	484	26-Dec
GENTLE DREAM f d Curryhills Specl-Newlands Lass Mar-93	1	2	100	450	6-Dec
GENTLE TIMES bew d lm Slippy-Zee Zee Apr-92	2	5	250	400	14-Oct
GENTLE WARNING be d Glenpark Dancer- Gentle Sarah Apr-90	1	5	200	484	13-Jan
GIGGS GIRL bd b Bucks Blast- Millrace Lady Jul-91	1	8	80	686	20-May
GIGGSY bk d Early Vocation-Lisacahane Echo Feb-93	2	5	155	458	19-Oct
GIGLIS MIRAGE bk d Odell King -Witches Blast Nov-89	1	1	100	450	20-Sep
GILTI SEAN wf d Ardfert Sean -Ridgedale Madam Jan-92	1	3	120	645	26-Mar
GINGERMAN GEORGE f d Future Band-Patches Girl Mar-91	8	46	975	945	17-Dec
GIRL FRIDAY bdw b Tapwatcher-Jofie Jun-92	2	9	210	548	29-Aug
GIS A SMILE wf d Flashy Sir-Desert Pearl Apr-91	19	30	6,310	460	25-Oct
GLACIAL ARCTIC bd d Whisper Wit-Knocklucas Daisy Jun-92	1	2	125	290	25-Nov
GLEANNRUE PIPER bd d Adraville Bridge-Cecelia One Nov-91	1	5	120	484	14-Oct
GLENGALL BADGER bd d Greenpark Fox-Manx Violet Dec-90	1	5	100	256	9-Sep
GLENGAR DESIRE bd d Kanturk Chipper-Glengar Moss Mar-90	1	6	100	450	12-Jul
GLENGAR JET bk d Kanturk Chipper-Glengar Moss Mar-90	1	4	100	450	24-May
GLENHOLM LADY f b Make History-Spring Season Nov-91	1	7	100	555	25-Aug
GLENHOLM TIGER bd d Manorville Major -Quare Gold Dec-91	10	25	2,150	470	16-Aug
GLENSIDE ROSE bk b Tip For Glory-Strobes Tigress Apr-91	4	15	370	628	13-Jun
GLENSIDE TED f d Bad Intentions-Acacia Jun-90	1	4	100	450	31-Jan
GLIDEAWAY FOX f d Greenpark Fox-Cute Betty Dec-91	16	26	1,580	292	5-Sep
GLIDEAWAY JIM bebd d lm Slippy-Tarbrook Spark Jun-91	3	22	375	494	21-Sep
GLIDEAWAY TOBY f d Greenpark Fox-Cute Betty Dec-91	4	9	1,300	263	31-Aug
GLINROAD JOCK bk d Kildare Ash-Flying Touch Oct-91	1	3	150	400	26-Mar
GLUE VIXEN wbd b Greenpark Fox-Glow My May-92	1	2	50 4	80	6-Dec
GOLD DEMPSEY bk d Dempsey Duke -Another Dancer Oct-92	5	21	315	474	16-Jul
GOLD DOON f d Top Flash-Doon Duchess Oct-90	8	24	2,700	456	1-Dec
GOLD SPLASH bk d Whisper Wishes-Locket Lisa Nov-89	1	13	100	660	2-Aug
GOLD SYNDICATE wbd d lm Slippy-Ballinderry Gold May-91	1	9	75	480	2-Sep
GOLDMAN wf d Daleys Gold-Tri Nitro Mar-91	2	17	150	269	22-Aug
GOOD CHAMPAGNE wf d Daleys Gold-Fosshill Prince Aug-90	1	3	100	278	7-Feb
GOOD LUCK CHARM bd b House Hunter-California Belle Aug-90	2	21	620	802	31-Mar
GOOD TOUCH bd d Odell King-Manor House May-92	1	5	100	465	1-Dec
GORDONS JILL f d Whisper Wishes-Penmaric Jan-90	1	4	250	484	28-Apr
GORSE GREEN bd d Green Gorse-Trout Stream Jul-90	1	6	75	480	12-Jul
GORTMORE EXPRESS bk d Nightpark Lad-Eugenes Girl Jan-90	9	39	1,880	596	29-Jul
GRANARD BETTY wbk d Satharn Beo-Egmont Betty Jul-92	1	10	100	500	4-Apr
GRANGE FIRE bk d Glencorbry Celt-Cuddly Jul-91	1	3	75	270	19-Aug
GRANGE MORAL bd d Moral Support-Grange Grace Jun-91	3	15	350	312	22-Apr
GRANNYS BOY bk b Brownies Outlook -Lilian Grey May-91	8	28	920	682	19-Dec
GRANSHAGH JADE bk b Hygard-Ringview Bass Oct-91	1	4	100	484	27-May
GRANSHAGH MELODY bk d Hygard-Ringview Bess Oct-91	6	17	660	462	10-Nov
GREAT HOUSE f d Dukes Lodge-Shirleys Opinion May-92	13	39	1,370	488	30-Dec
GREAT OLD TIME bd d Waltham Abbey-Carvilles Hill Jul-91	1	7	125	640	11-Feb
GREEK COMMANDER bd d Manorville Sand-Aglish Rose Mar-92	3	5	660	457	20-Aug
GREEN ANCHOR bk b Meeniyan Prince-Glencoe Penny Sep-89	3	12	260	479	19-May
GREEN DENVER wf d Green Gorse -Denver Minnie Aug-92	1	6	100	480	13-Sep
GREENANE SQUIRE bd d Manorville Major -Endless Game Jun-91	9	13	8,450	480	23-Aug
GREENFIELD FAWN f d Arrow House-Greenfield Tune Jul-92	1	3	100	484	6-Apr
GREENWELL KIT wf b Lavally Oak -Cahills Gate May-91	3	8	350	643	14-Jun
GREYFRIARS RANDY wbk d Randy -Greyfriars Rose Jan-91	5	22	645	484	17-Dec
GROUND BAND f d Live Contender-Barron Rose Jan-92	1	10	75	509	16-Feb
GROVESHILL WISH wbd b Penny Less -Festive Queen Sep-90	2	5	200	275	10-Nov
GULLEEN SAINT wf d Whisper Wishes-Gulleen Style Jul-91	2	11	175	475	7-Nov
GUN FIGHTER bd d lm Slippy-Strange Manner Jul-92	3	12	3,250	400	27-Aug

A-Z STATISTICS

Greyhound			W	R	£	Ave D	Last Win
GUNS BLAZING	f d	Deenside Spark-Aghadown Heather Jul-90	1	3	100	290	22-Feb
GUYSWAY	wbk d	Daleys Gold-Winnie The Witch Aug-92	1	3	200	252	19-Nov
HADIES MASTER	wf d	Master Hardy-Clountie Nuxer Mar-92	1	4	85	440	18-Aug
HALL DOOR	wbk d	Galtymore Lad -Pulse Trail Aug-91	1	6	75	545	7-Mar
HANAHS CHOICE	f b	Ben G Cruiser-Kildare Birch Jul-91	1	1	100	675	3-May
HANDSOME DES	bd d	Oran Champion-Oran Velvet May-91	1	5	120	484	11-Nov
HANDSOME FELLOW	f d	Greenpark Fox- Kora Jul-92	1	2	120	605	19-Oct
HANG OVER		wbd d Im Slippy -Synone Crest Feb-93	1	6	75	450	19-Oct
HANS PAL	bd d	Odell King-Cuddles Sandy Oct-89	1	3	100	450	20-Sep
HARBOUR MOUNT	f d	Airmount Grand-Harbour Express Apr-91	3	6	150	440	29-Nov
HARD VOCATION	bd d	Early Vocation-Locklin Lady Jun-91	1	13	200	580	19-Feb
HAREDRESSER	wbk b	Slaneyside Hare-Daniels Dolly Nov-91	1	1	200	875	6-Oct
HARRIOTS CHOICE	f b	Murlens Hawk-Image Of Mam Oct-91	1	1	75	440	26-Aug
HARRY WHO	bd d	Cuggar-Sand Gift Jun-91	1	4	100	484	25-Jan
HARRYS LION	f d	Skelligs Tiger-Maggies Wishes Nov-91	8	32	1,535	540	12-Nov
HATIKVAH JAFFA	bd b	Hyper -Silverhill Lass Mar-92	2	13	295	769	8-Oct
HAVOC HOUSE	bk d	Westmead Havoc-House Of Hope Aug-91	2	13	255	470	5-Jul
HAVOC IS FORTUNE	f d	Westmead Havoc-Fortune Princess Mar-92	1	12	150	640	29-Oct
HAWKSTONE	bk d	Phantom Flash-Chocolate Satin Sep-91	1	11	100	400	5-Aug
HAWKSTONE STAR	wbk d	Phantom Flash -Chocolate Satin Sep-91	2	6	175	487	28-Jun
HAWTHORN DELL	bd d	Kyle Jack-Finnure Flyer Mar-91	3	27	275	310	13-Jul
HAWTHORN JACK	bk d	Kyle Jack-Finnure Flyer Mar-91	1	3	125	420	30-May
HAZY ROXY	f b	Greenpark Fox-Tullig Patsey Sep-92	3	11	300	547	31-Aug
HEAD FIRST	bk d	Druids Johno-Rahela Susie Jun-91	4	26	440	274	20-Jun
HEADLEYS BRIDGE	fw d	Murlens Hawk-School Road Maid Jan-92	2	12	225	573	21-Apr
HEAVEN SENT	bk b	Lodge Prince-Murlens Mandy Oct-92	2	7	225	575	25-Nov
HEAVENLY COMET	bk b	Daleys Gold-Black Sancisco Oct-91	10	20	2,750	474	10-Dec
HEAVENLY DREAM	f d	Whisper Wishes-Sail On Jenny Jul-90	13	36	6,245	479	28-Jul
HEAVENLY DUKE	f d	Whisper Wishes -Rhincrew Moth Mar-89	2	11	200	480	26-Mar
HEAVENLY JUJU	f b	Daleys Gold-Black Sancisco Dec-91	1	8	100	275	30-Jun
HEAVENLY LADY	bk b	Manorville Sand -Black Sancisco Jun-90	5	7	2,475	682	12-Mar
HEAVENLY SPIRIT	bk b	Daleys Gold-Black Sancisco Oct-91	13	51	1,415	609	17-Dec
HEDSOR STAR	bd d	Murlens Slippy-Westmead Hannah Sep-92	3	12	175	467	11-Aug
HELLO OCTOBER	f d	Ardfert Sean-Euro Princess Oct-92	1	14	150	475	13-Aug
HELLO TOWER	bk d	Adraville Bridge-Hello Flower Mar-93	1	1	125	480	19-Nov
HENRYS WORLD	be d	Kisba-Worlds Bobette Nov-91	1	2	100	480	15-Apr
HERES SEANIE	f d	Ardfert Sean-Mindys Miracle Jul-92	7	16	17,050	548	29-Sep
HEROIC MYTH	bd d	Manorville Major-Maireads Ruby Oct-90	3	16	400	312	15-Jul
HI BRAZIL SAM	bdw d	Lartigue Note-Hi Brazil Gypsy Mar-91	4	31	320	471	1-Oct
HI NOON REBEL	dk bd d	Dutch Delight-Cokeoben Bridie Dec-90	1	4	100	400	14-Jan
HI RA BOY	bd d	Leaders Best-Ra Ra Girl Feb-91	3	16	1,160	693	15-Jan
HI STREET DALEY	f d	Daleys Gold-Sandy Sentiment Jul-92	1	10	120	440	4-Nov
HIGH FIDELITY	bd b	Manorville Major-Special Gamble Dec-92	2	9	250	375	19-Oct
HIGH VELOCITY	bk b	Kilcannon Bullet -Special Gamble Jan-91	1	1	125	640	28-Oct
HIGHFLYING	wbd d	Pond Hurricane-Pixie Chime Aug-91	1	13	100	260	30-Sep
HIGHLAND BRIDGE	f d	Adraville Bridge-Kilbarry Lady Jun-91	3	11	300	412	6-Sep
HIGHWAY LEADER	bk d	Leaders Best-Highway Mystery Nov-91	13	25	19,225	425	1-Oct
HILLCREST BILL	wbd d	Murlens Slippy-Hillcrest Jose Jun-91	5	10	585	447	8-Dec
HILLDUN GARA	bd d	Curryhills Gara-Indian Flight Aug-91	2	13	300	475	14-Jun
HILLMOUNT JEAN	bd b	Curryhills Gara-Rockmount Mandy Jan-92	2	9	320	788	10-Mar
HILLVIEW HOUSE	wf d	O'Hickey Garden-Anhid Cross Apr-91	5	17	325	489	19-May
HILLVIEW SAND	bk d	Manorville Sand -Pretty Sally Feb-90	1	3	100	575	10-Sep
HOLD THE FORT	be d	Ardfert Mick-Lyns Fli Jun-93	1	2	75	450	19-Oct
HOLLIWIL BUSTER	wbk d	Murlens Slippy-Pond Spitfire Mar-91	1	7	125	640	30-Sep
HOME AT EIGHT	wbd b	Im Slippy -Home Alone Mar-90	2	9	200	660	10-Mar
HOME FROM HOME	bd d	Murlens Slippy -Home Alone Mar-92	4	18	550	474	1-Sep

A-Z STATISTICS

Greyhound		W	R	£	Ave D	Last
HOME TOWN	bk d Druids Johno-Dark Mixture Aug-91	1	4	75	484	4-May
HOMELOCATOR	dkbd b Manorville Magic-In Advance Jan-92	1	7	100	575	30-Dec
HONEST BRUTUS	bd d Im Slippy-Come On Duchess Sep-90	1	1	75	375	3-Jan
HONEYS MIRACLE	bd b Fair Hill Boy- Honeypound Lady Jan-91	1	9	75	440	28-Apr
HOT TIGER	bd d Coalbrook Tiger -Kilgobbin Lady Aug-92	1	2	75	440	5-Aug
HOWLING DARKIE	bk d Comeragh Boy-Culleog Molly Aug-91	2	5	175	486	23-Aug
HUGO BOSS	bk d Slaneyside Hare-Just Flash Mar-93	1	6	150	458	1-Dec
HUNTER	wbd d Hit The Lid -Mowgil Mutt May-90	1	12	100	605	19-Mar
HUNTSMANS FANCY f b React Fraggil -Huntsmans Blond Mar-90		2	5	200	484	1-Feb
HURLYBALL MARKIE f d Airmount Grand -Smoke Galore Aug-91		1	6	125	640	5-Nov
HYMENSTOWN BART	bk d Macs Lock-Hymenstown Lynn Feb-93	1	5	50	480	20-Sep
HYMENSTOWN MAC	bk d acs Lock-Hymenstown Lynn Feb-93	5	7	365	437	30-Nov
HYPNOTIC GOBLIN	wf b Fearless Champ- Hypnotic Sue Mar-92	1	10	100	462	12-Jul
SAY PATCH	wbk d Hit The Lid-Barefoot Miss Oct-90	3	6	255	555	24-Feb
ICE HOT	f d Deenside Spark -Optimum Girl Mar-93	2	3	120	492	19-Dec
IM ALIYSA	bk b Im Slippy-Droopys Aliysa Aug-91	2	20	200	490	8-Nov
IM FROM JAPAN	wbk b Storm Slave-Finnure Magic Aug-90	1	16	75	480	8-Jul
IM HOME	wbd b Im Slippy -Home Alone Mar-90	1	2	100	610	7-Oct
IM HOME MADE	bd b Murlens Slippy-Home Alone Mar-92	3	15	275	647	17-Aug
IM JOE	bk d Im Slippy-Minnies Siren Oct-92	8	14	1,350	432	14-Dec
IM SPECIAL	wbd b Im Slippy-Special Gamble Apr-92	1	18	100	675	31-Jan
IM THE FINEST	bd b Siostaloir-Pets Echo Jan-93	1	6	40	400	30-Nov
IMA SHABIN	bd d Murlens Slippy-Ballylynch Girl Jan-90	1	4	125	260	20-Jan
IN THE BACK	bk d Daleys Gold-Rooskey Critic Apr-91	2	7	150	450	14-Feb
IN THE ZIM	bd d Greenpark Fox -Murlens Ruby Jul-92	3	11	315	475	10-May
INFORMATION	bk b Concentration-Footpath Aug-92	2	6	200	400	2-Sep
IRISH PRIDE	wbk b Nightpark Lad -Garrenroe Pet Feb-91	1	9	110	700	17-Jan
ISLAND DOE	f d John Doe -City Border Mar-91	6	10	4,175	650	24-Feb
IVANS FLASH	wbk d Phantom Flash -Ivalog May-92	4	21	400	531	4-Nov
IVORY TIME	bk d Alpine Minister-Francies Chance Mar-92	1	1	75	220	9-Nov
IZA POSER	wbk d Ransom Crackers-Thats A Lady Mar-92	9	23	905	502	7-Nov
JACK OF SPADES	f d Lisamote Dawn-Modern Fiction Jul-92	2	9	150	460	24-Jun
JACK STANGER	bk d Pond Mirage -Special Sunday Jul-92	3	10	275	301	3-Nov
JACKBECK	bd d Bawndaw Slippy- Gero Jul-92	4	13	925	449	23-Dec
JACKIES BANANA	bd d Flashy Sir-Chicita Banana Oct-91	2	15	170	653	27-Oct
JACKS BIRTHDAY	bd d Kildare Ash-Moody Dream Jul-92	1	4	120	666	30-Sep
JACKS DALEY	wbk d Daleys Gold -Saints Tania Feb-92	1	8	50	740	10-May
JACKSONFLYBYNITE bk b Phantom Flash-Pennylane Black Sep-91		1	10	50	545	4-Apr
JAFFA LINE	wbd d Im Slippy-Bower Jewe l Sep-92	3	20	535	400	29-Aug
JAMESIE COTTER	wbd d Fearless Action -Irish Exchange Oct-90	3	24	310	448	21-Jun
JAMIE JIM	bk d Tapwatcher-Punters Pocket May-92	8	26	735	527	30-Dec
JEMS LARRY WISH	wbd d Whisper Wishes-Dream Impulse May-91	1	6	125	260	17-Feb
JENKS CHALLENGER	bd d Slaneyside Gold-Vida Jewel Mar-89	1	3	100	675	14-Feb
JESPERE JOEY	bk d Tain Solas-Kelsos Slinkey May-92	1	3	100	610	25-Mar
JESSE DU NORD	bk b One To Note-Moneypoint Moth Aug-90	1	2	75	220	10-Jan
JESSIES WAY fw b	Bankers Benefit-Margarets Joy Jan-93	1	5	75	460	12-Nov
JEWEL SAM	bd d Glenhill Blue -Inn Above Jan-92	2	7	300	339	14-Apr
JILL AIR	bk b Airmount Grand-Matter Of Honour Mar-91	3	9	250	568	22-Aug
JODES	bk d Lyons Dean -If Only Feb-92	3	21	300	514	26-Aug
JOES GREEN	bd b Green Gorse-Trout Stream Jul-90	1	2	50	460	8-Jul
JOESITA	wf b Bankers Benefit- Margarets Joy Nov-91	5	17	585	714	28-Oct
JOHN COLIN	wbk d Flashy Sir-Marita Sep-91	3	14	300	465	7-Jul
JOHNOS MAGIC	f d Druids Johno-Baby Doll Apr-91	3	28	300	392	9-Sep
JOHNS BANANA	bk d Flashy Sir-Chicita Banana Oct-91	1	15	150	640	6-Jan
JOHNSTOWN DANDY bd d Leaders Best-Johnstown Kay Apr-91		1	1	500	824	3-Sep
JOIN THE WIND	dk bd d Floating Champ-Orient Queen Mar-92	1	5	100	241	10-Feb

A-Z STATISTICS

Greyhound		W	R	£	Ave D	Last Win
JUBILEE RAMONA	bk b Pond Mirage-Lively Bid Feb-93	1	2	125	580	15-Oct
JUBILEE REBECCA	bkw b Pond Mirage-Lively Bid Mar-91	10	19	7,300	716	21-May
JUBILEE ROSANNA	bk b Pond Mirage-Lively Bid Feb-93	3	7	300	580	7-Dec
JULES COMET	wbd d Darragh Commet -Lady Alda Dec-91	1	2	75	460	18-Jan
JUNIORS BANANA	bk d Flashy Sir-Chicita Banana Oct-91	7	20	740	528	26-Dec
JURASSIC PARK	f d Skelligs Tiger-Fair Princess Jul-92	7	16	685	400	30-Dec
JUST AWESOME	f d Tapwatcher -Cranley Primrose Aug-91	2	11	150	270	27-May
JUST FRED	wf d Ransom Crackers-Kiltomey Ace Aug-91	1	10	100	480	28-Feb
JUST HANDY	bd d Manx Marajax -Genevey Slippy Jul-92	3	19	220	600	13-Dec
JUST PARKER	f d Ransom Crackers -Kiltomey Ace Aug-92	3	8	300	675	9-Dec
JUST RIGHT JET	bk d Daleys Gold-Kyle Jill Apr-92	7	34	675	325	12-Aug
JUST RIGHT JUMBO	f d Im Slippy -Chini Chin Chin Sep-91	1	11	75	480	26-Apr
JUST RIGHT KYLE	bk d Kyle Jack-Im A Duchess Sep-90	3	13	1,275	470	22-Jun
JUST RIGHT RUSTY	bd d Kyle Jack-Im Ugly Apr-91	1	10	100	310	24-Jan
JUST RIGHT SCOUT	bk d Whisper Wishes-Im Ugly Jun-92	3	32	1,155	460	13-May
JUST RIGHT SIR	bd d Whisper Wishes -Im Ugly Jun-92	2	5	250	241	7-May
JUSTRIGHT MAGIC	f d Ardfert Sean-Mineola Tara May-93	1	6	100	480	8-Nov
JUSTRIGHT MELODY	f d Farloe Melody-Farloe Mineola Dec-92	15	28	8,730	469	1-Dec
JUSTRIGHT RISKY	bd d Satharn Beo-Scandal Vandal Jan-93	3	10	275	537	16-Nov
KANE	bk d Soda Fountain-Shibumi Sep-91	3	10	350	486	5-Nov
KARENS WHISPER	bk b Whisper Wishes -Silver Shoes May-90	4	15	450	618	20-Oct
KASAMANTHA	f b Flashy Sir-Macs Jeannie Feb-91	1	7	125	640	17-Sep
KATALODGIC	wbk d Druids Lodge-Katabatic Apr-93	1	1	100	400	4-Nov
KATE SLIPPY	fw b Aulton Slippy-Fryers Whisper Sep-92	3	11	175	598	27-Dec
KEELEYS BANANA	bd b Flashy Sir -Chicita Banana Oct-91	11	32	1,550	645	6-Jul
KEEREEN WILL	wf d Aulton Slippy-Madam Rose Feb-91	2	10	300	658	21-Nov
KEIBERWOOD BOB	f d Ballyregan Bob -Broomwood Beauty Dec-91	7	31	1,000	644	31-Oct
KEIBERWOOD DAN	bebd d Carters Lad-Favourite Return Jun-91	4	14	420	704	16-Sep
KEIGHLEY LAD	be d Curryhills Gara-Drumrane Lady Feb-91	1	6	150	475	19-May
KELLSBORO KING	bd d Manorville Major -Galaxy Snowie Jun-92	3	9	260	600	31-Oct
KELLYMOUNT KID	wbk d Carters Lad -Kellymount Suzie Jun-91	6	28	750	472	28-Jun
KELLYMOUNT KUDOS	wbk b Craters Lad-Kellymount Suzie Jan-91	2	6	220	520	29-Aug
KENALOE	wbk d Phantom Flash-Ivalog May-92	3	15	320	333	12-Aug
KENTUCKY OAK	wbd b Im Slippy -Kentucky Storm Feb-91	2	8	115	375	12-Dec
KEROGUE IVY	bk b Lartigue Note-Kerogue Wish Apr-92	5	14	1,940	657	13-Aug
KESLAKE MOVER	wbd d Flashy Sir-Keslake Rose May-92	1	7	75	277	13-Dec
KEYNSHAM BLACK	bkw d Dempsey Duke-Castlelyons Moll Sep-92	1	7	120	460	25-Jun
KID ALL LAD	wf d Im Slippy-Frisky White Feb-92	1	18	100	400	20-May
KIEL EBONY	bk d Manorville Magic-Kiel Crazy Mar-93	1	6	100	480	1-Nov
KILBREEDY PUNCH	bd d Curryhills Gara-Kilbreedy Lassie Jun-92	1	3	100	620	2-May
KILCAROON LODGE	wbe d Druids Lodge-Shebas Lass Feb-93	1	3	400	460	3-Dec
KILCOLMAN RAMBO	f d Murlens Hawk-October Lady May-91	1	4	75	375	7-Nov
KILCOMMON PET	bd b Lavally Oak -Alfos Pal Jun-91	3	11	525	635	22-Apr
KILCORAN BLOND	bk b Bankers Benefit -Kylehill Bid Jun-91	1	6	75	659	13-Dec
KILCORAN DANCER	bd b Bankers Benefit-Kylehill Bid Jun-91	6	18	485	570	14-Nov
KILDAGON KITTY	bk b Waltham Abbey-Poor Kitty Feb-92	6	13	1,510	693	25-Apr
KILDRENAGH LAD	f d Macs Lock-Millies Chick Feb-92	3	7	400	420	14-Dec
KILELTON BILBO	bd d Skelligs Tiger-Monew Mutt Apr-92	1	2	150	666	28-Oct
KILFINNY SUZY	bk b Brownies Outlook-Ballea Treasure Sep-91	1	12	50	575	7-Feb
KILKENNY CHAMP	bk d Raely Vocation-Acraboy Baby Jun-92	1	3	100	575	5-Aug
KILLEENAGH BRUNO	bd d Im Slippy-Killeenagh Lady Jun-92	1	2	125	474	28-May
KILLEENAGH BIBI	bdw b Murlens Hawk-Killeenagh Lady Aug-91	1	11	150	855	19-Aug
KILLEENAGH JANE	bd b Murlens Hawk-Killeenagh Lady Aug-91	1	3	120	714	10-Sep
KILLEENAGH REBEL	bd d Murlens Hawk-Killeenagh Lady Aug-91	1	7	100	500	8-Aug
KILLENAGH DREAM	wbd d Dads Bank-Killeenagh Lady Mar-90	9	21	1,905	762	6-Jun
KILLILA BEO	bb b Satharn Beo-Cottesloe Beach Aug-91	2	4	210	510	6-Jun

A-Z STATISTICS

Greyhound		W	R	£	Ave D	Last
KILLILA PLACE	f b Ardfert Sean -Adams For Peace May-91	8	27	800	546	16-Nov
KILLOTTERAN ASH	bdw d Randy-Shebas Lass Sep-91	1	11	80	660	29-Mar
KILLOURAGH LUCY	bd b Murlens Slippy-Singside Lady Aug-92	3	7	740	718	17-Sep
KILLOWNEY DREAM	bd d Phantom Flash -Killowney Rose Dec-91	1	7	100	500	30-Jul
KILMACSIMON WAVE	bk d Ninth Wave-Honky Tonk Lady Jan-93	3	8	2,165	440	23-Dec
KILMEEDY ARROW	wbd b Arrow House-Lanrigg Lassie Jun-90	1	2	140	660	17-Aug
KILPATRICK CON	bd d Curryhills Gara -Kilpatrick Rose May-91	1	9	100	400	3-Jun
KILPIPE BIBI	wbd b Manorville Sand-Another Cheer Sep-91	4	19	525	759	23-Jun
KILRUSH CHAMP	bkw d Silver Ghost-Kilrush Beauty Sep-90	2	12	175	278	13-Apr
KILTOMEY LEADER	f b Adraville Bridge-Kiltomey Ann Jul-91	1	1	100	420	24-Aug
KILVIL FRIEND	bk d Mathews Gold-Keeleys Friend Jun-92	1	3	100	420	28-Nov
KINCORA SEAN	bdw d Ardfert Sean-Dark Alley Aug-92	1	4	100	660	17-Nov
KINCOURA GLORY	bd d Leaders Best-Little Queenie Apr-91	2	10	200	450	25-Jan
KINDO	bd d Skelligs Tiger-Junior Miss Jan-91	1	5	150	475	20-Oct
KING KEV	bk d Glebe Dasher-Grace Line Jan-92	1	13	120	695	8-Feb
KING OF GALES	fw d Manorville Magic-Fairy Mission Nov-92	1	4	75	545	19-Oct
KING SIZE	wf d Whisper Wishes-Supreme Miss Feb-91	5	23	575	456	12-Jul
KINGSMILL LODGE	wbk d Skelligs Tiger-Sheilas Court Jan-92	1	2	100	450	19-Jan
KINGSWELL ACE	bk d Easy And Slow-Hardy Ivy Dec-91	1	6	100	400	3-Jun
KINGSWELL LIMO	bk d Easy And Slow-Hardy Ivy Oct-90	4	14	400	529	1-Jul
KISH GALE	bk b Randy-Kishquirk Linda Apr-92	3	18	1,195	642	17-Jun
KISON SISTER	bkw b Balalika-Sand Fire Aug-91	1	7	100	675	15-Apr
KNEE LEVEL	bd d Amenhotep-Tobys Delight Aug-92	1	4	75	440	15-Apr
KNOCKMANT CINDY	bk b Flashy Sir-Knockmant Fire Aug-91	1	6	75	685	9-Feb
KNOCKROUR BRUNO	f d Adraville Bridge-Dear Liza Apr-92	4	19	495	409	30-Aug
KWENDA BELLA	f b Ballymadoe Ben-Celtic Swallow Jan-92	2	7	150	583	30-May
KWIK KWIK SLOW	f b Greenpark Fox-Kevalling Kwik Jul-91	1	3	50	460	22-Mar
KYLE JUDGE	bd d Daleys Gold -Kyle Jill Apr-92	3	18	340	511	11-Jul
LACKEN PRINCE	be d Live Contender-Afternoon Blue Sep-92	13	30	4,205	530	22-Dec
LACKENS MOTTO	dkbd d Greenpark Fox-Ramotto Sep-92	2	9	200	378	23-Sep
LADY DESMONA	wbk d Dereen Star -Pusher Bird Nov-92	1	7	20	485	16-Nov
LADY DRAGON	bdw d Greenpark Fox-Burgess Gypsy Nov-91	7	26	665	473	18-Aug
LADY GROVE	wf b Fly Cruiser-Ardnalee Anne Nov-91	3	25	150	407	16-Jul
LADY PEACH	bk b Manorville Major -Peach Supreme Jul-91	1	9	200	460	31-Mar
LADYS CHAMPION	wbk d Ransom Crackers-Thats A Lady Mar-92	1	4	110	380	30-May
LAGANORE SPARK	bebd d Deenside Spark-Celtic Cracker Aug-92	6	15	925	456	16-Nov
LAMMERMUIR LAD	bk d Dutch Delight-Black Moselle Jul-91	4	32	750	493	11-Nov
LANGKAWI	bk b Waltham Abbey -Mninga Multibet Apr-92	1	6	175	820	29-Oct
LANNIGANS GOLD	bebd d Carters Lad -Lannigans Twist Jun-92	1	9	125	290	16-Dec
LASSA JAVA	f d Lassana Champ -Fawn Java Jun-91	7	14	5,775	467	3-Jun
LASSIES HOUSE	f b Arrow House-Lanrigg Lassie Apr-91	2	10	175	233	8-Apr
LAST ACTION	bd b Chet-Sunshine Penny Oct-92	4	6	2,040	719	19-Dec
LAWLESTOWN PHIL	bd d Pond Hurricane -Gemini Duchess May-91	1	11	110	380	11-Jun
LEADERS SMILER	bd b Leaders Best-Ballyboggan Lady Jul-91	7	20	700	692	17-Dec
LEENANE SHEILA	bk b Greenpark Fox-I Know You Feb-93	1	6	75	460	29-Nov
LEESON ST LADY	wf b Skelligs Tiger-Circle Lady Jul-91	2	16	290	679	8-Oct
LEEVIEW FOX	f d Curryhills Fox-Skiddaw Jan-89	1	4	100	450	12-Jul
LEEVIEW JEWEL	wbd b Daleys Gold -Yellow Riband Nov-91	1	2	100	250	19-Apr
LEFT BACK	dkbd b Soda Fountain -Arma Flex Jul-90	3	15	270	757	21-Sep
LEITRIM BAND	bd d Curryhills Gara-Girls Band Oct-91	1	4	140	663	15-Oct
LEITRIM MANDY	bd b Manorville Sand -Girls Band Jul-92	2	9	185	785	28-Nov
LEMON FLASH	f d Willie Joe-Lemon Bid Jan-91	3	22	400	471	18-Aug
LEMON HERO	bd d Im Slippy-Lemon Miss Mar-92	2	10	165	430	10-Feb
LEMON NELL	bk b Greenpark Fox -Lemon Chill May-92	5	20	610	696	30-Aug
LEMON RAIDER	wf d Im Slippy-Lemon Miss Mar-92	5	12	1,090	392	12-Feb
LEMON ROB	wbk d Daleys Gold -Lemon Miss Nov-92	4	8	2,800	478	12-Dec

NGRC Greyhound Racing Yearbook 1995

A-Z STATISTICS

Greyhound		W	R	£	Ave D	Last Win
LEMON RUPERT	bk d Greenpark Fox-Lemon Chill May-92	2	4	225	467	23-Feb
LEMON SHAMROCK	bkw d lm Slippy -Lemon Chill Sep-91	1	6	100	450	22-Feb
LEMONFIELD WISH	bebd b Curryhills Brock-Peaceful Wish Aug-92	1	2	0	462	13-Jun
LENITY LAD	bk d Lyons Dean -Wonder Blonde Apr-92	1	1	100	465	7-Jul
LEPERSTOWN MOAT	f b Carmels Prince -Moat Jo Oct-92	1	4	110	540	20-Aug
LESTER	f d Whisper Wishes-Ferndale Class May-92	4	24	355	457	19-Oct
LETHAL EFFECT	bk d Daleys Gold-Little Effect Apr-92	1	1	100	480	8-Mar
LETS ALL BOOGIE	bd d Carters Lad-Princess Alucard Jun-89	1	15	120	695	8-Jan
LETS GO LADDIE	wf d Whisper Wishes-Gallant Beauty Apr-92	2	14	150	375	29-Aug
LEWDEN FLYER	bk d Lemon King-Celtic Sail Dec-92	2	9	170	462	14-Nov
LIAMS HOUSE	bd d Arrow House-Damh Nait Jun-93	1	1	100	420	26-Dec
LIBERAL ART	wbd d Skelligs Tiger-Pushy Princess Mar-91	1	5	100	400	20-May
LIBERAL IDEA	bk d Easy And Slow-Ballinvard Rose Mar-92	4	6	350	660	4-Nov
LIBRA JOHN	bk d Arrow House-Alexa Apr-92	1	9	110	385	4-Aug
LIBRARY SHEET	bk d Bold Rabbit-Red Rag Jun-91	2	10	225	484	25-Feb
LIGHTFOOT BOY	f d lm Slippy-Cadgers Loan Feb-91	1	6	100	400	14-Jan
LIKE A MOAN	wbk b Skelligs Tiger -Always Grumbling Apr-92	1	8	120	515	25-Jan
LILAC WONDER	wbd b Carters Lad -Miss Irene Aug-89	1	7	115	815	9-Jul
LINDAS SHADOW	bk b Slippy Blue -Little Shadow May-92	1	3	100	259	18-Jun
LING DORADO	bd d Murlens Slippy -Without Equal Jun-92	1	7	125	655	21-Oct
LISA MY GIRL	wbd b Murlens Slippy -Longvalley Lady May-92	5	12	5,325	606	2-Sep
LISNAKILL DAKOTA	wbd d Kildare Ash-Lisnakill Patty Feb-92	1	5	100	450	26-Jan
LISNAKILL HENRY	wbk d Airmount Grand- Lisnakill Lady Apr-91	1	19	120	460	28-Jan
LISNAKILL MOVE	bk b Westmead Harry-Boss Mans Girl Jul-91	1	13	100	620	3-Mar
LISSENAIR FOX	bd d lm Lizzys-Molls Share Sep-92	1	3	50	480	1-Dec
LISTEN TO DAN	f d Glenpark Dancer-Farloe Mineola Apr-91	3	16	325	433	12-Mar
LISTEN TO HIM	bk d Whisper Wishes-Belair Bronx Jan-93	4	21	425	460	12-Nov
LITTLE WASP	bd d Manorville Major-Slippy Helen Nov-91	2	16	200	613	29-Sep
LIVE TIP	bd b Live Contender-Some Tip Feb-92	2	6	185	445	3-Nov
LIZZIES CORNET	wf d Sir Gaylord-Jessia Apr-92	2	15	175	445	2-Nov
LLOYDS CORNER	wbd d Daleys Gold-Coragh Lady Jun-92	3	12	300	333	2-Aug
LOCH BO ALFIE	f d Druids Johno -Loch Bo Goldie Sep-91	1	10	75	400	4-May
LOCH BO ANCHOR	wbd d Murlens Slippy-Loch Bo Cheeky Mar-90	3	7	1,600	640	17-Feb
LOCH BO BEAUTY	f b Druids Johno-Loch Bo Goldie Sep-91	4	11	400	575	16-Dec
LOCH BO LUCKY	fw b lm Slippy-Loch Bo Goldie Jun-90	1	6	150	400	13-Jan
LOCH BO MISTY	f b Whisper Wishes-Loch Bo Mandy Jan-92	1	8	100	480	17-Jan
LOCH BO PEARL	f b lm Slippy -Loch Bo Cheeky Jun-92	1	5	100	278	25-Aug
LOFTY	fw d Aulton Slippy -Bouncing Barquet Nov-90	1	5	75	480	2-Sep
LONDON LEADER	bd d Leaders Best-London Anne Dec-91	1	1	100	476	4-May
LONELY DRIVE	bef d Live Contender-Ballybar Girl May-92	2	4	150	440	5-Aug
LONELY MIXTURE	bd d Another Mixture-Dunasbuig Sara Nov-89	1	3	75	220	31-Jan
LONGVALLEY MANOR	wbk d lm Slippy-Longvalley Lady Jul-91	10	32	1,155	460	30-Dec
LOOPHEAD ROSE	wbd b Aulton Slippy-Briscoe Jul-90	1	3	110	645	18-Jan
LOTHIAN LADDIE	f d Arrow House -Lanrigg Lassie Mar-92	2	13	350	500	26-Jul
LOTS OF JOLLY	bd d Whisper Wishes-Fair Hill Rose Oct-91	11	32	760	354	8-Oct
LOUISES LAD	bd d Greenpark Fox-Rosewood Lass Jun-93	1	2	75	462	26-Nov
LOVE OF YOU	bd d Manx Treasure-Smart Fairy Jan-93	1	9	50	660	27-Dec
LOVELY KAY	bk b Kyle Jack -Punters Pocket Jul-91	3	15	225	542	11-Aug
LOVERS DREAM	wbk b Randy-Snakes Whisper Sep-90	1	3	200	640	13-Jan
LOWFIELD ABBEY	bk b Galtymore Lad -Knockroe Abbey Jul-92	1	9	80	620	23-Sep
LUCKY GAMBLE	bd d Manorville Major-Special Gamble May-90	3	14	300	480	5-Mar
LUCKY TIMES	bd d Manorville Major -Touch The Sail Jul-91	5	19	750	766	30-Sep
LUKES CHOICE	wbk d Westmead Claim -Our Alma Sep-91	6	21	445	484	13-Dec
LUKES CREATION	bd b Murlens Slippy-Mountain Madam Apr-92	1	6	100	450	19-Jul
LULUS CHRISTIE	bd d Aghadown Timmy-Lulus Moth Sep-92	1	12	75	545	22-Aug
LULUS HEATHER	dkbd b Aghadown Timmy-Lulus Moth Sep-92	1	3	50	460	6-Dec

A-Z STATISTICS

Greyhound		W	R	£	Ave D	Last
LULUS ROSE	bk b Waltham Abbey -Lulus Moth-May-91	2	4	300	878	24-Dec
LULUS TIMMY	fw d Aghadown Timmy-Lulus Moth Sep-92	1	15	300	500	29-Aug
LUPI	bd b Dempseys Whisper-Coppertone Feb-92	1	12	200	888	29-Apr
LUXURY LODGE	bd d Druids Lodge-Luxury Girl Apr-91	1	5	100	400	11-Mar
LYACON	bd d Tapwatcher-To Manor Born Nov-92	6	23	625	358	9-Dec
LYONS BLACK	bk d Whisper Wishes-Lyons Lassie Aug-92	5	28	490	469	15-Dec
LYONS DOUBLE	wf d Castlelyons Gem-Lyons Lady May-91	4	28	480	517	21-Oct
LYRE RAMBO	bk d Childrens Champ-Barraduff Gold May-91	1	5	50	450	24-Jan
MA PETITE PET	bk b Curryhills Gara-Cute Pigeon Mar-92	1	3	250	631	30-Jul
MACSEA ROYAL	bd d Slaneyside Hare-Daniels Dolly Nov-91	4	18	920	467	25-Apr
MADAM CHIPI	bd b Murlens Slippy-Mountain Madam Apr-92	1	7	100	850	27-Oct
MAGICAL CHIEF	bd d Amenhotep-Tobys Delight Jun-91	3	24	400	508	24-Jun
MAGICAL CIRCLE	f d Wheres The Limo-Tobys Delight Mar-93	1	10	85	440	3-Nov
MAGICAL KYLIE	f b Kyle Jack-Crowes Meat Oct-90	3	5	225	488	19-Oct
MAGICAL MAGOO	wbeb b Catunda Flame-Bawnard Tess Apr-90	3	5	285	563	9-Jun
MAGICAL PIPER	bd d Amenhotep-Tobys Delight Jun-91	4	15	550	471	8-Mar
MAGLIN PRINCE	bd d Carmels Prince-Skiddaw Oct-91	1	5	125	415	5-Mar
MAGNETIC OCEAN	wbk d Airmount Grand-Patterdale Fairy Aug-91	2	8	200	480	25-May
MAGNUM DEBBIE	bd b Slaneyside Hare-Westmead Sarra Apr-92	2	4	325	730	16-Dec
MAGNUM FLASH	bk d Flashy Sir-Alvas Dream Aug-92	2	13	100	465	18-May
MAIREADS FOX	bk d Greenpark Fox-Bronze Ball Jun-91	2	9	175	388	31-Aug
MAIZIES BOY	bk d Dutch Delight-Black Moselle Jul-91	1	2	125	480	12-Nov
MAJOR THOMAS	bk d Flashy Sir-Mrs Thomas Apr-91	1	2	140	484	25-Feb
MALDEN FANCY	bkw b lm Slippy-Free Fancy Oct-92	1	3	200	460	15-Dec
MALL FUNCTION	bk d Curryhills Gara -Quality Count Aug-90	1	4	100	450	7-Feb
MANCUB	f d Greenpark Fox-Coolagh Fantasy May-92	4	11	450	460	30-Aug
MANDYS NURSE	bk b Fly Cruiser -Mandys Bar Sep-91	4	18	410	579	12-Oct
MANX CARPET	bk d Greenpark Fox-Flying Rita Aug-91	1	4	100	300	1-Sep
MANX FITIX	f d Greenpark Fox -Darian Ivy Feb-90	2	8	175	339	30-Sep
MARGOS CUTIE	bk b Odell Supreme-Aclamon Lady Jul-91	2	7	200	400	22-Apr
MARIGOLD	bk b Whisper Wishes-Fair Hill Rose Oct-91	1	13	120	515	8-Jan
MARINA DER	bk d Adraville Bridge-Der Tag Oct-91	1	5	100	474	12-Mar
MARIS PIPER	db d Tapwatcher-Coolelan Grand Mar-93	1	2	75	545	29-Aug
MARKET TAKE OFF	be d Balalika-Market Skite Jan-91	1	4	100	647	12-Jul
MARLENA	f b Satharn Beo-Kylemore Hem Jan-92	2	11	200	650	7-Jul
MARSHMALLOW	bd b lm Slippy-Sadie Sep-92	1	3	0	460	28-May
MASTER BUCK	bd d Tune In-Tame Duchess May-91	3	4	0	500	17-May
MASTER SLATER	bd d Tapwatcher-Coolelan Grand May-92	1	11	100	220	22-Apr
MASTER WESTLANDS	wbd d Lord Westlands-Handball Jan-91	2	12	1,120	515	12-Jul
MATCHLESS MATT	fw d Hit The Lid-Mowgil Mutt May-90	1	6	200	640	20-Jan
MATRONS PAL	bd d Princes Pal-Matrons Doll dec-90	1	5	75	277	3-Aug
MAYTREE GIRL	wbd b Skelligs Tiger-Always Grumbling Apr-92	1	5	110	645	8-Nov
MEADOWVALE MOON	bk b Glenpark Dancer-Wee Chance Aug-91	1	2	75	545	17-Jun
MEENG FLYER	bk b Whisper Wishes -Fortune Citizen Mar-91	4	20	570	676	14-Feb
MEGANS CHAMP	wbd d Fearless Champ-Davids Smokey Oct-92	1	2	150	458	8-Sep
MEHAVEWYN	dkbd d Ballyregan Bob-Broomwood Beauty Dec-91	1	6	150	640	21-Nov
MELLOW BOSS	f d Mid Clare Champ-Dancing Way Mar-92	4	22	375	281	14-Nov
MEMPHIS KING	bk d Dempseys Whisper-Bawnard Tess May-92	1	8	125	415	23-Jun
MERE FLAMINGO	wbk b lm Slippy-Pond Flamingo Apr-92	1	6	50	278	27-Jun
MERE FOXTROT	wbk d Murlens Slippy-Pond Flamingo Jan-93	1	2	100	450	17-Aug
MERE MISCHIEF	bk b New Level-Starlight Airway Mar-93	1	5	100	580	30-Nov
MERRY CAIN	wbd b Murlens Slippy-Tricias Gold May-91	1	5	40	575	11-Jul
MICHAELS IMAGE	f d Curryhills Lemon-Pineapple Beauty Apr-90	3	9	400	440	29-Oct
MICHAELS MACHINE	f d Satharn Beo-Sleepy Midget Jan-92	1	7	50	480	6-Apr
MICHIGAN MIDAS	bdw d lm Slippy-Michigan Moira Jun-90	4	18	350	273	24-Jun
MICKS ROVER	bk d Greenpark Fox-Lowfield Wishes Aug-91	15	29	1,560	430	19-Dec

A-Z STATISTICS

Greyhound		W	R	£	Ave D	Last Win
MIDWAY BEO VIEW	bd b Satharn Beo-Review Jul-92	4	10	525	596	30-Dec
MIDWAY GLORY	bd d Dark Wonder-Southrope Emily Nov-91	1	6	100	420	12-Dec
MIKEYS FAVOURITE	f d Fly Cruiser-Ardnalee Anne Nov-91	3	10	155	474	30-Sep
MILEHOUSE SPEEDY	wbd d Randy-Trans Linda Aug-91	1	16	50	655	31-Oct
MILES DEMPSEY	f d Dempseys Whisper-Coppertone Feb-92	11	33	1,640	674	19-Dec
MILNER CRESCENT	bd dFearless Ace-Worthy Choice Aug-91	2	11	200	510	4-Jul
MINNIES HAZEL	bk b Kyle Jack-Minnies Siren Feb-92	1	5	80	686	3-Nov
MINOR CRYSTAL	bk b Bold Rabbit-Newmans Mall Oct-90	6	8	675	818	19-Mar
MINT CONTROL	bkw d Im Slippy-Dream Orchid Jan-92	1	6	100	575	24-Jun
MISS PIGGY	bd b Deenside Spark-Miss Irene May-92	10	18	1,185	799	29-Nov
MISS SANDRA	bk bBallyard Hoffman-Every Second Sep-91	3	14	925	545	9-Apr
MISSISSIPPI JOE	wf d Carmels Prince-Armada Queen Sep-91	2	8	200	454	1-Mar
MISTER BRIDGE	wbd d Moon Dawn-Moving Again Dec-90	2	15	200	778	20-Sep
MISTER MAST	bd d Moneypoint Mast-Kinaglory Lydia Aug-91	2	6	200	471	2-Dec
MISTER NICK	bk d Glencorbry Celt-Darklawn Mist May-90	1	9	125	640	17-Jun
MISTER RANT	bk d Ardfert Sean-Fair Hill Rose Aug-92	3	9	370	541	28-Oct
MISTY DOON	wbk d Whisper Wit-Ginger Wings Sep-92	1	7	100	462	6-Sep
MISTY PHANTOM	bd d Phantom Flash-Twink Star Nov-92	6	18	640	463	5-Oct
MISTY SCORCH	bk d Slaneyside Hare-Boos Hobby Jan-92	1	13	100	450	1-Mar
MISTY SOOT	bk b Slaneyside Hare -Boos Hobby Jan-92	3	8	270	500	29-Sep
MITCHELLS TIGER	bd d Skelligs Tiger- Fortune Toinette Sep-92	1	7	100	375	17-Dec
MOANING LAD	f d Kyle Jack-Lady Bellamy Apr-92	10	24	1,125	485	11-Oct
MOCKERY	f b Westmead Havoc-Tailor Blackie Mar-92	1	4	300	610	25-Mar
MOLLIES DREAM	bd b Carters Lad -Knocksme Dream May-91	5	29	620	753	19-Dec
MOLLYS MAID	bk b Westmead Havoc -Rathkennan Mil Apr-92	1	9	120	385	29-Apr
MOMBASA TAXI	bd d Dark Mittens-Fair Una Dec-91	1	14	100	555	28-Jul
MOMENTUMS MADAM	bd b Manorville Sand-Momentum Express Mar-92	2	13	225	482	8-Feb
MON CHERRIE	bd b Skelligs Tiger-Linsella Jul-92	1	6	50	540	8-Aug
MONARD WISH	bd d Whisper Wishes-Solas An Maiden Aug-91	7	27	2,060	647	5-Jul
MONMORE CHAMP	bkw d Floating Champ-Wood Mego Nov-91	4	26	300	377	22-Aug
MONTEREY MARIA	wbk b Westmead Havoc-Abbeymore Darkie Jun-92	1	5	100	465	8-Feb
MOON IDOL	wbd d Moon Dawn-Shipyard Sally Jul-93	1	1	100	480	19-Dec
MOONCOIN MELODY	bkw b Kilcannon Hero-First Five Jul-92	1	1	100	450	18-Oct
MOOR BRIDGE	f b Adraville Bridge-Moorlough Magic Jun-91	3	15	360	420	24-Oct
MOORFIELD BLUE	be b Im Slippy-Westmead Harriet Jun-92	1	6	100	462	4-Apr
MOORSTOWN MELODY	bd b Willie Joe-Anemometer Jul-91	3	9	250	351	24-Nov
MORAL DIRECTOR	wbd d Double Bid-Moral Shadow May-92	6	27	6,115	481	10-Dec
MORAL STANDARDS	wbk d Flag Star-No Way Jose May-92	12	18	56,325	485	25-Jun
MORRIS MINOR	bk d Phantom Flash -Killeacle Gold Sep-92	1	4	85	440	21-Jul
MOS IMP	bk b Whisper Wishes-Celt CountryJun-91	8	34	3,275	482	18-Oct
MOSSFIELD FIRE	bk d Toy Boy-Upstream Girl Apr-91	3	24	350	811	6-Sep
MOSSFIELD SCOTTY	wf b Catunda Flame-Mossfield Terror Oct-90	3	10	520	851	9-May
MOSSFIELD SID	wbk d Catunda Flame-Speedy Maura Jun-92	2	13	240	655	16-Nov
MOSSROW MASCOT	wf b Satharn Beo -Corville Hill Jan-92	1	7	75	545	18-Jan
MOUNT FRISCO	wbe d Daleys Gold-Curragh Lady Jan-92	1	4	125	400	6-Jan
MOUNT ROYAL FOX	bd d Greenpark Fox -Spring Season Sep-92	1	7	75	277	13-Dec
MOUNT RUBY JET	bk d Adraville Bridge-Mount Ruby Jill Jul-91	5	18	500	273	3-Jun
MOVE ON SOUND	f d Whisper Wishes-Burnpark Vera Jun-92	4	17	1,075	464	15-Dec
MOVE ON WISHES	wbk b Whisper Wishes-Burnpark Vera Jun-92	1	2	110	450	29-Nov
MOVE OVER LAURA	dkbd b Macs Lock-Rustic Ripple Mar-92	1	6	100	250	19-Jul
MOVEALONG DANDY	bk d Manorville Magic-Movealong Peg Jul-92	1	8	100	660	18-Oct
MOVEALONG FLYER	bkw b Manorville Magic-Movealong Peg Jul-92	1	4	75	480	6-May
MOYBELLA HARARE	f d Arrow House-Brown Socks Jul-92	1	3	100	310	5-Dec
MOYLE KNIGHT	wbk d Daleys Gold-Still Knight Mar-93	1	4	150	458	1-Dec
MOYNEVILLA CHIEF	f d Greenpark Fox-Westpark Schull Nov-91	2	5	175	290	29-Mar
MOYNEVILLA ECHO	bdw d Murlens Slippy-Mutts Motto Jul-91	3	11	400	485	6-Jun

A-Z STATISTICS

Greyhound		W	R	£	Ave D	Last
MR BLUE SKY	bd d Curryhills Specl-Ballylarkin Mini Nov-91	1	20	150	640	5-Mar
MR MAGOS	wbk d lm Slippy-Aglish Dawn Jul-92	2	5	225	490	16-Sep
MR MAX	bk d The Other Risk-Yale Princess Aug-91	1	6	110	380	26-Mar
MR OSSY	bd d Curryhills Gara-Alley Lady Jun-91	3	32	1,600	513	25-Nov
MR TAN	bdw d Murlens Slippy-Without Equal Jun-92	6	31	2,600	506	11-Nov
MR VANDER BROOKE	bk d Whisper Wishes-Yama Pet Jan-91	2	9	150	570	8-Nov
MRS JONES	wbk b Farncombe Black-Proud To Run Oct-91	1	12	120	555	26-May
MRS NIGHTINGALE	bk b Midnight Hustle- Greenwood Ale Jan-92	1	5	50	460	3-May
MUCKY BUDD	bd d Greenpark Fox-Tracy Budd Mar-92	6	24	690	500	29-Jul
MULS BID	wbd d Double Bid-Hazelwood Shadow Nov-91	2	6	200	513	10-Jun
MUMS CHAMPION	be bd d lm Slippy-Mosseys Dream Apr-91	1	10	85	440	10-Mar
MUMS VISION	be bd d lm Slippy-Mosseys Dream Apr-92	1	13	85	440	16-Jun
MURLENS KATIE	wbd b lm Slippy-Lemon Chill Sep-91	4	7	430	391	11-Jul
MURLENS PARK	f b Greenpark Fox-Murlens Ruby Jul-92	1	16	100	460	24-Dec
MURLENS SON	wbk d Murlens Post-Summer Ruby Jun-92	1	5	100	480	28-May
MUSIC CHARMER	bd d Ramtogue Dasher-Paulas Charm Jul-92	3	6	150	467	10-May
MUSTANG ALLIE	bd b lm Slippy- Zee Zee Apr-92	2	13	400	562	17-Mar
MUTUAL CONSENT	wbk d Hello Blackie -Smart Slippy Feb-92	1	10	100	465	12-Apr
MY BOY SEVEN	bd d Westmead Claim-Fearsome Queen Sep-92	3	11	335	493	8-Jul
MY CIARA	be b Glencorbry Celt-Saol Fada Sally Oct-90	2	12	225	730	1-Feb
MY DAD GEORGE	bd d Westmead Havoc-Morans Lady Aug-92	2	18	220	575	28-Dec
MY LITTLE KING	bd d My Little Fox -California Queen Mar-92	1	6	100	545	14-Sep
MY LITTLE PIGS	f d Carmels Prince-Windove Aug-91	1	5	175	260	21-Mar
MY LOCKET	wbd b Galtymore Lad-Rosies Hope Oct-91	4	9	250	534	21-May
MY NAMES RACHEL	bd b Westmead Harry-Kileton Joy Aug-92	1	6	100	405	9-Nov
MY ROSIE LEE	bd b Westmead Havoc-Todis Tribe Feb-92	3	13	305	433	19-Aug
MY TEXETTE	bk b Waltham Abbey -Document May-90	4	18	275	795	19-Nov
MYSTICAL GALE	wbd d Gino II-Desmonds Gift Jun-91	3	11	275	633	28-Oct
NAE BOTHER	bd d lm Slippy-Bonnybrig Blonde Oct-90	1	3	100	241	27-Jan
NANNY STAGE	be b Ballygrowman Jim-Blue Stage May-91	1	6	500	1100	11-Mar
NARABANE COMET	bd d Alpine Minister-Narabane Gosh Aug-91	1	3	75	509	27-Apr
NARABANE MITCH	wf b Daleys Gold-Genny Cosh Mar-91	1	7	75	480	29-Apr
NAUGHTY BUT NICE	wbk d Torbal Duke-Guys Pal Mar-93	1	3	75	462	13-Dec
NEAT CHOICE	bk b Leaders Best-Neat Dish Apr-92	1	2	100	660	15-Dec
NEAT KELLY	bkw d Murlens Hawk-Neat Dish Dec-92	3	3	670	474	16-Nov
NEDS FLYER	bebd d Live Contender-Trout Stream Sep-92	3	10	225	432	28-Dec
NEW ROSE FOX	bd b Greenpark Fox -Lindas Solo Jun-92	4	17	310	378	24-May
NEW YORK EXPRESS	bd d Greenpark Fox-Shenick Lady Jan-92	4	30	520	502	18-Nov
NEW YORK WHISPER	bk d Whisper Wishes- Rockfield Eve Sep-91	2	9	225	253	18-Mar
NEWFORD RIFRAF	f d Satharn Beo-Much Adored Jul-91	2	9	175	470	12-Jul
NEWLAWN SUZY	bd b Murlens Slippy-Beaufils Jul-92	1	7	115	647	1-Jun
NEWLAWN WARRIOR	bd d Dutch Delight -Ardrine Carrie Jul-92	3	5	220	278	22-Nov
NEWRY TOWN	bk d Flag Star-Lady Tico Feb-90	13	22	1,960	797	9-Jun
NEXT TIME ROUND	bk d Randy-You Princess Sep-90	4	17	610	717	9-Jul
NICE MELODY	bk b Slippy Blue-Free Fancy Aug-91	3	9	250	376	7-Sep
NICE ONE JOLLY	bd b Moneypoint Coal-Freezer Jan-92	1	8	120	640	4-Feb
NICKYS SPIRIT	wbk b Westmead Havoc-Isolbella Jet Jan-91	1	6	75	476	18-May
NICOLAS AMEDEUS	f d Kylehill Cheeta-Zola Sep-90	1	8	150	475	5-Feb
NIGHT OF THE FOX	bd d Greenpark Fox-Easy Journey Nov-91	9	14	900	480	15-Jul
NIMBLE PIPER	bk d Tico-Fair Damsel Oct-92	2	3	400	440	3-Dec
NITE BOY	bk d Up For One-Lady Hamilton Nov-91	1	14	125	640	18-Jul
NO CAN	bk d Lartigue Note-Dainty Susan Jun-91	1	3	100	647	15-Nov
NO PROBLEM FOXY	f d Murlens Hawk-Coondara May-92	2	21	200	473	18-Aug
NO TRUTH	wbd d Satharn Beo-No Thanks Jul-91	1	5	100	480	6-May
NOBBYS FLIER	bk d Kyle Jack-Daleys Run Jul-91	2	6	150	440	15-Apr
NOELS EXCUSE	wf d Green Legend-Killala Queen Oct-91	1	4	150	458	28-Oct

NGRC Greyhound Racing Yearbook 1995

A-Z STATISTICS

Greyhound		W	R	£	Ave D	Last Win
NOIR BANJO	bk d Im Slippy-Gortbofinna Lady Apr-91	3	23	375	481	29-Jun
NORFOLK WHISPER	f d Whisper Wishes-Hasty Ann Jun-91	3	4	260	318	24-Jun
NORWOOD EARL	wbk d Daleys Gold-Geinis Gamble Mar-91	1	3	75	476	9-Mar
NOT MY GEORGIE	wbd d Ballyregan Bob-Josie Feb-92	1	9	50	515	26-Jul
NOT MY LINE	bd b Adraville Bridge -Odd The Line Sep-92	8	19	1,425	471	13-Dec
NOTED RETURN	bk d Lartigue Note-Muls Return Oct-91	2	9	450	400	28-Apr
NOVEMBER BLUE	be b Skelligs Tiger-Maggies Wishes Nov-91	1	8	250	450	30-Jul
NUDE GENERATION	bd b Mr John Dee-Celtic Shamrock May-91	1	1	100	545	14-Sep
O HICKEY RED	f d Kildare Ash-Lulus Wren May-91	1	6	120	515	12-Jul
OAKDENE EXPRESS	dkbd d Kyle Jack- Madeira Mad Jan-91	3	11	340	438	30-Nov
OAKFRONT DRIVE	bk d Druids Johno-Oakfront Magic Jun-91	1	1	125	260	13-Jan
OAST HOUSE	bd d Tapwatcher-Druids Darling Apr-92	1	6	0	460	2-Jun
OBITUR DICTUM	wbd d Ardfert Sean-Chance Skinomage Nov-91	1	8	200	555	26-May
ODELL DOUBLE	wbk d Double Bid-Odell Heather Feb-92	1	5	75	220	10-Oct
OFF OUR MINDS	wbd d Satharn Beo-Game Misty un-92	5	17	455	472	5-May
OLD JACK	bk d Westmead Claim-Well Timed Jun-91	1	9	75	545	31-Jan
OLD MONEY	bk d Waltham Abbey-Home Run Feb-91	5	18	475	669	17-May
OLIVERS MELODY	bk b Lartigue Note -Foretop Jun-91	3	8	390	655	2-Sep
OLYMPIC JIM	wbk d Daleys Gold-Darling Flash	6	12	535	356	5-Sep
OLYMPIC KNIGHT	bk b Glencorbry Celt-Dusky Knight Jul-91	3	9	300	459	16-Nov
ON THE BOUNCE	bd d Live Contender-Nippy Maid Jan-93	4	7	1,270	464	18-Nov
ON YOUR OWN	bd b Manorville Major-Touch The Sail Jul-91	1	11	175	820	1-Sep
ONE FOR LUCK	wbk d Greenpark Fox -Creighmore Jun-91	6	17	600	443	11-Nov
ONE MORE CHANCE	bdw d Druids Lodge-Damhnait Jun-91	1	5	100	450	22-Feb
OPEN FORUM	wf d Glenpark Ranger-Princess Alucard Oct-90	1	5	100	458	17-Feb
ORAN BRANDY	bd d Powerstown Pax -Oran Rosie Mar-92	1	7	75	440	6-May
ORIENT ANCHOR	bd d Satharn Beo -Yellow Riband Sep-92	6	16	620	488	6-Aug
ORIENT ARROW	wbk d Im Slippy-Siahg Aug-91	1	6	100	450	11-Jan
ORIZONTALS BEST	bk d Leaders Best-Lovely Lisa Jan-92	1	13	50	474	5-Oct
OUR CAPTAIN	f d Greenpark Fox-Perfect Stranger Sep-91	1	9	100	450	25-Jan
OUT IN THE DARK	bd d Gambling Shay-Shimsville Snow Mar-91	1	5	120	790	14-Mar
OUT OF SPEC	wbd b Aulton Slippy-Tout Lee Pip Oct-91	1	11	110	450	26-Jul
OUTCAST BID	bd d Double Bid-Outcast Lady Sep-92	2	5	250	618	30-Jul
OUTLAW ROBIN	bd d Early Vocation-Outlaw Kitty Oct-91	3	16	450	647	19-Nov
OYSTER COTTAGE	bk d Airmount Grand-Oyster Drop Aug-90	3	8	340	636	4-Aug
PADDYS BEGGAR	bd d Greenpark Fox-Fossabeg Rose Aug-92	3	14	700	385	9-Nov
PADDYS IVY	bd d Greenpark Fox -Manx Ivy Jun-91	2	5	75	370	24-Nov
PALMA RYDE	wbk d Al Zobbar-Nans Queen Aug-91	1	2	100	275	17-Dec
PALOOKA PRINCE	f d Midnight Hustle-Ballysally Tina Apr-91	5	22	635	472	13-Dec
PAMS MAGPIE	wbk d Manorville Sand-Ballintee Flash Jul-90	1	1	110	484	29-Apr
PAMS PANTHER	wf d Whisper Wishes- Summer Flower Oct-92	1	2	75	440	21-Oct
PAMS SILVER	wf d Skelligs Tiger -Cosy And Warm May-92	3	21	1,175	413	9-May
PAPER CRUISER	bew d Fly Cruiser -Paper Slippy Aug-91	1	7	150	400	17-Feb
PARADISE MELODY	wf b Will Dannagher-Paradise Whisper Jul-91	1	9	100	241	10-Feb
PARADISE SLIPPY	bk d Will Dannagher-Paradise Whisper Jul-91	19	44	2,265	491	24-Oct
PARANOIA	bd d Phantom Flash-River Suzy Oct-91	1	3	125	484	4-Feb
PARKWAY KATE	wbd b Murlens Slippy-Glenclare Dec-91	1	7	0	700	24-Oct
PARKWAY PILOT	bk d April Trio-Killua Gift Apr-91	1	16	100	310	9-May
PARQUET PADDY	wbd d Im Slippy-Bangor Style Aug-91	10	24	705	477	8-Oct
PARTNERS IN HOPE	f b Guiding Hope-Allglaze Alva Jul-91	2	15	200	570	28-May
PAT YOUR BACK	wbk b Flag Star-Take The Wean Aug-91	7	18	930	750	17-Jun
PATRIOT SAIL	bd d Manorville Major-Touch The Sail Jul-91	10	32	3,280	588	22-Dec
PATRIOT SLIPPY	wbd d Murlens Slippy-Kildinan Lass Mar-93	1	7	150	475	15-Sep
PATS HOPE	bd d Murlens Slippy-Off The Line Sep-92	1	4	120	484	11-Nov
PAULS PRIDE	bd d Westmead Havoc-Abbeymore Darkie Sep-91	2	15	200	465	29-Sep
PEARLS GIRL	fw b Flashy Sir-Desert Pearl Apr-91	10	23	9,100	497	28-Nov

A-Z STATISTICS

Greyhound		W	R	£	Ave D	Last
PEASEDOWN DALEY	bk d Daleys Gold-Audrey Rose May-91	4	13	350	501	2-Dec
PEMBURY GIFT	bdw b Farncombe Black-Proud To Run Oct-91	6	20	625	634	2-Dec
PENALTY SPOT	wbk d Greenpark Fox-Lyns Fli Jan-92	2	15	300	475	29-Oct
PENARE BEO	bdw d Satharn Beo-Sand Bucket Feb-92	1	6	100	450	18-Jan
PENARE DOUBLE	wbd d Double Bid-Catsrock Bubble Apr-92	1	2	100	256	7-Oct
PENNYS ARMANI	wbe b lm Slippy-Colorado Holly Sep-92	2	4	200	370	30-Nov
PENNYS DIANA	bk b Adraville Bridge-Colorado Holly Jul-91	1	1	1,000	474	26-Mar
PENNYS GLEN	wbk d Daleys Gold-Synone Crest Oct-91	1	4	100	500	30-May
PENNYS HOLLY	bef b lm Slippy-Colorado Holly Oct-90	1	2	40	474	14-May
PENNYS JAG	wbk d Daleys Gold-Synone Crest Oct-91	1	8	150	484	10-Mar
PENNYS JET	wbk d lm Slippy -Synone Crest Feb-93	1	5	1,000	500	24-Dec
PENNYS PRINCESS	bd b Adraville Bridge-Colorado Holly Jul-91	1	4	120	460	7-Apr
PEPSI JOE	wbd d lm Slippy-Pepsi Princess Jan-92	5	26	645	599	27-Jun
PEPSI PETE	bd d lm Slippy-Pepsi Princess Jan-92	9	29	1,045	529	1-Dec
PERRYS FANCY	be d Skelligs Tiger-Double Toe Aug-92	1	4	115	484	10-Nov
PERSIAN FANTASY	wf d Track Man-Tiny Catcher May-91	3	14	835	732	12-May
PET TREASURE	bd b Manx Treasure-Smart Fairy Jan-93	1	4	100	465	17-Dec
PEUTETRA	wbk b Manorville Magic-Im A Survivor Dec-91	1	11	50	555	18-Apr
PHANTOM ROSIE	bk b Phantom Flash-Tullig Rosie Apr-92	3	16	600	600	27-Dec
PHYSCHO CITY	bk d Hygard-Run Slave Aug-91	5	22	365	456	7-Oct
PICTURE GOLD	bk d Daleys Gold-Picture Card Apr-92	2	9	200	400	26-Jul
PIMLICO PAUL	bk d Zorro-Citywide Suzy Apr-92	1	10	125	640	18-Feb
PIPE DOWN	bk b Surge Home-Hildas Niece Jun-91	1	8	200	790	18-May
PIPER GARA	bk d Curryhills Gara-Tyrone Marion Jul-91	3	6	300	250	19-Jul
PLEASANT OUTLOOK	bk d Brownies Outlook-Leyland Bride Aug-91	3	28	450	380	20-May
POLAND BID	bkw d Double Bid-Polano Jul-92	1	9	120	666	30-Sep
POLAR WIND	bd d Manorville Major- Miss Kyle Nov-91	2	5	155	460	28-Oct
POLLYSBRAE BOY	f d Glenpark Dancer-Farloe Mineola Apr-91	3	18	100	461	7-Sep
POLNOON GOLD	f b Daleys Gold-Polnoon Lass Dec-91	1	9	100	400	23-Dec
POLO MITTENS	f b Dark Mittens-Avongate Polo Mar-92	1	15	100	400	25-Feb
POND APHRODITE	bk b Adraville Bridge-Pond Mosquito Apr-93	2	8	200	450	23-Nov
POND DIABLO	wbd d Murlens Slippy-Pond Mosquito Jul-91	7	14	850	258	11-May
POND HAMLET	bd d Tapwatcher-Pond Mosquito Apr-92	8	23	3,950	423	4-Nov
POND LUCIUS	bk d Tapwatcher-Pond Mosquito Apr-92	3	14	300	320	20-Jul
POND MACBETH	bk d Tapwatcher -Pond Mosquito Apr-92	1	7	100	450	1-Jun
POND MOTTO	bd d Macs Lock-Pond Jemima Aug-92	1	3	100	450	2-Feb
POND RACONTEUR	f d Macs Lock -Pond Jemima Aug-92	3	9	450	455	3-Sep
POND ROMEO	f d Fearless Champ-Pond Jemima May-90	1	7	0	640	19-Sep
PORTLAW	bdw d lm Slippy-Ballyard Monroe Feb-92	1	2	110	645	14-Jun
POTTO COBRA	f d Ballyard Hoffman-Slippery Peg Jan-93	4	14	375	418	4-Nov
POTTOS SAMPSON	bd d Ballyard Hoffman-Slippery Peg Jan-93	1	5	100	500	12-Sep
POUND RAFFLE	bk d Choice Of Game-Slaneyside Speed Apr-92	4	18	450	419	23-Sep
POWDER FINGER	wbe d lm Slippy-Coolgorman Mint Apr-91	1	6	100	458	28-Feb
POWYS GOLD	f d Daleys Gold-Diamias Damsel May-91	8	21	1,550	478	4-Jun
PRACTICAL KID	bd d Hello Blackie-Life Member Jul-92	3	6	350	467	28-Nov
PRESS COPY	f d Flashy Sir-Hogans Kizzy Jan-92	3	14	300	590	7-May
PRETTY LIVELY	bk d Live Contender-Solas An Maiden Jul-92	4	11	3,295	609	27-Aug
PRIMARY GREGORY	bd d Manorville Major-Twilight Slave Feb-91	1	2	100	575	25-Feb
PRINCE CHARLIE	wbk d Adraville Bridge- Rhincrew Lady Jul-91	1	5	110	380	19-Sep
PRINCESS PENNIE	bd b lm From Tallow-Greek Echo May-93	1	4	100	460	15-Nov
PRINTER PETE	wbk d Newhill Printer-Tax Free Mar-93	1	7	75	545	21-Sep
PRIVATE LEGEND	wf d lm Slippy-Minnies Countess May-92	2	14	350	480	5-Mar
PROUD GLEN	bd d Skelligs Tiger-Proud Magpie Jun-92	3	11	315	469	8-Oct
PROUD PRIZE	wbk b Skelligs Tiger -Proud Magpie Jun-92	1	3	100	647	4-Oct
PROVE THE POINT	wbk d Moneypoint Coal-Cregg Jennie Feb-92	2	18	170	558	21-Mar
PUBLIC APPEAL	wbd d Double Bid-Biddys Clover Aug-91	3	20	365	536	16-Jul

A-Z STATISTICS

Greyhound		W	R	£	Ave D	Last Win
PUBLIC POACHER	bkw d Balalika-Endless Game Feb-92	2	15	250	553	9-Aug
PURE CLASS	wbd b Vesington Soda-Rathkennaw Helen Nov-92	1	4	120	666	11-Aug
PURE PEPPER	bd b Carmels Prince-Pure Posh Dec-91	4	5	350	465	6-Dec
PYROMANIAC	wbd d Ravage Again-Smart Fairy Jul-91	1	4	125	260	4-Feb
QUALITY AWARD	f d Skelligs Tiger-Minorcas Tramp Jun-92	1	2	50	440	22-Dec
QUALITY MOON	bd d Daleys Gold -Darling Flash Jun-91	1	7	75	476	16-Mar
QUARRYMOUNT SCOT	f d Skelligs Tiger-Quarrymount Swan Jul-92	1	2	200	241	3-Sep
RABATINO	f d Poor James-Hymenstown Rose Jan-92	6	29	3,175	426	25-Jul
RACELINE SEAN	bd d Ardfert Sean-Slaneyside Glory Feb-92	2	7	210	462	23-Nov
RACELINE SLIPPY	bk d Slippy Blue-Catunda Helena Sep-92	4	15	465	460	6-Oct
RADBUG	bkw d Skelligs Tiger-Sheilas Court Jan-92	1	15	100	650	17-Feb
RAG BUSH	bebd d Coalbrook Tiger -Melville Chill Feb-92	1	9	125	484	8-Mar
RAHEEN ROGER	bd d Karens Champ-Mountleader Swan Jun-90	3	16	320	637	7-Jul
RAMBLING HEATHER	be b Airmount Grand-Rambling Delight Jul-91	5	22	975	551	19-Nov
RAMBOS KING	f d Odell King-Yellow Sash Nov-91	2	11	160	493	17-Jun
RANDY SAVAGE	bk d Randy-Sooty Foot May-91	6	18	6,395	470	15-Jul
RATHANGAN REGGIE	bd d Slippy Highland- Jambalava Sep-90	1	12	110	450	19-Mar
RATHBEG JOHNO	bk d Druids Johno-Rathbeg Crystal Apr-92	2	7	175	240	23-Dec
RATHDOVE BOY	bdw d Murlens Slippy-Mountain Dove Jul-92	1	6	100	450	5-Sep
RATTLESNAKE JAZZ	bd b Murlens Slippy-Lindas Dance Aug-90	1	3	100	484	28-Jan
RAY OF SUN	wbk d Randy-Dunmurry Lassie Sep-91	2	6	150	700	24-Aug
RAYS WILLOW	wbk d Crafty Roberto-Ardnalee Mary Mar-91	4	12	600	490	6-May
READY AGAIN	wf b lm Slippy-Ready Rubbed Jun-91	1	1	100	241	24-Feb
REAGROVE CHIEF	bk d Arrow House-Miss Gemma Mar-92	4	16	500	475	15-Dec
REAROUR CHIEF	bdw d lm Slippy-Another Whisper Apr-91	2	4	200	484	28-Jan
REDWOOD GIRL	bd b Ardfert Sean-Redwood Sue Mar-91	14	27	11,075	644	31-Oct
REDWOOD PIPPIN	bd b Ardfert Sean-Redwood Sue Mar-91	9	25	1,270	688	15-Dec
REDWOOD TIGER	bd d Ardfert Sean Redwood Sue Mar-91	3	16	400	640	5-May
REENARD ROCKET	be d Tapwatcher-Louise Champion Nov-92	6	22	625	453	29-Nov
REGENT LASS	bd b Murlens Slippy-Little Dancer Jul-90	1	7	100	660	4-Mar
REJECT JACK	bd d Curryhills Gara-Killila Bess Sep-91	1	7	100	450	2-Aug
RESULT LINE	wf b Track Man-Tiny Catcher May-91	1	3	200	640	10-Feb
RHEBOGUE TREATY	bd d Manorville Major-Anns Jam Jun-90	3	8	400	400	3-Jun
RICKYS MATE	bebd d Skelligs Tiger-Rathkennan Biddy Dec-90	5	27	410	402	15-Sep
RIDGEDALE SLIPPY	bd d Murlens Slippy-Naked Beauty Apr-92	1	2	50	460	28-Jul
RIGHT BUSTER	bk d Slippy Blue-Priceless Note Aug-91	5	8	525	289	6-Aug
RIGHT HENRY	f d Flashy Sir-Rashane Nimble Sep-91	4	19	550	599	30-Nov
RIGHT WISH	bk d Daleys Gold-Burnpark Wish Mar-93	2	10	245	450	17-Dec
RING DAMSEL	bd b Manorville Major-Ring Park Apr-91	1	4	100	700	24-Mar
RING MANOR	bebd d Manorville Major-Ring Park Apr-91	6	19	880	492	3-Dec
RING PATRIOT	bd d Kyle Jack-In Advance Jan-90	8	27	730	468	21-Nov
RINGSIDE CYCLONE	bk d Live Contender-Anti Cyclone Nov-91	2	13	350	470	6-Aug
RINGSIDE RETURN	wbk d Daleys Gold-No Way Jose Aug-91	11	29	1,450	340	19-Dec
RINGTOWN EXPRESS	bk d Ardfert Sean -Fair Hill Rose Aug-92	2	7	200	420	7-Dec
RIO GOLD	bd d Powerstown Pax-Derrymore Girl Feb-92	5	20	800	494	19-Nov
RIO REMEMBER	wbdd Ardfert Sean-Meadowbank Tip Jan-92	4	16	400	459	8-Oct
RISKY WAY	bd d The Other Risk-Killeacle Biddy Jul-90	2	9	200	400	11-Mar
RITAS GEM	f b Satharn Beo-Rita Rose Mar-92	1	3	100	575	16-Dec
RIVAL PENNY	bk d Westmead Havoc-Tribal Rule Oct-92	3	22	335	473	16-Jun
RIVER OF DREAMS	bd d Carters Lad-Miss Irene Feb-93	3	10	270	443	8-Dec
RIVER ROAD SWIFT	bd d Hello Blackie-Life Member Jul-92	4	18	500	462	5-Oct
RIVERDALE GLOW	bd d Skelligs Tiger-Westmead Glow Nov-92	2	4	150	475	3-Oct
RIVERMOUNT HOPE	wbd b lm Slippy-Millies Claddagh Apr-92	3	11	235	575	24-Oct
ROAMING EYE	wbk d Odell Supreme-Silver Linda Aug-90	2	4	75	277	26-Sep
ROBBING MONEY	bk d Leaders Best-Highway Mystery May-91	2	13	200	575	11-Feb
ROBERTS PAYING	bd b Moon Dawn-Always Paying Aug-92	1	6	125	714	17-Oct

A-Z STATISTICS

Greyhound		W	R	£	Ave D	Last
ROCK FLYER	bkw b Manorville Magic-Ballydaly Flyer Jul-92	1	7	100	555	25-Aug
ROCK TIGER	wbd d Skelligs Tiger-Woodview Bond Jun-92	1	4	100	640	10-Oct
ROCKGLEN DASHER	bd d Rugged Mick-Ballylinan Girl Nov-90	3	24	325	463	6-Dec
ROCKGROVE SAND	bd d Satharn Beo-Sheilas Bend Jun-91	2	14	140	409	9-Sep
ROCKMOUNT JEAN	wbd b Im Slippy-Rockmount Mandy Mar-92	1	11	150	640	24-Feb
ROCKY ARMOUR	bdw d Whisper Wishes-Dream Impulse May-91	2	8	300	475	12-Nov
RODMERSHAM FLASH	bk d Double Bid-Odell Heather Feb-92	2	14	200	480	8-Jul
ROGERSPARTYPIECE	wbe d Ballinderry Ash-Birdmans Spark Jan-93	1	4	100	250	20-Sep
RONDOR GRANGE	bd d Glatton Grange-Rondor Style Jul-90	5	10	385	678	18-Jul
RONNOCCO SILVER	bd d Manx Marajax-Ronnocco Jessica Jan-91	8	28	1,275	628	14-Oct
ROOFERS GAMBLE	f d Flashy Sir-Lonely Bird Sep-91	2	9	200	465	27-Aug
ROSCAHILL SUPER	bk d Airmount Grand-Gleannrue Hazel Jan-91	5	22	620	464	30-Dec
ROSEGREEN PIPPA	dk bd b Ravage Again-Westmead Kara Jun-92	1	6	60	480	10-Dec
ROSELEX	bk b Greenpark Fox-Naquita Jul-91	2	7	150	298	30-Dec
ROSES ROCK	bk d Druids Johno-Rose Surprise Oct-92	1	5	75	375	22-Aug
ROSES VOCATION	bk d Early Vocation-Shenick Lady Sep-92	1	6	175	484	27-Aug
ROSLO SPEEDY	bk d Captain Villa-Fast Girl Jan-92	4	14	845	372	9-Jul
ROSSTEMPLE GIFT	wbd d Murlens Slippy-Baurleigh Gift Aug-91	1	3	120	385	23-Jun
ROUGH COAT	bk b Carters Lad-Roman Countess Feb-91	2	8	275	830	11-Apr
ROVING BUNNIE	bd b Bold Rabbit -Roving Linda Aug-91	4	16	305	496	2-Jul
ROWLEAZE BOY	bk d Money Matters-Fleagh Artist Jun-91	1	11	100	480	22-Mar
RUEBAL	bk b Westmead Havoc-Tribal Rule Oct-92	1	3	85	440	29-Sep
RUGBY WISHES	bkw d Whisper Wishes-Burgess Ruby Jul-91	6	25	1,210	529	23-Jun
RUN A BIT	bk d Skelligs Tiger-Missed Again Mar-92	3	19	280	433	29-Apr
RUN ON MICK	bk d Ardfert Mick-Move Over Birdie Dec-92	3	14	200	463	14-Nov
RUN OVER RAINBOW	bk b Lartigue Note-Queens Anthem Aug-91	1	1	75	245	2-May
RUN SPARK	bk d Jamie Harmony-Run Slave Nov-90	3	21	300	353	14-Oct
RUN TO PADDY	f d Adraville Bridge-Super Risk May-92	4	15	520	264	7-Apr
RUN WITH BILLY	bk d Farncombe Black-Proud To Run Oct-91	5	8	435	461	19-Mar
RUNALONG BLACKIE	bk d Westmead Wish-Tuesdays Mint Feb-91	3	20	250	670	9-Aug
RUNNYMEADE RASCAL	be b Moneypoint Coal-Rosy Outlook Jul-92	1	12	100	580	20-Jul
RUSS IS ACOMING	bk d Manorville Major-Keltic Bimbo Sep-91	6	19	475	616	13-Dec
RUSSIAN FOX	bk d Greenpark Fox -Kinnanes Fancy Apr-92	1	4	0	500	14-May
RYLANDS BEST	bk d Manorville Magic-Movealong Peg Jul-92	1	6	100	480	14-Apr
SAFEPAC GEM	bd b Summerhill Gem-Killaha Whisper Aug-91	1	4	75	545	11-Jul
SAIL TO VICTORY	f b Odell King-Yellow Sash Nov-91	2	16	220	700	21-Feb
SAINTLY SPIRIT	f b Curryhills Specl-Saintly Things Jun-92	1	1	75	480	4-Nov
SAINTS CHARLIE	wbk d Aussie Flyer-Saints Tania Sep-92	1	6	1,000	645	19-Nov
SALCOMBE	bk d Hygard-Micks Susie Jun-91	4	18	420	406	12-May
SALLYPARK LAD	bkw d Nightpark Lad-Terrylane Sally Mar-91	2	13	400	475	5-Jul
SALTHILL CHAMP	wbd d Druids Lodge-Park Na Veena Jul-91	9	26	810	485	24-Sep
SAMS BULLET	f d Kyle Jack -Coolagh Fantasy- Apr-91	5	22	490	605	28-Sep
SAMS LEGEND	wbk d Bold Rabbit-Tortune Mill Feb-90	3	8	300	412	3-Jun
SANDANITA	bd d Ardfert Sean-Glynn Gold Sep-91	6	20	495	567	29-Nov
SANDFORD STAR	fw d Phantom Flash-Clounanna Apr-92	5	27	440	468	5-Oct
SANDOLLAR LOUIE	bk d Manorville Magic -Im A Survivor Dec-91	6	28	10,395	759	22-Nov
SANDOLLAR SOPHIE	wbd b Manorville Magic-Im A Survivor Dec-91	4	19	570	849	24-May
SANDY COURT	fw d Im Slippy-Wandering Nellie Apr-91	2	9	200	294	7-Mar
SANDY COVE	bd d Satharn Beo-Kylemore Gem Jan-92	1	3	100	260	3-Dec
SANTA LUCIA	bd b Adraville Bridge-Santa Rita Jul-91	5	34	480	458	9-Dec
SANTA PONSA BAY	wbk d Nightpark Lad-Ritva Jul-90	1	4	100	450	2-Feb
SAPPYS ACORN	bk b Moral Support-Curryhills Cooga Feb-91	1	3	100	575	23-Dec
SARACEN	bd d Amenhotep-Tobys Delight Aug-92	2	19	190	510	3-Oct
SATIN FLASH	bk b Phantom Flash-Chocolate Satin Sep-91	9	34	1,175	666	22-Dec
SAUCY CHILD	wbd d Childrens Champ-Coolruss Girl May-91	1	3	0	290	14-Jun
SAUCY SADIE	bebd b Im Slippy-Westmead May Nov-92	3	14	225	475	29-Oct

A-Z STATISTICS

Greyhound		W	R	£	Ave D	Last Win
SCHOOL PRINCIPAL	bk d Kilmeedy Kin-Tricias Gold Jun-92	3	12	260	459	14-Jun
SCINTILLAS PANSY	bd b Murlens Slippy-Scintillas Queen Apr-91	6	22	1,495	633	25-Jun
SCRABO ROSE	bk b Cast No Stones-Lady Major Feb-91	1	28	200	710	5-May
SEAMAN MIKE	wbk d Airmount Grand-Kerogue Wish Oct-90	3	12	300	465	24-Feb
SEANS BREEZE	bd d Double Bid-Last Breeze Mar-92	1	9	100	400	15-Apr
SEAVIEW	f d Druids Johno-Dromature Silver Jun-91	5	16	540	303	17-Aug
SECURITY CLARE	bd b Murlens Slippy-Security Susan Jun-92	1	6	120	845	18-Oct
SECURITY DAWN	wbk b Murlens Slippy-Security Susan Jun-92	1	6	110	645	13-Sep
SECURITY SPECIAL	wbk b Murlens Slippy-Security Susan Jun-92	2	8	185	665	22-Jun
SECURITY WILLOW	dkbd d Murlens Slippy-Security Susan Jun-92	1	3	110	645	19-Jul
SEE JAYS MURLEN	wbd d Murlens Slippy-See Jays Cannon Oct-92	1	5	0	460	28-May
SEE JAYS TIGER	bd d Murlens Slippy-See Jays Cannon Oct-92	7	14	420	376	5-Oct
SELD MADE	bk d Greenpark Fox-Who Dares Jan-93	1	1	100	450	6-Dec
SENLAC ROSE	wf b Satharn Beo-Liberal Girl Sep-92	2	4	1,090	820	15-Dec
SESKIN EVELYN	f b Bold Rabbit -Seskin Lady Jun-91	3	13	330	645	20-Aug
SETTLE	wbk d Darragh Commet-Stouke Pet Apr-91	3	24	1,100	467	20-Aug
SEVENTH LADY	f b Druids Johno-Seventh Dynamic May-91	1	5	120	484	2-Jul
SHAMROCK GOLD	bd d Live Contender-Mansion Gold Apr-93	1	2	85	440	24-Nov
SHANAKIEL	wbd d Fearless Champ-Hostile Witness Nov-91	1	3	120	645	6-Dec
SHANBALLY CROSS	wbd d Murlens Slippy-Lucky Ward Feb-91	1	5	150	640	3-Mar
SHEILAS QUEST	f b Slippys Quest-Yale Princess May-92	1	4	125	490	6-May
SHELL DREGHORN	be d Tico-Lucky Blackbird Jan-90	1	5	100	465	26-Apr
SHERIFF	bk d Whisper Wishes-Kalamity Kelly Oct-90	1	16	100	474	12-Mar
SHIMMERING SPOT	f d Westmead Claim-Well Timed Jun-91	3	18	295	474	3-Nov
SHOE HORN	bebd d Wise Band-Barneys Girl Mar-91	1	3	50	474	12-Nov
SHROPSHIRE DASH	bk d Flag Star-Shropshire Lass Jul-92	4	18	435	626	14-Dec
SHROPSHIRE NICK	f d Slippy Blue-Chocolate Satin Oct-90	11	24	1,065	639	23-Dec
SHY PARISIENNE	wf b Fearless Ace-Paris In Spring Oct-91	1	8	100	792	9-Sep
SIDE GLANCE	bd d Deenside Spark-Revelence Jul-92	1	5	100	310	12-Dec
SIGN HERE	fw d Kyle Jack-Lady Bellamy Apr-92	1	10	100	460	16-May
SILBURY CLOUD	f b Whisper Wishes-Ferndale Class May-92	6	22	3,550	653	8-Oct
SILBURY STORM	bk d Whisper Wishes-Ferndale Class May-91	5	23	440	622	14-Nov
SILENT GUY	wbd d Whisper Wishes-Gleansharoon Oct-90	3	19	210	457	10-Dec
SILVER DASH	wbk d The Other Risk-Moneypoint Peg Jan-91	1	1	110	380	4-Jul
SILVER DEW	bd b Daleys Gold-Yellow Riband Nov-91	1	10	100	460	4-Apr
SILVER ECLIPSE	dk bd b Toy Boy-Upstream Girl Apr-91	2	5	220	645	5-Jul
SILVER GLOW	bdw b lm Slippy-Frisly White Feb-92	6	20	735	594	15-Dec
SILVERHILL SUE	bd b Hyper-Silverhill Lass Mar-92	10	28	1,590	556	26-Aug
SILVERVIEW SIDNY	bd d Pennys Karl -Blonde Aishling Feb-93	1	3	75	375	10-Dec
SIMPLE EXCEL	bd d Double Bid-Simply Eilte Aug-92	1	8	100	465	15-Dec
SIMPLY FREE	bd b Daleys Gold-Rooskey Critic Apr-91	12	29	1,065	575	12-Sep
SIMPLY SHAMROCK	wbd d Murlens Slippy-Simply Elite Apr-93	3	5	300	442	17-Dec
SIMSONS LASS	wbd b Arrow House-Lanrigg Lassie Jun-90	1	2	100	575	18-Feb
SING THE BLUES	wbk d Daleys Gold-Shes Dainty Feb-91	3	25	325	478	27-Aug
SIR FREDERICK	wbd d Satharn Beo-Liberal Girl Sep-92	2	7	170	495	5-Oct
SIR JAMES	f d Flashy Sir-Mrs Thomas Apr-91	1	14	100	620	27-Oct
SIREENA BRONTE	bd b Manorville Major-Special Gamble dec-92	1	5	75	545	28-Sep
SITUATION	bk d Flashy Sir-Mrs Thomas Apr-91	1	6	100	484	28-Jan
SKIPTON BRIDGE	bk d Adraville Bridge- Coolavanny Band Jan-93	1	3	50	460	22-Nov
SLANEYSIDE REBEL	bd d Skelligs Tiger-Slaneyside Queen Feb-91	1	5	100	675	15-Apr
SLAPDASH CLUB	wbd d Ballyregan Bob-Josie Feb-92	1	8	100	480	1-Nov
SLIDEAWAY SLIPPY	bd b Murlens Slippy-More Boot Jul-90	3	11	325	662	23-Jul
SLIP BY SPOT	wbk d lm Slippy-Magnolia Miss Aug-92	3	19	265	467	16-Jul
SLIPAWAY JAYDEE	wf d lm Slippy-Ballyvalican Jan-92	7	13	850	289	17-Dec
SLIPMAN	bk d Slippy Blue-Kilquain Glow Oct-91	1	7	100	450	1-Feb
SLIPPED SOUL	wbd d Murlens Slippy-Sheffield Spirit Nov-91	2	15	175	509	6-Jul

A-Z STATISTICS

Greyhound		W	R	£	Ave D	Last
SLIPPERY HUNTER	fw d lm Slippy-Cheerful Beauty Mar-91	4	18	475	529	22-Apr
SLIPPERY KING	bdw d lm Slippy-Sheerful Beauty May-91	2	9	220	475	9-Nov
SLIPPING HOME	wbd b lm Slippy-Home Alone Mar-90	1	2	200	640	21-Apr
SLIPPY CORNER	bd d lm Slippy-Tiger Hart Jul-91	8	26	1,245	347	17-Oct
SLIPPY LAWN	fw d lm Slippy-Lawn Dancer Jan-91	2	10	200	275	24-Feb
SLIPPY MAX	bebd d lm Slippy-Deroon Ball Sep-91	1	16	100	438	25-Mar
SLIPPY MINT	wbe d lm Slippy-Coolygorman Mint Apr-91	1	2	0	500	10-May
SLIPPY NIGHT	f d Aulton Slippy-Bouncing Barquet Nov-90	1	3	0	500	5-Apr
SLIPPY THOUGHTS	wbd d Murlens Slippy-Atnama Oct-91	1	4	100	640	5-Jul
SLOODOO PRINCE	bk d Flashy Sir-Alley Bally Aug-91	1	12	125	420	18-Jul
SLYBOOTS GINGER	f d Kylehill Cheeta-lm Golden Mar-92	5	13	595	584	12-Dec
SMART DECISION	wbd b Carters Lad-Knockshe Dream May-91	23	34	6,310	844	8-Dec
SMART TREASURE	bd d Manx Treasure-Smart Fairy Jan-93	1	10	150	640	20-Oct
SMILE ROSE	bk b Kyle Jack-Feedwell Rose Apr-91	1	3	1,000	575	14-Jan
SMITHS DASH	f d Slippys Quest -Yale Heroine Feb-93	1	1	100	485	17-Dec
SMOKEY FRED	f d Greenpark Fox-Smokey Wizard Apr-93	3	9	150	418	6-Dec
SMOOTH FLYER	bd d Westpark Mansour-Little Support Mar-91	5	16	475	514	28-Mar
SNOW FLASH	wbk d Phantom Flash-Airport Lady Sep-91	5	9	4,025	480	19-Sep
SNOWIE RIVER	wbk d Adraville Bridge-Bower Bee Aug-91	2	7	150	509	23-Feb
SO FIZZY	wbk d Poor James-Soda Fizz Aug-91	3	14	290	484	19-Oct
SO I HEARD	wbd d Manorville Sand-Squire Jenny May-91	3	28	250	537	15-Nov
SOCIETY PRINCE	bk d Lodge Prince-Garryduff Lassie Sep-90	5	24	975	256	23-Jul
SOCKITOUM	bdw d Tico-Keltic Bimbo dec-90	2	5	175	270	30-Mar
SODAS SLIPPY	bkw b Aulton Slippy-Springfield Soda dec-92	6	14	1,855	450	15-Dec
SOLVA CHIEFTAIN	bd b lm Slippy-Active Touch Jul-92	1	10	150	475	8-Nov
SOLVA FLAME	bd d Lodge Prince-Miss Kyle Sep-92	4	24	225	528	15-Nov
SOLVA GUY	bk d Daleys Gold-Lemon Miss Nov-92	4	28	935	454	22-Dec
SOLVA PRINCE	bk d Lodge Prince-Miss Kyle Sep-92	4	24	435	445	24-Nov
SOLVA SONIC	wbk d Greenpark Fox-Kerogue Wish Jan-93	1	3	85	440	8-Dec
SOLVA TIGER	bd d Carmels Prince-Aglish Mandy Jun-92	8	21	685	484	6-Dec
SOME GAMBLE	bd d Greenpark Fox-Spring Season Sep-92	2	10	900	386	17-Sep
SOME PRETENDER	bd d Live Contender-Some Tip Jan-92	5	11	725	476	19-Nov
SON OF THE BEST	wf d Premier Calandra-Zitas Baby dec-89	1	3	75	480	12-Aug
SONIC BLUE	bebd d Daleys Gold-Drom Echo May-91	9	29	1,515	608	17-Dec
SORE POINT	f d Satharn Beo-White Milly Jul-91	1	2	100	400	28-Jan
SOVIET SOPRANO	bd b Randy-Forever Grateful May-90	1	2	110	645	25-Jan
SOVIET SUMMER	bk d Tico-Soviet Supreme Mar-93	2	4	190	472	29-Nov
SPEAKERS CHOICE	bk b Skelligs Tiger-Bold Bells Apr-92	3	26	300	700	12-Nov
SPECIAL TILLER	wbd d Rikasso Tiler-Piper Lilac Feb-90	2	4	220	450	8-Feb
SPENWOOD MAGIC	bk b Westmead Claim-Loopy Lill Jun-91	10	30	1,100	670	31-Oct
SPINNING SUN	bd b Whisper Wishes-KS Expressions May-92	3	20	500	658	29-Apr
SPIRAL DANCER	fw d lm Slippy-Spiral Skip Aug-92	3	13	320	501	14-Dec
SPIRAL GRAND	wbd d Ravage Again-Spiral MayOct-91	1	18	100	400	17-Jun
SPIRAL ZEE ZEE	bk d lm Slippy-Zee Zee Apr-92	3	11	330	483	13-May
SPIT IT OUT	bk d Phantom Flash-Ivalog May-92	5	20	10,345	494	29-Oct
SPOT THE SLIP	wbd d lm Slippy-Magnolia Miss Aug-92	1	4	100	462	9-Aug
SPRING ARTIST	bd d Greenpark Fox-Spring Season Sep-92	2	13	500	277	26-Nov
SPRING FAIRY	bk b Kyle Jack-Kahan Express Nov-92	1	7	75	620	28-Oct
SPRING MELODY	bebd b Farloe Melody-Rural Rover Dec-92	1	1	75	375	30-Nov
SPRING WELCOME	fw d Castleyons Gem-Jills Whisper Jul-91	1	10	100	575	11-Mar
SPRINGFIELD RORY	bd d Deenside Spark-Springfield View Jan-93	1	4	40	545	21-Nov
SPRINGWELL ROSIE	wbk b Moneypoint Coal-Springwell Amie Jul-91	2	7	100	573	7-Oct
SQUIRE DELTA	bd d Easy And Slow-Squire Jenny Apr-90	10	26	920	615	26-Aug
STAGE FRIGHT	be d Daleys Gold-Tiny Tolcas Oct-91	2	14	250	438	20-Sep
STAGECRAFT	wf d Aulton Slippy-Motos Dream Mar-90	6	16	850	585	21-May
STAPLERS JO	wbk d Dempsey Duke-Perfect Rhythm Jun-93	1	2	0	500	19-Dec
STAR ABBEY	bk d Waltham Abbey-Donaskeigh Star Dec-92	1	2	150	640	20-Oct

A-Z STATISTICS

Greyhound		W	R	£	Ave D	Last Win
STAR BLAST	bk d Flag Star-Fast Blast Aug-92	2	3	300	666	1-Dec
STAR GIRL	bd b Ballyard Hoffman-Star Approach Oct-91	7	26	700	688	31-Aug
STAR OF TYRONE	dkbd d Leaders Best-Aldens Support Aug-91	11	22	1,580	482	16-Nov
STAR SPIRIT	bd b Manx Treasure Star Approach Feb-93	1	3	75	460	12-Nov
STARLIGHT DREAM	bd d Brownies Outlook-Starlight Dancer Aug-92	4	15	480	333	25-Nov
START AFRESH	f d Airmount Grand-Blue Seskin ar-93	2	4	50	495	7-Nov
STAY GOING	b b Murlens Hawk-Neat Dish dec-92	2	14	2,050	480	19-Nov
STAY ON SHERRY	wbd b Whisper Wishes-Catsrock Hope Feb-92	1	10	75	659	26-Nov
STEADY MAJOR	bk d Manorville Major-Always Steady Feb-91	4	14	355	464	5-Mar
STEP OUT LADY	f b Aulton Slippy-Hi Me Lady Feb-91	1	4	100	259	13-Aug
STOCK ORDER	bk d Ravage Again-Leyland Bride Jul-92	3	6	300	400	23-Dec
STOP AT NOTHING	bd d Murlens Slippy-Jennys Orphan Mar-93	1	3	100	420	7-Dec
STORMY DRIFTER	bd d Kyle Jack-Stormy Sabrina Feb-91	1	5	75	375	24-Aug
STOUKE TANIA	wbk b Darragh Commet-Stouke Pet Apr-91	9	15	890	588	6-Dec
STOWAWAY MAGIC	bd d Im Slippy-Winsor Way Oct-91	6	11	110	380	29-Apr
STRADBALLY COVE	bkw d Moneypoint Coal-Emmas Whisper Jan-92	1	7	100	400	11-Nov
STRANGER PASSING	wbd b Skelligs Tiger-Always Grumbling Apr-92	2	7	220	685	12-Jul
STRAUSS	bdw d Lodge Prince-Maid Of Knock Mar-93	1	3	100	450	6-Dec
STRAWS FLASH	wbd d Fly Cruiser-Ardnalee Anne Nov-91	5	11	500	456	12-Apr
STRETCH YOURSELF	bd d Hot Sauce Yankee-All For Who Apr-90	2	12	275	500	22-Apr
STYLEFIELD GEM	wf d Castlelyons Gem-Avongate Tico Sep-91	2	7	150	462	19-Oct
STYLEFIELD LAW	bd d Darragh Commet-Shenick Lady May-91	4	19	425	485	12-Jul
SUBTLE SAM	f d Leading Flight-Quarrymount Hays May-91	4	12	775	480	2-Dec
SUMMER CHOICE	f b Greenpark Fox-Manx Violet Dec-90	2	13	400	545	7-Jun
SUNCREST SAIL	bebd d Low Sail-Sarahs Surprise Aug-92	4	7	355	562	1-Oct
SUNDOWN	bk d Flashy Sir -Skimmer Aug-92	1	4	150	278	8-Sep
SUNGLEN DOLLAR	bd b Satharn Beo-Ardrine Fluff Jun-92	5	12	605	612	14-Dec
SUNHILL MISTY	bd b Kyle Jack-Game Misty Oct-91	10	24	4,000	840	24-Sep
SUNKLEEP	bd d Flashy Sir-Skimmer Aug-92	1	10	100	460	29-Aug
SUNNYSIDE HAVOC	bk b Westmead Havoc-Sunnyside Bess Mar-92	4	7	425	615	3-Dec
SUNNYSIDE IMP	bk b Glencorbry Call -Nickies Pal Jan-91	1	13	150	484	24-Feb
SUNSHINE EVE	bk b Curryhills Fox-Lindas Pleasure Feb-90	5	8	375	230	18-Nov
SUNSHINE SANDY	f d Druids Lodge-Angie A Railer Jan-90	4	14	425	488	25-Nov
SUPER BLASTER	bd d Manorville Major-Turtulla Rose May-90	4	21	405	485	22-Jul
SUPER BRIDGE	bd d Adraville Bridge-Anhid Cross Mar-92	14	31	2,725	460	25-Aug
SUPER COOPER	wbk b Randy-Im A Cooper Feb-90	3	15	400	804	12-May
SUPER DOMINEE	wbk d Summerhill Super-Westmead Dominee Jun-92	1	8	50	460	6-Dec
SUPER FAGAN	bk d Glenpark Dancer-Alsa Nikita Jun-91	1	6	125	420	4-May
SUPER SPY	f d Super Mecca-Bluefield Spy Sep-91	4	34	310	471	16-Aug
SUPERSONIC DUKE	wbk d Dempsey Duke-Top Lady Dec-92	1	2	100	465	17-Nov
SURE AND CERTAIN	bd d Carmels Prince-Debs Tick Oct-92	1	9	100	420	5-Sep
SURE FANTASY	bk d Phantom Flash-Lively Spark Sep-90	10	22	1,925	494	22-Nov
SURGE AGAIN	wf d Surge Home-Cee Cee Girl Aug-90	1	2	200	438	27-Jul
SWALE BANDIT	bd d Double Bid-Odell Heather Feb-92	5	26	500	417	29-Jul
SWEDISH BELLE	f b Skelligs Tiger-Bold Belle Apr-92	1	3	200	484	3-Mar
SWIFT HILL	be d Summerhill Gem-Swift Lucy Sep-91	1	5	100	275	15-Apr
SWINDLING TOFF	bk d Manorville Magic-Cute Pigeon Jul-91	2	14	220	799	4-Mar
TABLE GLOBE	bd d Milltown Crest-Birdthistle Dame Sep-91	3	13	840	472	6-Jun
TAILORED HAVOC	bkw b Westmead Havoc-Tailor Blackie Mar-92	1	5	100	610	9-Sep
TAILORS NOEL	bk d Ballinderry Ash-Tailors Rush Jun-92	1	3	80	270	6-Oct
TAIN FLIP	f b Manorville Magic-Tain Bua Oct-92	1	3	100	827	29-Oct
TAKE A CHANCE	bk d Tapwatcher-Muls Return Jul-92	1	6	85	440	17-Feb
TAKE A FLYER	bd d Moral Support-Highway Manor Mar-92	5	18	475	682	12-Nov
TAKE IT HOME	bef d Hello Blackie-Home Mardi Sep-91	2	5	200	255	26-Jan
TALLYHO ACTION	f b Greenpark Fox-Burnpark Wish Apr-92	2	13	315	687	12-May
TALLYHO ATOM	fw b Dukes Lodge-Burnpark Wish Jun-91	1	7	100	660	3-Nov
TAMMYS DELIGHT	wbk b Waltham -AbbeyLulus Moth May-91	5	16	6,420	784	15-Jul

A-Z STATISTICS

Greyhound		W	R	£	Ave D	Last
TAMPA BAY	wbk b Wise Band-Malin Duff Jun-92	3	15	340	540	10-Sep
TANNAGHMORE	bk b Glencorbry Celt-Still Knight Jun-90	2	10	220	645	8-Feb
TARTAN TED	bd d Leaders Best-Picket Jan-91	1	11	100	575	10-Jun
TATANKA	bk d Arrow House-Flying Object May-92	1	4	150	278	1-Dec
TATTENHAM CORNER	bd d Guiding Hope-Allglaze Alva Jul-91	2	14	265	440	26-Dec
TAWNY FLASH	bk d Lartigue Note-Flashy Fiona Mar-92	7	17	2,050	333	22-Oct
TAWNY HARP	wbd b Kildare Ash-Tawny Fun Dec-92	2	9	150	298	24-Oct
TELEMATIC SLIPPY	wbd b Murlens Slippy-Sheffield Spirit Nov-91	5	21	490	530	2-Dec
TELFORD BOY	f d Penny Less-Fawn Music Jan-91	7	19	1,665	481	15-Nov
TELL THE YARN	fbd d lm Slippy-Duchess Of Erin Aug-91	9	33	2,320	687	24-Dec
TEMPLE WOOD	bk d Aghadown Timmy-Lyons Club Jan-93	1	13	200	460	19-Nov
TERESAS COLLAR	f b Greenpark Fox-Manx Chick May-92	1	5	250	484	14-Apr
TERRYDRUM BLUE	f d Glenpark Dancer-Farloe Mineola Apr-91	11	29	970	475	25-Nov
TERRYDRUM EMMA	bd b Double Bid-Im Ugly Nov-91	2	10	200	480	20-May
TERRYDRUM GLEN	bk d Leaders Best-Glenbrien Jazz Jan-93	4	13	770	632	26-Nov
THE GREAT GONZO	wbd d Flashy Sir -Move Over Bess Jun-91	6	22	950	672	19-Sep
THE HUSTLER	bd d Cutcutin-Ballybeg Crystal Sep-91	2	11	150	673	22-Sep
THE OTHER NUMBER	bk d Arran Court Duke-Green As Metro Feb-91	1	1	100	375	17-Dec
THERMOS	b d Skelligs Tiger-Summer Flower Feb-92	4	11	1,225	494	21-May
THOMPSON BLUE	be d Live Contender-Thompson Black Oct-91	1	7	100	255	5-Jan
THREE OF US	bd d Greenpark Fox-Babsies Girlie Oct-92	4	8	430	318	16-Nov
TICKLE TARTAN	wbd d Im Slippy-Moygara Kiwi Jan-91	2	13	300	475	28-May
TICOS LODGE	bd d Druids Lodge-Ticos Pet Nov-91	4	14	380	448	23-Jun
TIGER KHAN	bd d Ballybrack Manor-Seefin Lass Aug-92	1	7	100	260	23-Nov
TIGER WARRIOR	f d Round The Bend-Tigers Bridge May-90	2	12	250	475	30-Jun
TIMELESS PRAGADA	bd d Penny Less-Tracton Dawn Mar-92	3	12	150	480	8-Nov
TINAS CLAIM	bk b Westmead Claim-Black Tina Mar-92	1	5	115	692	8-Dec
TINAS DEPOSIT	bd b Kildare Ash-Cheerful Deposit Jun-91	10	30	1,335	715	9-Nov
TINTOWN ROCKY	f d Druids Johno-Fine Trade Aug-92	1	4	75	440	21-Oct
TIP THE TRIP	f d Satharn Beo-Yellow Riband Sep-92	2	12	190	492	20-Sep
TIPSY MINSTREL	wbd d Curryhills Gara-Come On Siggi Aug-91	1	10	100	465	18-Aug
TOBACCO ROAD	wbk d Rikasso Nippy-Gabriel Countess Jul-91	1	5	75	509	19-Jan
TOBY TWO NICKS	f d Bucks Blast-Torbal Blonde Jun-91	2	24	75	370	24-Nov
TOKEN BID	wbd d Double Bid -Cathys Air Oct-92	1	8	100	440	10-Sep
TOMBRICK LIKA	bkw b Rockmount Toff-Lika Rip May-91	5	22	575	606	29-Oct
TOMMYS PRIDE	bd b Slaneyside Hare-Sandras Pride Mar-92	1	1	85	440	28-Jul
TOMS CABIN KING	f d Surge Home-Timmies One Apr-91	6	23	2,375	555	18-Aug
TOMS LODGE	bk d Druids Lodge-Grannys Black Apr-91	1	2	75	290	29-Mar
TONDUFF CHOICE	bd d Greenpark Fox-Ballymullen Rose Aug-90	3	10	300	400	20-May
TOP IT ALL	be b lm Slippy-I Know You Feb-92	1	1	100	480	21-Jan
TORBAL KELLY	bd d Dutch Delight-Can Be Fun Oct-91	2	9	170	440	21-Apr
TORNAROY COPPER	f d Penny Less -Artoo Detoo Jun-91	8	21	1,405	466	6-Oct
TORRENT EXPRESS	bd d Make History-Spring Season Nov-92	1	9	200	484	7-Apr
TOUCH AGAIN	f d Ravage Again-Westmead Kara Jun-92	4	19	2,000	495	12-Aug
TOUCH OF JOY	f b Westmead Havoc-Kilelton Joy Nov-91	1	7	200	580	6-Apr
TOYBOX SCHOONER	bd d Odell Schooner -Pond Jemima Oct-91	10	31	2,475	490	8-Nov
TRACYS FLASH	f d Phantom Flash-Gate Pusher Apr-92	1	3	125	484	3-Feb
TRADE AMBASSADOR	fbd d Greenpark Fox -Trade Gold Nov-92	2	9	120	482	15-Nov
TRADE EXCHANGE	bd d Greenpark Fox-Trade Gold Nov-92	7	16	3,110	467	28-Oct
TRAMORE ASH	bebd b Kildare Ash-Locket Lisa Jun-92	2	10	150	605	16-May
TRANS DOMINO	bk b Dukes Lodge-Trans Linda Jun-90	2	15	200	563	27-Oct
TRAVELLING MAID	bdw b Arrow House-Parkswood Magpie May-92	1	2	175	260	24-Mar
TRICK SHOT	bd d Manx Marajax-Kevalnig Kite Dec-92	1	2	100	460	24-Sep
TROMORA MAYOR	bebd d Manorville Major-Born To Race Feb-91	10	23	1,350	540	14-Jul
TUBERCURRY SAM	bk d Skelligs Tiger- Classiebawn Rose Mar-91	1	11	100	250	19-Apr
TUFTON BEAU	f d Fearless Action-Tufton Lady Sep-91	1	3	200	590	15-Dec
TULLERBOY LADY	dkbd b Alpine Minister-Tullerboy Kate Jun-92	1	5	120	714	20-Aug

NGRC Greyhound Racing Yearbook 1995

A-Z STATISTICS

Greyhound		W	R	£	Ave D	Last Win
TULLIG BANK	wbd d lm Slippy-Tullig Patsey Nov-91	2	4	100	278	30-Jun
TULLIG MOUSE	f b Phantom Flash-Tullig Rosie Apr-92	2	15	260	555	4-Aug
TULLIG PHANTOM	bk d Phantom Flash-Tullig Rosie Apr-92	1	6	100	480	25-May
TULLIG ZAFONIC	bd d Greenpark Fox-Tullig Patsey Sep-92	2	5	90	474	19-Nov
TURTLEMOON	f d Curryhills Ron -Anna Maria Mar-92	1	9	50	555	5-Sep
TURTULLA FLIGHT	bk d Lyons Dean -Sadras Flight Feb-92	2	6	200	275	20-May
TWIN RAINBOW	wbk b Flag Star-No Way Jose May-92	4	16	375	645	7-Nov
TWIST CARD	wbd d Satharn Beo-No Thanks Jul-91	4	11	1,050	553	28-Jul
TYLERS CRYSTAL	bd b Greenpark Fox-Fort Leader May-92	1	10	150	630	19-Oct
TYRIAN BLUE	wbe d Additional Work-Daleys Pet Nov-91	2	6	230	484	1-Jun
UBIQUITOUS	bk d Glencorbry Celt-Dirty Pet May-90	2	8	200	620	12-May
ULTIMATE BOY	bk d Hygard-Bangor Whirl Jan-93	1	3	120	440	18-Nov
UNCLE KATO	be d Live Contender-April Dancer Oct-92	1	8	120	460	30-Aug
UNIQUE BAY	wf d Castlelyons Gem-Kenmare Bay Apr-91	14	35	4,470	499	12-Nov
UNIQUE SLIPPY	wbk d Murlens Slippy-Ego Trip Oct-92	2	9	175	438	29-Jul
UNLIKELY	bebd b Tapwatcher-Maninga Multibet May-90	1	9	125	640	2-Jun
UNWANTED COINS	bk b Captain Villa-Miles To Go May-90	1	2	150	640	10-Feb
UP AND OFF	fw d lm Slippy-Cheerful Beauty Mar-91	1	13	100	400	4-Feb
UP THE JUNCTION	bd d Slippys Quest-Elf Arrow Feb-92	3	6	375	480	11-Jun
URGENT MEETING	wbe b Daleys Gold-Coragh Lady Jan-92	9	27	940	414	28-Oct
VAN DIE QUEEN	bebd d Deenside Spark dougs Suzie Jul-91	7	16	610	456	29-Nov
VANCOUVER ROY	bd d Kildare Ash -Carrick Express Jan-91	7	25	750	554	29-Oct
VEGAS LIGHTS	bebd d Manorville Major-Kingdom Star Apr-91	1	10	50	490	21-Mar
VELVET SPARK	wf d Murlens Hawk-Bee Spark Oct-92	1	17	115	484	22-Jun
VICS QUEST	wf d lm Slippy-Vics Snowdrop Apr-92	1	9	100	260	7-Oct
VITAL RETURN	bk d Concentration-Footpath Aug-92	2	9	150	400	17-Oct
WACHOVIA ACE	be bd d Citizen Comet-Wee Sheena Apr-93	1	2	75	545	19-Oct
WANGOLA	wbd d Carters Lad-Fair Damsel Aug-91	1	4	75	440	25-Nov
WANT TO BE	bk d Early Vocation-Bower Bee Apr-92	1	10	100	484	1-Feb
WATCH ME VIC	bk d Tapwatcher-Punters Pocket May-92	2	6	370	484	21-Apr
WATERSHIP DOWN	wbdd Tune In-Banstead Lady Sep-92	1	3	85	440	18-Aug
WATH BLUBELL	bew b Ballygalda Glory-Wath Duchess Oct-92	5	12	600	621	7-Dec
WATH BRACKEN	be d Ballygalda Glory-Wath Duchess Oct-92	1	6	500	462	17-Jun
WATH LILY	wbe b Ballygalda Glory-Wath Duchess Oct-92	1	5	100	450	21-Sep
WAY UP SLIPPY	bk d lm Slippy -Way Up Wish Jan-93	1	8	75	450	19-Oct
WEAVE MCGREGOR	bk b Manorville Magic -Cute Pigeon Jul-91	6	20	1,250	858	10-Sep
WELFARE AMBER	bdw d Lodge Princ-Niamhs Gold Sep-92	1	24	75	375	15-Aug
WELFARE DIAMOND	bdw d lm Slippy-Welfare Lady May-92	1	12	120	714	7-Jul
WELFARE JADE	bk b Balalika-Springwell Suzie May-92	1	15	75	220	2-Nov
WELFARE PANTHER	bk d Balalika-Sappys Susie Jan-93	4	15	2,800	445	9-Dec
WELL DONE DAME	bk d Glenpark Dancer- Jills Pearl Apr-91	1	4	125	420	6-Jun
WELLARD GAMBLE	wbd d lm Slippy-Special Gamble Apr-92	1	9	100	450	27-Jan
WELLPAD FAIRY	f d Macs Lock-Roe Fairy Apr-92	1	11	100	500	10-Jan
WELSH WIZARD	f d Westmead Havoc-Fortune Princess Mar-92	7	36	2,025	475	25-Nov
WESTLAKE WONDER	bd d Aulton Slippy-Bronogue Motto Mar-92	4	19	1,335	471	20-Dec
WESTMEAD CHICK	bd b lm Slippy-Westmead Move Jan-92	17	33	21,010	489	17-Dec
WESTMEAD DASH	bk d Right Move-Westmead Chloe Aug-92	1	7	90	475	10-May
WESTMEAD FLIGHT	bk b Flashy Sir-Westmead Kim Mar-92	2	11	300	555	17-Sep
WESTMEAD FORCE	bk d Slaneyside Hare-Just Flash Mar-93	1	5	50	440	14-Nov
WESTMEAD HAZZARD	bd d lm Slippy-Westmead Move Jan-92	1	14	100	480	11-May
WESTMEAD JACK	bd d Murlens Slippy -Westmead Hannah Sep-92	3	20	225	481	5-Oct
WESTMEAD MADAM	bk b Right Move-Westmead Chloe Aug-92	2	16	185	530	30-May
WESTMEAD MERLIN	bd d Murlens Slippy-Westmead Hannah Sep-92	13	27	11,060	483	6-Dec
WESTMEAD MYSTIC	bk b lm Slippy-Westmead Move Jan-92	1	17	50	474	5-Oct
WESTMEAD ODD	bd d lm Slippy-Westmead Move Jan-92	3	11	370	415	8-Sep
WESTMEAD PADDY	bk d Airmount Grand-Westmead Move Sep-90	11	33	1,315	619	15-Dec
WESTMEAD SAYURI	bk b Aussie Flye-Just Flash Aug-92	1	2	120	845	8-Nov

A-Z STATISTICS

Greyhound	W	R	£	Ave D	Last
WESTMEAD SUNNY wbk d Im Slippy-Westmead Chloe Jan-92	5	14	500	266	15-Aug
WESTMEAD SUPRISE bk d Daleys Gold-Westmead Move Jan-90	5	12	570	687	26-Apr
WESTPARK PRIVATE bd d Manorville Major-Westpark Salamm Oct-91	1	4	50	575	22-Aug
WEXFORD MINX bd b Manorville Major-Ballarue Suzy Aug-91	17	33	11,450	623	26-Dec
WHAT BRIDGE bk d Adraville Bridge-Soviet Supreme Jun-92	2	7	255	500	29-Sep
WHERE WITHALL wbd b Quare Rocket -Floweasy Jo May-92	1	2	0	480	8-Nov
WHERES DUNAIT bebd b Carters Lad-Nells Mink Feb-90	2	9	375	933	26-Mar
WHISPERING ROSE wbd b Murlens Slippy-Elegant Dream May-92	6	19	680	659	15-Oct
WHITE DEREEN w b Dereen Star-Right Opinion Dec-91	2	10	150	700	28-Jun
WHITE INK wbd d Alpine Minister-California Blue Jul-92	5	15	495	481	16-Nov
WHITE WELL wf d Daleys Gold-Castlemary Druid Nov-92	1	5	200	460	15-Dec
WHOS MINNIE bd b Tipi Tip-Greenfield Madam Aug-92	4	12	560	626	17-Oct
WHOS RODNEY wbd d Randy-Rhincrew Moth May-92	5	16	490	494	7-Oct
WHOS SARAH wbk b Waltham Abbey-Dellatoe Wonder Mar-92	1	4	120	714	24-Jan
WHY JOSEPH bkw d Whisper Wishes-Why You Lady Jun-90	2	2	200	450	13-Dec
WILLIAM PET bd d Aulton Villa-Abbeycourty Duke Sep-91	3	12	225	697	12-Jul
WILLIAMS GLEN bd d Im Slippy-Tiger Hart Jul-90	1	5	100	465	12-Apr
WIND ISSUE bd d Never Issued-Aquaduct Wind May-93	1	9	50	500	1-Nov
WINDS OF AUTUMN wbk b Airmount Grand-Cleos Society May-90	1	5	110	540	30-May
WINDY wbk b Randy-Yellow Soda Feb-92	2	15	260	590	19-Sep
WINDY SPARK bd b Randy-City News Apr-92	1	13	110	540	15-Jan
WINETAVERN CELT bk b Ardfert Sean-Pamar Celt Jul-92	5	15	590	803	23-Dec
WINGHOUSE LODGE bdw d Slaneyside Hare-Wing House Lane Jan-93	3	17	1,125	458	4-Nov
WINSOR ABBEY bd d Waltham Abbey-Miss Fussy Jun-90	1	4	100	575	7-Jan
WINSOR DAN bk d My Tallyho Two-Winsor Aird Feb-92	4	22	450	403	18-Jul
WINSOR DREAM wbk d Whisper Wishes-Dream Impulse May-91	1	17	150	484	10-Feb
WINSOR GROVE bkw d Murlens Slippy-Millies Wish Aug-90	1	2	250	490	10-Jan
WINSOR NIKITA fw d Im Slippy-Winsor Aird Aug-92	1	8	100	400	27-May
WINSOR SALAM bd d Manorville Major-Westpark Salamm Oct-91	2	12	150	545	16-May
WINSOR SQUAW wbk d Whisper Wit-Wyoming Squaw May-90	2	3	270	472	28-Jan
WISE MOVE wbd d Im Slippy-Mixed Up Lady Sep-90	2	12	160	450	15-Aug
WITCHES BILLY wbk d Hit The Lights-Normas Leracro Aug-91	1	14	125	575	9-Dec
WITCHES DEAN bk d Lyons Dean-Witches Betty Feb-92	16	35	4,370	396	5-Dec
WITCHITA WONDER bd b Manorville Major-Nice Class Oct-90	1	2	150	655	21-May
WITTON STAR bd d Macs Lock-Pond Juliet Apr-92	8	19	2,455	500	25-Nov
WOLF MAN bk d Slaneyside Hare-Clongeel Liz Jul-92	3	16	5,050	465	5-Oct
WON BIG DEAL bd d Im Slippy-Special Gamble Apr-92	2	11	100	455	26-Jul
WOODFORD SARA f b Kyle Jack-Sahara Whisper May-91	1	8	200	484	21-Apr
WOODFORD SEAN fw d Ardfert Sean-Blackroad Lady Nov-91	5	25	500	555	11-Aug
WOODLAND ASH wbd d Kildare Ash-Landino Jul-92	1	1	100	465	1-Sep
WOODLAND SATHARN bd d Satharn Beo-Manorville Rose Jan-92	1	7	50	500	9-Dec
WOODVIEW BRANDY wbk d Randy-Forever Fresh Feb-91	1	10	125	490	20-Jun
WRESTIN TIME bk d Dempseys Whisper-Chiltern Meg Apr-92	2	8	200	620	2-May
WRETTON ACE bk d Curryhills Specl-Far Gone Oct-92	1	7	75	440	16-Sep
WRETTON PACE bk d Curryhills Specl-Far Gone Oct-92	1	12	75	480	12-Aug
WYN SOUTHEASTERN wbd d Phantom Flash-Dunasbuig Laura May-92	2	8	180	452	7-Mar
YACHT SAIL bd b Satharn Beo-Sand Melody Jun-91	1	7	200	685	24-Mar
YASMINS LUCK bd b Tapwatcher-To Manor Born Nov-92	1	1	100	450	20-Jun
YASOO VATOU bkw b Fair Boot-Lisieux May-92	1	4	125	640	5-Nov
YES SUPER be bd b Skelligs Tiger-Pick One You Aug-92	1	2	200	241	3-Sep
YOU LEAD bk d Aghadown Timmy-Leaders Blue Jul-91	4	9	350	263	18-Apr
YOUNG DOMINGO f d Placid Son-Peniarth Sand May-90	1	9	100	792	25-Mar
YOUNG TADGH bk d Darragh Commet-Mercy Lass Dec-92	2	4	215	492	9-Jul
YOUR EXACT bk d Easy And Slow-Meadowbank Pool Sep-89	4	12	350	596	3-Mar
YOUR RIGHT BENNY f d Ardfert Sean-Bann Queen May-92	5	20	550	341	8-Sep
ZAP wbk d Murlens Slippy-Synone Crest Aug-90	1	8	225	850	4-Apr

NGRC Greyhound Racing Yearbook 1995

NGRC Calendar

Race Dates 1995

Key: (H) Hurdles event. (B) Bitches only. (P) Puppies only. Br (British-bred greyhounds only.

Races shown in **BOLD CAPITALS** are Category 1 events.
Races shown in CAPITALS are Category 2 events.
All other races are Category 3 events.

Published by the National Greyhound Racing Club Limited, 24-28 Oval Road, London, NW1 7DA.

January

Monday	2	Romford TONY WILLIAMS CORONATION CUP (HEATS) (575m)
		Walthamstow Jim Davis Stakes (Heats) (640m)
		Romford Gerry Allen New Year Stayers Stakes Final (750m) (£1,500)
		Wembley William Hill New Year Trophy (Heats) (710m)
Friday	6	Romford TONY WILLIAMS CORONATION CUP (SEMI-FINALS) (575m)
		Wembley William Hill New Year Trophy Final (710m) (£1,590)
Saturday	7	Walthamstow Jim Davis Stakes Final (640m) (£2,715)
Monday	9	Hackney **EMBASSY GOLD CUP** (1st rd heats) (825m)
Tuesday	10	Canterbury P Harbour Bookmakers Dual Distance Trophy (Heats) (480m)
Friday	13	Romford TONY WILLIAMS CORONATION CUP FINAL (575m) (£4,000)
		Canterbury P Harbour Dual Distance Trophy Final (675m) (£1,000)
Saturday	14	Wimbledon FOSTERS GOLD CUP (HEATS) (660m)
Monday	16	Hackney **EMBASSY GOLD CUP** (2nd rd HEATS) (825m)
Tuesday	17	Wimbledon FOSTERS GOLD CUP (SEMI-FINALS) (660m)
		Sheffield Sunday Funday Five Hundred (Heats) (500m)
Thursday	19	Brough Park REGAL NORTHUMBERLAND GOLD CUP (HEATS) (480m)
Saturday	21	Wimbledon FOSTERS GOLD CUP FINAL (660m) (£5,890)
Sunday	22	Sheffield Sunday Funday Five Hundred Final (500m) (£1,000)
Monday	23	Hackney **EMBASSY GOLD CUP** (SEMI-FINALS) (825m)
		Ramsgate A P Amusements New Year Hurdle (Heats) (450m) (H)

Race Dates

		Romford Don James Memorial Hurdle (Heats) (400m) (H)
Tuesday	24	**Brough Park** REGAL NORTHUMBERLAND GOLD CUP (SEMI-FINALS) (480m)
		Canterbury K B Racing Bookmakers Cup (Heats)(480m)
Thursday	26	**Ramsgate** A P Amusements New Year Hurdle Final (450m) (H) (£1,000)
Friday	27	**Canterbury** K B Racing Bookmakers Cup Final (480m) (£1,000)
Saturday	28	**Hackney EMBASSY GOLD CUP FINAL** (825m) (£10,000)
		Brough Park REGAL NORTHUMBERLAND GOLD CUP FINAL (480m) (£4,150)
		Romford Don James Memorial Hurdle Final (400m) (H) (£1,000)
Monday	30	**Hackney** A R DENNIS MIDDLE PARK (HEATS) (484m)
		Catford William Hill Cup (Heats) (555m)
		Nottingham Know Something Stakes (Heats) (500m)
Tuesday	31	**Walthamstow** PEPSI COLA MARATHON (HEATS) (820m)

February

Wedn'dy	1	**Hackney** A R DENNIS MIDDLE PARK (SEMI-FINALS) (484m)
Thursday	2	**Nottingham** Know Something Stakes Final (500m) (£1,390)
Saturday	4	**Catford** William Hill Cup Final (555m) (£2,770)
Monday	6	**Crayford** Rose Bowl (Heats) (380m)
Tuesday	7	**Walthamstow** PEPSI COLA MARATHON (SEMI-FINALS) (820m)
		Canterbury M Duncan Bookmakers Cup (Heats) (480m) (H)
Wedn'dy	8	**Sunderland REGAL TEN THOUSAND** (HEATS) (450m)
Thursday	9	**Monmore Green** John Russell Staffordshire Knot (Heats) (484m)
Friday	10	**Canterbury** M Duncan Bookmakers Cup Final (480m) (H) (£1,000)
Saturday	11	**Sunderland REGAL TEN THOUSAND** (SEMI-FINALS) (450m)
		Wimbledon JOHN HENWOOD SPRINGBOK TROPHY (HEATS) (460m) (H)
		Walthamstow PEPSI COLA MARATHON FINAL (820m) (£4,120)
		Hackney A R DENNIS MIDDLE PARK FINAL (484m) (£4,000)
		Crayford Rose Bowl Final (380m) (£1,500)
		Monmore Green John Russell Staffordshire Knot (Final) (484m) (£1,500)
Monday	13	**Crayford LADBROKE GOLDEN JACKET** (HEATS) (714m)
		Romford George Marler Trophy (Heats) (575m)
Tuesday	14	**Wimbledon** JOHN HENWOOD SPRINGBOK TROPHFULL PAGEFY (SEMI-FINALS) (460m) (H)

NGRC Greyhound Racing Yearbook 1995   **163**

Race Dates

Friday	17	**Sheffield** Great Yorkshire Chase (Heats) (500m) (H) **Romford** George Marler Trophy Final (575m) (£1,500) **Sheffield** Gt Yorkshire Chase Final (500m) (H) (£1,000)
Saturday	18	**Sunderland REGAL TEN THOUSAND** FINAL (450m) (£15,100) **Crayford LADBROKE GOLDEN JACKET** (SEMI-FINALS) (714m) **Wimbledon** JOHN HENWOOD SPRINGBOK TROPHY FINAL (460m) (H) (£4,775)
Monday	20	**Wembley** Douglas Stuart Coronation Stakes (Heats) (850m)
Tuesday	21	**Walthamstow RACING POST ARC** (1st rd HEATS) (475m) **Canterbury** Keki Bookmakers Cup (Heats) (675m)
Friday	24	**Canterbury** Keki Bookmakers Cup Final (£1,000) **Wembley** Douglas Stuart Coronation Stakes Final (850m) (£1,475)
Saturday	25	**Crayford LADBROKE GOLDEN JACKET** FINAL (714m) (£11,000) **Walthamstow RACING POST ARC** (2nd rd HEATS) (475m)
Tuesday	28	**Walthamstow RACING POST ARC** (SEMI-FINALS) (475m) **Powderhall** SCOTTISH OAKS (HEATS) (465m) (B)

March

Friday	3	**Wimbledon** W J & J E CEARNS MEMORIAL TROPHY (HEATS) (660m)
Saturday	4	**Walthamstow RACING POST ARC** FINAL (475m) (£10,030) **Powderhall** SCOTTISH OAKS (SEMI-FINALS) (465m) (B)
Tuesday	7	**Wimbledon** W J & J E CEARNS MEMORIAL TROPHY (SEMI-FINALS) (660m) **Belle Vue** Gorton Cup (Heats) (460m) **Sheffield** March Hare Stirrup Cup (Heats) (660m) **Canterbury** P Harbour Bookmakers Cup Heats) (480m)
Friday	10	**Sheffield** March Hare Stirrup Cup Final (660m) (£1,000) **Canterbury** P Harbour Bookmakers Cup Final (480m)
Saturday	11	**Powderhall** SCOTTISH OAKS FINAL (465m) (B) (£5,000) **Wimbledon** W J & J E CEARNS MEMORIAL TROPHY FINAL (660m) (£4,375) **Belle Vue** Gorton Cup Final (460m) (£1,900)
Sunday	12	**Monmore Green** CARLING BLACK LABEL MIDLAND PUPPY DERBY (HEATS) (484m) (P)
Monday	13	**Romford** Coral Marathon (Heats) (750m)
Tuesday	14	**Oxford PALL MALL** (1st rd HEATS) (450m)
Thursday	16	**Monmore Green** CARLING BLACK LABEL MIDLAND PUPPY DERBY (SEMI-FINALS) (484m)

Race Dates

Friday	**17**	Romford Coral Marathon Final (750m) (£1,880)
Saturday	**18**	Oxford **PALL MALL** (2nd ROUND HEATS) (450m)
		Hall Green **DAILY MIRROR /SPORTING LIFE GRAND NATIONAL** (1st rd HEATS) (474m) (H)
Sunday	**19**	Monmore Green CARLING BLACK LABEL MIDLAND PUPPY DERBY FINAL (484m)(£4,000)
		Walthamstow Willis Builder Stakes (Heats) (475m)
		Walthamstow Polypipe Stakes (Heats) 640m)
Tuesday	**21**	Oxford **PALL MALL** (SEMI-FINALS) (450m)
		Canterbury K B Racing Bookmakers Trophy (Heats) (480m) (H)
Wednesday	**22**	Hall Green **DAILY MIRROR /SPORTING LIFE GRAND NATIONAL** (2nd rd HEATS) (474m) (H)
Friday	**24**	Canterbury K B Racing Bookmakers Cup Final (480m) (H) (£1,000)
Saturday	**25**	Oxford **PALL MALL** FINAL (450m) (£10,000)
		Hall Green **DAILY MIRROR /SPORTING LIFE GRAND NATIONAL** (SEMI-FINALS) (474m) (H)
		Walthamstow Willis Builder Stakes Final (475m) (£1,630)
		Walthamstow Polypipe Stakes Final (640m) (£1,630)
Monday	**27**	Wembley **WENDY FAIR BLUE RIBAND** (1st rd HEATS) (490m)
		Romford R Magnus Trophy (Heats) (575m)
Tuesday	**28**	Wimbledon Spring Cup (Heats) (660m)
Wednesday	**29**	Hall Green **DAILY MIRROR/SPORTING LIFE GRAND NATIONAL** FINAL (474m) (H) (£10,000)
Friday	**31**	Wembley **WENDY FAIR BLUE RIBAND** (2nd rd HEATS) (490m)
		Sheffield WILLIAM HILL STEEL CITY CUP (HEATS) (500m)
		Romford R Magnus Trophy Final (575m) (£1,500)

April

Saturday	**1**	Wimbledon Spring Cup Final (660m) (£1,250)
Monday	**3**	Wembley **WENDY FAIR BLUE RIBAND** (SEMI-FINALS) (490m)
		Hackney **JOHN POWER GYMCRACK PUPPY STAKES** (HEATS) (440m) (P)
		Crayford Spring Trophy (Heats) (714m)
Tuesda	**4**	Sheffield WILLIAM HILL STEEL CITY CUP (SEMI-FINALS) (500m)
		Shawfield Spring Cup (Heats) (480m)
		Canterbury M Duncan Bookmakers Dual Distance Trophy (Heats) (480m)
Friday	**7**	Wembley **WENDY FAIR BLUE RIBAND** FINAL (490m) (£12,400)
		Hackney **JOHN POWER GYMCRACK PUPPY STAKES** (SEMI-FINALS) (440m) (P)
		Sheffield WILLIAM HILL STEEL CITY CUP FINAL (500m) (£4,000)
		Canterbury M Duncan Bookmakers Dual Distance Trophy Final (675m) (£1,000)
Saturday	**8**	Walthamstow N G R C STEWARDS CUP (HEATS)

Race Dates

		Shawfield Spring Cup Final (480m) (£2,000)
		Crayford Spring Trophy Final (£1,000)
Monday	10	Romford J Magnus Trophy (Heats) (575m)
Tuesday	11	Walthamstow N G R C STEWARDS CUP (SEMI-FINALS) (640m)
Friday	14	Good Friday No Race Meetings
Saturday	15	Hackney **JOHN POWER GYMCRACK PUPPY STAKES** FINAL (440m) (P) (£10,000)
		Walthamstow N G R C STEWARDS CUP FINAL (640m) (£4,090)
		Romford J Magnus Trophy Final (575m) (£1,500)
Monday	17	Catford E COOMES GREENWICH CUP (HEATS) (555m)
		Peterborough WAFCOL PUPPY DERBY (HEATS) (420m) (P)
Tuesday	18	Reading **READING MASTERS** (1st rd HEATS) (465m)
Friday	21	Reading **READING MASTERS** (2nd rd HEATS) (465m)
Saturday	22	Catford E COOMES GREENWICH CUP (SEMI-FINALS) (555m)
		Peterborough WAFCOL PUPPY DERBY (SEMI-FINALS) (420m) (P)
Tuesday	25	Reading **READING MASTERS** (SEMI-FINALS) (465m)
Saturday	29	Reading **READING MASTERS** FINAL (465m) (£30,000)
		Catford E COOMES GREENWICH CUP FINAL (555m) (£5,080)
		Peterborough WAFCOL PUPPY DERBY FINAL (420m) (P) (£4,000)

May

Tuesday	2	Belle Vue Northern Oaks (Heats) (460m) (B)
		Sheffield May Puppy Cup (Heats) (500m) (P)
Thursday	4	Ramsgate Master Brewer Trophy (Heats) (590m)
Friday	5	Sheffield May Puppy Cup Final (500m) (P) (£1,000)
Saturday	6	Walthamstow MISTLEY TROJAN PUPPY STAKES (HEATS) (475m) (P)
		Belle Vue Northern Oaks Final (460m) (B) (£1,900)
Monday	8	Romford Quicksilver Stakes (Heats) (400m)
Tuesday	9	Shawfield **REGAL SCOTTISH GREYHOUND DERBY** (HEATS) (500m)
		Walthamstow MISTLEY TROJAN PUPPY STAKES (SEMI-FINALS) (475m) (P)
		Brighton COURAGE GREYHOUND OLYMPIC (HEATS) (515m)
Thursday	11	Ramsgate Master Brewer Trophy Final (590m) (£3,050)
		Bristol 57th Golden Crest (Heats)(460m)
		Monmore Green Midland Classic Potential (Heats) (484m)
Friday	12	Romford Quicksilver Stakes Final (400m) (£3,000)
Saturday	13	Shawfield **REGAL SCOTTISH GREYHOUND**

Race Dates

		DERBY (SEMI-FINALS) (500m)
		Brighton COURAGE GREYHOUND OLYMPIC (SEMI-FINALS) (515m)
		Walthamstow MISTLEY TROJAN PUPPY STAKES FINAL (475m) (P) (£4,010)
		Bristol 57th Golden Crest Final (460m) (£2,350)
		Monmore Green Midland Classic Potential Final (484m) (£1,750)
Monday	15	Peterborough JOHN SMITH BITTER CESAREWITCH (HEATS) (605m)
Wednesday	17	Hall Green John Smiths Bitter Midlands Oaks (Heats) (474m) (B)
Thursday	18	Brighton COURAGE GREYHOUND OLYMPIC FINAL (515m) (£5,600)
		Catford Bookmakers Hurdles (Heats) (385m) (H)
Saturday	20	Shawfield **REGAL SCOTTISH GREYHOUND DERBY** FINAL (500m) (£20,000)
		Peterborough JOHN SMITH BITTER CESAREWITCH (SEMI-FINALS) (605m)
		Hall Green John Smiths Bitter Midlands Oaks Final (474m) (B) (£2,500)
Monday	22	Romford B Edwards Trophy (Heats) (575m)
		Swindon Pride Of The West (Heats) 685m
Tuesday	23	Wimbledon **DAILY MIRROR /SPORTING LIFE GREYHOUND DERBY** (1st rd HEATS) (480m)
Thursday	25	Catford Bookmakers Hurdles Final (383m) (H) (£3,100)
Friday	26	Wimbledon **DAILY MIRROR! SPORTING LIFE GREYHOUND DERBY** (1st rd HEATS) (480m)
		Romford B Edwards Trophy Final (575m) (£1,500)
		Swindon Pride Of The West Final (685m) (£1,000)
Saturday	27	Wimbledon **DAILY MIRROR /SPORTING LIFE GREYHOUND DERBY** (1st rd HEATS) (480m)
		Peterborough JOHN SMITH BITTER CESAREWITCH FINAL (605m) (£4,000)
		Bristol 49th TWO-YEAR-OLD PRODUCE STAKES (1st rd HEATS) (460m)
Monday	29	Crayford Wafcol Kent Puppy Cup (Heats) (380m) (P)
Tuesday	30	Walthamstow CARLING BLACK LABEL TEST (HEATS) (640m)

June

Thursday	1	Bristol 49th TWO-YEAR-OLD PRODUCE STAKES (2nd rd HEATS) (460m)
Friday	2	Wimbledon **DAILY MIRROR /SPORTING LIFE GREYHOUND DERBY** (2nd rd HEATS) (480m)
Saturday	3	Wimbledon **DAILY MIRROR/SPORTING LIFE GREYHOUND DERBY** (2nd rd HEATS) (480m)
		Walthamstow CARLING BLACK LABEL TEST (SEMI-FINALS) (640m)
		Bristol 49th TWO-YEAR-OLD PRODUCE STAKES (SEMI-FINALS) (460m)
		Crayford Wafcol Kent Puppy Cup Final (380m) (P) (£1,330)

Race Dates

Thursday	8	Walthamstow CARLING BLACK LABEL TEST FINAL (640m) (£4,390)
Friday	9	Walthamstow A R Dennis Hurdle (Heats) (475m) (H)
Saturday	10	Wimbledon **DAILY MIRROR/SPORTING LIFE GREYHOUND DERBY** (3rd rd HEATS) (480m)
		Bristol 49th TWO-YEAR-OLD PRODUCE STAKES FINAL (460m) (£4,000)
Tuesday	13	Wimbledon **DAILY MIRROR/SPORTING LIFE GREYHOUND DERBY** (Qtr-finals) (480m)
		Brighton THE REGENCY (HEATS) (740m)
		Sheffield Northern Sprint Championship (Heats) (290m)
Friday	16	Walthamstow A R Dennis Hurdle Final (475m) (H) (£2,190)
		Sheffield Northern Sprint Championship Final (290m) (£1,000)
Saturday	17	Wimbledon **DAILY MIRROR/SPORTING LIFE GREYHOUND DERBY** (SEMI-FINALS) (480m)
		Brighton THE REGENCY (SEMI-FINALS) (740m)
Tuesday	20	Wimbledon Champion Hurdle (Heats) (460m) (H)
Thursday	22	Brighton THE REGENCY FINAL (740m) (£8,450)
Saturday	24	Wimbledon **DAILY MIRROR/SPORTING LIFE GREYHOUND DERBY** FINAL (480m) (£50,000)
		Wimbledon Champion Hurdle Final (460m) (H) (£2,100)
Monday	26	Monmore Green **LADBROKE GOLD CUP** (HEATS) (484m)
		Peterborough Evening Telegraph Grand National (Heats) (420m) (H)
Tuesday	27	Shawfield Puppy Cup (Heats) (480m) (P)
		Brighton Brighton Belle (Heats) (515m) (B)
Wednesday	28	Hackney EMBASSY IMPERIAL CUP (HEATS) (640m)
Thursday	29	Catford COURAGE BEST BITTER SCURRY GOLD CUP (HEATS)
Friday	30	Monmore Green **LADBROKE GOLD CUP** (SEMI-FINALS) (484m)
		Hackney EMBASSY IMPERIAL CUP (SEMI-FINALS) (640m)

July

Saturday	1	Catford COURAGE BEST BITTER SCURRY GOLD CUP (SEMI-FINALS) (385m)
		Shawfield Puppy Cup Final (480m) (P) (£2,000)
		Brighton Brighton Belle Final (515m) (B) (£1,940)
		Crayford Ladbroke Hurdle (Heats) (540m) (H)
		Peterborough Evening Telegraph Grand National Final (420m) (H) (£1,000)
Monday	3	Crayford JULY CUP (HEATS) (714m)
Wednesday	5	Hackney EMBASSY IMPERIAL CUP FINAL (640m) (£4,000)
Thursday	6	Crayford Ladbroke Hurdle Final (540m) (H) (£1,530)
Friday	7	Monmore Green **LADBROKE GOLD CUP** FINAL

Race Dates

	(484m) (£10,000)
Saturday 8	Catford COURAGE BEST BITTER SCURRY GOLD CUP FINAL (385m) (£4,820)
	Crayford JULY CUP (SEMI-FINALS) (714m)
	Monmore Green CHOICE FURNITURE MIDLAND St.LEGER (HEATS) (647m)
Monday 10	Romford **CHAMPION STAKES** (1st rd HEATS) (575m)
Tuesday 11	Wimbledon **WEY PLASTICS/TONY STANTON MEMORIAL** (1st rd HEATS) (480m)
	Sheffield The Ebor (Heats) (750m)
Thursday 13	Crayford JULY CUP FINAL (714m) (£4,000)
	Monmore Green CHOICE FURNITURE MIDLAND St.LEGER (SEMI-FINALS) (647m)
Friday 14	Romford **CHAMPION STAKES** (2nd rd HEATS) (575m)
	Sheffield The Ebor Final (740m) (£1,000)
Saturday 15	Wimbledon **WEY PLASTICS/TONY STANTON MEMORIAL** (2nd rd HEATS) (480m)
	Monmore Green CHOICE FURNITURE MIDLAND St.LEGER FINAL (647m) (£4,000)
Tuesday 18	Wimbledon **WEY PLASTICS/TONY STANTON MEMORIAL** (SEMI-FINALS) (480m)
Wednesday 19	Romford **CHAMPION STAKES** (SEMI-FINALS) (575m)
Thursday 20	Ramsgate KENT St.LEGER (HEATS)
Saturday 22	Romford **CHAMPION STAKES** FINAL (575m) (£13,560)
	Wimbledon **WEY PLASTICS/TONY STANTON MEMORIAL** FINAL (480m) (£12,200)
Monday 24	Peterborough **Q8 PETERBOROUGH GREYHOUND DERBY** (1st rd HEATS) (420m)
	Ramsgate KENT St.LEGER (SEMI- FINALS) (640m)
Tuesday 25	Oxford OXFORDSHIRE GOLD CUP (HEATS) (450m)
	Brighton SUSSEX CUP (HEATS) (515m)
Friday 28	Peterborough **Q8 PETERBOROUGH GREYHOUND DERBY** (2nd rd HEATS) (420m)
Saturday 29	Ramsgate KENT St.LEGER FINAL (640m) (£6,350)
	Crayford BASS GUYS & DOLLS (HEATS) (380m)
	Brighton SUSSEX CUP (SEMI-FINALS) (51 Sm)
Monday 31	Peterborough **Q8 PETERBOROUGH GREYHOUND DERBY** (SEMI-FINALS) (420m)

August

Tuesday 1	Walthamstow A R DENNIS SILVER COLLAR (HEATS) (640m)
	Oxford OXFORDSHIRE GOLD CUP (SEMI-FINALS) (450m)
	Wimbledon WILLIAM HILL LONG DISTANCE HURDLE (HEATS) (660m) (H)
	Shawfield St.Mungo Cup (Heats) (500m)
Thursday 3	Crayford BASS GUYS & DOLLS (SEMI-FINALS) (380m)
	Brighton SUSSEX CUP FINAL (515m) (£4,000)
Friday 4	Sheffield WILLIAM STONES SILVER COLLAR

Race Dates

Saturday 5	(HEATS) (500m) Peterborough **Q8 PETERBOROUGH GREYHOUND DERBY** FINAL (420m) (£10,000) Oxford OXFORDSHIRE GOLD CUP FINAL (450m) (£5,080) Crayford BASS GUYS & DOLLS FINAL (380m) (£4,580) Wimbledon WILLIAM HILL LONG DISTANCE HURDLE (FINAL) (660m) (H) (£4,220) Bristol Ernest Thornton Smith Trophy Heats) (855m) Shawfield St.Mungo Cup Final (500m) (£2,000)
Sunday 6	Walthamstow A R DENNIS SILVER COLLAR (SEMI-FINALS) (640m)
Tuesday 8	Sheffield WILLIAM STONES SILVER COLLAR (SEMI-FINALS) (500m) Brighton Sussex Puppy Trophy (Heats) (515m) (P)
Wednesday 9	Hackney **FLEETFOOT FUTURITY CHAMPIONSHIP** (HEATS) (484m)
Thursday 10	Bristol Ernest Thornton Smith Trophy Final (855m) (£2,350) Walthamstow O'Gorman Hurdles (Heats) (475m) (H)
Friday 11	Sheffield WILLIAM STONES SILVER COLLAR FINAL (500m) (£4,000)
Saturday 12	Hackney **FLEETFOOT FUTURITY CHAMPIONSHIP** (SEMI-FINALS) (484m) Walthamstow A R DENNIS SILVER COLLAR (FINAL) (640m) (£5,860) Brighton Sussex Puppy Trophy Final (515m) (P) (£1,250)
Monday 14	Hackney **FLEETFOOT FUTURITY CHAMPIONSHIP** FINAL (484m) (£10,000) Hackney HENDERSONS FESTIVAL MARATHON (HEATS) (865m) Yarmouth Wafcol East Anglian Challenge (Heats) (462m)
Tuesday 15	Shawfield William King Cup (Heats) (670m) Perry Barr Ladbrokes 1,000 Guineas Stakes (Heats) (500m)
Wednesday 16	Hall Green WILLIAM HILL MIDLAND SPRINGBOK (HEATS) (474m) (H) Yarmouth Wafcol East Anglian Challenge Final (462m) (£1,300)
Thursday 17	Nottingham **COLDSEAL PUPPY CLASSIC** (HEATS) (500m) (P) Milton Keynes SUMMER CUP (HEATS) (620m) Walthamstow O'Gorman Hurdles Final (475m) (H) (£1,630)
Saturday 19	Milton Keynes SUMMER CUP (SEMI-FINALS) (620m) Hackney HENDERSONS FESTIVAL MARATHON (SEMI-FINALS) (865m) Hall Green WILLIAM HILL MIDLAND SPRINGBOK (SEMI-FINALS) (474m) (H) Shawfield William King Cup Final (670m) (£2,000) Perry Barr Ladbrokes 1,000 Guineas Stakes Final (500m) (£1,940)

Race Dates

Monday	21	Nottingham **COLDSEAL PUPPY CLASSIC** (SEMI-FINALS) (500m) (P)
		Romford **STADIUM BOOKMAKERS ESSEX VASE** (1st rd HEATS) (575m)
		Crayford Peter Regan Memorial Stakes (Heats) (714m)
		Romford Steve Simmons Stakes (Heats) (750m)
Wednesday	23	Hall Green **WILLIAM HILL MIDLAND SPRINGBOK** FINAL (474m) (H) (£4,000)
Thursday	24	Milton Keynes SUMMER CUP FINAL (620m) (£4,045)
		Crayford Peter Regan Memorial Stakes Final (714m) (£1,500)
Friday	25	Romford **STADIUM BOOKMAKERS ESSEX VASE** (2nd rd HEATS) (575m)
		Romford Steve Simmons Stakes Final (750m)
Saturday	26	Powderhall **EDINBURGH CUP** (HEATS) (465m)
		Walthamstow TETLEY YORKSHIRE BITTER CIRCUIT (HEATS) (475m)
		Hackney HENDERSONS FESTIVAL MARATHON FINAL (865m) (£4,000)
Monday	28	Nottingham **COLDSEAL PUPPY CLASSIC** FINAL (500m) (P) (£12,375)
Tuesday	29	Powderhall **EDINBURGH CUP** (SEMI-FINALS) (465m)
		Walthamstow TETLEY YORKSHIRE BITTER CIRCUIT (SEMI-FINALS) (475m)
		Brighton National Hurdle (Heats) (515m) (H)
Wednesday	30	Romford **STADIUM BOOKMAKERS ESSEX VASE** (SEMI-FINALS) (575m)

September

Saturday	2	Powderhall **EDINBURGH CUP** FINAL (465m) (£12,000)
		Romford **STADIUM BOOKMAKERS ESSEX VASE** FINAL (575m) (£10,050)
		Walthamstow TETLEY YORKSHIRE BITTER CIRCUIT FINAL (475m) (£5,040)
		Brighton National Hurdle Final (515m) (H) (£1,950)
Wednesday	6	Yarmouth 49th **EAST ANGLIAN GREYHOUND DERBY** (1st rd HEATS) (462m)
Thursday	7	Walthamstow RON BAZELL PUPPY STAKES (HEATS) (475m) (P)
		Bristol Con John Trophy (Heats) (665m)
		Shawfield Daily Record Marathon (932m) (£1,500)
Friday	8	Sheffield Harry Holmes Memorial Trophy (Heats) (500m)
Saturday	9	Yarmouth 49th **EAST ANGLIAN GREYHOUND DERBY** (2nd rd HEATS) (462m)
		Bristol Con John Trophy Final (665m) (£2,350)
Monday	11	Catford **JOHN HUMPHREYS GOLD COLLAR** (1st rd HEATS) (555m)
		Yarmouth 49th **EAST ANGLIAN GREYHOUND DERBY** (SEMI-FINALS) (462m)
		Swindon Arkells Silver Plume (Heats) (476m)

NGRC Greyhound Racing Yearbook 1995

Race Dates

Tuesday	12	Belle Vue **COURAGE CESAREWITCH** (1st rd HEATS) (855m)
		Walthamstow RON BAZELL PUPPY STAKES (SEMI-FINALS) (475m) (P)
Wednesday	13	Swindon Arkells Silver Plume Final (476m) (£1,000)
		Yarmouth Pepsi Cola Sprint (Heats) 277m
Thursday	14	Yarmouth **49th EAST ANGLIAN GREYHOUND DERBY** FINAL (462m) (£11,500)
		Ramsgate JOHN BULL THANET GOLD CUP (HEATS) (450m)
Friday	15	Sheffield Harry Holmes Memorial Trophy Final (500m) (£2,000)
Saturday	16	Belle Vue **COURAGE CESAREWITCH** (2nd rd HEATS) (855m)
		Catford **JOHN HUMPHREYS GOLD COLLAR** (2nd rd HEATS) (555m)
		Walthamstow RON BAZELL PUPPY STAKES FINAL (475m) (P) (£4,010)
		Yarmouth Pepsi Cola Sprint Final (277m) (£625)
Monday	18	Catford **JOHN HUMPHREYS GOLD COLLAR** (SEMI-FINALS) (555m)
		Ramsgate JOHN BULL THANETGOLD CUP (SEMI-FINALS) (450m)
		Catford John Humphreys Diamond Stakes (Heats) (718m)
		Catford John Humphreys Platinum Hurdle (Heats) (385m) (H)
Tuesday	19	Perry Barr **ANSELLS BIRMINGHAM CUP** (HEATS)(500m)
Friday	22	Belle Vue **COURAGE CESAREWITCH** (SEMI-FINALS) (855m)
		Wimbledon PUPPY DERBY (HEATS)(460m) (P)
Saturday	23	Catford **JOHN HUMPHREYS GOLD COLLAR** FINAL (555m) (£12,440)
		Perry Barr **ANSELLS BIRMINGHAM CUP** (SEMI-FINALS) (500m)
		Ramsgate JOHN BULL THANET GOLD CUP FINAL (450m) (£5,165)
		Catford John Humphreys Diamond Stakes Final (718m) (£1,070)
		Catford John Humphreys Platinum Hurdle Final (385m) (H) (£1,000)
Monday	25	Crayford BASS VASE (HEATS)(540m)
		Romford Joe Magnus Rose Bowl (Heats) (575m)
		Peterborough Middle Eastern plc Marathon (Heats) (790m)
Tuesday	26	Walthamstow **LAURENT PERRIER CHAMPAGNE GRAND PRIX** (1st rd HEATS) (640m)
		Wimbledon PUPPY DERBY (SEMI-FINALS) (460m) (P)
Thursday	28	Perry Barr **ANSELLS BIRMINGHAM CUP** FINAL (500m) (£10,400)
		Crayford BASS VASE (SEMI-FINALS) (540m)
Friday	29	Wimbledon PUPPY DERBY FINAL (460m) (P) (£7,450)

Race Dates

Saturday	30	**Romford** Joe Magnus Rose Bowl Final (575m) Belle Vue **COURAGE CESAREWITCH** FINAL (855m) (£13,600) **Walthamstow** LAURENT PERRIER CHAMPAGNE GRAND PRIX (2nd ROUND HEATS) (640m) **Peterborough** Middle Eastern plc Marathon Final (790m) (£1,000)

October

Monday	2	**Crayford** BASS VASE FINAL (540m) (£5,080)
Tuesday	3	**Wimbledon IKE MORRIS LAURELS** (1st rd HEATS) (460m) **Walthamstow LAURENT PERRIER CHAMPAGNE GRAND PRIX** (SEMI-FINALS) (640m)
Wednesday 4		**Hall Green BREEDERS FORUM PRODUCE STAKES** (1st rd HEATS) (474m) **Peterborough** ALAN SPEECHLEY FENGATE COLLAR (HEATS) (420m)
Friday	6	**Sheffield** Yorkshire Oaks (Heats) (500m) (B)
Saturday	7	**Wimbledon IKE MORRIS LAURELS** (2nd rd HEATS) (460m) **Walthamstow LAURENT PERRIER CHAMPAGNE GRAND PRIX** (FINAL) (640m) (£12,450) **Hall Green BREEDERS FORUM PRODUCE STAKES** (2nd rd HEATS) (474m)
Monday	9	**Peterborough** ALAN SPEECHLEY FENGATE COLLAR (SEMI-FINALS) (420m) **Wembley** Arthur Stanley Trafalgar Challenge Cup (Heats) (490m) (P)
Tuesday	10	**Wimbledon IKE MORRIS LAURELS** (SEMI-FINALS) (460m) **Shawfield** Autumn Cup (Heats) (480m)
Wednesday 11		**Hall Green BREEDERS FORUM PRODUCE STAKES** (SEMI-FINALS) (474m)
Friday	13	**Peterborough** ALAN SPEECHLEY FENGATE COLLAR FINAL (420m) (£4,000) **Sheffield** Yorkshire Oaks Final (500m)(B) (£2,000) **Wembley** Arthur Stanley Trafalgar Challenge Cup Final (490m) (P) (£1,725)
Saturday	14	**Wimbledon IKE MORRIS LAURELS** FINAL (460m) (£12,920) **Hall Green BREEDERS FORUM PRODUCE STAKES** FINAL (474m) (£10,000) **Shawfield** Autumn Cup Final (480m) (£2,000)
Monday	16	**Nottingham PETER DERRICK ECLIPSE STAKES** (HEATS) (500m) **Romford** CORAL GOLDEN SPRINT (HEATS) (400m) **Romford** Stadium Bookmakers Mercury Trophy (Heats) (750m)
Tuesday	17	**Walthamstow** Douglas Tyler Dual Distance (Heats) (475m)
Wednesday 18		**Sunderland MAILCOM PUPPY DERBY** (HEATS) (450m) (P)
Friday	20	**Romford** CORAL GOLDEN SPRINT (SEMI-FINALS)

Race Dates

          (400m)
          Romford Stadium Bookmakers Mercury Trophy Final (750m) (£1,500)

Saturday 21 Sunderland **MAILCOM PUPPY DERBY** (SEMI-FINALS) (450m) (P)
          Walthamstow Douglas Tyler Dual Distance Final (640m) (£1,630)

Monday 23 Nottingham **PETER DERRICK ECLIPSE STAKES** (SEMI-FINALS) (500m)
          Crayford Crayford Marathon Stakes (Heats) (874m)
          Nottingham Keith Tomlin Puppy Trophy (Heats) (500m) (P)
          Nottingham Steve Charlesworth Stayers Trophy (Heats) (700m)

Tuesday 24 Oxford Oxfordshire Trophy (Heats) (450m)
Thursday 26 Nottingham Bill Bright Sprint Trophy (Heats) (310m)
Friday 27 Romford CORAL GOLDEN SPRINT FINAL (400m)
Saturday 28 Nottingham **PETER DERRICK ECLIPSE STAKES** FINAL (500m) (£12,050)
          Sunderland **MAILCOM PUPPY DERBY** FINAL (450m) (P) (£12,000)
          Crayford Crayford Marathon Stakes Final (874m) (£1,500)
          Oxford Oxfordshire Trophy Final (450m) (£1,270)
          Nottingham Keith Tomlin Puppy Trophy Final (500m) (P) (£1,250)
          Nottingham Bill Bright Sprint Trophy Final (310m) (£1,250)
          Nottingham Steve Charlesworth Stayers Trophy Final (700m) (£1,250)

Tuesday 31 Belle Vue NORTHERN FLAT CHAMPIONSHIP (HEATS) (460m)
          Powderhall SCOTTISH PUPPY CHAMPIONSHIP (HEATS) (465m) (P)
          Sheffield Autumn Puppy Cup (Heats) (500m) (P)

November

Friday 3 Sheffield Autumn Puppy Cup Final (500m) (P) (£1,000)
          Wembley Fosters Select Stakes (490m) (£3,950)

Saturday 4 Belle Vue NORTHERN FLAT CHAMPIONSHIP (SEMI-FINALS) (460m)
          Powderhall SCOTTISH PUPPY CHAMPIONSHIP (SEMI-FINALS) (465m) (P)

Monday 6 Wembley **WENDY FAIR GREYHOUND St. LEGER** (1st rd HEATS) (655m)

Tuesday 7 Hackney **A R DENNIS GUINEAS** (HEATS) (484m)
Friday 10 Wembley **WENDY FAIR GREYHOUND St. LEGER** (2nd rd HEATS) (655m)

Saturday 11 Hackney **A R DENNIS GUINEAS** (SEMI-FINALS) (484m)
          Belle Vue NORTHERN FLAT CHAMPIONSHIP FINAL (460m) (£5,025)
          Powderhall SCOTTISH PUPPY CHAMPIONSHIP FINAL (465m) (P) (£5,000)

Race Dates

Monday	13	Wembley **WENDY FAIR GREYHOUND St. LEGER** (SEMI-FINALS) (655m)
		Wembley Joseph Magnus Marathon (Heats) (850m)
		Wembley Tony Morris Challenge Cup (Heats) (490m)
		Wembley Interent Empire Hurdles (Heats) (490m) (H)
Tuesday	14	Wimbledon Puppy Oaks (Heats) (460m) (P)
Thursday	16	Catford William Hill First For Services Stayers Stakes (Heats) (718m)
Friday	17	Wembley **WENDY FAIR GREYHOUND St. LEGER** FINAL (655m) (£14,900)
		Wembley Joseph Magnus Marathon Final (850m) (£1,475)
		Wembley Tony Morris Challenge Cup Final (490m) (£1,100)
		Wembley Interent Empire Hurdles Final (490m) (H) (£1,100)
Saturday	18	Hackney **A R DENNIS GUINEAS** FINAL (484m) (£10,000)
		Hall Green FOSTERS MIDLAND FLAT CHAMPIONSHIP (HEATS) (474m)
		Wimbledon Puppy Oaks Final (460m)(P) (£2,750)
		Walthamstow Goodwood Cup (Heats)(475m)
Monday	20	Romford Triumph Hurdle (Heats) (575m) (H)
Tuesday	21	Brough Park ALL ENGLAND CUP (HEATS) (480m)
		Walthamstow Goodwood Cup Final (475m) (£2,715)
		Belle Vue Cock O'The North (Heats) (645m)
Wednesday	22	Hall Green FOSTERS MIDLAND FLAT CHAMPIONSHIP (SEMI-FINALS) (474m)
Thursday	23	Catford William Hill First For Services Stayers Stakes Final (718m) (£3,100)
Friday	24	Romford Triumph Hurdle Final (575m) (H) (£2,800)
Saturday	25	Hall Green FOSTERS MIDLAND FLAT CHAMPIONSHIP FINAL (474m) (£7,190)
		Brough Park ALL ENGLAND CUP (SEMI-FINALS) (480m)
		Belle Vue Cock O'The North Final (645m) (£1,900)
Monday	27	Romford PUPPY CUP (HEATS) (400m) (P)
Tuesday	28	Wimbledon Courage Key (Heats) (868m)
Thursday	30	Brough Park ALL ENGLAND CUP FINAL (480m) (£7,500)

December

Friday	1	Romford PUPPY CUP (SEMI-FINALS) (400m) (P)
Saturday	2	Wimbledon Courage Key Final (868m) (£2,375)
Monday	4	Wembley Spillers Winalot Puppy Cup (Heats) (490m) (P)
Tuesday	5	Wimbledon **SUNDAY MARKET OAKS** (1st rd HEATS) (480m) (B)
Thursday	7	Walthamstow Holt Marathon (Heats) (820m)
Friday	8	Romford PUPPY CUP FINAL (400m) (P) (£4,550)
		Wembley Spillers Winalot Puppy Cup Final (490m) (P) (£2,700)
		Sheffield Christmas Cup (Heats) (500m)
Saturday	9	Wimbledon **SUNDAY MARKET OAKS** (2nd rd HEATS) (480m) (B)

NGRC Greyhound Racing Yearbook 1995

Race Dates

Tuesday	12	Wimbledon **SUNDAY MARKET OAKS** (SEMI-FINALS (480m) (B)
Thursday	14	Belle Vue Manchester Puppy Cup (Heats) (460m) (P) Walthamstow Holt Marathon (Final)(820m) (£2,765)
Friday	15	Sheffield Christmas Cup (Final) (500m)(£2,000)
Saturday	16	Wimbledon **SUNDAY MARKET OAKS** FINAL (480m) (B) (£12,000) Belle Vue Manchester Puppy Cup Final (460m) (P) (£1,900)
Monday	18	Nottingham Peter Derrick Christmas Cracker (Heats) (310m) Catford Ray Dean Boxing DayMarathon (Heats) (718m) Catford Dean Bookmakers Boxing Day Trophy (Heats) (555m)
Tuesday	19	Wimbledon Schweppes Xmas Vase (Heats) (460m) (H)
Thursday	21	Milton Keynes Christmas Cracker Stakes (Heats) (440m)
Saturday	23	Nottingham Peter Derrick Christmas Cracker Final (310m) (£2,950) Wimbledon Schweppes Xmas Vase Final (460m) (H) (£2,500)
Monday	25	Christmas Day - No Race Meetings
Tuesday	26	Catford Ray Dean Boxing Day Marathon Final (718m) (£2,200) Milton Keynes Christmas Cracker Stakes Final (440m) (£1,680) Wimbledon Dell Nash Surrey Cup(Heats) (660m) Catford Dean Bookmakers Boxing DayTrophy Final (555m) (£1,100)
Wednesday	27	Romford Gerry Allen New Years Stayers Stakes (Heats) (750m)
Saturday	30	Wimbledon Dell Nash Surrey Cup Final (660m) (£2,500)

January 1996

Monday	1	Romford Gerry Allen New Years Stayers Stakes Final (750m) (£1,500)

MEET ME HALFWAY

(GAME BALL) x (DROOPY'S FIRST)
White/Black 82lbs

**T.R. Holder
Shelbourne Park**
360yds – 19.19

**Former National
T.R. Holder**
550yds – 29.80

**Winner Cork
Marts Puppy,**
beating
Summerhill
Super, 5 lgths

**Broke 29 secs 3
times at Cork**

THIS DOG IS OUTSTANDING IN EVERY RESPECT

Also the brilliant
PENNY LESS
(Murlens Slippy) x (Penny More)
Brindle 75lbs

Ran 19 times, won 14, second 3, 2 unplaced due to injury. He has consistently thrown open class puppies with early pace and staying power. His success ratio is second to none – check him out in *In The Blood*.

Both dogs £200 – free return to missing bitches.
**Contact Peter Onslow, Sanfield,
626 Leyland Lane, Leyland, Lancs**

**Tel: Day – 0772 627262 Evngs – 0772 434834
Mobile – 0831 272435**

OPEN RACE Statistics

Comparative times at Open Race circuits

Compiled by **Clive Lawrence**

THE FOLLOWING times compare the 'standard' Open Race time that you would expect a good class dog to record.

For example a dog that has clocked 27.80 over 460m at Wimbledon should, given a clear run, be able to complete the 480m trip at Sheffield in 28.70.

Different styles of running would suit certain tracks and not others but these timings below are designed to give you an idea of the relative merits of open race dogs that you may be seeing for the first time.

NB. Not all distances are stated due to the rarity of open races over certain trips.

Track								
BELLE VUE	250	14.50	460	28.20	645	40.20	855	55.50
BRISTOL	270	16.30	460	28.00	665	41.50	855	54.70
BROUGH PARK	290	17.50	480	29.00	500	30.50	640	39.40
	670	42.60	825	53.00				
CANTERBURY	275	16.60	480	29.50	675	42.10	880	56.80
CATFORD	385	23.60	555	34.90	718	46.50		
CRADLEY HEATH	231	14.60	272	16.00	462	28.40	647	40.80
	875	56.90						
CRAYFORD	380	23.70	540	34.20	714	45.90	874	57.40
HACKNEY	260	15.80	440	27.20	484	29.30	640	40.80
	825	53.50						
HALL GREEN	259	15.60	474	28.70	663	41.30	815	52.90
HENLOW	318	19.00	484	29.40	680	43.60	730	45.00
	890	57.50						
HOVE	285	16.70	515	30.50	695	41.70	740	45.00
HULL	290	17.70	460	28.80	490	30.20	655	41.60
MIDDLESBORO	266	16.50	462	28.60	640	41.00		
MILDENHALL	220	13.50	375	23.40	545	34.30	700	45.20

178   NGRC Greyhound Racing Yearbook 1995

OPEN RACE Statistics

Track								
MILTON KEYNES	245	14.90	440	26.80	620	38.40	815	52.20
MONMORE	277	16.90	484	29.70	647	40.60	692	43.60
	815	52.70						
NOTTINGHAM	310	18.50	460	28.10	500	30.30	700	44.00
	747	47.10						
OXFORD	250	15.30	450	27.20	645	40.10	845	53.90
PERRY BARR	275	16.70	460	28.20	500	30.20	660	41.40
PETERBOROUGH	235	14.50	420	25.80	605	37.80	790	50.70
PORTSMOUTH	256	15.70	438	26.90	610	38.90	792	51.00
POWDERHALL	241	14.70	465	28.00	650	40.60		
RAMSGATE	235	15.10	450	27.30	590	37.40	640	40.00
	855	54.60						
READING	275	16.60	465	28.30	660	41.50	850	54.70
ROMFORD	400	24.30	575	35.80	750	48.00	925	59.70
SHAWFIELD	300	17.70	480	29.90	500	30.30	670	41.50
	730	46.10						
SHEFFIELD	290	17.00	480	28.70	500	29.70	650	39.50
	730	45.20						
STAINFORTH	278	16.60	458	27.50	495	30.00	666	41.40
SUNDERLAND	255	15.80	450	27.50	580	36.60	631	39.70
	827	53.40						
SWAFFHAM	270	16.60	440	27.30	480	29.60	620	39.50
	686	43.50	856	56.00				
SWINDON	280	16.60	476	28.70	509	30.90	685	42.80
	737	44.90						
WALTHAMSTOW	415	25.30	475	28.80	640	39.70	820	51.90
	880	55.80						
WEMBLEY	275	16.30	490	29.20	655	39.80	710	43.50
	850	53.10						
WIMBLEDON	252	15.30	460	27.80	660	41.00	820	51.40
	868	55.10						
YARMOUTH	277	16.90	462	28.10	659	41.40	843	54.40

Jan's Greyhound Gifts

SPECIALIST MAIL ORDER GIFTS FOR THE GREYHOUND OWNER – ENTHUSIAST – STADIA

OUR BROCHURE IS OUR SHOWROOM

SEND NOW FOR YOUR COPY OF THE WORLD'S BEST COLOUR BROCHURE OF GREYHOUND GIFTS, ALL WITH THE GREYHOUND THEME.
FINE ARTS, JEWELLERY, HANDBAGS, STOP WATCHES, PENS, PRINTS, SWEATSHIRTS, MUGS AND MUCH MORE

Jan's Greyhound Gifts

PO Box 280, Rayleigh, Essex SS6 8EZ
Tel: 01268 745280
Fax: 01268 745280

NGRC Directory

Belle Vue

Kirkmanshulme Lane, Gorton, Manchester M18 7BA.
Telephone number: 0161 223 1266. Fax: 0161 2238432

Owner: GRA Group plc.
General Manager: Colin Delaney.
Racing Manager: Ian Travis.
Trainers (attached): R. Andrews, L. Branagh, P. McCombe, N. Saunders, F. Watson, J. Walton, R. Barber, B. Heaton.

Race nights: Tuesday and Thursday (7.26 pm), Saturday (7.26 pm)
Trial sessions: Before racing each night.
Distances: 250m, 460m, 460mH, 460mhcp, 645m, 645mhcp, 855m, 855mhcp.

> ### HOW TO GET THERE
> **BY BUS:** Nos. 210 or 211 from city centre.
> **BY TAXI:** five minutes from BR Piccadilly station or 10 minutes from BR Victoria.
> **BY CAR:** M6, M56 Didsbury turn-off

Grading times:
 460m: 29.60,
 645m: 42 50.
Greyhounds per race: Six.
Surface: All sand.
Type of hare: Outside Bramwich.
Circumference of track: 395m.
Distance to the first bend: 98m.
Width of track: 6m.
Layout of the track and how it runs: An all sand, galloping track with slightly banked bends. A good run to the first bend on all distances except 855m, which has a short run. Open race dogs usually run the track well without the advantage of a trial beforehand.
Usual method of track preparation: The tractor rakes and smooths the track before racing and also after each race. The track is watered the morning and afternoon of each race day and rolled on non-race days.
Winning traps: No specific trap is shown to any advantage.
Major competitions:
 The Northern Flat (460m), £2,000, July.
 The Cesarewitch (855m), £13,600, September.
Graded prize money: Bottom grade £30, top grade £60.
Number of bookmakers: Eight.
Totalisator: Computerised, win, place, forecast, trio.

NGRC Directory

Timing: Automatic timing with display on Totalisator board.
Facilities: Chromatography, vet in attendance, kennels for 100 greyhounds, car park for 350 vehicles, restaurant for 300 covers, five bars, fast food bar, executive suite, covered and glass-fronted stand, video replay.

Track Records

250m	Ravage Again	14.20	19-5-90
460m	Fearless Action	27.50	27-9-86
460mh	Greek Commander	28.60	2-8-94
645m	Aglish Blaze	39.64	16-8-94
815m	Laden Jennie	52.38	15-9-85
855m	Decoy Lynx	54.59	17-6-94

Major Races

WEBSTER'S YORKSHIRE BITTER CESAREWITCH (855m)

1	**SANDOLLAR LOUIE** 10-1	(6)

bk d Manorville Magic-I'm a Survivor Dec 91

2	Decoy Lynx	1-7f	(1)
3	First Defence	8-1	(3)
4	Double Polano	14-1	(5)
5	Lone Rider	33-1	(4)
6	Mossfield Fire	66-1	(2)

55.20 (+60) nk, 1½, 1¼, 3¼, 5¼, Connor, Canterbury

1970 Gleneagle Comedy (Maryville Hi-Her Nibs)
    R. Hookaway   Owlerton   33.25   10-1
1971 Whisper Billy (Crazy Society-My Goodness)
    C. Coyle   Private   33.45   50-1
1972 Weatmead Lane (Clonalvy Pride-Cricket Dance)
    N. Savva   Private   51.65   11-4
1973 Country Maiden (Spectre-Lazy Pet)   F. Baldwin   Perry Barr   52.46   5-2
1974 Westbrook Quinn (Myross Again-Abbey Holly)
    Coulter   Private   52.17   7-2JF
1975 Silver Sceptre (Maryville Hi-Trojan Silver)
    P. Young   Bletchley   52.31   4-1
1976 Moy Summer (Skyhawk-Meronome)   E. Bamford   Belle Vue   51.32   16-1
1977 Montreen (Moordyke Spot-Avondale)   E. Bamford   Belle Vue   51.64   4-6F
1978 Sportland Blue (Baylough Jet-Real Proud)
    H. Crapper   Owlerton   51.20   7-2
1979 Roystons Supreme (Supreme Fun-Greenhill Fairy)
    A. Jackson   Wembley   51.47   7-4

NGRC Directory

1980	Linkside Liquor (Westmead Champ-Derby Liquor)			
	G. Bailey	Yarmouth	51.22	3-1
1981	Kinda Friendly (Friendly Spectre-Angel Eyes)			
	E. Gaskin	Private	52.68	7-4F
1982	Liga Lad (Law Lad-Jims Girl) B. Vass	Private	51.83	6-4JF
1983	Jo's Gamble (Ballydonnell Sam-Fealeside Beauty)			
	J. Fisher	Reading	50.90	5-2
1984	Mobile Bank (Sand Man-Banks Best) G. Gaskin	Private	52.92	7-4F
1985	Scurlogue Champ (Sand Man-Old Rip) G. Drake	Private	54.62	1-3F
1986	Yankee's Shadow (Cosmic Sailor-Kings Lace)			
	G. Curtis	Brighton	54.90	4-7F
1987	Role Of Fame (Sand Man-Cashelmara) A. Hitch	Wimbledon	52.41	1-7F
1988	Proud To Run (Mathews World-Run With Pride)			
	H. While	Canterbury	56.23	7-1
1989	Minnies Siren (Easy And Slow-Fenmians Minnie)			
	K. Linzell	Walth'stow	56.03	6-4F
1990	Carlsberg Champ (Ballyregan Bob-Chocolate Satin)			
	B. Silkman	Private	55.50	5-4 F
1991	Wayzgoose (Manorville Major-Comerah Larch)			
	D. Hawkes	Walth'stow	55.30	20-1
1992	Zap (Murlens Slippy-Synons Crest) Honeyfield	Perry Barr	55.44	12-1
1993	Killenagh Dream (Dads Bank-Killenagh Lady) Lister	Stainforth	55.21	20-1

BELLE VUE

NGRC Directory

Bolton

BOLTON have applied to join the NGRC and hope to start racing under Permit rules once construction of the new kennel block is complete in late April or early May. The switch from Independent to NGRC should be smooth with no break in racing and individuals are invited to apply to the Racing manager for NGRC Permit licenses.

Raikes Park, Manchester Road, Bolton BL3 2RE. Telephone number: 01204 525181 / 01204 529099 (race line). Fax: 01204 387580

Owner: Bolton Greyhound Racing Co Ltd
General manager: Bill Williams.
Racing manager: Peter O'Dowd.

Race nights: Monday, Wednesday and Saturday.
Trial sessions: Before racing Monday and Wednesday evenings and Saturday mornings, 10.30.
Distances: 270m, 450m, 630m and 810m..
Grading times: Yet to be fixed.
Number of greyhounds per race: Five.
Surface: All sand.
Type of hare: Inside Sumner (changing to outside shortly).
Circumference of track: 361m.
Width of track: To be verified.
Graded prizes: Yet to be fixed.

Major competitions
   Guineas (270m), April
   Bolton Derby (450m), August
   St Leger (630m), September.

Number of bookmakers: Eight.
Timing: Omega Hawkeye Photo
Facilities: Restaurant seating 150 diners. Belmont Bar, Hare & Hounds Bar, Paddock Snack Bar..

Track Records

270m	Engers	16.12	11-5-92
450m	Well Lined	27.17	26-7-94
630m	John Henry	39.37	30-10-93

NGRC Directory

Bristol

Stapleton Road, Eastville, Bristol BS5 6NW.
Telephone number: 01272 520683. Fax: 01272 354386

Owner: BS Group plc.
General Manager: Brian Ludgate.
Racing Manager:
David Lawrence.
Trainers (attached)
Mrs J. Dickenson,
Mrs M Millard, G. Kibble,
V. Clapp, P. Wellon, P
Swadden, G. Clapp, A
Rowsell,
P. Ryan, J. Hicks. M. Osborne, A. Kovalev.

> **HOW TO GET THERE**
>
> **BY CAR:** Leave the M32 at junction 2. The track is close by.

Race nights: Saturdays and Thursdays (7.30 pm). BAGS as contracted.
Trial sessions: Tuesdays (10 am).
Distances: 270m, 460m, 620m, 665m, 855m.
Number of greyhounds per race: Six and eight.
Surface: Sand.
Type of hare: Outside Bramwich.
Circumference of track: 394m.
Width of track: 6m.
Layout of the track and how it runs: All sand, slight banking on bends.
Usual method of track preparation: Summer—watering when necessary. Winter— salt when necessary.

Major competitions:
  Golden Crest (470m), May.
  Two-year-old Produce Stakes (470m), May/June.
  Con John Trophy (620m), July
  Ernest Thornton Smith (874m), August.

Graded prize money: Bottom grade £28, top grade £100
Number of bookmakers: Seven.
Totalisator: Computerised win, place, forecast, trio and jackpot.
Timing: Automatic ray timing, split times on four and six bends.
Facilities: Chromatography, vet in attendance, kennels for

NGRC Directory

100 greyhounds, car park for 300 vehicles, restaurant for 90 covers, four bars, refreshment room, glass fronted stand, video replay.
Other activities at the stadium: Friday and Sunday market and retail superstores.

Track Records

270m	**Wheres The Limo**	16.24	19-2-92
460m	**Wolf Man**	27.82	11-6-94
620m	**Airmount Flash**	38.29	15-2-93
665m	**First Name Bart**	41.30	25-9-93
855m	**Decoy Lynx**	53.72	13-8-94
1015m	**Mossfield Scotty**	66.29	15-10-92

Major Races

COURAGE TWO-YEAR-OLD PRODUCE STAKES (470m)

1 **WOLF MAN**   4-5f   (6)
   bk d Slaneyside Hare-Clongeel Jul 92
2 Super Dominee   6-1   (1)
3 See Jays Tiger   7-4   (2)
4 Feltham Donald   16-1   (4)
5 Dast House   16-1   (5)
6 Moscow Morgan   66-1   (3)
   27.92 (+10) 7¼, 2, ½, hd, 5, Pugh, Hall Green.

1970 Peasedown Merang (Peasedown Magic-Maid)
                         Sayer   Bristol   28.22   11-4
1971 Arcon Blue (Ambiguous-Carmen Switch)
                         Mrs E. Baber   Bristol   28.89   7-2
1972 Marton Sarah (Discretions-Marton Jayne)
                         Russell   Private   28.89   6-1
1973 Pile Driver (Ballyseedy Star-Jadeite) Mrs Waldon Private   28.66   4-7 F
1974 Daemonic Gambol (Don't Gambol-Dusk Gambol)
                         McEvoy   Wimbledon   28.52   1-5
1975 Forest Storm (Newdown Heather-Forest Brown)
                         McEvoy   Wimbledon   29.37   10-11
1976 Angel Eyes (Craggs Flier-Morris Magpie)
                         Parker   Harringay   28.63   8-1
1977 Ballybryan Bolt (Westmead Lane-Maggies Heather)
                         McEntyre   Bletchley   28.78   1-3 F
1978 Ricky Q (Myrtown-Rolling Ridge) McEvoy Wimbledon 29.14   Ev F

NGRC Directory

1979 Feldon Squire (Sandispec-Feldon Lady)
Corely Bletchley 28.52 6-4 F
1980 Mr Candy (Sudden Start-Vals Candy) Mrs J.L. Green Swindon 28.45 7-4F
1981 Milo Gem (Carhumore Speech-Ollies Folly)
Markwell Bristol 28.27 5-1
1982 Donnas Dixie (Black Beetle-Bright Parade)
Kibble Bristol 28.54 1-5 F
1983 Balynjohn Lad (Balliniska Band-Phillistine)
Osborne Bristol 28.67 7-4 JF
1984 Ballybeg Steel (Minnesota Miller-Ballybeg Heather)
Mrs Holloway Oxford 28.41 4-6 F
1985 Chiltern Sam (Glenroe Hiker-Tina Monday)
Mrs P. Cope Milton K 28.49 10-11 F
1986 Fulwood Star (Gentle Star-Just Be Fair)
Moffat Whitwood 28.59 3-1
1987 Fearless Ace (Mt Keefe Star-Sarahs Bunny)
de Mulder Oxford 28.11 1-7 F
1988 The Aeroplane (Ron Hardy-Squiffy) de Mulder Norton C 28.58 11-10F
1989 Wiltshire Anne (Supreme Tiger-Berkshire Ann)
Plank Swindon 29.01 7-1
1990 Moscow Magic (Mollifrend Lucky-Moscow Miss)
Coleman Walth'stow 28.94 11-8 F
1991 Batsford Boy (Hit The Lid-Midnight Cassim)
Mann Swindon 28.86 16-1
1992 Ultimate Gamble (Manorville Major-Special Gamble) March, Unn. 27.90 11-4
1993 Cortman Jasper (Flashy Sir-Lonely Bird) Meek Oxford 28.36 4-1

NGRC Directory

Brough Park

The Fossway, Byker, Newcastle NE6 2XJ.
Telephone number: 091-265 8011. Fax: 091-265 1452.

Owner: Brough Park Greyhounds Ltd.
Managing Director: Kevin Wilde.
General Manager: Patricia Hutchinson.
Racing Manager:
Jimmy Nunn and Terry Meynell.
Trainers (attached):
N. Oliver, J. Williams, G. Rooks, R. Elliot, P. Davies, J. Taylor, G. Miller, Y. Bell, G. Calvert, T. Hart, J. Powell, A. Waggott

HOW TO GET THERE

Follow A187 towards Wallsend, from City Centre if travelling via A1, or, if via A19, A187 City Centre.

Race nights: Tuesday and Thursday, (7.30 pm), Saturday (7.20 pm) plus BAGS.
Trial sessions: Before racing.
Distances: 290m, 480m, 640m.
Grading times: 480m: 31.00, 640m: 41.50.
Number of greyhounds per race: Five, six or eight.
Surface: Sand.
Type of hare: Outside Sumner.
Circumference of track: 456m on hare rail, 415m inside.
Distance to the first bend: 90m.
Width of track: 7m.
Layout of the track and how it runs: A good galloping track, but it is a stiff test for a greyhound.
Usual method of preparation: Track watered during summer, salted during winter.

Major competitions:
Regal Northumberland Gold Cup (£5,000) January.
Regal All England Cup ((£5,000) December.

Graded prize money: Bottom grade £32, top grade £60.
Number of bookmakers: Six.
Totalisator: Computerised, win, place, forecast, trio, jackpot.
Timing: Automatic and ray timing.

NGRC Directory

Facilities: Chromatography, vet in attendance, kennels for 94 greyhounds, car park for 600 vehicles, restaurant for 130 covers, four bars, two refreshment rooms, (all facilities recently upgraded), glass-fronted stand, video replay.
Other activities at the stadium: Speedway.

Track Records

290m	**Hows Yer Man**	17.22	2-3-93
480m	**Just Right Melody**	28.72	26-7-94
480mhcp	**Village Star**	29.14	15-9-94
640m	**Stouke Tania**	39.16	19-4-94
640mhcp	**Village Star**	39.50	19-8-94
825m	**Newry Town**	52.02	10-5-94

Major Races

REGAL ALL ENGLAND Cup (480m)

1	**MORAL DIRECTOR**	4-1	(2)

wbd d Double Bid-Moral Shadow May 92

2	Westmead Merlin	6-6f	(4)
3	Just Right Melody	9-2	(5)
4	Carloway Dancer	8-1	(3)
5	Toybox Schooner	16-1	(6)
6	Westmead Jack	14-1	(1)

28.97 (+10) 1½, 2½, ½, 2, ¾, Gibson, Belle Vue

1970 Allied Banker (Greenane Flash-Glenogue)
　　　　　　　　　　　　M.B. Wilson　　Private　　30.64　3-1
1971 Spectre Jockey (Spectre-Jockeys Dream)
　　　　　　　　　　　　D. Power　　Private　　30.54　4-5 F
1972 Bright Tack (Newdown Heather-Annaclaive Queen)
　　　　　　　　　　　　G. Hodson　　White City　30.20　5-2
1973 Fly Dazzler (Kilbeg Kuda-Nualas Lovely)
　　　　　　　　　　　　N. Oliver　　Brough Pk　30.63　7-2
1974 not run
1975 Show Man (Monalee Champion-Crefogue Dancer)
　　　　　　　　　　　　K. Raggatt　　Brough Pk　29.21　4-5 F
1976 Houghton Rip (Spectre-Call Me Swallow)
　　　　　　　　　　　　B. Tompkins　Bletchley　29.93　2-1 F
1977 Prince Hill (Own Pride-Dainty Beauty) J. Kelly　Leeds　29.37　Ev F
1978 Champers Club (Patricias Hope-Ballypierce Girl)
　　　　　　　　　　　　S. Milligan　　Private　　29.30　5-4 F

NGRC Directory

Year	Winner (Sire-Dam)	Trainer	Track	Time	SP
1979	Burniston Jet (Jimsun-Davids Black)	R. Hookaway	Owlerton	29.45	5-1
1980	Jon Barrie (Clashing-Famous Heart)	B. Andrews	Leeds	30.37	5-2
1981	not run				
1982	Long Spell (Downing-Moss Drain)	T. Dartnall	Reading	30.92	4-6 F
1983	Squire Cass (Yellow Ese-Minus)	T. Dartnall	Reading	30.15	11-4
1984	not run				
1985	Moneypoint Coal (Yellow Band-Queens Hotel)	S. Graham	Ireland	30.00	5-4 F
1986	Lavally Oak (I'm Slippy-Lavally Time)	J. Glass	Powderhall	30.39	8-11 F
1987	Killouragh Chris (Moreen Rocket-Moreen Honey)	P Beaumont	Owlerton	30.57	4-5 F
1988	Pond Hurricane (Lindas Champion-Sodapop II)	H. Williams	Brough Pk	30.66	6-4 F
1989	Slippy Blue (I'm Slippy-Valoris)	Linzell	Walth'stow	30.39	11-4 F
1990	Alans Luck (I'm Slippy-Lindas Pleasure)	Andrews	Belle Vue	31.02	4-1
1991	Monaree Tommy (Ninth Wave-Maglass Model)	Copplestone	Portsmouth	30.75	3-1
1992	New Level (Murlens Slippy-Well Plucked)	Williams	Sunderland	28.73	8-11F
1993	Tom's Lodge (Druids Lodge-Grannys Black)	Johnson	N Canes	29.20	6-4F

BE FIRST PAST THE POST...

with this great Greyhound Racing book offer...

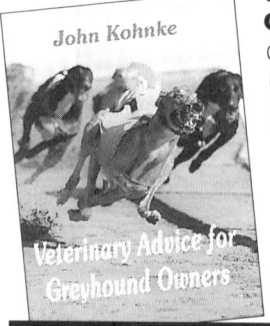

Veterinary Advice for Greyhound Owners

(£14.99, plus £2.50 post and packing)

Practical, easy-to-follow advice from **JOHN KOHNKE**, the vet who is Greyhound racing's leading columnist dealing with greyhound ailments.
Covers everything from the treatment and prevention of injuries to vital information on nutrition.

To order, send a cheque or money order to:
Ringpress Books, PO Box 8, Lydney, Glos., GL15 6YD
Access/Visa orders phone **0594 563800**. Prices are UK only. Eire add £2 per item.

NGRC Directory

Canterbury

Kingsmead Stadium, Kingsmead Rd, Canterbury, Kent CT2 7PH.
Telephone number: Racing office: 01227 761244.
Fax: 01227 762219

Owner: Kingsmead Sports Centre Ltd.
Racing manager: David Day.
Trainers: 35 attached plus 12 professional.

Race nights: Tuesday, Friday, Saturday and Sunday (7.30 pm).
Trial sessions: Wednesday (9 am, 1.30 pm).

> **HOW TO GET THERE**
>
> **A2 from Dartford Tunnel, run into M2 to Canterbury follow ring road to Margate, turn left into Kingsmead Road at roundabout, stadium 200 yds on right.**

Distances: 275m, 480m, 480mh, 675m, 675mh, 880m.
Grading times: 275m 17.15; 480m 30.80; 480mh 31.50; 675m 44.60.
Number of dogs per race: Six or eight.
Surface: All sand.
Type of hare: Outside Sumner.
Circumference of track: 400m.
Distance to the first bend: 100m.
Width of track: Straights 26', bends 30'.
Layout of the track and how it runs: Big galloping track with wide sweeping bend, very easy circuit to run.
Usual method of track preparation: Watering in summer, salting in winter.

Major competitions:
   Currently none

Graded prize money: Bottom grade £22, top grade £70.
Number of bookmakers: Seven.
Totalisator: Computerised with place, forecast, trio.
Timing: Ray timing, photo timing.
Facilities: Chromatography, vet in attendance, kennels for 82 greyhounds, car park for 100 vehicles, restaurant for 150, three bars, refreshment room, covered stand, video replay.
Other activities at stadium : Football, Sunday market.

NGRC Directory

Track Records

275m	**Cora Hill**	16.43
480m	**Paradise Slippy**	28.97
480mh	**Cassies Street**	29.54
675m	**Liberal Idea**	41.88
880m	**Back Before Dawn**	56.34

BE FIRST OUT OF THE TRAPS...
for these great Greyhound Racing video offers...

GREAT RACES OF 1994

(£19.99)

The video of the year – a must

1994 GREYHOUND DERBY

(£19.99)

Every race from the premier classic

Training Greyhounds with George Curtis

(£19.99)

Unique insights into his methods

To order, send a cheque or money order to:
Ringpress Books, PO Box 8, Lydney, Glos., GL15 6YD
Access/Visa orders phone **0594 563800**. Prices are UK only. Eire add £2 per item.

ON PARADE: Racing preliminaries at Adenmore Road.

Catford

Adenmore Road, Catford, London SE6 4RJ.
Telephone number: 0181 690 2261, (0181 690 2240, racing office). Fax: 0181 690 2433.

Owner: Belle Vue.
General Manager: Mike Raper.
Racing Manager: Jim Snowden.
Trainers (attached):
J. Horsfall, A. Boyce,
R. Peacock, P. Milligan,
A. Ellis, J. Gibbons,
T. Taylor, T. Gates,
D. Mullins.

Race nights: Monday, Thursday. Saturday (7.30 pm).
Trial sessions: Tuesday (10.30 am).
Distances: 222m, 385m, 385mH, 555m, 555mH, 718m, 888m, 1051m.
Grading times: 385m: 25.50, puppies

HOW TO GET THERE

Next to Catford and Catford Bridge Stations (BR). Buses 36, 36b, 47, 54, 108, 124, 141, 160, 108, 185, 199. Green Line 704.

NGRC Greyhound Racing Yearbook 1995

NGRC Directory

24.80, 385mH: 25.20, 555m: 36.80.
Number of greyhounds per race: Six.
Surface: Sand.
Type of hare: Outside McKee.
Circumference of track: 333m.
Distance to the first bend: 385m, 718m: 60m. 555m, 888m: 70m.
Width of track: 8m in straights.
Layout of the track and how it runs: Short straights, wide sweeping bends, almost circular in shape, suits railers.

Major competitions:
    The Greenwich Cup (555m), April.
    The Scurry Gold Cup (385m), July.
    The Gold Collar (555m), September.

Graded prize money: Bottom grade £35, top grade £80.
Number of bookmakers: Seven.
Totalisator: Computerised.
Timing: Automatic, split times on four bends and six bends.
Facilities: Chromatography, vet in attendance, kennels for 92 greyhounds, car park for 250 vehicles, private function room, two restaurants, two fast food bars, covered and glass-fronted stands, video replay.

Track Records

222m	**I'm From Tallow**	13.56
385m	**Bolt Home**	23.35
385mH	**Kildare Slippy**	23.73
517m	**Hello Blackie**	32.03
517mH	**Breeks Rocket**	33.23
555m	**Track Man**	34.47
555mH	**Freewheel Kylo**	35.34
718m	**Scurlogue Champ**	45.58
888m	**Scurlogue Champ**	57.60
1051m	**Cregagh Prince**	69.93

NGRC Directory

Major Races

JOHN HUMPHREYS GOLD COLLAR (555m)

1	**PEARL'S GIRL**	7-4jf	(6)
	fw b Flashy Sir-Desert Pearl Apr 91		
2	Decoy Cheetah	7-1	(5)
3	Heres Seanie	7-4jf	(2)
4	Decoy Holly	33-1	(4)
5	Westmead Mystic	20-1	(3)
6	Paradise Slippy	4-1	(1)

34.82 (N) nk, 3^4/$_4$, 3·3 2, Sykes, Wimbledon.

1970	Cameo Lawrence (Dusty Trail-Hack Up Titanic) A Smith, Catford	33.84	8-1
1971	Down Your Way (Printer Prince-Wonder Groves) H Warrell, Pvt	33.10	5-2
1972	Rathmartin (Kilbeg Kuda-Tyrone Lark) C Orton, Wimbledon	35.36	7-4
1973	Ramdeen Stuart (Sallys Story-Any Streak) N Oliver, Brough Pk	35.04	1-3F
1974	Leaders Champion (Monalee Champion-Little Leader) D Geggus, Wal'stow	35.02	8-11F
1975	Abbey Glade (Kilbelin Style-Abbey Groves) G Curtis, Brighton	34.97	11-4
1976	Westmead Champ (Westmead County-Hacksaw) P Heasman, Hckny	35.02	4-7F
1977	Westmead Power (Westmead County-Westmead Damson) N Savva, Bletchley	34.98	11-4
1978	I'm A Smasher (Rockfield Era-Kiltea Fawn) J Coleman, Wembley	35.31	7-1
1979	Gay Flash (Fiontra Frolic-London Child) S MIlligan, Catford	35.08	7-2
1980	Sports Promoter (Breakaway Town-Kensington Queen) P Mullins, Cam	35.06	8-15F
1981	Laughing Sam (Tullig Rambler-Sherrys Corner) B Goode, Hall Grn	35.50	4-1
1982	Donna's Trixie (Black Beetle-Bright Parade) H Kibble, Bristol	35.19	13-8
1983	Rathduff Tad (Ceili Band-Rathduff Gazelle) T Dennis, Southend	35.13	7-1
1984	Wheelers Tory (Glen Rock-Sandhill Fawn) P Wheeler, Pvte	35.05	11-4
1985	Black Whirl (Sand Man-Prince of Rocks) T Gates, Pvte	34.99	5-1
1986	Westmead Move (Whisper Wishes-Westmead Tania) N Savva Pvte	34.80	11-4
1987	Half Awake (Sand Man-Fenians Minnie) B Silkman, Pvte	34.90	4-1
1988	Sard (Manorville Sand-Knockroe Elm) J McGee, Canterbury	34.61	6-4
1989	Burgess Ruby (I'm Slippy-Burgess Emerald) A Boyce, Hackney	34.72	11-8F
1990	Dempseys Whisper (Whisper Wishes-Lemon Gem) P Byrne, Cant'by	34.84	9-4
1991	Appleby Lisa (Whisper Wishes-Moon Bran) H Dodds Norton Canes	34.67	5-1
1992	Westmead Surprise (Daleys Gold-Westmead Move) N Savva, M Kyns	34.75	6-4
1993	Ardcollum Hilda (Druids Johno-Seventh Dynamic) Byrne, Wimb'don	33.87	2-7F

WHAT A GIRL!: Pearl's Girl is the centre of attention after her John Humphreys Gold Collar victory.

NGRC Directory

Cradley Heath

Track's future under a cloud

CRADLEY HEATH has been the subject of intense speculation in the sporting Press in recent months, with its survival in doubt at time of publication. Owner Derek Pugh at one point told the track bookmakers that their contracts would not be renewed.

But Mr Pugh, who has been in charge at the West Midlands venue since 1976 said two parties had expressed an interest in the site. 'I told one to reconsider his bid.'

The interested parties are reported to be involved in the leisure industry and are keen to continue greyhound racing at the track.

Speedway has been axed at the track, which has been associated with greyhound racing for 47 years.

There was speculation that the entire Cradley Heath strength of 120 might be transferred to permit track Norton Canes, which was said to be on the verge of re-opening as an NGRC venue.

Dudleywood Road, Dudley, West Midlands DY2 0DH. Telephone number: 01384 66604. Fax: 01384 566089

Owner: Derek Pugh.
Racing Manager: Paul Griffiths.
Trainers (attached):
C. McNally, J. Barrett, A. Bloor, N. Dams, R. Green, H. Carpenter, R. Speck, B. Norris, R. Dix.

HOW TO GET THERE

By car: M5 Junction 2; from Dudley, take the Netherton Road for a mile and a half.

Race nights: Tuesdays and Fridays (7.30 pm).
Trial sessions: Wednesdays (10 am).
Distances: 231m, 462m. 647m.

NGRC Directory

Grading times:
462m: 30.00,
647m: 43.00.
Number of greyhounds per race: Five.
Surface: Sand.
Type of hare: Outside McKee.
Circumference of track: 413m.
Distance to the first bend: 80m.
Width of track: 6m
Layout of the track and how it runs: Easy-running track, bends not too sharp.
Usual method of track preparation: Four permanent ground staff all year round, watering summer, salting when necessary in winter.
Graded prize money: Bottom grade £18, top grade £35.
Number of bookmakers: Seven
Totalisator: Computerised win, forecast, tricast.
Timing: Automatic, ray timing and hand.
Facilities: Chromatography, vet in attendance, kennels for 100 greyhounds, car park for 200 vehicles, two bars, refreshment room, covered stand, video replay.

Track Records

272m	**Tea Punt**	15.97	24-7-81
462m	**Slender Boy**	28.12	8-11-83
647m	**Ballybeg Grand**	40.35	28-9-77
692m	**Ritas Hero**	42.40	23-4-82
875m	**Pineapple Choice**	55.73	20-7-82

THEY'RE OFF: Bursting from the traps at Crayford Stadium

Crayford

Ladbroke Stadium, Crayford, Kent DA1 4HR.
Telephone number: 01322 557836, 01322 522262 (racing office). Fax: 01322 524530.

Owner: Ladbroke Stadia Ltd.
General Manager: Barry Stanton.
Racing Manager: Paul Lawrence,
Trainers (attached): D, Luckhurst, P, Issac, G Lang, M. Mew, P Tompsett, B, O'Sullivan, S, Kennett, R. Steele, J. Reynolds, L. Sams, G. Ripley.

Race days: Saturday mornings (BAGS) and evenings, Monday evenings Thursday evenings (BAGS or BEGS) and Sundays (as advertised).
Trial sessions:

HOW TO GET THERE

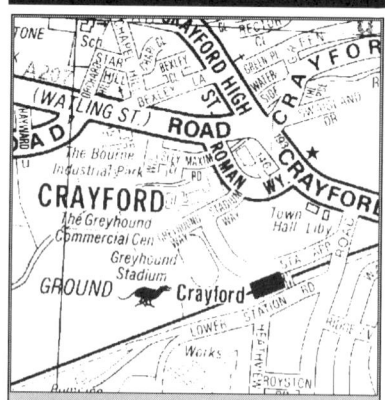

RAIL: BR to Crayford from Charing Cross.
BUS: No. 96 bus,
By Car: M25, M20, M2, or follow A207 (Watling Street) from London.

NGRC Directory

CRAYFORD

Tuesday 11am,
Distances: 380m, 380mH, 540m, 540mH, 714m, 874m,
Grading times: 380m 24,60; puppies 24,80; 540m: 35.70;
puppies 35.90; 380mH 25.20; 540mH 36.00.
Number of greyhounds per race: Six,
Surface: Sand,
Type of hare: Outside Sumner,
Circumference of track: 334m,
Distance to the first bend: 77m,
Width of track: 5,5m straights, 6.1m crown ot bends,
Layout of the track and how it runs: Safe sand surface with slightly banked bends. Does not favour rails or wide runners.
Usual method of track preparation: Weekly cut with powerharrow. Regular hydraulic plate use. Hand rake of bends.

Major competitions:
A.E. Bullard Rose Bowl (380m), January.
Ladbroke Golden Jacket (714m), February.
Wafcol Kent Puppy Cup (380m), May,
Tony Morris & John Humphreys July Cup (714m), July.
Bass Guys & Dolls (380m), July.
Bass Vase (714m), August

Graded prize money: Bottom grade £50, top grade £120 (varies with distance),
Number of bookmakers: Four (evenings), four (BAGS),
Totalisator: Computer—win, place, forecast, trio, jackpot,
Timing: Automatic, hand, sectional ray timing. All types used, split times available on four bends and six bends
Facilities: Chromatography, vet in attendance, kennels for 85 greyhounds, car park for 800 vehicles, restaurant for 180, two bars, twin-tier glass-fronted covered stand, video replay,
Other facilities at the stadium: Sports complex, including tennis. badminton, five-a-side football, weight training.

Track Records

380m	Genotin Laura	23.31	17-5-93
	Lots of Jolly	23.31	16-7-94
380mH	Ladys Champion	23.86	24-9-94
540m	Side Wink	33,46	9-1-92
540mH	Sunshine Sandy	34.32	11-3-93
714m	Heavenly Lady	45.25	8-2-93
874m	Astrosyn Trace	57.21	26-10-87

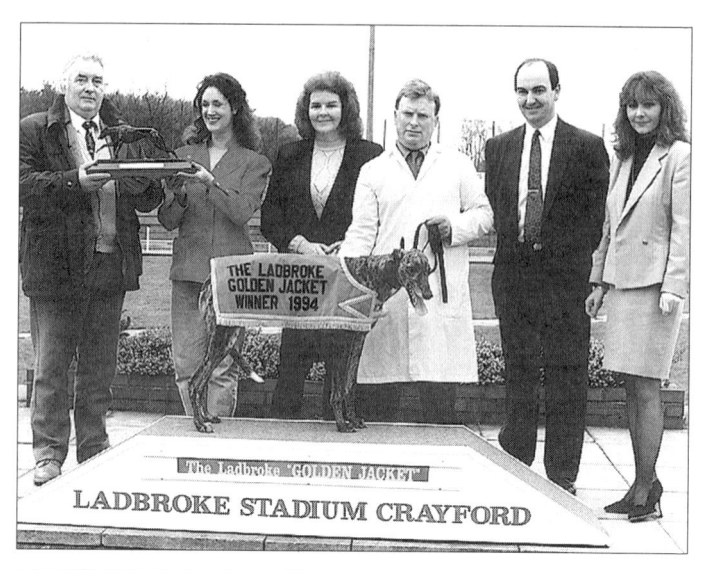

ALL YOURS: Author Laura Thompson presents owners Mr and Mrs E Furlong with the trophy after Wexford Minx's win. Also pictured are trainer Derek Knight; Barry Stanton, Crayford's General manager, and Karen Starkey of Ladbrokes.

LADBROKE GOLDEN JACKET (714m)

1. **Wexford Minx** bd.b. Manorville Major-Ballarue Suzy, (Aug 91) (T6) 11-4 JF
2. Heavenly Lady bk.b Manorville Sand-Black Sancisco, (June 90) (T5) 6-1
3. The Great Gonzo w.bd.d Flashy Sir-Move Over Bass, (June 91) (T2) 3-1
4. Jubilee Rebecca b.w.b Pond Mirage-Lively Bid, (Mar 91) (T4) 7-1
5. Killenagh Dream w.bd.d. (Dads Bank-Killeenagh Lady), (May 90) (T3), 8-1
6. Arrancourt Lord bk.w.d. (Ardfert Sean-Kilmorna Pearl (June 91) (T1) 8-1.

45.83 (Normal) $3^1/_2$, $1^1/_4$, shd, $4^1/_4$, $^3/_4$. Knight (Hove)

Year	Winner	Trainer	Track	Time	SP
1975	Nice One Cyril (Newdown Heather-Itsabet) Coyle	Private	40.86	11-4
1976	Glin Bridge (Spectre-Shore Susie) Curtis	Hove	40.59	9-4
1977	Sindys Flame (Monalee Champion-Dolores Rocket) Honeysett	Private	40.99	1-10 F
1978	Black Legend (Spectre-Nora Again) Dickson	Slough	41.09	7-4 F
1979	Westmead Bound (Westmead County-Attoulia Girl) Mrs N. Savva	Wembley	41.02	2-1
1980	Brainy Prince (Mortor Light-Move First) Mrs H.Hayward	Coventry	40.63	2-1JF

NGRC Greyhound Racing Yearbook 1995

NGRC Directory

1981 Just It (Itsachampion-Salubrious Lady)
Duggan — Romford — 40.67 — 7-2
1982 Try Traveiscene (Ballybeg Prim-My Dowry)
A.J. Mobley — Private — 40.61 — 7-2
1983 Minnies Matador (Sand Man-Virginia Chat)
Milligan — Private — 40.69 — 4-1
1984 Amazing Man (Glen Rock-Orchard Rock)
Knight — Hove — 40.88 — 5-2
1985 Keem Rocket (Decoy Sovereign-Keem Princess)
A.C. Meek — Swindon — 41.67 — 8-11
1986 Glenowen Queen (Yellow Ese-Rikasso Monica)
Hawkes — Walth'stow — 40.92 — 5-2
1987 Clover Park (Westpark Clover-Mullinakill)
Gibbons — Crayford — 35.40 — 10-1
1988 Decoy Princess (Glatton Grange-Decoy Lassie)
Lucas — Swaffham — 46.30 — 7-2
1989 Time Lord (Manorville Sands-Scintillas Tina)
Dickson — Wembley — 46.03 — 10-1
1990 Chicita Banana (Sail On II-Bonita Banana)
McGee — Hackney — 45.75 — 9-4
1991 Bobs Regan (Ballyregan Bob-Sandy Gem)
Timcke — Private — 47.00 — 6-1
1992 Bobs Regan (Ballyregan Bob-Sandy Gem)
Timcke — Private — 46.10 — 5-1
1993 Heavenly Lady (Manorville Sand-Black Sancisco)
Mullins — Walth'stow — 45.33 — 2-5F

Run at Harringay until 1985 then Hall Green, Monmore Green and Crayford from 1987, The 1988 competition was run over 718m.

ACTION OVER Hurdles at Crayford is always popular

NGRC Greyhound Racing Yearbook 1995

STOCK NUTRITION

Station Road, Yaxham, Norfolk, NR19 1RD Telephone 0362 694957

EXPERTS IN GREYHOUND HEALTH

Have you tried these exciting new products to help your dogs achieve their full poten-

FORMULA ONE
A tablet supplement containing creatine, carnitine ubiquinone and vitamins B1 and E. Formula One will assist sudden bursts of energy and help against muscle fatigue. Especially developed for the performance greyhound. £7.99 for a tub of 100 tablets, to be taken two per day.

The greatest advance in animal health since antibiotics.

MAGIC
MAGIC is the powerful symbiotic to support the protective gut flora of your dog. Used daily, MAGIC will assist digestion and stimulate natural immunity. Especially useful for use after antibiotics, for dogs under stress and in the face of digestive disturbance. £6.49 for a tub, lasts a single dog approximately 8 weeks.

TRY THESE SUPERB PRODUCTS TODAY – AND LET YOUR DOG'S PERFORMANCE BE THE JUDGE!

STOCK NUTRITION – SUPPLEMENTS THAT WORK

FOR FURTHER INFORMATION, CALL OUR HEALTH-LINE: 0760 440522. Open 1pm – 3pm daily.

Important news for our Irish customers: Due to increased demand, we now have an agent for Eire: John Phelan, Clare, Co. Kildare. Tel 045 68481

Order the following direct to the address at the top of this advert. Make cheque/PO payable to STOCK NUTRITION

FORMULA ONE (£7.99). The high-performance tablet for exceptional racing results (50 day course).
MAGIC (£6.49). Your dog's best bet for internal health. One tub will last one dog approx 8 weeks.
GENIE (£6.49, + $1.50 p&p if order is less than £20). The safe, powerful disinfectant.
CHECK (£5.49). For the effective control of animal odours.
DYNAMITE (£6.49). Safe herbal insect repellant. Makes 25 litres of solution.

NGRC Directory

Dundee

Dens Park Stadium, Sandeman St, Dundee DD3 7JY.
Telephone number: 01382 825404 Fax: 01382 832284.

Owner: Dundee Leisure.
General manager: Mr J Taylor.
Racing manager: Mr V. Taylor.

Race nights: Mondays, and Fridays (7.30)
Trial Sessions: Race nights.
Distances: 216m, 400m, 578m.
Grading times: 400m: 27.80; 578m: 41.50.
Number of greyhounds per race: Five and six.
Surface: Sand
Type of hare: Outside McKee.
Circumference of track: 400m.
Width of track: 5m.
Graded prize money: Bottom grade £30, top grade £70.
Number of bookmakers: Three.
Totalisator: Computerised. Win, place, forecast, trio, jackpot.
Timing: Automatic and ray timing.

Major Races:
   None

Facilities: Chromatography, kennels for 100 greyhounds, car park for 500 vehicles, restaurant for 60 covers, four bars, three refreshment rooms, video replay. Full restaurant and bars glass-fronted.
Other activities at the stadium: Bell's Scottish Premier League Football.

Greyhound Racing's European Flagship

The London Stadium Hackney, situated in the heart of east London, has been the home of greyhound racing for over 60 years. This superb track is currently undergoing a radical £7.5 million transformation into a dazzling entertainment arena.

Greyhound Racing is the second most popular spectator sport in Britain. Make the London Stadium Hackney your first choice for a great night of greyhound excitement.

Opened back in October 1993, the West stand with a capacity of 1000 persons, offering spectacular track views, 3 bars, a fast food diner and a 120 seat restaurant.

A magnificent towered East Stand opens in Autumn 1995 and will immediately become greyhound racing's European Flagship.

With a capacity of 3000 persons, this new facility will boast 6 licensed bars (including a pub and exclusive lounge bar), a 550 seat restaurant and fast food outlet.

All races are relayed via video monitors placed throughout the stadium, with slow motion action replays adding to the enjoyment of top quality racing.

The combination of Britain's largest on-course betting facility, the latest computerised tote facilities and an efficient tote messenger service offers you unrivalled betting opportunities.

Enjoy the racing from the comfort of the fabulous Fleetfoot Restaurant, where fine cuisine is available at affordable prices. Whether you are a first-timer or seasoned race-goer, there is simply no better choice for thrilling entertainment!

See the National Press for our latest **Special Night Out Promotions**

Racing is held Monday, Wednesday, Friday and Saturday. Stadium gates and bars open at 6.30 pm with 12 races between 7.45pm and 10.30pm.

LONDON STADIUM HACKNEY

For all promotional information and inclusion on our mailing list, please contact, London Stadium Marketing

0181 9863511

The London Stadium • Hackney • Waterden Road, E15 2EQ

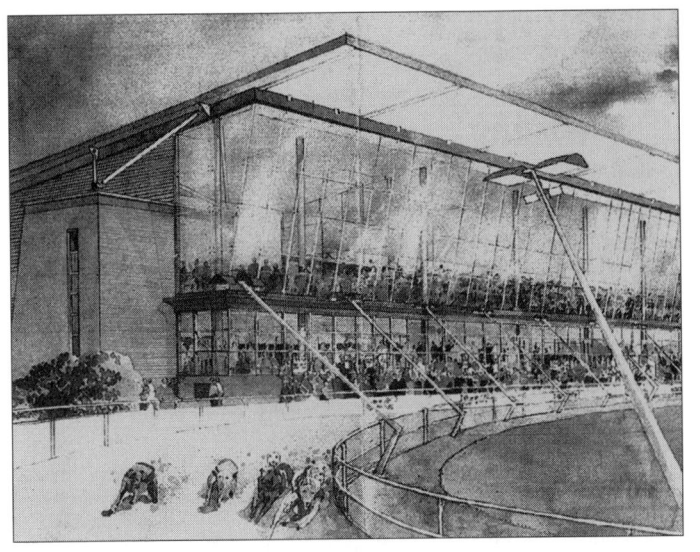

STATE OF THE ART: Hackney's new East Stand, as mocked up by KSS Architects, engaged in the design of the project.

New-look Hackney takes shape

THIS is the shape of things to come at Hackney— an artists' imoression of the new East Stand, due to open for business this summer.

Work has already begun on the foundations, and the steel frame will shortly be in place, says Stephen Rea, operations director of track owners Fleetfoot Racing.

Some late modifications were put in place to the original plans and will see huge sliding glass windows on the ground floor, which can be opened in summer. An absence of pillars will give spectators an onobscured view of racing.

There will be a special all-glass judges box suspended from the ceiling, with gantry access.

And that's not the end of the improvements that punters will notice. Rea says: 'We plan to have up-to-date photo-finish equipment and there will be instant results for the public— just as they have at Hove.

Staff training is under way well in advance of completion, a result of lessons gleaned from the building of the West Stand. 'Tote, bar and restaurant staff will be well prepared for when the new stand opens,' he said.

It all goes to show Hackney's confidence for 1995. The track saw a 32 per cent increase in tote turnover last year on the 1993 figures, with the number of meetings also up, from 114 to 348.

NGRC Directory

Hackney

London Stadium, Waterden Rd, Stratford, London. E15 2EQ
Telephone: 0181-986 3511
Fax: 0181 985 6922. 081 533 1969

Owner: Fleetfoot Racing Ltd.
General manager: Geoff Smith.
Racing managers: Michael Marks. (BAGS), Bill Glass
Trainers (attached):
L. Maxen R. York, Mrs J. Tite, P. Walsh, Mrs B. Bateman, D. Vowles, T. Lanceman, B. Lane, B. Clemenson, C. Duggan, J. Connolly, J. Simpson.

Race days: Monday, Wednesday, Friday, Saturday.
(BAGS Tuesday pm, Saturday am).
Trial sessions:

HOW TO GET THERE

236 bus Leyton Station (Central Line) to top of Waterden Road, 276 bus Stratford Broadway (Central Line) to bottom of Waterden Road.

Wednesday mornings (BAGS), Thursday mornings.
Distances: 260m, 400m, 440m, 484m, 640m, 685m, 820m, 909m.
Grading times: 440m: 28 30; 484m: 30.80; 640: 42.00.
Number of greyhounds per race: Six.
Surface: All sand.
Type of hare: Outside Sumner.
Circumference of track: 437m.
Distance to the first bend: 484m: 81m.
Width of track: 6m.
Layout of the track and how it runs: Big galloping track with long, wide straights and sweeping bends.
Usual method of track preparation: Regular watering whenever rnquired, even during racing. Rock salt mixed with sand whenever frost forecast. Motorised tractor used during

NGRC Directory

race intervals includes grader and roller.

Major competitions:
 Embassy Gold Cup
 John Power Gymcrack Puppy Stakes
 Hackney Fleetfoot Futurity Championship
 AR Dennis Guineas (484m)

Graded prize money: Bottom grade £40, top grade £150.
Number of bookmakers: Six.
Totalisator: Computer, win, place, forecast, trio pool, jackpot
Timing: Automatic, hand, sectional, ray timing, all types in use, sectional timing traps to line.
Facilities: Chromatography, vet in attendance, kennels for 90 greyhounds, car park tor 300 vehicles, restaurant for 50 covers, three bars, refreshment room, glassfronted stand, video replay.
Other activities at the stadium: *Speedway, Sunday market, greyhound sales.*

Track Records

260m	**Fast Copper**	15.52	20-4-94
400m	**Danesfort Slippy**	25.01	26-3-94
400mH	**Fancy Major**	25.44	25-11-94
440m	**Jurassic Park**	26.70	23-9-94
484m	**Lassa Java**	28.86	24-3-94
484mH	**Gis A Smile**	29.72	7-2-94
640m	**Coolmona Road**	39.95	22-8-94
640mH	**Freewheel Kylo**	41.84	27-12-93
685m	**Coolmona Road**	42.95	15-7-94
825m	**Winetavern Celt**	53.78	12-12-94
909m	**Smart Decision**	58.88	7-4-94

Major Races

EMBASSY MARATHON

EMBASSY PERMIT DERBY

AR DENNIS MIDDLE PARK PUPPY CUP
(Full results, see over page)

NGRC Greyhound Racing Yearbook 1995

NGRC Directory

EMBASSY MARATHON

1 **TAMMYS DELIGHT** 5-4f (1)
   wbk d Waltham Abbey-Lulus Moth May 91
2 Kilpipe Bibi 9-1 (4)
3 Lisnakill Move 6-1 (5)
4 Clonbrin Black 8-1 (2)
5 Deenside Fire 20-1 (6)
6 Killenagh Dream 9-4 (3)
   54.44 (+10) $2\frac{1}{2}$, $1\frac{1}{2}$, nk, 3, $\frac{3}{4}$. Meek, Hall Green

AR DENNIS MIDDLE PARK PUPPY CUP

1 **DRUIDS ELPRADO** 2-1 (4)
   bdw d Im Slippy-Druids Dalroy Mar 92
2 Kilpipe Bibi 10-1 (3)
3 Lisnakill Move 8-1 (5)
4 Clonbrin Black 11-10f (1)
5 Deenside Fire 10-1 (6)
6 Killenagh Dream 6-1 (2)
   29.60 (N) $1\frac{1}{4}$, sht-hd, sht-hd, $1\frac{1}{4}$, $2\frac{1}{2}$. McGee, Hackney.

EMBASSY PERMIT DERBY

1 **ANNAMORE KYLE** 7-4jf (6)
   bk b Kyle Jack-Velvet Doll Nov 91
2 Huntsmans Fancy 14-1 (5)
3 Rearour Chief 6-1 (4)
4 Great Old Time 16-1 (3)
5 Situation 6-1 (2)
6 Want To Be 7-4jf (1)
   29.79 (N) $5\frac{3}{4}$, $2\frac{1}{4}$, $1\frac{3}{4}$, $1\frac{1}{4}$, nk. Walsh, Henlow.

HALL GREEN: One of the country's premier tracks

Hall Green

York Road, Hall Green, Birmingham B28 8LQ,
Telephone number: 0121-777 1181.
Restaurant: 0121-777 8439. Fax: 0121-777 6860.

Owner: GRA.
General manager: Mrs Jean Feltham.
Racing manager: Mr G. Woodward.
Trainers (attached):
B. Bakewell, W. Cowans, B. Hall, P. Hancox, G. Lilley, J. Malcolm, M. Pugh, B. Smith, M Barlow, G. De Mulder, T. Meek.

Race nights:
Wednesday, Friday, Saturday (All 12-race cards). 1st race: 7.15 pm.

HOW TO GET THERE

From City Centre: Leave on the A34 (Stratford Road) starting from the Bull Ring/Rotunda. Pass through Sparkbrook and Sparkhill. Look for the College Arms pub, take left fork into B4271 (Shaffsmore Lane). Turn right into Cateswell Road, then first left, York Road.
From the Motorway (M6/M1): Take M42 from the M6, leave at Junc 4 and head for City Centre on the A34, passing through Shirley. At Bulls Head pub, turn right into Foxhollies Road. Then first left into York Road.

Trial sessions: Tuesdays; kennelling (9.30 am)
Distances: 259m, 474m, 474mh, 663m, 663mhcp, 815m, 881m.

NGRC Directory

Grading times: 259m: 16.10, 474m: 30.25, 663m: 43 30.
Number of dogs per race: Six.
Surface: All sand
Type of hare: Outside McKee.
Circumference of track: 404m.
Distance to the first bend: 85m.
Layout of the track and how it runs: A good all round test for a greyhound. The long run in demands some stamina.
Usual method of track preparation: Raking, rolling and watering, salted in winter.
Major competitions:
    Daily Mirror/Sporting Life Grand National, March.
    Courage Midland Flat Championship, November.
    Courage Midland Oaks, May.

Graded prize money: Bottom grade £30, top grade £85 (474m).
Number of bookmakers: 14.
Totalisator: Computerised, win, place, forecast, trio.
Timing: Automatic, with ray timing back-up.
Facilities: Chromatography, vet in attendance, kennels for 100 greyhounds, car park for 400 vehicles, two restaurants for 350 and 120 covers, seven bars, refreshment room, main grandstand extended, two glass-fronted stands, video replay, 51-bedroom motel adjacent to third and fourth bends.

ROOM WITH A VIEW: The Lodge is a 51-bedroomed model close to the third and fourth bends at Hall Green.

NGRC Directory

Track Records

259m	**Fearless Action**	15.46	30-11-85
474m	**Westmead Chick**	28.20	19-11-94
474mh	**Kildare Slippy**	29.14	22-4-91
663m	**Roseville Jackie**	41.37	9-4-88
815m	**Minnies Siren**	52.50	27-4-88

Other activities at the stadium: Stadium Snooker Club (members only).

Major Races

DAILY MIRROR/SPORTING LIFE GRAND NATIONAL (474mH)

1	**RANDY SAVAGE**	8-1	(5)
	bk d Randy-Sooty Foot Nov 91		
2	Heavenly Dream	5-2	(6)
3	Gis A Smile	11-10F	(2)
4	Jamesie Cotter	8-1	(3)
5	Super Spy	16-1	(1)
6	Hi Brazil Sam	12-1	(4)

29.50 (-10) 2, 2, 4, 3¾, ½, 2½. Connor, Canterbury

1970	Sherry's Prince (Mad Era-Nevasca)	4-6F	J. Shevlin W Ham	30.02
1971	Sherry's Prince (Mad Era-Nevesca)	1-3F	C. West W Ham	29.22
1972	Sherry's Prince (Mad Era-Nevasca)	5-4F	C. West W. City	29.80
1973	Killone Flash (Forward Flash-Dancing Barrier)	5-2	B.Singleton W. City	29.35
1974	Shanney's Darkie (Monalee Champion-Shannays Jet)	10-1	C.West W. City	29.43
1975	Pier Hero (Tender Hero-Helenas Girl)	EvF	F. Melville Har'gay	30.65
1976	Weston Pete (Monalee Champion-New Kashmir)	4-6F	C. West W City	30.60
1977	Salerno (Clerihan Venture-Fish Pond)	5-4F	J. Coleman Wem	30.43
1978	Topothetide (Westpark Mint-Ladyin Love)	8-11	F T. Forster Har'gay	30.23
1979	Topothetide (Westpark Mint-Ladyin Love)	6-4F	T. Lanceman S'end	31.60
1980	Gilt Edge Flyer (Monalee Expert-Proud Secretary)	4-6F	E.Pateman Unn.	30.22
1981	Bobcol (Westpark Mint-Black Katty)	1-2F	N. McEllistrim Wim	30.64
1982	Face The Mutt (Mutta Silver-Millroad Cast)	11-1	N.McEllistrim Wim	30.71
1983	Sir Winston (Myrtown-Kings Comet)	5-1	G. Curtis Brighton	31.00
1984	Kilcoe Foxy (Hume Highway-Aghadown Liz)	4-6F	G. Curtis Brighton	30.32
1985	Seaman's Star (Thurles Yard-Sleepy Nell)	14-1	A.Boyce Catford	30.08

NGRC Directory

1988 Breeks Rocket (Noble Brigg-Sandyville Lady) 5-1	Luckhurst Crayford	30.08
1989 Lemon Chip (Sinbad-Lemon Lisa) EvF	Rees Wim'don	29.64
1990 Gizmo Pasha (Whisper Wishes-If And When) 4-6F	Mullins Romford	29.62
1991 Ideal Man (Clayderman-Ideal Honeygar) 3-1	McGee Peterboro	29.81
Ballycarney Dell (Track Man-Ballycarney Blue) 14-1	Gittins Yarmouth	D/H
1992 Kildare Slippy (Im Slippy-Kildare Elm) EvF	Hancox Hall Green	28.52
1993 Arfur Daley (Pond Mirage-Blue Mint II) 5-4F	Meadows Oxford	28.89

FOSTERS MIDLAND FLAT (474m)

1 **WESTMEAD CHICK** 4-5f (2)
   bd b Im Slippy-Westmead Move Jun 92
2 Lacken Prince 10-1 (4)
3 Westmead Merlin 7-4 (6)
4 Tullig Zafonic 12-1 (5)
5 Sandford Star 14-1 (3)
6 Slipaway Jaydee 8-1 (1)
28.56 (N) $2^{3}/_{4}$, sht-hd, $1^{1}/_{4}$, $3^{1}/_{2}$, 6. Savva, Walthamstow.

1975 Sun Chariot (Kilbeg Kuda -Rocks Violet) Melville Harringay	28.87	25-1
1976 Westmead Border (Always Proud-Cricket Dance) Savva Bletchley	29.22	8-1
1977 Shiloh Jenny (Sole Aim-Shiloh Hope) Wilkes Hall Green	28.54	8-1
1978 Shiloh Jenny (Sole Aim-Shiloh Hope) Wilkes Hall Green	28.83	2-1 F
1979 Loughlass Champ (Itsachampion-Final Score) Kovac Pvt	28.94	6-1
1980 Creamery Pat (Monalee Hiker-Young Speech) Chamberlain Pvt	28.97	7-2
1981 Houghton Sinbad (Shamrock Sailor-Thank You ken) Tomkins Cov	29.05	5-2
1982 Rikasso Hiker (Glenroe Hiker-Lady Myrtown) Mentzis Camb	28.97	10-1
1983 Beau Geste (Desert Pilot-Faypoint Flyer) Pugh Hall Green	29.02	5-1
1984 Golden Sand (Desert Pilot-Sarahs Bunny) de Mulder Pvt	28.91	4-1
1985 Hi There Trina (Glenroe Hiker-Trina Ceili) Wearing Harringay	29.08	EF
1986 Leading Part (Rhincrew Rover-Leading Blonde) Hancox Hall Gn	29.00	5-2
1987 Ramtogue Dasher (Outer Mission-Ramtogue Witch) de Mulder, Ox	28.80	13-8F
1988 Parkers Brocade (Brief Candle-Parkers Morning) Gaynor Hall Gn	29.28	4-1
1989 Claddagh Heights (Rushwee Heights-Eightys Lady) Hancox Hall Gn	30.31	2-1
1990 Slaneyside Holly (Lodge Prince-Prince Of Rocks) Cobbold Pvt	29.21	7-2
1991 Awbeg Ball (Game Ball-Teeavan) McEllistrim Wimbledon	29.97	8-11
1992 Winsor Vic (Dukes Lodge-Winsor Aird) McGee Unnattached	28.61	9-2
1993 Just Right Kyle (Kyle Jack-Im A Duchess) Lister Peterboro	29.04	3-1

BREEDERS FORUM PRODUCE STAKES, 474m

1 **WESTMEAD MERLIN** 11-8F (6)
   bd d Murlens Slippy -Westmead Hannah Sep 92
2 Sandford Star 9-2 (1)
3 Fearless Leader 4-1 (3)
4 Decoy Cheetah 8-1 (5)
5 Welsh Wizard 9-1 (4)
6 Baby Dan 14-1 (2)
28.33 (+10) $5^{1}/_{4}$, $^{1}/_{2}$, hd, $2^{1}/_{4}$ $^{3}/_{4}$ Savva, Walthamstow.

PRIMED and ready for action, the new stadium at Harlow

Harlow

McGee Jr reported to be joining ranks at Harlow

HARLOW STADIUM opens its doors for business early in 1995. At the time of going to press there were no details available on the track facilities.

However, John McGee jr was reportedly one of the trainers to be represented at the track's first trials session.

Racing manager Stan Gudgin said: 'We have 102 greyhounds and we are already virtually full up.

'We hope to get under way some time in March, but we still need a few more dogs in order to be confident we can meet regular commitments.

'As a result, I'm not really certain yet whether we will be a permit or full NGRC track.

'But we are trialling once a week and if anyone wants to get in touch, our telephone number is 01279 426804, and our fax number is 0279 444182.'

The facilities in the Essex New Town certainly look impressive enough, with the all-sand track and tidy brick-faced stand in place.

NGRC Greyhound Racing Yearbook 1995

HARDY FAITHFULS: Henlow attracts a loyal crowd of regulars.

Henlow

Henlow Stadium, Bedford Rd, Henlow Camp, Beds. SG16 6EA. Telephone : (01462) 813608. Fax: (01462) 817040.

Owner:
J D McNaughton
General manager:
J D McNaughton
Racing manager:
David Smith.
Trainers (attached): M. Bass, K. Mellor T. Dilley, M. Westwood, J. Rogers, V. Beard, F. Morrow, D. Crosse, B Dash, H. Laver, J. Page, D. Puddy, L. Coleman, T. Trevis, L. Steed, V. Pateman.
Race nights: Friday (7.30 pm) and Sunday morning.

Trial sessions: Friday, Tuesday and Saturday.
Distances: 318m, 484m, 680m, 730m,.
Grading times: 318m: 20.00; 484m: 31.00;
Number of dogs per race: Six.
Surface: Sand.

HOW TO GET THERE

On A600 Hitchin to Bedford road, at Henlow Camp roundabout, Bedford side.

NGRC Directory

Type of hare: Inside Sumner.
Circumference of track: 412m.
Width of track: 18 ft
Layout of the track and how it runs: Good galloping track. The sprint first bend is better run with experience. Usual method of preparation: Summer watered, winter salted.
Graded prize money: Bottom grade £15, top grade £45, appearance £3.

Major competitions:
   None

Number of bookmakers: Six.
Totalisator: Computerised, win, place, forecast, trifecta.
Timing: Ray timing, photo timing (instaprint). Split times are available on tour bends and six bends on request.
Facilities: Vet in attendance, kennels for 72 greyhounds, car park for 400 vehicles, bar, refreshment room, two open stands,

Track Records

318m	**Chin No Nose**	18,97	12-4-91
484m	**Cannongrand**	29,08	25-10-89
680m	**Snow Shoes**	42.14	25-11-91
730m	**Chicita Banana**	44.96	13-6-90
890m	**Clydes Dolores**	57,20	22-2-88

JOCK MCNAUGHTON: Henlow's owner and general manager, who is profiled on page 64.

AERIAL VIEW of the well-appointed Hove Stadium.

Hove

Nevill Road, Hove, Sussex BN3 7BZ.
Telephone number: 01273 204601 *(all inquiries and restaurant bookings)*. Fax: 01273 820763.

Owner: Coral Stadia Ltd.
General manager: Peter Shotton (Managing Director).
Racing manager: Peter Miller.
Trainers (attached): Mrs D. Walsh, G. Hodson, D. Knight, J. Rouse, D. Barwick, W. F. Masters, A. Lucas, B. Clemenson, T. Townsend, R.V. Young.
Race days: Wednesday afternoons (times vary, see Sporting Press or phone stadium for details), Tuesday (7.30pm), Thursday (7.30 pm), Saturday (7.15 pm), Sunday (1.45pm).
Trial sessions: Normally Mondays (10.30 am) and usually before racing.

Distances: 285m, 515m, 515mh, 695m, 695mh, 740m and 970m.
Grading times: 515m: 32.00; puppies 32.20.
Number of greyhounds per race: Six.
Surface: Sanded bends, grass straights.
Type of hare: Outside McKee.
Circumference of track: 455m.
Distance to the first bend: 81.24m.
Width of track: 5.70m.
Layout of the track and how it runs: A safe circuit with

HOW TO GET THERE

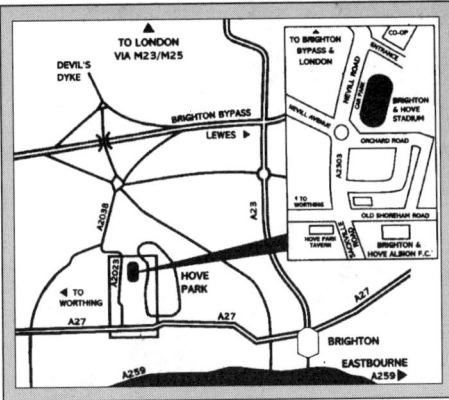

BR, Hove Station, then taxi or 10 minute walk. Buses: 5, 5a, 5b, 16. 25, 25a, 29 and 229. By car: From central Brighton, follow road along the Brighton seafront to the King Alfred Leisure Centre, turn into Hove Street and continue straight ahead for just over a mile.

wide sweeping bends and a good gallop all the way. The 695m distance is a true guide to a greyhound's ability to stay and a good judge will spot possible marathon performers.

Major competitions:
   Regency (740m), May.
   Courage Greyhound Olympic (515m), April.
   Brighton Belle (for bitches) (515m), June.
   National Hurdle (515mH), August.
   Sussex Cup (515m), £3.000, July/August.

Graded prize money: Bottom grade £56, top grade £100.
Number of bookmakers: Seven.
Totalisator: Computerised. Pools - win, place, forecast, trio, nugget, super jackpot.
Timing: Automatic .
Facilities: Chromatography, vet in attendance, kennels for 90 greyhounds, car park tor 365 vehicles, restaurant tor 460 covers, eight bars, two fast food outlets, video replay.

Other activities at the stadium: A squash and badminton club with various facilities such as sauna sun-beds, fully air-conditioned gymnasium and aerobics studio, pool tables, snooker, club bar, television, etc. is next to the stadium. Membership allows certain stadium facilities on race evenings such as tote, video race replays, and view of racing from club lounge.

Track Records

285m	**Ravage Again**	16.27	Sept 1990
515m	**Hit The Lid**	29.73	30-7-88
695m	**Waltham Abbey**	41.21	31-8-89
740m	**Mobile Magic**	44.24	1992
970m	**Saquita**	59.99	27-7-89
515mh	**Lord Westlands**	30.49	5-11-88
695mh	**Razmac Dancer**	42.95	1989

Purina Greyhound Meal

- Complete and balanced food for racing dogs.
- Specially formulated with 28% protein, moderate fat levels and the correct balance of vitamins, minerals and amino acids.
- Ensures the optimum development and maintenance of muscle, ligament and bone.
- World's No.1 Greyhound Food.

The Winning Difference

FOR INFORMATION PLEASE CONTACT THE SOLE UK DISTRIBUTORS
FLOWSYSTEMS
ANIMAL HEALTH PRODUCTS
Tel: 0191 5170701
Fax: 0191 5170920

NGRC Directory

SUSSEX CUP (515m)

1	**UNIQUE BAY**	7-2	(6)

wf d Castleyons Gem-Kenmare Bay Apr 91

2	Decoy Jaguar	6-4f	(1)
3	Not My Georgie	8-1	(2)
4	Solva Tiger	6-1	(3)
5	Parquet Paddy	10-3	(5)
6	Kyle Judge	20-1	(4)

29.98 (+50) sht-hd, 2½, 1¼, 4¾, hd, Mullins, Walthamstow

1973	Mickey Finn (Monalee Champion-Spring Shower) Milligan Private	28.65	5-4 F
1974	Clear Reason (Quiet Spring-Regal King) Clark Private	28.47	2-1
1975	Abbey Glade (Kilbeg Kuda-Abbey Groves) Curtis Brighton	29.63	7-2
1976	Gaily Noble (Monalee Champion-Noble Lynn) Coleman Wembley	29.55	10-1
1977	Linacre (Lively Band-Central) Dickson Slough	28.99	4-6 F
1978	Sandpiper Dolly (Broadlord Boy-Dolores Rocket) Honeysett Crayford	29.52	9-1
1979	Mondays Bran (Brave Ban-Mainly Personal) Rees Wimbledon	28.96	2-1
1980	Maplehurst Star (Tullig Rambler-Sparks Star) Curtis Brighton	29.21	10-3
1981	Black Armour (Tullig Doctor-Flying Pixie) Mrs March Ipswich	30.04	2-1 F
1982	Yankee Express (Pecos Jerry-Kings Comet) Curtis Brighton	30.06	4-5 F
1983	The Jolly Norman (Knockour Brandy-Breeze Valley) Curtis Brighton	30.31	3-1
1984	Sammy Bear (Mexican Chief-Lady Laurdella) Curtis Brighton	29.98	5-1
1985	Links Way (Hurry On Bran-Giglis Fancy) Peacock Harringay	29.95	9-4
1986	House Hunter (Tiger Jazz-Brass Tacks) Smith Brighton	29.97	9-4
1987	Sambuca (Pat Seamur-Lyons Flora) Smith Brighton	29.83	Ev F
1988	Hit The Lid (Soda Fountain-Cailin Dubh) McGee Private	29.73	8-11 F
1989	Slippy Blue (I'm Slippy-Valoris) Linzell Walthamstow	29.95	2-5 F
1990	Phantom Flash (Flashy Sir-Westmead Seal) Savva Milton Keynes	30.00	2-5 F
1991	Lyons Monks (The Other Risk-Mountkeefe Lady) Coleman Wal'stow	29.91	5-4
1992	Parquet Patch (Satharn Beo-Burgess Chimes) Hitch, Wimbledon	29.96	9-2

THE REGENCY

1	**DECOY COUGAR**	6-4f	(1)

bk bSlaneyside Hare-Easy Bimbo Jul 92

2	Wexford Minx	5-2	(6)
3	Decoy Lynx	7-2	(4)
4	Old Money	5-1	(2)
5	Tell The Yarn	33-1	(3)
6	Jacks Daley	33-1	(5)

45.00 (N) 2½ 1, 1¼, 3¼, 1¾, Cobbold, Unattached

NGRC Directory

Hull

Craven Park, Preston Road, Hull, HU9 5HE.
Telephone number: 01482 74131. Fax: 01482 789158.

Owner: Prentice Racing,
General manager: J. Prentice
Racing manager: K. Rushworth.
Trainers (attached): J. Tollafield, J. Seagrave, J. Bentley, T. Earles, G. Pearson, C. Savoury, K. Thomas, D. Morris, J. Smith, D. Barton, J. King, D. Haywood, L. Ashford.

> **HOW TO GET THERE**
>
> **BY CAR:** Via Hendon Road on to Preston Road.

Race nights: Thursday and Saturday (7.30 pm)
Trial sessions: Wednesday (1 pm).
Distances: 290m, 460m, 490m, 655m,
Grading times: 19.00, 31.00, 33.00, 45.00.
Number of greyhounds per race: Six,
Surface: All sand,
Type of hare: Outside Sumner.
Circumference of track: 400m,
Width of track: 6m
Layout of the track and how it runs: Big galloping track, needs stamina,
Usual method of track preparation: Watering, salting when necessary.

Major Competitions:
   Rossy Bookmakers Dean Jackson Memorial

Graded prize money: Bottom grade £20, top grade £50.
Number of bookmakers: Five.
Totalisator: Computerised, win, place, torecast, trio, jackpot.
Timing: Photo and ray timing.
Facilities: Vet in attendance, kennels for 72 greyhounds, car park for 500 vehicles, restaurant for 120 covers, three bars, refreshment room, glass-fronted stand. Restaurant booking available.

NGRC Directory

Middlesbrough

Cleveland Park, Stockton Road, Middlesbrough, Cleveland TS5 4AE.
Telephone number: 01642 211803 or 247381.
Fax: 01642 240576.

Owner: National Greyhounds. Middlesbrough Ltd.
General manager: John Taylor.
Racing manager: John Taylor.
Assistant racing manager: Dave Weatherall.
Trainers (attached): Professional: T. Jameson, D. Armitage, K. O'Neill, P. Wood, T. Wood, J. McNicholas, B. McDonald..
Owner-trainers: M. Allen, D. Smart, G. Sharp, J. Luke, G. Lynas, J. Simpson, D. Jordon, B. Stephenson, J. Thompson, R. Paterson, B. McMeekin, F. Branson, R. Jones, D. Spraggon, J. Mudd, R. Chambers.

Race nights: Monday, Wednesday and Saturday (7.30 pm).
Trial sessions: Before racing.
Distances: 266m, 462m, 640m, 774m, 836m
Grading times: 462m: 30.20; 30.40 Pups.
Number of dogs per race: Five and six.
Surface: All sand.
Type of hare: Inside Sumner,
Circumference of track: 374m.
Distance to the first bend: 100m approx.
Graded prize money: Top grade £25.
Number of bookmakers: Six.
Totalisator: Computer, win, forecast, trifecta and jackpot.
Timing: Ray timing.
Facilities: Vet in attendance, kennels for 72 greyhounds, car park, two bars, two refreshment rooms, two covered stands.

Track Records

266m	**Seaview**	15.97	1-8-94
462m	**Jubilee Rocco**	28.18	18-6-93
640m	**Keiberwood Bob**	40.26	23-9-94
774m	**Hollands Sand**	50.91	12-11-93
836m	**Dampit Pride**	54.94	25-7-90

ON PARADE: The runners on their way to the start as battle commences at Mildenhall.

Mildenhall

Hayland Drove, West Row, nr Mildenhall, Suffolk IP28 8QU. Telephone number: 01638 711777. Fax: 01638 510967.

Owner: Mr T. Waters
General Manager: Mr Richard Borthwick, Mr Michael Glynn.
Racing Manager: Mr Michael Hill.
Trainers (attached): B. Owen, V. Lee, C. Finch, L. Jones, G. Harding, D. Barret, V. Hawes, B. Boreham. F. Wiseman, R. Stringer, D. Andrews,

HOW TO GET THERE
A45 and follow signs to Norwich. Turn left at the Five Ways roundabout to Mildenhall. Follow signs to West Row, then to stadium.

Race nights: Monday, Wednesday and Friday (summer, 7.30p.m.); Monday, Friday and Saturday (7.30 pm, winter).
Trial sessions: Tuesday (kennel 6.30pm), limited trials after racing.
Distances: 220m, 375m, 545m, 700m, 870m, 1025m.
Grading times: 375m: 24.90, (puppies 25.10). 545m: 36.10.
Number of dogs per race: Six.
Surface: All sand.
Type of hare: Outside Sumner.

NGRC Directory

Distance to the first bend: 50m.
Width of track: 7m.
Layout of the track and how it runs: Small, tight track.
Usual method of track preparation: Sledging and regular watering.
Major competitions: None as yet.
Graded prize money: 375m: bottom grade £12., top grade £40; 545m: bottom grade £20, top grade £45.
Number of bookmakers: Four.
Totalisator: Computer tote.
Timing: Automatic, ray
Facilities: Vet in attendance, three bars, refreshment room, open stand, restaurant, snack bar, free parking. Restaurant booking on 01638 711777

Track Records

220m	**Lots of Jolly**	13.39	26-10-93
375m	**Lots of Jolly**	23.10	11-7-94
545m	**Decoy Panther**	33.90	12-12-94
700m	**Take A Flyer**	44.90	31-10-94
870m	**Hillmount Jean**	56.53	26-9-93
1025m	**Dusty Image**	67.49	11-11-94

MIDNIGHT MARVEL: If You Wish (left)) wins the first race with legal Sunday betting—at a minute past midnight.

NGRC Directory

Milton Keynes

Ashlands, Milton Keynes MK6 4AA.
Telephone number: 01908 670150 or 670006.
Fax: 01908 670504

Status: Permit.
Owner: Milton Keynes Stadium Ltd.
General manager: Mr D McCormick.
Racing manager: David Beckett.

> **HOW TO GET THERE**
>
> How to get there: Situated six miles to west of M1, Junction 13, on A421 city grid road.

Trainers (attached): Professional: Mrs J. A. Armstrong, B. Austin, Mrs V. J. Beard, Mrs F. H. Laver, Mrs F. Morrow, J Page, M. Westwood, G Knibb
Owner trainers: B. Booth, Mrs P. Cope, R. Tompkins, A. McCurg
Race nights: Thursdays and Saturdays (7.30 pm).
Trial sessions: Monday (7.30 pm).
Distances: 245m, 440m, 620m, 815m.
Grading times: 440m: 28.00, puppies 28 40; 620m: 40.30.
Number of dogs per race: Six.
Surface: All silica sand with banked bends.
Type of hare: Outside Sumner.
Circumference of track: 375m
Distance to the first bend: 80m
Width of track: 6m.
Layout of the track and how it runs: Bends are of a true radius of a 90m circle with straights of 85m in length.
Usual method of track preparation: Surface graded and prepared for watering when necessary.
Graded prize money: 440m: £20-£50, 620m £35-£50
Number of bookmakers: Eight.
Totalisator: Computerised, win, forecast, tricast.
Timing: Automatic ray and photo timing, split times available on all races.
Facilities: Vet in attendance, kennels for 72 greyhounds, car park for 1,000 vehicles, three bars, refreshment room, covered stand, video replay.
Other facilities at the stadium: Sunday market, and car boot sale. Car auctions Wednesdays and Fridays.

NGRC Directory

Monmore

Ladbroke Stadia Ltd, Monmore Green Stadium, Sutherland Avenue, Monmore Green, Wolverhampton WV2 2JJ.
Telephone number: 01902 452648.
Racing Office: 01902 456663. Fax: 01902 871 1C4.

Owner: Ladbroke Stadia Ltd.
General manager: Bob Harwood.
Racing manager: Jim Woods.
Trainers (attached): J. Anderson, P. Billingham, S. Buckland, M. Burt. J. Coxon, D. Edwards, B. Picton, S. Ralph, J. Searle, P. Stringer, J. Wileman.

> **HOW TO GET THERE**
> From M6 Junction 10 follow signposts to Wolverhampton, turn left at Cleveland Arms and follow signs for stadium and wholesale market.

Race nights: Thursday and Saturday (7.25 pm). BAGS most Mondays and Fridays, some Saturdays.
Trial sessions: Tuesday (kennelling 9.30 am).
Distances: 231m, 277m, 484m, 484mh, 484mhcp, 484m (eight dogs), 647m, 647mhcp, 692m, 815m, 8l5mhcp.
Grading times: 484m: 31.40.
Number of dogs per race: Six and eight.
Surface: Sand.
Type of hare: Outside Sumner.
Circumference of track: 412m.
Distance to the first bend: 138m (484m), 115m (462m).
Width of track: 7m.
Layout of the track and how it runs: Wide track with long straights, first class gallop.
Usual method of track preparation: 8-l0in sand, watered, graded and rolled. Salt liberally added and harrowed in winter.

Major competitions:
John Russell Staffordshire Knot (484m), £500, February.
Carling Black Label Puppy Derby (484m), £1,750. March
The Midland Classic Potential (484m), £500. May.
Monmore Green Choice Furniture St Leger (647m).
 £1,750. July.

NGRC Directory

Graded prize money: Bottom grade £50, top grade £125.
Number of bookmakers: Six
Totalisator: Computerised. all pools.
Timing: Automatic, hand and sectional ray timing, split times available on four bends and six bends.
Facilities: Chromatography, vet in aftendance, kennels for 96 greyhounds, car park for 1,000 vehicles, including owners' car park, restaurant for 160 covers, four bars, two refreshment rooms, glass-fronted stand, video replay. Restaurant booking available, 169 seats. Betting shop facility on site.
Other activities at the stadium: Speedway.

Track Records

227m	**Fearless Champ**	16.34	9-11-85
462m	**Fearless Champ**	28.12	18-1-86
484m	**Darragh Commet**	29.08	11-2-89
484mh	**Run On King**	30.04	10-8-91
647m	**Highmoor Glen**	40.10	10-7-93
647mh	**Tebroc Heathen**	42.60	20-4-89
692m	**Miss Bluebird**	43.57	29-10-85
815m	**Scurlogue Champ**	51.64	22-5-85
900m	**Lilac Wonder**	57.83	5-12-92
1067m	**Coverall**	70.34	29-10-90

NGRC Directory

Nottingham

The Racecourse, Colwick Park, Nottingham.
Telephone number: 0115 598231/2 (racing office).
Fax : 0115 580290

Owner: Nottingham Greyhound Stadium Ltd.
General manager: A. Littlewood.
Racing manager: P. Robinson.
Assistant Racing manager: R. Munton.
Trainers (attached): D. Bodell, M. Clarke, M. Cooper, W. Flint, K. Gebski, V. Green, M. Jones, D. Kenney, M. Lee, T. Munslaw, J. Orme, S. Poole, M. Roberts, E. Saville, M. Scahill, L. Syred, P. Timmins, D. Wheatley.

> **HOW TO GET THERE**
> By car: Follow signs to Colwick racecourse. By bus: No 21/22 from city centre.

Race nights: Monday, Thursday (7.15 pm), Saturday (7.30).
Trial sessions: Before racing and Tuesday 11.00am.
Distances: 310m, 460m, 500m, 700m, 747m, 900m.
Grading times: 500m: 32.00; 700m: 46.00.
Number of dogs per race: Mainly five.
Surface: Sand.
Type of hare: Outside Bramich.
Circumference of track: 437m.
Distance to the first bend: 90m
Width of track: 17ft.
Layout of the track and how it runs: Very good galloping track, long straights and banked bends. The longest run-in in the country on NGRC tracks and a true test of stamina.
Usual method of track preparation: Summer: harrowing, water and vibrating roller. Winter: when extremely cold salting and no roller.

Major competitions:
   Peter Derrick Eclipse (500m), £10,000, October.
   Joe Booth Memorial (500m), June.
   Coldseal Classic (500m) £1,000, August.

Graded prize money: Bottom grade: £20 top grade: £50.
Number of bookmakers: Four.

NGRC Directory

Totalisator: Computerised tote, win, place, forecast, trio, jackpot (7 legs).
Timing: Automatic and ray timing.
Facilities: Vet in attendance, kennels for 94 greyhounds, car park for 1,000 vehicles, restaurant for 150 covers, three bars, refreshment room, covered stand, video replay.
Restaurant Booking: Fontaine Restaurant, Tel: 0115 9598231
Other facilities at the stadium: Banqueting suite.

Track Records

310m	Cocktail Darkie	18.18	4-9-89
460m	Almost New	27.66	31-10-92
500m	Westmead Merlin	29.65	17-10-94
700m	Mobile Magic	43.06	28-1-93
747m	Miss Piggy	46.12	26-9-94
900m	Red Arrow Lady	56.76	24-10-91
937m	Deenside Fire	59.74	30.08.93

Major Races

PETER DERRICK ECLIPSE STAKES (500m)

1	**SPIT IT OUT**	14-1	(2)
	bk d Phantom Flash-Ivalog May 92		
2	Westmead Chick	5-4f	(1)
3	Westmead Merlin	5-2	(6)
4	Sure Fantasy	4-1	(3)
5	Anhid Blaze	25-1	(4)
6	Droopys Lanny	9-1	(5)

29.80 (+50) 5, 2½, 1½, ½, 3, Bacon, Perry Barr.

NGRC Directory

Oxford

Sandy Lane, Cowley, Oxford. OX4 5LJ
Telephone number: 01865 778222. Fax: 01865 748676.

Owner: Northern Sports Stadiums Ltd.
General manager: John Blake.
Racing manager: Gary Baiden.
Trainers (attached): J. Annett, R. Bicknell, M. Massey, T. Meek, J. Morgan, J. Peterson, L. Andrews, J. Cox, M. Mercer, P. Garland, L. Miller, B.Doyle, J. Ansell.

Race nights: Tuesday, Thursday, Saturday (7.45 pm), Friday afternoons (BAGS).
Trial sessions: Monday (afternoons).
Distances: 250m, 450m, 645m, 645mh. 845m, 1040m.
Grading times: 450m: 28.10, 28.40, puppies 28.40;
Number of dogs per race: Six.
Surface: Sand.
Type of hare: Outside Sumner.
Circumference of track: 395m.
Distance to the first bend: 145m.
Width of track: 6.8m straights, 7.6m bends.
Layout of the track and how it runs: Easy track to run, with long run to the first turn and wide bends. Drains exceptionally well, so no problems with surface water.
Usual method of preparation: Salted at first sign of frost.

Major competitions:
    Pall Mall (450m), £5,000, March.
    The Oxfordshire Gold Cup (450m), £3,000, August.
    The Oxfordshire Trophy (450m) £1,000, October.

Graded prize money: Bottom grade £35, top grade £70.
Number of bookmakers: Six.
Totalisator: Computerised, win, place, forecast, trio and Jackpot.
Timing: Automatic, ray timing.
Facilities: Chromatography, vet in attendance, kennels for 80 greyhounds, car park for 250 vehicles, restaurant for 250 covers (bookings taken), five bars, conference facilities, two covered and glass-fronted stands, video replay.
Other activities at the stadium: Speedway, Sunday market, sports and leisure complex.

NGRC Directory

Track Records

250m	**Debbies Lad**	14.96	28-10-88
450m	**Carmels Prince**	26.72	20-10-90
450mh	**Faoides Country**	27.47	24-08-91
645m	**Run Free**	39.46	11-11-86
645mh	**Cygnet Man**	40.96	7-2-89
845m	**Jaroadel**	52.91	30-8-86
1041m	**Honeygar Bell**	67.63	14-11-89

Major Races

ARTHUR PRINCE PALL MALL (450M)

1	**LASSA JAVA**	5-2	(6)
	f d Lassana Champ-Fawn Java Jun 91		
2	Ashford Boy	9-2	(4)
3	Silent Guy	33-1	(3)
4	Salcombe	7-2	(1)
5	Carraig Paws	7-4f	(2)
6	Listen To Dan	12-1	(5)

27.17 (N) 1$^3/_4$, $^3/_4$, 2$^1/_4$, nk, $^1/_2$, Meek, Hall Green.

NGRC Directory

Perry Barr

Perry Barr Greyhound Racing Club, Aldridge Road, Perry Barr, Birmingham. B42 2ET
Telephone number: 0121 356 2324. Fax: 0121 356 6704

Owner: Perry Barr Greyhound Racing Club Limited.
Racing manager: Ian Hillis
Trainers (attached):
B. Cook, B. Jennings, C. Hopkins, C. McNally, D. Exell, G. Normnan, G. Corbett, I. Williams, J. Walters, J. Ridley, K. Prince, K. Babe, K. Day, L. Cooper, L. Johnson, M. Williams, P. Ryan, R. Horwood, R. Kinsey, S. Chetwynd, S. Alexander.

Race nights: Monday, Tuesday, Thursday, Friday and Saturday. (Mon, Fri, permit nights)

HOW TO GET THERE

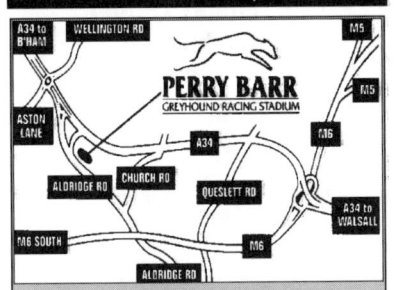

FROM BIRMINGHAM: Leave on A324 for the Bull Ring, Join A34 and then take the A453 under fly-over. Stadium is 100 yards on left.
FROM M6/M5: Turn off towards City centrre at Junct 6 of m6. Follow A34 and fork left at Perry Barr onto A453 (Aldridge Road). Large free parking at stadium.

Distances: 275m, 460m, 500m, 660mH, 710m and 895m.
Circumference of track: 435m.
Layout of the track and how it runs: Extremely wide track with sweeping bends. Good galloping circuit.
Number of dogs per race: Six and eight.
Surface: Sand.
Type of hare: Outside Sumner.
Graded prize money: Bottom grade £30, top grade £50.
Number of bookmakers: Seven.
Totalisator: Datatote.
Facilities: Chromatography testing, vet in attendance, kennels for 160 greyhounds, clubhouse and covered stand. Restaurant, private boxes and function room.
Bookings: 0121 356 3734.

NGRC Directory

Track Records

500m	**Westmead Spirit**	30.03	10-9-91
275m	**Blissful Piper**	16.61	4-6-91
	Motown Way	16.61	29-6-91
460m	**Torbal Ash**	27.97	13-11-90
660mh	**Olives Champ**	41.22	26-3-91
710m	**Dark Luke**	44.48	14-5-91
895m	**Shropshire Lass**	57.19	6-7-91

Major Races

ANSELLS BIRMINGHAM CUP (500m)

1 **HERE'S SEANIE** 6-4F (1)
  f b Ardfert Sean-Mindys Miracle Jul 92
2 Moral Director 5-1 (5)
3 Solva Tiger 10-1 (3)
4 Droopys Alfie 14-1 (2)
5 Droopys Craig 11-2 (4)
6 Salthill Champ 3-1 (6)
  30.13 (+20) 1³/₄, 2, 3, 1¹/₄, ¹/₂, Ryan, Perry Barr

FEN FANS can enjoy their racing from the comfort of the modern main stand at Peterborough.

Peterboro Greyhound

Fengate Stadium, First Drove, Peterborough. PE1 5BJ
Telephone number: 01733 343788 and 344674.
Restaurant bookings: 01733 555527. Fax: 01733 68576

Status: Permit.
Owner: Peterborough Sports Stadium Ltd.
Co-Promoters: Rex and David Perkins.
Racing manager: Mike Middle.

HOW TO GET THERE
Turn off the ring road (A1139) at Exit 5 for Eastern Industry and Fengate

Trainers (attached): Professional: D. Atkins, S. Brennen, N. Bradford, J. Counsell, R. Creckendon, D Steels, R. Drage, B. R. Ford, D. R. Pruhs, M. E. Westwood, N. Wills.
Owner trainers: V. Dearling, D. Carr, F. Grain, J. R. Hammond, G. F. Nightingale, M. S. Ross, Mrs Savage, R. Smith, C. Taylor. Plus about 60 permits.

Race meetings: Wednesday, Friday, Saturday (7.30 pm) and Sunday (12 noon)
Trial sessions: After racing on Wednesday, Tuesday and Thursday (10 am kenneling), followed by puppy schooling trials.
Distances: 235m, 420m, 605m, 790m, 975m.
Grading times: 235m: 15.20,; 420m: 27.30, puppies 27.60; 605m: 39.60.

NGRC Directory

Number of dogs per race: Six.
Surface: Silica sand.
Type of hare: Outside Sumner.
Circumference of track: 370m.
Distance to the first bend: 75m
Layout of the track and how it runs: Small, compact track with a well-kept running surface.
Usual method of track preparation: Water and vibrator roller, salted in winter.
Major competitions:
    Puppy Derby (420m), April.
    Cesarewitch (605m), June.
    Grand National (420mh), July.
    Derby (420m) July/August.
    Fengate Collar (420m), October.

Graded prize money: Bottom grade £30, top grade £40.
Number of bookmakers: Six
Totalisator: Computerised, win, place, forecast, trifecta.
Timing: Ray timing, photo finish.
Facilities: Vet in attendance, kennels for 81 greyhounds, car park for 400 vehicles, Restaurant for 200 covers (400 other seats at tables) six bars, canteen, fast-food servery, handicapped lift, air-conditioned glass-fronted stand.

Track Records

235m	**I'm From Tallow**	14.39	18-6-90
420m	**Highway Leader**	25.15	30-7-94
420mh	**Gis A Smile**	25.90	27-6-94
605m	**Simply Free**	37.24	12-9-94
790m	**Fortunate Man**	49.66	15-6-92
975m	**Lenas Cadet**	63.30	19-11-88

Q8 PETERBOROUGH DERBY (420m)

1 **HIGHWAY LEADER**   7-4jf (5)
    bk d Leaders Best-Highway Mystery Nov 91
2 Witches Dean   7-4jf (6)
3 Nice Melody   8-1 (4)
4 Rabatino   5-1 (1)
5 Ar Dream   14-1 (2)
6 Chadwell Charmer   8-1 (3)
    25.47 (+20) $1^{3}/_{4}$, $6^{3}/_{4}$, $1^{1}/_{4}$, $2^{1}/_{4}$, $4^{1}/_{2}$, Bacon, Perry Barr

UPGRADE: Lord Kimball recently opened the new kennels here.

Portsmouth

Target Road, Tipner, Portsmouth, Hants PO2 8QU.
Telephone number: 01705 663231 (general office),
01705 663232 (racing manager), 01705)660202 (restaurant).
Fax: 01705 673165

Owner: GRA Ltd.
General manager: Bill Francis.
Racing manager: Lee McAlpine.
Trainers (contract): Liz Redpath, Wendy Short, Jo Burridge, Keith Glaister, Doreen Barwick, C. Barwick, W. Short, D. Bunt, T. Lucas, P. Magill.

Race nights: Tuesday, Friday and Saturday (7 30 pm)
Trial sessions: Before racing (6.45-7.15)
Distances: 256m, 438m, 610m, 792m. 964m

HOW TO GET THERE

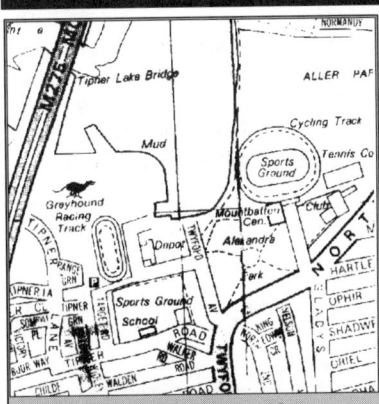

Enter Portsmouth on the M275. The Stadium can be seen on the left hand side. Take the hard left at the end of the motorway and follow signs for half a mile.

NGRC Greyhound Racing Yearbook 1995

NGRC Directory

Grading times: 438m: 28.40, 610m: 40.80.
Number of dogs per race: Five.
Surface: Sanded bends, turf straights.
Type of hare: Inside Sumner.
Circumference of track: 368m
Distance to the first bend: 92m.
Width of track: 21ft
Layout of the track and how it runs: Long straights —longer than the average 500m circuit. Very sharp bends but well cambered.
Usual method of track preparation: Straights cut and marked day before racing. Bends watered am and before racing. Winter: bends salted, straights protected by peat, hay and plastic sheets.
Major competitions: None
Graded prize money: Bottom grade £16, top grade £50.
Number of bookmakers: Nine
Totalisator: Brand new, computerised, colour.
Timing: Photo, ray
Facilities: Vet in attendance, kennels for 70 greyhounds, car park for 200 vehicles, restaurant for 100 covers, three bars, two buffets, two covered stands, video replay. Restaurant booking available on 01705 660204 or 663231.

Track Records

256m	**Lissadell Tiger**	15.55	9-6-89
438m	**Beaver Dip**	26.37	16-9-88
610m	**Crohane Lucy**	38.26	6-10-89
792m	**My Texette**	50.52	28-7-93
964m	**Wheres Dunait**	62.94	28-7-93

NGRC Directory

Powderhall

Address: Beaverhall Road, Edinburgh EH7 4JE.
Telephone number: 0131-556 8141. Fax: 0131 557 1443

Owner: Scottish Greyhound Racing Co Ltd
General manager: Edgar Ramsay.
Racing manager: Iain Woolley.

> **HOW TO GET THERE**
>
> **By car: 10 minutes from Edinburgh Airport.**
> **By rail: A mile and a half north of Waverley Station, Princes Street.**

Trainers (attached): E. Armstrong, N. Murdoch, H. Davies, J. Glass, S. Richards, I. Rodgerson, J. Flaherty, J. Reid, W. Russel.

Race nights: Tuesday, Thursday, Saturday and Sunday..
Trial sessions: Wednesday and before racing.
Distances: 241m, 415m 465m, 465mh, 650m, 824m.
Grading times: 465m: 29.70, puppies 29.70.
Number of dogs per race: Six.
Surface: All sand.
Type of hare: Outside Bramich
Circumference of track: 409m.
Distance to the first bend: l00m.
Width of track: 7m.
Layout of the track and how it runs: Average size track running from east to west that suits greyhounds with early pace.
Usual method of track preparation: Small tractor rotavators, sand then smooths with a roller for racing.
Major competitions:
　Scottish Oaks, February.
　Scottish Grand National (465mh), May.
　Edinburgh Cup (465m), August/September.
　Scottish Puppy Cup, October.

Graded prize money: Bottom grade £20, top grade £40.
Number of bookmakers: Six.
Totalisator: Computer, win, place, forecast, trio, jackpot
Timing: Photo, ray and hand timing..
Facilities: Chromatography, vet in attendance, kennels for

NGRC Directory

90 greyhounds, car park for 200 vehicles, restaurant for 100 diners, (bookable on 0131 556 8141), seven bars, tive refreshment rooms, four glass-fronted andcovered stands, video replay.
Other facilities at the stadium: Speedway and rally karting.

Track Records

241m	**Yes Super**	14.54	3-9-94
465m	**Toms Lodge**	27.53	August 93
465mh	**Kildare Slippy**	28.29	1992
650m	**Droopys Evelyn**	39.54	1993
824m	**Easy Bimbo**	51.43	1991

Major Races

EDINBURGH CUP (465m)

1	**HIGHWAY LEADER**	15-8f	(1)

bk d Leaders Best-Highway Mystery Nov 91

2	Faultless Buddy	33-1	(2)
3	Delmonte Lane	6-1	(3)
4	Big Cyril	10-3	(6)
5	Knockrour Bruno	7-1	(4)
6	Mancub	7-2	(5)

28.08 4, 1, 4½, ½, 1¾, Bacon, Perry Barr.

Year	Winner	Trainer	Time	SP
1973	Deelside Silver (Silver Hope-Dusty Prim)	Kane	28.14	9-2
1974	Bealkilla Diver (Sallys Yarn-Bealkilla Queen)	Mullins	28.20	7-i
1975	Tory Mor (Toms Pal-Melville Money)	Milligan	27.67	7-4
1976	Gaily Noble (Monalee Champion-Noble Lynn)	Coleman	28.24	6-1
1977	Linacre (Lively Band-Certral)	Dickson	27.91	11-10F
1978	Dale Lad (Bright Lad-Kerry Pal)	de Mulder	28.07	100-30
1979	Jon Barrie (Clashing-Famous Heart)	Andrews	28.25	3-1
1980	Jelly Crock (Lindas Champion-Mosey Ada)	Travers	28.35	4-5 F
1981	Deel Joker (Free Speech-Leaping Lady)	Gibbons	28.07	6-4F
1982	Brief Candle (Peruvian Style-Sky Banner)	Hancox	27.98	6-4
1983	Creamery Cross (Knockrour Slave-Creamery Alice)	Briggs	28.18	3-1
1984	Creamery Cross (Knockrour Slave-Creamery Alice)	Briggs	28.35	6-1
1985	Smokey Pete (Smokey Flame-Smokey Cotton)	Linzell	28.54	7-4
1986	Coolamber Forest (Cuolamber Tank-Coolamber Pet)	O'Sullivan	28.26	10-1
1987	Princes Pal (Cronins Bar-Balles Oshkosh)	Travers	28.32	11-10 F
1988	Pond Hurricane (Lindas Champion-Soda Pop)	Williams	28.92	4-9 F
1989	Intelligent Lad (Burn Park Black-Face The Dawn)	Milligan	28.21	5-1
1990	Social Circle (Nelson's Dasher-Gorgeous)	Mullins	28.22	4-5 F
1991	Glenpark Again (Whisper Wishes-Ballycrine Style)	Frew	28.09	7-1
1992	Murlens Abbey (Daleys Gold-Murlens Toe)	Copplestone	28.00	4-6F
1993	James John (Manorville Major-Frisky White)	Neil	27.69	12-1

NGRC Directory

Ramsgate

Hereson Road, Dumpton Park, Ramsgate, Kent, CT11 7EU.
Telephone number: 01843 593333. Fax: 01843 590710.

Owner: Northern Sports Stadiums Ltd.
General manager: Sheila Yandle.
Racing manager: W J Jeffcoate
Racing & Print Manager: J. Ross.
Trainers (attached): D. Ingram-Seal, P. Garland, B. McIntosh, S. Pilford, S. Mavrias, A. Bean, R. Bartlett, M. Cumner, S. Swaine, M. Trimmings, R. Duncan.

HOW TO GET THERE
By car: M2 and Thanet Way into Ramsgate.
By rail: Dumpton Park station is opposite stadium.
By bus: 8, 8a, 9, 9a from City Centre.

Race nights: Thursday (7.30 pm), Saturday (7.30 pm, 12 races). Sundays (from January 22, 1995), 12 noon.
Trial sessions: Tuesday (12 noon).
Distances: 450m, 450mh, 590m, 640m, 855m.
Grading times: 450m: 28.69, puppies, 28.89; 840m: 41.99.
Number of dogs per race: Six.
Surface: Sand.
Type of hare: Outside Sumner.
Circumference of track: 405m.
Distance to the first bend: 90m.
Width of track: 18ft
Layout of the track and how it runs: Long straights, sharp bends. Large track with a big gallop.
Usual method of track preparation: Automatic watering system in summer, salting in winter.

Major competitions:
   Master Brewer Trophy (450m), May.
   Kent St Leger (640m), July.
   Thanet Gold Cup (450m), October.

Graded prize money: Bottom grade £25, top grade £70.
Number of bookmakers: Four.
Totalisator: Computerised, win, place, forecast, trio, jackpot.

NGRC Directory

Timing: Automatic, ray timing and photo timing.
Facilities: Chromatography, vet in attendance, kennels for 88 greyhounds (all inside, most modern In the country), car park for 300 vehicles, restaurant for 150 covers. two bars, two refreshment rooms, two glass-fronted stands, video replay.
Other activities at the stadium: Friday market, garden centre, squash, snooker, gymnasium, night club.

Track Records

235m	**Oakfront Drive**	14.68	11-10-93
450m	**Poor Brian**	26.95	26-9-92
450mh	**Deerpark Jim**	27.49	1-8-92
590m	**Patriot Sail**	36.82	5-5-94
590mh	**Glenrobin**	37.59	16-3-92
640m	**Loch Bo Anchor**	39.68	11-10-93
640mh	**Freewheel Kylo**	40.82	11-10-93
855m	**Glenowen Queen**	53.95	2-12-85
1045m	**Wayzgoose**	68.11	10-5-92

BE FIRST PAST THE POST...

with this great Greyhound Racing book offer...

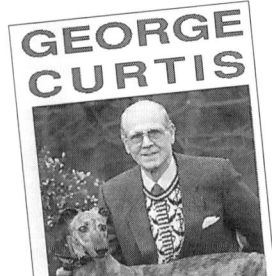

George Curtis: Training Greyhounds (£17.50)

Secrets of the maestro. The essential, classic guide for all those with an interest in Greyhounds. It chronicles the training methods of the great George Curtis, who came from the slums of pre-war Portsmouth to become Britain's leading trainer.

To order, send a cheque or money order to:
Ringpress Books, PO Box 8, Lydney, Glos., GL15 6YD
Access/Visa orders phone **0594 563800**. Prices are UK only. Eire add £2 per item.

PRE-RACE VIEW of the main stand at Smallmead Stadium

Reading

Smallmead Stadium, Bennet Road, Reading, Berks RG2 OJL. Telephone number: 01734 863161. Fax : 01734 313264.

Owner: Allied Presentations Limited.
General manager: William Dore.
Racing manager: Martyn Dore.
Trainers (attached): W. Black, W. Burrow, M. Cantrell, M. Cumner, B. Doyle, R. Gilling, T. Holtom, K. Howard, G. Mayhew, J. McGee Jnr, N. Mourning, M. Nierobisz, C. Packham, R. Stiles, D. Stinchcombe, M. Thomas, D. Vass, W. Walden, R. Yeates.

HOW TO GET THERE
By car: Junction 11 of M4. Bennet Road is five minutes from M4 off A33.

Race nights: Tuesday and Thursday (7.30 pm), Saturday (7.15 pm).
Trial sessions: Friday (10.30 am).
Distances: 275m, 465m, 465mh, 660m, 660mh, 850m, 1045m.
Grading times: 275m: 17.20; 465m: 29.60, puppies 30.00; 465mh: 30.80; 660mh: 43.30.
Number of dogs per race: Six.
Surface: Sand.
Type of hare: Outside Sumner.
Circumference of track: 385m.
Distance to the first bend: 85m.

NGRC Directory

Width of track: 20m
Layout of the track and how it runs: Good run to first bend and long run in to finish.
Usual method of track preparation: Prepared before each meeting and during racing, weather permitting. Salted from November and throughout winter.

Major competitions:
   Reading Masters (465m), £30,000, April.
   Hunt Cup (660m), £2,500, October/November.

Graded prize money: Bottom grade £20, top grade £100.
Number of bookmakers: Eight.
Totalisator: Computerised, win, place, forecast, tritecta, jackpot.
Timing: Automatic and sectional ray timing.
Facilities: Vet in attendance at all race and trial meetings, kennels for 94 greyhounds, car park, restaurant for 70 covers, three bars, refreshment room, covered stand, video replay.
Other activities at the stadium: Speedway.

Track Records

275m	**Greenfield Box**	16.32	23-10-82
465m	**Coomlogane Euro**	28.58	24-11-94
465mh	**Gis A Smile**	28.58	30-4-94
660m	**Waltham Abbey**	41.01	22-10-88
	Airmount Flash		1-12-92
660mh	**Gold Splash**	41.95	24-4-93
850m	**Ivory Lamb**	54.19	11-9-90
1045m	**Sandollar Sophie**	67.90	30-4-94

Major Races

THE MASTERS (465m)

1	**DRUIDS ELPRADO**	11-8f	(1)
	bdw d lm Slippy-Druids Dalroy Mar 92		
2	Longvalley Manor	10-1	(5)
3	Farmer Patrick	6-4	(4)
4	Salthill Champ	7-1	(3)
5	Lyons Double	7-1	(6)
6	Micks Rover	14-1	(2)

27.99 (+20) 2³/₄, ³/₄ sht-hd, 2¹/₂ sht-hd, McGee, Hackney.

NGRC Directory

Romford

London Road, Romford, Essex, RM7 9DU.
Telephone number: 01708 762345, Fax: 01708 744899.

Owner: Coral Stadia Ltd.
General manager: W. R. Hiscock.
Racing manager: Stephen Daniel.
Trainers (attached): K. Linzell, T. Dennis, P. Payne, E. Wiley, P. Rich, K. Marlow, M. Lucas, P. Rich.

Race nights: Monday, Wednesday, Friday (7.30pm), and Saturday (7.15 pm), and some Tuesday and Thursday Thursdays (BAGS). April-August, Monday evening BAGS.
Trial Sessions: April-August 31, Tuesdays; September 1-October 31, Thursdays.

HOW TO GET THERE

BY RAIL: Romford mainline station is about half a mile away.
BY CAR: A12 to Romford, turn towards town ring road and then follow A118 London Road, eastbound.

Distances: 400m, 400mh, 575m, 575mh, 750m, 925m, 1100m.
Grading times: 400m: 25.40, puppies 25.50. 575m; 37.50.
Graded Prizes: Bottom grade £55, top grade £90.
Number of dogs per race: Six.
Surface: All sand.
Type of hare: Outside McGee.
Circumference of track: 350m.
Distance to the first bend: 67m.
Width of track: Straights 15ff 6in, bends 18ff 6in (widest part).
Layout of the track and how it runs: A sprint circuit with tightish bends, but a very safe track. Ideally suited to a smallish, short coupled greyhound or small nippy bitch. Not ideal for the heavyweight, long legged type which requires half an acre in which to perform on the turns. Early pace is a must.

NGRC Directory

Usual method of track preparation: Topping up of sand where and when necessary, smoothing out ruts, foot marks etc, and regular watering. Applying salt during winter whenever frost is a danger.

Major competitions:
Sporting Life Marathon (750m), February.
The Champion Stakes (575m) July.
Stadium Bookmakers Essex Vase (575m), August.
Bailey Racing Golden Sprint (400m) October.
Triumph Hurdle (575m), November.
Puppy Cup (400m), November/December.

Number of bookmakers: Main enclosure, eight; Popular enclosure, three.
Totalisator: Computer, win, place, forecast, trio, nugget, super jackpot.
Timing: Automatic and hand. Sectional ray timing to winning line from starting traps. No split times available on bends.
Facilities: Chromatography, vet in attendance, kennels for 72 greyhounds, car park, restaurant for 250 seats, seven bars (four main enclosure, three popular enclosure), five refreshment rooms (two main enclosure, three popular enclosure), two glass-fronted stands, video replay, large video screen. Also, children's playground.
Restaurant booking: Tel: 01708 762345

Track Records

400m	**Right Move**	23.78	8-5-92
400mh	**Run With Billy**	24.41	18-2-94
575m	**Sard**	35.09	21-9-88
575mh	**Shanavulin Jacko**	36.20	10-4-93
715m	**Scurlogue Champ**	44.18	16.4.85
750m	**Keem Rocket**	46.70	2-3-85
925m	**Salina**	59.13	7-4-81
1100m	**Cregagh Prince**	72.59	10-3-87

NGRC Directory

STADIUM BOOKMAKERS ESSEX VASE (400m)

1	**LISA MY GIRL**	Ev f	(2)

wbd b Murlens Slippy-Long Valley Lady Mar 92

2	Solva Flame	5-1	(1)
3	Gortmore Express	10-1	(3)
4	Harrys Lion	7-2	(4)
5	Creamery Bridge	16-1	(5)
6	Pepsi Pete	6-1	(6)

35.69 (+20) 3¾, sht-hd, sht-hd, 1¼, 2¾, Coleman, Walthamstow.

Year	Winner	Time	SP
1971	Dolores Rocket (Newdown Heather-Come On Dolores) White, Pvt	36.06	EF
1972	Fit Me In (Myross Again-No Mable) Singleton, Harringay	36.59	8-1
1973	Kenneally Mowor (Moordyke Spot-Kenneally Tune) Orton W'don	36.91	4-1
1974	Cowpark Yank (Yanks Boy-Cowpark Late) Duggan, Romford	36.70	5-2
1975	Handy High (Handy Valley-Black High Bird) Milligan, Pvt	36.62	11-10F
1976	Westmead Myra (Myrtown-Weatmead Silver) Savva, Bletchley	36.69	7-4F
1977	Xmas Holiday (Supreme Fun-Marys Snowball) Rees, W'don	37.40	6-1
1978	Bermuda's Fun (Supreme Fun-Avondhu Lass) Ushe, Romford	35.15	4-1
1979	Black Haven (Blackwater Champ-Ahaveen Hunter) Payne, Romford	35.55	6-1
1980	Taranaki (Sole Aim-Honeymoon Band) Rich, Ramsgate	35.82	20-1
1981	Shandy Edie (Chain Gang-Out Of My Way) Ingram-Seal, Pvt	35.48	5-1
1982	Glenmoy Raven (Black Legend-Glenmoy Lily) Hitch, Pvt	36.03	12-1
1983	Winning Line (Some Skinomage-Small Bend) Foley, Pvt	35.36	2-1 F
1984	Wheelers Tory (Glen Rock-Sandhill Fawn) Wheeler, Pvt	35.45	4-1
1985	Ballyregan Bob (Ballyheigue Moon-Evening Daisy) Curtis, Brighton	35.15	1-2F
1986	Roseship Trish (Knockrour Slave-Rosehip Queen) Wiley, Hackney	35.49	11-10F
1987	Silver Walk (Noble Brigg-Annaghmore Slave) Gaskin, Pvt	35.56	5-1
1988	Double Bid (Gambling Fever-Deccaso) Rees, Wimbledon	35.27	10-11 F
1989	Poker Prince (Whisper Wishes-Proud Chill) Rees, Wimbledon	35.44	8-1
1990	No Doubt (Oran Jack-Supreme Cut) Payne, Romford	24.02	8-1
1991	Vics Snowdrop (Daleys Gold-White Ranger) Rees, Wimbledon	24.34	5-1
1992	Frost Hill (Glencorbry Celt-Ballycrine Spots) Mullins, Wal'stow	24.05	5-1
1993	Up And Off (Im Slippy-Cheerful Beauty) Coleman, Wal'stow	24.70	2-1F

MAGGIE BARTON CHAMPION STAKES (575m)

1	**HERES SEANIE**	6-4f	(3)

f d Ardfert Sean-Mindys Miracle Jul 92

2	Simply Free	7-2	(1)
3	Silver Glow	8-1	(3)
4	Wexford Minx	5-2	(5)
5	Mountain Wind	20-1	(4)
6	Gortmore Express	8-1	(2)

35.23 (+20) 4¾, 1¼, ¾, 1, ¾, Ryan, Perry Barr.

1992	Chic Mona (Gastrognome-Sirius Mona) Gaskin, Walthamstow	35.58	11-4
1993	Westmead Surprise (Daleys Gold-Westmead Move) Savva, M Keynes	36.05	3-1

RYEHOUSE STADIUM

RACING UNDER NGRC PERMIT RULES

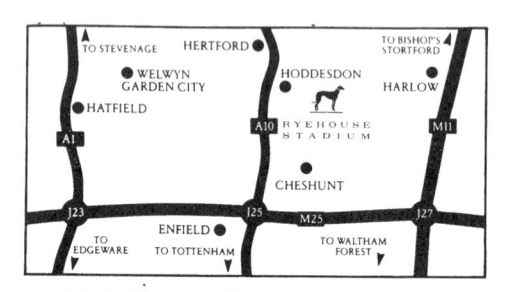

HOW TO GET THERE . .

By road
M25 JUNCTION 25, NORTH ON A10 TO HODDESDON, TURN OFF, FOLLOW SIGNS TO RYE PARK AND STADIUM

By rail
FROM LIVERPOOL ST, TOTTENHAM HALE, SEVEN SISTERS TO RYE HOUSE STATION. 1 MINUTE WALK FROM STATION. BRITISH RAIL PASSENGER ENQUIRIES TEL: 0171-928 7171

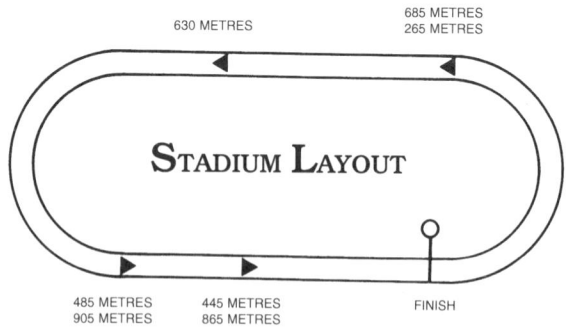

Stadium Layout

630 METRES

685 METRES
265 METRES

485 METRES
905 METRES

445 METRES
865 METRES

FINISH

ONE OF THE COUNTRY'S FINEST GALLOPS. LONG STRAIGHTS AND SWEEPING BANKED BENDS

RACING EVERY WEDNESDAY, SATURDAY AND OCCASIONALLY SUNDAY, FIRST RACE 7.45 pm

RYE HOUSE STADIUM, RYE ROAD, HODDESDON, HERTFORDSHIRE. TEL: 01992 464200

NGRC Directory

BAILY RACING GOLDEN SPRINT (400m)

1	**WITCHES DEAN**	4-1	(5)
	bk d Lyons Dean-Witches Betty Feb 92		
2	Countrywide Fox	2-1	(6)
3	Danesfort Slippy	11-2	(2)
4	Fly Wish	13-8f	(1)
5	Bassiano	16-1	(4)
6	Lots of Jolly	14-1	(3)

24.28 (+10) hd, $3/4$, $13/4$, 1, $83/4$,. Rich, Romford

NEW – THE BEST BOOK ON GREYHOUNDS EVER!

THE COMPLETE BOOK OF GREYHOUNDS

Edited by **Julia Barnes** and written by the world's TOP experts on every facet of the breed.

JOHN KOHNKE on **PHYSIOLOGY, FEEDING** and **NUTRITION**

NICK SAVVA on **BREEDING** and **REARING**

MALCOLM WILLIS on **GENETICS**

PATRICK SAWARD on **BLOODLINES**

GEOFF DE MULDER, LINDA MULLINS

and **MICHAEL O'SULLIVAN** compare **TRAINING** methods

with leading American and Australian handlers

OVER 100,000 WORDS....MORE THAN 150 PHOTOGRAPHS, MANY IN FULL COLOUR.

'A WONDERFUL BOOK AT A SENSIBLE PRICE'

£17.50 (PLUS £2.50 Postage and Packing)

To order, send a cheque or money order to:
Ringpress Books, PO Box 8, Lydney, Glos., GL15 6YD
Access/Visa orders phone **0594 563800**. Prices are UK only. Eire add £2 per item.

Rye House

Rye Road, Hoddesdon, Herts.
Telephone number: 01992 464200. Fax: 01992 464046

Status: Permit.
Promoter: Rye Racing Ltd
General Manager: Ray Spalding.
Racing Manager: Frank Baldwin
Trainers: 12 professional trainers and 100 permit trainers.

HOW TO GET THERE

By car: A10 to Hoddesdon (off the M25 Hertford turn off), then follow signs to Rye Park.

Race nights: Monday, Wednesday and Saturday (7.45 pm).
Trial sessions: Sundays.
Distances: 255m, 485m, 630m.
Number of dogs per race: Six.
Surface: Grass /Sand.
Type of hare: McKee.
Circumference of track: 420m.
Distance to the first bend: 90m.
Width of track: 5m.
Layout of the track and how it runs: Long galloping straights and reasonable, easy-running bends. A track where quality greyhounds may encounter early trouble and redeem

NGRC Directory

their position on the long straights.
Usual method of track preparation: Watered as required.

Major competitions:
Gold Vase, September.
Sovereign Stakes, September/October.
Cloth of Gold, October.

Graded prize money: From £15 to £50 win.
Number of bookmakers: Five.
Totalisator: Computerised, forecast, win and place.
Timing: Ray and photo-timing.
Facilities: Vet in attendance, kennels for 60 greyhounds, car park for 200 vehicles, restaurant for 40 covers, three bars, refreshment room, glass-fronted stand.
Other facilities available at the stadium: Speedway, go-kart racing.

Track Records

A new surface has been recently laid at Rye House and new track record data is to be established.

NGRC Directory

Shawfield

Ruthergien Road, Glasgow.
Telephone number: 0141 6474121. Fax: 0141 6477265.

How to get there: By car: A74 Glasgow south turn-off.
Owners: Greyhound Racing & Leisure Co.
General Manager: Robert Lithgow.
Racing Manager: Alex McTaggart

Trainers (attached): M. Bell, J. Spence, J. Flaherty, Y. Fvans, S. Douglas, W. Weir, G. Smith, A. Stirling, E. Scally, T. Sharkey.

Race nights: Tuesday, Thursday and Saturday (7.45 pm). Monday, Friday (permit).
Trial session: Wednesday (10.30 am).
Distances: 300m, 450m, 480m, 500m, 670m, 730m,
Grading times: 450m: 29.00; 480m: 31.00.
Number of dogs per race: Five.
Surface: Silicon sand.
Type of hare: Outside McKee & Outside Sumner.
Circumference of track: 432m.
Distance to the first bend: 120m.
Width of track: 8yds.
Layout of the track and how it runs: Good galloping circuit, banked bends.
Usual method of track preparation: Harrowing, rolling and watering, salting in winter.

Major competitions:
Scottish Derby (500m). £10,000, May.

Graded prize money: £45.
Number of bookmakers: Nine.
Totalisator: Computerised.
Timing: Ray and photo timing.
Facilities: Chromatography, vet in attendance, kennels for 90 greyhounds, car park for 150 vehicles, restaurant for 60 covers, six bars, including members club, covered stand, video replay.
Other activities at the stadium: Speedway and boxing

NGRC Directory

Track Records

SHAWFIELD

300m	**Ravage Again**	17.41	27-10-89
450m	**Fair Hill Boy**	26.85	27-10-89
480m	**Funny Enough**	29.32	10-9-94
500m	**Droopys Sandy**	29.39	21-5-94
500mh	**Face The Mutt**	31.07	25-5-82
670m	**Crack Of The Ash**	40.50	11-9-93
730m	**Decoy Princess**	45.40	20-2-88
932m	**Silken Dancer**	59.35	2-9-94

REGAL SCOTTISH DERBY (480m)

1	**DROOPYS SANDY**	Ev f	(6)

bk d Manorville Magic-I'm a Survivor Dec 91

2	Decoy Lynx	20-1	(4)
3	First Defence	6-1	(2)
4	Double Polano	7-1	(3)
5	Lone Rider	5-2	(5)
6	Mossfield Fire	25-1	(1)

29.39 (+20) 9, 1, 1¼, hd, 2, Murray, Ireland.

1970	Brilane Clipper (Faithful Hope-Brilane Parachute) 9-4	F Kelly, Leeds	29.46
1971	not run		
1972	Patricia's Hope (Silver Hope-Patsicia) 9-2	Jackson, Clapton	29.22
1973	Dashalong Chief (Monalee Champion-Hopeful Glen) 1-2	Jackson, W. City	29.60
1974	Cosha Orchis (Own Pnde-Monalee) 12-1	Meechan, Shawfield	29.20
1975	Dromlara Master (Own Pride-Monalee Last) 7-1	Gaynor, Perry Barr	29.30
1976	Flip Your Top (Own Pride-Whittle Off) 11-10F	Young, Private	30.56
1977	Amber Sky (Bright Lad-Quite Efficient) 6-4F	Beaumont, Private	29.08
1978	Pat Seamur (Tullig Rambler-Dainty Black) 11-4	de Mulder, Hall Grn	30.52
1979	Greenville Boy (Tullig Rambler-Greenville Lass) 6-4F	Mullins, Camb	30.49
1980	Decoy Sovereign (Westmead County-Ka Boom) 4-1	Cobbold, Ipswich	30.68
1981	Marbella Sky (Weston Blaze-Maries Kate) 12-1	Andrews, Belle Vue	30.66
1982	Special Account (Westmead County-Ka Boom) EvF	Savva, Milton K	29.99
1983	On Spec (Blushing Spy-On Pot) 2-1	Crapper, Owlerton	30.50
1984	not run		
1985	Smokey Pete (Smokey Flame-Smokey Cotton) 7-2	Linzell, W'atow	30.29
1986	not run		
1987	Princes Pal (Cronins Bar-Ballea Oshkosh) EvF	Tracers, Ireland	27.58
1988	Killouragh Chris (Moreen Rocket-Horeen Honey) 6-4F	Beaumont, Owlerton	28.75
1989	Airmount Grand (Daley's Gold-Airmount Jewel) EvF	Kiely, Ireland	30.03
1990	Weatmead Harry (Fearless Champ-Westmead Move) 5-4F	Savva, Mil Keynes	29.62
1991	Phantom Flash (Flashy Sir-Westmead Seal) 1-4F	Byrne, Wimbledon	29.77
1992	Glideaway Sam (Echo Spark-Cute Detty) 25-1	Compton, N Canes	30.26
1993	New Level (Murlens Slippy-Well Plucked) 3-1	Willams, Sunderland	30.22

NGRC Directory

Sheffield

Penistone Road, Owlerfon, Sheffield S6 2DE
Telephone number: 0114 2343074. Fax: 0114 2333631.

Owner: A & S Leisure Ltd.
Managing Director: David Proctor.
General manager: Jon Carter.
Racing manager: David Baldwin.
Trainers (attached): P. Beaumont, M. Wainwright, Elaine. Parker, P. Woodward, H. Crapper, S. Robinson, S. Clift, R. Warren, B. Draper, R. Hough, D Hopper, R. Carr.

> **HOW TO GET THERE**
> Leave MI at Junction 36, take A61 - Stadium is 7 miles down A61 on left (half a mile past the Hillsborough football ground).

Race nights: Tuesday, Friday and Saturday (7 pm), Sunday (12.15 pm)
Trial sessions: Monday (10 45 am).
Distances: 290m, 362m, 480m, 500m, 500mhcp, 660m, 730m, 800m and 932m.
Grading times: 500m: 31.40; 660m: 42.70.
Number of dogs per race: Mainly six.
Surface: All sand.
Type of hare: Outside Sumner.
Circumference of track: 437m.
Distance to the first bend: 65m.
Width of track: 5m
Layout of the track and how it runs: Shortish straights but wide sweeping bends make Owlerton a very good gallop. It is a true test of the ability of a greyhound to stay 500m.
Usual method of track preparation: Raking, levelling and watering. Salt mixed into sand before winter and increased during cold spells.

Major competitions:
   William Stones Northern Sprint Ch'ship (290m), June.
   The Dransfield (660m), July
   Nigel Troth Yorkshire Oaks (500m)
   Harry Holmes Memorial Trophy (500m), November.

Graded prize money: Bottom grade £19, top grade £50.

NGRC Directory

Number of bookmakers: Five.
Totalisator: Computerised, win. place, forecast, trifecta and jackpot.
Timing: Ray
Facilities: Vet in attendance, kennels for 100 greyhounds, car park for 500 vehicles, restaurant, four bars, one snack bar, covered stand, video replay.
Restaurant booking available, 140 seats.

Track Records

290m	Fearless Prince	16.78	13-8-80
	Melton Hill	16.78	19-10-90
362m	Check Out	20.97	3-5-89
480m	Cheeky Hero	28.07	
500m	Galtymore Lad	29.25	19-1-90
730m	Beano Blondie	44.63	22-8-86
800m	Change Guard	49.02	15-8-86

Sittingbourne

Telephone: 01795 420605. Fax: 01795 430776

DUE to come under starter's orders shortly in 1995, there were no directory details available at the time of going to press.

Stainforth

Regal Meadow Court Stadium, Station Rd, Stainforth DN7 5HS
Telephone number: 01302 351639/ 351204.
Fax: 01302 351650.

Owners: D. Hicken, J Brindley.
General manager: Mrs B Tompkins
Racing Manager: K Ward
Race nights: Thursday, Saturday, Sunday afternoon..
Trial sessions: Monday evenings.
Distances: 495m, 458m, 278m, 666m,
Grading times: 495m: 31.50; 458m 29.30; 278m 17.50..
Number of greyhounds per race: Six.
Surface: Sand.
Type of hare: Outside Sumner.
Circumference of track: 428m.
Width of track: 7.5m.
Graded prize money: Given to each graded greyhound.
Totalisator: Data tote.
Timing: Ray timing.
No. of Bookmakers: Four

Track Records

278m	Slippery Jaydee	16.44	1-12-94
458m	Super Bridge	27.46	2-7-94
495m	Jubilee Rocco	29.73	24-6-93
666m	Westwood Surprise	40.95	10-9-93

NGRC Directory

Sunderland

Newcastle Road, Sunderland.
Telephone number: 0191-536 7250 Fax: 0191-519 1151.

Owners: K. Wilde.
General manager: Mrs P. Hutchinson.
Racing Manager: Mr J Nunn

> **HOW TO GET THERE**
> Two minutes from A1M, off A19— A184 Boldon.

Race nights:
Wednesday, Friday and Saturday (7.30 pm). BAGS meetings some Thursdays and some Sundays.
Trial sessions: Before racing and on Thursdays when no BAGS meeting.
Distances: 255m, 405m, 580m, 631m, 782m, 824m.
Grading times: 450m: 29.40.
Number of dogs per race: Five or six.
Surface: Sand.
Type of hare: Outside McKee.
Circumference of track: 377m.
Distance to the first bend: 90m.
Width of track: Straights 6m, bends 7m.
Layout of the track and how it runs: Scaled down version of Harringay. Long straights, well-banked bends.
Usual method of track preparation: Watered and rolled before racing. Salted in winter when necessary.

Major competitions:
   The Regal 10,000, February
   Dranesfield Northern Puppy Cup (450m), October.

Totalisator: Computerised, win, place, forecast, trio and jackpot.
Timing: Ray timing.
Number of Bookmakers: Five
Facilities: Kennels for 118 greyhounds, car park for 500 vehicles, three bars, restaurant for 140 covers, four executive boxes, bistro in lounge bar, snack bar, video replay.

NGRC Directory

Track Records

255m	**Intelligent Lad**	15.64	12-9-90
405m	**Sunshine Slippy**	24.97	3-12-90
450m	**Gulleen Darkie**	27.29	19-12-90
450mhcp	**Willrose Street**	27.21	26-7-91
580m	**Tomijo**	36.00	16-6-90
631m	**Sir Alva**	39.59	16-6-90
782m	**Chitral**	49.91	25-8-90
824m	**Road Princess**	52.99	16-6-90

DRANESFIELD NORTHERN PUPPY CUP

1 **JUST RIGHT MELODY**   11-10f   (6)
f d Farloe Melody-Farlow Mineola Dec 92
2   Ettrick Blue   9-4   (2)
3   Canny Choice   5-1   (4)
4   Listen To Him   10-1   (1)
5   Potto Cobra   33-1   (5)
6   Pilot   33-1   (3)
27.79 (+10) $3\frac{1}{4}, 1\frac{1}{4}, 2\frac{1}{4}, 1\frac{1}{4}, 3\frac{1}{4}$. Robinson, Unattached.

PUPPY REGAL 10,000

1 **CARRIGEEN BLAZE**   11-4f   (5)
bk d Adraville Bridge-Carrigeen Lucky May 91
2   Killila Place   6-1   (3)
3   Fermaine Monarch   6-1   (6)
4   King Size   3-1   (2)
5   Mr Lucky   7-1   (4)
6   Slaneyside Jack   6-1   (1)
27.72 (N) hd, 1, $1\frac{1}{2}, 1\frac{1}{4}$, sht-hd, Hough, Sheffield.

BBC TV TROPHY 827m

1 **JUBILEE REBECCA**   2-1   (1)
bw b Pond Mirage-Lively Bid Mar 91
2   Killenagh Dream   7-2   (4)
3   Decoy Lynx   4-1   (6)
4   Newry Town   13-8F   (2)
5   Mossfield Fire   50-1   (3)
6   Tonduff Susie   12-1   (5)
53.13 (+30) $7\frac{3}{4}$, 1, $1\frac{1}{4}$, 4, 1. Rooks, Brough Park.

AWAY THEY GO: Action in front of the main stand at Swaffham.

Swaffham

Downham Road, Swaffham.
Telephone number: 01760 724761. Fax: 0176) 725081

Owner: Tom Smith (leaseholder).
General manager: Tom Smith.
Racing manager: Tom Smith.

HOW TO GET THERE

How to get there: By car: Swaffham Town by pass to Kings Lynn, turn into Downham Road A1122 at rear of Little Chef.

Race nights: Tuesday (free entry), Friday (7 30 pm), and Saturday).
Trial sessions: Wednesday 2.00 pm and after racing. Pups schooling Saturday am..
Distances: 270m, 440m, 480m, 620m, 686m, 856m.
Grading times: 440m 29.00 (allowances made for puppies).
Number of dogs per race: Six.
Surface: Silica sand.
Type of hare: Outside McKee.
Circumference of track: 41 6m.
Distance to the first bend: 88m.
Width of track: Straight 23ft, bends 27ft.
Layout of the track and how it runs: Very large galloping track. Wide, spacious, easy-running, banked bends.

NGRC Directory

Usual method of track preparation: Watered and rolled.
Number of bookmakers: Five.
Totalisator: Computerised. Win, place, forecast trifecta, jackpot.
Timing: Automatic.
Facilities: Vet in attendance, kennels for 84 greyhounds, car park for 2,000 vehicles, bar, retreshment room, covered stand, video replay. Restaurant for 54 patrons.
Other activities at the stadium: Stock car racing.

Track Records

270m	**Hot Hot**	16.31	14-9-93
270mh	**Ashgrove Gift**	16.97	29-10-91
418m	**Killee Stranger**	25.50	31-3-89
440m	**Dims Favourite**	26.85	4-4-90
480m	**Hit The Lid**	29.32	29-8-88
620m	**Tarnwood Emperor**	38.37	28-11-89
686m	**Decoy Cheetah**	43.55	22-11-94
834m	**Mullawn Rip**	54.22	13-2-90
856m	**Barefoot Queen**	24-5-93	55.50
1102m	**Stir About Biddy**	74.03	20-6-92

PUNTERS in the main stand at Abbey Stadium.

Swindon

Abbey Stadium, Blunsdon, Swindon, Wilts SN2 4DN.
Telephone number: 01793 721333 (racing office),
01793)721253 (restaurant). Fax: 0793 723038.

Owner: A.D.T. Auctions.
General manager: W. A. Chandler.
Racing manager: D. J. Stow.
Assistant racing manager: Miss C. S. Hurst.

HOW TO GET THERE

By car: M4 exit 15, follow A419 (Cirencester signs). Stadium is just off main road in Blunsdon.
By train: Swindon station, 10 minutes by taxi.

Trainers (professional): B. Baker, R. Barratt, A. Beale, Miss J. Christie, S. Davis, P. Foster, T. Gray, Mrs C. Gomersall, G. Holland, Mrs. P. Houseman, Mrs. M. Porter, S. Ray, D. Shallis, Mrs. R. Summers, D. Tucker, L. Wallington, Mrs R. Wood, M. Walsh, C. Wilkins, Miss. B. Woodley.

Owner trainers: M. Backhurst, Q. Bevan, R. Bibbins, N. Brent, R. Brimble, H. Burford, B. Dobbin, D. Egan, M. Ellis, R. Evans, P. Farmer, N. Frayling, G. Gillet, R. Harris, R. Hunt, R. Jeans, M. Jeans, R. JOnes, C. Kite, Mrs. C. Llewellyn, J. Little, A. Mann, Mrs D. Mann, C. Martin, Mrs. K. Massey R. Miluk, A. Motti, E. O'Regan, P. Owens, A. Passfield, Mrs P. Radley, C. Rhymer, Mrs. GH. Stringer, Mrs. T. Tungatt, C. Weare, D. O'Sullivan, E. Lane, D. Ace.

NGRC Directory

Race nights: Monday, Wednesday and Friday (7.30 pm).
Trial sessions: Tuesday (11.00 am) and before racing.
Distances: 280m, 476m, 476mh, 509m, 685m, 737m, 933m.
Grading times: 280m: 17.40, 476m: 30.35, 509m: 32.40, 685m: 4450.
Number of dogs per race: Six.
Surface: Sand.
Type of hare: Outside Sumner.
Circumference of track: 457m.
Distance to the first bend: 80m from 476m start.
Width of track: 4m on straights, 7-8m on bends.
Layout of the track and how it runs: The biggest galloping track in England. Stamina is essential.
Usual method of track preparation: Watering, graded between races. Salted in winter when needed.

Major competitions:
The Pride Of The West (685m), June.
Arkells Silver Plume (476m), September

Graded prize money: Bottom grade £14, top grade £50.
Number of bookmakers: Five.
Totalisator: Data tote.
Timing: Photo and ray timing.
Facilities: Vet in attendance at race meetings and trials, kennels for 78 greyhounds, car park for 4,000 vehicles, restaurant for 70 covers, four bars, refreshment room, covered and glass-fronted stand, video replay. Paddock bar and hospitality box available for group bookings.
Other activities at the stadium: Speedway.

Track Records

280m	**Mollifrend Tom**	16.19	5-10-88
476m	**Money Matters**	27.89	3-8-88
476mh	**Faoides Country**	29.11	18-9-91
509m	**Darragh Comett**	29.94	4-7-88
685m	**Black Port**	41.72	18-7-84
737m	**Wailea Flash**	44.62	3-8-88
933m	**Tartan Sarah**	58.52	23-7-84

Walthamstow

Chingford Road, London E4 8SJ.
Telephone number: 0181531 4255. Fax: 01815232747.

Owner: The Chandler family.
Managing Director: Jack Chandler.
Racing manager: Chris Page.
Trainers (attached): G. Baggs, J. Coleman, F. Gaskin, O. Hawkes, Mrs L. Mullins, M. Puzey, C. Duggan, N. Savva. G. Sharp, J. Sherry.

Race nights: Tuesday, Thursday and Saturday (7.30 pm), Sunday 12 noon, Friday BAGS.
Trial sessions: Monday (10.30 am).
Distances: 415m, 475m, 475mh, 640m,

HOW TO GET THERE

**By underground: Walthamstow Central Station. Victoria Line.
By bus: from Walthamstow Central to stadium. By road: Just off North Circular Road, Crooked Billet turn-oft**

NGRC Directory

640mh, 820m, 880m, 1045m.
Grading times: 475m: 30.00, puppies 30.20; 640m: 41.40.
Number of dogs per race: Six.
Surface: All sand.
Type of hare: Outside McGee.
Circumference of the track: 405m.
Distance to the first bend: Approx 100m.
Width of track: 5.5m.
Layout of the track and how it runs: Tight circuit, but has the compensation of long straights. Suits early-paced railers.
Usual method of track preparation: Undersoil heating system, so very little salting is requirnd in the winter. Watered am, pm and before racing in the summer.

Major competitions:
  Jim Davis Stakes (640m), £1,000, January.
  Pepsi Cola Marathon, £2 000 February.
  Racing Post Arc (475m), £5,000, February/March.
  NGRC Stewards Cup (640m), £2,000, April.
  Mistley Trojan Puppy Stakes (475m), £1,500, May.
  The Test (640m), £2,000, June.
  A.R Dennis Hurdle (475m) £1,000, June.
  The Circuit (475m), £2,500, August.
  A.R. Dennis Silver Collar (640m), £3,000, August.
  Ron Bazell Puppy Stakes (475m), £1,500, September.
  Laurent Perrier Grand Prix (640m), £7,500,
    September/October.
  Countrywide Steels Goodwood Cup (475m), £1,000,
    November.
  Holt Marathon (820m), £1,000, December.
  Graded prize money: Bottom grade £50, top grade £120.
  Number of bookmakers: 16.

Totalisator: Computerised. Win, place, forecast, trifecta, jackpot.
Timing: Automatic sectional ray timing, split times available on tour bends and six bends
Facilities: Chromatography, vet in attendance, kennels for 74 greyhounds, two restaurants, paddock grill for 180 covers, Stowaway for 300 covers, three private boxes, several bars, several refreshment rooms, video replay, children's playground, night club.
Other activities at the stadium: Charlie Chan's Nightclub (private members only).

NGRC Directory

Track Records

415m	**Roslo Speedy**	24.99	9-7-94
475m	**Connells Cross**	28.55	9-7-94
475mh	**Heavenly Dream**	28.96	19-5-94
640m	**Silver Glow**	39.41	31-5-94
640mh	**Freewheel Kylo**	40.49	8-10-94
820m	**Smart Decision**	51.59	9-7-94
880m	**Decoy Lynx**	55.65	8-10-94
1045m	**Wheres Dunait**	68.61	5-3-94

Major Races

RACING POST ARC (475m)

1	**WESTMEAD CHICK**	8-1	(3)
	bd b Im Slippy-Westmead Move Jun 92		
2	Paradise Slippy	16-1	(4)
3	Ardilaun Bridge	9-2	(2)
4	Flag The Fawn	12-1	(1)
5	Magical Piper	2-1jf	(5)
6	Glenholm Tiger	2-1jf	(6)

28.73 (+10) nk, 2$^3/_4$, 3$^1/_4$, 2$^1/_2$, hd. Savva, Hackney.

1987	Funny Oyster (Debbycot Lad-Cu Helen) Sherry	W'stow	28.98	9-2
1988	Foretop (Blue Train-Green Slieve) Linzell	W'stow	28.98	7-4F
1989	Kilcannon Bullet (Odell Supreme-Murlens Toe) Coleman	W'stow	28.58	33-1
1990	Brownies Outlook (Citizen Supreme-Hardi Hostess) Payne	Romford	28.94	5-1
1991	Fires Of War (Dipmac-Marys Silver) Meek	Oxford	28.82	2-1
1992	Murlens Abbey (Daleys Gold-Murlens Toe) Copplestone	Reading	28.61	3-1
1993	Bonney Seven (Airmount Grand-Powerstown Pine) Coleman	W'stow	28.82	10-11F

LAURENT-PERRIER CHAMPAGNE GRAND PRIX

1	**REDWOOD GIRL**	2-1	(1)
	bd b Ardfert Sean-Redwood Sue Mar 91		
2	Twin Rainbow	6-1	(4)
3	Decoy Lion	13-8f	(2)
4	Browside Pat	6-1	(1)
5	Sonic Blue	16-1	(5)
6	Speakers Choice	20-1	(6)

39.74 (+15) sht-hd, 1, $^1/_2$, nk, 1,$^1/_2$. Savva, Hackney.

BE FIRST PAST THE POST...

with these great Greyhound Racing book and video offers...

Books

Veterinary Advice for Greyhound Owners
£14.99 (plus £2.50 post and packing)
Practical, easy-to-follow advice from **JOHN KOHNKE**, the vet who is Greyhound racing's leading columnist dealing with greyhound ailments. Covers everything from the treatment and prevention of injuries to vital information on nutrition.

1994 Greyhound Stud Book
£20 (plus £2.50 post and packing)
The breeder's bible

George Curtis: Training Greyhounds
£17.50 (plus £2.50 post and packing)
Secrets of the maestro. The essential, classic guide for all those with an interest in Greyhounds. It chronicles the training methods of the great George Curtis, who came from the slums of pre-war Portsmouth to become Britain's leading trainer.

The Complete Book of Greyhounds
£17.50 (plus £2.50 post and packing)
Edited by **Julia Barnes** and written by the world's TOP experts on every facet of the breed.
JOHN KOHNKE on **PHYSIOLOGY, FEEDING** and **NUTRITION; NICK SAVVA** on **BREEDING** and **REARING; MALCOLM WILLIS** on **GENETICS; PATRICK SAWARD** on **BLOODLINES; GEOFF DE MULDER, LINDA MULLINS** and **MICHAEL O'SULLIVAN** compare **TRAINING** methods with leading American and Australian handlers

Videos

GREAT RACES OF 1994 (£19.99)
The video of the year – a must
1994 GREYHOUND DERBY (£19.99)
Every race from the premier classic
Training Greyhounds with George Curtis (£19.99)
Unique insights into his methods

Order the Curtis book and video together for £27.49 – SAVE £10!

To order, send a cheque or money order to:
Ringpress Books, PO Box 8, Lydney, Glos., GL15 6YD
Access/Visa orders phone **0594 563800**. Prices are UK only. Eire add £2 per item.

NGRC Directory

1970	Baton (Annard-Pine Blacktop) Durkin	W'stow	40.39	9-4	
1971	Breaches Blizzard (Maryville Hi-Breaches Blizzard) McNally	Perry Barr	40.00	4-5F	
1972	not run				
1973	Pendys Mermaid (Merry Newdown-Linnees Venture) Geggus	Walth'atow	40.65	11-8F	
1974	Ballyglass Hope (Faithtul Hope-Deise Ivory) Thornton	Pvt	40.58	7-1	
1975	not run				
1976	Manderlay King (Crazy Top-Shandaroba) de Mulder	Hall Green	40.21	9-2	
1977	Paradise Spectre (Spectre-Paradise Wonder) Mullina	Pvt	40.19	6-4F	
1978	Paradise Spectre (Spectre-Paradise Wonder) Mullins	Pvt	40.03	3-1 JF	
1979	Frame That (Ritas Choice-The Grand Love) Dickson	Slough	39.57	11-2	
1980	Sports Promoter (Breakaway Town-Kensington Dueen) Mullins	Cambs	40.17	2-IJF	
1981	Rathduff Solara (Ivy Hall Solo-Rathduff Gazelle) Dennis	Southend	40.71	2-1JF	
1982	Huberts Shade (Luminous Lad-Huberts Fate) Jackson	Wembley	39.73	11-8F	
1983	Flying Duke (GailyNoble-Shans Fantasia) Coughlan	Crayford	40.49	4-1	
1984	Sunrise Sonny (Armagh Rocket-Kerry Wedding) Curtis	Brighton	40.00	25-1	
1985	Slaneyside Gold (Sand Man-Prince Of Rocks) Sherry	W'stow	40.00	5-1	
1986	Westmead Move (Whisper Wishes-Westmead Tania) Savva	Pvt	39.35	10-11 F	
1988	Digby Bridge (Yellow Band-Ballylough Judy) Malcolm	Hall Green	40.14	50-1	
1989	Waltham Abbey (Manorville Sand-Mona Lisa) Gaskin	Pvt	39.91	2-1	
1990	Dempseys Whisper (Whisper Wishes-Lemon Gem) Byrne	Canterbury	39.07	4-11 F	
1991	Dempseys Whisper (Whisper Wishes-Lemon Gem) Byrne	Wimbledon	39.20	2-1	
1992	Westmead Darkie (Airmount Grand-Westmead Move) Savva	M Keynes	39.36	2-1F	
1993	Redwood Girl (Ardfert Sean-Redwood Sue) Gaskin	W'stow	39.89	5-1	

AR DENNIS SILVER COLLAR (640m)

1 **SILBURY CLOUD** 20-1 (3)
   f b Whisper Wishes-Ferndale Class May 92
2 Lyons Double 7-2 (6)
3 First Defence 9-2 (4)
4 Simply Free 7-4f (2)
5 Runalong Darkie 33-1 (5)
6 Gallys Lady 9-4 (1)
39.80 (+30) 1¼, ½, ½, 1½, 2½. Finch, Swindon.

NGRC Greyhound Racing Yearbook 1995

Greatest in Racing

**Belle Vue
Catford
Wimbledon
Portsmouth
Hall Green
Wembley**

**For information contact
Annette Hinton on
0121-778-6946**

Wembley

The Empire Stadium, Wembley, Middlesex HA9 0DW.
Telephone number: 0181 9028833. Fax: 0181-903 0048.

Owner: Wembley plc.
General manager: Mr J Rogers.
Racing manager: Mr M. Smith.
Trainers (attached): H. Dickson, J. Honeysett, P. Heasman, T. Johnston, W. Ginzel, T. Atkins, F. Greenacre, Mr T. Trevis, Mr C. Dolby, Mr. J. Haynes.
Race nights: Mondays, and Fridays
Trial Session: 12 trials before racing.
Distances: 275m, 490m, 655m, 710m, 850m, 925m.
Grading times: 490m: 31.00, 655m: 42.00.

HOW TO GET THERE

BY CAR: Five minutes from the North Circular Road. Follow signs to Wembley Stadium.
BY RAIL: Wembley Stadium Complex (3 mins). Wembley Central (15 mins) Wembley Park (10 mins).
BY TUBE: Wembley Park (Met. and Jubilee Lines).

NGRC Directory

Number of dogs per race: Six.
Surface: All sand
Type of hare: Outside McKee.
Circumference of track: 435m.
Distance to the first bend: 95m.
Width of track: Straights 4m.
Layout of track and how it runs: Big galloping track, bends are not banked. A true test of stamina.
Usual method of track preparation: Hand-watered and raked.

Major competitions:
Blue Riband (490m) March/April.
Select Stakes (490m), £1 400, September.
Wendy Fair St Leger (655m), November.

Graded prize money: 490m: bottom grade £35, top grade £100; 655m: bottom grade £60, top grade £100.
Number of bookmakers: 12.
Totalisator: Computer. Win, place, forecast, trio, jackpot.
Timing: Photo timing.
Facilities: Chromatography, vet in attendance, kennels for 78 greyhounds, car park for several thousand vehicles, restaurant for 280 covers, three bars, refreshment kiosks, covered stand, video replay, executive suites, carvery.
Other activities at the stadium: Pop concerts, Sunday market, football.

Track Records

275m	Flashy Rocket	15.99	17-10-88
490m	Phantom Flash	28.79	1-10-90
490mh (6F)	Castlelyons Cash	29.70	28-4-86
490mh (5F)	Ballinlough Hill	29.88	8-1-92
655m	Chicita Banana	39.41	5-5-89
655mh	Ellas Ivy	40.99	14-8-87
710m	Ballyregan Bob	42.63	11-12-85
850m	Pineapple Choice	52.53	26-7-82

NGRC Directory

Major Races

WENDY FAIR BLUE RIBAND (490m)

1	**ARDILAUN BRIDGE**	11-10f	(1)
	bk d Adraville Bridge-Celelia One Nov 91		
2	Drovers Road	5-1	(3)
3	Moral; Director	14-1	(2)
4	Lyons Double	8-1	(4)
5	Coast Is Clear	14-1	(5)
6	Druids Elprado	3-1	(6)

29.03 (+10) 3¾ hd, 7 5¾ dis. Duggan, Walthamstow

Year	Winner	Trainer	Track	Time	SP
1981	Arter Mo (Carhumore Speech-Monalee Roman) Honeysett	Crayford	29.47	20-1
1982	Master Darby (Sole Aim-Aglish Pilgnm) Fisher	Reading	29.88	7-2
1983	Cross Times (Violet Hall-Full Circle) Fisher	Reading	30.01	7-2
1984	Living Trail (Ivy Hall Solo-Flimron) Honeysett	Wembley	29.69	50-1
1985	Lulus Hero (Sail On II-Lulus Loner) Smith	Hove	29.23	3-1
1986	Fearless Champ (Special Account-Sarahs Bunny) de Mulder	Oxford	29.04	8-11 F
1987	Sambuca (Pat Seamur-Lyons Flora) Smith	Hove	29.08	16-1
1988	Pike Alert (Security Alert- PC Breda) Foster	W'don	29.18	7-1
1989	Ring Slippy (I'm Slippy-Westpark Chill)Millen	C'bury	29.64	3-1
1990	Westmead Harry (Fearless Champ-Westmead Move) Savva	M Keynes	29.09	5-4F
1991	Wuncross Double (Creamery Cross-Wuncoat) Knight	Hove	29.02	33-1
1992	Dempsey Duke (Shangarry Duke-Willowbrook Peg) Kibble	Bristol	29.87	2-1JF
1993	Hypnotic Stag (Greenpark Fox-Sister Moonshine) Coleman	Wal'stow	28.85	8-13F

WENDY FAIR ST LEGER (655m)

1	**BALLARUE MINX**	7-2	(4)
	wbd b Greenpark Fox-Ballarue Suzy May 92		
2	Twin Rainbow	3-1	(1)
3	Decoy Lion	5-1	(3)
4	Clongeel Fern	7-1f	(2)
5	Sandanita	5-1	(6)
	Trap Vacant		(5)

39.65 (N) 1, ¾ 2¾ hd, Masters, Hove.

| 1970 | Spotted Rory (Shanes Legacy-Dainty Flash) McEllistrim Wim'don | 40.26 | 2-1 |
| 1971 | Dolores Rocket (Newdown Heather-Come On Dolores) White | Pvt | 40.03 | 1-2F |

NGRC Directory

Year	Dog (Sire-Dam) Trainer	Track	Time	SP
1972	Ramdeen Stuart (Sallys Story-Any Streak) Oliver	Brough Pk	39.82	2-1
1973	Case Money (Backed Out-Jamboree Judy)Parker	Harringay	39.89	6-4JF
1974	Cute Caddie (RedBarrel-Fellside Tiney) Kinchett	W City	41.17	4-1
1975	Tartan Khan (Spectre-Chilled Sweet) Lynds	Bletchley	39.45	7-2
1976	Westmead Champ (Westmead Power-Hacksaw) Heasman	Hackney	39.90	9-4
1977	Stormy Spirit (Spectre-Nora Again) Pickering	W.City	40.22	10-1
1978	Westmead Power (Westmead County-Westmead Damson) Savva	Coventry	39.67	4-5F
1979	Kilmagoura Mist (Yanka Boy-Kumagoura Fair) Johnston	Wembley	40.04	9-2
1980	Fair Reward (Flip Your Top-Modest Style) YOung	Pvt	40.46	5-2
1981	Fox Watch (Ritas Choice-Queen of Morray) Hold	Pvt	40.17	5-2JF
1982	Huberts Shade (Luminous Lad-Huberts Fate) Jackson	Wembley	39.83	13-2
1983	Easy and Slow (Sand Man-Lucky Arnval) Jackson	Wembley	40.37	5-2
1984	Gizzajob (Knockrour Bank-Move 'n' Groove) Coleman	flomford	40.26	33-1
1985	Jet Circle (Jet Control-Kielduff Fun) Dickson	Wembley	40.14	11-4
1986	Lone Wolf (Yankee Express-Breeze Valley) Curtis	Brighton	39.99	9-2
1987	Life Policy (Lindas Champion-Lucky Friend) Young	Brighton	39.96	12-1
1988	Exile Energy (Gambling Fever-Princess Nora) Baggs	Wal'stow	39.76	9-2
1989	Manx Marajax (Easy And Slow-Darian Ivy) Saunders	Belle Vue	39.87	33-1
1990	Match Point (Tico-Cuddles Sandy) Kibble	Bristol	39.92	7-1
1991	Temps Perdu (Coolmona Man-Miss Tico) Hill	Linatt	40.16	9-4
1992	Airmount Flash (Mr John Dee-Airmount Mary) Gibson	Belle Vue	39.81	3-1
1993	Galleydown Boy (Flashy Sir-Annies Last) Copplestone	Unattached	40.06	13-2

BE FIRST PAST THE POST...

with this great Greyhound Racing book offer...

1994 Greyhound Stud Book

The breeder's bible

Price **£20** (plus £2.50 postage and packing)

To order, send a cheque or money order to:
Ringpress Books, PO Box 8, Lydney, Glos., GL15 6YD
Access/Visa orders phone **0594 563800**. Prices are UK only. Eire add £2 per item.

THEY'RE OFF: A big crowd and a big race night at Plough Lane.

Wimbledon

Plough Lane, London SW17 DBL.
Telephone number: 0181-946 5361. Fax: 0181 947 0821.

Owner: GRA Ltd.
General manager: Graham Ellis.
Racing manager: Simon Harris.

Race nights: Tuesday, Friday and Saturday (7.30 pm). Alternative Thursdays, BAGS.
Trial session: Monday (10.30 am).
Distances: 252m, 460m, 460mh, 480m, 660m, 660mh, 820m, 868m, 1068m.
Grade times: 460m 29.20 (Pups 29.30); 660m 42.60.
Number of dogs per race: Six.
Surface: All sand.
Type of hare: Outside McKee M S Cable.
Circumference of track: 408m.
Distance to the first bend: 90m
Width of track: 18ft straights, 22ft bends.
Layout of the track and how it runs: A medium-sized

HOW TO GET THERE

By underground: Northern line to Tooting Broadway. Free return coach from Shepherds Bush Green.

NGRC Greyhound Racing Yearbook 1995   **271**

NGRC Directory

racing circuit with moderately-banked bends and suited to the early-paced, compact runner. There is no distinct advantage from any starting position.

Usual method of track preparation: Fastidious preparation of the racing surface is maintained throughout. Regular salting of sand surface takes place from November until early Spring.

Major competitions:
   Foster's Gold Cup (660m), January.
   John Henwood Springbok (460mh), February.
   Mirror/Life Greyhound Derby (480m), May/June.
   Stantons Wey Plastics Winner Trophy (480m), July.
   Surrey Racing Puppy Derby (460m), September.
   Ike Morris Laurels (460m), October.
   Larry's Puppy Oaks (460m), November.
   St Mary's Hospital Oaks (480m) December.

Graded prize money: Bottom grade £50, top grade £100.
Number of bookmakers: Grandstand seven, back straight five.
Totalisator: Computerised: Win, place, forecast, trio, six-leg carry-over win jackpot. Turnover £16m.
Timing: Automatic, hand, ray timing, sectional times recorded on four, six and eight bends.
Facilities: Chromatography, vet in attendance, kennels for

PANORAMIC: Great viewing from the restaurant at Plough Lane

NGRC Directory

84 greyhounds, car park for 1,000 cars, restaurant for 320 covers and a further 180 grill room seats, eight bars, four refreshment rooms, stands (all covered, glass-fronted and heated areas available to all racegoers at no extra charge), video replay (previous meeting before racing, plus replays after every race).

Other activities at the stadium: Car racing, squash club, Sunday market (general), indoor specialist markets, private catering. HGV and motorcycle training.

Track Records

252m	**Dysert Moth**	15.08	10-12-82
272m	**Wheres The Limo**	16.23	11-5-91
412m	**Ballinahow Blue**	24.89	27-12-84
	Mr Plum	24.89	23-6-87
	Spiral Manor	24.89	25-6-87
412mH	**Pantile**	25.38	5-8-89
460m	**Double Bid**	27.33	25-6-88
460mH	**Unbelievable**	28.00	22-6-91
480m	**Lodge Prince**	28.34	29-5-86
660m	**Ballyregan Bob**	40.15	19-4-86
660mH	**Longcross Bruce**	41.52	6-8-82
820m	**Sail On Valerie**	51.16	30-12-89
868m	**Sandy Lane**	54.11	6-5-83

Major Races

DAILY MIRROR/SPORTING LIFE DERBY (480m)

1	**MORAL STANDARDS**	9-4f	(2)	
	wbk d Flag Star-No Way Jose May 92			
2	Ayr Flyer	3-1	(6)	
3	Moaning Lad	7-2	(5)	
4	Up The Junction		3-1	(1)
5	Flag The Fawn	16-1	(3)	
6	Callahow Daly	12-1	(4)	

28.59 (+20) 1¼, ½, sht-hd, 1½, 1½. Meek, Hall Green

☆ *See Derby Night pictures in colour section.*

1927 Entry Badge (Jamie-Beaded Nora)　　Harmon W. City F. Baster　29.01　1-4F
1928 Bother Ash (Over The Water-Honeybee II)
　　　　　　　　　　　　　　　　　　Johnston Phall Mrs.Stokes　30.48　5-1
1929 Mick The Miller (Glorious Event-Na Boc Lei) P. Horan Dublin A. Williams 29.96　4-7F

NGRC Greyhound Racing Yearbook 1995

NGRC Directory

1930 Mick The Miller (Glorious Event-Na Boc Lei)
　　　　　　　　　　S. Orton W'don Mrs Kempton　30.24　4-9F
1931 Seldom Led (Society Boy-Pity) Green W Ham Hammond/Flemming　30.04　7-2
1932 Wild Wolley (Hautley-Wild Witch) Rimmer W City S.Johnson　29.72　4-7f
1933 Future Cutlet (Mutton Cutle-Wany Guide) Probert Wemb W.Evershed　29.80　6-1
1934 Davesland (Kick Him Down-Hasty Go) Harvey Har'gay F. Brooks　29.81　3-1
1935 Greta Ranee (Doumergue-Parrein) Jonas W.City J. Lockhart-Mummery 30.18　4-1
1936 Fine Jubilee (Silver Seal II-Harissi) F Yate Pvte Mrs.Yate　29.48　10-11
1937 Wattle Bark (Secret Chance-Helena Kane) Syder Wembley Mrs.Dent　29.26　5-2
1938 Lone Keel (Lone Man-Lucky Plum) Wrlght Pvte J. Walsh　29.62　9-4
1939 Highland Rum (Rum Ration-Liagh Lady) Fortune Wdon J Harty　29.35　2-1JF
1940 G. R. Archduke (Ataxy-GayRevels) Ashley Har'gay O. Leach　29.66　100-7
1941-1944 Not run
1945 Ballyhennessy Seal (Lone Seal-Canadian Glory)
　　　　　　　　　　Marlin Wdon Mrs.Stow & A.Vivien　29.56　EvF
1946 Monday's News (Orlucks Best-Monday Next)
　　　　　　　　　　Farey Pvte O. Stewart　29.24　5-1
1947 Trev's Perfection (Melksham Nobody-Come On Biddy)
　　　　　　　　　　Trevillion Pvte F Trevllion　28.95　4-1
1948 Priceless Border (Clonahard Border-Priceless Sandhills)
　　　　　　　　　　Reynolds Wembley W. O'Kane　28.78　1-2F
1949 Narrogar Ann (Dutton Swordfish-Winnie Of Berrow)
　　　　　　　　　　Reynolds Wembley W. J. Reid　28.95　5-1
1950 Ballmac Ball (Lone Seal-Raging Tornado) Marlin W'don T. Nicholls　28.72　7-2
1951 Ballylanigan Tanist (Mad Tanist-Fly Dancer)
　　　　　　　　　　Reynolds Wembley A. Dupont　28.62　11-4
1952 Endless Gossip (Priceless Border-Narrogar Ann)
　　　　　　　　　　Reynolds Wembley H. Gocher　28.50　EvF
1953 Daw's Dancer (The Daw-Castleview Dancer) McEvoy Pvte O.Fitzgerald　29.20　10-1
1954 Paul's Fun (Sand Down Champion-All Fun)
　　　　F Reynolds Wembley T. Watford　28.84　8-I
1955 Rushton Mac (Rushton News-Rushton Panda)
　　　　　　　　　　Johnson Pvte F.&J.Johsson　28.97　5-1
1956 DunmoreKing (Shaggy Lad-Dunmore Dancer)
　　　　　　　　　　McEvoy Clapton J.McAllister　29.22　7-2
1957 Ford Spartan (Polonius-Harrow Glamour)
　　　　　　　　　　Hannafin W'donF Hill &S.Frost　28.84　EvF
1958 Pigalle Wonder (Champion Prince-Prairie Peg)
　　　　　　　　　　Syder Wembley A. Burnett　28.65　4-5F
1959 Mile Bush Pride (The Grand Champion-Witching Dancer)
　　　　　　　　　　Harvey Wembley N. Purvis　28.76　EvF
1960 Duleek Dandy (Flash Jack-Flower of Suleek)
　　　　　　　　　　Dash Pvte Mrs.Dash　29.15　25-1
1961 Palm's Printer (The Grand Champion-Palm Shadow)
　　　　　　　　　　McEvoy Clapton D. Heale　28.84　2-1
1962 The Grand Canal (Champion Prince-The Grand Duchess)
　　　　　　　　　　F Dunphy Ireland P. Dunphy　29.09　2-1
1963 Lucky Boy (Superman-Grange Maiden) Bassett Clapton S. Barrett　29.00　xxx
1964 Hack Up Chieftain (Knochhill Chieftain-Bunclody Queen)
　　　　　　　　　　Stagg B Vue Mrs. Donohue　28.92　20-1
1965 Chittering Clapton (Noted Crusader-Chittering Hope)
　　　　　　　　　　Jackson Clapton P.Leach　28.82　5-2
1966 Faithful Hope (Solar Prince-Millie Hawthorn)
　　　　　　　　　　Keane Clapton Miss Wallis & Sir B.Adeane　28.52　8-1
1967 Tric Trac (Crazy Parachute-Supreme Witch)

NGRC Directory

WIMBLEDON

	Hookway Sheffield Pinson	29.00	9-2
1968 Camira Flash (Prairie Flash-Duet Fire)			
	Singleton W.City Duke of Edinburgh	28.89	100-8
1969 Sand Star (Bauhus-Direct Lead) F Orr Ireland H. Orr		28.76	5-4
1970 John Silver (Faithful Hope-Trojan Silver) Tompkins Pvte B. Young		29.01	11-4
1971 Dolores Rocket (Newdown Heather-Come On Dolores)			
	White PA H. White	28.74	11-4
1972 Patricia's Hope (Silver Hope-Patsicia)			
	Jackson Clapton B Stanley & G.&B.Marks	28.55	7-1
1973 Patricia's Hope (Silver Hope-Patsicia)			
	O'Connor Ireland G.&B. Marks & J.O'Connor	28.66	7-2
1974 Jimsun (Monalee Champion-Lady Expert)			
	de Mulder Hall Green J. de Mulder & Miss Walker	28.76	5-2
1975 Tartan Khan (Spectre-Chilled Sweet) Lynds Bletchley D. Law		29.57	25-1
1976 Mutts Silver (The Grand Silver-Simple Pride)			
	Rees W'don B. Lancaster	29.38	6-1
1977 Balliniska Band (Lively Band-Certral) Moore Belle Vue B. Bacci		29.16	EvF
1978 Lacca Champion (Itsachampion-Highland Flinch)			
	Mullins Pvte Mrs.Pearce	29.42	6-4F
1979 Sarah's Bunny (Jimsun-Sugaloaf Bunny) de Mulder Hall Gn B. Hadley		29.53	3-1
1980 Indian Joe (Brave Bran-Minnatonka) Hayes Ireland J. McLean		29.68	13-8JF
1981 Parkdown Jet (Cairnville Jet-Gabriel Ruby)			
	McKenna Ireland Mrs.Barnett	29.57	4-5F
1982 Lauries Panther (Shamrock Sailor-Lady Lucey)			
	Duggan Romford L. James	29.60	6-4F
1983 I'm Slippy (Laurdella Fun-Glenroe Bess) Tompkins Covtry J. Quinn		29.40	6-1
1984 Whisper Wishes (Sand Man-Micklem Drive) Coyle M'stone J. Duffy		29.43	7.4F
1985 Pagan Swallow (Black Earl-Acres Of Apples) Bees W'don D. Hawthorn		29.04	9-1
1986 Tico (The Stranger-Derry Linda) Hitch Slough A. Smee		28.69	6-4JF
1987 Signal Spark (Echo Spark-Balbec Duchess)			
	Baggs W'stow Towfi Al-Aali	28.83	14-1
1988 Hit The Lid (Soda Fountain Cailin Dubh) McGee Canterbury F. Smith		28.53	3-1
1989 Lartigue Note (One To Note Lartigue Spark)			
	McKenna Ireland C. McCarthy	28.79	EvF
1990 Slippy Blue (I'm Slippy-Valoris) Linzell W'stow Mrs F.Fenn		28.70	8-1
1991 Ballinderry Ash (Kyle Jack-Ballinderry Sand) Byrne W'don H. Roche		28.78	5-1
1992 Farloe Melody (Lodge Prince-Chini Chin Chin) O'Donnell Ireland		28.88	6-4F
1993 Ringa Hustle (Midnight Hustle-Ring U Back) Meek Oxford		28.62	5-2

SURREY RACING PUPPY DERBY (460m)

1	**BONMAHON DARKIE**	2-1f	(5)
	bdw d Carmels Prince-Debs Tick Oct 92		
2	Droopys Joe	9-2	(1)
3	Deenside Dean	9-4	(3)
4	Solva Guy	14-1	(2)
5	Temple Wood	20-1	(4)
6	Misty Phantom	3-1	(6)

27.70 (+10) 1$3/4$, hd, 1$1/4$, 3, sht-hd. Dartnall, Wimbledon.

NGRC Greyhound Racing Yearbook 1995

NGRC Directory

1970 Cretogue Flash (Newdown Heather-Duffy Flash)
    Mitchell   Belle Vue 28.22
1971 Tawny Satin (The Grand Silver-Cathys Tiny) Johnston Wembley 27.78
1972 Seamans Pride (Own Pride-Stolen Tilley) Milligan Pvt 28.17
1973 Handy High (Handy Valley-Black Highbird) Milligan Pvt 28.40 4-5F
1974 Tory Mor (Toms Pal-Melville Money) Milligan Pvt 27.72 3-1
1975 Knockrour Bank (Clomoney Jet-Damsels Last) Coleman Wembley 27.65 11-10
1976 Carhumore Speech (Free Speech-Pats Glory) White Pvt 28.17 I-2F
1977 Ruakuras Mutt (Spectre-Areopagus) Coyle Pvt 27.65 9-4
1978 Purdys Pursuit (Aghawadda Flash-Fxchange Dolly)
    Bees Wimbledon 27.83 20-1
1979 Price Wise (Free Speech-Take The Lead) Baldwin Perry Barr 2770 12-1
1980 Desmonds Fancy (Sole Aim-Blissful Linda) Coker Oxford 28.22 7-1
1981 Special Account (Westmead County-Ka Boom)
    Mrs N. Savva Cambs 27.79 7-2
1982 Mountleader Mint (Cairnville Jet-Mountleader Cleo)
    Duggan Romford 27.82 2-1F
1983 Rhincrew Moth (Ballarat Prince-Skipping Fun)
    Miss Gwynne Ipswich 27.53 1-3F
1984 Bans Champion (Lacca Champion-Raffles Bridge)
    Pateman Wimbledon 27.61 4-6F
1985 Fearless Swift (Ron Hardy-Sarahs Bunny) de Mulder Oxford 27.67 4-5F
1986 Spiral Darkie (Lindas Champion-Spiral Three) Baggs Ramsgate 27.70 9-2
1987 Debby Hero (Debbycot Lad-Kisco) Kinchett Wimbledon 27.99 12-1
1988 Spring Band (Wise Band-Gentle Hearthrob) Sykes Wimbledon 28.13 3-1
1989 Newry Flash (Dran Flash-Townview Fuzz) Hitch Wimbledon 27.97 4-1
1990 Murlens Support (Moral Support-Murlens Chill) Meek Oxford 28.50 1-2F
1991 Right Move (Daleys Gold- Westmead Move) Savva Milton K 28.25 14-1
1992 Bixby (Murlens Slippy-Skylab) Black Reading 28.04 7-2

ST MARY'S HOSPITAL OAKS (480m)

1 **WESTMEAD CHICK** 8-11f (1)
   bk d Manorville Magic-I'm a Survivor Dec 91
2 Droopys Fergie 7-1 (5)
3 Egmont Joan 7-1 (2)
4 Twin Rainbow 16-1 (4)
5 Not My Line 7-2 (3)
6 Coomlogane Euro 8-1 (6)
28.60 (-10) 7½, sht-hd, 1½, 5, hd, Savva, Walthamstow.

1970 Perth Pat (Maryville Hi-Hiver Swanky) 13-8F Morgan Pvt 28.81
1971 Short Cake (The Grand Silver-She Is Landing) 5-1 Geggus W'stow 28.98
1972 Decimal Queen (Dusty Trail-Roamin Beauty) 6-4F Hawkins Pvt 28.60
1973 Miss Ross (Myross Again-Rich Life) 8-1 Johnston Wemb 28.63
1974 Lady Devine (Supreme Fun-Funny Flash) 3-1 Ryall Wemb 28.76
1975 Pineapple Grand (The Grand Silver-Pineapple Baby)
    8-11 F Baldwin Perry B 28.85
1976 Ballinderry Moth (Kilbelin Style-Skipping Chick)
    4-6F O'Connor W'stow 28.60

NGRC Directory

Year	Dog (breeding) Odds	Trainer	Track	Time
1977	Switch Off (Westpark Mint-Kudas Pinch) 6-4F	Singleton	H'gay	28.69
1978	Kilmagoura Mist (Yanka Boy-Kilmagoura Fair)10-1	Johnston	Wemb	28.55
1979	Sunny Interval (Itsachampion-Cloheadon Pussy) 12-1	Rees	W'don	28.77
1980	Devilish Dolores (Glin Bridge-Dancing Dolores) 20-1	Gaskin	Pvt	28.72
1981	Thanet Princess (Instant Gambler-Isle Of Thanet) 11-2	Hawkes	W'stow	28.82
1982	Duchess Of Avon (Ballintee Star-Duarry Blaze) EF	Jackson	Wemb	28.72
1983	Major Grove (Knockrour Tiger-Sandras Melody) 6-1	Pateman	W'don	28.59
1984	Sandy Sally (Sand Man-Ballyderg Moth) 9-2	Coker	Mil Key	28.69
1985	Spiral Super (Cooladine Super-Spiral Mint) 10-11f	Curtis	Br'ton	28.57
1986	Sullane Princess (Dran Jack-Muileann Amere) 20-1	Payne	Romf'd	28.79
1987	Lucky Empress (Citizen Supreme-Dark Empress) 2-1	Briggs	Pvt	28.43
1988	Wendys Dream (Tamarac-Up Town Girl) 4-5F	Foster	W'don	28.81
1989	Nice And Lovely (Plunket Tim-Luisa Daniella) 9-4	Tidswell	P'boro	29.02
1990	Liberal Girl (Easy And Slow-Ballinvard Rose)5-1	Knight	Br'ton	28.95
1991	Simple Trend (Moral Support-Wooodside Breeze) 2-1	Gaskin	W'stow	29.06
1992	Skelligs Smurf (Skelligs Tiger-Speedy Smurf) 11-8F	Gilling	Reading	29.71
1993	Pearls Girl (Flashy Sir-Desert Pearl) 8-11F	Sykes	W'don	28.55

IKE MORRIS LAURELS (460m)

1	**BONMAHON DARKIE**	6-4	(6)
	bdw d Carmels Prince-Debs Tick Oct 92		
2	Pearls Girl	11-10f	(1)
3	Raceline Sean	8-1	(2)
4	Longvalley Manor	10-1	(3)
5	Another Moment	14-1	(5)
6	Rio Remember	14-1	(4)

27.87 (N) 1¼, nk, 1¼, 1¼, ½, Dartnall, Wimbledon.

Year	Dog (breeding) Odds	Trainer	Track	Time
1972	Cricket Bunny (Printers Prince-Cricket Lady) 100-30	Booth	Pvt	28.11
1973	Black Banlo (Monalee Champion-Brook Densel) 5-2CF	B. O'Connor	W'stow	27.93
1974	Over Protected (Monalee Arkie-Spotlight Cindy) 7-4	Coleman	W'bley	28.00
1975	Pineapple Grand (The Grand Silver-Pineapple Baby) 3-1	Baldwin	P Barr	27.77
1976	Xmas Holiday (Supreme Fun-Marys Snowball) 3-1	Bees	W'don	27.66
1977	Greentield Fox (Burgess Heather-Skipping Chick) 4-5 F	Dickson	Slough	27.26
1978	Jet Control (Toms Pal-Morning Rose) 9-2	Gaynor	P Barr	27.45
1979	Another Spatter (Barbados-Small Spatter) 7-2	Pickering	W.City	27.75
1980	Flying Pursuit (Kudas Honour-Faiodes Look) 6-4F	Gibbons	Cr'ford	27.89
1981	Echo Spark (Liberty Lad-Lady Armada) 5-1	Cobbold	Ip'wich	27.84
1982	Lauries Panther (Shamrock Sailor-Lady Lucey) 9-2	Duggan	Romf'd	27.79
1983	Darkie Fli (Ballinmanan Sam-Star Fli) 2-1F	Stevens	Cambs	28.87
1984	Amenhotep (Aquaduct Coach-Ladys Lib) 7-1	Mullins	Cr'ford	27.82
1985	Ballygroman Jim (Knockrour Tiger-View Lady) 7-4F	Gaskin	Pvt	27.68
1986	Mollitriend Lucky (Lauries Panther-Top Princess) 4-6F	Packham	R'ding	27.48
1987	Flashy Sir (Sand Man-Cherry Express) 11-4	Savva	Mil Key	27.52
1988	Comeragh Boy (Moral Support-August Morning) 6-4F	Gaskin	Pvte	27.86
1989	Parquet Pal (Game Ball-Hollands Kay) 9-4	Hitch	W'don	27.68
1990	Concentration (I'm Slippy-Eliogarty) 4-7F	McKenna	Ireland	27.75
1991	Glengar Ranger (Carters Lad-Glengar Moss) 6-4F	Fletcher	Cant'by	27.47
1992	Balligari (Daleys Gold-Westmead Move) 6-4	Savva	M Keys	27.37
1993	Slipaway Jaydee (Im Slippy-Ballyvalican) 9-4	McGee	Reading	27.61

Yarmouth

Yarmouth Rd, Caister-on-Sea, Gt Yarmouth, Norfolk NR30 5TE.
Telephone number: 01493 720343. Fax: 01493 721200.

Status: Permit.
Owner: Norfolk Greyhound Racing Co Ltd.
General manager: Stephen Franklin.
Racing manager: Dick Keable.

HOW TO GET THERE

BY CAR: from Norwich or A12 from Ipswich, follow signs to Caister from Gt Yarmouth. Then follow brown Tourist signs to the stadium.

Trainers (attached): G. Lynds, I. Barnard, C. Smith, D. Mattocks, R. White, S. Riches, I. Mills, R. Pleasants, P. Wright, A. Rumbelow.

Race nights: Monday, Wednesday and Saturday in summer (7.30 pm). Tuesday, Thursday and Saturday in winter (7.30 pm). Will soon race Sundays, exact pattern to be decided.
Trial sessions: 10 am Wednesday (winter), 10am Thursday (summer), and before racing.
Distances: 277m (open only), 462m, 659m, 843m, 1041m.
Grading times: 462m: 30.40; 659m: 43.80.
Number of dogs per race: Six.
Surface: All sand.
Type of hare: Outside Sumner.
Circumference of track: 382m (1m from inner rail).
Distance to the first bend: 80m.
Width of track: 4m.

Layout of the track and how it runs: Oval shape, lett hand bends, long galloping straights, well-banked bends and excellent sanded surface.
Usual method of track preparation: Harrowing and sand leveller, salted only when necessary in winter.

Major competitions:
   East Anglian Derby (462m). September.
   Wafcol East Anglian Challenge (462m), August.
   Yarmouth Championship (462m), November.

Graded prize money: Bottom grade £21. top grade £68.
Number of bookmakers: Six..
Totalisator: Computerised. Win, place, forecast, trifecta.
Timing: Photo timing and hand timing, sectional times.
Facilities: Vet in attendance, kennels for 83 greyhounds, floodlit paddock area, car park for 600 vehicles, four bars (three with race view), covered stand, video replay with slow-motion, 60-seater Raceview Diner, 60-seater snacl bar.
Other activities at the stadium: Markets, stock car racing Tuesdays, Thursdays, Sundays, May-September, large amusement arcade, children's play area.

Track Records

277m	**Where's The Limo**	16.64	22-9-79
462m	**Dempsey Duke**	27.68	19-9-91
659m	**Big City**	40.79	24-9-88
843m	**Change Guard**	53.62	25-8-86
1041m	**Some Moth**	68.81	6-12-86

Major Races

EAST ANGLIAN DERBY (462m)

1	**FRANKS DOLL**	5-1	(1)
	bd d Kilbarry Slippy-Come On Mandy Dec 91		
2	Decoy Lynx	3-1	(6)
3	First Defence	5-1	(2)
4	Double Polano	10-1	(4)
5	Lone Rider	10-11f	(5)
	Trap Vacant (3)		

29.38 1, 4, 1½, 2¼. Scott, Canterbury

NGRC Greyhound Racing Yearbook 1995

For all your requirements . . .

TRACKSIDE KENNELS

Lingfield, Surrey

SCHOOLING AND RE-SCHOOLING

(450m sand, outside McGee)

VACANCIES FOR

Resters, in-season, injured, retired.

Facilities available also include muscle injury detection scanning, ultrasound, laser, Portamag etc.

PUPS, GRADERS and OPEN RACERS always for sale

STANDING AT STUD HERE . . .

AGHADOWN TIMMY

| Moral Support | Fastnet Heather |
| x Yellow Band | x Sand Man |

and introducing at stud . . .

SABRE DANCE

Brilliant early pace

and

PRESS COPY

strong running winner of Open Races up to 590m

BROTHERS FROM THE 1992 LITTERS BY

| Flashy Sir | Hogans Kizzy |
| x Sand Man | x Count Five |

Phone for further details call

01273 492344

NGRC Directory

Professional Trainers

Key: Transfer from OT— formerly on Owner/trainer listing;
Att: Attached

ADAM J S,	(Trans from OT) Meadowbank Bungalow, Northey Road, Peterborough, Cambs. PE6 7YX. (01832 223 527). (Att: Peterborough)
ADAMS Mrs N S,	28, Whitings Road, Barnet, Herts.ENS 2QY. (Kennels) The Thrift, Mays Lane, Barnet, Herts. (0181 441 1256).
ADAMS W T,	Bridge Cottage, 181, Castledon Road, Downham, Wickford, Essex. (01268 733293). (Att: Canterbury)
ALDEN M F,	Kelva, Highside, Parsons Drove, Wisbech, Cambs. PE13 4LH. (01945 700858).
ALLEN F,	(Trans from OT) Kellsacre Animal Holiday Home, Matchams Lane, Hurn, Christchurch, Dorset. BH23 6AW. (01202 482457).
ALLEN K H,	The Poplars, Barroway Drove, Downham Market. PE38 OAN. (03668 381). (Att: Peterborough)
AMYES F W,	Monza, Pinley Green, Claverdon, Warks. CV35 8LU. (01926 843 429).
ANDERSON J,	Caynton Manor, Newport, Salop. TF1O 8NF. (01952 550 425). (Att: Monmore Green)
ANDREWS Miss J,	Whinmoor Grange Farm, York Road, Leeds. LSl4 3AD. (01532 735 791). (Att: Belle Vue)
ANNETT J J,	1, Goose Green Close, Upper Wolvercote, Oxford. OX2 8OJ. (01865 59646). (Kennels): Cuckoo Pen Kennels, Winaway, Harwell, Didcot, Oxon. (01860 627978). (Att: Oxford)
ANSELL J L,	Glendale, 5, Northfield Road, Maidenhead, Berks. SL6 7JP. (01628 789 304). (Att: Swindon)
ANSELL L P P,	The Outlook, Little Chart, Forstall, Near Ashford, Kent. TN27 OPU. (0233 840 382). (Att: Canterbury)
ANSTES K M,	Greylands, Yarmouth Road, Melton, Woodbridge, Suffolk. 1P12 IQE. (01394 387820). (Kennels) Bramfield House School, Walpole Road, Bramfield, Halesworth, Suffolk. (01986 84235).
APPLETON A A,	2, Conifer Close, Ormesby, Great Yarmouth, Norfolk. (01493 731 640). (Kennels) Wood View,Tower Road, Fleggburgh, Gt Yarmouth, Norfolk. (01493 368110).
ARMITAGE D P,	(Trans from OT) Mount Farm, Whenby,

NGRC Directory

	Brandsby, York. Y06 4SE. (01347 878 457). (Att: Middlesbrough)
ARMSTRONG A,	Drumbeg Farm Kennels, Blackridge, Bathgate, West Lothian, Scotland. (01501 53224). (Att: Powderhall)
ARMSTRONG Mrs J A,	Journeys End, Singleborough, Milton Keynes. MK17 ORF. (0129 671 2523). (Att: Milton Keynes)
ARNOLD P.J. (Snr) -	(Trans from OT) "Rupen", Long Drove, Parsons Drove, Wisbech, Cambs. PE13 4JT. (01945 700 485). (Att: Peterborough)
ATKINS D J,	48, Cross Street, Farcet, Peterborough, Cambs.PE7 3DD. (01733 244 132). (Att: Peterborough)
ATKINS J F,	Greystones, Jarvis Gate, Sutton St James, Spalding, Lincs. PE12 OEP. (01945 85374).(Att: Peterborough)
ATKINS T,	Sunnymead Kennels, Dedworth Road, Oakley Green, Windsor, Berks. (01753 868801). (Att: Wembley)
AUSTIN B,	Forest Lodge Kennels, Forest Road, Quinton, Northampton. NN7 2EQ. (01604 862239). (Att: Milton Keynes/Peterborough)
BABE Miss K G,	The Old Covert, Muggington Lane, Muggington, Weston Under Wood, Derbys. (0177 389 280). (Att: Nottingham)
BACON M D,	(Home) 45, Greatfield Road, Wythenshawe, Manchester. M22 7RZ. (0161 436 1270). (Kennels): Mossfield Kennels, Drury Lane, Warmingham, Nr Crewe, Cheshire. CWl 4PN (0127 077 490). (Att: Perry Barr)
BAGGS G,	Rosewood Kennels, Sawyers Green Farm, Langley Park Road, Langley, Bucks. SL3 6D0. (01753 547895). (Att: Walthamstow)
BAILEY Mrs J A, -	Forge Farmhouse, Powdermill Lane, Southborough, Tunbridge Wells, Kent. TN4 9EG. (01892 534 384).
BAKER R,	White House Kennels, Beckley Road, Stanton St John, Oxford. OX9 lAF. (01865 351 274). (Att: Swindon)
BAKER V J,	The Old Forge House, Hall Lane, Crostwick, Norwich, Norfolk. NR12 7BB. (01603 737754).
BAKEWELL B J,	The Elms, Withybrook Road, Bulkington, Near Nuneaton, Warks. (01203 314 634). (Att: Hall Green)
BALLS J L,	Bridge House, Church Lane, Tydd St Giles, Wisbech, Cambs. PE13 5LG. (01945 870386).
BARBER R,	3, Victory Grove, Audenshaw, Manchester. (0161 370 8260). (Kennels) Chips Farm Kennels, Southport Road, Ormskirk, Lancs. (01695 570138). (Att: Belle Vue)
BARLOW M A,	890, Kingstanding Road, Kingstanding, Birmingham. B44 9RS. (0121 355 7516).

NGRC Directory

	(Kennels) Blackgreaves Farm, Blackgreaves Lane, Lea Marston, Sutton Coldfield, West Mids. (01675 470 661). (Att: Monmore Green)
BARNARD Mrs I J,	The Homestead, Low Road, West End, West Caister, Norfolk. (01493 721 227). (Att: Yarmouth)
BARRETT J,	Airport Kennels, Village Farm, Coventry Rd, Elmdon, Birmingham. B26. (0121 779 4335). (Att: Cradley Heath)
BARRETT R W,	Barretts Yard, Stone Lane, Lydiard Millicent, Near Swindon, Wilts. SN5 9LD. (01793 770071). (Att: Swindon)
BARTLETT Mrs R A,	Ransley Kennels, Kingsford Street, Mersham, Ashford, Kent. TN25 6PF. (01233 636476). (Att: Hackney)
BARTON D M,	20, Glebe Road, Scartho, Grimsby, Sth Humberside. DN33 2HL. (01472 870227). (Att: Stainforth)
BARWICK Mrs D E,	"Shimeon", New Park, Park Lane, Maplehurst, Sussex. (01403 891528). (Att: Brighton)
BATEMAN Mrs B W,	Novedene, Hovefields Avenue, Wickford, Essex. (0168 726251). (Att: Hackney)
BEALE A R,	(Trans from OT) School House Farm, Stoke Trister, Wincanton, Somerset. BA9 9PE. (01963 31840). (Att: Swindon)
BEARD Mrs V J,	The Brickyard Kennels, Hall End Road, Wootton, Beds. MK43 9HJ. (01234 852648).
BEAUMONT P,	Upper Woodhouse Farm, Emley, Nr Huddersfield, West Yorkshire. HD8 9QU. (01924 848121). (Att: Sheffield)
BEBBINGTON K M,	The Whitehouse, Moss Lane, Leighton, Nr Crewe, Cheshire. CWl 4RL. (01270 522278).
BELL Mrs E Y,	1, Bishops Close Cottages, Whitworth, Spennymoor, Co Durham. (01388 815113). (Att: Brough Park)
BENNETT D E,	33, Daisy Farm Road, Warstock, Birmingham. B14 4QA. (0121 604 6891). Kennels: Thistlegrove Farm, Quantry Lane, Belheath, Belbroughton, Stourbridge, Nr Kidderminster, West Midlands. (01562 710887). (Att: Cradley Heath)
BENSON Mrs D,	10, The Smallholdings, Woodmansterne Road, Carshalton, Surrey. SM5 4AL. (0181 643 5514). (Att: Reading)
BENTLEY J K,	45, Sutton Road, Askern, Doncaster. Kennels: Greenacre Farm, Hophills Lane, Off Bootham Lane Dunscroft, Doncaster. (01302 841652). (Att: Hull)
BENTLEY K J,	28, Doncaster Road, Askern, Doncaster. DN6 0AL. (01302 844377). Kennels: The Ridge, Green Lane, Scawthorpe,

NGRC Directory

	Doncaster. DN5 7UX.
	(01302 330138). (Att: Stainforth)
BERGIN P C,	265, Elm Park Ave, Hornchurch, Essex.
	RM12 4PG. (01708 450200). Kennels: Unit 2,
	Ockendon Road, Upminster, Essex.
	(01708 640242). (Att: Hackney)
BERRY Mrs L,	Highlow, 464, Redhill, Wateringbury,
	Maidstone, Kent. ME18 5BE. (01622 812572).
	(Att: Canterbury)
BETTERIDGE B F,	25, Castle Road, Rowlands Castle, Hants.
	PO9 6AP. (01705 412 871).
	Kennels: Old Park Farm, Hambledon Road,
	Denmead, Hants. (01705 269 421).
	(Att: Portsmouth)
BICKNELL R,	South Lodge, Ford Lane, Iver, Bucks.
	SL0 9LL. (01753 653580). (Att: Oxford)
BILLINGHAM P A,	Church Cottage Farm, Swindon, Dudley, West
	Midlands. DY3 4PH. (01902 896042).
	(Att: Monmore Green)
BLACK W J,	Horseshoe Paddocks, Old Odiham Rd, Alton,
	Hants. GU34 4BU. (01420 544085).
	(Att: Reading)
BLANCHARD Mrs E R,	Old Rectory Garden, Shillingstone, Blandford,
	Dorset. DT11 0SL. (01258 860410).
	(Att: Swindon)
BLOOR Mrs J B,	145, Lime Lane, Pelsall, Near Walsall, West
	Midlands. WS3 5AW. (01543 360 254).
	(Att: Cradley Heath)
BLUMIRE J G T,	The Foc'scle, Calcott Hill, Sturry, Canterbury,
	Kent. CT3 4ND. (01227 710440).
	(Att: Canterbury)
BODELL Mrs D M,	Prospect House, 53, Rose Valley, Newhall,
	Burton On Trent, Staffs. DE11 0ON.
	(01283 215315). (Att: Nottingham)
BOOSEY R C,	53, Swan Lane, Wickford, Essex. SS11 7DE.
	(01268 733153). (Kennels) 13, Inglefield Road,
	Fobbing, Stanford Le Hope, Essex. SSl7 9HW.
	(01268 51441). (Att: Rye House)
BOOTH B,	24, London Road, Newport Pagnell, Bucks.
	MK16 0AE. (01908 613014).
	(Att: Milton Keynes)
BOREHAM B V,	5, Silk Factory Row, Brook Street,
	Glemsford, Sudbury, Suffolk. CO10 7PL.
	(01787 280536). (Kennels) The Kennels,
	Shepherds Lane, Glemsford, Sudbury, Suffolk.
	(01787 281029). (Att: Mildenhall)
BOYCE A E,	Catford Stadium Kennels, Layhams Rd,
	Keston, Bromley, Kent. (01959 574 432).
	(Att: Catford)
BRADFORD Mrs N R,	Rossland, Cheal Road, Gosberton Risegate,
	Spalding, Lincs. PE11 4JQ.
	(01775 750451). (Att: Swaffham)
BRANAGH Mrs P A,	2, Reddish Vale Road, Stockport, Cheshire.

NGRC Directory

	SK5 7EU. (0161 477 5829). (Att: Belle Vue)
BRENNAN J J,	Orton Croft, Great North Road, Haddon, Peterborough, Cambs. (01733 244413). (Att: Peterborough)
BRIGHTON D H,	Highland Farm, Ilketshall St Margarets, Nr Bungay, Suffolk. NR35 INB. (01986 781 461). (Att: Swaffham)
BRINDLEY R V,	Silver Birch Farm, Monxton Rd, Monxton, Nr Andover, Hants. SP11 8BU. (01264 710239). (Att: Portsmouth)
BROOKS B G,	Overdale Boarding Kennels, Arterial Road, Wickford, Essex. SS12 9JF. (01268 727561). (Att: Hackney)
BROWN E,	291, Meadowhead Road, Wishaw, Lanarks. ML2 7UJ. (01698 357828). (Kennels) The Railway Cottage, 240, Thornley Bank Road, Glasgow. G46 7RQ. (0141 638 4260). (Att: Shawfield)
BRUNNOCK M K,	45, Meldon Terrace, Heaton, Newcastle Upon Tyne. (Kennels) Nenagh Kennels, Moor Lane, Cleadon, Sunderland. SR6 7TT. (0191 519 1279). (Att: Brough Park)
BUCKLAND S M,	Watford Gap Cottage, Watford Gap Road, Little Hay, Nr Lichfield, Staffs. WS14 00D. (021 308 2112). (Att: Monmore Green)
BURRIDGE Mrs J M,	"Kerstins", Tarrant Launceston, Blandford Forum, Dorset. DT11 8BY. (01258 830261). (Att: Portsmouth)
BURROW W G,	"Pla" Greyhound Kennels, Botley Road, Bishops Waltham, Southampton, Hants. SO3 1DR. (01489 893305/01489 892762). (Att: Reading)
BURT M J,	(Trans from OT) 5, Newfield Crescent, Halesowen, West Mids. B63 3SS. (0121 503 0823). Kennels: Woodside Farm, Duttons Lane, Sutton Coldfield, West Midlands. B75 5RJ. (0121 323 4137). (Att: Perry Barr)
BYRNE P,	14, Coombe Ridings, Kingston, Surrey. (0181 546 2450). Kennels: The Byrne Kennels, Pretty Lane, Hooley, Surrey. CR5 INS. (01737 550473). (Att: Hackney)
CALVERT G,	Sedgeletch Farm Kennels, Fencehouses, Houghton Le Spring, Co Durham. DH1 5PN. (0191 385 4041). (Att: Brough Park)
CANTRELL M R E, -	Winkfield Manor Farm, Forest Road, Ascot, Berks. SL5 8QU. (01344 890323). (Att: Reading)
CARMICHAEL A,	46/6, Captains Drive, Gracemount, Edinburgh, Scotland. EH16 6QL. Kennels: Liberton Greyhound Kennels, Standykehead Road, Near Alnwickhill Road, Edinburgh, Scotland. (0131 666 264). (Att: Powderhall)

NGRC Directory

CARPENTER H.D. (Trans from OT) Stirt Farm, Shelsley Kings, Stanford Bridge, Worcs. WR6 6SA. (01229 89 6421).

CARR P R, Hopeville, New Road, Little Burstead, Near Billericay, Essex. CM12 9TS. (01268 545903). (Att: Rye House)

CARR R, Moorhouse Farm, Locko Lane, Pilsley, Chesterfield. S45 8AW. (01246 850648). (Att: Sheffield)

CARTER D F, Shairlane Kennels, Shair Lane, Great Bentley, Essex. CO7 8OT. (01206 303 876).

CARTER Mrs J M, (Trans from OT) 47, Trapstyle Road, Ware, Herts. SG12 OBA. (0920 466265). (Kennels): The Wellhouse, Tonwell, Nr Ware, Herts. (01920 402684). (Att: Peterborough)

CECIL Mrs J E, Old School House, The Mount, Flimwell, East Sussex. TN5 7OP. (0158 087 352). (Att: Ramsgate)

CHALKLEY H, Midway Kennels, Swan Bridge Farm, Long Drove, Parsons Drove, Wisbech, Cambs. PE13 4JT. (01945 700612). (Att: Yarmouth)

CHAPMAN R H, Home Farm, Aston Abbotts, Aylesbury, Bucks. HP22 4LY. (01296 681 364). (Att: Milton Keynes/Reading)

CHETWYND R, 7, Hunters Park, Baddesley Ensor, Atherstone, Warks. CV9 2DE. (01827 715632). Kennels: Speedwell Farm, Speedwell Lane, Baddesley Ensor, Atherstone, Warks. (01827 718537). (Att: Nottingham)

CHRISTIE Miss J, - South View, King Lane, Over Wallop, Hants. SO2O 8JA. (01264 781778). Kennels: Lower Farm, Picket Twenty, Andover, Hants. (01264 353384). (Att: Swindon)

CLAPP G R C, The Meads, Common Mead Lane, Hambrook, Bristol. BS16 IQQ. (01272 567548). (Att: Bristol)

CLARKE M G, Hollinwood Farm, Hollinwood Lane, Calverton, Nottingham. NG14 6NO. (0115 9652 688). (Att: Nottingham)

CLEMENSON B A, 3, Honiley Avenue, Wickford, Essex. Kennels: Bersheda Kennels, Brookside, Arterial Road, Wickford, Essex. (01268 590 794). (Att: Brighton)

CLIFF Mrs S J, Croft Farm, Worksop Road, Aston Common, Sheffield. S31 0AD. (0114 2872382). (Att: Sheffield)

COBBOLD K J, New Bungalow, Sedge Fen, Lakenheath, Brandon, Suffolk. IP27 9LQ. (0135 375 297). Kennels: Decoy Kennels, Sedge Fen, Lakenheath, Brandon, Suffolk. (0135 375 365). (Att: Hackney)

COBBOLD Mrs P J, (Full PT issued Sept 1994) "Utopia", Cowles

NGRC Directory

	Drove, Hockwold, Thetford, Norfolk. IP26 4JO. (01842 828888).
COHEN Mrs J,	4, Bilney Lane, Felthorpe, Norwich, Norfolk. NR10 4ED. (01605 48730).
COLEMAN J J,	4, Claverhambury Kennels, Galley Hill, Waltham Abbey, Essex. EN9 2BL. (0199 289 2674). (Att: Walthamstow)
COLTON N,	(Trans from OT) Green Acres, Puxley Road, Deanshanger, Milton Keynes. MK19 6LR. (01908 264311).
COMPTON M J,	Platt Farm, Heatley Heath, Lymm, Cheshire. WA13 9SF. (0192 575 3268).
CONNOLLY J J,	Tinkersfield Kennels, Hullbridge Road, Rayleigh, Essex. SS6 9OS. (01702 230288). (Att: Hackney)
CONNOR D M,	30, Osprey Close, Norton, Stockton On Tees, Cleveland. (01642 531 043). Kennels: C.P. Kennels, Stockton Road, Middlesbrough. (01642 240831). (Att: Middlesbrough)
CONNOR K P,	Field Cottage, Junction Cross Roads, Bodiam, East Sussex. (01580 860767). Kennels: The Old School House Kennels, The Mount, Flimwell, East Sussex. TN5 70P. (01580 87750). (Att: Canterbury)
CONWAY D F,	East Lings, Stainforth Road, Barnby Dun, Doncaster. DN3 1AL. (01302 844 377). (Att: Stainforth)
COOK R,	29, Bestwood Road, Hucknall, Nottingham. NG15 7PR. (0115 9634345). Kennels: ABC Palletts, Plot 2, Pyebridge Industrial Estate, Derbyshire. DE55 4NX. (01773 608 244). (Att: Perry Barr)
COOPER Mrs L,	141, Woodway Lane, Walsgrave, Coventry, Warks. CV2 2EH. (01203 613 498). Kennels: Hawkesbury Kennels, Aldermans Green Road, Coventry, Warks. (01203 542 794). (Att: Perry Barr)
COPE J,	Woodview, Grange Road, Nailstone, Nuneaton, Warwickshire. CV13 OQW. (01530 260 670).
CORBETT G,	(Trans from OT) 82, Stechford Road, Hodge Hill, Birmingham. B34 6BH. (0121 783 3766) (Att: Perry Barr)
COTTEE F,	9, Seldon Road, Tiptree, Essex. COS 0HH. Kennels: Woodside Farm, Colchester Road, Tiptree, Essex. (01621 816085). (Att: Hackney)
COULTER J E,	The Traps, Whelpley Hill, Chesham, Bucks. HP5 3RL. (01442 833 425).
COUNSELL Mrs E M,	Richborough Kennels, Black Hall Farm, Common Gate Drove, Isleham, Ely, Cambs. CB7 5RF. (01353 720 154). (Att: Peterborough)

NGRC Directory

COWANS W,	9, New Row, Drayton Bassett, Tamworth, Staffs. (01827 288 760). Kennels: Beacon Park Farm Kennels, Barr Beacon, Bridle Lane, Aldridge, West Midlands. (0121 325 0059). (Att: Hall Green)
COX V J,	St Christoph, Carbinswood, Upper Woolhampton, Nr Reading, Berks. (01734 712297).
COXON Miss A,	(Transfer from OT) 34, The Bungalow, Dixon Estate, Shotton Colliery. DH6 2PZ. (0191 517 0012). Kennels: Dene View, Salters Lane, Shotton Colliery, Co Durham. (0191 526 4192). (Att: Sunderland)
COXON J A,	8, Cedar Close, Cheadle, Stoke On Trent, Staffs. ST10 ISE. (0538 755 500). Kennels: Herriot Hayes Farm, Codsall Wood, Wolverhampton, West Midlands. WV8 IRQ. (01902 374 064).
CRAPPER H,	Commonside Farm, Renishaw, Sheffield. S31 9UW. (01246 434475). (Att: Sheffield)
CRECKENDON R C,	Ivy House, Green Lane, Tilny All Saints, Kings Lynn, Norfolk. PE34 4RR. (01553 829 466). (Att: Peterborough)
CRONSHAW T J,	Blaxland Farm, Mayton Lane, Broadoak, Near Canterbury, Kent. CT2 0QN. (01227 711 807 & 713 439). (Att: Canterbury)
CROSS Mrs P I,	The Bungalow, Drury Square, Beeston, Kings Lynn, Norfolk. PE32 2NA. (01328 701 493).
CROSSE Mrs D,	New Wrights Farm, Holwell Road, Pirton, Nr Hitchin, Herts. SG5 3OZ. (01462 712 581).
CUMNER Mrs M A,	Stedlyn Farm, Lynsted, Sittingbourne, Kent. ME9 0RH. (01795 522 561). (Att: Reading/Canterbury)
CURTIS D J,	Drifters Lodge, Burrs Orchard, Cellar Hill, Lynsted, Sittingbourne, Kent. ME9 9OY. (01795 522360). (Att: Canterbury)
CUSACK P J,	Trans from OT) 2, St Heliers Road, Leyton, London. El0 6BH. (0181 556 0667). Kennels: 2b, Claverhambury Kennels, Galley Hill, Waltham Abbey, Essex. (01992 892429). (Att: Hackney)
DARNELL Mrs J,	Chestnut Tree Farm, Burwell, Cambs. CBS 0BH. (01638 742 958).
DARTNALL T,	Wild Briars, Horton Road, Stanwell Moor, Staines, Middx. TW19 6BD. (01753 685 363). (Att: Wimbledon)
DAVIDSON J A,	Yew Tree Farm, Copthorne Road, Felbridge, East Grinstead, Surrey. RH19 2QQ. (01342 328 258). (Att: Hackney)
DAVIES Mrs M A,	Roxtown Kennels, 25, Sedge Fen, Lakenheath, Brandon, Suffolk. IP17 9LQ. (0135 375 355) (Att: Swaffham)
DAVIES P E,	181, Scarborough Road, Byker,

NGRC Directory

	Newcastle Upon Tyne. Kennels: Brough Park Stadium Knls, The Fossway, Byker, Newcastle Upon Tyne. NE6 2XJ. (0191 265 1181). (Att: Brough Park)
DAVIS Mrs G E,	126, Brize Norton Road, Minster Lovell, Nr Witney, Oxon. OX8 5FQ. (01993 700835). (Att: Swindon)
DAVIS S G,	North Lodge, Cokethorpe Estate, Ducklington, Oxon. OX8 7PU. (01993 704513). (Att: Swindon)
DAY Mrs K D,	Wolvey Fields Farm, Wolvey, Hinkley, Leics. LE10 3HD. (01455 220 225). (Att: Perry Barr)
DE MEUR Mrs W Y	(Formerly Mrs W.Y. Cook) (Home/Kennels: Honeywick Farm, Honeywick Lane, Eaton Bray, Dunstable, Beds. LU6 2BJ. (01525 220896). Att: Milton Keynes)
DE MULDER G,	Redlum Kennels, Eaves Green Lane, Meriden, Coventry, West Midlands. CV7 7JL. (01676 22548). (Att: Hall Green)
DEACON D.	(Trans from OT) Las Vegas, Field Road, Peasemore, Nr Newbury, Berks. RG16 OJE. (01635 248323). Att: Reading)
DEBENHAM D G,	18, Ridgewell Road, Great Yeldham, Nr Halstead, Essex. CO9 4RG. (01787 237 840).
DENNIS T W,	Fallowfield Kennels, Northlands Approach, Langdon Hills, Basildon, Essex. SS16 5LP. (01268 542 061). (Att: Romford)
DICKENSON Mrs J B,	Lansdown Kennels, Stroud, Glos. GL5 IBU. (Att: Bristol)
DICKSON Miss H E,	Smoothfield Kennels, Winkfield Plain, Nr Windsor, Berks. SL4 4QN. (01344 882 791). (Att: Wembley)
DILLEY E,	"Fairbourne", Barton Road, Gravenhurst, Beds. MK45 4JP. (01462 711208). (Att: Henlow)
DIX R E,	2, Lime Kiln Cottages, Ubley Warren Farm, Nordrach Blagdon, Bristol. BS18 6XW. (01761 462 040). (Att: Cradley Heath)
DODDS H,	The Old Rectory, Appleby Magna, By Burton On Trent, Staffs. DE12 7BQ. (01530 270402/ 510273/ Fax 01530 271660).
DOLBY C A R,	Brickyard Farm, Lower Road, Croydon, Nr Royston, Herts. SG8 0HA. (01223 208 004). (Att: Wembley)
DOUGLAS Mrs S J,	New Barreman Farm, Barreman, Clynder, Helensburgh, Dunbartonshire. G84 0QN. (01436 831 902). (Att: Shawfield)
DOUGLASS M,	250, Higham Hill Road, Walthamstow, London. E17 5RQ. (0181 527 2746). Kennels: Wayside Kennels, Benskins Lane, Noak Hill, Romford, Essex. RM4 1LB. (017083 40865).
DOYLE B,	"Ramat Kennels", 89, Denham Way, Maple

NGRC Directory

	Cross, Rickmansworth, Herts. WD3 2SL. (01923 776754). (Att: Peterborough/Reading)
DRAGE R J,	Patch Lodge, Cranford Road, Great Addington, Kettering, Northants. (01536 78734). (Att: Peterborough/Reading)
DRAPER B,	71, Bramley Grange Crescent, Bramley, Rotherham, South Yorks. (01709 549222). (Kennels) Poultry Farm, Dalton Magna, Rotherham, South Yorks. (01709 851322). (Att: Sheffield)
DUCE K.	(Trans from OT) Elbony Kennels, Sandhouse Farm, Sand Lane, Susworth, Near Sth Humberside.DN17 3NR. (01724 783 068). (Att: Stainforth)
DUGGAN C,	Bodiam Farm, St Marys Lane, Upminster, Essex. RM14 3PB. (01708 222657). (Att: Walthamstow)
DUNCAN G,	32, Cliffs End Road, Ramsgate, Kent. CT12 5JD. (01843 591804). (Att: Canterbury)
DUNHAM Mrs A A,	The Bungalow, Chalk Lane, Walpole St Andrew, Wisbech, Cambs. PE14 7JU. (01945 780260).
DUNLOP A H R,	Wheatpark Farm, St Quivox, Ayr. KA6 5HG. (01292 282 116). (Att: Shawfield)
EARLES T,	Oakland Farm, General Lane, Melbourne, Yorks. YO4 4SY. (01759 318516). (Att: Stainforth)
EDWARDS D T,	The Bungalow, Stourbridge Road, Wombourne, Wolverhampton. WV5 0JH. (01902 893540). (Att: Wolverhampton)
ELLIOTT R J,	73, Whitefield Crescent, New Penshaw, Tyne & Wear. DH4 7QU. (0191 415 1801). (Kennels) Brough Park Stadium Kennels, The Fossway, Byker, Newcastle U Tyne. (0191 427 0864). (Att: Brough Park)
ELLIS B A W,	30, High Street, Farnborough, Kent. Kennels: Catford Stadium Knls, Layhams Rd, Keston, Bromley, Kent. (01959 574434). (Att: Catford)
ELLISON Mrs M,	Greenacre Kennels, 101, Mill Road, Allanton, Shotts, Strathclyde. ML7 5DD. (01501 821 648/mobile 0850 065 875). (Att: Shawfield)
FAINT J,	Laurel Park, Newgate Street Road, Cheshunt, Herts. EN7 5RY. (01707 875 771). (Att: Rye House)
FENWICK J J,	Coneygarth Farm, Bothal, Morpeth, Northumberland. NE61 6QN. (01670 855009/0860 759618). (Att: Sunderland)
FINCH C G,	Kiln Lane Kennels, Elmswell, Bury St Edmunds, Suffolk. IP30 9QR. (01359 240 750). (Att: Yarmouth)

NGRC Directory

FINCH Mrs P A,	The Grange Barrow, Beckhampton, Marlborough, Swindon, Wilts. SN8 IQR. (01672 3345). (Att: Swindon)
FIRMAGHER D P,	Glebe House, Scalford Road, Melton Mowbray, Leics. LE13 ILB. (01664 76404). (Att: Notts)
FITZGERALD M J,	Hillside Cottage, Moses Dell, Loom Lane, Radlett, Herts. WD7 8BP. (01923 856 510). (Att: Milton Keynes)
FLAHERTY J,	Greenwells Farm, 140, Netherhouse Road, Nr Bargeddie, Scotland. G69 6TU. (0141 771 5774). Att: Shawfield)
FLETCHER Mrs C P,	Low Farm, Wilden Road, Colmworth, Beds. MK44 2NN. (01234 376541).
FLINT W G,	"Rozel", 34, Shipley Common Lane, Ilkeston, Derbyshire. DE7 8TQ. (0115 9301481). (Att: Nottingham)
FORD B R,	52a, Sedge Fen, Lakenheath, Brandon, Suffolk. IP27 9LH. (0135375 276). (Att: Peterborough)
FOSTER F B,	Suncrest, Lydbrook, Gloucester. GL17 95D. (01594 61063). (Att: Swindon)
FOSTER P R,	(Trans from OT) Botany Farmhouse, Roman Way, Highworth, Wilts. SN6 7BU. (01793 861181). Kennels: Swindon Stadium Kennels, Blunsdon, Swindon.(Att: Swindon)
FOSTER T I,	Burhill Kennels, Turners Lane, Hersham, Walton On Thames, Surrey. (01932 226647). (Att: Wimbledon)
FOWLER R.B.	(Trans from OT) 35, Salcombe Road, Reading, Berks. RG2 7LH. (01734 862 757). (Att: Reading)
FREDERICKS D A,	(Home) 6, Soane Street, Pitsea, Basildon, Essex. SS13 IOU. (01268 726753). Kennels: Suffolk House Kennels, Ashwells Road, Coxtie Green, Brentwood, Essex. (01227 374863). (Att: Hackney).
FREW G L,	Elderslie House, Annandale, Kilmarnock. KA1 2RS. (01563 25537/28173). (Att: Shawfield)
FRITH Mrs G B	(Trans from OT) Hillside, Brock Hill, Wickford, Essex. SS11 7PD. (01268 710947).
GALLOWAY P E,	Buckholt Kennels, Buckholt Lane, Sidley, Bexhill On Sea, East Sussex. TN39 5AU. (01424 830666). (Att: Canterbury)
GAMMON S J,	43, Quex View Road, Birchington, Kent. CT7 0DZ. (01843 848472). Kennels: Valley Kennels, Valley Far, Valley Road, Manston, Kent. (01843 822978). (Att: Ramsgate)
GARLAND P R,	Birchgrove Kennels, Sun Hill, Fawkham, Kent. (01474 879 532). (Att: Ramsgate)
GASKIN E A,	Winston Farm, Hoe Lane, Nazeing, Waltham

NGRC Directory

	Abbey, Essex. EN9 7RJ. (0199 289 3172). (Att: Walthamstow)
GATES T,	Crows Hole Farm Kennels, Stalisfield Church Road, Charing, Kent. (01233 71 3128). (Att: Catford)
GEBSKI Miss K M,	10, William Street, Loughborough, Leics. (01533 375503). Kennels: Mayfield Grove Knis, Mayfield Grove, Long Eaton, Nottingham. (0115 9726760). (Att: Nottingham)
GENTLES T T,	(Trans from OT) 18, Princess Street, Bonnybridge, Stirlingshire, Scotland. (01324 813035). Kennels Loanhead Greyhound Kennels, Broomridge, Glasgow Road, Dennyloanhead, Stirlingshire, Scotland. (01324 815035). (Att: Dundee)
GIBBONS J P, (Jnr)	6, Vale Drive, Chatham, Kent. MES 9XD. (06134 686 625). Kennels: Redgate Kennels, Priestwood Green, Harvel, Meopham, Gravesend, Dartford, Kent. DA13 0DA. (01474 814768). (Att: Catford)
GIBSON J,	5, Town Brow, Leyland, Lancashire. PR5 2SY. (01772 431 715). (Att: Belle Vue)
GIFKINS A B,	"Elmcroft", London Road, Capel St Mary, Ipswich. Suffolk. IP9 2JJ. (01473 730584). (Att: Yarmouth)
GILBERT F,	(Trans from OT) Granby, Stafford Road, Darlaston, West Mids. WS10 8TZ. 0121 526 5275).
GILLING R J,	Ryehurst Kennels, Ryehurst Lane, Binfield, Bracknell, Berks. RGl2 SOY. (01344 423126). (Att: Reading)
GINTY P,	(Trans from OT) 250, March Road, Coates, Whittlesey, Peterborough, Cambs. PE7 2DE. (01733 840 578). (Att: Peterborough)
GINZEL W,	Hortondale Kennels, Horton, Near Leighton Buzzard, Beds. LU7 0QR. (01296 668379). (Att: Wembley)
GLAISTER K J,	Kennels: Old Oakleigh Kennels, London Road, Sunninghill, Nr Ascot, Berks. (01344 21332).
GLASS J K,	Cranstoun House, Ford, Pathmead, Midlothian. EH37 5UB. (01875 320701). (Att: Powderhall)
GODDARD A S,	The Hollies, Hepworth Road, Stanton, Bury St Edmunds, Suffolk. (01359 50159). (Kennels) A.G. Kennels, 6 1/2, Fen Street, Hopton, Diss, Norfolk. (Att: Swaffham)
GOMERSALL Mrs C S	,3, Grove Farm Cottages, Lady Lane, Blunsdon, Swindon, Wilts. SN2 4DY. (01793 729043). (Att: Swindon)
GOODALL Miss G H,	1, Saucheside Cottages, Edgehead, Mid Lothian. EH37 SRB. Kennels: Drumbank Kennels, Drumbank Stables, 612,

NGRC Directory

	Old Dalkeith Road, Edinburgh, Scotland. (0131 672 1201). (Att: Powderhall)
GOODWIN G P,	Ferrybank Farm, Northampton Road, Orlingbury, Kettering, Northants. NN14 1JF. (01933 401593/0604 or 39586/ or 0850 326556). (Att: Oxford)
GRAY T G,	"Elmcroft", 3, Ermin Street, Blunsdon, Swindon, Wilts. SN2 4DJ. (Att: Swindon)
GRAY W T,	14, Pollock Avenue, Eaglesham, Glasgow. (0135 53 3461). Kennels: 8, Field Road, Busby, Glasgow, Scotland. (0141 644 2201).
GREEN Mrs V A,	Oaks Farm, Ashby Road, Stapleton, Leics. LE9 8JE. (01455 290137). (Att: Nottingham)
GREENACRE Mrs F,	Harlingwood Kennels, Harlingwood Lane, Old Buckenham, Norfolk. NR17 IPT. (01953 860750). (Att: Wembley)
GRIEVE D I,	Blue Acres Boarding Kennels, East Pasture Farm, Cornforth Lane, Coxhoe, Co Durham. DH6 4ER. (0191 377 3711). (Att: Sunderland)
GRIFFIN H E,	Norfolk House Kennels, Stanton Mereway, Willingham, Cambs. CB4 SHJ. (01954 260445).
GRIFFIN R S,	"Ivanhoe", Arterial Road, Wickford, Essex. SS12 9JF. (01268 727208). (Att: Peterborough)
GRIGGS D.N.	(Trans from OT) Uplands Farm, Meggett Lane, South Alkham, Dover, Kent. CT15 7DG. (01303 89 2300). (Att: Canterbury)
HALL J R,	Sunnycroft, 222, The Longshoot, Nuneaton, CV11 6JW. (01203 383466). (Att: Hall Green)
HALL M C,	12, Ockendon Kennels, Ockendon Complex/Road, Upminster, Essex. RM14 3PU.
HANCOX Miss D N,	89, Kestrel Cres, Blackbird Leys, Cowley, Oxford. OX4 SEE. (01865 777538). - Kennels: Glebe Farm Kennels, Fringford, Bicester, Oxon. (01869 277679). (Att: Reading)
HANCOX P A,	Westview, Dadleys Wood, Wall Mill Road, Corley, Nr Coventry, West Midlands. (01676 40446). (Att: Hall Green)
HANSLOW R E,	Farmhill Kennels, Trueleigh Hill, Shoreham West Sussex. (01903 814690).
HARDING G,	D & D Kennels, Harding Sheet Metal, Bunns Bank, Attleborough, Norfolk. NR17 2NG. (01953 456721). Fax 01953 453 758.
HARDING Miss M J,	30, Barataria, Papercourt Lane, Ripley, Surrey. GU23 6DR. (01932 221 516). Kennels: Burhill Kennels, Turners Lane, Hersham, Walton On Thames, Surrey. (Att: Wimbledon)
HARRIS Mrs T,	St Thomas School Road, Tilny St Lawrence, Kings Lynn, Norfolk. PE34 4QZ. (01945 880940).
HART T,	60, Bassleton Lane, Thornaby, Cleveland. TS17 OAF. (01642 763108). (Att: Brough Pk)
HARVEY N.P.	(Home) 1, Woodside, Stony Stratford, Milton

NGRC Directory

	Keynes, Bucks. MK11 1DL. (0908 565072). Kennels: Sherington Bridge Farm, Bedford Road, Newport Pagnell, Bucks. MK16 9JA. (01908 218889). (Att: Milton Keynes)
HARWOOD R B,	52, Poplar Road, Dorridge, Solihull, West Mids. (01564 730045). (Kennels) Melbick Nursery Kennels, Chester Road, Coleshill, Warks. (0121 782 0571). (Att: Perry Barr)
HAWES Mrs V P,	Ash Tree Farm, Wicken, Ely, Cambs. CB7 5YE. (01353 720512).
HAWKE M J C,	The Stables, Lingfield Common Road, Lingfield, Surrey. RH17 6BU. (01342 835950).
HAWKE P S	Heath Grange Greyhound Training Centre, Tandridge Lane, Blindley Heath, Nr Lingfield, Surrey. (01342 834 634).
HAWKES D F,	Harmony Kennels, Brook House, Purleigh, Nr Chelmsford, Essex. (01621 828563). (Att: Walthamstow)
HAYNES J,	Fallowfield Kennels, Grays Avenue, Dry St, Langdon Hills, Basildon, Essex. SSl6 5LP. (01268 542 061). (Att: Hackney)
HEAD T.G.	(Trans from OT) Brooklyn Lodge, Burts Lane, Mannington, Wimbourne, Dorset. BH21 7JX. (01202 825 226). (Att: Portsmouth)
HEAP R,	East Farm, Stanhope Road, Middleton In Teesdale. DL12 0RR. (01833 40541). (Att: Sunderland)
HEASMAN Miss R P,	Denver Lodge Kennels, Nazeing, Waltham Abbey, Essex. EN9 2EB. (0199 289 3220). (Att: Wembley)
HEATON Mrs B,	Lynwood, Langley Road, Swinton, Manchester. M27 2SS. (061 736 6923). (Att: Belle Vue)
HELD P,	Turpin Cottage, London Road, Binfield, Bracknell, Berks. RG12 SAB. (01344 423382). (Att: Reading)
HICKEN D,	Meadow Court Kennels, Lands End Road, Thorn, Nr Doncaster. DN8 4JL. (01405 812189).
HICKS H A J,	21, Rex Road, Higher Odcombe, Nr Yeovil, Somerset. BA22 8XP. (0193 586 3666). Kennels: Southmead Farm, Common Lane, Keinton Mandeville, Somerset. (01458 223 093). (Att: Bristol)
HILL A C,	Meadow Sweet Kennels, Oak Ave, Crays Hill, Billericay, Essex. CMll 2YE. (01268 527587).
HITCH A J,	Nuf field Farm, Flaunden Lane, Bovingdon, Hemel Hempstead, Herts. (01442 832271). (Att: Wimbledon)
HODSON G,	(Home) 17, Priors Close, Upper Beeding, W Sussex. BN4 3HT. (01273 492874). Kennels: Albourne Kennels, Wheatsheaf Road, Albourne, Nr Henfield, Sussex.

NGRC Directory

	(01273 492722). (Att: Brighton)
HOLLAND G D,	Avon Park Kennels, 19, Ringwood Road, St Ives, Nr Ringwood, Hants. (0831 264 608). (Att: Portsmouth)
HOLTOM L G,	Well Place Farm, Ipsden, Oxford. OX9 6AD. (01491 680092). (Att: Reading)
HONEYSETT J,	Pendene Farm & Kennels, Pendell Road, Bletchingley, Redhill, Surrey. (01737 642125). (Att: Wembley)
HOPKINS C.J.	(Trans from OT) The Poplars, Alstone Road, Teddington, Nr Tewksbury, Glos. GL20 8JA. (Att: Swindon)
HOPPER D 5,	17, Greenside Road, Mirfield, West Yorks. (01924 492598). (Att: Sheffield)
HORSFALL J C,	(Home) Rother House, 271, Main Road, Biggin Hill, Westerham, Kent. Kennels: Catford Stadium Kennels, Layhams Road, Keston, Bromley, Kent. (01959 574 433). (Att: Catford)
HOUGH R,	Sand Rock Lodge Kennels, Bawtry Road, Tick Hill, Doncaster, South Yorks. DN11 9EZ. (01302 750834). (Att: Sheffield)
HOUSEMAN Mrs P A,	Beech Cottage, South Leigh Road, High Goggs, Witney, Oxon. OX8 6UW. (01993 703874). Kennels: Woodlands Kennels, Little Heath Farm, Tackley, Oxon. OXS 3EN. (01869 83608). (Att: Swindon)
HOWARD K H,	2, Farmwood Cottage, Broad Lane, Hedsor, Wooburn Common, Bucks. (01628 20197). Kennels: Ockwells Home Farm, Cox Green, Berks. SL6 3AB. (01628 782155).
HULME R H,	Highfields, Ruddle Lane, Micklebring, Rotherham. S66 7RT. (01709 818860). (Att: Sheffield)
HUNTER T W,	90, Woodfarm Bungalow, Salhouse, Norwich, Norfolk. (01603 721335). (Att: Yarmouth)
HUNWICKS Mrs T V,	Harrimans Farm Cottage, Old Knarr Fen Drove, Thorney, Peterborough, Cambs. PE6 0RJ. (01733 270066).
INGRAM Miss A J,	Croftview Kennels, Whitehorse Lane, Harvel, Meopham, Kent. (01474 815202). (Att: Ramsgate)
INGRAM-SEAL D,	Broomewood Kennels, Swingfield Street, Swingfield, Nr Dover, Kent. (01303 83271). (Att: Ramsgate)
ISAAC P D,	Sunhaven, Crocknorth Road, Ranmore Common, Dorking, Surrey. (01483 283363). (Att: Crayford)
JACKSON A M,	Fairyknowe, Stone Dyke Road, Carluke, Scotland. ML8 4BQ. (01555 772576). (Att: Sheffield)
JAGO R N,	Little Follies, Netherne Lane, Merstham, Redhill, Surrey. RH1 3AJ. (01737 555146). (Att: Reading)

NGRC Directory

JAMES R A,   22, Clatford Manor Estate, Upper Clatford Estate, Andover, Hants. SP11 7PZ. (01264 365946). Kennels: Lower Farm Kennels, Picket Twenty, Andover, Hants. (01264 337898). (Att: Portsmouth)

JAMESON T, (Snr)   (Trans from OT) 2, Fairholme Court, Hemlington, Middlesbrough, Cleveland. T58 9LD. Kennels: Cleveland Park Stadium Kennels, Stockton Road, Middlesbrough, Cleveland. (01642 598 955). (Att: Middlesbrough)

JEFFREY R N,   Kildara Kennels, Odiham Road, Ewshot, Farnham, Surrey. GU10 SAJ. (01252 850 384). (Att: Oxford)

JENKINS A K,   (Home) 437, Fox Hollies Road, Acocks Green, Birmingham. B27 7OA. (0121 604 3856). (Kennels) Church Farm, Church Lane, Bickenhill, Solihull, West Mids. B92 0DN. (01675 442641).

JENNINGS B E,   Wood Farm Kennels, Astley Lane, Astley, Nuneaton, Warks. CV10 7PU. (01676 41595). (Att: Monmore Green)

JOHNSON Mrs A L,   Beacon Park Farm, Barr Beacon, Aldridge, Nr Walsall, Staffs. WS9 0RG. (0121 325 0750). (Att: Perry Barr)

JOHNSON T,   1, Speedwell Cottages, Speedwell Farm, Long Drove, Coldham, Wisbech, Cambs. PE14 0NW. (01945 860377). (Att: Mildenhall)

JOHNSTON T,   Stilliters Farm, Moulsoe Road, Cranfield, Bedford. MK43 0BL. (01234 750362). (Att: Wembley)

JONES D,   Panda Cottage, Magpie Hall Road, Kingsnorth, Ashford, Kent. TN26 1HF. (01233 631507). (Att: Canterbury)

JONES J J F,   (Trans from OT) Marpo Nurseries, Stodmarsh Road, Canterbury, Kent. CT3 4AP. (01227 765 296). (Att: Canterbury)

JONES Mrs L E,   Imperial Kennels, 100, Undley Common, Undley, Lakenheath, Brandon, Suffolk. IP27 9BZ. (01842 860579).

JONES L J,   (Trans from OT) Winterfield Farm, Winterfield Lane, Hulme, Stoke On Trent, Staffs. ST35 SBG. (01782 304 762).

KAYE R A J,   (Trans from OT) Mallards, South Hanningfield Rettendon Common, Chelmsford, Essex. CM3 SHH. 01245 400064). (Att: Peterborough)

KEEGAN Miss E,   (Nee: Armstrong) South Lodge Kennels, Blair Adam, Kelty, Fife, Scotland. KY4 0JJ. (01383 830122). (Att: Powderhall)

KELLY M G,   Shamrock, 10, Redmoor Lane, Wisbech, Cambs. PEl4 ORN. (01945 584394). (Att: Peterborough)

NGRC Directory

KEMPSTER C J,	15a, Corkscrew Hill, West Wickham, Kent. BR4 9BA. (0181 777 4680). Kennels: Croftview Kennels, Whitehorse Lane, Harvel, Meopham, Kent. (01474 814285).
KENNETT S P,	46, Buckhurst Way, Buckhurst Hill, Essex. IG9 6HP. Kennels: The Kennels, Patches Farm, Galley Hill, Waltham Abbey, Essex. EN9 2AJ. (01992 767249). (Att: Crayford)
KENNEY D W,	Holly Hill Farm, Little Shaw Lane, Markfield, Leics. LE67 9PP. (01530 243557). (Att: Nottingham)
KIBBLE T,	36, Broadway Close, Witney, Oxon. Kennels: Hoskins Barn, Buckland Road, Bampton, Witney, Oxon. OX8 2AA. (01860 216034). (Att: Bristol)
KIMBERLEY Mrs R A,	The Cottage, Main Road, Ratcliffe Culey, Near Atherstone, Warks. CV9 3PD. (01827 716590). (Att: Perry Barr)
KINCHETT D F,	D. Kinchett Knls, Catford Stadium Kennels, Layhams Road, Keston, Bromley, Kent. BR2 6AR. (01959 574428). (Att: Wimbledon)
KING J R,	Garth Gate, Rillington Fields, Scragglethorpe, Malton, Nth Yorks. YO17 8EB. (019442 8868). (Att: Stainforth)
KING Mrs L M,	Sunnymead, Mill Lane, Potton Road, Everton, Sandy, Beds. SG19 2LH. (01767 692610).
KINSEY R J,	Mossfield Boarding Kennels, Drury Lane, Warmingham, Nr Crewe, Cheshire. CW1 4PN. (0127 077 249). (Att: Perry Barr)
KNIBB G I,	Toms Cabin Kennels, 1, Vale View, Tring Hill, Tring, Herts. HP23 4LD. (01442 890 144). (Att: Milton Keynes)
KNIGHT D D,	20, Peacock Lane, Brighton. Kennels: Albourne Kennels, Wheatsheaf Rd, Albourne, Nr Henfield, Sussex. (01273 494737). (Att: Brighton)
KOVALEV A,	1, Limekiln Cottage, Nordrach Blagdon, Bristol. BS18 6XW. (01761 462044). (Att: Bristol)
KUERES O D,	Lakeside Kennels, 60, Church St, Wincham, Northwich, Cheshire. CW9 6EP. (01565 733812). (Att: Norton Canes)
LANCEMAN T L,	Suffolk House Kennels, Ashwells Road, Coxtie Green, Brentwood, Essex. (01277 355485/374554). (Att: Hackney/Rye House)
LANE B W,	40, Harrowgate Road, Hackney, London. E9 5ED. Kennels: Hackney Stadium Kennels, Waterden Road, London E15 2EQ. (0181 985 2528) (Att: Hackney)
LANG G A,	The Dawn Ranch, Blind Lane, Botney Hill Rd, Billericay, Essex. CM12 9SN. (01277 651809). (Att: Crayford)

NGRC Directory

LARGE M,	(Trans from OT) Highfield, 1, Cranfield Road, Moulsoe, Milton Keynes. MK16 0HL. (01908 614836). (Att: Milton Keynes)
LAVER Mrs F H M, -	Hunters Bungalow, 1a, Hatch, Nr Sandy, Beds. (01767 681 191). (Att: Milton Keynes)
LAWLOR M,	Lower Hortondale Kennels, Horton, Near Leighton Buzzard, Beds. LU7 0OR. (01296 662834). (Att: Oxford)
LAWRENCE L J,	45, Peartree Close, South Ockendon, Essex. RM15 6PR. (01708 852450). Kennels: Ockendon Kennels, Ockendon Road, Upminster, Essex. (01708 224593). (Att: Hackney/Rye House)
LAWRENCE T,	Greystone Kennels, Holbeach St John, Near Spalding, Lincs. PE12 8RJ. (01406 540382). (Att: Peterborough)
LEA Mrs M,	166, Battram Road, Ellistown, Leics. LE7 1GB. (01530 230557). (Att: Nottingham)
LEA V A,	Ivycombe, Catley Cross Road, Pebmarsh, Near Halstead, Essex. CO9 2PD. (01787 29331). (Att: Mildenhall)
LEYDEN J M,	(Trans from OT) 77, Seymour Court Road, Marlow, Bucks. SL7 3BQ. (01628 471118). (Att: Reading)
LIDDLE Miss T,	Oakgrove Kennels, Sedge Fen, Lakenheath, Suffolk. IP27 9LE. (0135 375 234). (Att: Hackney)
LILLEY G.D. 1	Watch Kennels, Stave Hall Fm, Monks Kirby, Nr Rugby, Warks. CB23 0RL. (01788 833213). (Att: Hall Green)
LINDSAY A E,	(Trans From OT) 9, Saywell Road, Luton, LU2 0TJ. (05182 416122).
LINLEY Mrs S,	South View, N Otterington, North Allerton, North Yorks. DL7 9JQ. (01609 776788). (Att: Sunderland)
LINZELL K W,	Burton Lodge, Borwick Lane, Wickford, Essex SS12 0QA. (01268 733945). (Att: Romford)
LISTER C R,	Mudross, Main Road, North Clifton, Newark, Notts. NE23 7AZ. (01777 228 247). (Att: Peterborough)
LITTLE Mrs J A,	Lower Wath, Silloth, Cumbria. CA5 4PH. (016973 31387). (Att: Sunderland)
LOADER K G,	The Kennels, Lower Farm, Picket Twenty, Andover, Hants. SP11 6LF. (01264 333437). (Att: Reading/Portsmouth)
LOVERIDGE A,	143, Viola Avenue, Stanwell, Staines, Middx. TW19 7RZ. (01784 242794). (Att: Reading)
LOWE E W,	Aramona Greyhound Kennels, Seats Hill, Hull Road, Seaton, Nr Hull, Nth Humberside. HU11 5RN. (01946 534088). (Att: Hull)
LUCAS A M,	20, Fentum Road, Guildford, Surrey. GU2 6SA (01483 36598). Kennels: Hillside Kennels, Shere Road, Clandon, Guildford, Surrey.

NGRC Directory

	(01483 224018). (Att: Brighton)
LUCAS Miss M E,	12, Long Lynderswood, Basildon, Essex. Kennels: Jessamine, Hovefields Ave, Wickford, Essex. SS12 9JR. (01268 591027). (Att: Romford)
LUCKHURST D E,	Home Farm, Staplehurst, Tonbridge, Kent. TN12 0RU. (01580 891579). (Att: Crayford)
LYNDS C E G,	South Walsham Kennels, South Walsham Hall, Ranworth Road, South Walsham, Norfolk. NR13 6DQ. (01605 49601). (Att: Yarmouth)
MADDEN J A,	Clarnella, Short Lane, Fotherby, Louth, Lincs. LN11 OTE. (01507 608296). Kennels: The Newlands, Wash Road, Fosdyke, Boston, Lincs. PE20 2DJ. (01205 85272). (Att: Swaffham)
MAGNASCO L LG,	Fairview, Old London Road, Milton Common, Oxford. OX9 2JR. (01844 279 480). (Att: Swindon)
MARCH Mrs J J,	Wheatsheaf Farm, 41, Straight Road, Boxted, Nr Colchester, Essex. CO4 5HN. (01206 272245).
MARKHAM Mrs P M,	Birdbeck Cottage, Gillsbridge, Outwell, Wisbech, Cambs. PE14 8TQ. (01945 773442). (Att: Peterborough)
MARLOW Miss K A,	Waterdell Kennels, Waterdell Farm, Springwell Lane, Harefield, Middx. UB9 6PG. (01895 825057). (Att: Romford)
MARTIN B R,	Homelands, Morley St Peter, Wymondham, Norfolk. NR18 9ST. (01953 607380).
MASON M W E,	(Trans from OT) 88, Lashford Lane, Dry Sandford, Abingdon, Oxon. OX13 6EB. (01865 739958). (Att: Reading)
MASSEY M H,	Windmill Cottage, Blackthorn, Nr Bicester Oxon. OX6 OTJ (01869 253187). (Att: Oxford)
MASTERS W F,	Sake Ride Field, Wineham Lane, Nr Henfield, West Sussex. BN5 9AG. (01273 494098). (Kennels) Albourne Kennels, Wheatsheaf Road, Albourne, Nr Henfield, West Sussex. (01273 492874). (Att: Brighton)
MATTOCKS K D,	33, High Bungay Road, Loddon, Norwich, NR14 6DZ. (0508 20310). (Att: Yarmouth)
MAVRIAS M,	Sandhurst Farm Kennels, Crouch Lane, Sandhurst, Kent.TN18 SPA. (0580 850464). (Att: Hackney)
MAVRIAS Spencer:	(Thornton Farm Kennels, Tilmanstone, Deal, Kent. (01304 620085). (Att: Ramsgate)
MAXEN L,	80, Mabley Street, London E9. Kennels: Hackney Stadium Kennels, Waterden Road, London E15 2EO. (0181 533 2548). (Att: Hackney)
MAY G F,	The Acres, Durfold Farm, Fisher Lane, Dunsfold, Godalming, Surrey. GU8 4PH. (01483 200467). (Att: Reading)

NGRC Directory

MAYES G T,	8, Stratford House, Earlsdon Street, Southsea, Portsmouth, Hants. PO5 4BX. (01705 733602). Kennels: Whitehouse Kennels: Whitehouse Farm, Birdham, Wittering, Sussex. PO20 7HU. (01243 513 814). (Att: Portsmouth)
MAYHEW G E,	Redfield Kennels, Old Forge, Redfield Lane, Church Crookham, Aldershot, Hants. GU13 ORB. (01252 851040). (Att: Reading)
McAULIFFE J J,	Allerds Farm, Crown Lane, Farnham Royal, Slough, Berkshire. SL2 3SF. (01753 644664). (Att: Milton Keynes)
McCOMBE W P,	Spring Garden Farm, Aldervale Kennels, Dean Lane, Lumb In Rossendale, Lancs. BB4 9RD. (01706 214500). (Att: Belle Vue)
McDERMOTT E J,	Hurle House, Wynard Road, Wolviston, Cleveland. TS22 SNE. (01740 644232). (Att: Sunderland)
McDONALD B A,	Middlesbrough Stadium Kennels, Stockton Rd, Middlesbrough, Cleveland. TS5 4AE. (01642 230845). (Att: Middlesbrough)
McELLISTRIM Miss N,	Hillside Farm, Ruxbury Road, Lyne, Chertsey, Surrey. Kennels: Burhill Kennels, Turners Lane, Hersham, Walton On Thames, Surrey. (01932 221545). (Att: Wimbledon)
McGEE J F, (Snr) -	"Brookside", Arterial Road, Wickford, Essex. SS12 9JF. (01268 726583). Also: Peaceful Kennels, Ockendon Road, Upminster, Essex. RM14 3QJ. (01708 224156). (Att: Canterbury)
McGEE J F, (Jnr)	Peaceful Kennels, Ockendon Complex/Road, Upminster, Essex. RM14 3OJ. 01708 224156).
McGINTY Miss J A,	"Linton Kennels", Briardale Farm, Scarborough Road, Norton, Malton, N Yorks. (Knls 01653 600198/House 01653 692152). (Att: Sunderland)
McINTOSH B F,	Cherry Tree Farm, West Hougham, Nr Dover, Kent, CT15 7AT. (01304 211154). (Att: Ramsgate)
McKENNA A,	Underhill Farm, Underhill Lane, Wadley Br., Sheffield. S6 1NL. (01742 853889). (Att: Stainforth)
McNALLY C D,	Bridge Farm Kennels, Bretford, Rugby, Warks. (01203 542124). (Att: Cradley Heath/Perry Barr)
McNICHOLAS Mrs A J,	31, Ayresome Green Lane, Middlesbrough, Cleveland. TS5 4DT. (01642 828905). Kennels: Middlesbrough Stadium Kennels,
Stockton Road,	Middlesbrough, Cleveland. (01642 211803). (Att: Middlesbrough)
McSEVENEY W,	(Trans from OT) 42, Wells House, Spa Green Estate, Roseberry Avenue, Islington, London. EC1R 4TR. (0171 278 8046). Kennels: Block 4,

NGRC Directory

	Ockendon Kennels, Ockendon Road, Upminster, Essex. (01708 223 850). (Att: Hackney)
MEADOWS F H,	Crossleigh Kennels, Narcot Lane, Chalfont St Giles, Bucks. HP8 4DX. (01494 873455). (Att: Oxford)
MEEK A C,	Yew Tree Cottage, Upper Carterspiece Farm, English Bicknor, Nr Coleford, Glos. GL16 7ES. (01594 861083). (Att: Hall Green)
MELLOR K,	35, Station Road, L. Stondon, Henlow Camp, Beds. (01465 813608). (Att: Henlow)
MENTZIS T,	Rikasso Kennels, Stablebridge Road, Aston Clinton, Aylesbury, Bucks. HP22 5ND. (01296 630638). (Att: Milton Keynes)
MERCER M J,	102, Drovers Way, Dunstable, Beds. LU6 1AW. (01582 607924). Kennels: Horsendon Hill Farm, Judds Lane, Tetsworth, Oxon. (01836 269781). (Att: Oxford)
MEW M F,	Berrycourt Kennels, Cooling Street, Cliffe, Rochester, Kent. (01634 220459). (Att: Crayford)
MILLARD Mrs M D,	Priory Farm, Dauntsey, Nr Chippenham, Wilts. (01249 890423) (Att: Bristol/Swindon)
MILLEN D R,	Valley View Farm, Stockbury Valley, Newington, Sittingbourne, Kent. ME9 7QP. (01795 842915). (Att: Canterbury)
MILLER Miss C,	10, Tremaine Close, Brockley, London SE4 1YF. (Kennels) Croftview Kennels, Whitehorse Lane, Harvel, Meopham, Kent. (04174 815 273). (Att: Canterbury)
MILLER Mrs F,	The Old Nursery, Horton Cum Studley, Oxon. OX33 IDA. (01865 351423). (Att: Oxford)
MILLER G W,	Deerness Racing Kennels, Mill Road, Langley Moor, Co Durham. (0191 378 9543). (Att: Brough Park)
MILLIGAN Mrs D H,	Furzehill House, Woodhill, Ponteland, Newcastle Upon Tyne. NE20 0JA. (01661 823731).
MILLIGAN S R,	Beaverwood Kennels, Perry Road, Chislehurst, Kent. BR7 6HF. (0181 300 8365). (Att: Catford)
MILLS E W,	2, Hare And Hounds Corner, Hemingstone, Ipswich. Suffolk. IP6 9RW. (01473 785840).
MILLS I W,	The Bungalow, Low Road, Norton Sub-Course, Norfolk. (01508 548353). (Att: Yarmouth)
MOODY K F,	15, Deerswood Ave, Oxlease, Hatfield, Herts. AL10 8RX. (01707 267130). Kennels: Bushwood Farm, Dixons Hill Close, Service Road, Welham Green, Nr Hatfield, Herts. (01707 273837). (Att: Milton Keynes)
MORGAN J,	"Burwood", Menmarsh Road, Worminghall, Aylesbury, Bucks. HP18 9UP.

NGRC Directory

	(01865 351 627). (Att: Oxford)
MORLEY M J,	Kenley, 17, Cressex Road, High Wycombe, Bucks. HP12 4PG. (01494 534066).
MORRIS B H,	(Trans from OT) 47, Coppice Lane, Short Heath, Willenhall, West Mids. WV12 5BT. (01922 476630). (Att: Cradley Heath)
MORRIS D G,	8, The Orchard, Marfleet Lane, Hull. HU9 4EW. (Kennels) Woodlands Kennels, Thirtleby Lane, Thirtleby, Coniston, Nr Hull. (01482 815616). Att: Hull)
MORRIS R B,	Thorndon Cottage, Warley Gap, Little Warley, Brentwood, Essex. CM13 3DP. Tel No's: (01277 200738/202185/220299). (Att: Rye House)
MORROW Mrs F,	Popes Farm, 19, Tempsford Road, Sandy, Beds. SG19 2AE. (01767 680620). (Att: Milton Keynes)
MORTIMER Mrs M ,	(Trans from OT) 189, Havant Road, Hayling Island, Portsmouth, Hants. PO11 0LG. (01705 467550). (Att: Portsmouth)
MOURING N W,	7, Priors Court Cottages, Priors Court, Chievely, Newbury, Berks. RG16 8XL. (01635 247086). (Att: Reading)
MOYS B,	20, Sweechgate, Broad Oak, Canterbury, Kent. CT2 0OX. (01227 712667). Kennels: Broomewood Kennels, Swingfield St, Dover, Kent. (01303 83601). (Att: Canterbury)
MULLINS D,	D. Mullins Knls, 10a, Potton Road, Everton, Sandy, Beds. (01767 651751). (Att: Catford)
MULLINS Mrs L,	Old Hall Kennels, Green Lane, Mistley, Manningtree, Essex. (0120 639 2165). (Att: Walthamstow)
MUNSLOW M T,	Hilly Bank Kennels, Chevin Side, Belper, Derbyshire. (0177 382 2169). (Att: Nottingham)
NASH Mrs L,	114, Kings Chase, East Molesey, Surrey. KT8 9DG. Kennels: The Elms Kennels, Three Bridges Farm, Gambles Lane, Send, Surrey. GU23 7LQ. (01483 223268 or 0181 941 4281). (Att: Reading)
NEARY S,	45, Keycol Hill, Sittingbourne, Kent. ME9 8LZ. (01795 842182). (Att: Canterbury)
NEWMAN M T,	(Trans from OT) 8, Portmeers Close, Lennox Road, Walthamstow, London. E17 8PT. (0181 520 9481). Kennels: Valley View Kennels, Claverhambury Road, Waltham Abbey, Essex. (01992 893692). (Att: Hackney)
NIEROBISZ Miss M ,	Station House Knls, Cadley, Collingbourne, Ducis, Marlborough, Nr Swindon, Wilts. SN8 3EB. (01264 850188). (Att: Reading)
NORMAN G S,	5, Springs Avenue, Catsmill, Bromsgrove, Worcs (01527 579 073) Kennels: Lock Cottage

NGRC Directory

	Kennels, 254, Kingsbury Road, Marston, Warks. (01675 470 999). (Att: Perry Barr)
OCKENDON Mrs L,	2, Hill Terrace, Corringham, Stanford Le Hope, Essex. SS17 9BP. (01375 672345).
OLIVER N,	24, Barrett Road, Walkergate, Newcastle Upon Tyne. Kennels: Brough Park Stadium Kennels, The Fossway, Byker, Newcastle Upon Tyne. (0191 265 1741). (Att: Brough Park)
O'NEILL K P,	(Trans from OT) Low Moors Cottage, Ramshaw, Evenwood, W Auckland. DL14 0NG. (01388 834732). (Att: Stainforth)
ORME J,	(Trans from OT) Church Farmhouse, Barrow Village, Nr Oakham, Leics. LE15 7PE. (01572 812205). (Att: Nottingham)
OSBORNE M F,	Glan-y-Rhosog Farm, Peterstone, Wentloog, Nr Cardiff. CF3 8TN. (01222 795536/796729). (Att: Bristol)
O'SULLIVAN B D,	Hazelwood Kennels, Sun Hill, Fawkham, Near Dartford, Kent. DA3 8NU. (01474 872263). (Att: Crayford)
OWEN S C,	Nuclear Kennels, Flint House, 7, Wangford, Brandon, Suffolk. IP27 0SJ. (01842 813435).
PACKHAM C W,	Mollifrend House, Mollifrend Lane, Farmborough, Nr Bath, Avon. BA3 1BY. (01761 470555). (Att: Reading)
PAGE Mrs J A,	2, Wrestlingworth Road, Potton, Nr Sandy, Beds. SG19 2DP. (01767 261177).
PALMER A B,	(Home) Criston, Lower Platts, Ticehurst, East Sussex. TN5 7BU. (01580 201 275). Kennels: Whents Farm, Lower Road, Teyham, Kent. ME9 9LP. (01795 522270). (Att: Canterbury)
PARKER Mrs E T,	Russanda, Station Road, Hensall, North Humberside. DN14 0QU. (01977 662052). (Att: Stainforth)
PARKER I D,	8, Chapel Gardens, Whaplode, Spalding, Lincs. PE12 6UG. (01406 371464). Kennels: Blueberry Kennels, West Road, South Drove, Spalding, Lincs. (01775 761863). (Att: Peterborough)
PARKINS J,	(Trans from OT) Cynthia Cottage, Station Rd, Old Leake, Boston, Lincs. PE22 9RR. (Att: Peterborough)
PATTINSON R,	The Hazels, London Road, Vange, Basildon, Essex. SS16 4PX. (01268 553196).
PAYNE P F,	Brooklyn Kennels, Blackbush Lane, Horndon On The Hill, Stanford Le Hope, Essex. SS16 4PX. (01375 891614). (Att: Romford)
PEACOCK R K,	121, Sunningvale Ave, Biggin Hill, Kent. TN16 3XG. Kennels: R. Peacock Kennels,

NGRC Directory

	Catford Stadium Kennels, Layhams Road, Keston, Bromley, Kent. (01959 571926). (Att: Catford)
PEARCE K,	Dellrise Kennel, Waterdell Farm, Springwell Lane, Harefield, Middx. UB9 6PG. (01895 825034). (Att: Oxford)
PERKINS B J,	2, Timlett Cott, Stanton Rd, Shifnal, Shrops. TF11 8NX. (01952 461479). (Att: Monmore Green)
PETERSON Mrs G E,	Binwell Lane Farm, Woodham, Aylesbury, Bucks. HP18 OQE. (01296 658604). (Att: Oxford)
PETT T P,	62, Heath Road, Crayford, Kent. DA1 3NZ. (01322 274 997). Kennels: Culvey Down Kennels, Castle Hil, Hartley, Kent. (01831 665651). (Att: Canterbury)
PHILPOTT P B,	Valley View Kennels, Reevesgate Farm, Claverhambury Road, Waltham Abbey, Essex. (0199 289 2704).
PICKETT Miss D,	Mount Lodge Kennels, Oak Road, Crays Hill, Billericay, Essex. CM11 2YL. (01268 521714). (Att: Hackney)
PICTON B,	The Woodlands, Coppice Lane, Middleton, Staffs. (0121 323 2968). (Att: Monmore Green)
PILFOLD S J,	Pippins, Apple Pie Farm, Benenden, Cranbrook, Kent. TN17 4EU. (01580 240291). (Att: Ramsgate)
PLATTS Mrs D,	(Trans from OT) 12, Birchwood Rd, Wilmington, Kent. DA2 7HE. (Att: Hackney)
PLEASANTS R A,	7, Taylors Buildings, Magdalen Road, Norwich, Norfolk. NR3 4AW. (01603 424 649). Kennels: Malthouse Farm, Scotton, Near Norwich, Norfolk.
PORTER Mrs M J, -	12, Riverside, Hanham, Bristol. BS15 3NL. (01272 600765). (Att: Swindon)
PORTER Mrs S,	Stewarts Hill Farm, By Abernethy, Perth, Scotland. (01374 477 079). (Att: Powderhall)
POUNTNEY D G,	Delo Kennels, Heath Farm, Cowles Drove, Hockwold, Norfolk. IP26 4JQ. (01842 828750). (Att: Mildenhall)
POWER M W,	Vale Lodge, Swainsthorpe, Norwich, Norfolk. NR14 8PT. (01508 78433).
PRENTICE G,	(Trans from OT) Whinhill Bungalow, Daisy Hill, Burstwick, Nr Hull, Humberside. (01964 670115). (Att: Hull)
PRICE Mrs R A,	"Meadowside", French Mill Lane, Shaftesbury, Dorset. SP7 0EW. (01747 854042). (Att: Reading)
PRINCE Mrs K,J,	Stave Hall Farm, Fosse Way, Monks Kirby, Rugby. CV23 0RL. Kennels: Lenton And Bray, Blackhorse Lane, Bedworth, Coventry. CV6 6DN. (01203 364 047). (Att: Perry Barr)
PRUHS A M,	Pixies Lodge, Dowsdale Bank, Shepeau Stow,

NGRC Directory

	Whaplode Drove, Spalding, Lincs. PE12 0TZ. (01406 330198). Kennels: Horseshoe Lodge, Birds Drove, Sutton St James, Lincs. (0194 585 490). (Att: Peterborough)
PRUHS D,	The Willows, Burr Lane, Spalding, Lincs. PE12 6AZ. (01775 724446). (Att: Peterborough)
PUDDY D,	33, Rydons Lane, Old Coulsdon, Surrey. CR5 ISU. (0181 668 2953). (Att: Rye House)
PUGH M L,	Robin Mill Farm, Stony Lane, Tardebigge, Bromsgrove, Worcs. (01527 74381). (Att: Hall Green)
PUZEY M,	1, Claverhambury Kennels, Galley Hill, Waltham Abbey, Essex. (01992 893 188). (Att: Walthamstow)
QUINN J J,	Ellis Barn Farm Kennels, Kenardington, Ashford, Kent. TN26 2LP. (01233 861 429). (Att: Hackney)
RAGGATT L,	12, Shrewsbury Drive, Backworth, Tyne & Wear. (0191 268 8583). Kennels: 1, Bishops Close Cotts, Whitworth, Spennymoor, Co Durham. (01388 815113). (Att: Sunderland)
RALPH Miss S,	23, Peter Avenue, Bilston, West Mids. (01992 495971). Kennels: Newtack Farm, Walsall Road, Great Wyrley, Cannock, Staffs. (01992 417017). (Att: Monmore Green)
RAMAGE G,	10g, Mary Street, Paisley, Renfrewshire, PA2 6JF. (0141 887 4530). Kennels: West Caplaw Farm, Shilford Road, By Neilston, Glasgow. G78 3AW. (Att: Shawfield)
RAWDING P C,	Three Ways, South Drove, Spalding Common, Lincs. PE11 3BD. (01775 761863). (Att: Swaffham)
RAY I C,	Riverside Villa, Walham, Longford, Glos. GL2 9NG. (01452 526952). (Att: Swindon)
RAYMENT T M,	51, Scrattons Terrace, Scrattons Farm, Barking, Essex. IG11 OUG. (0181 593 4975). (Kennels) Terrys Kennels, Ockendon Road, Ockendon, Upminster, Essex. (01708 220332). (Att: Canterbury)
RAYNER V R,	35a, Bellegrove Road, Welling, Kent. DA16 3PB. (0181 304 3568). Kennels: Upper Thruxted Farm, Pennypot Lane, Waltham, Near Canterbury, Kent. CT4 7HA. (01227 738 555). (Att: Canterbury)
REDPATH Miss E,	Court Barn, Rake, Liss, Hants. GU33 7JQ. (01730 893255). (Att: Portsmouth)
REES P C,	51, Lonesome Lane, Reigate, Surrey. Kennels: Burhill Kennels, Turners Lane, Hersham, Walton on Thames, Surrey. (01932 222637). (Att: Wimbledon)
REID J,	23, Ardgour Parade, Carfin, Motherwell, Scotland. ML1 4HL. (01698 61536).

	Kennels: Briarfield, Easter Moffat Plains, Airdrie. (01236 842250). (Att: Powderhall)
REYNOLDS J W,	33, Wells Gdns, Basildon, Essex. SS14 3QS. (01268 533366). Kennels: Unit 11, Ockendon Kennels, Ockendon Road, Upminster, Essex. (01708 640218). (Att: Ramsgate)
RIBBENS Mrs Tina.	30, Whitebeam Ave, Bromley, Kent. BR2 8DL. Kennels: Hazelwood Kennels, Sun Hill, Fawkham, Dartford, Kent. (01474 874052). (Att: Reading)
RICH P J,	1, Upper Horton Farm, New House Lane, Chartham, Kent. (01227 731500). (Att: Romford)
RICHARDS S,	Norton Farm, Kelty, Fife, Scotland. (01383 830690). (Att: Powderhall)
RICHES Mrs S,	County Kennels Farm, Moorfield House, Mattishall Road, East Dereham, Norfolk. NR20 3BS. (01362 697841). (Att: Swaffham)
RIDLEY D C,	Sunningdale, Horsham Road, Steyning, West Sussex. BN44 3AA. (01903 813495). (Att: Portsmouth)
RIDLEY Mrs J,	Two Trees Farm, Coventry Road, Aldermans Green, Coventry. CV2 1NT. (01203 313442).
RIORDAN D C,	(Trans from OT) (Home) 127, Ashburton Avenue, Ilford, Essex. IG3 9EP. (0181 590 7140). Kennels: 3, Crow Lane, Romford, Essex. (01708 758892). (Att: Hackney)
RIPLEY G, Snr,	Glebe Retreat, Shadoxhurst, Ashford, Kent. TN26 1LT. (01233 73 2576). (Att: Ramsgate)
ROBINSON Miss S,	35, Ramsgate, Lofthouse, Wakefield, West Yorks. (01924 824134). (Kennels):- Sheffield Stadium Kennels, Penistone Road, Sheffield. S8. (0114 2340374). (Att: Sheffield)
ROOKS G,	34, Moor Cres, Ludworth, Co Durham. (01429 820 892). (Kennels) Brough Park Stadium Kennels, The Fossway, Byker, Newcastle Upon Tyne. (0191 2650542). (Att: Brough Park)
ROUSE J W,	Little Rowfold, Billingshurst, West Sussex. RH14 9DF. (01403 784748). (Att: Brighton)
ROWELL Mrs J,	(Trans from OT) Woodside Farm, Durham Lane, Haswell Moor, Co Durham. DH6 2BD. (0191 526 5979). (Att: Middlesbrough)
ROWSELL Mrs A,	Cross Roads Farm, Hazelbury Bryan, Sturminster Newton, Dorset. DT10 2BH. (01258 817215). (Att: Bristol)
RUMBELOW Mrs A ,	(Trans from OT) Matchbox Farm, Aslacton, Norwich, Norfolk. NR15 2JR. (01379 77739). (Att: Yarmouth)
RUSSELL W G,	109, Saughton Mains Gardens, Edinburgh, EH11 3QA. (0131 443 0295). Kennels:

	Butlerfield Kennels, Cockpen Road, Bonnybrigg, Scotland. (01875 21406). (Att: Powderhall)
RYAN P,	Shaws Cottage, Shaws Lane, Shifnall, Shropshire. (01952 462489). (Att: Bristol/Perry Barr)
SALVIN S,	Warminster Lodge, 165, Warminster Road, Norton, Sheffield. S8 8PP. (01742 586928).
SAMS Miss L D,	143, Leytonstone Road, Stratford, London E15 1LH. (0181 534 6964). Kennels: 3, Ockendon Kennels, Ockendon Road, Upminster, Essex. RM14 3PU. (01708 251446). (Att: Rye House)
SAUNDERS N J,	Springcroft, 45, Hall Moss Lane, Bramhall, Cheshire. SK7 1RB. (0161 439 2639). (Att: Belle Vue)
SAVILLE Mrs E,	(Home & Kennels) Two Acres, Dunholme Road, Scothern, Lincoln. LN2 2UE. (01673 860 300). (Att: Nottingham)
SAVORY C J,	25, Firth Park Avenue, Sheffield. S5 6HF. (01742 437 475). (Att: Sheffield)
SAVVA Mrs N,	Westmead Kennels, Cow Lane, Edlesborough, Nr Dunstable, Beds. LU6 2HU. (01525 220450). (Att: Hackney)
SEAGRAVE J,	Rainbow Kennels, Westgate Lane, Old Malton, North Yorks. YO17 0SG. (01653 692623). (Att: Stainforth)
SEARLE J,	Mons Hill Cottage, 1, Mons Hill, Woodsetton, Dudley, West Midlands. DY1 4LT. (01902 679470). (Att: Monmore Green)
SHALLIS D F,	Yew Tree Farm, Potters Hill, Felton, Bristol. BS18 7XB. (01275 474246). (Att: Swindon)
SHARP G L,	3, Hilltop Cottages, Theydon Mount, Epping, Essex. Kennels: Peaceful Kennels, Weald Bridge Road, North Weald, Essex. (0137 882 2317). (Att: Walthamstow)
SHARPUS A,	Tower Lodge, Remenham Hill, Henley On Thames, Oxon. RG9 3HG. (01491 575666) (Att: Reading)
SHAW L,	(Trans from OT) 37a, Summerleaze Road, Maidenhead, Berks. SL6 8EW. (01628 36700).
SHEARMAN K V,	Rose Cottage, Sookholme Lane, Mansfield Woodhouse, Notts. NG20 0DW. (01623 847247).
SHERRY J J,	Alders Farm, Willingale Road, Fyfield, Ongar, Essex. (01277 899 374). (Att: Walthamstow)
SHINKWIN R V,	(Trans from OT) 131, Furzehill Road, Borehamwood, Herts. WD6 2DP. (0181 207 2613). (Att: Hackney)
SHORT Mrs W E,	3, Daux Road, Billingshurst, West Sussex. RH14 9TF. (01403 785474). Kennels: "Little Rowfold", Billingshurst, West Sussex. RH14 9DF. (01403 782686). (Att: Portsmouth)

SILKMAN B,	2, Claverhambury Kennels, Galley Hill, Waltham Abbey, Essex. EN9 2BL. (0199 289 2779).
SIMMONS L C,	(Trans from OT) 11a, Radlett Road, Watford, Herts. WD2 4LH. (01923 239 446). (Att: Reading)
SIMMONS T,	The Old School House, Corby Road, Irnham, Grantham, Lincs. (01476 550308). (Att: Swaffham)
SIMPSON J S J,	34, Friars Road, East Ham, London E6 1LL. (0181 470 5992). (Kennels) The Barn, Suffolk House Kennels, Ashwells Road, Brentwood, Essex. (01277 374853). (Att: Hackney)
SINGLETON Mrs D	Rose Croft, Oxford Road, Dinton, Aylesbury, Bucks. (01296 747170). Kennels: Riverside Kennels, 105a, Kennington Road, Kennington, Oxford. (01865 739 221). (Att: Oxford)
SMITH Mrs B,	Lavender Hall Farm, Lavender Hall Lane, Berkswell, Nr Coventry, Warks. (01676 34790). (Att: Hall Green)
SMITH Mrs C E,	Seven Oaks Farm, Heywood Road, Tibenham, Norwich, Norfolk. NRl6 IPB. (01379 77512). (Att: Yarmouth)
SMITH James	17, Second Street, Tannochside, Uddingston, Glasgow. G71 6AT. (01698 815187). Kennels: Monard Kennels, Woodlands Road, Bargeddie. G69 7TY. (01236 433660). (Att: Shawfield)
SMITH Joseph	(Trans from OT) 1, Sheldon Gardens, Reading, Berks. RG2 8AU. (01734 863613). (Att: Reading)
SMITH J S,	Norton Kennels, Norton, Sheffield. S8 8BA. (01942 745 002). (Att: Sheffield)
SMITH Mrs K,	(Trans from OT) 44, Northway, Guildford, Surrey. GU2 6SB. (01483 39252). (Att: Portsmouth)
SMITH N.	(Trans from OT) 237, Skellow Road, Skellow, Doncaster, Yorks. (01302 725800). (Att: Hull)
SMITH R W,	Wych Farm, Wych Lane, Adlington, Macclesfield, Cheshire. SK10 4NB. (01625 829761).
SMYTH R B,	Sun Valley Farm, Shere Road, Clandon, Guildford, Surrey. GU4 8SH. (01483 222 832).
SNELL T,	Farnsworth Farm, Sporehams Lane, Danbury, Chelmsford, Essex. CM3 4AQ. (01245 225 881).
SPALDING Mrs K J,	White Lodge, Sewardstone Road, London E4 7SA. (0181 529 2029).
SPENCE J,	46, Millands Road, Frankerton By Biggar, Lanarkshire. (018993 686). Kennels: West Side Farm, Symington By Bigar, Lanarks. (Att: Shawfield)
SPIERS Miss S,	Upper Thruxted Farm, Pennypot Waltham, Nr

	Canterbury, Kent. CT4 7HA. (01227 730276). (Att: Canterbury)
STEED L F,	4, Sarcel, Stisted, Braintree, Essex. Kennels: Alfa Kennels, Water Lane, Stisted, Braintree, Essex. CM7 8AT. (01376 325319). (Att: Hackney)
STEELE R W,	23, Albion Road, Lordswood, Chatham, Kent. Kennels: Moorshill Kennels, Rushenden Road, Shatterling, Wingham, Kent. (01277 728376). (Att: Crayford)
STEELS Mrs D 1,	48, Quakers Drove, Turves, Peterborough, Cambs. PE1 2DR. (01733 840534). (Att: Peterborough)
STEVENI B,	Netherhall Farm, Netherhall Road, Roydon, Essex. CM19 5JP. (01279 793529).
STILES R C W,	Hall Farm, Chalk House Green, Nr Reading, Berks. RG4 9AD. (01734 722011). (Att: Reading)
STINCHCOMBE Mrs D,	Normanhurst, Church Lane, Upper Beeding, Steyning, Sussex. BN44 3HP. (01903 815833) Kennels: Deneholme Kennels, Wheatsheaf Road, Henfield, Sussex. BN5 9BD (01273 494857). (Att: Reading)
STOCKDALE Miss J	106, Wingfield Road, Sutton Trust Estate, Hull. HU9 4QD. (01482 704220). Kennels: Little Weighton Kennels, Highfield House, Neatmarsh Rd, Preston, Hull. (01482 897637). (Att: Hull)
STONE Mrs J E,	The Caravan, Opp Rayleigh Downs Road, Arterial Road, Rayleigh, Essex. SS9 4DT. (01702 521289). (Att: Hackney)
STRINGER R A,	Longtail Kennels, 54, Church Road, Emneth, Wisbech, Cambs. PE14 8AA. (01945 581221).
STROUD M,	28, Brookfield Road, Wooburn Town, Wooburn Green, High Wycombe, Bucks. HPl0 0PZ. (01628 526 859). (Att: Reading)
SUMMERS Miss R,	Hazelwood, Ratford Hill, Bremhill, Calne, Wiltshire. SN11 9LA. (01249 813266). (Att: Swindon)
SWADDEN P V,	Model Farm, Hilmarton, Nr Calne, Wilts. (01249 76360). (Att: Bristol)
SWAINE Mrs S E, -	Red Oak Kennels, Bladbean, Nr Canterbury, Kent. CT4 6LX. (01303 840541). (Att: Canterbury)
SYKES S,	64, Arch Road, Hersham, Surrey. (Knls) Burhill Kennels, Turners Lane, Hersham, Walton On Thames, Surrey. (01932 224918).(Att: Wimbledon)
SYMONDS C J G,	Drogheda, 2, Lynn Road, Tilney All Saints, Kings Lynn, Norfolk. PE34 4SA. (01553 829529). Kennels: The Kennels, Tower End, Middleton, Kings Lynn, Norfolk. PE32 1EE. (01850 297765).

NGRC Directory

SYRED Mrs L,	Knotbury Farm, Quarnford, Buxton, Derbyshire. SK17 0TO. (01298 71965). (Att: Nottingham)
TAYLOR , (Tony)	Catford Stadium Kennels, Layhams Road, Keston,Bromley, Kent. (01959 574420). (Att: Catford)
TAYLOR Mrs J,	54, Davis Cres, Langley Park, Co Durham. (0191 373 1538). (Att: Brough Park)
TAYLOR Mrs K J,	Whybrows Farm, Maltings End, Nr Newmarket, Suffolk. (01638 730403).
TAYLOR Miss Sherida	(Trans from OT) Cedar House, Emms Lane, Brooks Green, Horsham, West Sussex. RH13 8QR. (01403 741373). (Att: Portsmouth)
TERRY P J,	P & B Kennels, South Road, Woodhouse Down, Almondsbury, Near Bristol. BS12 4HU. (01454 616434).
TESTER K J,	Grasmere, Church Lane, Burstow, Surrey. (01293 784 302). (Att: Reading)
THOMAS A M C,	Surrey Hill Kennels, Tandridge Hill Lane, Godstone, Surrey. RH9 8DD. (01883 744382). (Att: Reading)
THOMAS Mrs K M,	Braemar House, Fields End Lane, Elstronwick, Nr Hull, Nth Humberside. HU12 9BX. (01964 670626). (Att: Hull)
THOMPSON Miss P,	65, Broomfield Road, Swanscombe, Kent. DA10 0LU. (01322 384819). (Kennels):- Nestledown Kennels, Blindley Heath, Near Lingfield, Surrey. (01342 832693). (Att: Canterbury)
THWAITES G V,	The Retreat, Comp Lane, Offham, W Malling, Kent. (01732 841308). (Att: Ramsgate)
THWAITES K J,	Barrybank Farm, Ugthorpe, Nr Whitby, Nth Yorks. YO21 2BO. (01947 840853). (Att: Sunderland)
TIDSWELL D,	3, Inghead Cottages, Brighouse Road, Lower Shelf, Nr Halifax, Yorks. HX3 7LD. (01422 202193).
TIMMINS Mrs P,	117, Thornborough Road, Coalville, Leics, LE67 3TN. (01530 832957). (Att: Nottingham)
TITE Mrs J,	Sunnyside, Wellington Road, (Off Lower Rd), Hockley, Essex. (01702 204130). (Att: Hackney)
TOMKINS Miss D,	Brunswick, Lower Dunton Road, Bulpham, Upminster, Essex. RM14 3TD. (01268 544467).
TOMPSETT P A,	Park Farm, Horsmonden, Kent. TN12 8EP. (0189 272 2550). (Att: Crayford)
TOWNER R J,	Ivy Farm, Lidsing, Chatham, Kent. NE7 3NL. (01634 232733). (Att: Canterbury)
TOWNSEND T N,	Foxdown Road, South Woodingdean, Brighton, Sussex. (01273 307181). Kennels: Lowlands Kennels, Freaks Lane, Burgess Hill, Sussex. RH15 8DO. (Att: Brighton)

NGRC Directory

TREVIS T D J,	1, Poplars Green, Near Hertford, Herts. (01438 717649). (Att: Henlow)
TRIMMINGS M C,	(Trans from OT) "Tipsy Greyhound Kennels", Rock House, Main Road, Sellindge, Kent. TN25 6AO. (01303 814097). (Att: Canterbury)
TRINDER W J,	(Home) 156, Sandy Lane, Littlemore, Cowley, Oxford. OX4 5LQ. (0865 777420). Kennels: Hinksey Hill Farm, Hinksey, Oxford. (01865 327812).
TUCKER D C,	(Trans from OT) Feltham Fm, Feltham, Frome, Somerset. (Att: Swindon)
TUGWELL T,	Sayers Farm, Adversane, Billingshurst, Sussex. RH14 9JH. (01403 784738). (Att: Reading)
TURVEY A G,	116, London Road, Cowplain, Waterlooville, Hants. PO8 8HB. (Knls 01705 593672/office 01705 591708). (Att: Portsmouth)
VASS D C,	56, The Causeway, Staines, Middx. TW18 3AX. (01784 456237). (Att: Reading)
VINE A M,	Gentian, Heath Road, Boughton Monchelsea, Maidstone, Kent. (01622 743453). (Att: Canterbury)
VOWLES D H,	Windmill Hill House, The Street, Ramsey, Nr Ramsey, Harwich, Essex. CO12 5HW. (01255 880413). (Att: Hackney)
WAGGOTT Mrs A,	26, Boyne Street, Willington, Crook, Co Durham. DL15 OEW. Kennels: Oakvali Kennels, Oakenshaw, Crook, Co Durham. DL15 OSX. (01388 746333). (Att: Sunderland)
WAINWRIGHT Mrs M,	White Farm Kennels, Broadcut, Calder Grove, Wakefield, Yorks. (01924 274329). (Att: Sheffield)
WALDEN Mrs H M,	Foxhold Farm, Thornford Road, Crookham Common, Nr Newbury, Berks. (01635 268544). (Att: Wembley)
WALLINGT0N L D,	Bridge Field, Sal ford, Near Chipping Norton, Oxon. 0X7 5YQ. (01608 642739). (Att: Swindon)
WALSH Mrs D,	49, Gladstone Place, Brighton, Sussex. BN2 3QE. (0127 695113). Kennels: Albourne Kennels, Wheatsheaf Road, Albourne, nr Henfield, Sussex. (01273 494272). (Att: Brighton)
WALSH J,	Whittingham Kennels, 6, Claverhambury Kennels, Galley Hill, Waltham Abbey, Essex. (0199 289 3734)
WALSH M,	Bampton Kennels, Buckland Road, Bampton, Oxon. (01993 850671). (Att: Swindon)
WALSH S A,	(Trans from OT) Sacred Heart Cottage, Oxford Rd, Horndon On The Hill, Essex. SS17 8PX. (Att: Hackney)
WALTERS Miss A J,	Rose Cottage, Morrilow Heath, Leigh, Stoke On Trent, Staffs. ST10 4PF. (01889 505489).

NGRC Directory

WALTON John	(Att: Perry Barr) (Trans from OT) Redhythe Farm, Portsoy, Banffshire, Scotland. AB45 2TT. (01261 843351). (Att: Dundee)
WALTON J M,	29, Audley Street, Ashton. Under Lyne, Lancs. OL6 6RB. (01611 330 8680). Kennels: Blackrock Training Kennels, 15, Boundry Close, Mossley, Lancs. (01457 835681). (Att: Belle Vue)
WARBY J M J,	36, Michael Cliffe House, Skinner Street, London. EC1R 0WW. (0171 278 7034). (Kennels): Maxens Yard Kennels, Galley Hill, Waltham Abbey, Essex. (0199 271 2168). (Att: Hackney)
WARD D C,	Fir Tree Farm, Sand Lane, West Heslerton, Malton North Yorks. YO17 8SG. (01944 728262). (Att: Hull)
WARD P,	The Cottage, (Off Green Lane) Fitton End, Leverington, Wisbech, Cambs. PE13 5EJ. (01945 870 590). (Att: Peterborough)
WARDEN B J,	(Trans from OT) 8, Belt Drove, Begdale, Elm, Nr Wisbech, Cambs. (01945 860 673). (Att: Peterborough)
WARREN R,	42, Alport Avenue, Hackenthorpe, Sheffield. S12 4RR. (0114 2392075). (Kennels) Sheffield Stadium Kennels, Penistone Road, Sheffield. S6. (0114 2343074). (Att: Sheffield)
WATKINS N W,	"Maubern", Cwm-Yr-Alt, Hengoed, Mid Glamorgan,CF8 8AW. (01443 832996).
WATSON O F,	Greenfield Kennels, Chapel Lane, Bronington, Nr Whitchurch, Shropshire. SYl3 3HR. (0194 873 274). (Att: Belle Vue)
WEARING Mrs E D,	Cravenia, Great North Road, North Mymms, Hatfield, Herts. AL9 5SD. (017072 63803). (Att: Hackney)
WEIR W,	42, Hartfield Terrace, Allanton, Shotts, Lanarks. ML7 SAD. (01501 821494). Kennels: 120, Dura Road, Allanton, Shotts, Lanarks.(Att: Shawfield)
WELLON P,	Shady Hollow, Compton Green, Redmarley, Glos. (01531 820520). (Att: Bristol)
WESTWOOD Mrs,	1, Hatch, Sandy, Beds. SG19 1PT. (01767 692345). (Att: Peterborough)
WHEATLEY Miss D,	Hawthorne Cottage, Fosters Bridge, Nr Ketton, Stamford, Lincs. PE9 3UU. (01780 720321). (Att: Nottingham)
WHITE J A,	298, Nuneaton Road, Bulkington, Nuneaton, Warks.CV12 9RQ. (01203 310501). Kennels: Overstone Lodge Kennels, Overstone Road, Withybrook, Nr Coventry, Warks. CV7 9LY. (01455 220241).
WHITE M J,	Great Jobs Cross Kennels, Hastings Road, Rolvenden, Kent. (01580 241044).

NGRC Directory

WHITE M R,	(Att: Hackney) 27, Hinkler Close, Wallington, Surrey. SM6 9JG. (0181 773 4139). (Kennels) Redroof, Small field Road, Home, Nr Horley, Surrey. RH6 9JX. (01342 844676). (Att: Reading)
WHITE R J,	Lyon House, Hulfords Lane, Hartley Wintney, Hants. RG27 8AG. (01850 978969). (Att: Reading)
WHITE R P, (Robin)	The Hills, Reedham, Norwich. NR13 3TN. (01493 701120). Kennels: Harts Hill, Holt Road, Horsford, Norwich, Norfolk. (01603 401979).
WHITE W E,	25, Rainham Road, Rainham, Essex. RM13 8ST. (01708 558670). Kennels: Haven Kennels, Ockendon Kennels, Ockendon Road, Upminster, Essex. (01708 223433). (Att: Canterbury)
WILEMAN J,	(Trans from OT) 2, Mount Cottages, Warton Lane, Grendon, Atherstone, Warks. CV9 3DT. (01827 897592).
WILEY E V,	The Gables, Borwick Lane, Wickford, Essex. (01268 732039). (Att: Romford)
WILKES R J,	Honeybrook Kennels, Bridgnorth Rd, Kidderminster, Worcs. DY11 5RR. (01562 754076).
WILKINS C W R,	(Trans from OT) 23, Bryn Glas, Laleston, Nr Bridgend, Mid Glamorgan, South Wales. CF31 4ES. Kennels: The Kennels, Tan-Y-Lan Farm, St Marys Hill, Nr Bridgend, Mid Glamorgan, South Wales. CF35 5BY. (0656 768572). (Att: Swindon)
WILLIAMS Mrs G,	Skylark, Arundel Road, Ashington, Rochford, Essex. SS4 3JU. (01702 207813). (Att: Hackney)
WILLIAMS H F,	Whitegates House, Witton Le Wear, Bishop Auckland, Co Durham. DL14 OBP. (01388 488 446). (Att: Sunder0and)
WILLIAMS I J,	Windyridge Farm, Commonside, Norton Canes, Staffs. WS11 3PY. (01543 71031/371030). (Att: Perry Barr)
WILLIAMS Mrs J,	179, Scarborough Road, Byker, Newcastle Upon Tyne. (01632 658011). Kennels: Brough Park Stadium Kennels, The Fossway, Byker, Newcastle Upon Tyne. (0191 265 5612). (Att: Brough Park)
WILLIAMS Mrs M,	Rosedene, Sandy Lane, Wildmoor, Bromsgrove, Worcs. B61 0QU. (0121 453 8928). (Att: Perry Barr)
WILLS N I,	3, Broad Street, Brinklow, Rugby, Warks. CV23 0LS. (01788 832148). Kennels: Dolfach, Smeaton Lane, Stretton Under Fosse, Rugby, Warks. (01788 832186). (Att: Peterborough)
WILSON Mrs H,	Stables Cottage, Dalkeith Park, Dalkeith,

NGRC Directory

	Midlothian. EH22 2NA. (0131 663 4510).
WILSON W M,	Nestledown Kennels, Blindley Heath, Nr Lingfield, Surrey. (mobile 0850 396911). (Att: Canterbury)
WISEMAN F R,	Moat Farm, Thorpe Road, Felsham, Bury St Edmunds, Suffolk. IP30 0QW. (01284 828612).
WOOD J G,	Fairview, Kirkgate Road, Tydd St Giles, Nr Wisbech, Cambs. PE13 5NE (01945 870058).
WOOD P,	6, Eton Road, Stockton On Tees, Cleveland. TS18 4DL. (01642 676061). Kennels: Burnhope Farm, Durham Lane, Nr Elton, Stockton On Tees, Cleveland. (01642 586422).
WOOD Mrs R M,	Cleeve Bungalow, Rodley, Westbury On Severn, Glos. GL14 1RF. (01452 760486). (Att: Swindon)
WOOD T,	8, Cleveland Avenue, Darlington, Co Durham. DL3 7HE. (01325 351189). (Att: Middlesbrough)
WOODLEY Miss R,	The Kennel Bungalow, Somerford Keynes, Nr Cirencester, Glos. GL7 6DT. (01285 862045). (Att: Swindon)
WOODS C J,	(Trans from OT) White Rocks Farm Kennels, Under River, Sevenoaks, Kent. TN15 0SI. (01732 762 913). (Att: Hackney)
WOODWARD P,	71, Station Road, Royston, Barnsley, South Yorks. S71 4HL. (01226 723058). Kennels: Springwood Farm, Cowley Lane, Holmesfield, Sheffield. S18 5SD. (0114 2891296). (Att: Sheffield)
WRIGHT Mrs P,	(Trans from OT) 73, Honeycombe Road, Salhouse, Norwich, Norfolk. NR13 6JR. (01603 720 433). (Att: Yarmouth)
YEATES R F,	Greentrees, 185, Wycombe Road, Prestwood, Nr Great Missenden, Bucks. HP16 0HJ. (01240 63685).(Att: Reading)
YEOMANS J,	(Trans from OT) 55, Stambourne Way, West Wickham, Kent. BR4 9NE. (0181 776 1857). (Att: Rye House)
YORK R B,	Croftview Kennels, Whitehorse Lane, Harvel, Meopham, Kent. (01474 814 892). (Att: Hackney)
YOUNG P W,	3, Gate Lodge Square, Noak Bridge, Basildon, Essex. SS15 4AP. (01831 357817). (Kennels) Inglenook Kennels, Honiley Ave, Off Arterial Road, Wickford, Essex.
YOUNG R V,	Buncton Manor, Buncton Lane, Bolney, West Sussex. RH17 5RE. (01444 881 533). Kennels): Cosmic Greyhound Kennels, Runtingdon Manor Farm, Heathfield, West Sussex. (01435 868 021). (Att: Brighton)

NGRC Directory

Owner Trainers

Key: Att—Attached; Alterations to the list are published in the NGRC Calendar

ABRAHAMS B C,	7, Leasway, Westcliff On Sea, Essex. SS0 8PA. (01702 75106). (Att: Henlow)
ACE D C,	113, Ryddwen Road, Craig Cefn Parc, Swansea, West Glamorgan. SA6 5RG. (01792 845241).
ADAWAY D J,	Long Acre, Bimbury Lane, Detling, Nr Maidstone, Kent. ME14 3HY. (01622 736233).
AGNEW A,	5, Castlehill Crescent, Ferniegair, Hamilton, Scotland. ML3 7TZ. (01698 428591).
ALBISTON Mrs C,	35, Vicarage Hill, Flitwick, Beds. MK45 IJA. (01525 712848).
ALEXANDER S L,	"Wainsbeck", 23, Brackley Gate, Morley, Ilkeston, Derbyshire. DE7 6DJ. (01332 880741). (Att: Perry Barr)
ALLEN M,	18, Wordsworth Road, Easington, Peterlee, Co Durham. SR8 3DP. (0191 527 1404). (Att: Middlesbrough)
ANDREAS G,	125b, Goodrich Road, East Dulwich, London. SE22 0ER. (0181 299 6786). (Att: Henlow)
ANDREWS D A,	63, Manderton Road, Newmarket, Suffolk. CB8 0NL. (01638 667427). (Att: Mildenhall)
ANDREWS T M,	White Farm, Coxes Farm Road, Gt Burstead, Billericay, Essex. CM11 2UB. (01277 657167). (Att: Mildenhall)
ANGEL G R J,	73, Park Road, Kingston, Surrey. KR2 6DE. (0181 546 6020).
AYEGUN O P,	406, Manchester Rd, Bolton, Lancs. BL3 2PG. (01204 35192).
BACKHURST M G,	Strawberry Farm, Glaziers Lane, Normandy, Guildford, Surrey. GU3 2DF. (01483 811534). (Att: Swindon)
BAILEY K B,	69, Grange Park Avenue, Winchmore Hill, London N21 2LN. (0191 364 1318).
BALLERIN0 J,	22, Rutherwyck Road, Chertsey, Surrey. KT16 9JF. (01932 569430).
BANDURAK M A,	"Red Roof", High Hill, Essington, Wolverhampton. WV11 2DP. (01922 476897).
BARNES H,	Black Cottage, London Road, Upper Harbledown, Nr Canterbury, Kent. CT2 9AL. (01227 767995). (Att: Canterbury)
BARRETT D A,	Glebe Farm, Horsford, Norwich. NR10 3AG. (01603 898263).
BARRON K,	13, Myrtle Road, Palmers Green, London N13 5QX. (0181 807 6825).

NGRC Directory

BASS M P, Balmaha, Sand Rd, Flitton, Beds. MK45 5DT. (01525 715247). (Att: Milton Keynes)

BATTERBEE T, Suffolk Hunt Kennels, Copy Farm, Great Whelnetham, Bury St Edmunds, Suffolk. IP30 0UF. (01284 386292).

BEADLE G J, 31, Hall Lane, Wacton, Norfolk. NR15 2UH. (01508 32155).

BEAN A A, 33, Lyttleton Road, London. E10 5NQ. (0181 539 5991). (Att: Ramsgate)

BELL R, 180, Albyn Road, Deptford, London. SE8 4JQ. (0181 692 6837). (Att: Canterbury)

BERRY K A, Manor Farm, Easterfields, East Malling, Kent. ME19 6BE. (01732 849 402).

BEVAN O P, 31, The Brow, Haydon Wick, Swindon, Wilts. SN2 3HT. (01793 694103). Kennels: Downfield Farm, The Pry, Purton, Swindon, Wilts. (01793 770917). (Att: Swindon)

BIBBINS T R, 28, Rydal Avenue, Tilehurst, Reading, Berks. RG3 6XT. (01734 423213/01850034813). (Att: Swindon)

BIRTLES D G, Bronte Kennels, Halifax Road, Briercliffe, Burnley. BB10 3RB. (01282 428 504). (Att: Hull)

BLOOMFIELD H, 1, Sculthorpe Lodge Farm, Sculthorpe, Nr Fakenham, Norfolk. NR21 9NN. (01328 862925). (Att: Swaffham)

BOLTON B M, 9, Hanscombe End Road, Shillington, Herts. SG5 3AN. (01462 711035). (Att: Henlow)

BONNER Mrs S K, 1, Beyers Ride, Hoddesdon, Herts. EN11 9PZ. (01992 445564). Kennels: Midnite Kennels, Valleyview, Reevesgate Farm, Claverhambury Rd, Waltham Abbey, Essex. (01850 507505). (Att: Mildenhall)

BOREHAM M L, Nowton Lodge, Nowton, Bury St Edmunds, Suffolk. IP29 5ND. (01284 768388).

BRABON G T, Foley House, Stockbury Valley, Stockbury, Sittingbourne, Kent. ME9 7QJ. (01795 842550). (Att: Canterbury)

BRANSON F A, 1, Barton Crescent, Wolviston Ct, Billingham, Cleveland. TS22 5HJ. (01642 556 289). (Att: Middlesbrough)

BRENT N J, 49, Trelleck Road, Coley Pk, Reading, Berks. RG1 6EN. (01734 576 971).

BRIGGS A H, The Hollies, 36, Whitehall Lane, Buckhurst Hill, Essex. IG9 5JG. (0181 504 4199).

BRIMBLE R A, 4, Brown Street, Trowbridge, Wilts. BA14 7AS. (01225 760914). (Att: Swindon)

BRINE Mrs C A, 66, Gorse Hill, Fishponds, Bristol. BS16 4HS. (01272 653989). (Att: Swindon)

BROOKES J J, 30, Layton Cres, Waddon, Croydon, Surrey. CR0 4EA. (0181 688 3201).

BROWN D S, 36, White Post Court, Corby, Northants. NN17 2AG. (01536 407546). (Att: Peterborough)

NGRC Directory

BROWN Derek	Bulls Head Kennels, St Johns St, Netherton, Dudley, W Mids. DY2 0PU. (01384 259672).
BROWN I H,	1, Broadside Cottage, Decoy Road, Ormesby, Gt Yarmouth, Norfolk. NR29 3LX. (01493 730177). (Att: Yarmouth)
BROWN J P,	2, Wayside Cottage, Colby Corner, Colby, Near Aylesham, Norfolk. NR11 7EB. (01263 734073). (Att: Yarmouth)
BROWN K M,	Sea View, Coast Road, Walcott, Norfolk. NR12 0ND. (01692 650108). (Att: Yarmouth)
BRYCE F,	Greylands, Deerland Road, Llangwm, Haverfordwest, Dyfed, Wales. SA62 2NG. (01437 891487).
BUCKLEY T,	(Temporary Licence) "Sandiacres" Skelton Road, Beck Row, Bury St Edmunds, Suffolk. (01638 717024).
BUDD D J,	41, North La., Marks Tey, Colchester, Essex. (01206 212899). (Att: Hackney)
BULLEN A R,	346, White Hart Lane, London N17 8LN. (day 0181 801 4422/eves 0181 801 3134).
BURFORD H F,	The Croft, Witcombe, Glos. GL3 4SZ. (01452 862 311). (Att: Swindon)
BURRAGE S C,	Cutlers, Marlow Rd, Lane End, High Wycombe, Bucks. HP14 3JW. (01494 882 176). (Att: Rye House)
BUTLER R W,	"Foxdene" Rumstead Lane, Stockbury, Near Sittingbourne, Kent. ME9 7QL. (01627 80610) or (01622 880374). (Att: Canterbury)
CAPALDI B R,	40, Beckford Avenue, Easthampstead, Bracknell, Berks. RG12 7NJ. (01344 862989).
CARN B,	Bridge Hse, Alconbury Weston, Huntingdon, Cambs. PE17 5JD. Kennels: Silks Farm, St Ives Road, Somersham, Cambs. (01480 890197/0860 712940). (Att: Swaffham)
CATCHPOLE D I,	572, Foxhall Road, Ipswich, Suffolk. IP3 8LT. (01473 713328/0860 396791).
CHAMBERLAIN R,	Huntsmans House, Kennel Lane, Billericay, Essex. CM12 9RT. (01277 658411). (Att: Hackney)
CHAMBERS M,	135, Berkeley Road, Hay Mills, Birmingham. B25 8NJ. (0121 782 1547).
CHAMBERS R,	32, Park Ave, Thornaby, Cleveland. TS17 6JN. (01642 671530). (Att: Middlesbrough)
CHAPMAN F W,	48, Woodlands Ave, Sidcup, Kent. DA15 8HA. (0181 302 0655). (Att: Rye House)
CHRETIEN J C J,	60, Crow Lane, Romford, Essex. RM7 0EP. (01708 704152). (Att: Hackney)
CLACK Mrs H R,	Bramblemere, 27, Station Road East, Ashvale, Aldershot, Hants. GU12 5LY. (01252 373127). (Att: Hackney)
CLARK E N,	57, Fair-A-Far, Cramond, Edinburgh. EH4 6OB (0131 336 1953).

OWNER TRAINERS

NGRC Greyhound Racing Yearbook 1995   **317**

NGRC Directory

CLARKE A A, 57, Colenso Road, Seven Kins, Ilford, Essex. IG2 7AH. (0181 599 4778). (Att: Rye House)
CLIFTON D S, Ashmead, Bell Lane, Nuthampstead, Herts. SG8 8ND. (01763 848553).
CODD R, 16, Clitterhouse Crescent, London. NW2 IDD. (0171 455 1486).
COLEMAN R T, The Bungalow, Cuckolds Cross, Kimpton, Hitchin, Herts. SG4 8HL. (01438 832798).
COLLINS P J, Brushwood Hse, 56a, Chichester Rd, Arundel, West Sussex. BN18 OAD. (01903 882039). (Att: Portsmouth)
COOK A F, 204, St Andrews Avenue, Elm Park, Hornchurch, Essex. Kennels: Jacksonville Kennels, Ockendon Complex, Ockendon Road, Upminster, Essex. (01708 459989). (Att: Hackney)
COOKE M, 22, Church Street, Chasetown, Walsall, Staffs. WS7 8QL. (01543 684907).
COOMBES G T, 9, Rounces Lane, Carlton, Colville, Lowestoft, Suffolk. NR33 3AJ. (01502 573376). (Att: Yarmouth)
COOPER B P, 66, Wootton Avenue, Fletton, Peterborough, Cambs. PE2 9EG. (01733 343 600). (Att: Peterborough)
COOPER M, 90, Spring La., Swannington, Coalville, Leics. LE67 4QQ. (01530 835788). (Att: Nottingham)
COPE Mrs P, Straws, Hadley Farm, Lower End, Wingrave, Aylesbury, Bucks. HP22 4PG. (01296 681222). (Att: Milton Keynes)
COPSEY P, 27, Rede Road, Whepstead, Bury St Edmunds, Suffolk. IP29 4ST. (01284 735557).
COSTELLO J, Thorn Cottage, Mill Lane, Snelson, Nr Chelford, Cheshire. SK11 9BN. (01625 860535). (Att: Stainforth).
COWLEY M J, 24, Rodes Ave, Gt Houghton, Barnsley, South Yorks. S72 OBA. (01226 752485).
COX C 7a, Manor Yard, Fringford, Nr Bicester, Oxon. OX6 9QD. (01869 277 537). Kennels: Ardley Kennels, Bucknell Road, Ardley, Oxon. OX6 9HP. (01869 345 384). (Att: Milton Keynes)
COX R H, 25, Lynwood Close, Woodham Lane, Woking, Surrey. GUl2 5TJ. (01932 341079). (Att: Portsmouth)
CROSS W F, Sandyacre, 97, Whitchurch Road, Chester, Cheshire. CH3 5QN. (01244 332394).
CROSSE P, 71, Woodhead Road, Tintwistle, Via Hadfield, Cheshire. SKl4 7JX. (01457 867554).
CROWE Mrs C, 127, Upwell Road, March, Cambs. PE15 ODE. (01354 59191). (Att: Peterborough)
CURTIN D M, 22, Devonshire Drive, Greenwich. SE10 8JZ. (0181 691 2285). (Att: Canterbury)
DAMS K, 35, Longwood Rise, Willenhall, W Mids.

NGRC Directory

	WV12 4AZ. (01902 608 968).
DAMS N,	26, Mounts Road, Wednesbury, West Mids. (0121 556 6370). (Att: Cradley Heath)
DANCE Mrs G J,	2, Whiterock, Whipsnade Rd, Dunstable, Beds. LU6 2NB. (01582 603632).
DAVEY G C,	Oakdene, Hopton Rd, Garboldisham, Nr Diss, Norfolk. IP22 2RO. (0195 381 326).
DAVIES B T,	64, Edmund Street, Tylorstown, Rhonnda, Sth Wales. CF43 3HW. (01443 731349).
DAVIS Mrs M V,	41, Purfleet Road, Aveley, South Ockendon, Essex. RM15 4DP. (01708 865100).
DAY L N,	Amberleigh, Cosmoor Lane, Elm, Wisbech, Cambs. PE14 OEG. (01945 860 532).
DEANUS E,	21, Mead Plat, Neasden, London. NW10 OPD. (0181 459 2715).
DEARLING Mrs V,	Broadacres, Lower Road, Westerfield, Ipswich, Suffolk. IP6 9AR. (01473 225669). (Att: Mildenhall)
DENNING J C,	Rose Cott, Micheldever, Winchester, Hants. SO21 3DF. (01962 774 268). (Att: Portsmouth)
-8-DEVANE M,	35, Park Drive, Winchmore Hill, London N21 2LU. (0181 360 7116). (Att: Milton Keynes)
DEWBERRY W G,	61, Old Nazeing Road, Broxbourne, Herts. EN10 6RW. (01992 441997).
DIMMOCK S G,	3, Winslow Road, Granborough, Bucks. MK18 3NJ. (01296 67504/0831 617 223).
DOBBIN H B,	241, Overdown Road, Tilehurst, Reading. RG3 6NX. (01734 429 165).
DOBSON K B,	61, Harsley Road, Hartburn, Stockton, Cleveland. TS18 5DJ.(01642 584420). (Att: Stainforth)
DODD D A,	69, Churchfield Road, Poole, Dorset. BH15 2QW. (01202 671641). Kennels: 25, Upton Rd, Fleetsbridge, Poole, Dorset. BH17 7AA (01202 672179). (Att: Portsmouth)
DOWDEN Mrs F,	"Snedwod", Burrowmoor Rd, March, Cambs. PE15 OYT. (01354 56778). (Att: Henlow/Mildenhall)
EGAN D J,	Oak View Farm, Forest Rd, Wokingham. RG11 5SA. (01734 776597/891159).
ELLIOTT D C,	Franklyn, Dobbs Weir Road, Roydon, Harlow, Essex. CM19 5JX. (01992 442403). (Att: Mildenhall)
ELLIS G R,	Carr Farm Cott, Low Road, Norton Subcourse, Norwich. NR14 6SD. (01508 548 265). (Att: Yarmouth)
ELLIS M A,	Langate, Duntisbourne Abbots, Cirencester, Glos. GL7 1JW. (01285 821537). (Kennels):- 20, Berry Hill Crescent, Cirencester, Glos. (01285 657380). (Att: Swindon)
ELLISON C,	Bobbing Lodge, Bobbing Lodge Farm, Chartham, Near Canterbury, Kent.

OWNER TRAINERS

NGRC Directory

	(01227 738074). (Att: Canterbury)
ELVIN B G,	162, North Walsham Road, Norwich, Norfolk. NR6 7QJ. (01603 483137). (Att: Yarmouth)
EMBERTON A,	Westfield Bridge House, Kirkhouse Green, Stainforth, Doncaster, Yorks. DN7 5TF. (01405 785640). (Att: Stainforth)
EVANS M J,	336, Stroud Road, Tuffley, Gloucester. GL4 0DH. (01452 303784). (Att: Swindon)
EVANS R J,	8, Crossgate Road, Woodside, Dudley. DY2 OSY. (01384 78214).
EVANS R R,	81, Callicroft Road, Patchway, Bristol. BS12 5BU. (0116 2759137). (Att: Swindon)
EXELL D C,	(Trans from PT) Buck & Bell, North Bar, Banbury, Oxon. OX16 0TH. (01295 251 390). - 46, Twyford Road, Adderbury, Oxon. (01831 369898). (01831 369898). (Att: Perry Barr)
FANOUS B C G	602, Moor Road, Bestwood Vill, Nottingham. NG6 8TE. (0115 9278609). (Att: Stainforth)
FARMER P K,	10, Durlett Road, Bronham, Wilts. SN15 2HY. (01380 850434).
FARRELL T,	5, Strensall Close, New Marske, Cleveland. TS11 8BG. (01642 471975). (Att: Middlesbrough)
FINAL A D,	1, Blenheim Place, Aylesbury, Bucks. HP21 8AH. (01296 415418).
FLETCHER J A,	Sapphire Kennels, Headcorn Road, Sutton Valence, Nr Maidstone, Kent. ME17 3EH. (01622 843185). (Att: Canterbury)
FOLEY M W,	Fawn Cott, Oxmadyke Crossing, Gilberdyke, Brough, North Humberside. HU1S 2UY. (01430 441196). (Att: Stainforth)
FOOT M F,	Burcott Grange, Soulbury Rd, Burcott, Wing, Beds. LU7 0JU. (01296 681497/682049). (Att: Milton Keynes)
FORDHAM M J P,	Buncton Court, Buncton Lane, Bolney, West Sussex. RH17 5RE. (01444 881 755).
FOSTER Mrs B J,	390, Hull Road, Woodmansey, Nr Beverley, Nth Humberside. HU17 0RU. (01482 871854). (Att Hull)
FRANCIS J T,	Harvel Stud, (Hilltop), Woodhill, Meopham, Kent. DA13 0DA. (01474 815013). (Att: Canterbury)
FRASER R,	11, Ogilvie Road, Stirling, Scotland. FK8 2HG. (01786 472773) Kennels: Broomhill Farm, Dunnipace, By Dennyloanhead, Stirling, Scotland. (01831 608081).
FRAYLING N D,	21, New Road, Chiseldon, Swindon, Wilts. SN4 0LX. (01793 740810). (Att: Swindon)
FRIEND C G,	Knowle Lodge, Knowle, Fareham, Hants. PO17 6DT. (01329 833235). (Att: Portsmouth)
GAIN R G,	Flightline, Adsborough, Taunton, Somerset. TA2 8RR. (01823 413089). (Att: Perry Barr)

NGRC Directory

GALLOWAY T N,	Merehead, 75, East End, Walkington, Beverley, N Humberside. HU17 8RX. (01482 869716). (Att: Hull)
GIBSON J M,	The Bungalow, Coxhill Farm, Coxhill Road, North Burlingham, Norwich, Norfolk. NRl3 4EN. (01493 751948). (Att: Yarmouth)
GILLESPIE Mrs M,	Mayfield, Stich Hill, Kelso, Roxburghshire. TD5 7TD. (01573 470262). (Att: Shawfield)
GILLETT G,	Flat 1, Sezincote House, Moreton-in-Marsh, Glos. GL56 9AW. (01386 701035).
GILLIAR J A,	The Cottage, Roundhouse Farm, Puddock Rd, Warboys, Cambs. PE17 2UE. (01354 77656).
GINN P J,	12, Redmere, Shippea Hill, Ely, Cambs. CB7 4ST. (01353 752111).
GLANVILLE F J,	32, Groff Green, Dunstable, Beds. LU6 lEG. Kennels: The Firs, East End, Houghton Regis, Nr Dunstable, Beds. (01582 865688).
G0DDEN G L,	6, Station Road, Eccles, Quidenham, Norfolk. NR17 2JG. (01953 87466). Kennels: 31, Heath Cottage, Quidenham, Norwich. (01953 87786). (Att: Yarmouth)
GOWER G J,	2, Lavender Close, East Malling, West Malling, Kent. ME19 6EA. (01732 873028).
GRAINGE D J,	Willow Garth, Patrick Brompton, Nr Bedale, North Yorks. DL8 1JR. (01677 50322).
GRAY J R,	13, Sutton Crescent, Barnet, Herts. ENS 2SW. (0181 449 9855). (Att: Rye House)
GREAVES I C,	1/3, Strawberry Cottages, Stakeford Lane, Stakeford, Choppington, North'land. NE62 5HU. (01670 812255).
GREEN A G,	10, Pentrich Avenue, Enfield, Middx. (0181 367 0864). Kennels: J.J. Stables, White Webb Lane, Enfield, Middx. (0181 363 1268). (Att: Hackney)
GREEN C J,	15, High Street, Haversham, Milton Keynes. MK19 7DU. (01908 315656). (Att: M. Keynes)
GREEN J G,	8, Eton Way, Orrell, Wigan, Lancs. WN5 8PN. (01942 214458).
GREEN R E,	10, Hillbank, Tividale, Warley, West Midlands. B69 2HJ. (0121 552 1230). (Att: Cradley Hth)
HADFIELD D J,	Denton House, Stilton Fen, Peterborough, Cambs. PE7 3SB. (01487 830190). (Att: Swaffham)
HALE D B T,	Church Farm, Lower Road, Wretton, K. Lynn, Norfolk. PE33 9QN. (01366 500231). (Att: Swaffham)
HALL Mrs L M,	98, Stonehouse Drive, St Leonards, East Sussex. TW38 9DN. (01424 428220).
HALL Mrs S M,	31, Limetree Lane, Bilton, Hull. HUll 4EA. (01482 813775). (Att: Hull)
HAMILTON S J,	1, The Dells, Church End, Edworth, Biggleswade, Beds. SG18 9TJ.

NGRC Directory

	(01767 315308).
HANCOX G A,	13, Wainbody Ave N., Green Lane, Coventry, West Midlands. CV3 6DD. (01203 417022).
HARRIS A G,	4, Elm Gdns, East Finchley, London. N2 OTF. (0181 883 1756).
HARRIS M F,	22, Oak Avenue, Blidworth, Mansfield, Notts. NG21 0TN. (01623 797861).
HARRIS M J,	16a, Heath Farm Road, Red Lodge, Bury St Edmunds, Suffolk. IP28 8LG. (01638 750729). (Att: Mildenhall)
HARRIS R E,	Mill Hse, Henford Marsh, Warminster, Wilts. BA12 9PA. (01985 219977). (Att: M. Keynes)
HARRISON Miss J,	12, Barrinton Avenue, Beith, Ayrshire. KA15 2BX. (0150 550 3657). Kennels: 7b, Means Road, Beith, Ayrshire. (0150 550 6161).
HARTLEY Mrs P,	117, Cecil Road, Hertford, Herts. SG13 8HS. (01992 581 607). (Att: Rye House)
HATCHER D A,	4, Pound Lane, Kingsnorth, Ashford, Kent. TN23 3JE. (01233 611301). (Att: Canterbury)
HEANEY J J,	Chartis Kennels, Hawthorn Cott, Coach Lane, Hazelrigg, Newcastle Upon Tyne.
HEMMINGS Mrs J	25, Dirdene Gdns, Epsom, Surrey. KT17 4AZ. (01372 724 136). (Att: Hackney)
HENDERSON Mrs K,	12b, Ravenshead Close, Selsdon, S Croydon, Surrey. CR2 8RL. (0181 657 6903).
HEYES A P,	1, Mount Pleasant Cottages, Barmhouse Lane, Godley, Hyde, Cheshire. SK14 3BX. (0161 368 1662). (Att: Stainforth)
HIGHTON Miss S	Lovitts Farmhouse, 1, Leicester Road, Shilton, Nr Coventry, Warks. CV7 9HU. (01203 610254).
HITCH P A,	24, Cannon Lane, Stopsley, Luton, Beds. LU2 8BJ. (01582 29413).
HODSON G,	18, Morris Cl., Yardley, Birmingham. B27 6SP. (0121 706 1562).
- 13 -HOLMES R R,	2, Carisbrooke Ave, Bexley, Kent. DA5 3HS. (0181 300 1420).
HOLT Mrs P A,	17, Cowpe Road, Cowpe, Rossendale, Lancs. BB4 7DQ. (01706 220396). (Att: Stainforth)
HOOLEY J,	30, Sandown Road, Mickleover, Derby. DE3 5QQ. (01332 511830). Kennels: 11, Roehampton Drive, Derby. (01332 366980).
HOUGHAM K J,	Keiberwood, Thornden Wood Road, Herne Bay, Kent. CT6 7NX. (01227 742750). (Att: Canterbury)
HOWARD E H,	13, Newgate, Shephall, Stevenage, Herts. SG2 9DS. (01438 356188).
HUBBLE R M,	Hurst Wickham, Upper Wield, Near Alresford, Hants. SO24 9RP. (01420 562 478).
HUDSON J H,	Brow Side Farm, Medley Lane, Northowram, Halifax. HX3 7SX. (01422 201396/206557). (Att: Stainforth)

NGRC Directory

HUNT D A,	New House Farm Stud, Saw Pit Lane, Apperley, Glos. GL19 4DW. (01452 780741).
HUNT R P,	Shades Farm House, Ashton Road, Minety, Malmesbury, Wilts. SN16 9QP. (01285 862121). (Att: Swindon)
HURST M B,	High Breck Fm, E Markham, Newark, Notts. NG22 OSM. (01777 870270). (Att: Stainforth)
HYLAND M R,	14, Shipman Avenue, Canterbury, Kent. CT2 8PD. (01227 456743). (Att: Rye House)
HYSLOP W J,	Fenceside, Crofthead Road, Kilmaur, Ayrshire, Scotland. KA3 2RX. (01563 38748).
IRONS B J,	66, Ampthill Road, Flitwick, Beds. MK45 1AY. (01525 712382). (Att: Mildenhall)
ISAACS R A,	48, Mayfield Road, Dunstable, Beds. LU5 4AP. (01582 608616). (Att: Milton Keynes)
IVORY R J,	Napiers Farm Bungalow, Colchester Rd, Tiptree, Essex. C05 0EX. (01621 815906). (Att: Hackney)
JACKSON G,	45, Bank St, High Wycombe, Bucks. HP13 7DT. (01494 464 930). (Att: Milton Keynes)
JACKSON Mrs N J,	168, Station Rd, Lower Stondon, Beds. SG16 6JQ. (01462 850615). (Att: Peterborough)
JEANS M W,	28, Turnpike Road, Blunsdon, Nr Swindon, Wilts. SN2 4EA. (01793 706683). (Att: Swindon)
JEANS R A,	20, Elgin Drive, Swindon, Wilts. SN2 6DN. (01793 692916). (Att: Swindon)
JENNISON D,	54, Common Ing Lane, Ryhill, Wakefield, Yorks. WF4 2DQ. (01226 727860). (Att: Stainforth)
JEWELL D H,	75, Oscar Street, Deptford, London SE8 4QJ. (0181 692 9324). (Att: Canterbury)
JONES Mrs M H,	246, Boulton Lane, Alvaston, Derby. DE24 OBB. (01332 757339). Kennels: Kempton Park Close, Ascot Drive, Derby. (01332 293121). (Att: Nottingham)
JONES R A,	Oakleigh, Yorkley Wood, Lydney, Glos. GL15 4TU. (01594 563903). (Att: Swindon)
JONES R J,	171, Darlington Lane, Stockton On Tees, Cleveland. TS19 0NF. (01642 601793). (Att: Middlesbrough)
JORDAN D,	450, Thornaby Road, Stockton, Cleveland. TS17 8QH. (01642 672395). (Att: Middlesbrough)
JOYCE S R,	Valley View, 250, Traverham Rd, Traverham, Traverham, Norwich, Norfolk. NR8 6SX. (01603 867045). (Att: Yarmouth)
KAVANAGH W,	34, Bracknell Road, Camberley, Surrey. GU15 4BG. (01276 20848).
KEARNEY F,	21, Derewent Street, Blackhill, Consett, Co Durham. DH8 8LP. (01207 502919).
KELLY P,	Clay Pits Farm, Spellowgate, Driffield, North Humberside. YO25 7UP. (01377 256 823).

NGRC Directory

KELSEY B H,	(Att: Stainforth) Kelfarm Kennels, Jerry Bog Farm, Laughton, Near Gainsborough, Lincs. DN21 3PU. (Att: Stainforth)
KEMP Mrs H P,	169, Thorpe Rd, Kirby Cross, Frinton On Sea, Essex. (Telephone Number Unknown). (Att: Mildenhall)
KENNEDY D A,	30, Miswell Lane, Tring, Herts. HP23 4DD. (0144 282 4334). (Att: Milton Keynes)
KINANE J,	19, Meadway, Seven Kings, Ilford, Essex. IG3 9BQ. (0181 590 0304).
KING S W J,	66, Beach Road, Scratby, Great Yarmouth, Norfolk. NR29 3AJ. (01493 384 008). (Att: Yarmouth)
KITE C R,	The Tunnel House Inn, Coates, Cirencester, Glos. DL7 6PW. (01285 770280). (Att: Swindon)
KNELL L,	16, Rockingham Place, Herne Bay, Kent. Kennels: Hill Farm, Bilsington, Nr Ashford, Kent. (Att: Canterbury)
LAMBE J P,	14, Montpelier Road, Erdington, Birmingham. B24 8EA. (0121 350 8133). Kennels: The Raconer, Weeford Rd, Sutton Coldfield, W Mids. B75 5RF. (0121 323 3212). (Att: Perry Barr)
LANE E W E,	5, Hyde Road, Upper Stratton, Swindon, Wilts. SN2 6RT. (01793 825579). (Att: Swindon)
LARBY D L,	19, The Oval, Wood Street, Guildford, Surrey. GU3 3DH. (01483 235314). (Att: Portsmouth)
LAVERY J M,	9, Forrestors Close, Bickershaw, Wigan, Lancs. WN2 STY. (01942 861 428). Kennels: Morris Farm, Bickershaw, Wigan, Lancs. (01942 865 330).
LAW D M,	Tollgate Hse, Leighton Rd, Wing, L Buzzard, Beds. LU7 0PW. (01296 688454).
LENG W T,	30, Grange Rd, Belmont, Durham. DH1 1AL. (0191 384 7180). (At: Sunderland)
LETHABY Mrs C,	13, Nairn Cl., Heath Pk, Nuneaton, Warks. CV10 7LG. (01203 340695). (Att: Perry Barr)
LIDDINGTON R W	39, Morton Crescent, Towcester, Northants. NN12 6DW. (01327 350019). (Att: M.Keynes)
LIGHTFOOT G,	17, Well Lane, Weaverham, Northwich, Cheshire. CW8 3PE. (01606 851752).
LITTLE J K,	33, Linslade Street, Swindon, Wilts. SN2 2BL. (01793 485795).
LLEWELLYN Mrs C,	16, Delius Grove, Innscourt, Knowle, Bristol. BS4 1XP. (0117 9871448). (Att: Swindon)
LODZIAK Mrs M E,	104, Folly Rd, Mildenhall, Bury St Edmunds, Suffolk. IP28 7BT. (01638 714958).
LOVE V,	Halfpenny Green Stables, Manor Lane, Bobbington, Stourbridge, W Mids. DY7 SEG. (01384 221531).
LUKE J D,	3, Queen Elizabeth Drive, Easington Lane,

NGRC Directory

	Houghton Le Spring. DH5 0NW. (0191 526 2673). (Att: Middlesbrough)
LYNAS G,	11, Hallimond Road, Escomb, Bishop Auckland, Co Durham. (01388 604700). Kennels: Escomb Poultry Fm, Hallimond Rd, Escomb, Co Durham. (01388 603 087). (Att: Middlesbrough)
MABBS F A,	12, Greenhills Park, Bloxham, Banbury, Oxon. OX15 4TA. (01295 720830).
MAGENNIS M,	17, Wellhurst Court, Carshalton Road, Sutton, Surrey. SM1 4SD. (0181 643 5640). - Kennels: Burnt Oak Farm, Burnt Oak Lane, Newdigate, Surrey. RH5 5BJ. (01293 862254).
MANN A W,	"Patone", Huddox Hill, Peasedown St John, Bath, Avon. (01761 432 342). (Att: Swindon)
MANN Mrs D,	Batsford, Failand Lane, Lower Failand, Nr Bristol. B28 3ST. (01275 372600). (Att: Swindon)
MARCHANT P,	The Maples, Gay Street Lane, Pulborough, W Sussex. RH20 2HW. (01798 875429).
MARRIOTT J A,	Hesley Farm Cott, Rear Of Ball Inn, Thorpe Hesley, Rotherham. S61 2SD. (0114 2455092). (Att: Stainforth)
MARSHALL A,	Sandhouse Farm, Sand Lane, Messingham Common, Susworth, S Humberside. DN11 3UR. (01724 783075). (Att: Stainforth)
MARTIN C D,	23, New Road, Chisledon, Swindon, Wilts. SN4 0LX. (01793 740 808). (Att: Swindon)
MARTIN D P F,	Tome Gatehouse, Epworth, Nr Doncaster. DN9 ILE. (01427 875004). (Att: Stainforth)
MASON Mrs R,	Southburgh Manor, Thetford, Norfolk. IP25 7TG. (01953 850 295). (Att: Swaffham)
MASSEY Mrs K P,	47, Newquay Road, Knowle, Bristol. BS4 1ED. (0117 9879016/779575).
MATTHEWS G D,	22, Codrington Hill, Forest Hill, London. SE23 1LW. (0181 690 8304). (Att: Rye House)
McCLENAGHAN J,	80, Eastfield Rd, Princes Risborough, Bucks. HP27 0HZ. (01844 346937).
McCLURG Mrs A,	The Old School House, Potsgrove, M Keynes. MK17 9HG. (01860 536 277). (Att: M Keynes).
McDERMOTT Mrs M,	Lowlands, High Rd, Gorefield, Wisbech, Cambs. PE13 4DJ. (01945 870 834).
McDONALD J,	41, Acton Lane, London NW10 8UX. (0181 961 1009).
McGARRITY T,	"Ashfield", 1, Station Road, Old Kilpatrick, Glasgow, Scotland. G60 5LT. (01389 74493).
McGILL J, (Snr)	37, Finhaven Street, Tollcross, Glasgow. G32 8SG. (0141 554 0696).
McGOLDRICK T J,	Moor House Farm, High Stt, Walkeringham, Doncaster, South Yorks. DN10 4LJ. (01427 891 270). (Att: Stainforth)
McLAUGHLAN R,	106, Hawthorn Drive, Wishaw, Lanarks. ML2 8JN. (01698 359184). (Att: Shawfield)

NGRC Directory

McLAUGHLIN P,	3, Wisbech Close, South Fens, Hartlepool, Cleveland. TS25 2LW. (01429 870482). (Att: Hull)
McMAHON R,	16, Stuart Road, Rowley Regis, Warley, West Midlands. B65 9JA. (0121 559 9147).
McMEEKIN W K,	24, Rosedale Gr, Dormanston, Cleveland. TS10 SHR. (01642 476 455). (Att: Middlesbrough)
McMINIMEE J,	Whitehill Farm, Glassford, Strathaven, Scotland. ML10 6TR. (01693 791819). (Att: Powderhall)
McNIVEN R,	48, Crichton Avenue, Pathead, Ford, Midlothian. (01875 320001). (Kennels):- The Kennels, Edmonstone Road, Danderhall, Dalkeith, Midlothian. EH22 (01836 589525). (Att: Powderhall)
MEIKLE A B,	"The Retreat", Malton Rd, Orwell, Royston, Herts. SG8 5QR. (01223 208005).
MELBOURNE Mrs J,	62, Wesley Road, Kiveton Park, Sheffield. South Yorks. S31 8RJ. (01909 7723232). (Att: Stainforth)
MELVILLE Mrs V	490a, City Way, Rochester, Kent. ME1 2TW. (01634 407984).
MILAN R J,	19, Church Rd, W Kingsdown, Kent. TNl5 6LG. (01474 85 3144). (Att: Hackney)
MILLER N,	Chilton Grange Fm, Gypsy Lane, Ferryhill, Co Durham. SL17 0LF. (01388 721565/091 410 9696).
MILLS Mrs L,	Langholme Farm, Tindlebank Rd, W Woodside, Doncaster. DN9 2ET. (01427 890356).
MILUK R G,	33, Queens Club Gardens, Trowbridge, Wilts. BA14 0DR. (Att: Swindon)
MOGG J,	144, Watermead Rd, Limbury Mead, Luton, Beds. LU3 2TF. (01582 583879).
MOORE A R,	32, Northview Road, Luton, Beds. LU2 7LF. (01582 413372).
MOORE R D,	92, High Street, Sandhurst, Near Camberley, Surrey. (01252 872393).
MOORE Miss W,	39, Hawton Lane, Balderton, Newark, Notts. NG24 3DH. (no telephone number). (Att: Peterborough)
MOTTI A,	12, Wheat Hill, Off Romney Road, Tetbury, Glos. GL8 8RG. (01666 503225). (Kennels):- Underbridge Cottage, Tetbury, Glos. (Att: Swindon)
MUDD J L,	Reivax House, High Lane, Maltby, M'Boro, Cleveland. (01642 595445). Kennels: Maltby Grange Farm, Roger Lane, Middlesbrough, Cleveland. (01642 593104). (Att: Middlesbrough)
MUIR H C,	6, Queens Road, Elderslie, Renfrewshire. PAS 9LJ. (01505 326242). Kennels: Craig Muir Farm, Paisley, Scotland. PA2 8UT.

NGRC Directory

	(01505 320 482). (Att: Shawfield)
MUNRO P J F,	The Nook, Goldsmith Drive, Rayleigh, Essex. (01268 780981).
NASH M, (Snr)	31, Hillside Croy, Kilsyth Road, Glasgow. G65 9HJ. (01236 825807). (Att: Shawfield)
NAYLOR A,	5, Queen Street, South Normanton, Alfreton, Derby. DE55 2AL. (01773 811148).
NEIL D P,	(Trans from PT) 57, Gateside Ave, Bonnybridge, By Falkirk, Scotland. (01324 815 301). Kennels: Loanhead Kennels, Glasgow Road, Dennyloanhead, Scotland. (01324 815 035). (Att: Powderhall)
NICHOLSON L,	10, Byfield Close, Luton, Beds. LU4 0BX. (01582 594018).
NIGHTINGALE G,	179, Noak Hill Road, Billericay, Essex. CM12 9UL. (01277 651 387).
NOBLE F,	29, The Fairway, Darlington, Co Durham. DL1 1ES. (01325 466707).
OAKHILL B H,	Leaze Farm, Leonard Stanley, Stonehouse, Glos. GL10 3PE. (01453 821248). (Att: Swindon)
O'CONNOR C N,	Mossdale, Sevenoaks Way, Orpington, Kent. BR5 3JE. (0181 300 0629).
O'FLAHERTY A R,	11, Carberry Road, Leeds, W Yorks. LS6 1QQ. (01532 743356/0532 302069). (Att: Stainforth)
O'HARA S,	Tollhouse, Carlisle Road, Cleland, Motherwell, Lanarkshire. ML1 5LR. (01698 860380).
O'REGAN E R,	29, Prestly Wood Road, Rudloe, Corsham, Wilts. SN13 0LR. (01225 810255). Kennels: Pickwick Lodge Farm, Pickwick, Corsham, Wilts. (Att: Swindon)
O'SULLIVAN D,	145, Oxford Road, Stratton St Margaret, Swindon, Wilts. SN3 4JA. (01793 823070). (Att: Swindon)
OWENS P R,	Broadleaze House, Purton Road, Cricklade, Swindon, Wilts. SN6 6HU. (01793 750310). (Att: Swindon)
PARKER Mrs C L,	2, Airey House, Scocles Road, Minster On Sea, Sheerness, Kent. (01795 872717). (Att: Canterbury)
PASFIELD Mrs S,	27, Harts Close, Grovelands, Kidlington, Oxon. OX5 1AZ. (01865 378455). Kennels: Wildwood Kennels, Upper Farm, Middleton Stoney, Bicester, Oxon. OX6 8RY. (01869 343308). (Att: Milton Keynes)
PATERSON R,	114, Dovecote Street, Stockton, Cleveland. TS18 1HG. (01642 607576). Kennels: 23, Mary St, Oxbridge, Stockton, Cleveland. (01642 601611). (Att: Middlesbrough)
PECKHAM J S,	38, Maurice Road, Kings Heath, Birmingham. B14 6DL. (0121 444 2594). (Att: Perry Barr)
PECKHAM Mrs P,	40, Paynes Lane, Feltwell, Thetford, Norfolk. IP26 4BB. (01842 828370).

OWNER TRAINERS

NGRC Directory

PECKOVER R H,	32, Salthill Drive, Slough, Berks. SL1 3TH. (01753 524472).
PHILLIPS R,	18, The Courts, Westbrook, Margate, Kent. CT9 SHP. (01843 832718). (Att: Canterbury)
PILGRIM S R,	94, Junction Road, Hamworthy, Poole, Dorset. BH16 SAB. (01202 677297). (Att: Swindon)
PLEECE C G,	Bunnywood Kennels, Midways, Weare St, Ockley, Surrey. RHS SNW. (01306 711216).
PLUMB S E,	99, Millfields Road, Hackney, London. E5 OAB (0181 533 3502). (Att: Hackney)
POOLE Mrs 5,	138, Moira Road, Swadlincote, Derbyshire. SE11 8EY. (01283 211931). (Att: Nottingham)
POOLEY I,	The Cringles, Station Road, Potter Heigham, Great Yarmouth, Norfolk. NR29 SHX. (01692 670 279).
PRINCE L,	30, Doddington Rd, Benwick, March, Cambs. PE15 0UT. (01354 77384).
PROBERT D J,	Rutland Quarantine Kennels, Ashwells Road, Oakham, Rutland, Leics. LE15 7QH. (01572 756656). (Att: Peterborough)
PRYDDERCH M C,	Harewood Halt, Long Parish, Andover, Hants. SP11 7AJ. (01264 72458).
RADLEY Mrs P M,	Whiitingtree Farm, Dymock, Newent, Glos. GL18 2AB. (01531 890 207). (Att: Swindon)
RANCE C W,	Greenacres, Nickley Wood Road, Shadoxhurst, Ashford, Kent. TN26 1LZ. (01233 733296). (Att: Canterbury)
RATCLIFF B,	West House Farm, Coxhoe, Co Durham. DH6 4PA. (0191 377 3557).
RAWLINSON D,	Welwyn, Rainhall Crescent, Barnoldswick, Colne, Lancs. (01282 816659). (Kennels):- 6, Warren Road, Orford, Warrington, Cheshire. WA2 9AL. (01925 240290). (Att: Stainforth)
RAY P A,	56, Stocks Lane. Gamlingay, Sandy, Beds. (01767 50866). Kennels: 3, Wrestlingworth Rd Potton, Sandy, Beds. (01767 260626). (Att: Henlow)
RAY S,	Black House Fm, Page Bank, Spennymoor, Co Durham. (01388 811 457).
REDDEN C,	Bracken Croft, Shotton La., Shotton Colliery, Co Durham. DH6 2RA. (0191 526 4845).
REED R J,	40, Fortescue Road, Colliers Wood, SW19 2EB. (0181 641 7415). (Att: Rye House)
RHYMER C L,	Highfields, 44, Greenlands Rd, Peasedown St John, Bath, Avon. BA2 8EZ. (01761 432014). (Att: Swindon)
RICHARDS M C,	182, Reservoir Road, Selly Oak, Birmingham. B29 6TE. (0121 472 7141). (Att: Norton Canes)
RILEY M J,	66, Harley Road, Gt Yarmouth, Norfolk. NR30 4JT. (01493 856283). (Att: Swaffham)
ROBERTS Mrs M A,	231, Main Rd, Westwood, Nottingham. NG16 SJB. (01773 602217). (Att: Nottingham)

NGRC Directory

ROBERTS W E,	7, Lairs Close, North Rd, Holloway, London N7 9TF. (0171 607 0912). (Att: Hackney)
ROBINSON D J,	119, Mile Cross Road, Norwich, Norfolk. NR3 2LG. (01603 419613). (Att: Yarmouth)
ROBINSON T,	Fair View House, Browney Lane, Browney, Co Durham. DH7 8HU. (0191 378 9638).
ROSS M S,	The Lodge, Off Melton Road, Uxbridge Road, Leics. LE4 7ST. (01533 680061). (Att: Peterboro)
ROWELL Mrs J,	Woodside Farm, Durham Lane, Haswell Moor, DH6 2BD. (0191 526 5979). (Att: Middlesbrough)
RUMNEY B,	Chez Nous, Thorne Road, Stainforth, Nr Doncaster, Sth Yorks. DN7 SBT. (01302 842300). Kennels: 1, Racing Yard, Haggswood Stables, Stainforth, Near Doncaster, South Yorks. DN7 SPS. (01302 842857). (Att: Stainfroth)
RYAN Mrs F M,	6, Russell Road, Walthamstow, London E17 6QY. (0181 923 4879). (Att: Hackney)
SAIT R,	22c, Moore Avenue, Bournemouth, Dorset. (01202 570909). Kennels: Dorset Window Co, 78, Alma Rd, Winton, Bournemouth BH9 1AN. (01202 533 126).
SAKER K J,	5, Orwell Cottages, Whitwell, Reepham, Norwich, Norfolk. NRlO 4RF. (01603 870978). (Att: Yarmouth)
SAMUELS Mrs E G,	Anvidale, 79, Yarmouth Rd, Ormesby, Nr Caister, Gt Yarmouth, Norfolk. NR29 3QF. (01493 384065).
ASSANKEY D,	Tanglewood, Rhododendron Ave, Meopham, Kent. DA13 0TT. (01474 814106).
SAVAGE Mrs S J,	31, Common La., Southery, Nr Downham Mkt, Norfolk. PE38 0PB. (01366 6436). (Att: Mildenhall)
SAVIGAR J,	8, The Meadows, Aldridge, Walsall, Staffs. WS9 OLB. (01922 57856).
SCAHILL M J,	14, Archer Crescent, Wollaton, Nottingham. NG8 1HB. (01602 288056). Kennels: The Barn, Main Oxton Road, Claverton, Nottingham. (01374 413215). (Att: Peterborough)
SCALLY E,	6, Douglas Avenue, Carmyle, Glasgow. (0141 641 8549).
SCHOFIELD Mrs S,	Southlands, Wormersley Rd, Knottingley, W. Yorkshire. WF1 0DJ. (01977 672152). (Att: Stainforth)
SCOTT A,	Coopers Shop, Bothal, Morpeth, Northumberland. (01670 853687).
SCOTT J,	7, Lees Terr, Old Wives Lees, Chilham, Kent. CT4 8AN. (01227 731184). (Att: Canterbury)
SCRIVENS R W,	2, Selina Close, Sundon Park, Luton, Beds. LU3 3AW. (01582 579770).
SCURR J,	1a, Thurloe Court, 117, Fulham Court,

NGRC Directory

	London. SW3 65B. Kennels: 76, Galworthy Rd, Cricklewood, NW2 25H. (0181 450 0308). (Att: Rye House)
SEERY H J,	29, Liverpool Rd, Watford, Herts. WD1 8DW. (01923 460849) (Att: Milton Keynes)
SHARP G,	237, Harrowgate Lane, Bishopsgarth, Stockton On Tees, Cleveland. TSl9 8UD. (01642 583609). Kennels: Whitton Moor Farm, Stillington, Co Durham. (01740 31013). (Att: Middlesbrough)
SHAW Ms C Z,	The Old Garage, Old Warwick Rd, Lapworth, Warwickshire. B94 6LN. (01564 782535).
SHAW D A,	23, Stamford Avenue, Seaton Delaval, Northumberland. NE2S OPA. (0191 237 7035).
SIBLEY F J,	11, Clacton Rd, Weeley, Clacton, Essex. CO16 9DN. (01255 830954). (Att: Hackney)
SIMMS S,	62, Low Row, Darton, Barnsley, S Yorks. S75 5JF. (01226 388491). (Att: Stainforth)
SIMPSON J,	27, Mardale Street, Hetton Le Hole. DHS 0DH. (0191 526 2703). (Att: Middlesbrough)
SMART D P,	66, Chalford Oaks, Acklam, Middlesbrough, Cleveland. TS5 8QQ. (01642 817724). (Att: Middlesbrough)
SMITH B K,	Miltescens House, Mole Drove, Gedney Hill, Spalding, Lincs. PE12 0PA. (01406 330436)
SMITH R,	8, Oak End, Alconbury, Huntingdon, Cambs. PE17 SEE. (01480 890600). (Att: Peterborough)
SMITH R F S,	16, Banks Close, Marston, Beds. MK43 0NP. (01234 768322).
SMITHERS P D,	40, Pipewell Rd, Carshalton, Surrey. SM5 IEY. (0181 715 1546). (Att: Canterbury)
SOPPITT E,	64, Woodlands Crescet, Kelice, Co Durham. DH6 4LX. (0191 377 2930).
SPECK R,	Blythe Cottage, Priory Farm, Blithbury, Rugeley, Staffs. WS15 3JA. (01889 22 224). - Kennels: 2/4, Prestwood Rd West, Wednesfield, Wolverhampton. WV11 1RJ. (01902 731443). (Att: Cradley Heath)
SPENCER Miss K,	Foan Hill Lodge, 11, Spring Lane Lane, Swannington, Nr Coalville, Leics. LE67 8QR. (01530 835024).
SPINKS D G,	Woodlands, 19, Yarmouth, Ormesby St Margaret, Gt Yarmouth. NR29 3OB. (01493 730433). (Att: Yarmouth)
SPRAGGON D,	The Old Vicarage, South Hetton, Durham. DH6 2SW. (0191 526 6726). (Att: Middlesbrough)
STANDING J H,	26, Mitcham Road, Old Dean Est, Camberley, Surrey. GU15 4AP. (01276 61000).
STARLING E,	41, Tavistock Street, Middlesbrough, Cleveland. TS5 6AX. (01642 827266).

NGRC Directory

STEPHENSON J R,	(Att: Middlesbrough) 21, Leinster Rd, Middlesbrough, Cleveland. TS1 4RA. (01642 850249).
STIRLING Mrs A,	(Att: Middlesbrough) 25, Blairbeth Place, Rutherglen, Glasgow. G73 4LR. (0141 631 3388). (Att: Shawfield)
STONE A,	71, Watling Street, Nuneaton, Warks. CV11 6JJ. (01203 386908).
STRINGER Mrs G F,	Shellgrove Farm, Horton Cum Studley, Oxford. OX33 1DE. (01865 351 757).
STRINGER P J,	(Att: Swindon) The Willows, Eardington, Bridgnorth, Shrops. WV16 5JT. (01746 765601).
STROUD J P,	Brindle Lodge, Sledmere Road, Langtoft, Nr Diffield, East Yorks. YO25 0BT. (01377 267471).(Att Hull)
STUART I B,	105, Barkby Road, Syston, Leics. LE7 2AH. (01533 695583).
SWAIN R P,	1, Butely Road, Leagrave, Luton, Beds. LU4 9HE. (01582 505885).
SYLVESTER W,	74, Coalhill Lane, Farsley, Pudsey, Leeds. LS28 5NA. (01532 566 140).
TALBOT D,	43, Waverley Road, Bolton, Lancs. BL1 6NW. (01204 303522). (Att: Norton Canes)
TASKER H D,	1a, West Avenue, Castle Bromwich, Birmingham. B36 0EB. (0121 747 4302).
TATE E G,	40, Shawfield Road, Ash, Surrey. GU12 6QX. (01252 311799). (Att: Hackney)
TAYLOR C,	46, High Street, Warboys, Cambs. PE17 2TA. (01487 822430). (Att: Peterborough)
THOMPSON J,	Pomona Cottage, Livertown, Mill Bank, Moorsholm, Cleveland. TS12 3JW. (01287 650281/643794).
THOMPSON J G,	(Att: Middlesbrough) Killingwold, Graves Lane, Bishop Burton, Near Beverley, Yorks. HU17 8OX. (01964 550868/550340). (Att: Hull)
THORN R,	33, Howard Road, Sompting, West Sussex. BN15 0LW. (01903 767664).
THORN R R,	127, Main Street, Clenchwarton, Kings Lynn, Norfolk. PE34 4AN. (01553 692093).
THORPE S,	249, Edenfield Road, Rochdale, Lancs. OL11 5AG. (01706 461116).
TIGHE G,	11, Hazelwood Ave, Southwick, Sunderland, Tyne & Wear. (0191 548 1513).
TILLETT R B,	(Att: Sunderland) Skylark, Springtime Nursery, Gt North Road, Stotfold, Hitchin, Herts. SG5 4BL. (01462 834 300). (Att: Henlow)
TIMCKE B A,	Foxden Farm, Claygate Road, Laddingford, Nr Yalding, Kent. M18 6BD. (01892 730515). Near Beverley, Yorks. HU17 8QX. (01964 550868/550340). (Att: Hull)

OWNER TRAINERS

NGRC Directory

TINGEY B C, 9.12.93.	The Shires, Thetford Road, Coney Weston, Bury St Edmunds, Suffolk. IP31 IDN. (01359 221606). (Att: Mildenhall)
TODD M,	54, Cheney Rd, Faversham, Kent. ME13 8DG. (01795 533306). (Att: Canterbury)
TOMPKINS R,	39a, Gold Street, Hanslope, Milton Keynes, Bucks. MK19 7LU. (01908 510021). (Att: Milton Keynes)
TOURLE G J,	89, Cranbourne Pk, Hedge End, Southampton, Hants. SO3 4NY. (01489 783303). (Att: Swindon)
TOWNER D P,	7, Burrell Road, Compton, Near Newbury, Berks. RG16 0NP. Kennels: Apple Pie Farm, Compton, Nr Newbury, Berks. (01635 578175/578902). (Att: Swindon)
TRANT P,	Stoneham Park House, Stoneham, Eastleigh, Hants. SO5 3HT. (01703 762255).
TRUE R,	Maitland, 78, Wragby Rd East, North Greetwell, Lincoln. LN2 4QZ. (01522 754405/ A/Phone 754380). (Att: Hull)
TUNGATT Mrs T	7k, Hillsley Road, Paulsgrove, Portsmouth, Hants. PO6 4LE. (01705 321034). (Att: Swindon)
TURNER A F,	Keepers Cott, Saltby, Near Melton Mowbray, Leics. (01664 65239). (Att: Peterborough)
TYERS D R,	48, Eastlands Rd, Moseley, Birmingham. B13 9RG. (0121 449 4038).
VENN Miss M J,	Overend Green Farm, Heath And Reach, Leighton Buzzard, Beds. LU7 9LD. (01525 237304). (Att: Milton Keynes)
WAINWRIGHT H,	Deans Farm, Wretton Fen Road, Wretton, Kings Lynn, Norfolk. PE33 9QP. (01366 500593). (Att: Swaffham)
WALKER Mrs N,	Airdrie Hill Farm, Airdrie, Lanarkshire. ML6 7SE. (01236 762534).
WALLACE H W I,	Millbank, 10, Kirkhill Terrace, Gorebridge, Midlothian. EH23 4LL. (01875 821 681).
WALLOND I C,	Ouorum, Ashford Road, Hithe, Kent. CT21 4JD. (01831 631 884). (Att: Hackney)
WALSH J J,	17, Page Street, Mill Hill, London. NW7 2EL. (0181 203 0249). (Att: Hackney)
WALSH M,	Thirlstane, Newby West, Carlisle. CA2 6QU. (01228 514000). Kennels: Peter Lane, Newby West, Carlisle. CA2 6BZ. (01228 591 833). (Att: Shawfield)
WARD A J,	35, The Parade, Colchester Road, Harold Park, Romford, Essex. RM3 0AQ. (01708 342594).
WARD D A,	9, Redmoor Lane, S Brink, Wisbech, Cambs. PE14 0RN. (01945 582 335). (Att: Peterborough)
WARREN Miss B	Addition House, Whale Drove, Whaplode Drove, Spalding. PE12 0UB. (01406 330964).

NGRC Directory

WARWICK D J,	10, Richmere Road, Didcot, Oxon. OX11 8HT. (01235 818 735). (Att: Reading)
WASS J A,	151, High Street North, Stewkley, Leighton Buzzard, Beds. LU7 0EX. (01525 240677).
WEARE C E,	34, Bath Road, Frome, Somerset. BA11 2HH. (01373 474 105). (Att: Swindon)
WEBSTER P,	44, Besom Lane, Millbrook, Stalybridge, Cheshire. SK15 3EZ. (0161 338 3641).
WEEKS M G,	40, Greenacres, Westfield, East Sussex. TN35 4QT. (01424 754235). (Att: Canterbury)
WELLS J E,	28, Park Rd, Bury St Edmunds, Suffolk. IP33 3QL. (01284 703 892).
WEST G, (Jnr)	3, St Leonards Road, Horsham, West Sussex. RH13 6EH. (01403 254014).
WEST T M,	Woodcott, Downley Comm, H. Wycombe, Bucks HP13 5YQ. (01494 438397).
WESTLAKE M J,	7, Blackthorn Close, Pennington, Lymington, Hants. SO41 8AY. (01590 679404).
WHEATER Miss S	Arden House, 80, High St, Norton, Stockton On Tees, Cleveland. TS20 1DR. (01642 552 355).
WHEELER R G,	Nuggetts, Valebridge Road, Burgess Hill, Sussex. RH15 0RT. (01444 236303).
WHITE H,	24, Pembury Cres, Sidcup, Kent. DA14 4OD. (0181 302 4292). (Att: Hackney).
WHITE J W,	48, Heather Road, Lee, London SE12 0UQ. (0181 857 6395). Kennels: B & J Kennels, Ockendon Complex, Upminster, Essex.
WILEMAN B P,	47, Watling Street, Dordon, Tamworth, Staffs. B78 1SY. (01827 895666).
WILKINSON B,	The Poplars, Wellington Road, Donnington, Telford, Shrops. TF2 8AB. (01952 605436).
WILSON J V,	Little Parndon Lodge, Parndon Mill Lane, Harlow, Essex. CM20 2HB. (01279 428372). (Att: Rye House)
WILSON Miss N,	Tylersley Fm, Tylers Causeway, Newgate St Village, Herts. SG13 8ON. (01707 875952).
WOOD Mrs H F,	8, Copperfield Drive, Langley, Sutton Valence, Maidstone, Kent. ME17 1SX. (01622 862019). (Att: Canterbury)
WOODCOCK Ms M	Brooklands Kennels, The Lindens. Mill Road, Walpole Highway, Cambs. PE14 7QW. (01945 780096). (Att: Swaffham/Hackney)
WOODROOF G J,	24, The Holt, Hainault, Essex. (0181 501 5071). Kennels: 34, Devonshire Hill Lane, Tottenham, London. N17.
WRAY F W,	7a, Bridge St, Moulton, Newmarket, Suffolk. CB8 8SP. (Att: Swaffham)
WRIGHT R,	3, Higher Stubbin, Stubbin Road, Rotherham, Sth Yorks. S62 7RY. (01709 524448). (Att: Stainforth)
YATES M J,	Fourwinds, Clacton Road, Weeley, Clacton On Sea, Essex. (01255 830 774).

Focus on BREEDING

Slippy rules, but litter numbers still on the slide

By P R Saward of the Racing Post

THERE was no let-up in the downward spiral of British breeding activity in 1994. Volume 113 of the Greyhound Stud Book, published in September, reported falls in litters (867) and registrations (6,292), with the latter down by nearly 12 per cent on the previous year.

Litters decreased only marginally from the last total of 880, but it would be optimistic to describe this as a glimmer of hope; one year's litters are largely the following year's registrations, so the depressing trend looks set to continue.

On the NGRC open scene, it was often the dead and departed stud dogs who made the headlines.

I'm Slippy, who died over two years ago, dominated in terms of quantity, the 371 races won by his offspring placing him well clear of Daleys Gold's tally of 236.

Quality was also evident as his daughter Westmead Chick brought off a magnificent Category One four-timer: Arc, Olympic, Midland Flat and Oaks.

Depressing downward spiral in new registrations looks set to continue in 1995 and beyond

Breaker also of Hall Green's 474 metres track record during the Midland Flat, the heavyweight brindle left journalists groping for new superlatives as she cut down one top class field after another.

Flag Star, who died from cancer at the beginning of 1994, sired the Derby victor Moral Standards, along with top marathon per-

Focus on BREEDING

I'M SLIPPY, left, with his son Murlens Slippy and Richard O'Regan.

former Newry Town and others who regularly gained winning brackets. Indeed, their consistency gave him the highest wins-from-runs strike rate among the leading stud dogs. His progeny scored 43 wins from 125 runs, a superb 34.4 per cent success rate.

Early September saw the death of Whisper Wishes, just before his son Joyful Tidings secured Irish Derby honours at Shelbourne Park.

The season's end brought Whisper Wishes another title when he became champion brood-bitch sire for the first time.

His daughters produced well over 100 winners, who ran up a score of more than 300 open race victories.

Ardfert Sean, another casualty among the stud dogs, sired the brilliant Scottish Derby winner Droopys Sandy, who broke Shawfield's 500 metres track record in the final with an amazing return of 29.39sec. Later on, the black set new figures for

Focus on BREEDING

TOP TEN BREEDERS OF NGRC OPEN & INVITATION RACE WINNERS 1994

	BREEDER	WINNERS	WINS	MOST PROLIFIC (WINS)
1	**Trevor Cobbold** (late)	11	98	Decoy Lynx (18)
2	**Nick Savva**	13	56	Westmead Chick (18)
3	**Sean Dunphy** (Ire)	10	39	Droopys Craig (11)
4*	**Mrs Joan Brennan** (Ire)	6	36	Druids Omega (12)
4*	**Mrs Breda Kennedy** (Ire)	4	36	Wexford Minx (17)
4*	**Harry Williams**	9	36	Toybox Schooner (10)
7	**Denis Lennon** (Ire)	9	33	Solva Guy (7)
8	**Mrs Ann Bourke** (Ire)	12	31	Jurassic Park (7)
9*	**Jim Donohoe** (Ire)	5	30	Heavenly Spirit (12)
9*	**Gerard Hayes** (Ire)	3	30	Super Bridge (14)

Continued from page 335

Dunmore's 435 yards. With such as Coolmona Road, Here's Seanie (Champion Stakes, Birmingham Cup) and Redwood Girl (Grand Prix) also figuring among Ardfert Sean's stock, breeders can but rue his passing.

The late Greenpark Fox got the St Leger heroine Ballarue Minx, and rattled up a double century of wins with his numerous offspring.

Turning now to those sires still in the land of the living, Slaneyside Hare achieved a table-topping winners-from-runners strike rate of 50 per cent, backed by an excellent wins-from-runs ratio of 26 per cent.

These figures pinpoint him as a remarkably efficient sire of consistently successful trackers.

And none more so than the July 1992 litter he sired out of Easy Bimbo. The produce included such prolific winners as Decoy Lynx, Decoy Cougar and Decoy Cheetah, and were instrumental in making their beeder, the late Trevor Cobbold, the season's most successful breeder of open winners.

On the following pages, are tables dealing with stud dogs. The conventional method of ranking the sires is by number of races won by their progeny, but I have never thought that to be entirely satisfactory. I know that regular readers of my column are interested by strike rates, and this is the basis of the breakdown that is shown.

Continued on page 353

The joys of greyhound racing

Colour Special on a great night out at the track

Above all it's about the thrill of the race

IN a harsh economic climate, greyhound racing, like every other sport, cannot be seen looking to its laurels (except, of course, the Ike Morris variety).

So many NGRC tracks are doing their utmost to widen their appeal; restaurant facilities, like this one at Hall Green, offer quality service at affordable prices. Customer needs are uppermost...

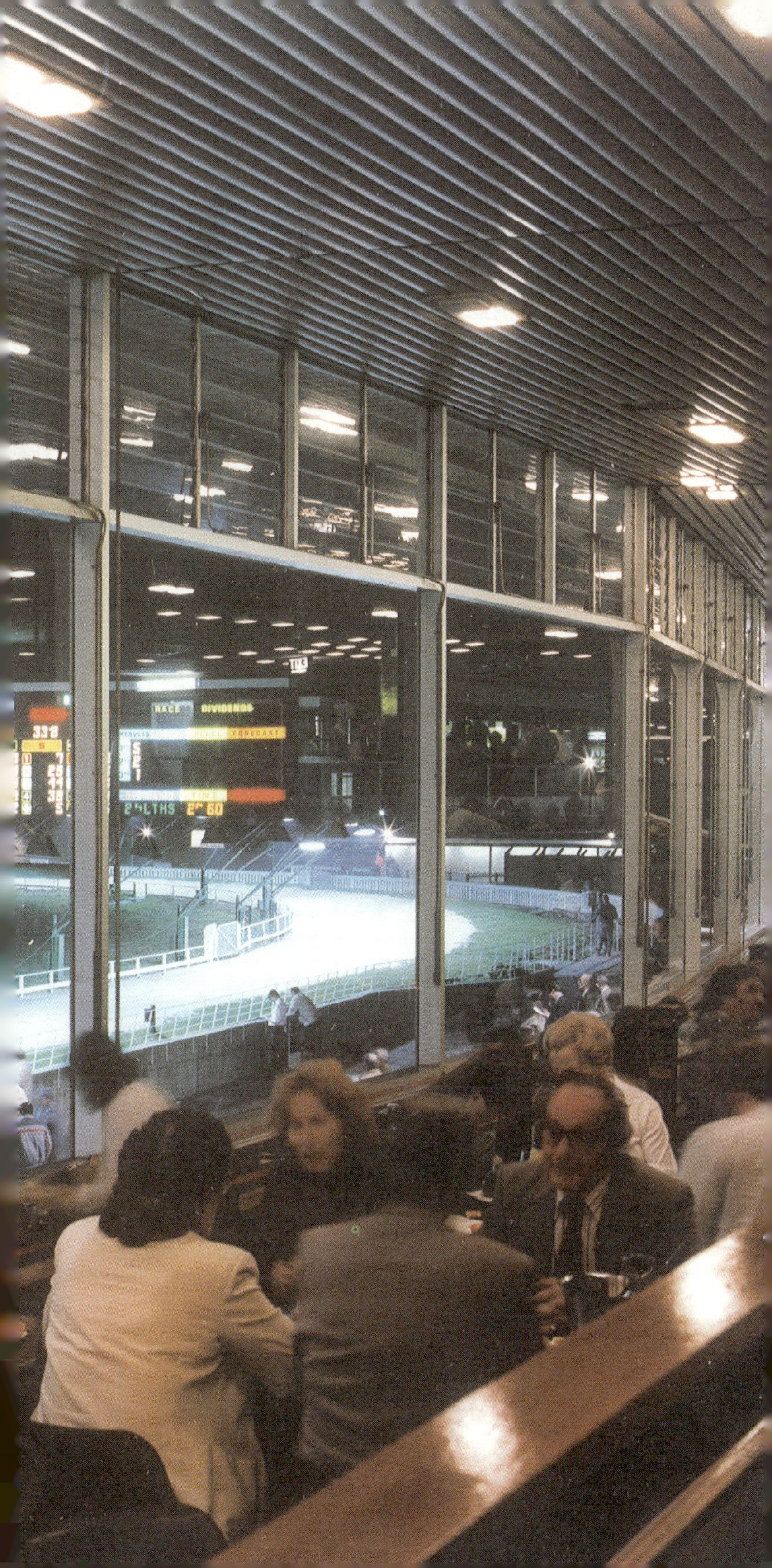
RACE
DIVIDENDS
FORECAST

A place for all occasions . . .

Attention to detail is a watchword at the tracks these days and means that every effort is made to make your night a special one—whether it be an anniversary dinner . . . or that first date.

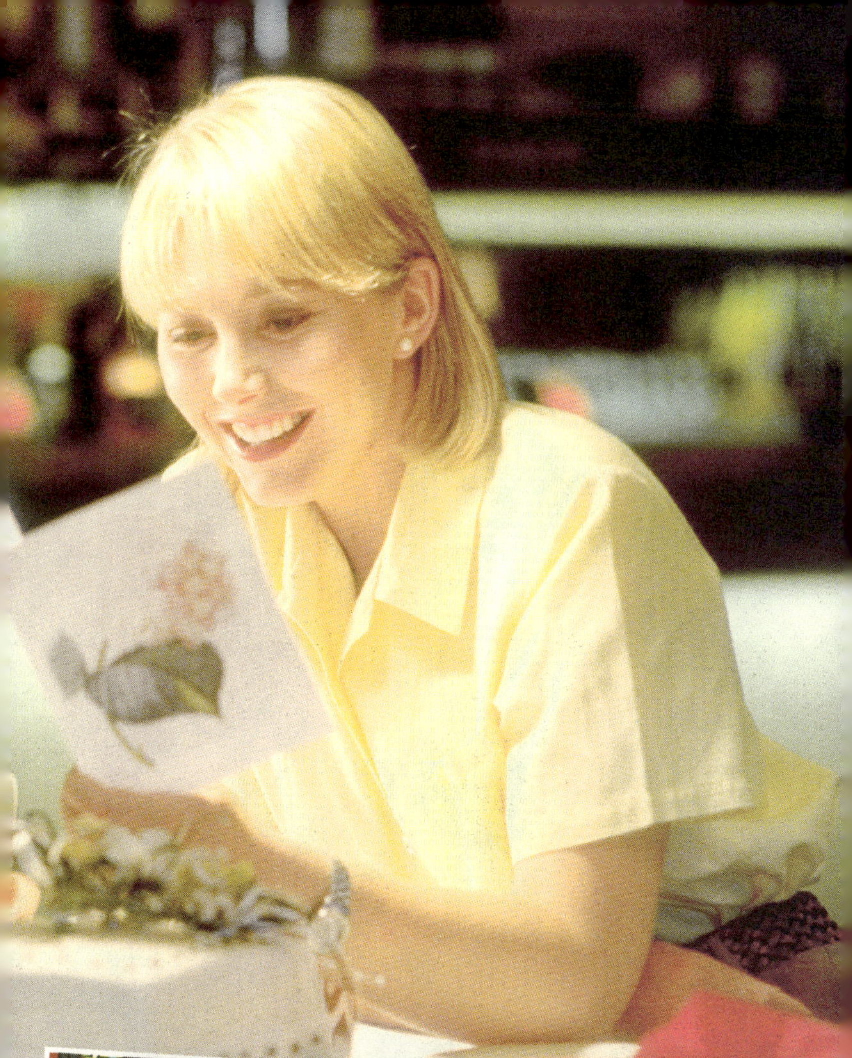

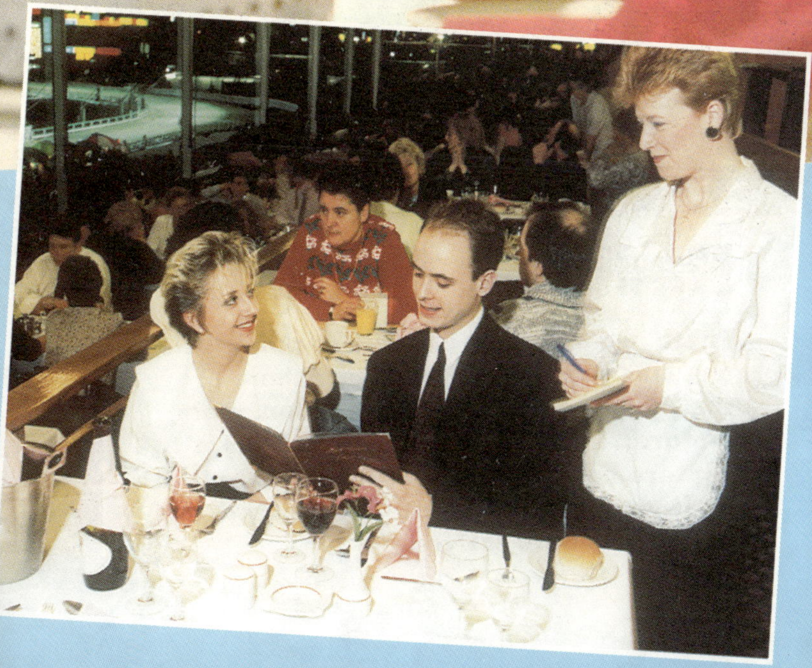

Having a flutter

There are a variety of ways to put a little on what you fancy. For a start there are the rails bookmakers (Wimbledon, main picture). But for those who don't want to venture outside, tote booths are plentiful or, if you are dining, Tote runners will place your bets for you.

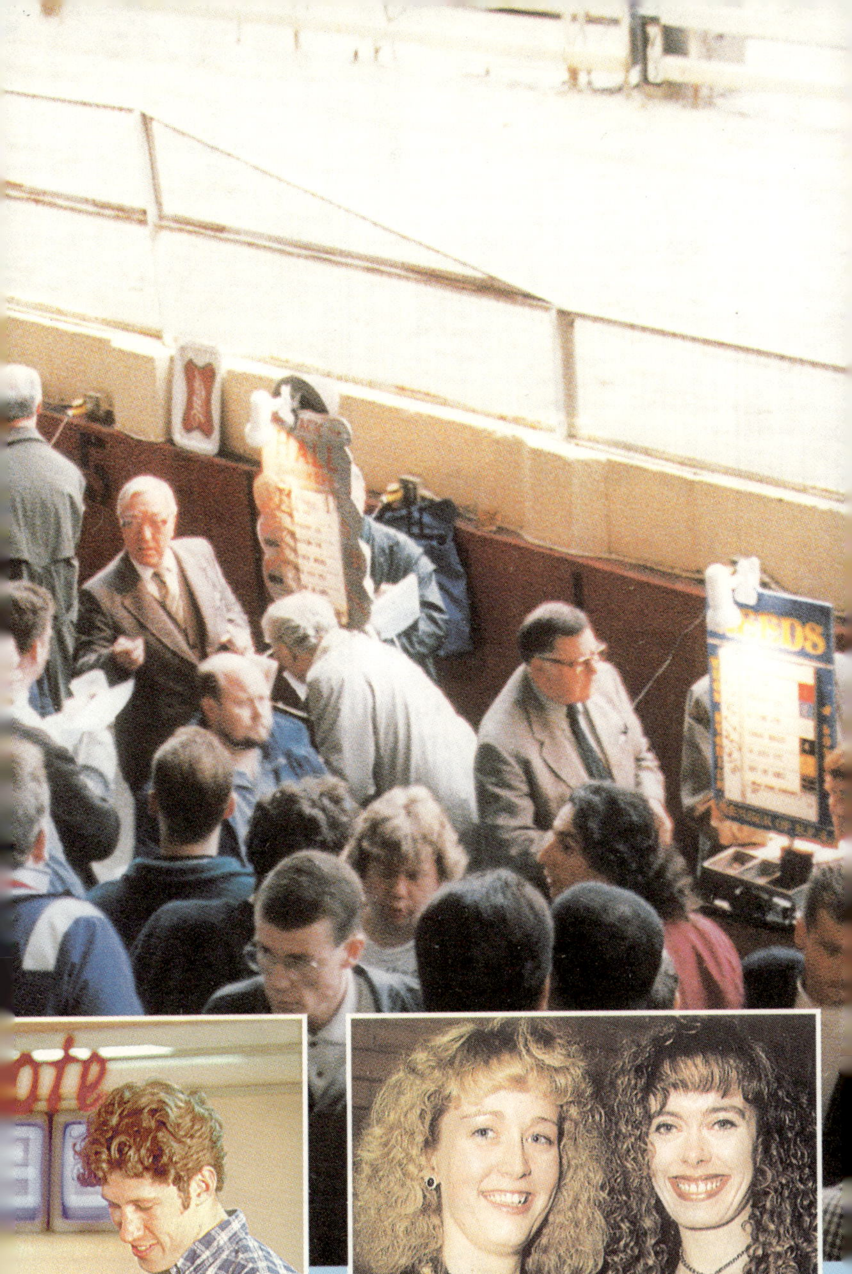
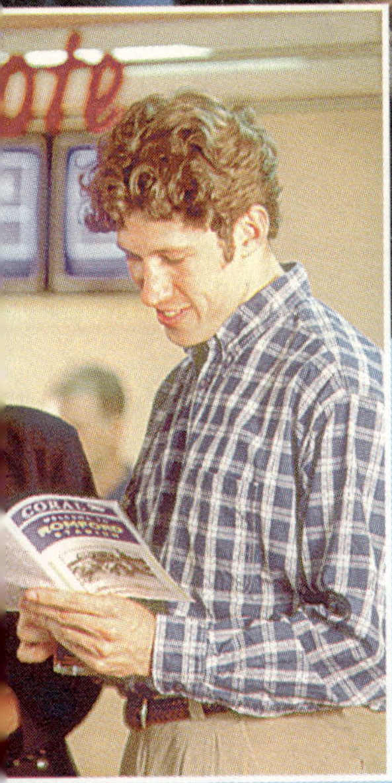
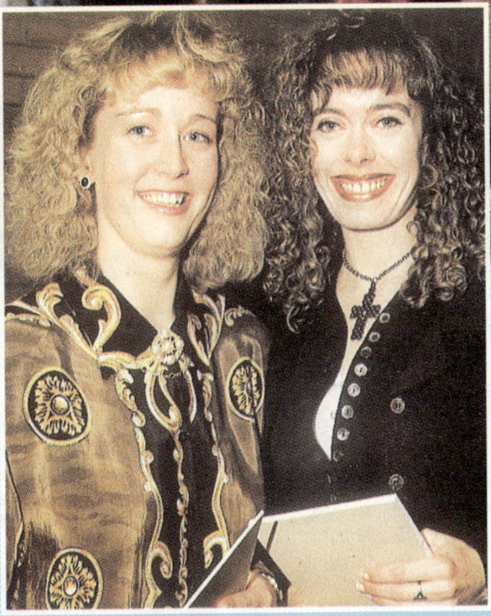

Keeping their feet on the ground...

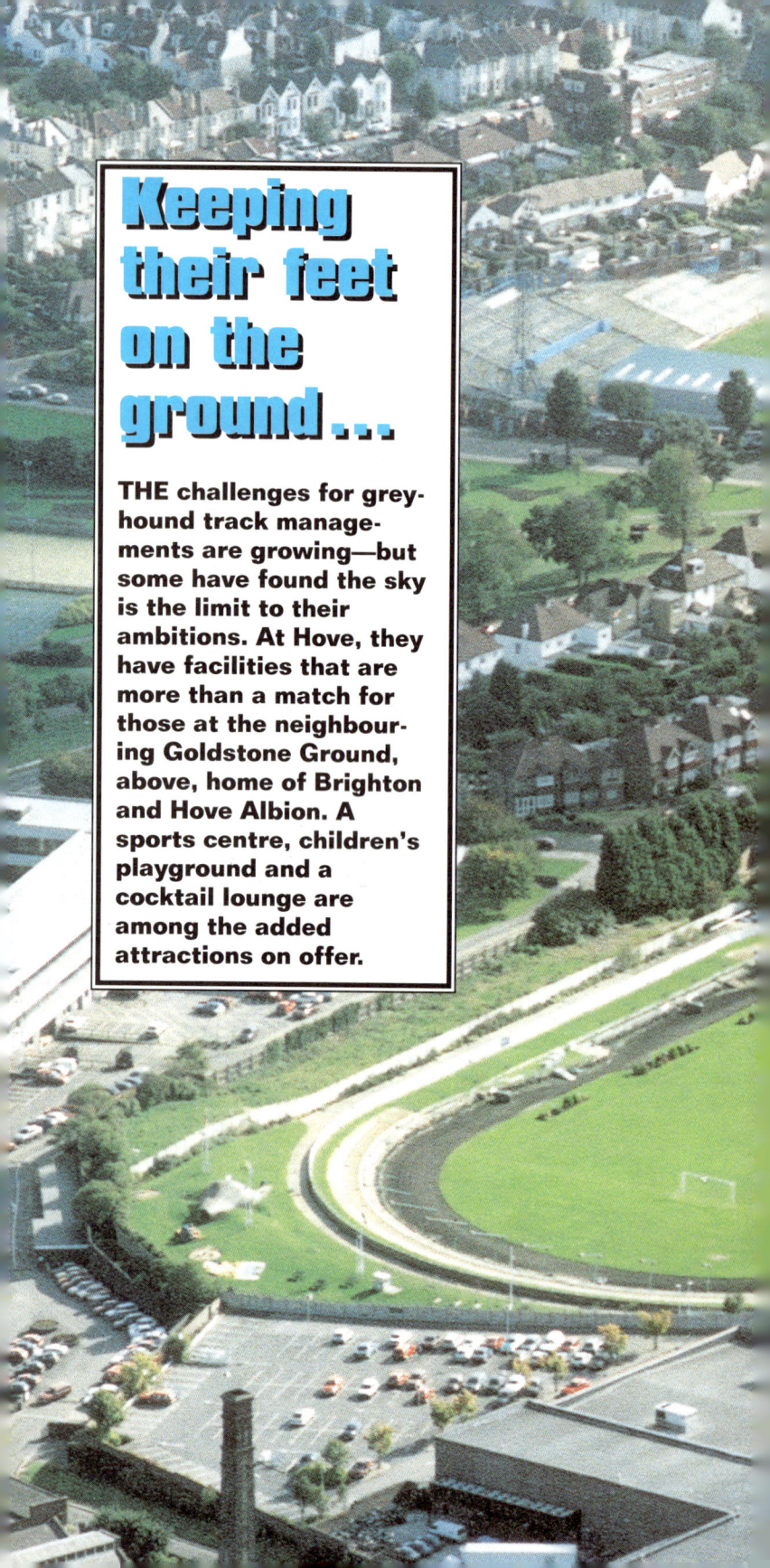

THE challenges for greyhound track managements are growing—but some have found the sky is the limit to their ambitions. At Hove, they have facilities that are more than a match for those at the neighbouring Goldstone Ground, above, home of Brighton and Hove Albion. A sports centre, children's playground and a cocktail lounge are among the added attractions on offer.

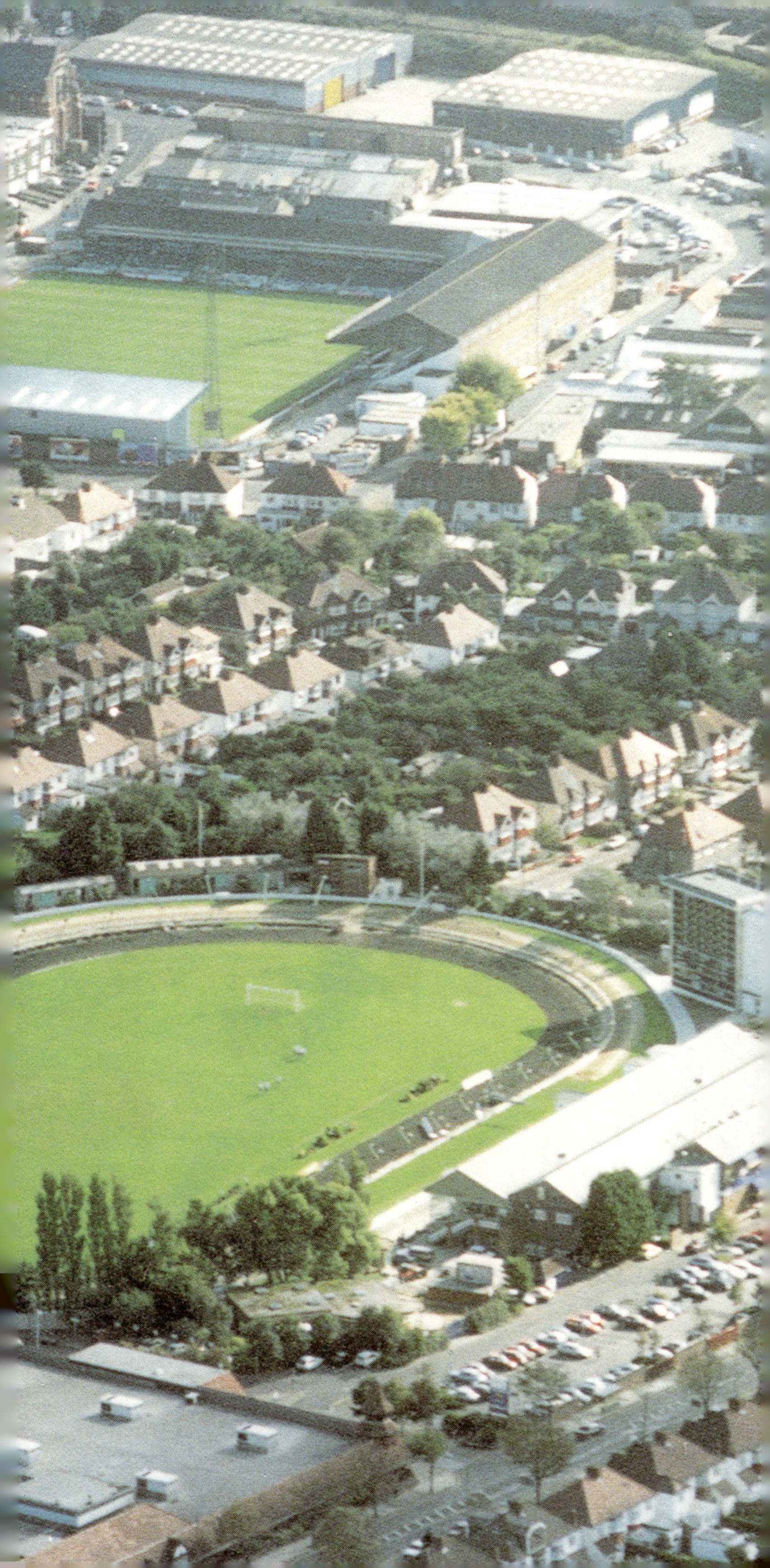

Menu

A'La Carte Menu

Starters
Your Chef's Soup of the Day
(Served piping hot with Bread Roll & Butter)
Crispy Coated Mushroom
(Pounded Mushrooms, deep fried & served with Garlic Dip)
Atlantic Prawn Cocktail
Garnished with a crispy Salad & Served with Brown Bread & Butter
Our Indian Selection
(Onion Bhaji & Vegetable Samosa with a Mint & Yoghurt Dip)
Miami Cocktail
(Orange, Grapefruit & Melon pieces)
Smooth Chicken Liver Pate
(Garnished with a Crisp Salad & served with Warm Toast)
****

Your Choice from the Grill
8oz Sirloin Steak
10oz Rump Steak
12oz T-Bone Steak
(Accompanied with Grilled Tomato, Buttton Mushrooms & Deep Fried Onion Rings)
& To Compliment your Steak a choice of Chasseur, Bordelaise or Au Poivre Sauce
****

Fish Dishes
Poached Salmon Steak
(Served with a Prawn & Dill Sauce)
Grilled Halibut Steak
(With Lemon & Herb Butter)
****

Vegetarian Dishes
Mushroom Stroganoff
(Served on a bed of Brown Rice)
Vegetable Lasagne Provencale
(Assorted vegetables cooked on layers of lasagne, covered in Cheddar Sauce)
****

for more tempting choices and details of our
Dessert Menu, please see next sheet

PERRY BARR
GREYHOUND RACING STADIUM

Wine LIST

Perry Barr Restaurant Wine List

PRICE

House Wine
			per Bottle	per Glass
1.	RED	(Smooth, Mellow)	6.50	1.20
2.	RED	(Full bodied, dry)	6.50	1.20
3.	WHITE	(Medium, dry)	6.50	1.20
4.	WHITE	(Dry)	6.50	1.20

Champagne
5. MOET & CHANDON BRUT IMPERIAL — 25.00
6. MERCER DEMI-SEC — 20.00

Selected White Wines
7. SOAVE — 7.75
Dry, light, fresh and subtly fruity
8. PIESPORTER MICHELSBERG — 7.00
Medium bodied, fragrant and fruity
9. LIEBFRAUMILCH — 6.50
Medium dry, soft, light and fruity
10. MUSCADET — 7.50
Light, dry fragrant wine from the Loire Valley

Drivers Delight
11. MICHEL SCHNEIDER — 7.50
Blanc/Light Medium
2% Volume for the driver

Selected Red Wines
12. COTES DU RHONE — 7.50
Full bodied, robust and well balanced
13. BEAUJOLAIS — 7.50
Light, refreshing and very fruity
14. MATEUS ROSE — 7.50
Medium dry, light and refreshing

Sparkling Wines
15. ASTI SPUMANTE — 10.00

PERRY BARR
GREYHOUND RACING STADIUM

Variety on the menu

They know how to dine in style in Birmingham: the restaurant at Hall Green is well appointed, and menu at Perry Barr (left) appealing.

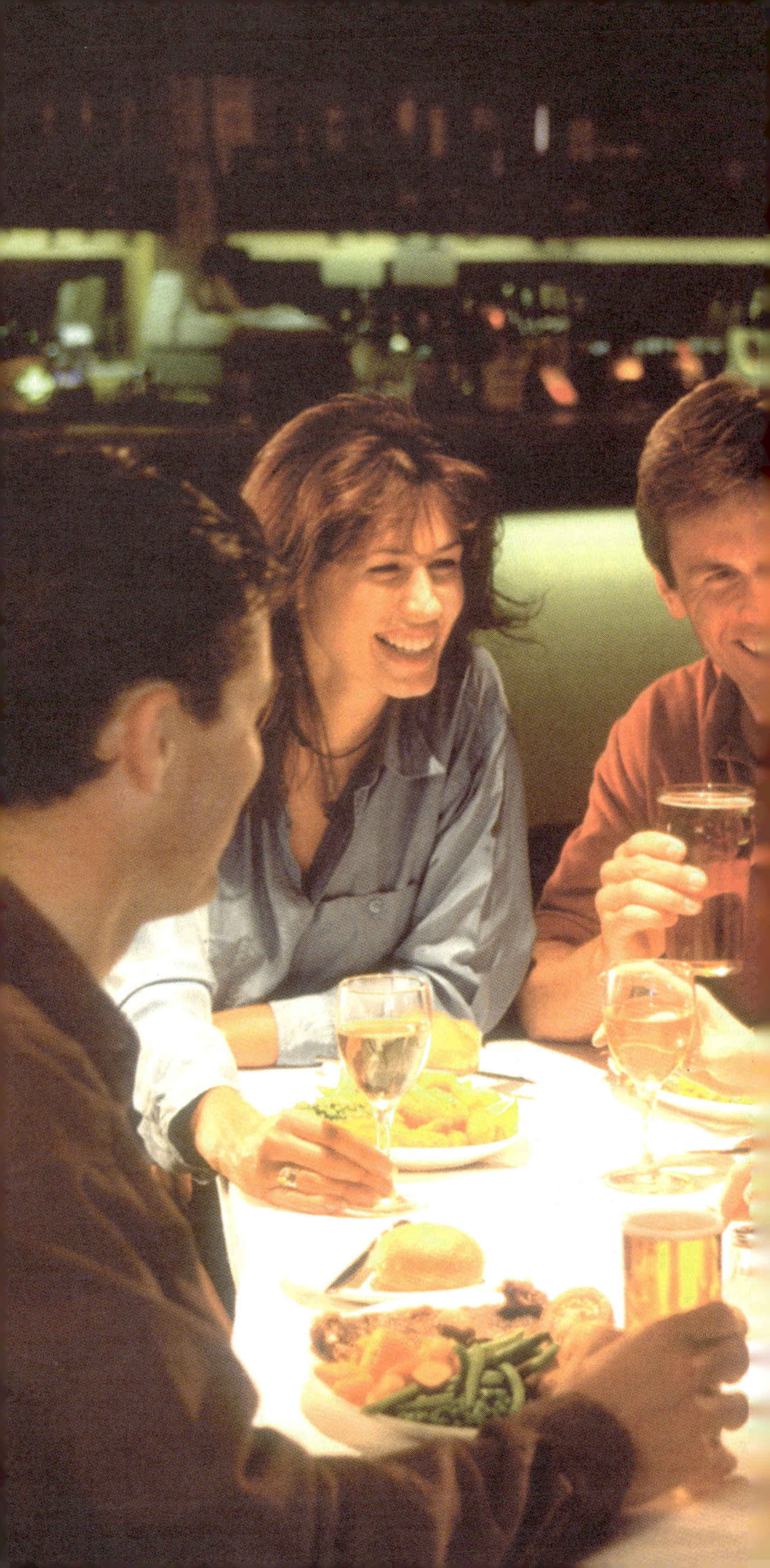

A night out tailored to suit all pockets

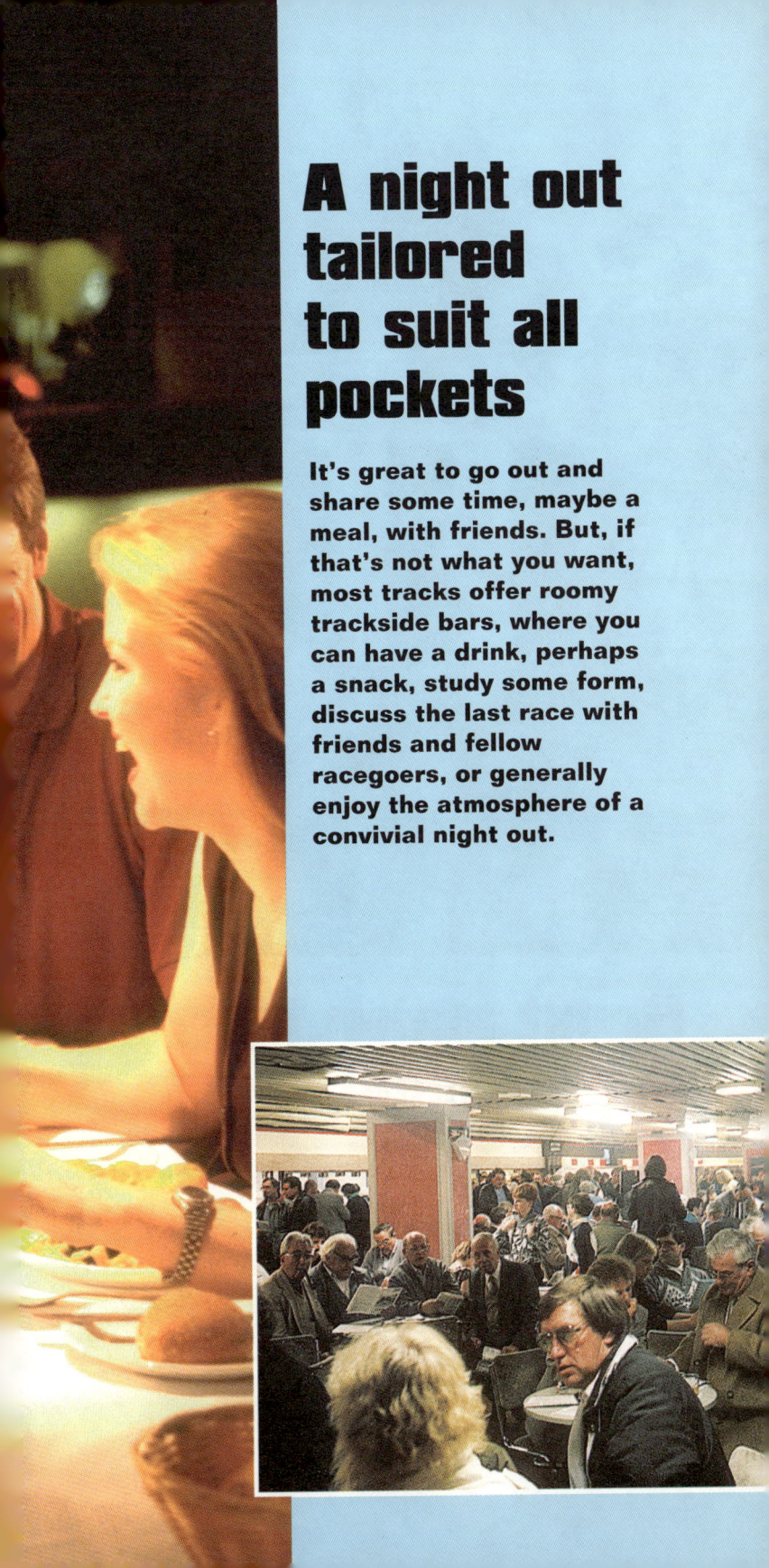

It's great to go out and share some time, maybe a meal, with friends. But, if that's not what you want, most tracks offer roomy trackside bars, where you can have a drink, perhaps a snack, study some form, discuss the last race with friends and fellow racegoers, or generally enjoy the atmosphere of a convivial night out.

Great action by day or night...

There is plenty of opportunity to go greyhound racing, with demand for meetings fuelled by the recent increases in betting shop hours. Fourteen tracks will feature regularly in the afternoon BAGS programme, which will be beamed direct to betting shops by SIS. But, as regular racegoers will tell you, there's no substitute for being there.

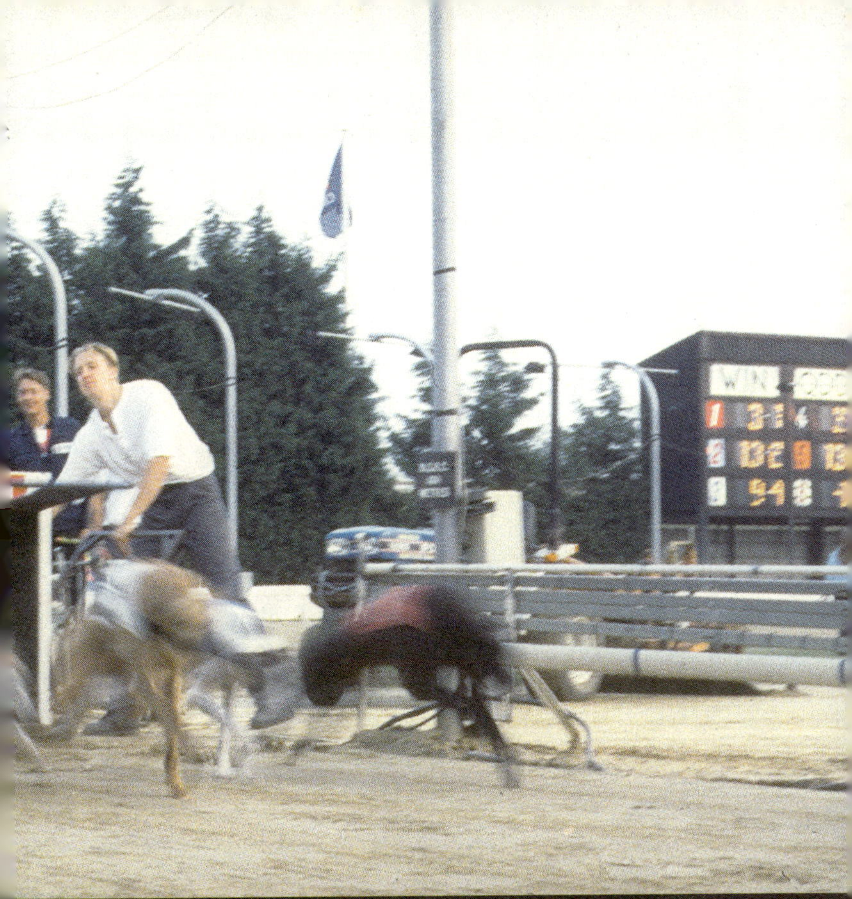
WIN

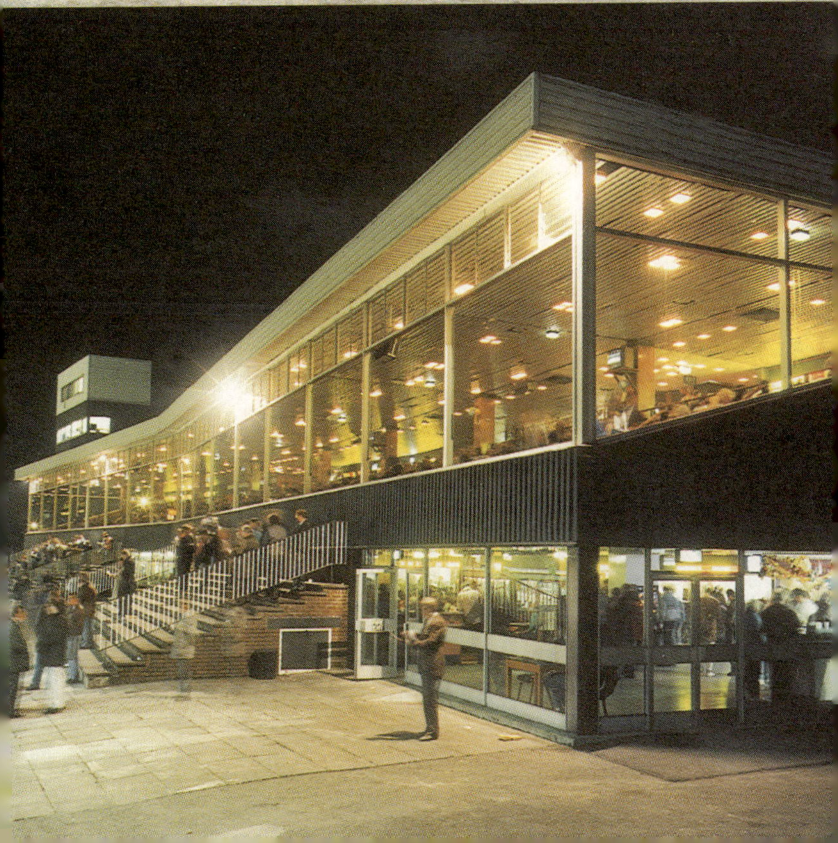

Outside track . . .

Well, it's alright for you punters, sitting in the warm while we dogs brave all weathers for your sport! Munster Confusion always refuses to parade, so there's only one answer to get him to the start on time . . .

Focus on BREEDING

Continued from page 336

Strike-rates of Sires represented by 15 or more runners in NGRC Open and Invitation races

Table 1: Ranked by winners/runners strike rate

		Winners	Runners	Wins	Runs	Winners/Runners	%Wins/Runs
1	Slaneyside Hare	20	40	110	423	50.0	26.0
2	Ballyard Hoffman	8	17	34	139	47.0	24.5
3	Slippys Quest	7	15	16	82	46.7	19.5
*4	Adraville Bridge	36	78	115	513	46.1	22.4
*4	Live Contender	18	39	48	211	46.1	22.7
6	I'm Slippy	126	274	371	1,944	46.0	19.1
7	Arrow House	21	47	38	194	44.7	19.6
8	Tapwatcher	25	56	64	328	44.6	19.5
*9	Aulton Slippy	11	25	28	141	44.0	19.9
*9	Glencorbry Celt	11	25	23	147	44.0	15.6
*11	Murlens Hawk	14	32	33	192	43.7	17.2
*11	Tlco	7	16	11	58	43.7	18.9
*13	Castlelyons Gem	9	21	55	202	42.8	27.2
*13	Early Vocation	9	21	12	92	42.8	13.0
*13	Manorville Magic	15	35	32	205	42.8	15.6
16	Easy And Slow	8	19	35	132	42.1	26.5
17	Daleys Gold	63	151	236	1,096	41.7	21.5
18	Carters Lad	20	49	61	288	40.8	21.2
19	Flashy Sir	34	84	111	606	40.5	18.3
20	Macs Lock	11	28	29	149	39.3	19.5
21	Manorville Major	40	102	140	696	39.2	20.1
22	Double Bid	23	59	50	370	39.0	13.5
23	Ardfert Sean	32	84	133	579	38.1	23.0
24	Glen Park Dancer	17	45	49	289	37.8	16.9
25	Druids Johno	20	53	67	337	37.7	19.9
26	Randy	19	51	49	316	37.2	15.5
27	Satharn Beo	36	97	85	499	37.1	17.0
*28	Flag Star	7	19	43	125	36.8	34.4
*28	Galtymore Lad	7	19	11	70	36.8	15.7
30	Skelligs Tiger	45	123	87	636	36.6	13.7
31	Murlens Slippy	57	156	150	874	36.5	17.2
*32	Aghadown Timmy	8	22	15	124	36.4	12.1
*32	Manorville Sand	16	44	40	233	36.4	17.2
34	Curryhills Gara	18	50	32	236	36.0	13.5
35	Phantom Flash	21	59	67	391	35.6	17.1
*36	Carmels Prince	11	31	29	159	35.5	18.2
*36	Lartigue Note	11	31	37	187	35.5	19.8
38	Alpine Minister	7	20	11	100	35.0	11.0
39	Whisper Wishes	56	165	181	1,113	33.9	16.3
*40	Catunda Flame	6	18	13	98	33.3	13.3
*40	Hello Blackie	5	15	13	85	33.	15.3
*40	Kyle Jack	24	72	89	423	33.3	21.0
*40	Nightpark Lad	6	18	20	123	33.3	16.3
44	Druids Lodge	18	57	60	342	31.6	17.5
45	Greenpark Fox	66	211	203	1,109	31.3	18.3
46	Manx Treasure	5	16	7	57	31.2	12.3
*47	Darragh Commet	6	20	20	97	30.0	20.6

Focus on BREEDING

		Winners	Runners	Wins	Runs	Winners/Runners	%Wins/Runs
*47	Fly Cruiser	15	50	40	288	30.0	13.9
49	Willie Joe	8	27	19	144	29.6	13.2
50	Leaders Best	12	41	47	207	29.3	22.7
51	Waltham Abbey ..	17	59	39	256	28.8	15.2
52	Airmount Grand	20	70	61	407	28.6	15.0
53	Westmead Havoc	17	61	40	312	27.9	12.8
54	Deenside Spark	14	51	45	211	27.4	21.3
55	Bold Rabbit	7	26	25	137	26.9	18.2
*56	Ballyregan Bob	5	19	12	109	26.3	11.0
*56	Fearless Champ	5	19	5	55	26.3	9.1
*56	Kildare Ash	15	57	34	229	26.3	14.8
*59	Lodge Frince	8	31	22	175	25.8	12.6
*59	Ravage Again	8	31	14	145	25.8	9.6
61	Lyons Dean	6	24	24	128	25.0	18.7
62	Slippy Blue	12	49	36	233	24.5	15.4
63	Moneypoint Coal .	7	29	22	163	24.1	13.5
64	Green Gorse	5	21	6	72	23.8	8.3
65	Balalika	15	66	30	275	22.7	10.9
66	Fearless Ace	6	28	22	114	21.4	19.3
67	Westmead Claim	6	29	24	115	20.7	20.9
68	Coalbrook Tiger	7	34	20	163	20.6	12.3
69	Soda Fountain	3	16	8	56	18.7	14.3
*70	Ballinderry Ash	4	24	4	75	16.7	5.3
*70	Dereen Star	3	18	8	79	16.7	10.1
*70	Moral Support	7	42	29	215	16.7	13.5
73	Dukes Lodge	3	21	16	90	14.3	17.8
74	Westmead Harry	2	18	2	52	11.1	3.8

'Runs' includes runs by winners and non-winners

Table 2: Ranked by wins/runs strike rate

		Winners	Runners	Wins	Runs	Winners/Runners	%Wins/Runs
1	Flag Star	7	19	43	125	36.8	34.4
2	Castlelyons Gem .	9	21	55	202	42.8	27.2
3	Easy And Slow ..	8	19	35	132	42.1	26.5
4	Slaneyside Hare	20	40	110	423	50.0	26.0
5	Ballyard Hoffrnan	8	17	34	139	47.0	24.5
6	Ardfert Sean	32	84	133	579	38.1	23.0
*7	Leaders Best	12	41	47	207	29.3	22.7
*7	Live Contender	18	39	48	211	46.1	22.7
9	Adraville Bridge	36	78	115	513	46.1	22.4
10	Daleys Gold	63	151	236	1,096	41.7	21.5
11	Deenside Spark	14	51	45	211	27.4	21.3
12	Carters Lad	20	49	61	288	40.8	21.2
13	Kyle Jack	24	72	89	423	33.3	21.0
14	Westmead Claim	6	29	24	115	20.7	20.9
15	Darragh Commet	6	20	20	97	30.0	20.6
16	Manorville Major	40	102	140	696	39.2	20.1
*17	Aulton Slippy	11	25	28	141	44.0	19.9
*17	Druids Johno	20	53	67	337	37.7	19.9

Focus on BREEDING

		Winners	Runners	Wins	Runs	Winners/Runners	%Wins/Runs
19	Lartigue Note	11	31	37	187	35.5	19.8
20	Arrow House	21	47	38	194	44.7	19.6
*21	Macs Lock	11	28	29	149	39.3	19.5
*21	Slippys Quest	7	15	16	82	46.7	19.5
*21	Tapwatcher	25	56	64	328	44.6	19.5
24	Fearless Ace	6	28	22	114	21.4	19.3
25	I'm Slippy	126	274	371	1,944	46.0	19.1
26	Tico	7	16	11	58	43.7	18.9
27	Lyons Dean	6	24	24	128	25.0	18.7
*28	Flashy Sir	34	84	111	606	40.5	18.3
*28	Greenpark Fox	66	211	203	1,109	31.3	18.3
*30	Bold Rabbit	7	26	25	137	26.9	18.2
*30	Carmels Prince	11	31	29	159	35.5	18.2
32	Dukes Lodge	3	21	16	90	14.3	17.8
33	Druids Lodge	18	57	60	342	31.6	17.5
*34	ManorvilleSand	16	44	40	233	36.4	17.2
*34	Murlens Hawk	14	32	33	192	43.7	17.2
*34	Murlens Slippy	57	156	150	874	36.5	17.2
37	Phantom Flash	21	59	67	391	35.6	17.1
38	Satharn Beo	36	97	85	499	37.1	17.0
39	Glen Park Dancer	17	45	49	289	37.8	16.9
*40	Nightpark Lad	6	18	20	123	33.3	16.3
*40	Whisper Wishes ..	56	165	181	1,113	33.9	16.3
42	Galtymore Lad	7	19	11	70	36.8	15.7
*43	Glencorbry Celt . .	11	25	23	147	44.0	15.6
*43	Manorville Magic	15	35	32	205	42.8	15.6
45	Randy	19	51	49	316	37.2	15.5
46	Slippy Blue	12	49	36	233	24.5	15.4
47	Hello Blackie	5	15	13	85	33.3	15.3
48	Waltham Abbey	17	59	39	256	28.8	15.2
49	Airmount Crand	20	70	61	407	28.6	15.0
50	Kildare Ash	15	57	34	229	26.3	14.8
51	Soda Fountain	3	16	8	56	18.7	14.3
52	Fly Cruiser	15	50	40	288	30.0	13.9
53	Skelligs Tiger	45	123	87	636	36.6	13.7
*54	Curryhills Gara	18	50	32	236	36.0	13.5
*54	Double Bid	23	59	50	370	39.0	13.5
*54	Moneypoint Coal	7	29	22	163	24.1	13.5
*54	Moral Support .	7	42	29	215	16.7	13.5
58	Catunda Flame	6	18	13	98	33.3	13.3
59	Willie Joe	8	27	19	144	29.6	13.2
60	Early Vocation	9	21	12	92	42.8	13.0
61	Westmead Havoc	17	61	40	312	27.9	12.8
62	Lodge Prince	8	31	22	175	25.8	12.6
*63	Coalbrook Tiger .	7	34	20	163	20.6	12.3
*63	Manx Treasure	5	16	7	57	31.2	12.3
65	Aghadown Timmy	8	22	15	124	36.4	12.1
*66	Alpine Minister .	7	20	11	100	35.0	11.0
*66	Ballyregan Bob	5	19	12	109	26.3	11.0
68	Balalika	15	66	30	275	22.7	10.9
69	Dereen Star	3	18	8	79	16.7	10.1
70	Ravage Again	8	31	14	145	25.8	9.6

NGRC Greyhound Racing Yearbook 1995

Professional Bodies

NATIONAL GREYHOUND RACING CLUB
24/28 Oval Road, London NW1 7DA
Telephone: 0171-267 9256
Fax: 0171-482 1023

THE National Greyhound Racing Club (NGRC) is the judicial body responsible for the discipline and conduct of greyhound racing at all major greyhound tracks. The NGRC is a member of the Central Council of Physical Recreation together with the controlling bodies of all other major sports in Britain.

Preserving the Integrity of the Sport

After the introduction of greyhound racing as a spectator sport in June 1926, its popularity grew rapidly. The need for central control soon became apparent and the NGRC came into being on 1 January 1928.

The Club's main objectives have stood the test of time. As in 1928, its prime role is still the orderly conduct and operation of greyhound racing so that the public is protected from cheating and dishonest practices. The NGRC continues to set the standard, and administer the code of rules for all the tracks which race under its banner.

The Power of the Stewards

Those appointed as NGRC Stewards usually meet twice a month and must be independent persons of recognised standing and integrity who are unconnected with the promotion or management of greyhound racing.

The Stewards act as the disciplinary arm of the NGRC and it is they who draw up and amend the Rules of Racing. The first Stewards, when drafting the rules took into account the principles upon which the Jockey Clubs Rules of Racing were based. It is a testimony to the sound judgement of the NGRC Stewards in the early years of the Club that their Rules still provide the bedrock for the modern-day sport of NGRC greyhound racing.

Among the wide disciplinary powers of the Stewards is the right to disqualify or warn off, suspend or withdraw a licence from any person who infringes the Rules of Racing. They can also disqualify any greyhound which they decide has been connected with fraudulent practice.

In addition to the NGRC Stewards there are seven full-time Area Stipendiary Stewards each of whom has responsibility for a region of the country. They inspect all licensed premises and supervise the duties of all licensed track officials, trainers arid kennel staff. They are also empowered to hold local inquiries an can impose penalties subject to limits and report their findings to the NGRC Stewards.

Professional Bodies

Continued from page 356

Security of Racecourses

An important aspect of the work of the NGRC is the co-ordination of security around the country, watched over by a Head of Security who is a former senior police officer. The services of the Horseracing Forensic Laboratory at Newmarket are retained for the analysis of samples taken from the greyhounds both before and after races.

A team of NGRC security (sampling) officers visits tracks in all parts of the country at random to obtain samples from greyhounds engaged in races or trials and these are sent to Newmarket for analysis, Valuable financial Support is provided by the British Greyhound Racing Fund.

Greyhound Welfare

In 1974 the Retired Greyhound Trust was established to assist owners and trainers at NGRC tracks to find homes for retired greyhounds when their own efforts had been unsuccessful.

The Retired Greyhound Trust was awarded charitable status and is the only charity of its kind in the world. The Trust has found homes for more than 10,000 retired greyhounds.

Financing the NGRC

Governments have persisted in denying to greyhound racing a proper Statutory funding of the sport as enjoyed by horse racing. The NGRC executive continue to support the British Greyhound Racing Board in its vigorous pursuit of a levy for greyhound racing based on the £1.7 billion of off-course betting on NGRC-registered greyhounds.

The NGRC is financed primarily by its registration and licence fees but in the past two years much of the enhanced drug testing programme has been financed by the BGRF. The NGRC issues annual licences to racecourses, officials, trainers and kennel staff and keeps a register of all owners and greyhounds All persons licensed or registered agree to be bound by the NGRC Rules of Racing.

NATIONAL GREYHOUND RACING CLUB OFFICIALS AND COMMITTEES

Executive

Archie Newhouse (Chief Executive/Secretary)
Frank Melville (Head of Racing)
David A Davies (Head of Security)
Colin Betteridge (Registrar and Computer Supervisor)

Professional Bodies

KEEPING UP WITH THE GAME: Geoffrey Thomas (right) and Archie Newhouse, both tireless and long-serving members of greyhound racing's governing bodies.

Stipendiary Stewards

Peter Field (South and West)
Les Halverson (North of Thames)
Irene McNally (South of Thames)
Jack Robinson (Midlands)
Adrian Smith (East Anglia)
Eric Vose (North and)
Karen Vose (Scotland)

NGRC Disciplinary & Management Committee (The Stewards)

Mr W Cooke (Chairman)
Mr J L W Crittall, BVSc MRCVS
Mr D A Brooks
Mr A C Hall
Mr J H C Nicholson
Mr J Taylor, OBE
Mr A H Newhouse (Secretary)

NGRC COMPLAINTS PROCEDURE
Stage One

An NGRC licence holder is alleged to be in breach of Rules of acing far a variety of reasons. For example: A greyhound finds or loses what is deemed to be an unacceptable amount of time, or a positive analysis of a drug test carried out on a greyhound in a trainer's care.

Professional Bodies

Stage Two
Local stewards conduct a preliminary investigation and if considered necessary request a local inquiry to be held by the Area Stipendiary Steward. The Area Stipendiary Steward has the authority to call for a local inquiry on any matter Such inquiries are usually held at the racecourse premises.

Stage Three
A local inquiry is held at a racecourse by the Area Stipendiary Steward The Area Stipendiary Steward may deal with the matter directly within limits of penalty unless:

(i) The defendant opts to go before the Stewards in London.
(ii) There is an allegation of breach of certain of the Rules of acing over which the Area Stipendiary Steward is not empowered to adjudicate In such circumstances, it will be referred to the NGRC Stewards.

Stage Four
The Area Stipendiary Steward reports to NGRC secretary. Either:

(i) the result of the local inquiry or
(ji) that he/she is referring the matter to the NGRC for inquiry in London.

All papers and statements taken will then be sent to NGRC head office.

Stage Five
Notice is given to the defendant of an NGRC Stewards inquiry in London and he/she is advised of rights and procedures.

NGRC VETERINARY & SCIENTIFIC PANEL

Mr J L W Crittall, BVSc MRCVS (Chairman)
Mr L N Anderson, MRCVS
Mr C H Chandler
Mr W Cooke   Mr D A Davies
Mr N Dunnett, C.Chem. FRSC   Mr F Melville
Mr A H Newhouse   Mr A J Westaway, MRCVS

This important committee provides a link between the British Greyhound Racing Board, the NGRC, racecourse veterinary surgeons and the Horseracing Forensic Laboratory. Problems relating to drug testing, research, veterinary and all integrity matters are discussed and recommendations go to the Stewards.

Inoculations
All greyhounds in licensed NGRC kennels must have inoculations against:

Professional Bodies

1   Distemper.
2.   Viral Hepatitis.
a.   Leptospira Canicola.
4.   Leptospira Leterhaenorrhagiae.
5.   Parvo virus.

Booster inoculations are required to be administered every 12 months.

NGRC TRAINERS

PROFESSIONAL TRAINERS. Licensed to train greyhounds in any ownership. The majority of professional trainers are attached to an NGRC track and are under contract to supply greyhounds for graded racing. Kennel accommodation and security must come up to the standards stipulated by the NGRC.
Fee £65 including one year's subscription to the NGRC Calendar.

OWNER TRAINERS: Licensed to train greyhounds in the ownership of themselves, their wife/husband or their children over the age of 18. A maximum of 12 racing greyhounds permitted. Greyhounds may be owned in partnership with up to three other named persons, but the owner trainer must own at least 2 per cent of each greyhound. Kennels and security must be to NGRC standards.
Fee £65 including one year's subscription to the NGRC Calendar

PERMIT TRAINERS: Licensed to train a maximum of four racing greyhounds for racing at permit racecourses only Ownership provisions are the same as for owner trainers.
Fee £20 (non inclusive of NGRC Calendar).

NGRC TRIALS

QUALIFYING TRIALS: To be accepted for grading at an NGRC full member track a greyhound must run three trials which satisfy the racing manager. Two of the trials must be run with at least two other greyhounds.
WEIGHT VARIATION: If a greyhound's weight varies by more than one kilogram from the weight shown in the last trial or race recorded in the identity Book it will be withdrawn from racing and must run at least one trial before it races subsequently.
WITHDRAWALS: If a greyhound is withdrawn from racing by the local stewards the greyhound in mot instances would have to run a satisfactory trial before it races subsequently.
RUNNING OUT: if a greyhound deviates from the defined racecourse during a trial or race, even if it returns and crosses the winning line, it will be disqualified from that race/trial ans will be required to run a tiral before racing subsequently.
IN SEASON: A bitch may not trial or racer after coming into season, for a minimum period of 10 weeks. If a bitch has been spayed, whelped a litter or had a season suppressed, the racing manager must be informed and the details entered in the Identity Book.
FIGHTING: This means aggressive interference by a greyhound in a

Professional Bodies

race or a trial. The dog will be disqualified by local stewards and reported to the NGRC and must run three clearing trials on three separate days before it can be reinstated. The clearing trial must be run with at least three other registered greyhounds of approximately equal grade.

If a greyhound is disqualified a second time the NGRC Stewards may declare it a Confirmed Fighter. This means it will not be allowed to run on any NGRC licensed racecourse.

NGRC REGISTRATIONS

Every greyhound that races on an NGRC track must be registered in a recognised Greyhound Stud Book.

British breds must be registered at the litter stage within one month of whelping and at a later stage each greyhound must be registered individually

A greyhound's name must have no more than 16 letters. Spaces between words or punctuation count as one letter. An owner can register a prefix which may be used in connection with all greyhounds running in his or her ownership.

A greyhound is not allowed to trial or race on an NGRC track until it is 15 months old. At this stage an Identity Book is issued and the greyhound Is marked up by a racecourse official. The book will include details of sex, colour, earmarkings and inoculations. It will record every trial and race of the greyhounds career and the name of the licensed trainer who has charge of the dog.

NGRC FEES

Professional and owner trainer licence £65 (including Calendar)
Owner trainer £65 (including Calendar):
Permit trainer £20 (Calendar optional extra).

Racecourse official £6:
Head kennel hand £8:
Kennel hand £6:
Parader £6:
Permit paraders £3.

Kennel inspection fee for new trainers £65 (including £5 rule book).
Transfer from owner trainer to professional £25.

Earmarking 1-4 pups £25: five or more in litter £5 per pup.

Calendar £25 annual subscription.

Registration of greyhound £20 (per single). Thereafter £5 each additional part-owner.

Permit registration £11 (per single owner). Thereafter £3 each additional part-owner.

Transfer of greyhound from permit to fully licensed track £10 (per

Professional Bodies

single owner). Thereafter £2 each additional part-owner. Maximum of four part-owners.

Syndicate registration (without ICC transfer) £50.

Company registration £25.

NGRC change of greyhound's name £25.

BRITISH GREYHOUND RACING BOARD

The Board came into being in April 1979 as an elected representative body to represent the commercial, political and welfare interests of greyhound racing under NGRC rules. It has been successful in promoting a large number of legislative amendments to remove the statutory restrictions which have hindered greyhound racing since the 1934 laws were enacted governing betting and gaming.

The ten years since 1985 have seen greyhound racing freed from the shackles which bound it for half a century involving restrictions on the number of days a track might race, deductions permitted from totalisator betting, removal of on-course taxation, improvements to on-course bookmaker betting facilities, moves to introduce track-to-track betting, revision of accountancy procedures and much more.

The 1991 report by the Home Office to the Government on the financing of greyhound racing, which was spawned by the Select Committee inquiry into the sport, accepted many of the points made in the British Greyhound Racing's Board written and oral submissions and this led to the Chancellor of the Exchequer at that time including greyhound racing as a recipient of the quarter of a per cent deduction he made from off-course betting duty to help support the horserace statutory levy.

The Government, for the first time, thus recognised greyhound racing's large contribution to off-course betting revenues and this brought about the formation of the British Greyhound Racing Fund, on which the sport is represented by six directors of the British Greyhound Racing Board plus its chief executive, together with six representatives drawn from the off-course betting industry. The Board believes it has also opened the door for the introduction of a statutory betting levy for greyhound racing in the foreseeable future.

Functions of the BGRB
The BGRB exists to promote the interests of greyhound racing in England, Scotland and Wales by:
    *Giving legislative and public bodies and other facilities to confer with and ascertain the views of persons engaged in or otherwise interested in greyhound racing;
    *Actively seeking improvements through Parliament in the laws governing the sport;

Professional Bodies

*Actively seeking improvements through Parliament in the laws governing the sport;
 *Promoting or opposing legislative and other measures affecting or likely to affect greyhound racing;
 *Providing a vehicle to consult with the NGRC over changes and improvements to the NGRC Rules of Racing and the levels of licence fees and registration fee charged by the NGRC;
 *Widening the public knowledge of greyhound racing; and
 *Improving the care and welfare of the greyhound.

Relationships with the NGRC

The NGRC acts as greyhound racing's police force, judiciary, registrar and licensing authority. The BGRB acts as the sport's commercial manager, parliamentary consultants, publicity managers and advisers. Although their functions are separate, they share the same full-time administrative staff and operate from the same London offices.

Membership of BGRB

The Chairman and Deputy Chairman of the BGRB are not permitted any direct or indirect financial or commercial interest in greyhound racing. The present Chairman 0£ the Board is Lord Newall who succeeded Lord Mancroft on 1st July 1985.

Also on the Board are the Senior Steward and Chief Executive. Elected representatives include five members of the NGRC Racecourse Promoter Association and one representative each of greyhound breeders and professional trainers and two greyhound owners.

Elections for the BGRB and for the Greyhound Consultative Body, a forum for consideration and discussion of any matter affecting greyhound racing which submits its recommendations direct to the Board, are held every two years. All relevant interests are given the opportunity of nominating qualified persons. A ballot is held when there are more nominations than vacancies.

Professional Bodies

THE BOARD OF DIRECTORS
(at January 1995)

Lord Newall	Chairman
Mr E W Cooke	Senior Steward NGRC
Mr C Chandler	
Mr W King	)
Mr K Wilde	) representing NGRC Racecourse
Mr C Osborne	) Promoters Ltd
Mr J Carter	)
Mrs L Mullins	representing NGRC Breeders
Mr S R Milligan	representing NGRC Trainers
Mr R V Hall	) representing NGRC Owners
Mr A Hammond	)
Mr A H Newhouse	Chief Executive
Mr G C Thomas	Executive Director

GREYHOUND CONSULTATIVE BODY
Consists of the members of the Board of Directors, plus:

Mr J J Sherry	representing NGRC licensed Trainers
Mr R Gilling	representing Breeders
Mr D Tyler	representing On-Course Bookmakers
Mr D Anderson MRCVS	representing NGRC licensed Veterinary Surgeons
Mr F Melville	NGRC Senior Stipendiary Steward
Mr D Poole	National Organiser, Retired Greyhound Trust

BGRB FINANCE AND GENERAL PURPOSES COMMITTEE

Lord Newall (Chairman)
Mr C H Chandler
Mr A H Newhouse
Mr C Osborne
Mr E W Cooke
Mr J H C Nicholson
Mr G C Thomas

GREYHOUND RACING INFORMATION TECHNOLOGY COMITTEE

Mr G C Thomas (Chairman)
Mr C Betteridge
Mr C Bissett
Mr S Franklin
Mr E Osborne
Mr P G T Shotton
Mr C Bissett
Mr C H Chandler
Mr F Melville
Mr R J Rowe

Professional Bodies

OPEN RACE CALENDAR PLANNING COMMITTEE
Mr F Melville (Chairman)
Mr C J Blake
Mr W Hiscock
Mr S Rea
Mr K Wilde
Mr C H Chandler
Mr C Betteridge
Mr R J Rowe
Mr G C Thomas

BRGB PRIZEMONEY COMMITTEE

Mr G C Thomas (Chairman)
Mr C H Chandler
Mr B Gilling
Mr A Hammond
Mr P Milligan
Mr M Glennerster
Mr R Hall
Mr F Melville
Mr R J Rowe

TRUSTEES OF THE RETIRED GREYHOUND TRUST

Mr E W Cooke (Chairman)
Miss J Beurner
Lord Newall
Mr R J Rowe
Mr C H Chandler
Mr A H Newhouse

RGT MANAGEMENT GROUP

Mr R J Rowe (Chairman)
Mr D Poole (National Organiser)
Miss J Beumer
Mr C H Chandler
Mrs A Dockray
Mr F Melville
Mr G C Thomas
Mrs M Brown
Mr E W Cooke
Mrs H Lawrence
Mr A H Newhouse
Mr A J Westaway MRCVS

BGRB/RGT STRATEGY GROUP

Mr G C Thomas (Chairman)
Mr C H Chandler
Mr W Hiscock
Mr S Rea
Mr R J Rowe
Mr S Franklin
Mr D Poole
Mrs I Reptowskl
Mr A J Westaway MRCVS

NATIONAL INTERTRACK COMMITTEE

Mr F Melville (Chairman)
Mr C; Bissett
Mr C Feltham
Mr W Hiscock
Mr G C Thomas
Mr C H Chandler
Mr S Franklin
Mr R J Rowe

NGRC Greyhound Racing Yearbook 1995

Professional Bodies

THE GREYHOUND STUD BOOK
16 Clocktower Mews, Newmarket, Suffolk CB8 8LL
Phone: 0638 667381. Fax: 0638 669224

THE Greyhound Stud Book was founded in 1882 by the National Coursing Club as the original breed register of the greyhound. From that date, only registered greyhounds were permitted to run at coursing meetings affiliated to the NCC. When track racing started in this country and the National Greyhound Racing Club was formed, the NGRC insisted that all greyhounds running on its tracks should be registered in a national stud book, and so in this country the greyhound breed has been closed effectively since 1882.

In 1923, the Irish Coursing Club was formed and established its own stud book. The stud books of Britain, Ireland, the United States of America, Australia and New Zealand make up the International Alliance of Greyhound Registries. To ensure the purity of the breed, these stud books permit transfers of greyhounds only between themselves. No greyhounds are permitted to enter the four stud books from outside sources.

The Greyhound Stud Book records are fully computerised. Greyhounds are identified by earmarking at three months after the litter has been registered within a month of being whelped. Greyhounds can be named only after earmarking. Identity cards are issued after the greyhound has been named and the greyhound has been marked up.

The Greyhound Stud Book keeps the only complete record of greyhounds bred in this country. Its ability to trace from an earmark within seconds the identity of a greyhound has proved of enormous help to the Retired Greyhound Trust and other animal welfare organisations.

The Stud Book itself is published in September each year, and is recognised as the essential handbook for all greyhound breeders. As well as the registrations for the relevant period, it includes articles on racing, coursing, and breeding, as well as information on stud dogs, extended pedigrees of champion greyhounds, and breeding statistics.

Charles Blanning Keeper of the Stud Book

GREYHOUND STUD BOOK REGISTRATIONS

Year	Total Registrations	Re-Registrations	Litters
1992	6984	1297	880
1993	6262	1256	867

STUD DOGS

Every sire shall be registered annually at a fee of £20 before the first mating takes place. Form No 4 for this purpose remains unchanged.

Professional Bodies

MATING, VETERINARY & WHELPING FORMS

ON RECEIPT of a stud dog registration, a supply of Mating, Veterinary & Whelping forms in four parts: 1a, 1b, 1c and 1d, will be issued. (Part 1a) is the top copy and includes the mating certificate. This shall be completed by the owner or authorised agent (as previously notified to the "Keeper") and returned to the "Keeper" within FOURTEEN DAYS of the date of mating with the fee of £5. No litter will be considered for registration without this certificate. (Part 1b) is a duplicate copy of Part 1a which shall be retained by the owner of the stud dog. (Part 1c) is the top copy of a register of whelping and includes a triplicate copy of the mating certificate and incorporates a top copy of the Veterinary Certificate which shall be completed by the Veterinary Surgeon who will retain the whole of Part 1c. (Part 1d) is a duplicate copy of Part 1c and includes a quadruplicate copy of the mating certificate (Part 1a). The whole of Part 1d shall be completed by the breeder and returned to the "Keeper" with the fee of £8 within one month of the date of whelping.

REGISTRATION OF NAME

Breeders of registered litters will be supplied with GREEN forms for the naming of the progeny.

The BREEDER is required to complete the colour, sex and breeding before signing as "breeder" and handing to the prospective owner for completion. The OWNER must select a name, plus several alternatives, sign the form, personally, and return to the "Keeper" as early as possible with the appropriate fee.

Owners who submit valid applications will be issued with the formal Certificate of Registration, Naming and Identification. Fines will be levied against applicants for registration of progeny aged over one year.

EAR MARKING

All litters must be earmarked and will only be registered if the registration form is accompanied by a completed earmarking application form.

REGISTRATION OF IDENTIFICATION

The DIAGRAMS on the reverse side of the WHITE CERTIFICATE must be completed in full detail by a Racing, Kennel or Training Official and returned to the "Keeper" within ONE YEAR of the date of whelping. The details supplied will be incorporated in an OFFICIAL IDENTITY CARD and given the SEAL of the GREYHOUND STUD BOOK.

OFFICIAL IDENTITY CARD

The Official Identity Card is in book form and includes: 1. Certificate of Registration, Naming and Identification. 2. An official record of Transfer of Ownership.

TRANSFER OF OWNERSHIP

EVERY transfer of ownership must be recorded in the "GREYHOUND

Professional Bodies

STUD BOOK". A BLUE Re-registration and Transfer form is required for this purpose and must be signed by the last registered owner in the presence of a witness. The form must be returned to the "Keeper" together with the IDENTITY CARD and appropriate fee for endorsement. On receipt of the IDENTITY CARD the new owner must sign the Identity Card where indicated.

GSB COSTS

Registration of Mating
£5.00 within 14 days of mating taking place.
Additional fines thereafter of £10.00 for each (or part month) over the 14 days limit.

Registration of Litter
£8.00	within one month of the date of whelping.
£20.00	thereafter, up to three months of whelping.
£10.00	to register breeder other than owner of the dam in addition to the registration fee.

Registration of Naming
(including £2 for subsequent issue of an Official Identity Card).
£10.00	Up to one year of age.
£17.00	thereafter, up to two years of age.
£32.00	over two years minimum of age (plus additional fines if permission to register is granted by the Standing Committee).

Transfer of Ownership
£10.00	within 28 days of change of ownership.
£15.00	thereafter, up to 6 months.
£20.00	after six months.

Stud Dogs
£20.00 annually, between 1 January and 31 December.

Transfer of Greyhound from Irish Greyhound Stud book
(or from International Alliance)
£10.00 for breeding or coursing purposes.

Partnerships
£4.00 per owner, in addition to registration fee, to be paid on each registration.

Authorised Agent
£10.00 annually, between 1 January and 31 December.

Duplicate Certificates
£5.00 each.

Duplicate Official Identity Cards
£10.00 each (issued at the discretion of the keeper).

Prefix
£25.00 For the duration of five years.

Extended or Export Pedigrees
£5.00 each.

Company Names
£25.00 annually, between 1 January and 31 December.

IRISH Directory

Clonmel

Davis Road, Clonmel. Co Tipperary.
Telephone number: (052) 21118.
(Code from UK 010 35352)

How to get there: Track is on the Waterford Road, going out of town.
Trainers (attached): M. O'Donnell. M. O'Sullivan, D. Stanbridge. F.Black, S. Bourke, A. Coyle. P.Brady. K. Barry, M. Fox. F. Wade, J.Heelan, A. Wade, G. McKenna, J.Reddan.
Race nights: Monday and Thursday (8.15 pm).
Trial sessions: Friday morning, including unofficial trials.

Distances: 300yds. 525yds. 550yds, 730yds. Grading times: 300yds: 17 80; 525yds:31.30.
Number of greyhounds per race: Six.
Surface: Sand.
Type of hare: Two wheel drive system.
Circumference of track: 593yds.
Width of track: 22ff.
Layout of the track and how it runs: Big galloping track. A good test for a greyhound.
Usual method of track preparation: An 8ft rake and roller attached to the back of a tractor prepares the surface. The track is raked and rolled after every trial and race session.
Winning traps: Favours trap one.

Major competitions:
National Meeting Festival ot Racing, February.
National Breeders Produce Stakes (525yds), April/May.
Munster Puppy Cup, October.

Number of bookmakers: 17 at busy times of year, decreasing to eight.
Totalisator: Win, place and forecast.
Timing: Automatic timing.
Facilities: Chromatography testing, vet in attendance, kennels for 54 greyhounds, car park for 200 vehicles, two bars, stand, video replay.

Other activities at the stadium: Horse show (June), dog show (August), Boy Scout day (August), Circus (May-September).

IRISH Directory

Track Records

300yds	**Greenpark Fox**	16.12	1-2-89
525yds	**Arran Court Duke**	28.38	13-4-89
550yds	**Meet Me Halfway**	29.80	1-8-89
730yds	**Mid Clare Lass**	40.88	3-2-90
1025yd	**Cute Way**	59.34	30-1-89

Principal Race Results, 1994

Event	Dist	Date	Winner	Breeding
Barney O'Connor Memorial Stk	525	1-Feb	Move On Passion	Whisper Wishes-Burnpark Vera
Owner: Rory Ryan, Limerick				Time 29.53 Prize £ 1,000
Airmount Flash Open 525	525	6-Oct	Murlens Link	Deenside Spark-Murlens Dale
C O'Sullivan, Dublin				29.38 2,000
Slaneyside Hare Stake	525	9-Jun	Hit The Hay	Hit The Lid-Exile Energy
George Walker, Eng				29.50 750
Stop Inn 30.20 Stake	525	13-Feb	Spit It Out	Phantom Flash-Ivalog
T. Condon, Newcastlewest				28.91 1,000
Murlens Post Stake	525	15-Aug	Glandore Girl	Fire Height Boy-Rose Bloom
Mrs M O'Connell, Charleville				29.88 900
Ladbroke Unraced Stake	525	15-Aug	Spare The Rod	Murlens Slippy-Come Calling
Miss Carey Harney, Clonmel				29.64 650
Kasco Supreme Unraced Stks	525	17-Mar	Come On Ranger	Greenpark Fox-Mandies Handbag
J O'Connor, Dungarven				28.64 1,000
Drangan Cross Open Bitch Stk	525	21-Mar	Brooklawn Vickie	Greenpark Fox-Shenick Lady
S Locke-Hart, Eng				29.08 700
Moral Right Stk	525	21-Apr	Mystery Novelist	Whisper Wit-Merry Song
Pat Dalton, Cashel				28.84 500
Greyhound Bar Stk	525	23-Jan	Generous Jet	Castleyons Gem-Mogeely Dawn
D O'Dwyer, Golden				29.58 1,000
Munster Puppy Cup	525	23-Oct	Local Manx	Manx Treasure-Local Pegaleen
R Leahy, Kilkenny				29.46 1,200
Ballinderry Ash Stk	525	27-Oct	Petal	Adraville Bridge-Mollifrend Jam
D Wren, Tarbert				29.38 700
Hit The Lid Stk	525	28-Mar	Brookpark Rory	Whisper Wishes-Burnpark Vera
Miss T Murphy, Cork				29.14 1,000
Country Pork Nat Breed Prod. Stk	525	28-Apr	Come On Ranger	Greenpark Fox-Mandies Handbag
J O'Connor, Dungarven				28.82 8,000
Come On Ranger Stk	525	28-Apr	Just Pride	Skelligs Tiger-Lauragh Pride
Mrs A Bourke, Clonmel				29.58 900
Country Pork Cons Prod. Stk	525	29-Sep	Murlens Park	Greenpark Fox-Murlens Ruby
J Murphy, Waterford				29.16 800
Princess Bar Stk	525	30-Jan	Slick Maid	Skelligs Tiger-Slick Irene
L & T Butler, Enniscorthy				29.26 1,000

IRISH Directory

Cork

Western Road, Cork.
Telephone number: (021) 543013/543095.
Code trom UK (010 35321)

How to get there: No. 8 bus from city centre.
Owner: Bord na gCon.
Racing manager: Noel Holland.
Race nights: Monday, Wednesday and Saturday.
Trial sessions: Thursday morning, Wednesday after racing.

Distances: 300yds, 525yds, 525yds, 700yds, 745yds, 970yds.
Grading times: 525yds: 31.50; puppies 300yds: 17.75.
Number of greyhounds per race: Six.
Surface: Grass straights, sanded bends.
Type of hare: Outside McKee Scott.
Circumference of track: 445yds.
Distance to the first bend: 105yds.
Width of track: 15ft 6in.
Layout of the track and how it runs: Tight circuit, fast trappers have the advantage.
Usual method of track preparation: Sand is raked, rolled and watered, grass is rolled.

Major competitions:
    Guinness Trophy (525yds), £4,000, April.
    Irish Laurels (525yds), £15,000, July.
    O'Flynn Memorial (525yds) £3,500, May.

Graded prize money: Top grade £65.
Number of bookmakers: 15.
Totalisator: Computerised tote win, place and forecast.
Timing: Ray timing.
Facilities: Vet in attendance, kennels, bar, refreshment room, glass-fronted stand, video replay.
Other activities at the stadium: Soccer.

IRISH Directory

Track Records

300yds	**Saras Moth**	16.35	29-9-89
525yds	**Live Contender**	28.50	17-11-90
525ydsH	**Race Riot**	29.75	7-7-73
700yds	**Kilcommon Cross**	39.70	14-7-90
745yds	**Experience**	42.80	5-9-81

Principal Race Results, 1994

Event	Dist	Date	Winner	Breeding
Newry Town Open Bitch Stk	525	1-Oct	Woodford Chick	Satharn Beo-Woodford Wish
	Owner: A O'Conner, C Dearing, Kerry			Time 28.96 Prize £ 1,400
The Shandrum Stks	525	3-Sep	Woodford Chick	Satharn Beo-Woodford Wish
	A O'Conner, C Dearing, Kerry			29.48 1,500
Spina Bifida Stk	525	4-Apr	Brownies Bridge	Adraville Bridge-Angelas Delight
	J Dillon, Clonakilty			30.13 500
Hennessy Welding Supplies Stk	525	5-Mar	Knockrour Bruno	Adraville Bridge-Dear Liza
	D Lynch, Aghabullogue			29.50 1,000
ZZ Services Stk	525	6-Aug	Lively Maggie	Kyle Jack-Leeview Jill
	H Ashcroft, Cork			29.28 500
Eugene Carey Stk	525	7-Jun	Marble Joe	Willie Joe-Lissaniskea Gold
	M Buckley, Limerick			29.26 500
Cork GOBA Past Presidents Stk	500	8-Oct	Castleyons Ice	Castleyons Gem-Alans Rose
	B Fitzgerald, Rathcormac			27.88 750
Michael Crowley Cons Laurels	525	9-Jul	Rockhill Boyo	Whisper Wishes-Ballylinch Girl
	T Brennans, Castlemartyr			29.48 500
Michael Crowley Irish Laurels	525	9-Jul	Clounmellane Oak	Ravage Again-Rosehip Joy
	TJK Syndicates, Cork			29.28 10,000
Guinness Trophy	525	10-Apr	Kildrenagh Lad	Macs Lock-Millies Chick
	T Barbour, Galway			29.58 2,000
Macroom Motor Services Stk	525	11-Jun	Emmett Robert	Murlens Slippy-Long Valley Lady
	P McCarthy, Clonakilty			29.24 1,800
Pat Banbury Bookmakers Stk	525	12-Feb	Cottesloe House	Adraville Bridge-Shanavulin Rose
	N Twomey, Cork			31.10 500
Clounmellane Oak Stk	525	12-Oct	Long Valley Star	Murlens Slippy-Longvalley Lady
	D Collins, Cork			29.52 600
Phantom Flash Stk	525	12-Nov	Lochbo Glen	Whisper Wishes-Lochbo Goldie
	M Spillane, Bantry			29.52 700
Triple-A Golden Maverick Stk	525	16-Jul	Marble Joe	Willie Joe-Lissaniskea Gold
	M Buckley, Limerick			29.20 1,500
O'Regan Nat. & Inter Transport Stk	525	20-Aug	Ritas Ash	Ballinderry Ash-Theresas Black
	Miss A Cotter, Mallow			29.47 1,000
Donal O'Brien Bookmakers Stk	525	21-Feb	Faultless Vixen	Greenpark Fox-Tracy Budd
	P Kiely, Cork			30.38 550
Red Mills Stk	525	22-Jan	Chief Commander	Whisper Wishes-Ferndale Class
	P Walsh, Cork			30.24 800
Kasco Stk	525	23-Apl	Newtown Ellen	Never Issued-Newtown Eliza
	Miss J Barry, Youghal			29.64 600
Freewheel Kylo Stk	525	26-Nov	Calder Gold	Tapwatcher-Mystical Jewel
	J O'Connor, Upton			29.36 600
Castle Hotel Stk	525	30-Apl	Costa Nostra	Marcus McGee-One O Two
	T O'Sullivan, Cork			29.12 500
Wilton Bar Stk	525	30-Jul	Supplement	Ardaville Bridge-Under The Clock
	T Brennan, Cork			29.46 500
Pat O'Brien Racing Stk	525	10-Oct	Sweeping Wish	Whisper Wishes-Still Spirit
	B Lynch, Upton			29.10 1,000

IRISH Directory

Derry

Brandywell Stadium, Lonemoor Road, Londonderry.
Telephone number: (0504) 265461.

How to get there: M2 from Belfast.
Owner: Licensed by the Irish Coursing Club.
Racing manager: Michael McLaughlin.
Race nights: Monday and Friday (8 pm)
Trial sessions: Public trials after racing, unrecorded trials Wednesday (6 pm).
Distances: 300yds, 500yds, 525yds, 600yds, 720yds, 920yds, 1020yds.
Grading times: 300yds: 18.00.
Number of greyhounds per race: Six.
Surface: Grass straights, sanded bends from inside to halfway across track.
Type of hare: Outside McKee Scott.
Circumference of track: 420yds.
Distance to the first bend: 90yds.
Layout of the track and how it runs: Tight circuit, suits fast starters.
Usual method of track preparation: Grass cut and rolled, sand watered and levelled.
Number of bookmakers: Seven.
Timing: Hand.
Facilities: Vet in attendance, kennels for 60 greyhounds, car park, refreshment room, covered stand.
Other activities at the stadium: Derry City Football Club.

Track Records

300yds	**Piper's Gold**	16.43	22-9-79
500yds	**Central Supreme**	27.85	24-8-90
525yds	**Westpark City**	29.04	15-6-84
600yds	**Pusher Bird**	33.99	29-7-95
720yds	**Miss Jahousy**	41.20	16-8-85

IRISH Directory

Dundalk

The Ramparts, Dundalk, Co Louth.
Telephone number: (042)34113/35019. Fax: 35019

How to get there: 50 miles north of Dublin, 50 miles south of Belfast. From Dublin turn right at Dundalk Shopping Centre and from Belfast turn left at Court House town centre and take second right hand turn and turn right again.
Owner: Private Limited Company.
Racing manager: John McComish.
Race nights: Monday, Friday and Saturday (8 pm).

Trial sessions: Monday (2-4.15 pm and 945-10.15 pm).
Distances: 320yds, 500yds, 550ydsH, 760yds.
Grading times: 320yds: 18.95, 525yds: 31.75.
Number of greyhounds per race: Six.
Surface: Grass, sanded ends.
Type of hare: Outside McKee Scott.
Circumference of track: 440yds.
Distance to the first bend: 100yds
Width of track: 20ft.
Layout of the track and how it runs: Sharp bends, early pace an advantage.
Usual method of track preparation: Watering in summer and sand is salted in winter.
Winning traps: Traps 1 and 6 all distances.
Major competitions:
   Toals Bookmakers International, 525, August

Graded prize money: Bottom grade: 1st £50, 2nd £20 (entry fee £2), top grade: 1st £100, 2nd £30 (entry fee £5).
Number of bookmakers: 14.
Totalisator: Win, place, forecast, 50p unit.
Timing: Ray timing.
Facilities: Chromatography testing, vet in attendance, kennels for 72 greyhounds, restaurant for 100 covers, three bars, refreshment room, two stands (one glass-fronted), video replay.
Other activities at the stadium: Junior football.

IRISH Directory

Track Records

320yds	**Eden Castle**	17.76	15-8-91
500yds	**First Officer**	28.04	15-8-90
500ydsH	**Tivoli Valley**	29.26	17-8-74
525yds	**Hit The Lid**	29.28	15-8-88
550yds	**Silver Ball**	30.68	15-8-88
550ydsH	**Pick Me**	31.90	30-7-77
760yds	**Rush For Silver**	43.78	19-5-90

DUNDALK

Principal Race Results, 1994

Event	Dist	Date	Winner	Breeding
Dundalk Junior Cup	525	2-Apl	Absolutely Foxed	Greenpark Fox-Quare Wish
	Owner			Time Prize £
	L McCabe, Clones			30.12 1,000
Paddy Glynn Memorial	760	4-Apl	My Jenny	Druids Lodge-Warm Jenny
	P Brady, Waterford			44.90 600
Frank Rooney Memorial	550	4-Apl	Rathcannon Lodge	Druids Lodge-Crown House
	W Frazer, Belfast			31.70 3,000
Michael Kerley Memorial	760	7-May	Windsor Abbey	Waltham Abbey-Miss Fussy
	A Dean, Essex			44.22 500
Gerry Boyle Mem. Sprint	320	11-Jul	Lemonition	Greenpark Fox-Lemon Chill
	T Waite, Carrick			17.82 1,000
Newry 550 Stk	550	11-Jul	Skip Pass	Mis Clare Champion-The Other Lass
	T Smith, Cashell			30.98 2,000
Toals Bookmakers Inter. 525	525	14-Aug	Ayr Flyer	Ardfert Sean-Slaneyside Glory
	Mrs H Halbert, H Roche, Scotland			29.46 7,500
Conomara Sprint Stk	320	19-Jun	Claude Rains	Glenpark Dancer-Meadow Dancer
	R Fulton, Ballygowan			17.90 500
Setanta Open 550	550	19-Jun	Gaelsman	Daleys Gold-No Way Jose
	Miss G Carroll, Dundalk			31.00 750
Bothar Moal Open 525 Stk	525	19-Jun	Ask The Lord	Curryhills Gara-Shes Smashing
	D Nelson, T Cantwell, Navan			29.72 500
Scoti Chriost Rl Open Bitch Stk	525	19-Jun	Mountaylor Fuss	Curryhills Gara-The Other Point
	Miss F O'Donnell, Killenaule			29.70 1,000
Bernard Barry Novice Selling Stk	525	24-Sep	Ice Crystal	Perfect Whisper-Downview Girl
	Miss S Ferran, Belfast			29.68 600
Bernard Barry Novice Sprint	320	27-May	Mossrow Silver	Curryhills Gara-Silver Tip
	K Nugent, Dsarkley			18.38 500

IRISH Directory

Dungannon

Oaks Road, Dungannon, Co Tyrone BT71 4AS.
Telephone number: (08687) 22023/23577.

How to get there: 40 miles from Belfast on the M1. Two minutes from hospital roundabout in the centre of Dungannon.
Owner: M. Mooney.
Racing manager: S. Campbell.
Race nights: Wednesday, Thursday and Saturday (7.30 pm)

Trial sessions: Monday (2-4 pm), Thursdays after racing.
Distances: 297m, 457m, 480m, 503m, 716m.
Grading times: 297m: 18.65; 457m: 29.40.
Number of greyhounds per race: Six.
Surface: Sand.
Type of hare: Outside Sumner.
Circumference of track: 485yds.
Distance to the first bend: From 525yd traps: 75 yds.
Width of track: 25ft.
Layout of the track and how it runs: Long straights, generally benefits inside runners.
Usual method of track preparation: Raked, rolled, and watered.
Graded prize money: £33 per race.
Number of bookmakers: 7.
Totalisator: Straight and forecast.
Timing: Hand timing
Facilities: Bar, vet can be contacted by phone if not present, kennels for 60 greyhounds, car park for 250 vehicles, snack bar, stand, video replay (competition nights only).

Track Records

297m	**Hard Ecu**	17.27	17-10-91
349m	**Belmont Villa**	33.55	13-6-90
457m	**Praidora**	27.50	14-8-91
480m	**Glenhill Pride**	28.70	14-8-91
503m	**Glenhill Pride**	29.75	9-10-91
549m	**Brookvale Pride**	33.57	11-6-81
716m	**Braccan Connie**	43.95	9-10-91

IRISH Directory

Dunmore

*Alexandra Park Avenue, Antrim Road, Belfast BT15 3ED.
Telephone number: Belfast 776232.*

How to get there: Antrim Road and Shore Road from city centre, branch off Alexandra Park Avenue.
Owner: Belfast Sporting and Leisure.
Racing manager: Sam Young.
Race nights: Tuesday, Thursday and Saturday (8 pm).

Trial sessions: Friday (12 noon 2 pm) public, Wednesday and Saturday (9-11.30 am) schooling
Distances: 360yds. 410yds, 435yds, 525yds, 550yds, 575yds, 600yds. 625yds 700yds, 1005yds.
Grading times: 435yds: 25.50. 525yds: 31.50.
Number of dogs per race: Six.
Surface: Sand.
Type of hare: Australian Bramich.
Circumference of track: 575yds.
Distance to the first bend: Sprints: 200yd, 525yd: 50yd
Width of track: 22ft.
Layout of the track and how it runs: One of the biggest circuits in existence, recognised as a tough galloping track.
Usual method of track preparation: Rake and smooth, apply sprinklers.
Graded prize money: Bottom grade £12, top grade £30.
Number of bookmakers: 15.
Totalisator: Forecast and jackpot.
Timing: Automatic ray timing.

Track Records

360yds	**Toss Pit**	19.60	1 9-5-90
410yds	**Wellpad Pal**	22.12	20-11-90
435yds	**Curryhills Fox**	23.11	13-8-85
525yds	**Drapers Autumn**	29.19	31-5-86
550yds	**Perfect Whisper**	30.08	17-7-91
575yds	**Murlough Flash**	32.18	31-8-91
600yds	**Toy Boy**	33.48	25-8-88
700yds	**Graigue Ring**	39.12	7-11-87

NGRC Greyhound Racing Yearbook 1995

IRISH Directory

Enniscorthy

Showgrounds, Ross Road, Enniscorthy.
Telephone number: (054) 33172. Fax: 34941.
Code from UK (01035354).

How to get there: Situated on main Rosslare-Dublin road.
Owner: Enniscorthy Greyhound Racing Co Ltd.
Racing manager: Stephen Cullen.
Race nights: Monday and Thursday (8 pm).

Trial sessions: Monday (2 pm), Thursday after racing.
Distances: 350yd, 525yd, 550yd, 600yd, 830yd, 1005yd
Grading times: 525yd: 31.30.
Number of greyhounds per race: Six.
Surface: Sanded bends, grass straights.
Type of hare: Outside (Two-wheel drive system).
Circumference of track: 480yds line to line.
Distance to the first bend: 85yds.
Width of track: 5.5 yds
Layout of the track and how it runs: A wide galloping track with a rise from the last bend to the winning line.
Usual method of track preparation: Permanent groundsman.

Major competitions:
April Stakes (525yds), April to May.
The Leger (550yds), June.
Grand Prize (525yds), August.
Leinster Champion Open Puppy (525yds), October.
Graded prize money: 525yds: £45-£50, 550yds: £48-£50.
Number of bookmakers: Seven.
Totalisator: Win, place, forecast (computerised).
Timing: Ray timing.
Facilities: Vet in attendance, kennels for 68 greyhounds, car park for 600 vehicles, bar refreshment room, covered stand.

Track Records

Distance	Record Holder	Time	Date
350yds	Luggers Speedy	18.57	1-9-94
525yds	Michaels Machine	28.92	12-11-93
550yds	Kilcloney Chief	30.22	19-7-93
600yds	Kiltrea Celt	33.24	7-10-91
830yds	Tonduff Susie	47.32	31-10-94
1005yds	Greenfield Salt	60.14	15-7-93

IRISH Directory

Principal Race Results, 1994

Event	Dist	Date	Winner	Breeding
Sam McCauley Stk & Slaney Cup	525	5-May	Westlyn Dawn	Lyons Dean-See The Light
	Owner			Time Prize £
	Mrs Jean Fox, Arklow			29.18 1,000
Colourworld Carson Tri-Distance	600	6-Oct	Three Points	Alans Champion-Lawn Park
	T Gordon, Enniscorthy			33.74 500
Bookmaker 29.70 Stk	525	8-Dec	Clonmore Breeze	Curryhills Gara-Clonmore Rose
	Mrs E Cowan, Clonmore			29.90 1,100
AIB Leinster Champion Puppy Stk	525	10-Nov	Summerhill Joy	Low Sail-Grange Joy
	Mrs T Enright, Enfield			29.13 1,000
Phil Turner Memorial Leger	550	11-Jul	Droopys Fergie	Manx Treasure-Star Approach
	S Murphy, Waterford			30.73 1,200
Pettits Supermarkets Unraced	525	14-Jul	Volcano Jack	Deenside Spark-Volcano Dream
	D McDonald, Carlow			29.41 750
Cry Dalcash Unraced Stk	525	15-Aug	Monbeg Twirl	Aquaduct Thuder-Monbeg Smart
	Miss M Doyle, Enniscorthy			29.93 500
Red Mills Grand Prize & WK Cup	525	18-Aug	Skeard Lass	Druids Lodge-Burgess Chimes
	J Scully, Kilmacow			29.63 1,350
Creane & Creane Open 600	600	20-Oct	Cool Survivor	Lodge Prince-Gunboat Ann
	M Fortune, G King, Dublin			33.66 700
Joannes Hot Bread Shops Open	550	23-Jun	Volcan Queen	Deenside Spark-Volcano Dream
	F O'Hara, Carlow			30.83 700
Heineken Open	600	25-Aug	Active King	Im Slippy-Active Touch
	P Foley, Knockgraffon			33.54 1,000
St Martins Open	600	27-Sep	Dodder Taxi	Fly Cruiser-Purple Rain
	Mrs D Gallagher, London			33.29 1,000

Galway

College Road, Galway.
Telephone number: (091)62273.
Code from UK (01035391)

How to get there: From the Dublin Road. turn left at Ryans Hotel roundabout.
Owner: Bord na gCon.
Racing manager: Luke Colleran.
Race nights: Tuesday and Friday (8.15 pm).
Trial sessions: After racing Tuesday, Wednesday (6.30 pm).
Distances: 325yds, 525yds, 550yds, 8iOyds.
Grading times: 325yds: 9.00; 525yds: 31.00.
Number of dogs per race: Six.
Surface: Grass straights, sanded bends.
Type of hare: Outside (two-wheel drive system).
Circumference of track: 500yds.
Distance to the first bend: 100yds.
Width of track: 16ft.
Layout of the track and how it runs: Oval shaped with long straights. A tough gallop.
Usual method of track preparation: Sand is watered,

IRISH Directory

raked and levelled, grass cut and rolled.

Major competitions:
Galway Festival, August.

Graded prize money: 525yds £34-50 (winter), £46 (summer).
Number of bookmakers: Nine.
Totalisator: Computerised. Win, place, forecast.
Timing: Ray timing.
Facilities: Vet in attendance, kennels for 60 greyhounds, car park for 130 vehicles, bar, refreshment room, covered stand. video replay (summer only).

Track Records

325yds	**The Duffer**	17.79	27-8-82
525yds	**New Line Bridge**	29.46	12-7-85
550yds	**Ollies Missy**	30.74	31-7-86
810yds	**Deerwood**	46.80	29-7-85

Principal Race Results, 1994

Event	Dist	Date	Winner	Breeding	Time	Prize £
O'Droighnean Cup	525	4-Nov	Fountain Slippy	Murlens Slippy-Fountain Lass	30.00	1,000
	Owner: J Hogan, Tipperary					
Springs Nigh Club Stk	525	5-Aug	Dabler	Fly Cruiser-Self Belief	29.82	500
	Owner: M Walsh, Headford					
September Stk	525	9-Sep	Ballygaloa Sugar	I'm Slippy-Ballygloa	30.18	500
	Owner: C Hennigan, Roscommon					
Collins Wayside Rest Stk	525	11-Feb	Milltown Skippy	Freenpark Fox-Rikie	30.90	700
	Owner: T Crowe, Milltown Malbay					
Flaherty Markets Corrib Plate	525	28-Jul	War Games	Phantom Flash-No Can Do	30.56	1,200
	Owner: P Houlin, Loughrea					
O'Droighnan Cup Final	525	20-Oct	Ballyregan Flash	I'm From Carrig-Ballyregan Ellen	29.40	1,000
	Owner: M Kennedy, Newcastlewest					
College Road Florist Final	325	29-Jul	Pet	Moneypoint Coal-Black Risk	18.26	500
	Owner: P Tynan and A McCarthy, Loughrea					

IRISH Directory

Harolds Cross

Harolds Cross Park, Dublin 6W.
Telephone number: (01) 4971081/4971523. Fax: 4977110.
Code from UK (0001)

How to get there: Buses 16 and 16A stop at the track.
Owner: Dublin Greyhound and Sports Association Ltd.
Assistant General Manager: Paul Murphy.
Racing manager: George Deegan.
Race nights: Tuesday, Thursday and Friday (8 pm). Plus at least six Sundays, 7.30pm.
Trial sessions: Day trials Monday (2 pm), hurdle trials Monday (3 pm). Night trials Tuesday (9.50 pm), unrecorded trials Monday (10.30 am).
Distances: 330yds, 525yds. 525ydsH, 550yds, 580yds, 580ydsH, 750yds, 830yds, 1025yds.
Grading times: 525yds: 31.20, raced greyhounds 330yds: 19.00.
Number of greyhounds per race: Six.
Surface Grass straights, sanded bends.
Type of hare: Outside McKee Scott.
Circumference of track: 500yds
Distance to the first bend: 92yds approx.
Width of track: 30ft minimum.
Layout of the track and how it runs: Good galloping straights and well-banked bends.
Usual method of track preparation: Polythene sheeting used in winter to protect from frost.
Winning traps: Traps 1 and 6 favoured.

Major competitions:
   Red Mills Racer Derby (525yds), October
   Red Mills Puppy Oaks (525yds), August.

Graded prize money: Bottom grade: 525yds - winner £60, top grade 525yds winner £62.
Totalisator: Computerised. Win, place forecast, trio and jackpot.
Timing: Automatic ray timing.
Facilities: Random and routine testing in operation, vet in attendance, kennels for 60 greyhounds, car park for 400 vehicles, restaurant, bar, refreshment room, glass-fronted stand video replay.
Other facilities: Soccer on Sunday and market.

IRISH Directory

Track Records

330yds	**Ballyoughter Lad**	17.72	5-4-91
	Williams Glen	17.72	11-5-93
525yds	**Wheres Carmel**	28.78	26-6-85
	Pulse Tube	28.78	6-8-85
525ydsH	**Run On Tar**	29.52	20-3-90
550yds	**Barneys Alarm**	30.20	2-8-91
580yds	**Rail Ship**	31.82	21-9-73
580ydsH	**Dark Cowboy**	32.88	16-5-75
750yds	**Azuri**	42.00	24-6-83
830yds	**Wishpark Miss**	46.82	30-4-93
1025yds	**Bodies Lisa**	59.52	4-12-92

Principal Race Results, 1994

Event	Dist	Date	Winner	Breeding
Castlethorn Construction Stk	525	6-May	Musette	Airmount Grand-Angel Passing
	Owner: R Catterson, Dublin			Time 29.70 Prize £ 500
Buckleys Garveys Stk	580	6-May	Savannah Tree	Manorville Major-Savannah Queen
	G Murphy, Wicklow			32.38 500
Shay Healy Memorial Stk	525	17-Jun	Playful Eddie	Murlens Post-Playful Lady
	Mrs K Cooney, Dublin			29.64 1,000
Harolds Cross Open Sprint	330	18-Feb	Big Cyril	Im Slippy-Bangor Style
	G Agnew, Dublin			18.10 1,000
The Corn Cuchulainn	750	22-Jul	Arrancourt Lass	Ardfert Sean-The Other Toss
	J. Houlihan, Eng			42.22 1,500
Exec. Transport Svcs 525	525	25-Mar	Newry Duchess	Macs Lock-Lady Tico
	B Matthews, Down			29.50 1,000
T R Motors Marathon	830	28-Apr	Savannah Tree	Manorville Major-Savannah Queen
	G Murphy, Wicklow			47.50 800
Pitman Moore Stk	525	29-Apr	Flashing Light	Live Contender-Some Tip
	M O'Dwyer, Kildare			29.68 1,000
Clery & Doyle Stk	580	29-Apr	Blue Bird	Lively Ton-Black Jagger
	W Byrne, Wicklow			32.80 500
ODC Chemists Stk	525	29-Apr	Carloway Dancer	Greenpark Fox-Prize Dancer
	Ms C Crane, M Kane, Scot			29.30 1,000
Red Mills Racer Derby	525	7-Oct	Glasskenny Echo	Lodge Prince-Rons Echo
	Nick Byrne, Dublin			28.80 7,000
Red Mills Racer Consolation	525	7-Oct	Likely Wish	Greenpark Fox-Kerogue Wish
	B Sweeney, Cork			29.00 500
Paddy Keane Memorial	580	9-Sep	Springwell Bride	Im Slippy-Springwell Flo
	D Hannon, Athlone			32.94 1,000
Red Mills Puppy Oaks	525	12-Aug	Cool Survivor	Lodge Prince-Gunboat Ann
	M Fortune, A King, Dublin			29.44 1,500

IRISH Directory

Kilkenny

James's Park, Freshford Road, Kilkenny.
Telephone number: (056)21214. Fax 62388
Code from UK (01035356).

How to get there: Half a mile from city centre on Freshford Road.
Owner: Kilkenny Agricultural Society.
General manager and Racing Manager: John O'Flynn.
Race nights: Wednesday and Friday (8.15).

Trial sessions: Thursday (11 am-12.30 pm) and Wednesday after racing.
Distances: 300yds, 525yds, 700yds.
Grading times: 300yds: 17.80; 525yds: 31.40.
Number of greyhounds per race: Six.
Surface: Grass straights, banked bends (sand and clay mixed).
Type of hare: Outside McKee Scott.
Layout of the track and how it runs: .10 or .20 spots behind Shelbourne Park. Long straights, but suits a dog experienced at the track.

Major competitions:
Red Mills Unraced Stakes, June.
Red Mills Stake and Kilkenny Cup, May.
Totalisator: Win, place, forecast.
Timing: Ray timing.
Facilities: Vet in attendance, kennels for 54 greyhounds, car park, bar.
Other activities at the stadium: Show-jumping.

Track Records

300yds	**Greyfriars Rose**	16.28	11-10-89
525yds	**Lax Law**	28.98	21-9-79
700yds	**Deenside Mist**	40.47	5-7-91

IRISH Directory

Principal Race Results, 1994

Event	Dist	Date	Winner	Breeding
AIPB Open Stk	525	3-Jul	Mountaylor Boss	Skelligs Tiger-Maggies Wishes
		Owner: F ODonnell, Rathmoyle		Time 29.54 Prize £ 800
Brosnan Scaffolding Tri Dist.	745	3-Jul	Curisers Breeze	Fly Cruiser-Bally Breeze
		E Murphy, Castleisland		43.77 600
Dobbs Oil Novice Stk	525	3-Jul	Demolition Dog	Manorville Major-Quiet Welcome
		T Leahy, Cuffesgrange		29.62 700
CLG Builders 30.30 Stk	525	3-Jul	Kickhams Town	Manx Marajax-Genevey Slippy
		J Murphy, Ballyhale		30.11 900
O'Dwyer Dog Food GOBA Stk	525	4-Nov	Advantage Rule	Moral Support-African Lovebird
		W McKenna, Thurles		29.72 500
Red Mills Champion Unraced Stk	525	5-Jun	Local Jasper	Wise Band-Local Kauth
		R Leahy, Grovine		29.30 2,000
Slippy Quest Stk	525	8-Apr	The Other Hope	Ardent Sean-Metal Merry
		M O'Donnell, Killenaule		29.85 800
Singing Forever Stk	525	11-May	Altesse Og	Adraville Bridge-Atlesse Emerald
		P Finn, Gorey		30.03 1,000
Red Mills Stake & Kilkenny Cup	525	13-May	Up The Junction	Slippy Quest-Elf Arrow
		G Firmager, Eng		29.08 6,000
Up The Junction Stk	525	16-Dec	Galaxy Man	Hit The Lid-Galaxy Snowie
		D Darrer, Mooncoin		30.11 600
Glen Home 29.70 Stk	525	29-Jul	Level Quay	Double Bid-Orlando Sand
		F & D Richardson, Doon		29.59 650

Lifford

Reelin Urney Road, Strabane, Co Tyrone.
Telephone number: (074) 41083/0805 04-883523.
Code from UK (010 353 74).

How to get there: Lifford is on Tyrone-Donegal border, 14 miles from Derry City.
Owner: The Magee family. Shelane, Co. Tyrone.
General manager: Seamus Magee.
Racing manager: Cathal Magee.
Race nights: Tuesday, Thursday and Saturday.

Trial sessions: Thursday (2-3.30 pm), after racing Tuesday and Thursday.
Distances: 325yds, 525yds. 550yds, 575yds, 790yds.
Grading times: 325yds: 1930; 525yds: 31.50.
Number of greyhounds per race: Six.
Surface: Grass, sanded bends.
Type of hare: Outside McKee Scott.
Circumference of track: 505yds.
Width of track: Bends 23ft, straights 21ft.
Layout of the track and how it runs: Rated as a fair galloping track.
Usual method of track preparation: Complete track

IRISH Directory

rolled before each meeting, bends raked and rolled.
Winning traps: 325yds: T6; 525yds: T1; 575yds: T3.

Major competitions:
Lauras Silver Trophy (525yds), March.
Duffy Greenbrae Sweepstake (525yds), August.
White Horse Trophy (525yds), August.
Seaborn Border Trophy (525yds), September.
James Magee Memorial Trophy (525yds), October.
East Antrim District Puppy Cup (325yds), November.

Number of bookmakers: 10.
Totalisator: Win, place, forecast.
Timing: Automatic timing.
Facilities: Vet in attendance when possible, kennels tor 58 racing greyhounds and 25 trial dogs, car park for 300 vehicles, restaurant for 20 covers, bar, two refreshment rooms, glass-fronted stand, video replay.

Track Records

325yds	**Eden Castle**	17.62	20-7-91
525yds	**Fair Hill Boy**	28.92	15-7-89
550yds	**Bowe Princess**	31.08	17-4-62
575yds	**Quare Whisper**	31.87	22-6-91
790yds	**Barrack Maid**	45.03	17-8-78

Principal Race Results, 1994

Event	Dist	Date	Winner	Breeding	
Lifford Novice Stk	525	12-Nov	Grovehill Comet	Darragh Commet-Beach Jewel	
	Owner			Time	Prize £
	J Kervick, Buncrana			29.48	800
Tennents Spring Stk	525	16-Apr	Hillcrest Laura	Moral Support-Moiras Pet	
	Mrs A Nolan, Lifford			29.58	600
James Magee Memorial Trophy	525	22-Oct	Bealin Pa	Curryhills Gara-Smerla Gara	
	R Gilroy, Belfast			29.54	800
Red Mills Puppy Stk	325	26-Nov	Shear Eater	Whisper Wishes-Ardcarn	
Heather	Mrs I Stevenson, Ballymote			18.22	500
North West Derby	550	28-May	Colorado Duke	Satharn Beo-Dolly Debate	
	J Ferris, Carrickfergus			30.82	750
Danny McCool Memorial	575	30-Jul	Hasten To Ask	Skelligs Tiger-Westmead Glow	
	Mrs T O'Sullivan, Thurles			31.96	600
Sean Donnelly Mem. Sprint	325	9-Jul	Duffys Gem	Tico-Ma Hand	
	J Duffy, Lisburn			17.93	700

IRISH Directory

Limerick

Markets Field. Limerick.
Telephone number: (061) 45170/47808.
Code from UK (010 353 61)

Racing manager: Brendan O'Connell.
Race nights: Monday, Thursday and Saturday (8 pm).

Trial sessions: Tuesday (10 am-12.00 noon, 2.30-4.00 pm).
Distances: 300yds. 525yds, 550yds, 700yds.
Grading times: 525yds: 31.20.
Number of greyhounds per race: Six.
Surface: Grass, sanded bends
Type of hare: McKee Scott.
Distance to the first bend: 80yds.
Width of track: 15h.
Layout of the track and how it runs: This track is recognised as one of the best tests of a dog in the British Isles. Long run to the first bend. A good gallop.
Usual method of track preparation: Straights re-sodded when required.
Winning traps: Trap 6 has had the most winners for a number of years.
Graded prize money: £60.
Number of bookmakers: 20.
Totalisator: Win, place, forecast.
Timing: Automatic timing.
Facilities: Vet in attendance, kennels for 60 greyhounds, bar, refreshment room, covered overhead stand, video replay.

Track Records

300yds	**Fionntra Favour**	16.34	3-10-83
525yds	**Aulton Slippy**	28.94	15-4-88
525ydsH	**Silver Light**	30.10	15-9-76
550yds	**Morans Beef**	30.06	20-10-84
700yds	**Game Misty**	39.53	20-9-90

IRISH Directory

Principal Race Results, 1994

Event	Dist	Date	Winner	Breeding
Castle Oaks Hotel Open	525	1-Aug	Rocky	Randy-Kishiquirk Libra
	Owner			Time Prize £
	Mrs J Daly, Clare			29.49 800
Ringa Hustle Stk	525	2-Apr	Fawn Rambler	Whisper Wishes-Pretty Londis
	T Cournane, Tarbert			29.65 550
Sponsored Open 525	525	2-May	Marble Joe	Willie Joe-Lissaniskea Gold
	M Buckley, Limerick			30.10 800
30.40 Ballysimon Sweep	525	4-Jul	Like A Winner	Greenpark Fox-Creans Cyclone
	D Crean, Bruree			30.17 800
Golden Marts Open	525	7-Jul	Marble Joe	Willie Joe-Lissaniskea Gold
	M Buckley, Limerick			29.81 1,000
Xmas Stake	525	8-Jan	Dromtransa Mist	Greenpark Fox-Urban Princess
	J Foley, Abbeyfeale			29.98 700
Limerick & Clare GOBA Sweep	525	10-Sep	Adare Spark	Deenside Spark-Warm Jenny
	R Savage, Milford Open			29.96 1,500
Ivans Caherdavin Open	525	11-Apr	Handsome Duke	Mid Clare Champ-The Other Lass
	S Hamett, D Murphy			29.61 800
JP McManus Sportsman Stk	525	13-Sep	Tullig Zafonic	Greenpark Fox-Tullig Patsey
	M Ahern, Abbeyfeale			30.00 1,000
Dore Aluminium Open	525	14-Nov	Rushing Magpie	Macs Lock-Evans Magpie
	P Geoghegan, Glin			29.83 800
Geraldines Open	525	15-Aug	Paddys Fox	Greenpark Fox-Manx Ivy
	P Hurney, S Dunne, Dublin			29.59 800
Pedigree Chum Formula Race	525	16-Jun	Up He Flew	Manorville Sand-Sheer Valvet
	J Ryan, Knocklong			29.81 800
O'Malley Pharmacy Stk	525	19-Feb	No Method	Alpine Minister-Francies Chance
	W Windrim, T Murphy, Limerick			30.53 1,000
Woodlands House Hotel Open	525	21-May	Marble Joe	Willie Joe-Lissaniskea Gold
	M Buckley, Limerick			29.43 1,000
Red Mills Racer Stk & Kennedy Cup	525	21-May	Linnad	Nadja-Cinmark
	D Fleming, Kerry			29.95 1,750
Estuary Fuel Open	525	24-Apr	Rockys Ivan	Adraville Bridge-Game Misty
	D Kiely, Dungarvan			29.65 2,000
Ace Homes Stk	525	26-Sep	Kilvil Skinner	Mathews Gold-Keeleys Friend
	Mrs M McMillan, Templemore			29.71 800
Red Cow Inn Classic	525	28-Mar	Rocky	Randy-Kishiquirk Libra
	Mrs J Daly, Limerick			29.11 1,000
Claughaun GAA Open	525	26-Dec	Kish Storm	Randy-Kishiquirk Libra
	Miss J Cahir, Limerick			29.63 800
Kerry Agribusiness Open	525	28-Nov	Radical Prince	Lodge Prince-Garryduff Lassie
	T Brennan, Cork			29.55 800
Golden Vale St Leger	550	29-Oct	Kilvil Skinner	Mathews Gold-Keeleys Friend
	Mrs M McMillan, Templemore			30.84 11,000
Tom Kilroy Open	525	30-May	Marble Joe	Willie Joe-Lissaniskea Gold
	M Buckley, Limerick			29.39 800

LIMERICK

IRISH Directory

Longford

Longford Sports Stadium, Park Road, Longford.
Telephone number: (043) 46441/45501.
Code from UK (010 353 43).

Owner: Longford Sports Ltd.
Racing manager: Jim Conroy.
Race nights: Monday and Friday (8 pm).
Trial sessions: Tuesday (3.30-4.30 pm), after racing on Monday, schooling trials Wednesday (7-9 pm).
Distances: 330yds. 525yds, 550yds.
Number of greyhounds per race: Six.
Surface: Grass straights, sanded bends.
Circumference of track: 485yds.
Layout of the track and how it runs: Difficult circuit to run, with tight bends.
Number of bookmakers: 3 (average).
Totalisator: Win, place. forecast.
Timing: Ray timing.
Facilities: Vet in attendance, kennels for 48 greyhounds, bar, covered stand.

Track Records

330yds	**Cast No Stones**	18.22	24-5-85
	Tubbercurry Lad	18.22	12-7-85
525yds	**Pepsi Princess**	28.82	1-9-89
550yds	**Bermadaghs Shay**	30.80	17-7-85
805yds	**Thanks Jim**	46.98	8-91

Principal Race Results, 1994

Event	Dist	Date	Winner	Breeding	
Jimmy O'Brien Memorial	525	26-Jun	Ringtown Express	Ardfert Sean-Fair Hill Rose	
	Owner			Time	Prize £
	P Rea, Longford			29.22	750
Red Mills Longford Derby	525	26-Aug	Moygara Perry	Greenpark Fox-Moygara Kim	
	B Hunt, Gurteen			29.40	1,200

IRISH Directory

Mullingar

Ballinderry, Mullingar, Co Meath.
Telephone number: (044) 48348.
Code from UK (010 353 44).

How to get there: By car: N4 from Dublin.
Owners: Mullingar Greyhound Racing Co Ltd.
Racing manager: Peter Kenny.
Race nights: Tuesday and Saturday.
Trial sessions: Day trials (2.30-4.30 pm).
Distances: 325yds 525yds, 525ydsH, 550yds 550ydsH, 600yds, 805yds.
Number of dogs per race: Six.
Surface: Grass, sanded bends.
Type of hare: Outside McKee Scott.
Circumference of track: 498yds.
Distance to the first bend: 100yds from 600yd traps.
Width of track: 15yds.
Layout of the track and how it runs: A difficult test for a greyhound, with long straights and very tight bends.
Totalisator: Computerised. Win, place, forecast.
Timing: Automatic and hand timing.
Facilities: Vet in attendance, kennels for 49 greyhounds, bar, refreshment room, covered and glass-fronted stand, video replay.

Track Records

Distance	Name	Time	Date
325yds	**Portrun Flier**	18.36	7-7-90
525yds	**Rex Again**	29.55	16-5-64
550yds	**Crory County**	30.78	22-6-91
600yds	**Butterfly Billy**	33.61	26-10-65
805yds	**Lady Erin**	47.12	14-5-88

Principal Race Results, 1994

Event	Dist	Date	Winner	Breeding	Time	Prize £
Slaneyside Hare Midland Oaks	525	2-Jul	Nitrol Lady	Daleys Gold-Tri Nitro	29.64	750
			Owner: Mrs G Loughrey			
Beamish Mid Sprint	325	9-Oct	Up He Flew	Manorville Sam-Sheer Velvet	18.48	750
			J Ryan, Limerick			
Red Mills/McHughs Mid Ces'tch	600	19-Nov	Maglin Manor	Manorville Sand-Cute Vixen	N/A	750
			T Delaney, Ballincollig			
Tennents Midland Derby	550	21-May	Glenclose	Im Slippy-Glenivy	31.90	2,000
			L Kirley, Geashill			

NGRC Greyhound Racing Yearbook 1995

IRISH Directory

Navan

Limekiln Hill, Trim Road. Navan, Co Meath.
Telephone number: (046) 21739/28436.
Code from UK (010 35346).

How to get there: 30 miles from Dublin on N4.
Owner: Boyne Valley Greyhound Racing Co Ltd.
General manager: Richard Brennan.
Racing manager: Paddy Barry.
Race nights: Wednesday and Thursday (8 pm).

Trial sessions: Tuesday (11 am-12 noon), Wednesday after racing.
Distances: 350yds, 525yds. 550yds, 600yds, 850yds
Grading times: 350yds: 20.40; 525yds: 31.40.
Number of greyhounds per race: Six.
Surface: Part sand, part grass.
Type of hare: Outside McKee Scott.
Circumference of track: 500yds.
Distance to the first bend: 80yds.
Width of track: 10yds.
Layout of the track and how it runs: Long straights, sharp bends.
Usual method of track preparation: Sand is raked and rolled manually after each race or trial session, eight hours per week to check pulleys.
Graded prize money: 550yds and 600yds: £50, 525yds: £46.
Number of bookmakers: Seven.
Totalisator: Computerised.
Timing: Ray timing.
Facilities: Vet in attendance, kennels for 54 greyhounds, car park for 200 vehicles, bar, covered stand with glass sides, video replay on big nights only.

Track Records

350yds	Princes Pal	18.76	23-7-87
525yds	Trip To Arran	29.10	25-9-86
550yds	Lispopple Story	30.26	29-7-99
600yds	Choice Model	32.92	19-8-82
850yds	Tiny Tolcas	48.80	23-7-87

IRISH Directory

Principal Race Results, 1994

Event	Dist	Date	Winner	Breeding
Red Mills Irish Cesarewitch	600	7-Jul	Roan Hurricane	Leaders Best-Roan Elf
Owner: B Mallon, Tyrone				Time 33.04 Prize £ 4,000
Daniel Reilly Open Sprint	350	8-Sep	Killoran Lass	Satharn Beo-Kildallon Sally
T Clyne, Roscommon				19.08 1,500
Ashcon 525	525	12-Jun	Exclusive Gem	Greenpark Fox-Exclusive Lady
M Kearns-Balbriggan				29.50 500
Ashcon 550	550	12-Jun	Droopys Mossie	Phantom Flash-Droopys Stranger
D Foley, M Murphy, Eng				30.58 500
Irish Auctioners 550	550	28-Jul	Louisianna Queen	Aussie Flyer-Armada Queen
R Cullivan, Stradone				30.54 700
Paddy Barry Mem. Cup	525	26-May	Droopys Mossie	Phantom Flash-Droopys Stranger
D Foley, M Murphy, Eng				30.56 1,000

Newbridge

Newbridge, Co Kildare.
Telephone number: (045) 31270/31660/34331.
Code from UK (010 353 45).

How to get there: Turn right at third set of traffic lights from Dublin, go straight on for approx a mile and a half.
Owner: Private Limited company.
Racing manager: Tom Broderick.
Race nights: Monday and Friday.
Trial sessions: Tuesday (2-4 pm), after racing Monday.
Distances: 300yds, 525yds, 525ydsH, 550yds, 600yds, 820yds.
Number of greyhounds per race: Six.
Surface: Grass straights, sanded bends.
Type of hare: Outside two-wheel drive system.
Circumference of track: 520yds.
Distance to the first bend: 90yds approx.
Width of track: 6yds approx.
Layout of the track and how it runs: Short run to the first bend, which benefits fast trappers.
Graded prize money: 300yds: Winner £55, second £15. 525yds; Winner £60, second £16. 600yds and others: Winner £63, second £17.
Number of bookmakers: 12.
Totalisator: Win, place, forecast, jackpot.
Timing: Ray timing.
Facilities: Vet in attendance, kennels for 60 greyhounds, car park for 500 vehicles, two bars, tea room, covered stand, video replay.

IRISH Directory

Track Records

300yds	**Joannes Treasure**	16.44	31-8-90
525yds	**Ardfert Mick**	28.68	22-6-91
525ydsH	**No Promises**	29.92	3-7-87
550yds	**Carlow County**	30.18	23-9-88
600yds	**Guess Twice**	32.86	28-6-91
820yds	**August Blossom**	46.90	4-10-91

Principal Race Results, 1994

Event	Dist	Date	Winner	Breeding		
Red Mills Unraced Stk	550	2-May	Lanigans Beo	Satharn Beo-Lanigan Ball		
	Owner: M Lennon, Kilkenny			Time 30.86	Prize £ 600	
Cox Cup	525	3-Jul	Valais Express	Daleys Gold-Carrick Express		
	J Ryan, Dublin			28.96	3,000	
John Greeley 750	750	3-Jul	Loch Bo Anchor	Murlens Slippy-Loch Bo Cheeky		
	J Smith, Eng			42.34	500	
AIB Stakes	600	3-Jul	Jurange	Ardfert Sean-Here Comes Rachel		
	P Lynch, Clare			33.20	500	
Gentle Warning Stk	550	3-Jul	Droopys Mossie	Phantom Flash-Droopys Stranger		
	Mrs D Jolly, M Dunphy, Eng			29.96	500	
Sara Emma Stk	525	3-Jul	Poets Dream	Moral Support-Expectations		
	B Cross, Newbridge			29.32	500	
Ray O'Brien Car Hire Stk	525	3-Jul	Cooma Kev	Cooma Slave-Cooma Girl		
	J Loughlin, Dublin			29.84	500	
Maginn TV Supreme Novice Stk	525	4-Nov	Cill Dubh Sam	Adraville Bridge-Cill Dubh Villa		
	S Locke-Hart, Eng			29.08	2,000	
Track Supporters Unraced	525	11 Apl	Lassana Dean	Lyons Dean-Mid Clare Lass		
	S Barratt, J Molloy, Clare			29.80	500	
Athgarvan Stk	525	16-Sep	Fifth of November	Skelligs Tiger-Maggies Wish		
	Mrs A Shawfield, Eng			29.20	500	
August Stk	525	19-Aug	Kalaster	Dereen Star-Kalazena		
	A Claydon, Eng			29.00	500	
John Casey Memorial	525	25-Mar	Celts Knight	Glencorbry Celt-Duskey Knight		
	J Melia, Naas			30.06	500	
Friends of Allen Stk	600	27-May	Ballydowel Boy	Manorville Major-Glennace		
	Mrs B Byrne, Wicklow			33.52	500	
Professionals Stk	525	27-May	Black Pavilion	Slippy Blue-Pavilion Girl		
	J Carty, Portlaoise			29.30	500	
Esso Stk	550	27-May	Lodgefield Pal	Greenpark Fox-Snow Panther		
	P Traynor, Naas			31.00	500	
ESB Win Electric Stk	550	27-May	Whitehood Hudini	Randy-Whitewood Shadow		
	M Smith, Eng			30.52	1,000	
Ace Construction & Lacey Roofing	525	27-May	Anticipation	Moral Support-Expectations		
	B Cross, Rathangan			29.48	500	
Quinns of Baltinglass Stk	525	27-May	Beneficial	Powerstown Pax-Lady of Close		
	Ms S Barratt, D O'Connor, Dublin			29.44	500	
Comerford Brothers Stk	300	27-May	Big Cyril	Im Slippy-Bangor Style		
	G. Agnew, Dublin			16.68	500	
Dee Morrin Stk	525	27-May	Mountaylor Boss	Skelligs Tiger-Maggies Wishes		
	Mrs E O'Donnell, Tipperary			29.50	750	
Beamish 525	525	28-Oct	Glenlyre	Greenpark Fox-Glenmoira		
	L Kirley, Offaly			29.06	600	

IRISH Directory

Shelbourne

Shelbourne Park, Ringsend, Dublin 4
Telephone number: (01) 6683502/6684040/6683503/685535.
Code from UK (0001).

General manager: Noel Hynes.
Racing manager: Pat Ryan.
Race nights: Monday, Wednesday and Saturday (8 pm). Trial sessions: Thursday (2 pm), Mondays after racing.
Distances: 360yds, 525yds 525ydsH, 550yds, 575yds, 600yds, 750yds.
Grading times: 525yds: 31.20.
Number of greyhounds per race: Six.
Surface: Grass, sanded bends.
Type of hare: Outside McKee Scott.
Circumference of track: 500yds.
Distance to the first bend: 75yds from 525 traps.
Width of track: 8yds and 10yds at bends.
Layout of the track and how it runs: A good galloping circuit, bends are on the sharp side and are better run with experience. Wide runners have a distinct advantage.
Usual method of track preparation: Normal grass maintenance with sanded bends.
Winning traps: Trap six consistently produces most winner over all distances.

Major competitions:
　　Easter Cup (525yds), April.
　　Guinness 600.(600yds) May.
　　Bord na gCon TV Trophy (750yds), August.
　　Irish Greyhound Derby, £97,000 (wnr £50,000)
　　　(550yds), September.
　　Champion Stakes (575yds), July.
　　Grand National (525ydsH), October.

Graded prize money: £65 to £200 per race.
Number of bookmakers: 18.
Totalisator: Computerised. Win place, forecast, trio and jackpot prizes.
Timing: Ray timing.
Facilities: Vet in attendance, kennels for 48 greyhounds, car park for 200 vehicles, restaurant for 100 covers, three bars, two refreshment rooms, glass-fronted stand, video replay.

IRISH Directory

Track Records

360yds	**Meet Me Halfway**	19.19	18-8-90
525yds	**Tantallons Gift**	28.73	24-7-76
525ydsH	**Sand Blinder**	29.46	4-10-86
550yds	**Lodge Prince**	30.03	9-8-86
575yds	**Popov**	31.58	15-10-94
600yds	**Deerfield Pier**	32.99	25-4-94
750yds	**Rush For Silver**	42.19	22-10-90
1025yds	**Ruscar Dana**	59.91	6-8-88

Principal Race Results, 1994

Event	Dist	Date	Winner	Breeding
Cry Dalcash 32.70	575	5-Mar	Kiwi Nick	Kyle Jack-Barneys Girl
	Owner: M McElhatton, Tyrone			Time 32.36 Prize £ 2,000
Rohcon Puppy	525	6-Aug	River Lad	The Other Knight-Wolesleys Commet
	F Campion, Tipperary			29.15 1,000
Guinness 600	600	7-May	Tip Top	Im Slippy-Dream Orchid
	T Moloney, M Enright, Limerick			33.16 8,000
DJ Reilly Easter Cup	525	9 Apl	Valais Express	Daleys Gold-Trade Express
	J Ryan, Newbridge			29.13 2,500
Sporting Press Cons Irish Oaks	525	11-Jun	Nicotine	Slippy Blue-Gleannrua Wood
	Mrs M Curtain, Limerick			29.34 500
Sporting Press Irish Oaks	525	11-Jun	Shimmering Wings	Alpine Minister-Narabane Gosh
	J McCarrick, Longford			29.23 12,500
Shelbourne Open	525	12-Mar	Rathcannon Lodge	Dukes Lodge-Crowded House
	W Frazer, Antrim			29.62 800
Frightful Flash 525	525	15-Oct	New Theme	Lodge Prince-Lady Barrister
	M Heeney, Louth			29.32 1,000
Corals Open	575	29-Jul	Popov	Fly Cruiser-Super Flow
	J Robinson, Tyrone			31.58 700
Ras Mor Na Gaeilge	550	18-May	Ramblers Bridge	Airmount Grand-Greenville Sand
	Mrs M Galvin, Kerry			30.75 2,000
Ladbrokes Anglo-Irish Int'l	525	20-Aug	Velvet Rocket	Manorville Sand-Sheer Velvet
	G Golden, Mayo			28.93 3,000
Febo Champion Stakes Consolation	550	27-Jul	Emmett Robert	Murlens Slippy-Long Valley Lady
	P McCarthy, Vork			30.46 1,000
Febo Select Open	525	23-Jul	Pluckey Punter	Skelligs Tiger-Minorcas Tramp
	P Ryan, Limerick			29.33 1,000
Febo Champion Stakes	550	23-Jul	Velvet Rocket	Manorville Sand-Sheer Velvet
	G Golden, Mayo			30.39 10,000
Respond Irish Derby	550	24-Sep	Joyful Tidings	Whisper Wishes-Newmans Mall
	M Carmody, Tarbert			30.35 50,000
Toyota 525	525	25-Jun	Old Maid	Moral Support-Rolan Rose
	R Roberts, Kildare			28.96 500
George Roe Memorial	550	25-Jun	Viscount Hustle	Midnight Hustle-Keltic Bimbo
	P Heffernan, Tipperary			30.48 750
Peter Sheridan Memorial	575	25-Jun	Melville Lace	Coalbrook Tiger-Melville Chill
	Mrs J Freyne, Wicklow			32.20 750
Bookmakers 750	750	26-Feb	Tonduff Susie	Wise Band-Redwoos Susie
	J McDermott, B Shea, Carlow			43.81 600
Bookmakers Open	525	29-Jan	Silver Hare	Slaneyside Hare-Cheerful Lover
	G Stephens, Dublin			29.64 1,000

IRISH Directory

Thurles

Town Park, Thurles. Co Tipperary.
Telephone number: (0504) 21003.
Code from UK (010353504).

How to get there: Thurles Town (Nenagh Road).
Owner: Share holders.
Manager: Eamonn Bourke.
Trial sessions: Official trials Tuesday (10.30 am to 12.00 noon), after race nights. Unofficial trials Thursday (1030am to 12noon) and (7-830 pm).
Distances: 330yds, 525yds. 550yds, 575yds, 750yds, 840yds.
Grading times: 330yds: 19.40, 525yds: 31.50.
Number of greyhounds per race: Six.
Surface: Grass, sanded bends.
Type of hare: Outside McKee Scott.
Circumference of track: 509yds.
Distance to the first bend: 90yds.
Width of track: 20ft.
Layout of the track and how it runs: Very long run to the first bend, particularly on the sprint trip. Runs on the slow side, but rated a first class gallop, probably the best test of a dog in the country.
Usual method of track preparation: Grass cutting and hand raking bends.
Graded prize money: £60 to £70.
Number of bookmakers: Six.
Totalisator: Computerised.
Timing: Ray timing.
Facilities: Vet in attendance, kennels for 60 greyhounds, car park for 150 vehicles, bar, covered stand.
Other activities at the stadium: Soccer.

Track Records

Distance	Name	Time	Date
330yds	**Lemon King**	17.94	28-7-90
525yds	**Smokey Sopine**	29.14	13-8-94
525ydsH	**Special**	29.75	15-9-73
550yds	**Kilvil Skinner**	30.36	5-7-94
575yds	**Gastrognome**	31.76	16-6-84
840yds	**Glengall Star**	47.62	21-8-93

IRISH Directory

Principal Race Results, 1994

Event	Dist	Date	Winner	Breeding
Kasco Unraced	525	5-Nov	Ballyhoe Fox	Greenpark Fox-Merry Moments
	Owner			Time Prize £
	P McCarthy, Freshford			29.48 1,000
Lyons Dean Stk	525	16-Apr	See The Future	Coalbrook Tiger-Firm Mist
	R Dwan, Holycross			30.02 600
Slippys Blue Unraced	525	20-Aug	Lemon Rob	Daleys Gold-Lemon Miss
	T Lennon, Threecastles			29.44 750
Tom Harvey Champion Bitch Stk	525	22-Oct	Glue Vixen	Greenpark Fox-Westmead Glow
	Mrs A Landin, Sweden			29.44 1,500
Tipperary Cup	550	24-Jul	Viscount Hustle	Midnight Hustle-Keltic Kimbo
	P. Heffernan, Tipperary			30.66 3,000
Red Mills Marathon	840	27-Aug	Molls Line	North Line-Lissaroon Fairy
	D O'Meara, Thurles			48.10 1,000
Thurles 575	575	28-May	Rathmangan Blue	Moral Support-Expectations
	P Stoner, Eng			32.06 1,000

Tralee

Oakview, Tralee, Co Kerry.
Telephone number (066) 24033/25416.
Code from UK (01035366).

How to get there: 80 miles Shannon Airport, 75 miles Cork Airport, 20 miles Killarney, 70 miles Limerick.
Owner: Kingdom Greyhound Racing Company.
Track directors: P. Healy, S. P. Flanagan, S. Collins, P. O'Neill, C. O'Leary.
Racing manager: John Ward.
Top trainers: D. O'Regan, J. Kelly, P. McMahon, M. Reidy, C. O'Callaghan, B. Fitzgerald, D. O'Sullivan, L. Connolly, J. Moriarty.
Race nights: Tuesday and Friday (8 pm).

Trial sessions: Official: Monday (2.30-4 pm), Tuesday night after racing. Unofficial: Wednesday (10.15 am-noon).
Distances: 325yds, 525yds, 550yds, 750yds, 812yds.
Grading times: 325yds: 19.20. 525yds: 31.40.
Number of greyhounds per race: Six.
Surface: Grass.
Type of hare: Outside hare (two-wheel drive system).
Circumference of track: 495yds.
Distance to the first bend: 10yds.
Width of track: 25ft.
Layout of the track and how it runs: Very short run to the first bend, favours inside runners.

Irish Directory

TRALEE

Major competitions:
Austin Stacks (550yds), April-May.
Rose Of Tralee Cup (550yds), £1,500.
Kingdom Puppy Cup (525yds).

Graded prize money: Top grade £61.
Number of bookmakers: 12.
Totalisator: Win, place, forecast.
Timing: Automatic.
Facilities: Vet in attendance, kennels for 60 greyhounds, car park, bars, refreshment room, stand, video replay.

Track Records

Distance	Name	Time	Date
325yds	**Michigan Maurice**	17.52	30-8-91
525yds	**Castleland Mac**	28.69	26-9-91
525ydsH	**Ballyard Hurdler**	29.85	18-8-73
550yds	**Ardfert Sean**	30.18	2-12-88
570yds	**Sirius**	31.34	8-4-69
750yds	**Slow Motion**	42.40	29-5-81
812yds	**Kertogue Sarah**	45.90	22-7-83

Principal Race Result, 1994

Event	Dist	Date	Winner	Breeding
Kerry Agri Business & Respond	525	1-Jul	Emmett Robert	Murlens Slippy-Long Valley Lady
Owner: P McCarthy, Clonakilty				Time 30.23 Prize £ 1,000
Feal Valley Plant Hire	525	14-Jul	Teevee Dancer	Kildare Ash-Teevee Vision
P O'Donnell, Duagh				29.17 1,500
Boyne Walk/Lixnaw Supp. Stk	525	15 Apl	Not My Line	Asraville Bridge-Off The Line
D Keane, Rathmore				29.44 2,000
Tom Bambury Memorial	525	17-Jun	Mystery Dream	Boveens Slippy-Tara Minstrel
K Savage, Tralee				29.87 1,000
Kellihers Garage Toyota Bitch Stk	525	19-Aug	Nanos Best	Leaders Best-Little Queenie
M O'Gorman, Tournafulla				29.37 1,000
Red Book Stk	525	20-Sep	Bower Sandy	Olives Champ-Fairy Fingers
J Saunders, Headford				29.30 1,000
Tossie Roe Memorial	525	21-Sep	Misty Treasure	Manx Treasure-City Border
M Egan, Tarbert				29.49 1,000
Paddy Byrne Memorial	550	22-Jul	El Dorado	Murlens Slippy-Without Equal
W O'Dowd, Ballyduff				30.23 3,000
Phantom Flash Stk	525	22-Jul	Ruby Mist	Pagan Pine-Rockpapra
M Egan, Listowel				29.94 1,150
Kasco Derby	525	22-Sep	Pilgrim	Im Slippy-Heartbreak Hill
P Stoner, Eng				29.15 1,400
J Myles Stk	525	24-Aug	Thorny Stake	Thorney Tip-Stakehill Fox
C O'Leary, Mallow				29.83 1,000
Kerry Ingredients Stk	550	25-Aug	Knocknaseed Macs	Lacs Lock-Lucky Slip
N Cronin, Gneevnaguilla				30.66 1,300
Dawn Milk Stk	525	25-Aug	Fear Sasta	Greenpark Fox-Trans Duchess
M Scanlon, Killorglin				29.45 1,000
Rose of Tralee Stk	525	26-Aug	Son of Sandles	Meet Me Halfway-Lennai Murt
P Fernane, Tralee				29.58 1,000

NGRC Greyhound Racing Yearbook 1995

IRISH Directory

Waterford

RACING started June 8 1948. The best-manicured track in the country and the only one of Ireland's seaside tracks to survive. Others existed at Ballybunion, Arklow, etc.

Kilcohan Park, Waterford.
Telephone number: (051) 74531.
Code from UK (010 353 51).

Owner: Bord na gCon.
Racing manager: Michael Higgins.
Race nights: Tuesday and Saturday.

Trial sessions: (Recorded) Tuesday after racing and Wednesday 10am-noon.
(Unrecorded) Monday 10am-noon and Wednesday 7-9pm
Distances: 290yds, 525yds, 700yds, 770yds.
Grading times: 525yds: 31.40.
Number of greyhounds per race: Six.

Surface: Grass straights. sanded bends.
Type of hare: Outside two-wheel drive system.
Circumference of track: 460yds.
Distance to the first bend: 110yds.
Width of track: 21ft bends, 17ft straights.
Layout of the track and how it runs: A fair circuit. Bends easy to run. The going is significantly slower in the winter months.

Major competitions:
  Waterford Crystal Sweepstakes, March
  Phil Rees Memorial Unraced, May.
  Red Mills Guineas, May
  MA Molloy Oaks, July

Graded prize money: Bottom grade £34.50- 525 yds.
Number of bookmakers: Six.
Timing: Ray timing.
Facilities: Kennels for 48 greyhounds, car park for 70 vehicles, bar, glass-fronted stand.
Other activities at the stadium: Soccer.

IRISH Directory

Track Records

290yds	**Concentration**	15.84	20-4-91
525yds	**Whitewood Hudini**	28.69	6-11-93
700yds	**Rockys Raisa**	39.37	7-7-92
760yds	**Fly Smasher**	42.94	2-10-93

Principal Race Results, 1994

Event	Dist	Date	Winner	Breeding
Waterford Crystal Stk	525	2 Apl	Greenane Gigolo T Nugent, Clonmel	Lodge Prince-Borris Chat 29.50 1,600
TJK Syndicate Open	525	6-Aug	Perrys Charmer Mrs Newman, Eng	Moral Support-Bar Snowie 29.31 500
Red Mills Guineas	525	15-May	Valais Express J Ryan, Dublin	Daleys Gold-Carrick Express 29.30 4,000
Snowcream Open	525	15-May	Whitehood Houdini J Smith, Eng	Randy-Whitewood Shadow 29.72 1,000
Phil Rees Memorial	525	23 Apl	The Other Joe M O'Donnell, Killenaule	Willie Joe-The Other Linda 29.80 1,600
Waterford Crystal Open Bitch	525	26-Jun	Dalcash Visa M Meade, Co Clare	Whisper Wit-Burnpark Vixen 29.09 1,000
Waterford Crystal Open 700	700	26-Jun	LIberal Idea C McCarthy, Drimoleague	Easy And Slow-Ballinvard Rose 39.83 1,000
MA Molloy Munster Oaks	525	31-Jul	Gun Um Down T Hegarty, Dublin	Ballyard Hoffman-Aghadown Heath 29.27 2,500
Parish Traders Open	760	15-May	My Jenny P Brady	Druids Lodge-Warm Jenny 43.93 1,000

Youghal

Youghal, Co Cork.
Telephone number: (024) 92305.
Code from UK (01035324).

How to get there: On the N25 (Cork-Rosslare route).
Owner: Bord na gCon.
Racing manager: Finbarr Coleman.
Race nights: Tuesday and Friday.
Distances: 325yds, 525yds, 550yds, 700yds, 790yds. 900yds.
Grading times: 325yds: 1900, 525yds: 31.50.
Number of dogs per race: Six.
Surface: Grass, sanded bends.
Type of hare: Outside two-wheel drive system.
Circumference of track: 464yds.
Layout of the track and how it runs: A fast circuit with

IRISH Directory

a short turn to the first bend, top class running surface.

Major competitions:
The Paddy Whiskey Stakes (550yds), June.
John O'Mahony Bookmakers Stakes (525yds), August.

Number of bookmakers: Eight.
Totalisator: Win, place and forecast.
Timing: Ray timing.
Facilities: Kennels for 48 greyhounds, car park for 70 vehicles, bar, glass-fronted stand.

325yds	**Greenane Catcher**	17.46	7-9-90
525yds	**Gabriel Wonder**	28.82	20-8-91
525ydsH	**Super Fellow**	30.70	17-7-62
550yds	**Lispopple Tiger**	30.20	31-5-85
700yds	**Blondie Brown**	39.68	26-8-83
	Barbery Glade	39.68	13-8-89
790yds	**Fen Tiger**	44.92	4-7-86
990yds	**Queenies Fire**	59.14	15-6-90

Principal Race Results, 1994

Event	Dist	Date	Winner	Breeding	
Barry Bros Southern Sprint	325	2-Sep	Super Senor	Greenpark Fox-Burgess Gypsy	
	Owner			Time	Prize £
	V Browne, Cork			17.22	500
Youghal 550	550	3-Jun	Move On Passion	Whisper Wishes-Burnpark Vera	
	R Ryan, Ballysimon			30.18	1,800
Bob Daly Memorial	525	10-Jun	Paper Warrior	Ravage Again-Paper Edition	
	Mrs M Barry, Kill			29.80	600
Kasco Stk	525	22 Apl	Upton Rover	Whisper Wishes-Island Flag	
	D O'Connor, Co Cork			29.80	500
Red Mills Ted Fitzgerald Stk	525	29-Jul	Mindys Friend	Murlens Slippy-Cassiebiancababy	
	Mrs S O'Donoghue, Cork			29.52	700